Pacific
Turning Point

USS *Gwin*

PACIFIC TURNING POINT

The Solomons Campaign, 1942–1943

Charles W. Koburger, Jr.

PRAEGER

Westport, Connecticut
London

Library of Congress Cataloging-in-Publication Data

Koburger, Charles W.
    Pacific turning point : the Solomons campaign, 1942–1943 / Charles
W. Koburger, Jr.
        p. cm.
    Includes bibliographical references and index.
    ISBN 0–275–95236–3 (alk. paper)
    1. World War, 1939–1945—Campaigns—Solomon Islands. I. Title.
D767.98.K63   1995
    940.54'26—dc20   95–5314

British Library Cataloguing in Publication Data is available.

Library of Congress Catalog Card Number: 95–5314
ISBN: 0–275–95236–3

First published in 1995

Praeger Publishers, 88 Post Road West, Westport, CT 06881
An imprint of Greenwood Publishing Group, Inc.

Printed in the United States of America

∞™

The paper used in this book complies with the
Permanent Paper Standard issued by the National
Information Standards Organization (Z39.48–1984).

10 9 8 7 6 5 4 3 2 1

For my seagoing friends
American
British
French
past and present, and for those who come after us

Contents

Illustrations		ix
Introduction		xi
1.	Prologue	1
2.	Collision Course	13
3.	The Southern Solomons	23
4.	Tokyo Reacts	35
5.	Control of the Sea	51
6.	Guadalcanal Ends	67
7.	The Central Solomons—New Georgia	79
8.	The By-Pass Strategy Arrives—Vella Lavella	93
9.	The Northern Solomons—Bougainville	103

10. Conclusion   115

Appendix A: Ships and Craft   127

Appendix B: Equipment   131

Appendix C: Personalities   135

Appendix D: Abbreviations, Acronyms, and Code Words   137

Bibliography   141

Index   145

Photographs follow page 91

Illustrations

DRAWING

1. PT-Boat   129

MAPS

1. Papua, the Bismarcks, and the Solomons   6
2. Guadalcanal and Tulagi   28
3. Central and Northern Solomons   81

TABLES

1. Naval Losses in the Naval Battle of Guadalcanal   65
2. Naval Losses in the Guadalcanal Campaign   77
3. Japanese Losses to Allied Mines in the Solomons Area   85

Introduction

The U.S. Navy in the Second World War fought in the Pacific two essentially distinct if closely interrelated kinds of war. One was the well-known fast fleet carrier war, fought by its famous large flat-deck aircraft carriers (the *Essex*-classes) and its lighter stand-ins (the *Independence*-class), led to glory by Admirals Halsey, McCain, and Mitscher. The other was the amphibious—or expeditionary—war, fought by almost unknown Admirals Turner, Wilkinson, and Barbey, along with the better-known Marines, especially at first. In these two kinds of war, campaign objectives, leadership mind-sets, and tools were—had to be—different in each case. Echoes of these differences persist today, making another serious look at our Second World War experience worthwhile, especially in today's world.

The hazards inherent in these two kinds of war are markedly different. Supercarriers operating offshore work on an essentially plain table, as far as navigation goes. Not so the amphibians, who must beach to land their troops, and who therefore must move close inshore, to shallow, constricted waters, full of reefs and shoals. To the dangers of navigation must be added those of the enemy, in both situations. But many of the prospective enemies today cannot reach offshore. Inshore, mines appear and become a major threat. The book that follows is a close look at and analysis of the first of these lesser-known amphibious campaigns—the Solomons Campaign—fought early in World War II.

Fought between August 1942 and December 1943, the far-off South Pacific Islands here saw what was, for its type, the U.S. Navy's most bitter fight since the Civil War (1861–1865). In today's jargon, this represents power projection under less than ideal conditions. Public positions notwithstanding, we are going to see more of this sooner or later, most likely sooner.

The thesis of this book is that the Solomons Campaign—not the Battles of the Coral Sea or Midway—represents the real turning point of the Pacific naval war. Until then, the Japanese were superior. At the close of the Solomons, they were not. In these pages the Solomons Campaign is described, the whole of it, not just Guadalcanal. Against this descriptive history I play concepts of war in a narrow sea, making generalizations where possible. "Lessons" are abstracted. I intend to make very explicit the strategy and tactics implicit in these events, and, therefore, the reasons behind them.

Wars are the great auditors of navies, and the U.S. Navy (USN) is no exception. In the Solomons, we made our share of mistakes, but we also learned from them. And we did some things right from the start—enough, at any rate. In the Solomons Campaign, the USN relearned how to fight inshore and at night, something it had forgotten. Leaders were found. The Navy refined its amphibious warfare techniques, developed in the interwar period but never previously tried out on a large scale, and refined its air and surface combat tactics in the light of experience with this particular enemy. The Navy tested much of its equipment, retaining peacetime models which worked, discarding—sometimes with difficulty—those which did not, and developing new ones. Here big ships were big targets. The Navy learned about the enemy, quickly getting disabused of the thought that they were second-class fighters.

Today (1994) the Navy is supposedly giving much lip service to a concept called "From the Sea . . . ," and is supposedly reorienting a more important part of itself toward "littoral warfare." Yet it was unable in 1994 to enforce a total blockade of Haiti, despite weeks in which to prepare for it. Fuel and other contraband were successfully smuggled into Port au Prince as well as other places by a fleet of small coasters which hugged neutral shores and mixed in with the multitude of local fishing boats. The same navy had been totally unable to intercept a freighter bringing North Korean antiship missiles into Iran several years earlier, despite adequate alert. The Navy is cutting Marine strength. It continues to build supercarriers, hoping at the same time to keep a total of twelve. The Navy could profit from rereading more of its own history.

This author is fully aware that he is entering a world where Neptune is god, Mahan his prophet, and the U.S. Navy his only true church. None of what follows is meant to diminish that navy's achievements in any way.

None of what follows is meant to indicate that at least minimal sea control—however obtained—does not remain a sine qua non—an absolutely necessary prerequisite—of successful maritime expeditionary operations. What it does mean is that our Navy's strategic and tactical emphasis ought to shift from the massive semiindependent fast fleet carrier forces to the formerly subsidiary tactical forces, prepared for deft power projection, or force projection, whatever the buzzword of the day is. Both efforts will still go on. It is just that fewer assets will have to be devoted to supercarriers and significantly more to the ships and craft used in lower intensity—probably amphibious—operations. Doctrine, attitudes, and hardware will all have to make this difficult shift.

This should not be taken to mean that the author does not think we still require some number of supercarriers—eight active plus one or two training carriers, perhaps, plus those in the reserve. These would provide cover for the low-intensity operations. They would also keep the carrier art alive to be expanded as needed from the reserves. The remaining monies, however, ought to be diverted to meet the challenges we immediately face. It is in the narrow seas that the smaller ships and craft—kept off the high seas by limitations on sea-keeping ability and range—come into their own. In these waters, high speed, maneuverability, shallow draft, and great firepower or good carrying capacity, are what count. If large ships made large targets—which in narrow waters they do—the reverse is also true, and there can be more of them. Unlike deep-draft ships—restricted to known fairways—the smaller ships and craft are free to go almost wherever they want, whenever they want.

Expeditionary wars are fought mostly with aircraft—shore-based as well as carrier-based—fast attack surface craft (FACs), escorts, small diesel-electric (or air independent) submarines, landing ships and craft, mine warfare ships and craft, missiles, and mines. Two-thousand ton destroyers become capital ships. All are needed in large numbers. Without an inventory of sufficient relevant force with which to effectively counter opposition, the Navy will be irrelevant, again.

Amphibious wars can be improvised, of course, fought with untrained and inexperienced troops, and make-do equipment. This old practice is extremely expensive, and becoming more so. It requires assets better used elsewhere, more time than it should, and is bloodier than it needs to be. But amphibious wars are integral to projecting power from the sea. Should we not be most prepared to fight the most likely—and most immediate—kind of war we face?

The U.S. Navy's obsession with carrier warfare appears to the attentive public to approach that of a collective "Queeg" syndrome, similar to that exhibited by the captain of the fictional World War II destroyer *Caine*. The Navy has several times in the past—the U.S. Civil War and the Second World War come first to mind—been forced into becoming a world-class expert on expeditionary war. But each time the need was over it has dismantled this expertise as rapidly as possible, even in indecent haste. Some at least among the Navy's leadership today do recognize that this specter is once again haunting the Pentagon's corridors, demanding attention. But what is actually taking place there? And in the fleet? Many of us among the public see only mixed signals, and to us it is worrisome.

In both of the two kinds of naval warfare we have sketched—carrier war and amphibious war—leadership mindsets present the bigger long-term problem. What is the Navy's role in waging these two types of combat? Simply put, attaining strategic command of the sea usually calls for the big battle against the enemy's main force, and its capture, scuttle, neutralization, or destruction. Exploiting this command here calls ultimately for an expeditionary force—its preparation, its safe and timely arrival, its insertion against a hostile shore, and its long-term support. It may even require its extraction, under fire. Pursued one at a time, there seems no theoretical conflict at all between these ideas. But pursued simultaneously, these ideas are often in conflict. Guadalcanal (1942) and Saipan (1944) offer good examples of this. In one case (Guadalcanal), long-term command of the sea was held to be the primary goal, even at serious risk to the landed forces. In the other (Saipan), while sea control was admittedly necessary, defense of the landing forces was held to be the overriding aim, even if this allowed the enemy's main force to escape. Both decisions are still argued today.

Today, the first aspect of our Pacific maritime wars—the fast overriding carrier war—no longer has any real purpose. There is for the moment no one super enemy—the Japanese, the Russians—to fight, at that level. In its place, there are a number of smaller essentially land-based opponents, sometimes with fairly large armies but only small navies, if any. Today, however, even small navies must be considered to possess sea mines—moored and bottom—and to understand their use. Think of Iraq (1990–91), where enemy mines played a large role in our decision not to attempt any major amphibious landing off Kuwait, and on which we in any case lost an improvised mine-sweeping helicopter carrier (*Tripoli*) and a cruiser (*Princeton*), both severely damaged. The Iraqis laid at most several thousand mines, with who knows what craft. A lone Iraqi minesweeper kept on laying mines—sixty to eighty a night—until the end. We should expect to see this again.

The U.S. military—including the Navy—apparently sees the Persian Gulf Campaign of 1991 as its model for future operations. That would be nice, indeed. But there the U.S. had an exceptionally complete, preplanned shore infrastructure—airfields, roads, terminals, ports—already in place. Even so, it took us six months to get ready to eject the Iraqis from Kuwait.

It is especially worth noting that in the Persian Gulf adventure the Navy's two on-scene carriers really earned their pay in the first few days. At that time, they and a brigade of Marines provided the only real immediate obstacle to Iraq's seizure of all of Arabia. Once the Air Force and Army could be brought in to shore bases—behind the carriers and Marines—the carriers became just extras to the affair. The Navy's real contribution then became the maintenance and protection of the sea lanes over which the other services came. Once moving, Desert Shield became the overwhelming Desert Sword. That obviously very desirable situation, however, is not likely to be repeated. The need almost certainly will be. The Solomons provides us with—in my opinion—a better model of what the U.S. is likely to face in the future.

NUTS AND BOLTS

Almost no historian writing today about World War II can claim to be writing original research totally out of his own head. Too many others have preceded us. The major research has been done, the facts have been laid out, and some, at least, of the acceptable conclusions set forth. This book, too, draws extensively (and appreciatively) on these earlier authors. This I freely acknowledge.

But this book goes further, with an analysis of what was done or not done in the Solomons, and where possible why, all within a conceptual framework called "war in a narrow sea." This frame was first set out in detail in my *Narrow Seas, Small Navies, and Fat Merchantmen* (New York: Praeger, 1990). A lot of the operational problems thereby became clearer, reinforcing the governing concepts of such warfare, and producing ideas for the future.

This book does not pretend to be an exhaustive history of the Solomons Campaign. There are several of these already. Here many things—repetitive or peripheral—have been left out. The book does include enough, I think, to give the reader an understanding of the thrust of the campaign, and enough detail to give a fair taste of what went on in these hectic, dangerous days, as well as a coherent narrative of events.

Before anyone writes me a letter explaining that—technically speaking—expeditionary war and amphibious war are not exactly the same thing, let me add a note. The amphibious aspect is indeed a lesser included aspect of the expedition. But to the outsider they seem loosely the same thing, and are used almost interchangeably all through the book.

Few sources agree exactly as to numbers. Most early sources depend for Japanese figures on U.S. intelligence estimates, and they are just that, estimates. Later figures integrate Japanese sources and can be different. Where there has been a choice, I have usually used the latter. Also, there are chapter endnotes, and an extensive bibliography.

All ranks are USN or USNR unless otherwise specified. They are those carried at the time. Those in open text are spelled out, those in parentheses are abbreviated in service fashion. The photographs are all courtesy of the U.S. Naval Institute at Annapolis, Maryland. No matter what, any errors of fact, analysis, or conclusion this book may contain must be mine and mine alone.

Most readers who are quite familiar with the story of the Solomons Campaign know what happened, but not necessarily why. Many here should find themselves in the position of the would-be poet who suddenly found that he had been speaking prose all his life, without being aware of it. Let us have a good look.

Pacific
Turning Point

1

Prologue

By August 1942, Americans were fighting desperate, bloody battles in a far-off, heretofore unknown to us chain of islands in the South Pacific—the Solomons. For a balanced view of how this came to be, let me explain.

Few people in today's America can have any real idea of how insular and disarmed—both mentally and otherwise—the United States had been only two years earlier. The business of America was then still business, and people were most concerned with recovery from the Great Depression. Disillusion with the results of the United States' first foray on the world scene—World War I—ran strong. The America First movement was a real one, a grass roots cry to keep the United States out of the conflict increasingly being waged around us. Out in the jungles and at sea, the Australians, New Zealanders, and British knew why they were there—they were defending their corner of the British Empire, or taking back their own. The United States had even been in the process of pulling out of the Philippines up north, and were turning them over to their people. So what brought Americans to the Solomons?

THE ENEMY

Japan's World War II strategic plans saw Tokyo as the ultimate leader of a so-called Greater East Asia Co-Prosperity Sphere. This integral economic unit was to include Burma, Malaya, Thailand (Siam, already an ally), Indochina, Indonesia, China (already partially overrun), and the Philippines. Southeast Asia would give Japan Malayan tin and rubber, Borneo's mercury, Indochinese and Burmese rice, Indonesian oil, and Philippine sugar. Bauxite from the Indies would give Tokyo a whole new aluminum industry. To all this, Japan would contribute management and the industrial base. Particularly, Tokyo wanted control of Malaya's rubber and tin, Indochina's rice, and Indonesia's oil. They only wanted the United States out of the Philippines.

As far as the Imperial Japanese Navy (IJN) was concerned, the oil fuel situation was the governing one. In 1940, Japan was producing domestically about 400,000 tons a year. At the same time, the country was consuming five million tons a year. The Netherland's East Indies that year alone produced some eight million tons, 160 percent of Tokyo's total needs. But the Allied oil embargo of July 1941 cut off East Indian oil, as well as the oil purchased from the U.S. and Britain.

By the fall of 1941, Japan's total national oil reserves amounted to seven million tons. Of this, the IJN had 3.6 million. Two years earlier the reserve had been 8.5 million. The IJN was using up 12,000 tons of fuel a day, or 4.4 million tons a year. War with the Allies could be expected to markedly increase this rate. If the IJN did not move soon, it would be unable to fight at all. As it was, in the war's first days, the IJN used up a four months' supply of fuel.[1]

By 1940 and 1941, Japan's master plans were admittedly logical and well thought out. These plans were divided into three phases, the first of which—the military ones—were firmer than the last.

Phase I had been executed with great efficiency, and aided by not a little luck. It was itself divided into three stages. Phase I's stage one included the occupation of Thailand and the landings in Malaya, the Philippines, and North Borneo. Not until the first week of November 1941 had the attack on the U.S. fleet at Pearl Harbor been officially incorporated into the plan, to neutralize the only real possible threat to Tokyo's dreams of empire. Stage two entailed the destruction of Allied air strength and landings in Dutch Borneo, Celebes, and other islands including southern Sumatra, culminating on Java, the strategic key to the Indies. Stage three was to be one of stabilization, mopping up, reestablishing order, reopening trade, and especially, getting access to Indonesian oil.

Phase II was described as the consolidation and strengthening of the perimeter thus gained. Trade patterns were to be reoriented with Japan as the center.

Phase III called for Japan to assume the strategic defensive, exploit its gains, and wait the rest of the world out inside a fortified Co-Prosperity Sphere. Once the United States saw the cost of running the Japanese out, its will to fight was expected to disappear. Had Tokyo been allowed to stick to this plan, it would have been very difficult to halt, much less reverse.[2]

THE FIRST PHASE

In Phase I, Japan, already entangled in the China tar baby, took on three major new enemies: the United States, the Dutch, and the British. Its own estimates located some 70,000 troops in Malaya, 42,000 in the Philippines, 85,000 in the Indies, and 35,000 in Burma. As most of these forces were made up of "colonials," they were with some justice regarded as inferior. They were supported by only inadequate numbers of mainly outdated aircraft. There was a British task force at Singapore, and a small Dutch colonial fleet in the Indies.

There was also the matter of the U.S. Navy (USN), which overall outnumbered the Imperial Japanese Navy (IJN) by four to three in modern ships. The USN was formed into a token Asiatic Fleet, based in Manila; a larger Atlantic Fleet; and the main or Pacific Fleet. The latter was based at Pearl Harbor and had been for several years, to help keep things damped down along the Pacific rim.

Against all this, the Japanese threw eleven army divisions and special units, up to 200,000 men. Japan committed 7,100 aircraft. It employed its entire fleet. It worked on interior lines, and it had the initiative. The Allies were always out of position and too late. Only a massive accumulation of land-based airpower assembled in advance could have staved off defeat. The hard-pressed British could not spare it, the Dutch did not have it, the Americans were still not ready. Then the Japanese became victims of a cruel fate. Tokyo sent Washington a war message. Due to arrive before any further military action was taken, the message was held up by the clumsy deciphering of the Washington embassy staff. What followed was "a day that would live in infamy," effectively mobilizing the American people in a way nothing else could have.

Pearl Harbor

During the first week of December 1941, a Japanese force of six fast fleet aircraft carriers (*Akagi* (flag) and *Kaga; Shokaku* and *Zuikaku; Hiryu* and *Soryu*) steamed east through the storms, fog, and mist of the North Pacific. It was headed for the United States' Pacific Fleet, then based at Pearl Harbor, on Oahu in Hawaii. Early on the seventh, it altered course to due south, reaching a point 275 miles north of Pearl Harbor. There it launched a strike of torpedo bombers, high-level bombers, and dive bombers along with a fighter escort. Just before 0800 on Sunday, December 7, these planes hit Pearl Harbor's "Battleship Row" as well as its Navy and Army airfields. A second strike of 170 planes arrived at 0840, with the same naval targets.

A planned Japanese third strike targeted against Pearl Harbor's fuel tanks and other shoreside facilities was, however, never launched. The IJN's carriers quit while they were ahead, and ran. Destruction of Pearl Harbor's support facilities would have rendered the base useless, and driven the U.S. fleet back to the West Coast, over 2,000 miles to the east. And when the raid was all over and losses could be counted, the United States had received another break it did not really earn. None of its Pacific fleet carriers were in port that morning, so not one of the precious carriers was lost. They would soon be put to work.

In all, the Japanese left behind eighteen U.S. ships either sunk or badly damaged, including four battleships on the bottom and four others no longer combat worthy. A total of 164 U.S. planes were destroyed and another 124 damaged. The Japanese lost only twenty-nine planes and crews. One of the world's two most powerful fleets had been reduced for the moment to that of a minor power. As such it was no longer a threat to Japan's ambitions in East Asia.[3]

Tokyo Harvests The Spoils

In the Philippines, once they had crippled U.S. airpower, the Japanese descended on Luzon. There they made three separate preliminary landings to seize the necessary air strips from which to provide cover for the main landings. These took place at Lingayen (December 21) and Lamon Bay (December 24). As Homer Lea pointed out long ago, that left the Americans no choice but to evacuate Manila, the base of their Asiatic Fleet. This was done by New Year's Eve. All of the fleet's major combatants got away, as did 200,000 tons of Allied merchant shipping.

Next came Mindanao—to the south of Luzon—where there was a large population of Japanese workers. Davao in the south of the island—a useful base for operations against North Borneo—had been captured on December 20, the Japanese landing having been covered by two light carriers and three cruisers. A seaplane base was set up at once.

Back on Luzon, the Americans fell back on the Bataan Peninsula, west of Manila. This fell on April 8, 1942. Corregidor, off its southern tip, fell May 6, and the remainder of the Philippines were mopped up. For the average American of the time, this was the greatest surrender in U.S. history. This is what brought the United States to the Solomons.

Meanwhile, the Japanese conquest of the East Indies, which began on December 17 with the landing on Borneo, ended on March 8 with the surrender of Java. On January 23, the Japanese had seized the great natural harbor and Australian administrative center of Rabaul, on New Britain in the Bismarck Archipelago at the top of the Solomon Sea. They immediately began building it up into a major naval and air base. Rabaul was to become the point d'appui of a two-pronged drive further south. One was to cross Papua to seize Port Moresby. The other was to move down the Solomons, the chain of islands which closed the Solomon Sea from the east (See Map 1).

THE FUTURE

What surprised everybody was the speed with which the enemy moved. They were in Tulagi—at the bottom of the Solomons chain—by April.

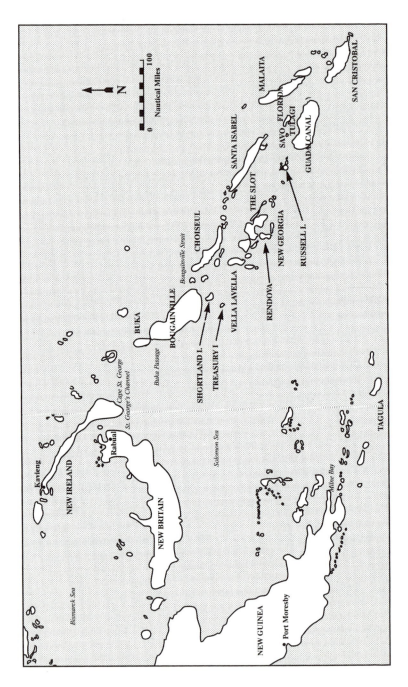

Map 1
Papua, the Bismarcks, and the Solomons

The seizure of Rabaul was seen by Tokyo as a Phase II operation—the consolidation and strengthening of Southeast Asia's defensive lines. At first, the Japanese Navy had hoped to secure participation of the Army in a final jump—an invasion of Australia, which everyone realized would sooner or later be necessary. The Army—overextended already—demurred, preferring for the moment to finish off China. The IJN then fell back on means of neutralizing Australia. Essentially, this meant cutting it off from the United States. Australia—too big and too far away—would therefore for the moment be isolated through the seizure of Port Moresby, in southeastern New Guinea (Papua), and Tulagi, at the southern end of the Solomons. Land-based bombers flying out of these two areas would be able to dominate northern and eastern Australia—the politically significant parts—at will.[4] Even this, the Allies could not allow.

U.S. WAR PLANS

During the previous interwar period (1919–1941), Washington's military staffs did what such staffs are supposed to do in the halcyon days of peace—they planned for war. In these contingency plans, they diplomatically tagged possible opponents with individual colors—black, red, etc. Japan was Orange. These war plans initially dealt with one country at a time.

War Plan Orange envisaged a thrust across the Central Pacific by the U.S. Fleet to relieve the Philippines, meeting and defeating the Japanese fleet along the way. It did not mention the Solomons. When it became possible that the United States would face more than one enemy at a time—the Axis (Germany, Italy, *and* Japan), for instance—these plans were melded into a Rainbow series. Rainbow 5 became the basis of the United States' overall World War II strategy, modified in light of unexpectedly limited resources with an emphasis on "Germany First."[5]

Pacific vs. Atlantic

Washington at this point was faced with a series of not very good choices. Though U.S. ground and air commitments to Europe were in the long run much greater than to the Far East, by mid-1942 nearly a quarter of a million troops had arrived in the Pacific, and the dispatch of two hundred thousand more was seen. Clearly, "Germany First" was a strategic but not yet implemented view. There was never any question of a purely defensive, holding operation in the East. Several diverse factors guaranteed this. There was America's severely wounded national pride. There was the jockeying for position among the three armed services. The Army saw its future in Europe, defeating Germany. The Navy had to have a major role of its own, and the Pacific was the obvious choice.

Admiral Ernest J. King had by now become the United States' Chief of Naval Operations as well as Commander-in-Chief of the U.S. Fleet. Arrogant, brilliant, rude, crude, King successfully bulldozed his way to an Allied agreement that thirty percent of our combined resources be devoted to the war against Japan. This thinly masked a higher allocation of assets to the Pacific from America, becoming in every sense the "Arsenal of Democracy." The U.S. Navy never allocated less than two-thirds of its strength to the Pacific at any point.

Assigned as a result of the disaster at Pearl Harbor, U.S. Admiral Chester W. Nimitz was Commander-in-Chief Pacific (CINCPAC). In many ways the direct antithesis of King, Nimitz was quietly and politely just as able and strong-minded as King, his boss, and seldom got run over in differences with "Main Navy."

The Pacific Fleet was beginning to receive its first major new ships. Carrier *Wasp* arrived from the Atlantic, restoring the total available to four. Fast battleship *North Carolina*, more cruisers and destroyers also joined CINCPAC's flag soon after the Imperial Japanese Navy was halted in the Coral Sea and off Midway.

General Douglas MacArthur, who on President Roosevelt's order had quit the Philippines for Australia before the surrender, was now Supreme Allied Commander Southwest Pacific. In spite of a number of initial clangers in the Philippines, the public saw him as a hero and he would have to be counted in any Pacific strategy. His personal public relations guaranteed that.

CARTWHEEL (Rabaul)

The Bismarck Archipelago strategically dominates Eastern New Guinea (Papua) and the Solomons. It is the hub from which run all roads south. This archipelago essentially is made up of two main islands—New Britain (370 miles by 50 miles) and New Ireland (220 miles by 30 miles). Rabaul sits on the top of the former and Kavieng—its satellite—on the latter. Anyone going north had to pass them, too.

The Japanese seizure of Rabaul was seen by the Allies primarily as the first step in a drive, via the Solomons and New Hebrides, to block any substantial flow of men and arms from the United States to Australia. For Tokyo, Australia had to be too near its newly acquired Indies oil. But the strategic situation was in fact more complicated than that. No matter, the Japanese had to be stopped and steps began to be taken.

Both King and MacArthur had their eyes on Rabaul. On February 18, King proposed to his Army opposite a plan, whereby jumping off from the New Hebrides they could establish advanced bases in the Solomons and on Northeastern New Guinea (Papua) in order to take back the Bismarcks. In June, MacArthur submitted a plan for seizing Rabaul in just three weeks—that is, if he could just have a Marine division and a carrier or two.

Both plans were at least as much concerned with obtaining the largest possible slice of the logistic cake at the expense of the other service as with Pacific strategy. The Navy had so far only a single Marine division, not yet complete or fully trained for amphibious warfare. It was also not about to let any of its carriers get caught in narrow waters within reach of so many Japanese airfields.

MacArthur held an ace, however. Whatever was decided, this was going to be an amphibious operation, obviously a naval matter. But the objectives were almost wholly in SOWESPAC, MacArthur's command. It took the Joint Chiefs of Staff in Washington to settle the issue, and so CARTWHEEL was born.

The drive on Rabaul was divided into three tasks. Nimitz would first take Tulagi; to this end, the dividing line between CINCPAC and SOWESPAC—originally set at 160 degrees east from the equator south—was moved one degree of longitude to the west. Task two was seen as a subsequent advance along the Northern New Guinea coast and up the Solomons. Task three was the ultimate attack on Rabaul itself. These last two tasks fell to MacArthur.[6] The Joint Chiefs would allocate the Navy and Army contributions to each task. In this the Joint Chiefs earned their salt. The problem of command was byzantine, the solution as it worked out a good one.

The Solomons

East of the two major South Pacific islands of New Guinea and Australia, and north of New Zealand, lies a barrier of smaller volcanic and coral islands which extend from the Bismarck Archipelago to New Caledonia. As a chain of potential air and surface force bases, these islands offered Tokyo the attractive possibility of cutting deep into the South Pacific and from there of severing Australia and New Zealand's communications with the U.S. west coast. For much of this route, the barrier was called the Solomons, a 600-mile double chain offering a 300-mile sheltered inside passage. Conversely, the islands provided a ladder by which the Allies might climb north to the enemy bases in the Carolines, bypassing the Gilbert and Marshall Islands. The Philippines lay just west of there. This was not—at first—part of the immediate Allied plan. In a sense, they were forced into it by the enemy as the result of a strategic meeting engagement.

Tokyo was the first to attempt to exploit this strategic island route. As early as January it was in possession of New Britain in the Bismarcks and the Northern Solomons, both then under Australian mandate. There they were busily establishing air and naval bases. In April, Japan moved farther south to Tulagi, a small island in the Southern Solomons, a British colony. This minor move of a pawn represented Japan's high water mark in the South Pacific.

The Japanese had hardly arrived in paradise. Even before one ripe corpse rotted in the jungle, the Solomons stank. The miasma they gave off was a queasy mixture of too lush vegetation, swift to rot, growing on a bed of primeval slime humming with malarial mosquitoes, black with flies, and breeding nameless bacteria. They were hot. They were rich only in mud and coconuts. They were wet from May to October, rainy from November to April, and humid all the time.

The native Melanesians—workers on the copra plantations—were uniformly hostile to the brutal Japanese who treated them badly. The Melanesians—as well as the Australian "coast watchers" who hid out in the Japanese-held Central and Northern Solomons—were to be an important factor in the eventual Allied victory. Fifteen-thousand islanders lived on Guadalcanal alone. More on this as we go.

NOTES

1. Stephen Howarth, *Morning Glory* (London: Hamish Hamilton, 1983), pp. 254, 257.

2. Dan van der Vat, *The Pacific Campaign* (New York: Simon and Schuster, 1991), pp. 120–22.

3. Samuel Eliot Morison, *The Two-Ocean War* (Boston: Little, Brown, 1963), pp. 46–69.

4. *The Landing in the Solomons 7–8 August 1942* (Washington, DC: Naval Historical Center, 1994), pp. 1–4.

5. Edward S. Miller, *War Plan Orange* (Annapolis, MD: Naval Institute, 1991), passim.

6. van der Vat, p. 200.

2

Collision Course

THE U.S. AND ITS ALLIES

The United States' task one—a campaign in the Solomons to shield their tenuous lines of communication to the all-important major bases of Australia and New Zealand by seizing Tulagi—was envisaged by the Allied Combined Chiefs of Staff as early as April 1942. For a time it amounted to little more than an idea. But with the gradual repair of the damage done to the fleet at Pearl Harbor, and with the consolidation of the remnants of the Allied forces left in the South Pacific (SOPAC), and their reinforcement, the project began to appear feasible. It was duly christened WATCHTOWER. At this point, of course, Japan still had the superior fleet, but even the IJN could not be strong everywhere. And any battle in the Solomons would take place on a minor fringe of Tokyo's new empire. If everything went well, the Allies could expect to meet only minor opposition. But surprise would be essential. All other things being equal the enemy could concentrate forces there faster than the Allies could.

Partly as a result of the way intelligence was reported—these reports regularly omitted any reference to the presence of major combatants in or near Solomons waters, considering them to be only transients— it was reasonably believed that IJN forces there consisted almost exclusively of planes, submarines, and small surface craft. At this point, the IJN was known to have seaplane (patrol) bases in the Solomons themselves, at Tulagi now, and at Gizo, Rekata Bay, Kieta, and on Buka Passage. Planes operating out of these bases would keep the enemy well informed of any Allied activity in the area, but otherwise these bases posed no real offensive threat. They could, however, always call up help.

Admiral King back in Main Navy had proposed using Efate (New Hebrides), 300 miles northeast of Noumea as a forward base. U.S. troops were garrisoning Efate before the end of March. A second advanced base was built on Espiritu Santo, at the northern end of the Hebrides. The Allies were thus also positioning themselves for whatever came. By the end of July, there were eight Allied island bases—apart from Australia and New Zealand—ready.[1] All would be needed.

SOPAC (GHORMLEY)

In order to organize what was to become the first major Allied offensive in the Pacific, a new command was created in April. Heading it up was Vice Admiral Robert L. Ghormley, who had recently returned from London, where he had served as special naval observer. He became SOPAC.

Admiral Ghormley departed Washington on the first of May. Passing through Pearl Harbor, he reviewed the situation with Admiral Nimitz (CINCPAC), and satisfied Nimitz as to his plans. Ghormley arrived in New Zealand on the eighth. Japanese seizure of Guadalcanal/Tulagi had markedly increased the need for prompt action on the part of the Allies. The primary element of any amphibious operations—the First Marine Division—had been sent out with a year to get ready. But it was becoming apparent that if the Allies did not act soon the enemy would end up so entrenched that it would be extremely difficult to dislodge him from the area.

Ghormley soon established his headquarters afloat, in USS *Rigel*, at Aukland. He then proceeded to Wellington, where he conferred with the Dominion's civil and military leaders. Subsequently, he was recognized as commander of all Allied land, sea, and air forces in the South

Pacific area, with the exception of those land forces specifically assigned to the defense of New Zealand itself. Ghormley moved forward from Aukland to Noumea (New Caledonia) on May 17, so as to be nearer the coming operational area. Things now began to move.

Ghormley must have been very conscious of his role as the leader of a military coalition, as a politico-military commander. In any case, he was not the most forceful of men. The Navy had already learned that modern warfare called for staffs too large to be totally afloat. But Ghormley allowed himself and his staff to be kept on USS *Argonne* rather than offend the sensibilities of the Free French administration by requisitioning offices ashore. The irritation of cramped spaces added to the multitude of his other worries.[2]

TWO-MILE-LONG TULAGI

Two-mile-long Tulagi lay on the north side of the inside passage (the Slot), just under the belly of larger Florida Island. It was too small for anything other than a seaplane base, but as the seat of the British resident commissioner it held various rudimentary signs of life, including a golf course. The IJN soon put Tulagi's various facilities to use, adding to them. On May 4, U.S. carrier-borne planes bombed the harbor.

Hearing of the Japanese seizure of Tulagi only late on the 3rd, Rear Admiral Frank Jack Fletcher had brought carrier *Yorktown*'s task group to within range, masked by bad weather. *Yorktown* launched twenty-eight dive bombers and twelve torpedo bombers against the enemy landing force, retaining his eighteen fighters as combat air patrol (CAP), to protect the task group. The first strike damaged a destroyer and sank three minesweepers. The second destroyed two seaplanes and damaged some of the shipping. The third sank four landing craft. One American plane was lost and two were forced down.[3] On this basis, Tulagi did not seem too hard a nut to crack.

GUADALCANAL

On July 4, Allied interest in the area jumped an order of magnitude up. The IJN landed a force of marines and civilian laborers on

Guadalcanal, and the fat was in the fire. Guadalcanal lay just south of Tulagi, across the Slot. Several days later, Allied reconnaissance found that what was at least an air strip was being built on the north coast of the larger island, not far from Lunga Point. As land-based planes flying out of Guadalcanal would immediately threaten Allied control of the New Hebrides and New Caledonia area, the Allies decided to take over that island as well as Tulagi. It was estimated then that the Japanese could have Guadalcanal ready to base sixty bombers by August 1, and by the end of the month be able to base a whole air flotilla there.

Ninety-miles long by twenty-miles wide, peanut-shaped Guadalcanal covers some 2,500 square miles. The island is mountainous—some mountains are over 8,000-feet high—and covered with dark green rainforest jungle. Like the rest of the Solomons, this jungle was spotted with patches of light green kunai grass whose tall, saw-toothed blades can cause a nasty cut. Along the northern coast—where the Japanese were building their landing strip—there was a narrow plain where the Australians had planted coconut palms.

ENEMY ORDER OF BATTLE

Estimated IJN strength in the Bismarck-New Guinea-Solomons area was eleven cruisers, thirteen destroyers, fifteen or more submarines, twelve submarine chasers, one seaplane tender (at Rabaul), and fifteen to seventeen troop transports and cargo ships. The best information put Japanese air strength at about 150 planes. Intelligence received up to July 30 indicated that the enemy had 1,850 men in the Tulagi area. The bulk of these forces was concentrated on Tulagi and its appendages Tanambogo and Gavutu, and across on the southern shores of Florida. Most were base staff or aviation personnel, the rest IJN marines.

On Guadalcanal, the enemy was believed to have some 5,275 troops, including a labor unit (900 men). By the time of the U.S. landing, the air strip southeast of Lunga was apparently completed, with a 3,600-foot runway. Another strip at Tetere and possibly one at

Tenaru were already under way. So were all necessary support facilities for a full-scale airfield complex.[4]

NEW CALEDONIA

French New Caledonia was the principal base for what follows. It is a large island 250-miles long, located 900 miles east of Australia and 800 north of New Zealand. In February 1942, concerned with the security of its South Pacific lines of communication, Washington recognized the London-based Free French as responsible for the administration of all French possessions in the Pacific. American troops were sent to defend New Caledonia and it became an early seaplane base. Tender *Tangier's* Catalina PBYs regularly watched the Coral Sea and the Lower Solomons. Before long, however, even before many staff planners became aware of it, Noumea mushroomed into a 20,000-man operating base.

When the United States first occupied the island, it found at Noumea an excellent, spacious anchorage. It offered, however, relatively few port facilities. So fast and totally unexpectedly did NOB Noumea grow that port conditions became chaotic, almost gridlocked. The anchorage became so congested that as many as one hundred ships at a time lay in the roads awaiting discharge or acting as floating storage.

As U.S. officers setting up advanced bases in the South Pacific islands all learned, supply-wise there was just nothing there. Everything they ate, everything they wore, everything used for building had to be brought in from elsewhere. There was no such thing as living off the country there, unless one lived off coconuts alone. The same applied to fuel, ammunition, equipment, and engineering supplies. Knowledge and appreciation of logistics was at this point, in the Navy, rudimentary. "I don't know what the hell this logistics is," Admiral King is supposed to have remarked during the first months of the war, "but I want some of it."

In the entire SOPAC area there were no ports nearer to Tulagi than New Zealand that had the docks, labor, and equipment needed to handle the transshipment of the mass of supplies that would be called for. The nearest deep-water port was Noumea, some 900 miles away.

At the receiving end there were no dock facilities at all, no cranes either. There were even very few good beaches to which to bring supplies by landing craft. Heavy engineering equipment had to be brought ashore before anything was built. That meant manhandling it, requiring tremendous manpower. The trade-off was time. Some balance between manpower and speed always had to be struck, watching out that so large a labor force was not built up that it itself consumed all that it built or brought in.[5]

FIRST MARINE DIVISION

Steady, hard-working, intelligent U.S. Marine Major General Alexander A. Vandegrift was to play a primary—even heroic—shore role in what follows. As commanding general of the newly formed First Marine Division, he was designated to lead any prospective landing party. He had been told on leaving the States that he could expect no combat assignment until sometime in 1943.

The first echelon of the division— one regiment—reached Vandegrift in New Zealand only on June 14. A second was in Samoa as a base defense force. The third was on the high seas not even scheduled to arrive until July 11. None of them was as yet fully trained as a unit in the art and science of the Marines' specialty—amphibious landings on a hostile shore. On June 26, Vandegrift received the official orders for WATCHTOWER from Ghormley. When Ghormley briefed him on the Joint Chiefs' directive, the general was stunned. D-Day was set for August 1. There was no time! As the objective area widened—to include Guadalcanal—Vandegrift's division was reinforced with a number of miscellaneous units, which just added to the chaos.[6]

Still in his role as a military diplomat, on July 7, Ghormley flew to Melbourne (Australia) for a two-day meeting with General Douglas MacArthur, Supreme Commander Southwest Pacific Area. During this difficult visit, agreement for the effective cooperative employment of all available Navy, Army, and Air forces was worked out. Everything was scarce, and reluctantly shared.

MacArthur, who had just previously offered to take Rabaul in three weeks with one assault division, now urged the postponement of WATCHTOWER. Although a much more limited operation, WATCHTOWER in his opinion lacked adequate preparation, training, or logistic support. In any case, we were committing large new resources to the Solomons when they were desperately needed in Papua—his command, of course. King was scathing, roughly dismissing all arguments, as was his wont. But the need for some additional time became clear. The Joint Chiefs therefore agreed to postpone the Solomons landing for one week, until August 7. Transports and cargo ships kept arriving.

On July 16, Admiral Ghormley issued WATCHTOWER's basic operation plan. In it, Ghormley reserved to himself overall command of the operation, coordinating from his headquarters ship at Noumea. This last he neglected to tell Nimitz, and for it the operation would suffer. Personal leadership was to be lacking.

Cooperating friendly forces were covered first. Commander SOWESPAC would provide for the interdiction of enemy air and naval activities west of the one-hundred fifty-ninth meridian, and his submarines would operate off Rabaul. For further insurance, five CINCPAC submarines would patrol off Truk. It was not a lot of help.

Tactical command of Ghormley's own forces was assigned to now Vice Admiral Fletcher, riding in specially formed Task Force 61, flying his flag from *Saratoga*. Task Force 62—virtually autonomous—was the South Pacific Amphibious Force led by Richmond Kelly "Terrible" Turner, a rear admiral, who as Chief of the War Plans Division back at Main Navy had fathered the whole thing.

The forces under his command, Ghormley continued, would seize, occupy, and defend (1) Tulagi and adjacent areas, and (2) the Santa Cruz Islands (specifically Ndeni), for the purpose of denying these areas to the enemy and in preparation for further offensive action. Everything in the Pacific Fleet apart from the older battleships and *Hornet's* Task Force 17 was committed to the Solomons, either under Fletcher or escorting convoys. This gave Fletcher a total of fifty-four American and three Australian combatants, including three carriers, a battleship, and eleven heavy cruisers. There were also six submarines, twenty-three transport and supply ships, and five oilers. Some of these would go to Turner.

Task Force 61 (Rear Admiral Leigh Noyes) was to provide the close carrier support (CAP, strike) for the landings. It was built around *Saratoga, Enterprise,* and *Wasp.* Task Force 62 (Turner) was to make the actual assault, transporting and landing the Marine occupying force and defending the transport convoys against surface attack.

Australian Rear Admiral V.A.C. Crutchley (seconded from the Royal Navy) led the screening group of cruisers and destroyers for Turner. He had two Australian heavy cruisers and one light cruiser, four U.S. heavy cruisers, and nineteen destroyers. On the ground side, Vandegrift now had about 19,000 marines. They were embarked in nineteen transports and would be Turner's responsibility until they were established ashore.[7]

South Pacific Air Forces (Rear Admiral John S. McCain) was to supply aerial surveillance, scouting, and observation and advance bombing of the operational area with its land-based planes and flying boats. Although effectively a third task force, McCain's element remained directly responsible only to SOPAC. On July 26, the assault force assembled south of Fiji, preparatory to holding a rehearsal there. Coming from half a dozen ports across the Pacific, only doctrine and the experiences of peacetime service held them together.

Fletcher called a conference on *Saratoga* the next day, marked mostly by a terrific row between Fletcher and Turner about tactics. Turner was an able tactician, but he had a temper, and he objected strongly to Fletcher's plan to withdraw all the carriers after only two days. Ghormley as their mutual superior officer should have settled this matter, but he was not there. Neither was he present at any of the other rows—almost invariably involving Turner—which brewed up. Ghormley would be missed.

REHEARSAL (JULY 28–31)

The full dress rehearsal of the coming assault, as accurate and complete a simulation as could be provided, was in fact held. The whole force proceeded to Koro Island, in the Fijis, for a two-day exercise. Orders for the approach to Koro, for the preliminary bombardment and bombing, and for the landing of troops were prepared as for the real thing. The rehearsal itself included two complete practice landings. On July 30, the carrier groups joined in, with a full schedule of sorties which began at 0530. Rehearsal did not include the actual landing of supplies, an omission that proved serious later. In the words of one officer, the dress rehearsal "stank." On the twenty-eighth, for instance, the weather was so foul as to endanger the ship's boats and tank lighters, and the exercise had to be cancelled for the day. Strict radio silence had to be kept, preventing practice in air-ground communications, something which also would have helped greatly later.

In spite of this, much was learned. At the close—on the afternoon of the thirty-first—Turner convened a conference of senior officers at which he went over his plans again, in detail. Vandegrift similarly went over his plans. Since the rehearsal had demonstrated that a large percentage of the boats involved would probably fall out for one reason or another, a boat pool plan was worked out. Also learned was the value of the Landing Force Manual. The Marines had spent the years between the wars searching for a specific role for their corps in modern war. In amphibious warfare they had found it. They had spent the 1930s developing the manual and practicing the doctrine inherent in it. They did not have to invent all the answers as they went.[8] So much for the six months to a year to get ready the Marines had been promised when they went out.

SOPAC's admiral was getting a real workout, but as a junior vice admiral he had in the end to take what he got. Nimitz would have mediated, but on the Solomons he basically agreed with King. Somehow, things fell together. WATCHTOWER would be a close-run thing. Most crisis campaigns are.

The U.S. Forces were still relearning—after twenty years of peace—how to actually fight. There had been no amphibious landing since the Spanish-American War, forty years earlier. As is always the case in such situations, there were officers who shone in peace but failed to measure up in war. Lifetime careers had to be wrecked, friendships ruined. These people had to be weeded out. There is some suspicion that there was not enough time for this, either.

Few commanders ever feel that they have sufficient troops and equipment on hand for the tasks they have been given. These officers were no exception. Preparations were so hasty and the forces available so scanty that some officers called this expedition Operation "SHOE-STRING."

What concerned the Allies most—assuming the absence of enemy aircraft carriers—was the major land-plane base complex which the Japanese had established at Rabaul, 675 miles from Guadalcanal, and the new air bases which they were building at Kieta only about 300 miles from Guadalcanal, and on Guadalcanal itself. The thought of an Allied expeditionary force being exposed to attack by large numbers of land-based fighters, bombers, and torpedo planes kept the staffs awake at night. The enemy had the initiative and was on the offensive. Japan's lines of communication and supply were interior. Three of its major bases—Rabaul, Truk, and Kwajalein—were within 1,200 miles of the target area; the United State's own nearest base—Pearl Harbor—was 3,000 miles away. Yet the presence of land-based aircraft only 555 miles from Espiritu Santo was a threat the United States had to parry at once, and did so.

NOTES

1. *The Landing in the Solomons 7–8 August 1942* (Washington, DC: Naval Historical Center, 1944), p. 4.

2. Ibid., pp. 2–3.

3. Dan van der Vat, *The Pacific Campaign* (New York: Simon and Schuster, 1991), p. 173.

4. *Landing in the Solomons*, pp. 4–5.

5. Ronald H. Spector, *Eagle Against the Sun* (New York: Free Press, 1984), p. 208.

6. *Landing in the Solomons*, pp. 2, 9.

7. Ibid., pp. 5–9.

8. Ibid., pp. 21–22.

The Southern Solomons

SHORE- AND TENDER-BASED AIR

Throughout July the aircraft and personnel of Admiral McCain's shore- and tender-based South Pacific Air Forces were assembling at or relocating to ready support airfields in the New Hebrides, New Caledonia, Samoa, the Tongas, and the Fijis. U.S. Navy, Army, and Royal New Zealand Air Force fighters, scouts, long-range patrol planes, and bombers were poising themselves for a week of intensive surveillance of the battle area and its approaches. They had the week before actually entering the Solomons to find out what was going on there. Where possible, jungles had been flattened and the ground hardened for the landing of heavy planes. Where time or terrain did not permit, pierced steel planking (PSP) was sometimes laid. In addition, the ground control environment had to be built up. Communications by which intelligence was sent back and new orders sent down quickly and safely were set up.

To conduct normal surveillance operations and to cover U.S. ships' approach to the objective area, McCain controlled a total of some 290 aircraft. The Navy intended to dominate the air in the Tulagi area, if nothing else. Carriers being in short supply, McCain was given everything that could be scraped up.

Ndeni (Santa Cruz Islands) not being occupied, tender *McFarland* was sent there during the first week of August, to mother five Catalina PBYs. Extensive searches of the operations area and toward enemy bases to the north were laid on. Happily, there was nothing unusual to report. On August 7 (D-Day itself), tender *Mackinac* with nine PBYs was transferred from Espiritu Santo to the Maramasike Estuary on Malaita, a large island just to the east of Florida. They were to provide another, nearer eastern patrol for the coming combat area.[1]

CARRIER-BASED AIR

Saratoga, Enterprise, and *Wasp* together with their ships played a more direct role in the coming events. As they together constituted the air support force, they were ordered by Admiral Fletcher to proceed to the Guadalcanal/Tulagi area to cooperate with Admiral Turner's amphibious force. They were there to provide air CAP and strike, and to make such air searches as were ordered or might seem useful. From this most general directive Admiral Noyes developed a quite precise operation plan, paying attention to minute detail. Noyes' plan listed the time of departure of the various squadrons from the three carriers and their return, their tasks, their ordnance, their fuel, and their communication frequencies.

The three carriers between them mustered twelve squadrons of planes—three of fighters (one each), two of dive bombers (*Wasp* had none), four of scout bombers, and three of torpedo bombers (one each). Especially of note—they were to prove the key to what followed—there was a total in the three squadrons of ninety-nine fighter planes. Navy carrier-borne fighter, bomber, and torpedo aircraft types in this era carried VHF two-way voice radios with a range of about fifty miles. They carried no radar, however, and were not expected to fight at night, a fact which was to have serious impact. The coming campaign was to see the first large-scale American use of naval fighter direction centers. Development of radar coupled with that of VHF voice radio allowed a central agency to allocate fighter strength, vector planes to targets, and shift them as need arose. Fighter direction made a much more efficient use of available aircraft strength.

The three carriers were to operate from an area southwest of Guadalcanal and were to remain available there for forty-eight hours, until the field ashore could be put into use. *Saratoga* (flag)—the guide ship—was to have a center lane, with *Wasp* to the west and south and *Enterprise* to the north and east at distances of 8,000 to 12,000 yards. As primary fighter control ship, *Enterprise* was to furnish the CAP for all three carriers. CAP for the transports and their screens was to come from the air support flights, and was to be directed from cruiser *Chicago* which would have a fighter direction unit provided by *Saratoga* aboard.

Air support flights were to be under the tactical control of two air group commanders, one in the air over Guadalcanal, the other over Tulagi. These two would receive information and requests by voice radio from Commander Amphibious Force (in *McCawley*) or Commander Landing Force (in *Neville*) directly.[2]

ORGANIZATION OF THE LANDING FORCE

The 19,000-man U.S. Marine landing force was divided into two groups: "X" for Guadalcanal under General Vandegrift himself, and "Y" for Tulagi under Brigadier General William H. Rupertus. This matched the landing force's basic organization to the ground and to the relative importance and estimated difficulty of the force's two objectives.

Assembly of these two groups was well under way by the last of June. Ships were arriving in the various assembly ports *administratively* loaded—that is, stowed so as to carry the largest feasible tonnage of men or equipment, with no regard for readiness for combat. They at best were arriving *unit* loaded; that is, elements were loaded on ships together with their own equipment and supplies, but still not ready for combat. Everything had to be offloaded and *combat* reloaded, with men, equipment, and supplies ready to hit a hostile beach, fighting. First needed under these conditions meant last in.

Reloading work had to be carried out under the most difficult conditions. Berthing spaces were few. Facilities even once in were inadequate. There was never enough time. Matters were made worse by the weather—cold and extremely rainy—a "southerly" blowing out of the Antarctic. The rain soaked thousands of cardboard containers, causing them to fall open and spill out their contents. Working parties were chilled and wet.

Ships were loaded on the general principle that each transport would carry one combat team together with all the equipment and supplies needed to put that team ashore and keep it in action for thirty days. For every three combat teams there was loaded a cargo ship with supplies sufficient for thirty additional days. In this way, the Marines were prepared for sixty days action, if necessary, without further support. But nothing other than what was absolutely necessary could be taken.

Transports and supply ships were scheduled to lay off the beach-heads for ninety-six hours. Commanding officers of troops were made responsible for the complete unloading of their ships, working all holds on a twenty-four-hour basis. Basic priorities for landing supplies and material were established. Traffic in beach areas was to be controlled by shore parties, inland traffic by military police.[3]

D-DAY

Everything went off well on August 7, for a time. Surprise was complete. The landings on Guadalcanal were effected in full daylight against slight and scattered opposition, the defenders here withdrawing into the bush. The still incomplete airstrip was occupied at 1600. Tulagi, where the bulk of the Japanese were concentrated and where there was no place to run, took a day's more time and effort. It, too, was more or less secure by the morning of the eighth. But that is just the bottom line. At 061615, August 1942, Admiral Turner's amphibious force assumed approach dispositions for entering the operational area. The formation adopted was a column of squadrons, with Squadron "Y," destined for Tulagi, in the lead. Squadron "X" headed for Guadalcanal, was six miles astern.

Guadalcanal's debarkation area was located 9,000 yards off Beach "Red," between Koli and Lunga Points. At 070650 the traditional signal "land the landing force" was made. The line of departure for the small craft was 5,000 yards off the beach. Meanwhile, across the bay at Tulagi similar arrangements were under way.

U.S. plans contemplated roughly simultaneous dawn landings in the Tulagi area and on Guadalcanal (see Map 2). The debarkation schedule was carefully worked out so as to utilize all the boats and landing craft carried by the transports and cargo ships. Including a number of amphibious tractors, there were about 500 small craft of all types. Bos'ns began calling the boats away. The frictions of war now set in. Some of Squadron "Y's" transports were slow in arriving in its transport area. Boats were late at their rendezvous. Resistance was (on Tulagi) unexpectedly strong. Material piled up on the beaches. Beach-masters waved boats off, or kept them in holding areas (see Map 2).

Although a smaller number of vessels and troops was involved in the Tulagi area, operations there were considerably more complex than on Guadalcanal. On the latter it was merely a matter of pouring first troops and then supplies onto a single beach. At Tulagi, several landings had to be made, necessitating a more elaborate schedule for both landing craft and for fire support. In neither case could things have gone in combat exactly as planned. Unloading, however, had been slowed by an unfortunate combination of reasons. The major part of the time was used up in awaiting orders to close the shore after a beachhead had been secured, ceasing unloading on orders from the beach, getting underway and coming to anchor, maneuvering to avoid the enemy, manning general quarters stations, scattering and recalling ships' boats, and diverting boats to assist in unloading other ships.[4]

FIRST RESPONSE

Rabaul responded to all this with professionalism and speed. A new Japanese Eighth Fleet under Vice Admiral G. Mikawa had just been formed for the drive down the Solomons. On hearing of the landings, Admiral Mikawa took immediate and proper action. An air response could be sent off first, and it was. Even though MacArthur's B-17s struck Rabaul on the seventh, that same day forty-three bombers in two groups escorted by eighteen fighters attacked various targets in the area. The Americans lost twelve and the IJN sixteen planes.

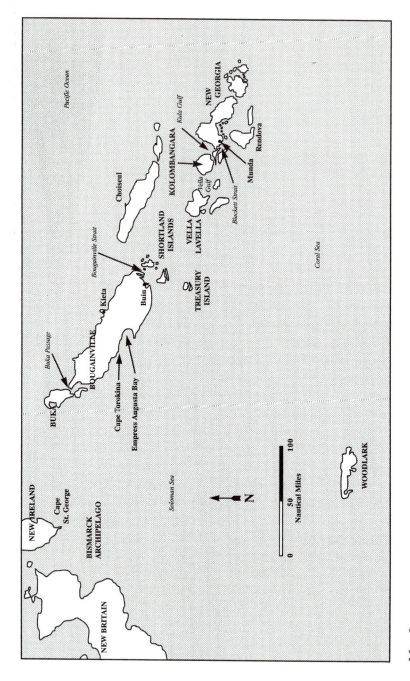

Map 2
Guadalcanal and Tulagi

On the eighth, Mikawa tried torpedo bombing. Twenty-six torpedo planes came in, but only nine went out again. They and a follow-on dive bomber attack were frustrated by USN professionalism. At 1038 Admiral Turner received a dispatch announcing that enemy twin-engine bombers were passing Bougainville, flying southeast. He immediately ordered all ships to move out of the transport areas and assume a cruising formation. By the time the planes appeared, almost precisely at noon, the transport groups and screens were in formation and maneuvering at top speed. The United States' very effective antiaircraft fire and Turner's two 30-degree turns away achieved the rest. The Americans did lose one transport (*George F. Elliott*) and one destroyer (*Jarvis*).

Mikawa's second response was to send six transports of troops to reinforce existing garrisons to the south. These transports were sighted by the USN's submarine *S38* (LCDR H. G. Munson) in the Solomon Sea, about fourteen miles off Cape St. George, shortly before midnight on the eighth. Munson sank one of the transports (*Meiyo Maru*). The rest were called back to base. It was too easy.

Mikawa's next step was a different story. He now decided to take personal command of what surface combatants he could scrape together and attack the invasion force while it was most vulnerable, in the act of putting the troops ashore. Mikawa boarded heavy cruiser *Chokai* (flag), collected four other heavy and two light cruisers plus a single destroyer, and tore south. With this squadron, Mikawa came within an ace of a major rewriting of the battle for the Solomons.[5]

INTELLIGENCE FAILURE

On the afternoon of the eighth, scattered intelligence reporting a possible new threat kept coming in to various staffs. Admiral Turner had received a warning stating that at 1127 a force of two Japanese destroyers, three cruisers, and two gunboats or seaplane tenders had been sighted off the east coast of Bougainville, 300 miles from Guadalcanal. This force was headed south down the Slot at a speed of fifteen knots. This warning had been sent out by Melbourne radio at 1821, but there had been earlier ones. The sighting patrol plane—an

RAAF Hudson—misidentified some of the ships, but this was Mikawa's cruiser force.

The very things that make an officer a good commander at sea—tightly centralized authority, strong personality, iron will—coupled with operations-heavy naval staffs, tend to get intelligence trampled on. Only admirals of truly broad view can really overcome this. We are about to see an example of what I mean.

Admiral McCain's shore- and tender-based South Pacific Air Forces was responsible for the comprehensive surveillance of the Solomon Islands area. Unfortunately, weather over the northern Slot that day was vile, and many areas were only partially covered. That should have alerted Fletcher's own reconnaissance, but it apparently did not. Fletcher's carrier-based air failed totally to sight and track this particular hostile group. Having been bombed, torpedoed, and strafed from the air for two days, the warnings' mention of seaplane tenders must have thrown Turner off. Shortly before midnight he sent Admiral McCain a message, alerting him that this enemy force might intend operating torpedo planes out of Rekata Bay (Santa Isabel Island), some 150 miles north up the Slot from Savo Island, the next day. Turner recommended that McCain strike Rekata the next morning early. Turner saw no other threat. He did not expect Mikawa to come through that night.[6] Fletcher was in overall command, but neither, apparently, did he. From their actions, what they were both expecting was another air attack before noon the next day.

FLETCHER PULLS OUT

At 1807 on the eighth, however, Admiral Fletcher dispatched Admiral Ghormley at Noumea, recommending immediate withdrawal of the air support group. He stated that carrier fighter strength had been reduced to seventy-eight planes (true) and that fuel for the carriers was running low (not true). Turner's force had endured a number of air attacks, and there was an unexpectedly large number of enemy torpedo planes and bombers in the vicinity. There was an inherent danger in remaining in such a limited area, tied to the beach. Ghormley allowed himself to approve the recommendation. The carriers had already begun retiring to the south. Fletcher went with them.

Information of this devastating decision precipitated a conference just before midnight aboard Admiral Turner's flagship. Attending aboard *McCauley* were Admiral Crutchley and General Vandegrift. In view of the carriers' withdrawal and the fact that the airfield ashore was not yet ready to use, the amphibious force was now dangerously exposed to attack from the air. It was therefore decided to move the still only partially unloaded ships out at 0600 the next day. In the event, this departure was extended to 0630, at which time the transports did begin to pull out. The last, however, did not actually leave until after noon. Meanwhile, the ships continued to land supplies, both at Guadalcanal and Tulagi. Supplies were particularly needed in the latter area because it had been necessary to land the Second Marines (the reserve) to reinforce depleted forces there. In any case, U.S. ships departed without having unloaded all of their cargo. On at least one ship (*Betelgeuse*), an estimated fifty percent remained on board. Some men and boats were also unavoidably left behind. The 7,500 Marines now in the Tulagi area were left with 39,000 rations, 3,000,000 rounds of .30 caliber ammunition, and 30,000 rounds of .45 caliber. The 10,900 Marines in the Guadalcanal area were left 567,000 rations, 6,000,000 rounds of .30 caliber, and 6,000,000 rounds of .45 caliber.[7] The Japanese had left large stocks of rice, which was eaten for days, and in the beginning, trucks were fuelled on captured gas.

Answers to the seemingly inevitable logistic problems had, however, begun to be worked out, largely through trial and error. The first of these was boat pools. The first pool had been initiated in the Guadalcanal/Tulagi plans. It turned out to be just the thing. These cox'ns earned their salt. Assault transports and supply ships carried their own tank lighters and ship's boats, of course, but the ships moved in and out, anchored and shifted berth, and sometimes were sunk. Boats got lost. They were always in short supply. So once an actual assault was over, these craft were based and maintained in a single shore pool and allocated by a single office.

Another answer was the formation of Construction Battalions (CBs). The famous Seebees were recruited directly from experienced construction personnel, with commissions and warrants granted as appropriate. They were given the best equipment and some basic military training. They worked in remote combat areas, often under atrocious conditions and under fire, as well as in the rear echelons. They were worth many times their number.

By midnight August 8–9, the beachheads and air strip on Guadalcanal and the whole Tulagi area were secure. Tulagi had cost the United States 248 casualties. Japanese casualties were virtually 100 percent, or about 1,500. Guadalcanal had cost the United States few casualties. It had a fairly firm hold on the northern shore from Kokum to Koli Point. Ship losses had been slight: one transport and one destroyer sunk. Aircraft losses—twenty-one out of ninety-nine fighters on the three carriers—were considerable but not excessive.

Ashore on both islands, with few tools and no barbed wire, Vandegrift's Marines were busy establishing themselves for the long haul. In the Tulagi area, Rupertus had occupied the whole complex of islands, taking over the seaplane base, siting antiaircraft artillery, and digging in for base defense. On Guadalcanal, Vandegrift himself had decided he had troops enough only to occupy a nine-mile by three-mile beachhead, centered on the not yet operational air strip. He also prepared his perimeter for defense. Commitment of the Second Marines to Tulagi had soaked up Vandegrift's reserve. The planned parallel full-scale occupation of Ndeni therefore had to be postponed.

Tulagi's stubborn and unexpectedly bitter resistance had prevented the one-day completion of the U.S. landing operation, as had been planned. Furthermore, the unloading of transports and cargo ships had been considerably delayed by Japanese air action. The delays these caused were to have a serious impact on events.

Two tactical developments had arisen the evening of the eighth which should have indicated that the situation was reaching a crisis. The significance of one—the unexpectedly early withdrawal of the three carriers—was appreciated at once. The importance of the other—reports of the approach of a significant enemy surface force—does not appear to have been realized at all. Then, shortly after midnight, the Battle of Savo Island was fought, probably the worst defeat ever inflicted on the U.S. Navy in a straightforward fight.

NOTES

1. *The Landing in the Solomons 7–8 August 1942* (Washington, DC: Naval Historical Center, 1994), pp. 13–17.

2. Ibid., pp. 6–7, 17–19.

3. Ibid., pp. 9–13, 19–21.

4. Ibid., pp. 38–54.

5. Ibid., pp. 54–63, 74–81.

6. Ibid., p. 89.

7. *The Battles of Savo Island 9 August 1942 and the Eastern Solomons 23–25 August 1942* (Washington, DC: Naval Historical Center, 1994), pp. 43–44.

Tokyo Reacts

SAVO ISLAND (AUGUST 8–9)

As the Japanese Eighth Fleet's Admiral Mikawa raced south down the Slot, U.S. Admiral Turner's amphibious force lay off the beachheads building up ashore as fast as they could. Responsibility for protecting Turner's transports lay with Admiral Crutchley and his Australian and American cruiser and destroyer force. The threat in general came from the north. Right at the northern end of what was to become Ironbottom Sound—between Guadalcanal and Tulagi—lay a small island called Savo. Savo was about to put its name on the worst defeat the U.S. Navy suffered in 130 years.

Geography prompted Crutchley to divide his force. Determined to make use of Savo to help block off the sound, he placed part of his ships (Northern Force, heavy cruisers *Vincennes, Astoria,* and *Quincy,* screened by destroyers *Helm* and *Wilson*) on one side of it, and a smaller one (Southern Force, heavy cruiser *Chicago* together with Australian *Canberra,* screened by destroyers *Patterson* and *Bagley*) on the other. Two more destroyers (*Ralph Talbot* and *Blue*) were pushed out beyond Savo to act as radar guard and ASW patrol. A third part (Eastern Force, light cruiser *San Juan* and Australian *Hobart*) was assigned to provide close-in protection to the transport area itself.

One hour after receiving news of the U.S. landing at Tulagi, the IJN's Admiral Mikawa in Rabaul had begun collecting a pickup force of five heavy cruisers—*Chokai* (flag), *Aoba, Kako, Kinugasa,* and *Furutaka*—two light cruisers—*Tenryu* and *Yubari*—and even one destroyer—*Yunagi.* Coming from Kavieng as well as Rabaul, the ships rendezvoused in St. George's Channel around 1900 on the seventh and headed south. Mikawa himself led them.

Mikawa's battle plan—perforce a simple one, sent by blinker light to each ship as they went—was to enter the sound between Guadalcanal and Florida in single column during the small hours of the ninth. There he would sink or drive off the Allied screen guarding the still unloading expeditionary force, shoot up the transports, and retire. Night fighting was an IJN specialty, and the risks of American air attacks were considered slight.[1]

Just counting cruisers, it would be Mikawa's seven versus Crutchley's seven (an eighth—Crutchley's heavy cruiser *Australia*—was not that night in the line). But using surprise and speed, Mikawa's plan was a good one. The chances of detection during his approach, however, amounted almost to a certainty. Mikawa had to steam in full daylight down the Central Solomons' Slot before night gave him cover. But once again, he who dared, won.

INTELLIGENCE

Code breakers and radio traffic analysts in Melbourne, Pearl Harbor, and Washington were providing SOPAC with detailed and accurate information on Tokyo's movements and plans. The Allies had broken JN25, the naval code. Indications of major enemy activity in the Solomons were plentiful, if sometimes oblique. There were, however, also other sources.

U.S. submarine *S38* (LCDR Munson) on patrol in St. George's Channel—between New Britain and New Ireland—sighted Mikawa the evening of August 7. Munson's report reached Turner's force at 080738, early the next morning. An RAAF PBO Hudson sighted Mikawa heading down the Bougainville coast about 340 air miles from Tulagi, on the morning of August 8, at 1027. It immediately radioed a warning that was common knowledge throughout the Allied fleet by that afternoon. Even Mikawa's *Chokai* picked the warning message up. A little more than half an hour later—at 1100—a second RAAF Hudson sighted Mikawa, as he temporarily reversed course to gain time to think things over.

Admiral Turner, as we have seen, controlled no air of his own. He did consider two courses of action. One was to send surface forces out that night to intercept Mikawa. That he dismissed, as it would have left the transports naked to attack. The other was to wait until the transports had pulled out as scheduled now for the next morning, then go after Mikawa. This he held in abeyance pending events. But hard intelligence was slow in reaching Turner. Intelligence coordination was bad. Communications between MacArthur's SOWESPAC, Ghormley's SOPAC, and Turner's command were poor. To top it all off, that bad weather up north apparently kept McCain's long-range surveillance from sighting anything more. Yet even several of the American cruisers (*Astoria, Quincy, Vincennes*) had picked up scraps of the picture.[2]

PRELIMINARY MOVES

Late on the evening of the eighth, a Japanese catapult plane—clearly identifiable by its floats as coming from a cruiser—was sighted by the Americans over Savo. Turner was not told, even when the first scout was joined by a second. Midnight came and went. There was no moon on the night of 8–9 August, and low-hanging clouds, moved by a 4-knot breeze from the northeast, drifted across the sky. Occasional thundershowers swept across the otherwise calm sea. Mist and rain hung heavily about Savo, and visibility in that direction was especially bad. Planes continued to fly over at intervals during the next hour and a half. *Quincy, Astoria,* and *Canberra* all heard them. But General Quarters was not sounded, nor—at least, so it seems—was any warning broadcast to other ships. Neither of the radar guard—*Ralph Talbot* or *Blue*—picked up the approaching Mikawa on their scopes. No one has ever established why. Technically, they should have.

THE ENGAGEMENT

Then about 0145, around Savo, several things happened in short order. First, enemy ships appeared without warning around the southern corner of Savo. No more than half an hour later they ceased fire and passed back out the other side of Savo. In that short interval they crossed ahead of our Southern Force, putting *Canberra* completely out of action in the first minute or two and damaging *Chicago*. They then crossed astern of our Northern Force, battering our cruisers so badly that all three sank—*Vincennes* and *Quincy* within an hour.

The action opened with two almost simultaneous events—contact by Southern Force with the enemy surface force, and the dropping of flares by those float planes over Guadalcanal's transport area. Mikawa in *Chokai* led his ships in single column behind her. *Canberra's* lookouts sighted her as a strange ship dead ahead. Destroyer *Patterson* sounded a general alarm by radio. Two torpedoes and twenty-four 8-inch shells landed on *Canberra*. *Chicago* saw flashes and flares ahead. By 0149, *Canberra* was dead in the water and burning. *Chicago* had her bow blown off by a torpedo.

Mikawa was already giving serious attention to Northern Force, located now ahead of him as he swung north around the east of Savo. At 0148 *Chokai*—still leading—fired a salvo of four torpedoes as his other ships opened fire, at ten thousand yards, with their guns. *Astoria*—last in line—opened fire on *Chokai*. The latter returned the fire, setting *Astoria* ablaze and lighting up the scene for the Japanese gunners. *Chokai* took a few hits but fought on. *Astoria* became her own funeral pyre.

Next up the line for the Japanese cruisers was *Quincy*, which was pounded to pieces from both sides of her. Although soon on fire, she managed to get off more rounds than any other Allied ship that night. Towards the end, she was using ranges of two thousand yards.

Mikawa's next and last target was *Vincennes*, soon dead in the water, on fire. *Vincennes* and *Quincy* were gone before 0300. *Canberra* had to be sunk the next morning, after the crew was taken off. *Astoria* sank at noon in spite of all attempts to save her. Ironbottom Sound was acquiring its name.

Mikawa then did a most remarkable thing. He had effectively eliminated almost all the Allied ships that stood between him and the frantically unloading transports. He knew it was the transports he was after; their destruction would put an end to the American attempt to seize the Tulagi area. In the confusion of the night, his ships, though only lightly damaged if at all, had lost their cohesion. But he could have now taken the few minutes he would have needed to rally them. Instead, he simply completed his circle of Savo and headed back north. The transport area—where the vessels were now preparing to leave, anyway—was never touched.

The Allied cruisers and destroyers had therefore—at great cost—done their job. Their sacrifice had saved the fat, slow, vulnerable transports.[3] A consolation prize was claimed by submarine *S44* (LCDR John R. Moore). On the tenth, as Mikawa was steaming back to port, *S44* put four torpedoes into heavy cruiser *Kako*. She sank within five minutes.

If the truth be told, the Allies at Tulagi were not pacing themselves. Most of the officers and men had been on their feet, working or at general quarters since before dawn on the seventh. The whole force was exhausted and groggy from lack of sleep. Bravery was the norm, but as the Japanese were showing, that was not enough. Thinking on U.S. ships was not clear, at any level. In situations like this, more realistic extended-term watch conditions had to be set.

ADMIRAL CRUTCHLEY

Rear Admiral Victor Alexander Charles Crutchley was the personification of the senior Royal Navy officer. Promoted rear admiral in June, the Briton was new to the Pacific and to his role as rear admiral commanding the Australian squadron, having taken up the post only two months before. As officer in tactical command of the screening and fire support group, Crutchley had Turner's complete confidence. But Crutchley had never met his American captains, and had barely had time to make himself known to his own. He had never commanded a squadron in action.

Among other things, Savo clearly brings out the difficulties of mixed commands. When Turner was informed of Fletcher's decision to pull out, he called a conference on board his *McCawley*, to include both Crutchley and Vandegrift, to work out the implications of it. Crutchley came, riding *Australia*. When in the midwatch Mikawa struck, Crutchley was still gone. Admiral Crutchley was therefore not present on the Savo line during the fight. Neither was *Australia*.

Admiral Crutchley correctly, I think, did not attempt to rejoin his force once the shooting started, but assumed a patrol line of his own behind it. He saw nothing, and from there he sent messages in a cypher not generally used. Able to obtain only the most fragmentary information about what was going on, at 0545 Crutchley was reduced to ordering the escort forces to prepare to defend the transport area.[4]

Aside from defective command and control, there were other technical errors. There had generally been communications deficiencies, faulty damage control, poor fire-fighting, and then above all unreadiness for battle. All were addressed, now, grimly. While in an untested fleet mistakes are probably inevitable, there was much to learn. Savo was a shock.

SLUGGING IT OUT

The U.S.'s recent experience in the Philippines was fresh in the minds of many of the Marines left in the Tulagi area once the Navy pulled out. In the event of war with Japan, U.S. plans (called "Orange," then Rainbow 5) had called for the Army to defend the islands as best it could, falling back into Bataan if necessary. The Army was to hold out there for an estimated three to four months until the Pacific Fleet could fight its way across the Pacific and relieve them. Relief never came.

The 10,900 Marines now on Guadalcanal thought it possible that they were about to relive the Philippine experience. They found themselves alone, with very little food, heavy equipment, or ammunition ashore. They were cut off by an enemy who apparently controlled sea and air, with half rations for five weeks and ammunition for just four days of combat. They had no radar, heavy guns, planes, or prospects of relief. They had to put up with high-level bombing from beyond the range of their light antiaircraft guns, and bombardment from Japanese ships out of range of their own light artillery.

In fact, Admiral Fletcher, having pulled back southeast for twelve hours without yet receiving permission from Ghormley, had reversed course on hearing of the massacre at Savo. Fletcher's planes could still catch Mikawa, withdrawing up the Slot. Two and a half hours later, when Ghormley's approval of the withdrawal finally arrived, Fletcher put about once more.

Wasp's Captain Forrest Sherman begged for permission to continue back north, if necessary alone. Such permission was refused. Even Japanese headquarters in Rabaul, unaware of just how many Marines had gone ashore, unaware that this was not just a raid, thought that the Allies had given up the whole idea, once the carriers left.

CACTUS (HENDERSON FIELD)

But for the Americans, things soon began to pick up. On the night of August 15, four old U.S. destroyers stripped down and converted into fast transports arrived with aviation supplies for the planes to be based on the Guadalcanal's air strip (CACTUS) once Marine engineers completed it. An amphibious PBY had already tested the strip.

On the twentieth, the first Marine planes—nineteen fighters of VMF-223 and twelve dive bombers of VMSB-232—flown off escort carrier *Long Island* to the south—pulled in. It may be that as few as two of the air group's original pilots left the Canal standing up.

A second delivery of supplies was made the same day. Ground crews were already in place. There were shelters for the planes and fuel dumps in the jungle. Air operations were established in the "Pagoda," the control tower built by the enemy. CACTUS was in business.

Fuel was always in short supply, limiting air operations. C-47 (R4D) transport aircraft brought in supplemental amounts of aviation gas, but each C-47 delivered only sufficient gas to keep twelve fighters over CACTUS for an hour. An airborne CAP was therefore a luxury, the CAP being kept on strip alert, at the end of the runway, ammunitioned, fuelled, pilot in the cockpit, ready to take off.

Despite the fact that an hour's rain turned CACTUS into a marsh, these planes quickly established and grimly held on to local air supremacy by day, forcing the Japanese to reinforce and resupply after dark. Japanese destroyers, small transports, and later barges dashed in at night, dumped their cargoes, and sped back north with such regularity that the Marines began calling them "the Tokyo Express."

The Guadalcanal matter was getting serious. The IJN's Fleet Admiral Isoroku Yamamoto, Commander-in-Chief (C-in-C) Combined Fleet, shifted the fleet to Truk in the Carolines to be nearer the operational theater. Large enough to support the entire Combined Fleet, Truk was 700 miles north of Rabaul.

DARK DAYS

The period following the successful landing in the Lower Solomons on 7–8 August and the severe losses in the night action off Savo was thus one of intense but small-scale activity by both sides. The USN carried out reinforcing operations for the Marines, while IJN surface and air units attacked the small convoys carrying supplies and munitions to the seriously beset troops.

Meanwhile, General Vandegrift on Guadalcanal decided to concentrate on his perimeter defense, built around the air strip. Patrols would be sent to find out where the main Japanese forces on the large island might be. Fighting was deadly. The Japanese Army reduced atrocity to routine, so the Marines were not inclined to take prisoners, even on those few occasions when they could have.

Larger IJN forces continued to come down the Slot from time to time. They gave many a fearful night shooting up the airstrip—or airfields, as CACTUS steadily grew. To protect the field and to put a stop to the Tokyo Express, U.S. naval forces were again and again to challenge the enemy. So many battles were fought, and so many ships of both sides sunk, in the sound between Guadalcanal and Tulagi that Ironbottom Sound stuck for good.

On the U.S. side, the few merchant-type bottoms were becoming fewer almost daily. The U.S. lacked the escorts necessary to protect them. There were no defended bases in the Tulagi area where they could shelter, no open water permitting evasive tactics. Enemy submarines were think and active. The Tulagi run was an expensive one.

The problems of supplying the Marines as they beat off successive Japanese attacks, each bigger than the last, were never ending. McCain's staff worked out how much aviation fuel would be needed for the first two weeks at CACTUS. Then they doubled it to be sure. With great effort, it was put into drums and delivered by destroyer. It ran out in ten days. Meanwhile, backlogs built up back at the bases. At the same time, the Japanese were working to bring powerful reinforcements to Rabaul for a major attack on the newly won Allied footholds in the Solomons. Intelligence kept the Allies aware of the steady accumulation of enemy forces in that strategic center.

HENDERSON FIELD (CACTUS)

The IJN never retook full control of the Solomons or the waters around them once CACTUS was going. They would first have to retake CACTUS and use it themselves, basing there the aircraft required to help mop up U.S. remnants throughout the rest of the Tulagi area. Only then would they be able to pick up the threads of the original campaign south, isolating Australia and New Zealand from the United States.

Once operational, CACTUS kept growing. The Japanese air strip completed, the U.S. enlarged it, and built others to achieve more dispersion, to acquire a reserve field, to base the additional Navy, Army, and even New Zealand aircraft that came to help the Marines out.

The GIs already had their enemies tagged. There was "Washing Machine Willie" (a plane whose engine sounded like one), and "Mayday Charlie" (his engine sounded like it was on its last legs). There was a gun called "Pistol Pete" which shelled CACTUS regularly. Guadalcanal was becoming "the Canal," where a plane called "Louie the Louse" kept you awake at night.

Marine F4F Wildcat fighters and SBD Dauntless dive bombers were in action on August 21, the day after they arrived. They were the first of the Marine, Army, Navy, and RNZAF squadrons that fought from CACTUS—the military's code for what became the Henderson

Field complex. These were the days of the first swirling dogfights between U.S. Grumman F4F Wildcat fighters and the enemy's Mitsubishi A6 Zeros. The Zeros were lighter, longer range, faster, more maneuverable. The Wildcats were stronger, dove faster, had some armor around the pilot and self-sealing fuel tanks (which Zeros did not). In gross oversimplification, once alerted, the heavier American fighters would claw for altitude and a position up sun. They would then plan for one diving pass on the enemy, and keep going until they could climb back over him for another. It was grim work.[5] Early warning was critical.

EASTERN SOLOMONS (AUGUST 23–25)

In a sense, the Battle of the Eastern Solomons toward which all this led was the strategic (major, long range) other half of the tactical (immediate, short range) Battle of Savo. It came two weeks later. In it, the IJN was not aiming directly at transports, but at the SOPAC fleet. Only secondarily did it cover a run of the Tokyo Express.

On the Japanese side, two large fleet carriers (*Shokaku* and *Zuikaku*, escorted by two battleships and three heavy cruisers), were to trail their coasts from east of the Solomons. Rear Admiral Raizo Tanaka now appears on the scene. Covered by the carrier action, he was simultaneously to lead a large reinforcement convoy (light cruiser *Jintsu*, eight destroyers, four destroyer transports, and a large merchantman) from Rabaul down the Slot. The Japanese could not lose. If there actually was a fleet action, they expected to win it. If not, they expected Tanaka to successfully deliver his convoy.

Adding a plum to the rice was a diversionary group—light carrier *Ryujo*, a battleship, cruisers, destroyers, and a seaplane tender, *Chitose*—which was also to operate from east of the Solomons, but closer in. They were to strike CACTUS, pounding it down and attracting attention away from Tanaka. They were at the same time to act as bait for the American carrier groups, luring them away from the Japanese fleet carriers.

On the American side, Admiral Fletcher was again ordered out with his three carriers (*Saratoga, Enterprise,* and *Wasp*). Nimitz sailed *Hor-*

net, his fourth carrier, plus two battleships and supporting forces, from Pearl Harbor, as distant cover. At the critical moment, Fletcher detached *Wasp* and her escorts to the south to refuel, so she played little part in what follows.

On 231040 August 1942, Admiral Fletcher received the first hard indication that the Japanese were moving—a heavily escorted enemy transport force sighted coming down the Slot. Comprising four transports supported by two cruisers and three destroyers (DDs), it was located by long range search planes 250 miles north of Guadalcanal, standing south at an estimated 17 knots. From east of the Solomons, *Saratoga* launched against it, to no end. Some of *Saratoga's* strike—short on fuel—remained overnight at CACTUS, returning the next morning.

On the twenty-fourth, light carrier *Ryujo* duly launched the strike on CACTUS. This was of little note, easily beaten off by Marine fighters. *Ryujo* herself then east of Malaita came under attack in her other assigned role as bait for the American fliers. Planes put up by *Saratoga* and *Enterprise* attacked her at 1620, duly sinking her.

While planes from the two American carriers were thus engaged, their carriers were in turn struck by planes from *Shokaku* and *Zuikaku*. Fletcher's CAP went to work. Battleship *North Carolina* managed to evade the bombs while putting up a volcano of antiaircraft fire. *Enterprise* was soon hit by three bombs. Miracles of improvisation by damage control parties had her more or less operational again within the hour. The enemy pilots then played hide-and-seek in the heavy clouds. They finally withdrew for lack of fuel. Some *Enterprise* planes were forced to land at CACTUS, providing it with a welcome if temporary reinforcement. Others from *Enterprise* crippled seaplane tender *Chitose*. The twenty-fifth was taken up by some ineffectual sparring by both sides, after which they both pulled out.[6]

Eastern Solomons was marked by American communications failures. On the twenty-third, during their approach, the IJN's convoy in the Slot (a feint?) altered course to the northwest at about 1300. This information—based on a PBY contact—was not received by *Saratoga* until around 240100. *Saratoga* had already on the twenty-third launched a useless strike against the lost Japanese.

On the twenty-fourth, a search located the enemy's main force, but the news never got back to Fletcher. He did know where the bait—*Ryujo*—was, and at 1435 he launched against her. The main Japanese force would have been the proper target. It was also, in fact, nearer. Moreover, another kind of communications failure—overloaded VHF voice radio circuits—prevented really satisfactory fighter direction. This last could be and eventually was corrected, by enforcing better radio discipline on the pilots and adding more radio nets.

EVALUATION

So was fought the Battle of the Eastern Solomons, most of which took place on August 24. The "battle" had been less a tremendous clash of arms than a series of skirmishes. Strategically, for the Americans it must be considered a partial failure—over the next few days Admiral Tanaka succeeded in landing large numbers of troops on Guadalcanal.

The first thing that strikes the eye about the Eastern Solomons is the inadequacy of the U.S. reconnaissance effort. Neither shore- nor tender-based air came through when it was really needed. McCain's planes should have tracked the enemy first and best, but did not. When their patrols failed to come up with what was needed, carrier-borne planes should have. They did not. Communications inadequacies only aggravated the situation. Submarines contributed little. They might have filled the reconnaissance gap.

Most pronounced in this battle was the Americans' ability to destroy enemy planes, whether in air combat or by antiaircraft fire. Air losses decided the issue. The USN lost a total of seventeen carrier planes in the confused, hesitant, and inconclusive clash, the IJN several times that. In the end, the IJN—all but stripped of carrier aircraft although their powerful surface force was still largely intact—broke off the fight.

The IJN's loss of *Ryujo*, on the other hand, gave the USN—which saved damaged *Enterprise*—a slight tactical victory. *Chitose* also survived. Tanaka's Guadalcanal reinforcement convoy did not even come under attack until later.

Admirals Ghormley and Fletcher were nearing the end of their time. They had carefully conserved carriers, risking everything else, and yet had hung on to their foothold in the Solomons. But now they had to get more positive results, to "go for broke." Eastern Solomons showed that for this new men were needed.

TANAKA'S CONVOY

Eastern Solomons was not yet really over. Not at all. Samurai Admiral Tanaka—like Admiral Mikawa—was a natural born seagoing fighter. He joined courage with brains, dangerous in an enemy. CACTUS' Marine pilots found Tanaka's convoy on the twenty-fifth. They set the merchantman—a troop transport—on fire, and damaged *Jintsu*. Tanaka hung on. He was tenacious. On the same day, eight B-17s up from Espiritu Santo scored rare direct hits on a destroyer—*Mutsuki*—which sank, and damaged another. That did it. Tanaka was ordered to withdraw his convoy and reorganize it for another run on the twenty-eighth. He pulled back to a Shortlands anchorage and regrouped.

Tanaka's Tokyo Express was sighted before dark on the twenty-eighth, as again it steamed down the Slot. CACTUS dive bombers attacked that evening. One escorting destroyer was sunk and two were damaged. Tanaka turned back. But on the twenty-ninth he landed a part of the original troops and on the thirtieth he landed the rest. On the thirty-first he apparently landed another large lot.[7]

THE EXPRESS

On board the unlovely, four-funnelled *Jintsu* at Truk on August 15, Admiral Tanaka had received an order from Commander Eighth Fleet at far-off Rabaul. This order named Tanaka commander of the Guadalcanal Reinforcement Force. Under him would be Destroyer Divisions 4 and 17 and destroyer-transports (converted old destroyers) 1, 2, 34 and 35. Americans dubbed them the Tokyo Express. They ran nightly. Responsibility for the reinforcement and resupply of the enemy on Guadalcanal during these early days—for the Express—

thus belonged to Tanaka and his Destroyer Squadron 2. Organic to his squadron was light cruiser *Jintsu*, acting as destroyer-leader, and eight destroyers. Originally, there had been ten DDs in the squadron, but here as elsewhere, replacements seldom kept up with losses. *Jintsu* damaged, Tanaka transferred his flag to *Kagero*. His squadron, however, was kept together and as a consequence fought as a finely trained and tuned team. Tanaka kept them top of the line. In a given situation, each knew what the other was apt to do. Tanaka was strengthened from time to time for specific missions, both with cruisers and more DDs, but his squadron was the Express' hard core.[8]

SUCCESS

Maneuver from the sea was not news to the IJN. The Japanese staff in Rabaul planned this time a truly major attack on Guadalcanal, to hit General Vandegrift's perimeter simultaneously from the west, south, and east. Tanaka landed his troops and cargo accordingly, some to the west, some to the east of the Marines, positioning them for the coming all-out ground assault. In any case, the Marines beat them off.

During the night of September 4–5, an Express bringing more men and supplies fought an extra nasty little night action. A PBY patrolling over the island saw gun flashes. These turned out to come from three escorting Japanese destroyers which were at the moment bombarding the shore to mask the landing of the cargoes. The PBY proceeded to drop flares, revealing to the Japanese the presence of destroyer transports *Little* and *Gregory*. The two U.S. ships were sunk.[9]

Toward the end of September, some 200 Marines landed west of the Matanikau River to establish a patrol base. These Marines were attacked by an overwhelming enemy force, pushed back to the beach, and threatened with being overrun. Coast Guard Petty Officer First Class Douglas A. Munro was cox'n of a 36-foot Higgins boat, one of a dozen landing craft assembled to rescue them. Directed by Munro—who gave covering fire from one of his boat's two machine guns—the landing craft succeeded in pulling all of the Marines—including 23 wounded—off. Minutes after getting the last man aboard his boat,

Munro was fatally wounded. He was awarded a Congressional Medal of Honor.

The Problem

The Allies' fundamental problem could at this point be made quite clear. They did not have sufficient sea control to be really secure on land. Neither did the enemy, however, even though some of their equipment and tactics were markedly better suited to the kind of war being fought.

During the day, aircraft from CACTUS now controlled the air and therefore the water around the Canal. But planes of that era were blind at night. At night, therefore, Japanese surface forces (the Tokyo Express) took over, bringing in troops, equipment and supplies and shelling Allied positions.

The Tokyo Express customarily left the Shortlands—its usual marshalling area—each afternoon, its destroyers loaded with up to 1,000 troops. By 1800 or so—a half hour before darkness—the Express would arrive within 200 miles of the Canal. This gave Allied planes perhaps one attempt before dark. But a maneuvering destroyer at speed in open water is hard to hit, and few were.

The Express would arrive at the Canal about midnight and unload its cargo. This was usually covered by a simultaneous nuisance bombing by enemy planes or a shelling of CACTUS by surface forces.

Within two or three hours at most, the enemy DDs would have cleared their decks and pulled back north. By daylight, they were again out of range—beyond 200 miles away—headed for their Shortlands.

The Tokyo Express—not always run by Tanaka, but a continuing fixture until the end—kept Japanese forces ashore on Guadalcanal alive, if sometimes only barely. It provided the base-line support. It contributed to the various build-ups. The Allies usually could not find it, much less stop it.

American ships had radar, but radar was not a lot of help. These early models were crude—SCs. There was always a radar shadow of some land for the enemy to hide in. Frequent very heavy storms or rain showers greatly increased the electronic clutter. The thick tropical nights and vile weather made the Express difficult to spot even by eye.

Admiral King back in Main Navy was furious. The United States had air superiority. How could the enemy get away with this? But a pattern had developed. The Americans could do more or less what they wanted during the day. The night belonged to the IJN. It would take the Allies many months to overcome this.

NOTES

1. *The Battles of Savo Island 9 August 1942 and the Eastern Solomons 23–25 August 1942* (Washington, DC: Naval Historical Center, 1994), pp. 2–4; Bruce Loxton with Chris Coulthard-Clark, *The Shame of Savo* (Annapolis, MD: Naval Institute, 1994), pp. 123–33.

2. *Battles of Savo and the Eastern Solomons*, pp. 1–2, 4–5.

3. Ibid., pp. 5–35.

4. Denis and Peggy Warner, with Sadao Seno, *Disaster in the Pacific* (Annapolis, MD: Naval Institute, 1992), p. 44; *Battles of Savo and the Eastern Solomons,* p. 37.

5. Barrett Tillman, *Wildcat* (Annapolis, MD: Naval Institute, 1990), passim.

6. *Battles of Savo and the Eastern Solomons*, pp. 49–71.

7. Samuel Eliot Morison, *The Two-Ocean War* (Boston: Little, Brown, 1963), pp. 179–82.

8. Tameichi Hara, *Japanese Destroyer Captain* (New York: Ballantine, 1961), passim.

9. Morison, p. 183.

Control of the Sea

WAR IN THE NARROW SEA

In retrospect, there were six recognized major naval engagements, at least ten pitched land battles, and too many bombardments, minor land and sea clashes to list, during the Guadalcanal Campaign. At sea, there was Savo Island (August 8–9), the Eastern Solomons (August 24), Cape Esperance (October 11), Santa Cruz Islands (October 26), Guadalcanal (November 11–15), and Tassafaronga (November 30). The first two we have already dealt with, the last we shall leave for later.

We shall here review the other Guadalcanal-related major naval engagements, tracing major developments in narrow sea tactics and technique as we go. We shall also develop operational patterns for what they tell us about control of these narrow waters.

Eastern Solomons was followed by a six-week hiatus in the war at sea, lasting through September. In this time, the IJN of course kept the pressure on. Skirmishing in the Slot continued every night—bitter, small-scale actions. On the morning of August 31, *Saratoga* was torpedoed (I26, CDR Yokota) and sent home for repair. Tokyo also used this time to attempt to understand the, to them, irrational scale of Washington's reaction to the Solomons affair. In this they were always behind the curve. They never succeeded in gaining the upper hand, although on several occasions they did come close to doing so.

The Japanese failure to capture CACTUS in the Battle of Bloody Ridge (September 12–14) led them to step up deliveries down the Slot, and to step up bombardment of CACTUS. Their efforts were now not to go unchallenged. On the night of October 11, an American cruiser-destroyer force finally advanced to try conclusions with them. In all this, one point stands out very clearly: the strong, continuous interaction between our position on land and that at sea. Without CACTUS—or at least sufficient carrier strength—we could never have controlled Solomons waters, not by day or night. The Allies had to hold CACTUS, and the IJN had to get it back.

REINFORCEMENTS ARRIVE

On September 14, the Seventh Marines left Espiritu Santo to reinforce Vandegrift. Turner himself commanded the convoy, covered by the only two battle-worthy carriers in the Pacific Fleet—*Wasp* and *Hornet*, with their usual surface escort. On the afternoon of the fifteenth, IJN submarine I19 (LCDR T. Kinashi) caught *Wasp* in her sights. I19 fired four torpedoes. Two struck *Wasp*. The third hit battleship *North Carolina*, and the fourth tore the bow off destroyer *O'Brien*. The latter two U.S. ships were escorting *Hornet*, a good six miles farther away from I19 than *Wasp*. *Wasp* was abandoned an hour later and had to be sunk by the Americans after dark. *North Carolina* patched herself up and proceeded to Pearl Harbor for repair. *O'Brien* finally broke in two on the way home for repair.

Turner now coolly decided that, having come so far, he had no choice but to press on, in spite of all. He deservedly got away with it. Turner's convoy continued north. The four thousand fresh Marines went ashore at dawn on the eighteenth at Lunga Point, as if on maneuvers. USN destroyers covered the landing by pounding Japanese coastal positions on either side of the perimeter. CACTUS also flew cover.

On October 9, Turner put to sea with the first U.S. Army troops for Guadalcanal, three thousand men of the Americal Division. The two transports and eight destroyers of the convoy were this time covered at a distance by three task groups, everything SOPAC had.

NAVAL FORCES SOPAC

Saratoga and *North Carolina* home for repairs, *Wasp* gone, Nimitz's Pacific Fleet was now down to one operable carrier (*Hornet*) and one newly arrived battleship (*Washington*). SOPAC got them both. Nimitz's head was on the block, too. Still, these plus two heavy and two light cruisers, destroyers, and other escorts were all there were.

SOPAC's major assets were organized into three task forces—one built around *Hornet* and her escorts; one, *Washington* and escorts; and one around the four cruisers. All three came north escorting Turner's latest convoy.

The cruiser-destroyer force was formed into Task Group 64 and commanded by Rear Admiral Norman Scott. Scott was determined to gain control of Solomons waters, mastering night action by surface ships. His orders were to shut down the Tokyo Express, or at least to disrupt it. On October 11, Scott heard from air reconnaissance that a large Japanese force was approaching down the Slot. He raced north to meet it. Scott's hoped-for encounter took place northwest of Savo and northeast of Cape Esperance, a promontory of Guadalcanal after which the ensuing battle was named.

CAPE ESPERANCE (OCTOBER 11)

Two Japanese forces were active in the Slot that night, one to bring down troops and supplies, the other—three heavy cruisers and eight destroyers—to cover the first and to shell the Marines while they were at it. This had by now become the typical IJN arrangement of forces. It also confused the American intelligence picture.

Catapult float planes from USN cruisers as well as radar picked up two separate Japanese forces all right, but it was not at first possible to tell which was which. The cruisers could have led the way into the sound, or the convoy might have gone ahead, leaving the cruisers northwest of Savo. Scott positioned himself between the two. He conformed with previous practice in adopting a "line of battle" formation for the coming fight. This was the expected single column, but this time the DDs were not to be just scouts in the van and guards in the rear. They were actually integrated tightly in the line, still at the head and rear, with his four cruisers in the center.

The Engagement

Scott's flagship—heavy cruiser *San Francisco*—did not light off her old SC radar for fear of Japanese detectors. Light cruiser *Helena* carried the latest SG model and she reported a large target to the west. Light cruiser *Boise* in a garbled message seemed to be reporting another to the northeast. The general radio signals mix-up told *Helena* she was free to open fire on her persistent contact, which she did at 2345, from five thousand yards. Heavy *Salt lake City* followed suit from ahead at only four thousand yards. Soon all Scott's ships were blazing away at whatever was to their right, northeast of their line. Scott apparently did not realize it, but he had succeeded in steaming across the enemy's bow—he had "crossed the T." All of his guns would bear, but only the enemy's forward ones. He should have been able to annihilate them. Even as it was, his ships fired at the enemy for seven minutes before the enemy returned a shot. Scott, however, was not certain that he was not firing on his own destroyers and ordered a cease-fire. The enemy was in the same situation. Leading from heavy cruiser *Aoba*, the Japanese admiral signalled a starboard turn. This had the unfortunate—for him—effect of setting his cruisers up one by one as they successively followed the flag around the corner. Scott reopened fire before most of his ships had even obeyed his order to check fire. Catching fire, *Aoba* took the brunt of the shells.

Cape Esperance demonstrated sharply several of the basic aspects of fighting in a narrow sea. The engagement took place at night. Radar played a role, if a somewhat limited one. The fighting was sudden, violent, short, and brutal, as quickly over as begun. Identification of friends and foes was a continuous problem. But in the end, Scott understood this better than his enemy, well enough to give a tidy win. It could have been more.

U.S. destroyer *Duncan* had been fired on by both forces, and was sunk. Destroyer *Farenholt*—shelled by the Americans—was damaged. *San Francisco* shot IJN destroyer *Fubuki* out of the water. IJN heavy cruiser *Aoba*, burning fiercely, fell out, later sinking on the far side of Savo. USS *Boise* caught fire and fell out to save herself.

By 0030 it was all over. The IJN had lost one heavy cruiser out of three and one destroyer out of the two engaged. Another cruiser was badly damaged. The USN suffered serious damage to one light cruiser (*Boise*). Heavy *Salt Lake City*—which had interposed herself to save *Boise*—showed moderate damage. The USN lost one destroyer. Another was crippled.[1]

EVALUATION

Some fallacious conclusions were drawn from this battle: that the single column was a good battle formation, and that gunfire could master any night battle. Actually, Scott's formation was dangerously unwieldy. It prevented his DDs from exploiting their proper weapon, the torpedo. Since the surprised enemy did not get off his usual torpedo attack, we assumed that to be no longer a serious threat. One learns more from defeat than from victory, unless one is careful.

In the midst of all this brawl, the other enemy force—that night's Express—went about deliberately landing its troops and supplies.

Cape Esperance was an American victory, but not a disastrous Japanese defeat. While Turner landed his Army regiment, the IJN successfully landed its troops and supplies. Worse, before its escorts left, the IJN shelled American positions with fire so obviously unhurried as to be an insult.

SOLOMONS CRESCENDO

The Battle of Cape Esperance unfortunately did not settle anything. Rather, it introduced a period of sharply intensified fighting. Both sides reinforced on a large scale, on land as well as on sea. The Japanese continued to attack, the Americans to hang on. To the Americans on the ground, lacking strong personal leadership at the top, it seemed the fighting would never end. Morale was bad and the prospects worse.

The Japanese still had control of the sea. In the early morning hours of October 14, two IJN battleships—*Kongo* and *Haruna*—turned their 14-inch guns on CACTUS. For those who experienced it, this remained *the bombardment*, no matter how long they served on the island. The battleships destroyed half of the field's ninety planes. With daylight, Japanese bombers appeared, adding to the damage and closing down the main strip. When a new reserve strip was opened up, enemy land-based artillery shelled it. The Americans had no monopoly of airpower, even by day. At times, CACTUS counted only one dive bomber able to fly, at other times, no aviation fuel. Some pilots were so weak from incessant combat, sleepless nights, and scanty food that they would land, crawl under the wings of their planes, and pass out.

The night of the fifteenth, IJN heavy cruisers took over. Two of them expended 750 8-inch shells. The night of the sixteenth, half as many. In between, six enemy transports unloaded troops in broad daylight, in full view of the dazed GIs. American ships, barges, and planes stole in whenever they could to deliver ammunition, food, fuel, and other supplies. For this, the price was high. The IJN sometimes exacted a terrible, brutal toll. Sufficient supplies got through, however.

On October 15, destroyer *Meredith* was off the Canal escorting tug *Vireo* and two barges loaded with aviation gasoline destined for CACTUS. Thirty-eight aircraft from carrier *Zuikaku* came across and attacked the tiny convoy, sinking all of it.

The survivors took to the water, only to be strafed by the planes. The rest—many wounded and burned—were left among the wreckage and burning oil. They drifted for three days, being eaten by sharks, dying from exposure and their injuries. Only 81 men lived to tell about it, out of 318 men.

It was during this time that Marine Sergeant John Basilone won the Congressional Medal of Honor. Basilone led a heavy machine gun section, part of the force holding the western approaches to CACTUS. All during one long frantic night, his section held off a Japanese thrust. Basilone himself carried a heavy machine gun, firing it from the hip.

He delivered ammunition to guns that ran out. Finally, he and his men were fighting with rifles and pistols. By morning, there was one belt of ammunition left at his position.

This period also produced the story of Marine Master Sergeant Lou Diamond, another one of the "old breed." Sergeant Diamond apparently led a mortar platoon, at one time supposedly dropping a mortar round down the funnel of a bombarding IJN destroyer. Also supposedly, the sergeant every morning sent a recruit down to the shore to pick up a case of beer.

CHANGING THE GUARD

Things in SOPAC could not remain as they were. Admiral Nimitz—CINCPAC—came out himself to survey the situation on the ground. Inevitably, he decided that Ghormley—exhausted and perhaps demoralized—was not acting aggressively enough. On October 18, he replaced Ghormley with Vice Admiral William F. Halsey. Halsey was a carrier admiral, but more important than that, he was a pugnacious fighter, known to the fleet.

Admiral Halsey commanded SOPAC from October 18, 1942, until June 15, 1944. At the time he took it over, the command was a hot potato. Aside from the Solomons—and probably in part because of it—New Zealand was clamoring to get its troops back from Africa for home defense. Australia was ready to withdraw halfway down the continent to "the Brisbane Line." Pacific Fleet had lost a carrier, three heavy cruisers, five destroyers, and four transports in the area since August. The fleet was jubilant. With Halsey, there would be no Bataan.

If aggression was the missing ingredient in the U.S. campaign, the deficiency was more than made good. Halsey's first order—and his slogan—was "Kill Japs, kill Japs, kill more Japs!" Under Halsey's leadership, the Americans in the Guadalcanal area—on land, at sea, and in the air—took a series of costly but calculated risks that in thirty extraordinary days and nights reversed the course of the fight, finally throwing the enemy on the defensive. President Roosevelt's "hold-Guadalcanal" message to the Joint Chiefs of Staff underscored how high the political stakes had become. Washington's huge and still growing effort to hold an island hardly anyone could find on a map could be justified only by positive results. Halsey brusquely commandeered adequate office space ashore, from the difficult Noumea French. From Nimitz he got the Army's 25th Infantry Division, long stationed in Hawaii. He also got more submarines, Army fighters, and heavy bombers. Finally, he went out to see for himself what was going on. Personal leadership still counted.

Halsey soon had his chance. The Japanese had assembled a powerful fleet to the north. At a minimum, it comprised four carriers (two fleet, two light), four battleships, four heavy cruisers, more than two dozen destroyers, and supporting ships. Halsey had the Third Fleet. It then comprised two small task groups. Admiral Scott commanded the first—survivors of Cape Esperance—one heavy cruiser, one light cruiser, and three destroyers plus, this time, battleship *Washington*. Rear Admiral George D. Murray commanded the other—carrier *Hornet*, heavy cruisers *Northampton* and *Pensacola*, light cruisers *San Diego* and *Juneau*, and six destroyers. A potential third task group built around repaired *Enterprise*, and including battleship *South Dakota*, heavy cruiser *Portland*, light cruiser *San Juan*, and eight destroyers was en route from Pearl Harbor. Commanded by Rear Admiral Thomas C. Kinkaid, it arrived in the proverbial nick of time, joining on the twenty-fourth.

All was set for another battle. Carrier power varies as the square, two carriers being four times more powerful than one. Counting *Enterprise*, Halsey had a force to be reckoned with. Halsey sent the combined force north to a position off the Santa Cruz Islands, beyond the reach of the enemy's land-based air yet able to hit the flank of any force closing the Guadalcanal area.

Preliminary clashes between light forces on Ironbottom Sound cost the Japanese a light cruiser. They cost the Americans a tug and a patrol boat. The IJN was waiting for the news that never came—the recapture of CACTUS. American forces under the tactical command of Admiral Kinkaid on *Enterprise* kept looking for the Japanese main force. Halsey stayed ashore in Noumea, like his predecessor, but he issued one order, "Attack, repeat attack."[2]

SANTA CRUZ ISLANDS (OCTOBER 26)

On the twenty-sixth both forces were in waters north of the Santa Cruz Islands, well to the east of the Solomons. Their morning searches finally succeeded in locating each other. The carriers were some two hundred fifty miles apart, Kinkaid to the southeast, the enemy to the northwest. Each launched an air strike, the enemy first with sixty-five, Kinkaid with seventy-three twenty minutes later. As the Japanese strike approached Kinkaid, *Enterprise* was lucky once again, running under a concealing squall. Only *Hornet* could be seen. All the incoming enemy therefore concentrated on *Hornet*. She finally went dead in the water, in spite of the downing of twenty-five enemy planes. *Enterprise's* planes damaged light carrier *Zuiho*. *Hornet's* planes badly damaged fleet carrier *Shokaku* and heavy cruiser *Chikuma*.

The Japanese were now fully aware of *Enterprise's* presence, and they went after her. *Enterprise* was hit three times in two major attacks, but withdrew in her own good time later that day. One U.S. destroyer was sunk, another damaged. *Hornet* could not be saved. The USN tried to sink her themselves and failed. In the end, the enemy came up, drove the Navy off, and sank her with four torpedoes. The USN had fired sixteen torpedoes and nine had hit. To the pain of losing *Hornet* was added the shame of knowing their torpedoes were still so poor.

Once again, the U.S. was left with only one fleet carrier at sea— *Enterprise*—and she was damaged; so was battleship *South Dakota*, in a collision with a destroyer as they both dodged torpedoes. The U.S. appealed to the British for the loan of a fleet carrier, but it was months before the request could be met.[3]

GUADALCANAL (NOVEMBER 11–15)

Fought over an area of two-hundred fifty-thousand square miles the Battle of Guadalcanal was the most complex naval engagement of the whole Guadalcanal Campaign. Beginning on November 11, it lasted for five days and was the culmination of everything that had gone before. During this time, the campaign went through four distinct phases: preliminary enemy air attacks, a cruiser night action, a carrier action, and a battleship night action. It was one of the war's major turning points.

The IJN precipitated the battle by launching another determined effort to land major reinforcements and finally seize CACTUS. The United States countered that effort. Both navies suffered heavy losses, but the IJN failed to seize control of Solomons waters or significantly to increase the strength of their forces ashore. This was the last major effort by the IJN in this area.

As November opened, both sides were as determined as ever to dominate Guadalcanal and its surrounding waters. The Tokyo Express came in and went out at night almost with impunity, bringing twenty-thousand fresh troops. Cruisers and destroyers shelled each other's shore positions. Dogfights continued in the air. Skirmishes kept erupting on the ground. On the afternoon of November 9, returning from an inspection trip which included the Tulagi area, Halsey received news that another enemy offensive was brewing. Intelligence estimated that enemy aircraft would in a maximum effort, bomb Guadalcanal on the eleventh; a major surface force would shell CACTUS on the night of the twelfth; and after a day-long working over by carrier air on the thirteenth, troops would land. First reports credited the combined assault fleet with two carriers, four battleships, five heavy cruisers, about thirty destroyers, and possibly twenty transports and cargo ships. Intelligence was close.

To defeat this plan, Halsey had a fleet that would have been inferior even if two of its heaviest units were not crippled. Moreover, not only was it dispersed, but some of it was already committed to delivering Vandegrift additional support. The exact situation was as follows:

- One light cruiser and four destroyers under Admiral Scott were escorting three cargo vessels from Espiritu Santo to Guadalcanal. There Scott was due to arrive on the eleventh.

- One heavy cruiser, one light cruiser, and four destroyers under Admiral Turner were escorting four transports from Noumea, due to arrive on the twelfth.

- Two heavy cruisers, one light cruiser, and six destroyers under Rear Admiral Daniel J. Callaghan—a newcomer—were to sail from Espiritu Santo on the tenth, joining up with Turner on the eleventh.

Enterprise, South Dakota, and *Washington,* one heavy cruiser, one light cruiser, and eight destroyers under Admiral Kinkaid were still at Noumea, where *Enterprise* and *South Dakota* were still under repair.

Kinkaid almost immediately turned over the two battleships and four of the destroyers to Rear Admiral Willis A. Lee—another newcomer, a gunnery expert—retaining for himself only *Enterprise* and escorts.[4]

FIRST PHASE: ENEMY AIR ATTACKS

The first phase of the Battle of Guadalcanal—the major Japanese air effort—lasted not one day, but two, although it did not appear to have been such an all-out effort. At 0905 on the eleventh, some ten dive bombers escorted by fifteen fighters from Rabaul's land-based 11th Air Fleet were reported coming south. All of the Japanese were downed, at a cost to the United States of six fighters and four pilots. At 1127, twenty-five medium and heavy level bombers protected by five Zeros (fighters) attacked shore facilities. Eight of the Japanese were shot down, for sure, at a cost of one fighter. At 1317 on the twelfth, more enemy bombers and fighters were reported. These turned out to be twenty to twenty-five torpedo bombers escorted by eight Zeros. All except one bomber were downed. The United States lost four fighters.

The principal effect of all this was to harass and delay U.S. troop and cargo unloading operations. Admiral Turner successfully brought in another three thousand men of our Americal Division on the twelfth. Close cover was provided him by Admiral Callaghan, distant cover by Kinkaid's patched-up carrier and Lee's two battleships. There was, after all, a lot of enemy buzzing around out there. Cargo ship *Zeilin* took three near-misses.[5] She was worst damaged. Two others took slight damage. Heavy cruiser *San Francisco* and destroyer *Buchanan* were also hit.

Turner pulled out his transports after dark on the twelfth, ninety percent emptied, leaving Callaghan his remaining cruiser. Callaghan was glad to get it. A little later Scott arrived, bringing with him his light cruiser (*Atlanta*) and two more destroyers.

SECOND PHASE: CRUISER NIGHT ACTION

The IJN raiding force (two battleships, a light cruiser, and fourteen destroyers) came down the Slot in three columns. Battleships *Hiei* and *Kirishima* were led by two destroyers and light cruiser *Nagara*. The battleships were flanked by destroyer columns on both sides. It did not seem the USN had anything big enough and near enough to stop them.

American radar (it was improving) picked up the Japanese at 130124, some fourteen miles to the northwest. Visual contact was made twenty minutes later. Aware of Scott's successful formation at Cape Esperance, Callaghan repeated it—four destroyers led five cruisers, then came four more destroyers. Although surprised, the radar-less Japanese reacted with the speed of experts. In the acrid dark their searchlights found *Atlanta* first, killing Scott almost at once. Callaghan on *San Francisco* soon followed him.

At such short—essentially point-blank—4,500-yard range, and in these confined waters, the two IJN battleships became little more than large targets. They could not maneuver, neither could they exploit the longer range of their 14-inch guns. The U.S.'s heavy cruisers' 8-inch guns pounded their upperworks, turning them into a shambles.

The final losses from this ferocious and disorderly action were—for the USN—two light cruisers and four destroyers sunk. Every surviving ship except one was damaged. For the IJN, two destroyers were sunk. *Hiei* was badly damaged, vulnerable to the inevitable daylight air strike.

On the morning of November 13, the Japanese reentered the Slot, to rescue *Hiei*, and to shell CACTUS again. Tanaka prepared to take his Express— a dozen transports escorted by eleven destroyers (held up by the cruiser action)—into Ironbottom Sound. Both these activities were to be covered by a force of two battleships and the two light carriers on hand. In any event, pounded all that day by CACTUS' pilots as well as others, *Hiei* sank late that day. It was, after all, Friday the thirteenth.

That night, two cruisers shelled CACTUS, making a lot of noise with 500 rounds of 8-inch. The remnants of Callaghan's force being in no shape to fight another battle, defense was up to a squadron of PT boats (Lt. Hugh M. Robinson). From their base on Tulagi, the PTs harried the cruisers until they broke off. At CACTUS, three planes had been wrecked and seventeen damaged. Cruiser *Kinugasa* was caught in the Slot by U.S. planes headed north the next day, and sunk.[6]

Halsey did not want to send Lee and his battleships into the Sound. Its narrow, treacherous waters were utterly unsuitable for the maneuvering of capital ships, especially in the dark. In addition, he needed those battleships to help defend his carriers. *Hiei's* fate must have reminded him of all this. But he had no choice. He now sent them in.

THIRD PHASE: CARRIER STRIKES OF THE THIRTEENTH AND FOURTEENTH

Admiral Kinkaid took *Enterprise* north early on the thirteenth, in response to information that Tanaka had started his run down the Slot. Halsey's instructions were that Kinkaid was to keep one hundred miles west of the Solomons axis while Admiral Lee took a parallel course midway between her and the chain. This would permit *Enterprise* to strike across the battleship screen. Halsey told Kinkaid, "Your objective transports." There may have been as many as 13,500 Japanese troops aboard Tanaka's transports. Halsey threw in every plane that could take the air. Their attacks began at 1000 and continued until twilight. They would strike, return to base, rearm and refuel, and strike again. When the "Buzzard Patrol" was done, seven transports had been sunk and four damaged. This in spite of interference from Zeros sent in from the enemy carriers.

The four remaining damaged troopships straggled down to Guadalcanal. When Tanaka finally reached Tassafaronga the next day it was turning daylight. More air attacks were expected. Unloading by lighters and barges as usual was out. Tanaka therefore simply ran the four transports aground on the beaches. He sent the troops over the side via nets and the supplies using the ships' own booms. With daylight, these troopships were shelled by U.S. artillery, bombed and strafed by planes, and finally shot up by destroyer *Meade*. Tanaka had already written them off. The United States was simply administering the coup de grace to empty hulks. Some 2,000 enemy troops reached shore, along with limited equipment and supplies. All eleven transports involved in this expensive effort were lost. Tanaka had already taken his DDs back out, headed north. He would be back another day.[7]

FOURTH PHASE: BATTLESHIP NIGHT ACTION

This fourth phase opened at 150016 November 1942. It lasted just fifty minutes. The enemy force consisted of two heavy and two light cruisers, nine destroyers, plus battleship *Kirishima*. Admiral Lee had his two battleships (*Washington* and *South Dakota*) and four destroyers. *Washington* was flag. The two main opposed surface forces approached Ironbottom Sound from opposite directions. Their screens had already clashed south of Savo. All four U.S. destroyers were soon out of action (two sunk, one fatally and one moderately damaged). The IJN lost one. Lee was now left with his two battleships to face *Kirishima* and two heavy cruisers (see Table 1).

Veteran battleship *South Dakota*, lit up by enemy searchlights, drew all the enemy's fire, leaving *Washington* to blast *Kirishima* from the darkness at will, forcing *Kirishima* out of the fight in little more than five minutes. She went down northwest of Savo at 0300. The rest of the enemy were driven off.[8]

Washington drove the enemy north, absolutely alone, until she was quite sure the enemy had pulled out. With no further targets, she turned south, rejoining *South Dakota* the following morning.[9] The battle was over.

Evaluation

The Naval Battle of Guadalcanal was a strategic victory for the United States. They had gotten all their reinforcements ashore, the enemy no more than a few troops, a little ammunition and food. This cost the USN two light cruisers, seven destroyers and much damage. It cost the IJN two battleships, one heavy cruiser, and three destroyers.

Table 1

Naval Losses in the Naval Battle of Guadalcanal (November 11–15, 1942)

| | IJN | | USN | |
	sunk	*damaged*	*sunk*	*damaged*
Battleships	2	-	-	1
Heavy Cruisers	1	2	-	2
Light Cruisers	-	1	2	1
Destroyers	3	6	7	4
Transports/Cargo Ships	12	-	-	1
Totals	18	9	9	9

It cost them a dozen transports, seventy thousand tons of precious, top-quality shipping. The IJN took heavy punishment in the air, where they were beginning to feel the continuing large losses. Halsey was made a full admiral.

But the battle was more than that, by not being more. This was Tokyo's chance to win that Mahanian "decisive battle" Yamamoto was always seeking. At Midway in June, he had failed in this. Here the opportunity had come again. Here he was still overwhelmingly superior, again. Almost everything the United States had in the Pacific was here. Yamamoto was well-positioned, free to maneuver. Halsey was tied to defending CACTUS. If Halsey could be annihilated, CACTUS would fall by itself. But in this case, Yamamoto allowed the opportunity to pass. He failed to commit more than a part of his available fleet, he failed to force the issue, and missed his chance. He would never have another.

NOTES

1. *The Battles of Cape Esperance 11 October 1942 and Santa Cruz Islands 26 October 1942* (Washington, DC: Naval Historical Center, 1994), pp. 1–20.

2. William F. Halsey and J. Bryan III, *Admiral Halsey's Story* (New York: McGraw-Hill, 1947), pp. 108–21.

3. *Battles of Cape Esperance and Santa Cruz Islands*, pp. 29–68.

4. *The Battle of Guadalcanal 11–15 November 1942* (Washington, DC: Naval Historical Center, 1994), pp. 1–9.

5. Ibid., pp. 9–15.

6. Ibid., pp. 15–36.

7. Ibid., pp. 37–59, 80–84.

8. Ibid., pp. 60–79.

9. For a command view of this battle, see Halsey and Bryan, pp. 124–33.

6

Guadalcanal Ends

WHERE YOU BEEN, JOE?

In the wider view, it could be seen that the campaign aimed at Rabaul was now indeed making progress. MacArthur's Americans and Australians in a mainly Army operation advanced from the south via New Guinea and New Britain. Halsey's Americans and New Zealanders in a Navy-dominated operation advanced from the southeast via the Solomons. The two-pronged campaign—so far island by island, basically on a shoestring—was intended to be mutually supporting, and it was. But things were getting even better.

The Battle for Guadalcanal had now been reduced to one of attrition. In this—as their own Admiral Isoroku Yamamoto, C-in-C Combined Fleet and the driving brain behind Pearl Harbor, had told them—they could not win. When the U.S. lost ships, these were getting replaced by more and better. When Japan lost ships, these might be painfully and slowly replaced, but seldom one for one. Tokyo began searching for a way out.

Ground forces continued to hammer each other in the jungle around the American perimeter. Vandegrift now held it with thirty-five thousand men—two divisions of troops—against barely twenty thousand starving enemy troops. Tanaka's Tokyo Express was kept busy; only destroyer types could now be used to deliver troops and supplies, supplemented by barges over short runs. There was no question of anyone living off the land, except on coconuts. Meanwhile, a shipload of turkeys reached U.S. forces in time for the Thanksgiving holiday.

The First Marine Division was relieved by the Second, and the Americal Division now had all three of its regiments. The "CACTUS Air Force"––officially AIRSOLS—now counted 124 aircraft of all types, all operating from one bomber and two fighter strips. As the Army reinforcements arrived, Marines would shout out, "Where you been, Joe?"

Carrier *Saratoga*—completely repaired and modernized—had rejoined *Enterprise* to rebuild the carrier force. Halsey now happily counted five battleships. Rear Admiral Carleton H. Wright—new to the area—took over a stronger cruiser-destroyer group. SOPAC was on a roll.

TASK FORCE 67

But everything was not well in SOPAC. Its aircraft carriers had done wonders, as everyone knew. The battleships had done well. But the cruisers and destroyers had not, as everyone also knew. Now that a little slack in the line was showing, it was perhaps time to do something about that. CINCPAC had prepared the ground, on paper at least. SOPAC was given a nudge.

On October 10, Captain Morton L. Deyo of CINCPAC staff had sent Admiral Nimitz a memorandum. In it he commented on the defeat at Savo and the far from satisfactory events that followed. He wrote that the training of cruisers and destroyers was unrealistic. He noted that their almost exclusive employment in convoy escort had prevented the development of the attitudes required in the Solomons fighting. He ended by suggesting the formation of a semipermanent South Pacific cruiser-destroyer group, to be given a solid month of training—especially in night fighting—and then thrown into the Slot to break up Admiral Tanaka's Tokyo Express.[1] Belatedly, Admiral Halsey did just that, some time in the first ten days after the Naval

Battle of Guadalcanal had shown him how necessary it was. This force was made up of heavy cruisers *Minneapolis, Pensacola, New Orleans,* and *Northampton,* light cruiser *Honolulu,* and four destroyers.

Wright's Task Force 67 staff had no time to work up an operation plan, or for the officers to get to know each other. Wright went through the change of command one day and went into battle the next. The resulting Battle of Tassafaronga was the last of the six major naval battles fought over the Southern Solomons, but probably not for the reasons you think.

THE "TIN CAN" NAVY

The destroyers were the real crux of the matter. U.S. destroyer squadrons were usually comprised on paper of two DD divisions, one of five DDs and one of four. They were, however, seldom fought this way. DD tactical squadrons (task groups) were made up of whatever divisions or even individual ships were available, according to the task in hand. Lucky was the squadron commander whose own division even stayed as a unit. A few comparisons seem in order here.

The USN sent out what were at the time its best DDs—the 2,050-ton *Fletchers.* They were armed with ten torpedo tubes, designed for 21-inch two-mile torpedoes, and five 5-inch guns. See Appendix A.

For forty years, Tokyo had studied and fought naval warfare, neglecting no aspect of it. It had made choices, putting much thought and great effort into new, improved torpedoes, night fighting (its night glasses enabled a lookout to pick out a ship in the dark at four miles), and torpedo tactics. Even the IJN's old 2,300-ton *Fubuki*-class DDs carried nine torpedo tubes, fitted for their deadly 24-inch ten-mile Long Lances as well as six 5-inch guns. Crews were trained to reload these big torpedo tubes in ten minutes, twice as fast as in the USN. Japan's commanding officers were all career "tin can sailors" and torpedo experts. Squadrons stayed as units. Tanaka's Squadron 2 is an example of this.

The USN armed its destroyers with those 21-inch slow, short-range, still unreliable torpedoes. The USN's "tin cans" were trained in ASW and in Jutland-style massed fleet tactics. They were not ready for night fighting in close waters. They were not assigned in permanent tactical squadrons but, always in short supply, were shifted around to meet the demands of the moment. Commanding officers were not specialist destroyer men except by accident. The DDs had guts, but that was not enough, as we have already seen.[2]

TASSAFARONGA (NOVEMBER 30)

In any case, the Tokyo Express had by now already been reduced to a very marginal effort. The destroyers' cargo was now loaded into rubber-wrapped drums. These drums were then roped together. Each destroyer would carry some combination of troops and\or drums (up to a hundred or more) each run. Combat capability had to be degraded—decks were piled so high with supplies now that the DDs could only carry half allowances of ammunition and torpedoes—but they were still fast enough to make the run down the Slot and back during darkness, small enough to take shelter among the islands, and large enough to carry a significant load.

Delivery consisted of jettisoning the strings of drums and dropping the troops into the water within 200 or 300 yards of a shore. No more anchoring and offloading directly into barges. Rather, the recovering troops would boat, swim, or wade out to retrieve the drums and pick up the incoming troops from the water. Once hauled ashore, the drums would be stored in jungle dumps, hidden from air attack. Wastage was severe, but the DDs' decks could be cleared within twenty minutes.

Tanaka was to run another Express the night of the thirtieth, and the USN had word of it. This run was to be a comparatively modest one. On this particular night, Tanaka had six destroyers crammed with troops and supplies, and two more without cargo. Destroyers only. Off Tassafaronga, Tanaka was to jettison his rubber-wrapped supply drums and drop his troops into the water, both to be recovered by small craft from the shore. He was then simply to depart back north.

Wright's five cruisers were formed into two divisions *Minneapolis* (flag), *New Orleans*, and *Pensacola*, then *Honolulu* and *Northampton*, in that column order. He had four DDs. Two more DDs picked up from a passing convoy followed astern. They got lost and played no part in the coming fight.

Wright and his captains quickly ran over the admiral's plans. His cruisers were to form in column, with van destroyers in their own column to port. First contact was expected on radar, probably by a DD. On contact the DDs were to attack with torpedoes. They were then to fall back to the cruisers' off side, prepared to fire star shells on order. The cruisers were to keep off at least 12,000 yards until after the torpedo attack. Cruisers were then to open fire under radar control the minute any of the torpedoes struck home. Use of searchlights was forbidden. "Fighting lights" were to be employed only if and when there was risk of "friendly fire." Wright's plan seemed a considerable improvement over previous ones. But it was unpractised, and the admiral and captains did not know each other.

Ironbottom Sound was dead calm that night. American float planes detailed to illuminate the Express were unable to take off. Destroyer *Fletcher* in Wright's van carried radar, and at 302316, November 1942, she saw Tanaka on her scope. He was broad on the port bow, steaming slowly along the shore toward the dumping area. The destroyer squadron commander, in *Fletcher*, asked Wright's permission for his four van destroyers to fire torpedoes. Wright hesitated for four minutes before granting it, and so lost the battle.

By the time Wright's van destroyers had fired their torpedoes—about 2321—Tanaka's column—on a contrary course—had passed Wright's, and the range was too great for the feeble U.S. torpedoes to overtake them. Wright immediately ordered his cruisers to open fire, and the flashes of his guns awoke Tanaka to what was going on. In spite of his being surprised and having six of his decks cluttered with troops and cargo, Tanaka's reaction was automatic and fast. IJN doctrine and training said to launch torpedoes and not to use guns but to turn away at speed. That is just what he did. Gun flashes and searchlights would only have given the USN aiming points.

Lead destroyer *Takanami*, however, showed up best on Wright's radars. She drew the brunt of the gunfire. She replied in self-defense, which only brought more shells down on her. She was the only Japanese ship sunk in the battle. Tanaka's line crumpled as individual ships took evasive action. Some of his destroyer-transports were already committed to releasing their drums. Nonetheless he managed to launch a total of twenty-four torpedoes. They had the range.

Not one of the twenty or so torpedoes the USN fired found its target. But at 2327 the Japanese "Long Lances" began to take out theirs. Two of Tanaka's torpedoes struck *Minneapolis* almost severing her bow. Next in line, *New Orleans*, took only one torpedo but had her bow ripped off by an internal ammunition explosion. *Pensacola*, third, hit amidships, was badly hurt. Smart ship-handling on the part of her officer of the deck (LCDR George F. Davis) enabled *Honolulu* to avoid being hit. *Northampton*, last, took two hits. She was the only one to sink, the others all eventually making their way back for repair.

For the Japanese their victory was merely tactical. By shear weight of numbers the Americans now had control of Solomons waters. But the Americans still had a lot to learn about the best use of destroyers, and about fighting at night. The IJN had once again demonstrated its superior destroyer material, technique, and training.[3]

Hardy, ever-dependable Tanaka was soon refuelled, rearmed, and ready for further runs of his Express. Successful trips were made on the nights of December 3–4, 7–8, and 11–12. But at Tassafaronga he had failed to properly deliver his load, and for this he was in considerable disfavor in Rabaul. Headquarters tend to be all the same. Tanaka soon went to other duty.

Allied intelligence duly noted Tanaka's efforts—and those of his successors—and evaluated them as another enemy build-up. Nothing could have been farther from the truth. The enemy was still dangerous, indeed, but he was barely hanging on. Even so, small groups of Japanese kept infiltrating through the jungle, assembling at a given point, and then jumping unwary American outposts.

It remained for the Americans to dispose of the increasingly hungry and sick enemy troops in the jungle. Their naval lifeline had now all but withered away. Evidently, the IJN was reduced to using even submarines as supply vessels. But CACTUS could not be considered secure until those troops were cleaned up.

On December 9, General Vandegrift was relieved of command in what was now the American XIV Corps by Major General Alexander

M. Patch. The new corps was composed of one Marine division (the Second) and two Army. Protocol decreed that an Army officer should lead it. Vandegrift went back to Washington, slated to be Commandant of the Corps.

During all this time, U.S. advanced bases were gradually increased in number and pushed farther and farther forward. The first new naval one was built on Efate, another on Espiritu Santo, and finally a proper one on Tulagi. As soon as these forward ports were ready, PTs, destroyers, and even cruisers were based there, enabling the USN the better to block off the Tokyo Express, to defend its own shipping, and to make offensive forays up the Slot.

One place where things were not really going better now was at CACTUS. To the three fields in operation was being added a fourth. Operating from them was a synergistic mix of Corsairs, Wildcats, Avengers, Catalinas, and various Army and RAF types. Combat was continuous. Living conditions were awful. But no one was paying much attention to that side of things.

Little noticed at the time, on December 23 Rear Admiral Marc A. Mitscher arrived to take over as Commander, Fleet Air, Noumea, relieving McCain. This was the administrative unit for SOPAC's shore-based planes and flying boats. Mitscher did well enough there to become marked for bigger things.[4]

TOKYO EVACUATES

Meanwhile in December 1942, in Tokyo, after bitter arguments between the Navy which wanted to pull out of Guadalcanal and the Army which wanted to dig in, the admirals won. A series of war games convinced the staffs that there was no longer any option. The games showed that this had been true since about the middle of October. The huge tonnage of irreplaceable shipping lost in supporting the troops had all been wasted. Evacuation was duly ordered. Tokyo's plan was to fight a spoiling action, to step up air raids from the Central and Northern Solomons, and to evacuate what was left. For Tokyo, this was a first, not just for this war, but in all of its military history.[5]

By the end of 1942, Tokyo maintained a force on Guadalcanal merely to keep the Allies at bay until it could prepare a new line of defense built on Central Solomons air bases. On the night of January 29, 1943, a dozen land-based naval twin-engined bombers from these new enemy fields attacked an American Guadalcanal-bound troop convoy. They torpedoed heavy cruiser *Chicago*, sinking her. Two days later, bombers from the same fields sank destroyer *DeHaven*. Enemy planes, either originating from or staging through these two new fields, continued to bomb the Guadalcanal area, occasionally even hitting more distant Espiritu Santo. AIRSOLS worked with little success to keep the fields too cratered for use.

By now, dependable radar (SGs, later SJs) had become generally available to the fleet and they were still finding ways to exploit it. One of these ways was in shipboard combat information centers (CICs). Here radar contacts were plotted. Other information—from radio and lookouts, for instance—was correlated there. The CICs greatly strengthened U.S. ships' ability to go in harm's way.

One night in early January, an American cruiser-destroyer force steamed up the Slot and gave the nearer field—Munda on New Georgia, some 175 miles northwest of CACTUS—an hour's heavy shelling. Toward the end of the month, another such force, also at night, shelled the other field—Vila on Kolombangara, across Kula Gulf from New Georgia. Ashore, General Patch began his drive to clean up Guadalcanal on January 10, 1943, moving west along the north coast, flushing out the ragged but still dangerous enemy. It was slow work.

FINAL DAYS

During the first week in February, Allied planes on three separate occasions flashed warnings of a score of enemy destroyers headed down the Slot, covered by swarms of fighters. This renewed enemy activity generated a great deal of speculation and some anxiety among the Allies. Radar-equipped PBYs ("Black Cats") used as night patrol-cum nuisance raiders were one Allied means of keeping a close watch on this activity.

On February 5, Allied surveillance spotted a powerful enemy force standing down from Truk—two carriers, four battleships, six heavy cruisers, two light cruisers, and twelve destroyers. These ships added a master touch to Tokyo's evacuation plan. The by-now desperate plight of enemy troops on Guadalcanal, and the long period of time since the enemy's last attack, had led Halsey to expect a final, supreme IJN effort. He disposed his forces just south of Guadalcanal and waited, ignoring the to-ing and fro-ing of the Express. So the Japanese threat worked. They had given the evacuation cover, and that was all they ever intended. Their main force activity was only a feint.

The Express had in fact gone into reverse, not bringing in more troops and supplies but rather taking out everything it could. In three high-speed night runs, it succeeded in bringing out every one of the 12,000 survivors of a garrison that at one point had numbered 30,000. Covered by the feint, the Express made its last run the night of February 7, six months to the day after the initial Allied landing. When Patch and his men got to the western tip of Guadalcanal, on February 8, they found nothing but abandoned barges floating offshore. The enemy had got clean away. Patch had expected to take eight weeks longer to do the job. In the late afternoon of February 9, Admiral Halsey's South Pacific headquarters received General Patch's radio report: "Total and complete defeat of Japanese forces on Guadalcanal effected 1625 today. . . . Express no longer has terminus." Pride dripped from every fine word.[6]

THE RUSSELLS (OPERATION CLEANSLATE)

The campaign for Guadalcanal ended with a final minor flourish. The Russells are a splatter of small islands thirty miles off the northern tip of Guadalcanal, fifty-five miles northwest of CACTUS. They were tactically and strategically an integral part of the U.S.'s brand new base. Halsey's drive took him over there. Halsey scraped together a force large enough to take them—9,000 men—and did. He landed unopposed, on February 21. SOPAC then built a pair of airstrips there that would extend the reach of U.S. planes that much further north, and at the same time provide them with handy emergency landing strips. He also installed early warning radar for the same reason.[7]

EVALUATION

The capture of the Tulagi area ended the first of three phases into which the Solomons Campaign was split. Geographically, operations so far represented the southern phase. Militarily, this was the defensive phase. The second phase would be fought in the Central Solomons, and would be offensive in nature.

The Guadalcanal/Tulagi Campaign was one of the most difficult campaigns of World War II. While it began well for Allied forces, the battle quickly degenerated into a contest of wills that lasted almost exactly six months. During this time, the tide of battle ebbed and flowed as both sides threw more and more resources into the struggle. By the time of the decisive five-day Naval Battle of Guadalcanal, almost the whole of CINCPAC's fleet was in or off the Canal. The key to the entire campaign was the control of Solomons waters. The first of many IJN challenges to U.S. sea power was the Battle of Savo Island, one of the worst defeats ever suffered by the USN. That short engagement provided U.S. naval forces with a bitter lesson in the initial superiority of IJN night surface tactics. For the Allies, however, Savo was not an unmitigated disaster—the IJN failed to get at the vulnerable but most important transports. But the cost was heavy. The sound between Tulagi and the Canal had begun to earn its name—Ironbottom Sound. Most of the iron was to be the USN's (see Table 2).

UNFINISHED BUSINESS

In the six months since the USN had entered the narrow Solomon Seas, it had been wrestling with the problem of night fighting tactics. For this they were totally unprepared. The night surface warfare picture was still a sad one. The DDs were obviously being mishandled. They were not playing a full night role. No single final answer would ever be possible, of course. The enemy played a large part in determin-

Table 2
Naval Losses in the Guadalcanal Campaign (six months)

	IJN (sunk)	USN (sunk)
Battleships	2	-
Aircraft Carriers	1	2
Heavy Cruisers	2	5
Light Cruisers	2	2
Destroyers	12	15
Totals	19	24

ing that equation, and his cooperation could not always be counted on. However, it was time to make some progress here.

The Japanese had begun in the Solomons with superior night fighting tactics, better training, and better equipment, particularly torpedoes and night glasses. The Americans were now beginning to master radar. It was the tactic they most needed to work out.

The night fighting problem was being passed to the Central and Northern Solomons. These tactics were really two related problems. There was the one problem of what to do with the DDs in a mixed cruiser-destroyer force, and then what to do with the DDs when they operated on their own. But the latter can be seen as a lesser included problem of the former.

COASTWATCHERS

Allied operations had long exploited the Australian coastwatcher corps. These Australian, New Zealand, and British prewar island residents—former civil servants, traders, missionaries, planters—were equipped with radios, a few supplies and weapons, and returned to the islands. Each coastwatcher recruited a network of native scouts; they would report to him and he would pass the information on by radio. Their information covered such things as how far along the new airfield at Vila was; where the enemy's barges laid up at night; how many planes had flown over going south; how many came back. They rescued downed fliers and kept them safe until they could be picked up. Especially, they were to give warning of ship movements up or down the Slot. They were very effective agents.

More coastwatchers were recruited as time went on and some of the original team had to be evacuated or were captured and killed. The IJN knew about the coastwatchers and tried every means of capturing them. They bribed and tortured the natives, combed the islands with patrols, even hunted the men down with dogs.[8] To discourage use of Munda and Vila (actually Vila-Stanmore) as air and surface way stations north and south, and to prepare for the next Allied move north, American surface forces had begun to raid them. Munda was shelled for the first time as early as January 4–5, by Rear Admiral Walden L. Ainsworth's light cruisers and destroyers (DDs). Vila across from Munda was also bombarded, on January 23–24 by Ainsworth. These were early harbingers of things to come.

NOTES

1. Samuel Eliot Morison, *The Two-Ocean War* (Boston: Little, Brown, 1963), p. 208.

2. Tameichi Hara, Fred Saito, and Roger Pineau, *Japanese Destroyer Captain* (New York: Ballantine, 1961), passim.

3. Theodore Roscoe, *United States Destroyer Operations in World War II* (Annapolis, MD: Naval Institute, 1953), pp. 206–09.

4. Theodore Taylor, *The Magnificent Mitscher* (Annapolis, MD: Naval Institute, 1954), pp. 141–43.

5. Dan van der Vat, *The Pacific Campaign* (New York: Simon and Schuster, 1991), pp. 244–45.

6. Morison, pp. 213–14.

7. William F. Halsey and J. Bryan III, *Admiral Halsey's Story* (New York: McGraw-Hill, 1947), pp. 153–54.

8. Eric A. Feldt, *The Coast Watchers* (New York: Doubleday, 1979), passim.

The Central Solomons— New Georgia

THE STRATEGIC SITUATION

Up to now, Halsey had been SOPAC, SOWESPAC's equal, responsible only to CINCPAC. From here on out, the overall strategy for the U.S.'s two-pronged assault on Rabaul was in MacArthur's hands. Only tactical command of the forces in the Solomons remained in Halsey's hands. To discuss plans for New Georgia—the next objective in the Solomons—Halsey flew across from Noumea to Brisbane early in April. Nimitz had always controlled Halsey's troops, ships, and supplies. Now MacArthur controlled his strategy, too. According to Halsey, the two great captains of war got along well together, then and from then on. That was fortunate for all. They must have respected each other, they did need each other, and the U.S. national interest demanded that they work together well. But they were both strong personalities in their own right.

Up to now, Rabaul had only been a distant, hazy, not quite real planning objective the great captains and their war plans staffs dreamed about. Guadalcanal had been essentially a self-contained fight for survival. Now suddenly Rabaul loomed over everything, a very real, attainable objective. But first there had to be Munda.

New Georgia was fifty miles long by twenty miles at its widest. Not terribly big, but in the right place. MacArthur accepted Halsey's plan for taking New Georgia and its associated islands (see Map 3). L-Day was set for May 15, to coincide with MacArthur's occupation of Woodlark and the Trobriand Islands. The combined operation was to be called ELKTON. Locally, it was known as Operation TOENAILS. It was, in the end, carried out on June 30.

RABAUL/KAVIENG

By February 1943, the Bismarck Archipelago—New Britain and New Ireland, Rabaul and its satellite Kavieng—represented Tokyo's main South Pacific defense line. Everything south, in the Solomons, was expendable. But the Japanese would, as forced into it, make a fighting withdrawal, island by island. Both Halsey and MacArthur still agreed that as long as Rabaul was tenable as a base, and as long as Truk was prepared to feed it with ships and planes, neither Papua nor the Solomons could be considered secure. Rabaul remained CARTWHEEL's ultimate Allied objective.[1] Halsey's problem was, Rabaul was 436 miles from MacArthur's bases at Port Moresby, from which some help was still coming. It was 515 miles from the Russells. Both of these were too distant from Rabaul for us to provide fighter escort. Munda was 175 miles closer for Halsey, if nothing else.

Halsey would have preferred to make the really important 150-mile leap to capture New Georgia right away, and he had ample means to do it. Seizing Munda would remove a constant threat to U.S. facilities in the Tulagi area, and from Munda Allied planes could keep the nearby Vila air strip pounded down while continuing on north. On it, the Allies could even build a bomber strip. This leap he could not take. The remainder of the Rabaul thrust had been planned so that MacArthur and Halsey would remain mutually supporting. Mac Arthur was held up, awaiting the arrival of the modest naval force he needed. Halsey therefore had to wait, too. Meanwhile, he kept "pushing the Japs around."

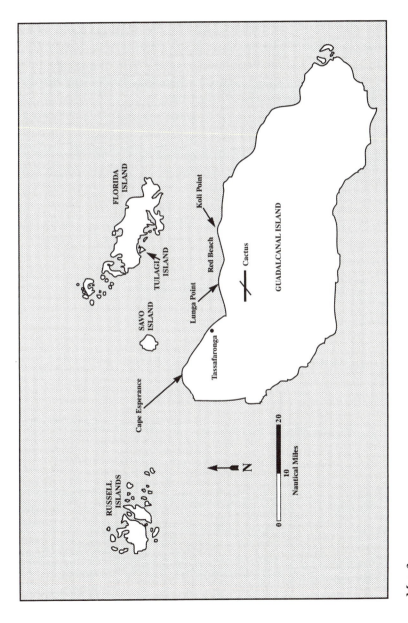

Map 3
Central and Northern Solomons

WOODLARK ISLAND

Halfway between Munda and Port Moresby, in the center of the south Solomon Sea, lay Woodlark Island, only 300 miles from Rabaul and just over 200 from Bougainville. Fighters based there easily could themselves, even with their limited range, strike Bougainville, Munda, or Rabaul, or fly bomber escort. Halsey needed Woodlark, and MacArthur was willing to take it, but MacArthur lacked the forces necessary to do so. Halsey had them. Woodlark was indisputably located at 153 degrees east longitude, deep in MacArthur's SOWESPAC area. Only after specific approval from the Joint Chiefs was obtained could Halsey send SOWESPAC those forces. When Washington approval was obtained Halsey sent over an Army regiment as an occupation force, some CBs as a construction force, enough shore-based Navy to organize and operate the port facilities, and the fighter planes to station there. Woodlark became part of ELKTON.[1]

MITSCHER

At this point—February 1943—some of the most furious air battles the Solomons would see were yet to come. Admiral Mitscher was detached from Noumea and sent to Guadalcanal to command all aircraft in the Solomons, as COMAIRSOLS. Included under him now were Navy, Marine, Army, and Royal New Zealand Air Force pilots and planes. COMAIRSOLS was strictly a combat job, and Mitscher loved it.

Guadalcanal itself was a depressing place. Tons of equipment lay rusting in stream beds. Twisted, burnt-out hulks that once were transports and cargo ships lined the beaches from Cape Esperance south. Former Japanese bivouac areas were deserted and maggoty. It was a dead island. Over it—in the air— the struggle was savage. Guadalcanal's three airfields were in operation. The fourth was still under construction. There was a fighter command, a bomber command, a strike command, and an intelligence section. Combat was continuous. There was no real letup.

In AIRSOLS, this continuous pressure was taking a severe physical and mental toll. The place was losing its edge. In his first hectic week of command, Mitscher therefore paid more attention to improving living conditions than to the Japanese. Then he moved to personnel, weeding out the unfit. People were the key to all else. With his AIRSOLS shaping up, Mitscher went to work on broad plans to pound down Munda, Vila, Buin, and Kahili (both on Bougainville) using all the bombs he could get. Meanwhile, the Japanese were hitting back, almost every night and day. Mitscher was to fight that battle until the day he left.

In any triservice command, some disagreement is built in. Mitscher disagreed continually with the Army over the need for long-range patrols. He knew that ninety percent of the results were negative, but the positive ten percent he had to have. The Army preferred to bomb. Dealing with three radically different service cultures, leadership was at a premium. Mitscher had it.[2]

SOFTENING UP FOR MUNDA

Mitscher continued to build up his existing three fields and to press for completion of the fourth. Meanwhile, he was hitting the enemy at Munda and Vila and beginning to work on Buin and Kahili. In theory, he could muster some 300 aircraft, but only one third of these were operational at any one time. Nonetheless, strike by strike, Mitscher gradually beat the enemy air down. Munda remained the primary target. Vila was only a fighter strip supporting Munda, much as the Russells did CACTUS. Buin and Kahili in the north were both bases in their own right. They were also way stations for planes staging between Rabaul and the Lower Solomons.

The IJN had its patrols out, too. It was fully aware of the build-up for Operation TOENAILS. Beginning April 7, the IJN finally struck back, launching a massive series of air raids. It used at a minimum 300 planes, some of which were seen to be carrier types. Those pilots were good, but they too were used up.

Admiral Yamamoto in Truk had stripped his fleet carriers of some 200 planes as temporary reinforcements for his decimated land-based

naval air. He hoped thus to check the deterioration of his situation
and to blunt the forthcoming Allied advance. When Yamamoto flew
to Bougainville on an April 18 inspection trip, the Allies shot him
down. Admiral Mineichi Koga succeeded Yamamoto as C-in-C Combined Fleet. He continued the tactics of his predecessor. Destroyers
and light cruisers were committed piecemeal into battle, scoring
occasional local victories but unable to stem the Allied tide. The major
part of the fleet was husbanded for the Mahanian great final battle
(which never took place).

In all this time, Mitscher's air offensive was being supported from
the surface, too. Munda was shelled again on March 5–6 by Captain
Robert P. Briscoe, and on May 12–13 by Captain Colin Campbell.
Vila was also bombarded again on March 5–6 by Rear Admiral Aaron
S. Merrill, on March 15–16 by Commander Francis X. McInerney,
and on May 12–13 by Ainsworth again. These raids marked a gradual
improvement in the Allies' ability to operate at night. As far back as
the night of March the fifth, there had been a minor technological
turning point. Enemy DDs *Minegumo* and *Murasame* were returning
north from a small Kolombangara supply run when Merrill's task
group caught them. Merrill had tracked the enemy with radar and had
opened fire under radar control. Both DDs were sunk, all by radar.[3]

MINE WARFARE

After the shelling of Munda and Vila, the most effective surface
activity in the Solomons was the sowing of several minefields (see Table
3). There had been a minesweeper group (five sweepers) assigned to the
amphibious force from the start. They duly swept off Tulagi and
Guadalcanal, but it does not appear that any enemy mines were met.
The sweepers ended up as gunboats, tugs, and escorts, but that was all.

Minelaying operations in the Solomons were something else. Tactical moves mostly in support of other offensives, they dislocated
enemy ship traffic. They sank a few of them. They forced the enemy
to sweep. Mining here began right away. In August 1942, Maramasike
anchorage off Malaita was mined by a destroyer-minelayer (DM). This
successfully prevented the anchorage from being used by the enemy,

Table 3
Japanese Losses to Allied Mines in the Solomons Area

	ships			
location	*sunk*	*tonnage*	*damaged*	*tonnage*
Blackett Strait	3	4,950		
Buin-Kahili (Bougainville)	3(?)	7,390(?)		
Guadalcanal	1	1,500		
Kavieng	5	8,233	7	20,701
Kula Gulf	1	1,200	1	3,000
Shortland Islands	1	750 (plus 2 submarines?)		
Simpson Harbor (Rabaul)	1	100		

although the field sank no known vessels. In February 1943, as the enemy evacuated his troops from the northern end of Guadalcanal, three DMs planted a field across the Express' route out. One enemy DD (*Makigumo*) was sunk.

Early in May 1943, Halsey decided to plug the Slot north of New Georgia. He ordered a field laid in Blackett Strait, between Kolombangara and Arundel. Three DMs led by a modern DD for navigation assistance did the job. Admiral Ainsworth at the same time took his three light cruisers and four more DDs to Vella Gulf to cover them. The enemy was taken completely by surprise. Three enemy DDs were sunk on the mines. Mine plants were not always that successful. On May 13, the DMs again headed north, covered again by Ainsworth. The DMs laid their mines with precision and dispatch. But this time, within twenty-four hours the Japanese had them up.

Surface mining of the Kula and Vella Gulfs and of the Shortlands followed in a series of operations lasting through November 1943. The Kula Gulf field sank one enemy merchantman. The Shortlands field accounted for two enemy submarines and a merchant vessel. Mining by aircraft was coordinated with surface laying. Navy and

Marine Avenger torpedo bombers mined Kahili and Buin harbors (both Bougainville) in March 1943. Replenishment of this field followed in May. Faisi harbor (Shortlands) was mined at the same time. Buka Pass (between Bougainville and Buka) was mined later.

The last mining operation carried out from the Solomons was by Navy Avengers, in Rabaul's Simpson Harbor, in February 1944. Navy aircraft losses there were high. Only one small ship was sunk in this field.[4] Mining in Rabaul should have been a worthwhile effort, but B.17s with their greater capacity were needed for this.

AIRSOLS AGAIN

Just when it appeared that New Georgia and Bougainville had been pounded down, the enemy air commander decided to go for broke. Just before noon on June 16, 1943, a 120-plane enemy strike headed for Guadalcanal in one last desperate gamble. No one thought the enemy had that many planes left there. Mitscher sent around 100 fighters to meet them. What followed was the largest air battle of the Solomons war, and the largest kill. One hundred and seven enemy planes were downed, the remainder fled. All at a cost of six American planes.

AIRSOLS was not the only force being regularized and prepared for the future. Guadalcanal was being turned into one huge staging and training area. Amphibious Force headquarters was now ashore on Koli Point, at Camp Crocodile. AIRSOLS was asked to destroy an important enemy facility on Greenwich Island, 700 miles away, too far for fighter escort. Lieutenant Commander Bruce A. Van Voorhis volunteered to go. Van Voorhis did not return, but the facility was wiped out. Forced low by Zeros, he had made six tree-level runs on the target, and was finally caught in his own bomb blast. Another medal of honor.

NEW GEORGIA (OPERATION TOENAILS)

For the New Georgia operation, three principal task forces were designated. From his headquarters in Noumea, Admiral Halsey himself retained overall command of the covering forces. These last were led by Admirals Ainsworth and Merrill, and provided both surface protection and fire support. The amphibious force was again commanded by Admiral Turner, relieved by Admiral Wilkinson after the first two weeks. AIRSOPAC again constituted the third task force, with Admiral Mitscher exercising tactical command of the land-based planes.

Mitscher's flyers having softened up New Georgia, it was coming time for the fat amphibious ships to run into the beaches. Small preliminary Marine landings took place on June 21 and 30, and on July 2 and 3. Each one was a success.

Admiral Merrill led one of the covering forces—light cruisers, destroyers, and minelayers—in another preliminary operation, up the Slot. He went as far north as the Buin-Shortland area, 200 miles further on. Two of the destroyers fell out to shell Vila; the minelayers laid their cargoes across the southern entrance to Bougainville Strait to seal it against raids against U.S. forces off Munda; and the remainder shot up enemy positions as they went.

Rabaul was somehow taken by surprise. When IJN submarine *RO103* reported Turner's main amphibious force approaching from the south on the thirtieth, most of its Solomons air had been pulled back to Rabaul bases. Other enemy submarines, however, sank two American freighters.

Munda was protected by reefs, so the Allies used Rendova Island—seven miles offshore—as an interim staging area and a site for their artillery. Two hours after six Allied transports began unloading, howitzers were exchanging fire with the enemy. The principal objectives—Munda (especially) and Vila fields—were expected to be soon taken. The landing on New Georgia was all but over by the time an enemy air raid showed up. All it did was torpedo Turner's flagship—transport *McCawley*. *McCawley* was abandoned, then sunk in error by U.S. PT boats. Ashore, where things had begun so well, they soon fell apart. Halsey sent two more divisions into the fight. As Halsey looked back on ELKTON, the smoke of charred reputations "made him cough."[5] War is the personnel registers' great auditor.

KULA GULF (JULY 5–6)

In the Battle of Kula Gulf—the first of six major sea actions in this second phase of the Solomons affair—the IJN showed once again that its people were dangerous in a night brawl. This battle was an indirect result of Munda. Seeing a threat to its other holdings in the central islands, Rabaul decided to reinforce Kolombangara, just to the north of New Georgia. Rabaul organized an Express and sent it in on the night of July 4–5. Included were seven destroyer-transports and three destroyers. But Ainsworth's three light cruisers and four destroyers were already there, on a bombardment mission. The Express was pulled back, first sinking destroyer *Strong*, at such long range that the USN thought the torpedo came from a submarine.

The following night, the Express came back. Ainsworth came out to meet them between Kolombangara and New Georgia. Ainsworth picked up the Express on his radar before the radarless Express saw him. The Navy proceeded to give itself away by opening with its guns at some six miles. The enemy responded with torpedoes. Three torpedoes hit light cruiser *Helena*, tearing off her bow and folding her in two. She went down in three minutes. The enemy lost one destroyer to gunfire, and another, which ran aground landing troops, to bombing the next day. Three more were damaged. But perhaps two thousand troops were in the end dropped off, as planned, by the enemy. Nearly two hundred of *Helena's* crew were left in the water. One hundred sixty-five of them eventually made shore on Vella Lavella, north of Kolombangara. They hid in the jungle until ten U.S. destroyers dashed up the Slot and picked them up on July 16.[6]

KOLOMBANGARA (JULY 12–13)

The two navies clashed again in the Battle of Kolombangara when an Express (light cruiser *Jintsu* with five DDs and four destroyer-transports) met up with Ainsworth, again. New Zealand light cruiser *Leander* had replaced *Helena*, bringing Ainsworth's force back up to three light cruisers. By now, he had ten DDs.

The enemy still carried no radar, but they had just acquired a radar detector. The enemy was thereby enabled to locate Ainsworth by the emissions of his radar before his radar found them. The enemy had therefore already launched their torpedoes before the USN opened up with its own torpedoes and guns. *Jintsu* was literally blown out of the water by 2,600 rounds of 6-inch from the USN's light cruisers, but the enemy's Long Lances sank destroyer *Gwin* and heavily damaged all three cruisers. The enemy nonetheless managed to land twelve hundred troops on Kolombangara's west coast in the early hours of the thirteenth, as planned. They then returned to Buin (Bougainville).[7] The IJN's destroyer leaders were taking Tanaka's loss of face to heart.

In retrospect, these two battles could hardly be called American victories. Obviously, the USN could not match the IJN's night surface tactics. In both of his battles, Ainsworth determinedly came in close, making him an easy visual target. He then waited too long to open fire, thus allowing the enemy time to deliberately aim and fire his torpedoes. In each case, these reached Ainsworth just as he was belatedly turning away.

WILKINSON, BURKE, MITSCHER, ET AL.

Brilliant, quiet, studious Rear Admiral Theodore S. Wilkinson relieved Turner in mid-July and now commanded the amphibious force. Wilkinson's assets included an ad hoc destroyer force known as DesSlot, the commander of which now was Captain Arleigh Burke. DesSlot became the incubator and testing unit for some badly needed new ideas.

Burke, as COMDESSLOT, commanded whatever Third Fleet DDs were available for independent tasks in waters of the Central Solomons, supplementing Merrill's and Ainsworth's task groups. It was while serving here under Wilkinson that Burke developed his fighting concepts for DDs in narrow seas. He obviously studied every post-action report he could get his hands on. Building on a year of every predecessor's mistakes—and listening to young officers around him—his ideas finally reversed what had been a very grim picture. Burke's ideas would grow and gradually gain acceptance through trial and error, as we shall soon see.

Late in July, Admiral Mitscher was relieved and sent home. His health had given out. Mitscher had relieved a rear admiral. He was relieved by an Air Force Major General. Jointness in action worked then, too. In any event, Mitscher had done his job. The enemy air threat in the Solomons had been chewed up and spit out. His box score was 340 enemy fighters and 132 bombers destroyed, seventeen ships sunk and eight damaged. He had dumped 2,083 tons of bombs on the enemy. One hundred thirty-one of his pilots had been snatched from enemy waters and jungle by his rescue planes.[8]

It took U.S. troops ten days short of three months to complete the conquest of New Georgia and its adjacent islands. The main objective—Munda airfield—actually fell only on August 5.

Marine air-ground support was available, but little was used. Pilots were usually briefed a day ahead for air support missions. Targets ordinarily were supply dumps, bivouac areas, and artillery positions. This proved too inflexible, not responsive to unexpected crises. In any case, the available maps were inaccurate and lacked sufficient detail. Troops had difficulty designating targets. They had little idea of what they could and could not get from their air. They themselves were sometimes strafed by their own air. Troops preferred to use their own mortars on close-in targets, or the division's artillery.

One significant innovation here was the first organization of a system of forward air controllers. Although rudimentary, it was aimed at really close air support of the ground troops. Air-ground liaison parties of two Marine pilots and two enlisted radiomen each were given a vehicle, communications, various visual means of target designation and of identifying the front line, and sent out. They did help.

The whole affair turned into an inch-by-inch struggle over truly appalling terrain. Shore-based artillery, naval shore bombardment, and supporting air expended mountains of ammunition. But the well-dug-in enemy always managed to recover to launch another bayonet attack. It took another six weeks of mopping up before the last enemy was killed by the numerically much superior U.S. troops. At New Georgia, the U.S. suffered 1,000 men killed in action, and 4,000 wounded in action. Japan lost perhaps 10,000, killed, wounded, and missing.[9]

Naval fighter direction techniques—which had first made their appearance in the Solomons during the Guadalcanal landings—had by now been worked up into a fine art. Radar had been hugely improved, as had our VHF communications nets. Capital ships and major airfields boasted full-blown fire direction centers. DDs had fighter-direction teams aboard. This all materially increased the Navy's ability to operate ships in daylight, ever nearer enemy bases, ever further into harm's way. So did the adoption of VT (proximity-fuzed) shells for the Allies' larger guns. Introduced into SOPAC the preceding January, this fuze was a miniature radar. Rather than depending on time or contact, the fuze set off the shell whenever it came within seventy feet of a solid target. Deadly for AA work, the fuze could also be used against surface targets. Also helpful was adoption of the 40-millimeter gun. Director-controlled, twin and quadruple 40s proved just the thing for close-in AA defense. These guns were useful against thin-skinned surface targets, also.

The logistics problems were getting solved as well. Another major advance was signaled when the first of the new landing ships and craft began to arrive in the theater. Both ships and craft had ramped, shelving bows, enabling them to nose into beaches to unload. Landing ships enabled operations to be shore-to-shore, loading at a base and unloading on the objective beach. Landing craft were usually identified with larger vessels and were employed carrying troops and cargo to and from ships and shore, but they could for short distances also work shore-to-shore. Together they represented a major increase in amphibious capability.

NOTES

1. William F. Halsey and J. Bryan III, *Admiral Halsey's Story* (New York: McGraw-Hill, 1947), pp. 153–55.

2. Theodore Taylor, *The Magnificent Mitscher* (Annapolis, MD: Naval Institute, 1954), pp. 144–60.

3. Theodore Roscoe, *United States Destroyer Operations in World War II* (Annapolis, MD: Naval Institute, 1953), pp. 216–17.

4. Ellis A. Johnson and David A. Katcher, *Mines Against Japan* (White Oak, MD: Naval Ordnance Laboratory, 1973), pp. 103–06.

5. Halsey and Bryan, pp. 159–61.

6. Roscoe, pp. 225–29.

7. Ibid., pp. 230–32.

8. Taylor, pp. 160–61.

9. Halsey and Bryan, pp. 161–65.

HIJN *Furutaka* (heavy cruiser): six 8-inch guns, eight 24-inch torpedo tubes on 9,150 tons; 33 knots (as reconstructed).

HIJN *Jintsu* (old light cruiser used as destroyer leader): seven 5.5-inch and two 3-inch guns, eight torpedo tubes on 5,950 tons; 33 knots. Early in the war, she carried a catapult and one plane in place of the after guns.

HIJN *Nowaki* (*Kagero*-class destroyer): six 5-inch guns, eight 24-inch torpedo tubes on 2,033 tons; 35 knots.

Zero (single-seat single-engined fighter): two 20-millimeter cannon, two .30 caliber machine guns; 340 miles per hour; wartime markings.

USS *Enterprise* (aircraft carrier): 80+ aircraft, eight 5-inch guns; 19,900 tons; 34 knots.

Wildcat (single-seat single-engined fighter): six .50-caliber machine guns; 318 miles per hour; as fighter-bomber carried two 250-pound bombs; early war markings (the red ball in the center of the star was removed beginning Spring 1942 to avoid confusion with the enemy).

Dauntless (two-place single-engined scout bomber): two fixed .50-caliber and one twin .30-caliber machine guns; 230 miles per hour; carried up to 1,600 pounds of bombs. Note air brakes used in dive-bombing.

USS *South Dakota* (battleship): nine 16-inch and sixteen 5-inch guns on 35,000 tons; 28 knots.

USS *Helena* (light cruiser): fifteen 6-inch and eight 5-inch guns on 10,000 tons; 34 knots.

USS *Young* (Fletcher-class destroyer): five 5-inch guns, ten 21-inch torpedo tubes on 2,050 tons; 35 knots.

USS *Gillespie* (Benson-Livermore-class destroyer): four 5-inch guns, ten 21-inch torpedo tubes on 1,630 tons; 37 knots.

USS *Mayrant* (Craven-Mccall-class destroyer): four 5-inch guns, sixteen 21-inch torpedo tubes on 1,500 tons; 36.5 knots (as built).

USS S 42 (submarine): four 21-inch torpedo tubes; one 3-inch gun; 870/1,135 tons; 15/11 knots, surface and submerged.

USS PT-552 (Elco 80-class motor torpedo boat): four 21-inch torpedoes, automatic cannon and machine guns; 80 feet long; 40 knots; depth charges or mines could replace two of the torpedoes.

USS *Zeilin* (transport): 14,123 tons; 20 knots; up to 1,500 troops.

USS *Sicard* (old destroyer converted into minelayer): three 3-inch guns; 1,160 tons; 30 knots; up to 80 mines.

USS LST 265 (landing ship, tank): 1,490 tons; 11 knots; up to over 1,800 tons of cargo, less if beached.

U.S. landing craft at beachhead on Guadalcanal.

Japanese transport (gutted, beached).

The By-Pass Strategy Arrives—
Vella Lavella

RABAUL—THE PRIZE

As Halsey saw it, the second phase of the climb up the Solomons had opened with the occupation of the Russells. By doing so, the Allies gained a toehold that much closer to the enemy's base at Munda, on New Georgia. Munda blocked the path to Bougainville in the Northern Solomons. Bougainville blocked the way to Rabaul. Munda was now in Allied hands.

Rabaul sat on a magnificant natural harbor—Simpson Harbor, ten miles across—at the north end of New Britain, at the entrance to the Solomon Sea. Japan had overwhelmed its small Australian garrison only seven weeks after Pearl Harbor. Tokyo began immediately to develop the town into its major South Pacific base, second only to Truk. It built five airfields, fortified the steep surrounding hills, and poured in troops and supplies. The great Japanese South Pacific naval base of Truk in the Carolines was yet another 700 miles to the north. Truk could be contained. If Rabaul could be either captured or neutralized, the Allies would have opened a gap in Japan's defenses through which they could reach northwest for the Philippines and beyond.

When in Kula Gulf on July 5, DD *Strong* was torpedoed, and she left survivors. One of them was a Lieutenant Hugh B. Miller, hurt but eventually to make Arundel Island. After giving up his shoes and survival gear to three others, he was left to die. Recovering, he found a dead enemy infantryman, complete with uniform, rations, and hand grenades. On August 5, or thereabouts, he succeeded in ambushing an enemy patrol, killing them all. Now relatively well-equipped, Miller built himself a lean-to in the jungle from which he continued to harass the enemy. By the time he was seen from the air and picked up, he had killed about thirty enemy and gathered much useful intelligence. For this, he received a Navy Cross.

PT-BOATS (MOTOR TORPEDO BOATS)

The first PT-boats had arrived in the theater under their own power, pulling into Tulagi's Government Wharf on October 12. They had been much in evidence since. They participated actively in the Battle of Guadalcanal, annoying two IJN cruisers enough so that they stopped shelling CACTUS and left. The PTs had also hampered but obviously not defeated the Express. It had been a continuous, running battle, every night. PT59 (LTjg John M. Searles) had sunk a blockade-running 2,000-ton submarine—I3—on December the ninth. Three PTs led by Lieutenant (jg) Lester H. Gamble sank Tanaka's newest flagship, light cruiser (*Jintsu's* replacement, DD *Teruzuki*, on the twelfth.

The PT squadrons were now organized into a task group (TG 30.3, COMO Edward J. Moran). Besides some fifty PTs, Moran controlled two PT tenders, six motor gunboats, a variety of gun-armed supporting landing craft, and one small coastal supply ship used to carry priority cargo from base to base.

After New Georgia, the PTs had their last actions with enemy DDs and their first with armored barges. These barges were too small and too shallow of draft to use torpedoes on. They were also more heavily armed than the PTs. The whole affair just moved into shallower water, closer to shore. PTs escorted by motor gunboats reconnoitered up enemy rivers before minelaying operations designed to disrupt this barge traffic. USN landing craft would then foul these rivers with mines, forcing the barges away from the shore into the open where PTs could get at them.[1]

VELLA GULF (AUGUST 6–7)

Commander Frederick Moosbrugger was a friend of Captain Burke's and knew of his work on destroyer fighting doctrine. Moosbrugger led six destroyers against the Express on the sixth, in the Battle of Vella Gulf. There were four enemy destroyers, three of them Kolombangara-bound transports. Vella Gulf was a clear victory for Moosbrugger's well-drilled DDs and Burke's ideas.

Amphibious Force's Admiral Wilkinson had told Moosbrugger to fight the battle as he saw fit. With six DDs (*Dunlap, Craven, Maury, Lang, Sterett,* and *Stack,* the last three under CDR Roger Simpson) he did. Moosbrugger's division had operated as a unit since May 1941. Further, their specialty was night torpedo attack using radar fire control.

DDs in these days carried two principal weapons—guns and torpedoes. Moosbrugger's main armament—5-inch guns—were fine, sturdy weapons. The same could not be said of the torpedoes. There had been technical troubles with them since the war began. Their depth-setting mechanism was erratic. They were equipped with a magnetic exploder which tended to fire too soon or not at all. When firing, the torpedo tubes flashed, not as badly as guns but enough to be seen, especially at night. Moosbrugger had done what he could to minimize these problems. His torpedoes were tended with great care. He had deactivated his torpedoes' cranky magnetic exploder, relying instead entirely on the contact pistol. His torpedo batteries were equipped with new flash hiders.

Against shallow-draft barges, torpedoes were wasted. Moosbrugger's DDs carried as secondary armament the new twin 40-millimeter guns, deadly against barges. Moosbrugger's technical improvements were about to pay off. But they alone would not be enough. He also had to know how to put it all together, and he did.

Moosbrugger's plan was for the two destroyer divisions to team up, steaming in separate columns two miles apart, Simpson's a little astern of Moosbrugger's. If the target proved to be DDs, Moosbrugger's division would take them on, using torpedoes. If barges were met, Simpson's—armed with the new 40-millimeters—would take them.

Moonset had turned the night into a coal-hole. A rain squall managed to make it worse. Surface visibility was less than 4,000 yards. At 062333 August 1943, *Dunlap* made the first radar contact. At 2336 Moosbrugger prepared to fire. Simpson headed for the enemy's disengaged bow, ready to join in. The enemy was in column. Alerted, the enemy tried to reverse course, turning to his right away from the Allies. Fired at 4,000 yards, the USN's twenty-four torpedoes could not miss. All three enemy destroyer-transports along with the 900 troops they were carrying were sunk by torpedoes at no loss to the Allies. Only the escorting DD got away. As usual, the enemy refused rescue.[2]

BY-PASSING BEGUN—VELLA LAVELLA

Nonetheless, at this rate the schedule for the recapture of enemy-held South Pacific islands could be torn up and thrown away. Given the chance of defense in depth, a few thousand dedicated enemy could tie the Allies down for months. Considering the current casualty rates and the gains, the enemy strategy—sapping the American will to fight—still might work. On the Allied side, fresh thinking was in order.

Amphibious forces Admiral Wilkinson, a long-time student of naval strategy, had long been eager to take advantage of Pacific geography, by-passing the strongest Japanese garrisons, sealing them off by air, land, and sea, and leaving them to "wither on the vine." Captain Harry R. Thurber of Halsey's staff had advocated by-passing Munda early in 1943. The Allies ended up having to take it anyway, simply because there had been nowhere else satisfactory for them to go to.

The next island targeted by ELKTON was Kolombangara. There had long been a fighter strip at Vila. On the island now were some 10,000 troops. But Allied experience on New Georgia had made them shy of taking on another such defended island. There is some argument about where the idea of by-passing strongly defended enemy outposts originated. But there can be no doubt that in the end, Kolombangara was by-passed in favor of Vella Lavella, thirty-five miles farther on, an easier if just as useful target. SOWESPAC approved the change.

THE LANDING

Vella Lavella at this point had a garrison of only some hundreds, and its shoreline offered ground for at least one air strip as well as a PT base. The Allies completed a thorough reconnaissance before the end of July and assembled a mixed Marine and Army force, setting L-Day as August 15.

On the fifteenth, the landings at Barakoma Bay on the eastern foot of the island achieved complete surprise. They were uncontested except from the air. Enemy planes did interfere with the second and third waves but caused little damage. By sunset of L-Day 4,600 troops were ashore. During the two weeks following the landings, Admiral Wilkinson delivered 2,000 more men and 8,626 tons of cargo to the island, fought off scores of enemy air raids, and turned back one enemy reinforcement effort. The air strip site of course had priority status. The site was cleared by September 3, and operational by the twenty-seventh.[3]

BASE HORANIU

The only drawback in the plan to by-pass Kolombangara was that there were not enough ships to seal it off altogether. Rabaul decided now to evacuate first its Kolombangara garrison, then the little one on Vella Lavella, to Bougainville, the expected next battlefield on the Allied road to Rabaul. This would again shorten its perimeter, and make it easier to defend.

Rabaul's evacuation plans had the effect—fortunately or otherwise—of requiring that Japanese lines of communication running south to Kolombangara overlap and cross the Americans' north to Vella Lavella. The result was a whole series of intense brawls between the respective light forces. American DDs and PTs duelled with their barges nearly every night. Nonetheless, during the nights at the end of September and early October, Rabaul succeeded in extracting some 9,000 men from these islands. They would soon be faced again.

To ease their problem, Rabaul set up a troop assembly area and staging point for its barges at Horaniu, on the northeast tip of Vella Lavella. By August 19, the staging point was established by a small detachment covered by four DDs, despite a skirmish at sea on the way. The Allies continued mopping up Vella Lavella, advancing slowly over the rest of the island. The Allies were in vastly superior numbers (6,300 men now), but were still using firepower to save lives. Horaniu was obliterated on September 14.[4]

BARGE TRAFFIC

The price exacted from Japan for all this resort to barge traffic was a terrible one. On September 9, Corsair fighters alone sank nine enemy troop and supply barges. On the fourteenth, PTs sank five. On the twenty-eighth, DDs sank four; on the twenty-ninth, three; on the thirtieth, six. On October 1 and 2—moonless—the Allies sank twenty barges a night. On the fourth, they got sixteen. This last brought up the known total to some 598 barges in three months. Many carried troops.

These barges traveled in convoys here, for self-protection. They were escorted by specialized gun-barges as well as submarine chasers. They were defended with machine gun and artillery fire from nearby beaches. They were even given some air cover by night-flying float planes.

By this time, more than fifty PT boats were causing major disruptions in enemy troop and supply runs. Allied coastwatchers noted these swarms of enemy barges creeping up and down the Slot and reported them. By day, the enemy pulled into lagoons, or hid in jungle-screened bays. By night, the barges chugged and putted along the channels carefully hugging the shore.

But for the enemy there were fewer and fewer places to hide. Over the Slot patrolled Allied planes, by night as well as day. Up it steamed U.S. DDs. PT boats covered the areas closer in. Both had the task of finding and sinking those barges. As during the last days at Guadalcanal, the enemy was paying a fierce price for very little.[5]

DD NIGHT TACTICS

The USN started out in the solomons using combined cruiser-destroyer forces. Typically, for major engagements these moved in column, using a "line of battle": van DDs—cruisers (main body)—and rear DDs. This line was intended for gun actions, mini-Jutlands. In the USN, cruisers did not even carry torpedoes. The DDs acted as the fleet's torpedo craft. So far, in battle this formation had only caused trouble. In the van, the DDs were usually the first to sight the enemy. If they could have fired at once, their torpedoes could have done much damage to the enemy. But cruiser admirals were loath to turn the DDs loose, much less let them fire on a target until identification was absolutely certain. By the time permission to fire was received, the opportunity had passed. The DDs ended up simply scurrying to get and keep out of the way of the others. Sometimes, U.S. DDs ended up targets of both sides or were sunk by friendly fire. Searchlights just drew fire.

All throughout this time, U.S. destroyers and small craft prowled, fought with the enemy, won some, lost some. There were many routine convoys to escort, many independent minor DD actions. ASW was practised, barges were shot up. There was no shortage of hard-charging young officers. But as events were soon to prove, the USN still had not really got the hang of large-scale DD actions, especially at night. That would take a while yet.

THE SOLUTION

Surface night warfare was the last and least tractable Solomons problem to be really solved. Captain Burke's destroyer fighting concept brought some imagination and flexibility to the raw courage the DDs had shown all along. His plan was based on DDs hitting the enemy with some sudden surprise after another, maneuvering, using radar and both his main weapons (guns, torpedoes) to their best advantage. Working with cruisers or not, Burke split his DD force into two divisions, moving them not in one long column but in two shorter but more maneuverable parallel columns. Against Japanese DDs—the usual and most dangerous enemy—the nearest American division—the one expected to first pick up the enemy—would under cover of night or smoke immediately attack, launch its torpedoes, and duck back out. Ordinarily it would not at this point yet have opened with its guns. As Burke saw it, the enemy at night aimed his torpedoes at gun flashes. Therefore the first reaction after firing torpedoes should be to turn away, bringing guns to bear only when the second section was in position to finish off the damaged and disorganized enemy.

Unfortunately, American torpedoes were still a problem, still unreliable both as to running and as to exploding. But to maintain course after firing torpedoes or (especially) guns was to invite the deadly Long Lances. Therefore, the Navy had to turn away at once. When the torpedoes hit or the enemy had otherwise located and opened fire on the first division, the second half of the team would suddenly open fire from a different side. When the surprised enemy turned to meet this new attack, the first division would slam back in again, this time using its guns. These tactics would be repeated as often as called for.[6]

It is interesting to note that as the USN worked out this solution, the IJN came up with a similar answer. It too went from the long single column as a fighting formation to the parallel short ones. But by now, for them, it was too late to exploit it.

The Solomons area was ideally suited to these tactics; its many islands—which had long sheltered the enemy—would now help hide the Allies from lookout or electronic detection until battle. Against barges, of course, guns would remain the primary weapon. Otherwise, Burke's tactics would apply. Ironically, Burke's ideas would be tried out by others before he had his own chance to test them. On September 18, the American troops on Vella Lavella were relieved by a New Zealand division, letting them finish the job. The New Zealanders pushed a pincer movement up both coasts.

The last of the 600 enemy on Vella Lavella were bottled up by October 1. Horaniu no longer usable, Rabaul sent in DDs to bring them out. The result was another naval clash—the Battle of Vella Lavella.

VELLA LAVELLA (OCTOBER 6)

Rabaul was still salvaging what it could. To rescue the less than a battalion of troops left on Vella Lavella, the enemy sent nine DDs from the IJN's dwindling and now effectively irreplaceable stock, three of them destroyer-transports. Militarily, they should not have bothered, especially having lost almost forty DDs in the past year, but honor was apparently at stake. So was the USN's, when three U.S. DDs took on six of theirs, knowingly, trying to stop them.

The overcommitted and dispersed Americans scraped up a division of three DDs under the command of Captain Frank R. Walker, and added a distant three more, all that could be spared from convoying troops. Walker's force was thus divided into two parts. The second three of his DDs, under Commander Harold O. Larson, was still twenty miles away coming up when action was joined.

The two forces met in the Slot off Vella Lavella before midnight on October the sixth. Both were fully aware of the other's approach and they swung parallel to each other on opposite courses. Walker opened fire first with his torpedoes, then his guns, at 7,000 yards. The Japanese DDs answered in kind. Within minutes, one enemy DD (*Yugumo*) and one U.S. DD (*Chevalier*) were sinking. *O'Bannon* collided with *Chevalier*. Larson arrived with the other three DDs just after midnight, and was left to pick up the pieces.

Under cover of the clash, the enemy had been able to load up and carry off their rescued troops. The enemy had to abandon sinking destroyer *Yugumo*, but notched up a clear if sterile small tactical victory in their stock-in-trade, the night action. What had happened was magnificent, but it was not war. Torpedoed *Selfridge* was saved, but had to be scuttled later. *Chevalier* sank.[7]

There were other things going on, however. The Americans found that inshore teams made up of a PBY "Black Cat," a DD, and one or more PTs together did good work. The Black Cats—orbiting overhead—found and on request illuminated the target. The PTs then flushed it or even took it on. If help was needed, the DD turned her guns on the enemy from deeper water. This team was used often now.

EVALUATION

Occupation of Vella Lavella was now complete. Its seizure concluded the Central Solomons Campaign. This campaign had cost the USN six men o'war, the IJN seventeen. Vella Lavella had cost the Allies less than 150 dead and had validated the by-pass strategy. The Allies now had the strategic initiative. On the other hand, the Allies had spent five months preparing for, and three months executing, their advance just 250 miles up a chain of islands that were 2,500-3,000 miles from Tokyo. Things should go more quickly now.

By-pass strategies were, however, only an option open to the Allies because of their sufficient control of the sea (and air). Within limits, this gave them the freedom to do as they wished. They could go around enemy-held islands. These could no longer hurt them, and they no longer needed them. Those islands by-passed by U.S. forces were kept isolated (real blockaded), and allowed to wither, starve, and die. Any further action taken depended as much on political or administrative convenience as anything else. Usually, none was taken. Bougainville, the main island in the Northern Solomons, was to be next. It could not be by-passed. And on Bougainville the enemy was digging in for what promised to be the toughest defense yet. These defenses, at least, could be by-passed.

NOTES

1. Robert J. Bulkley, Jr., *At Close Quarters* (Washington, DC: Naval History Division, 1962), pp. 85–165, passim.

2. Theodore Roscoe, *United States Destroyer Operations in World War II* (Annapolis, MD: Naval Institute, 1953), pp. 233–37.

3. William F. Halsey and J. Bryan III, *Admiral Halsey's Story* (New York: McGraw-Hill, 1947), pp. 170–71.

4. Dan van der Vat, *The Pacific Campaign* (New York: Simon and Schuster, 1991), pp. 283–84.

5. Halsey and Bryan, p. 172.

6. E. B. Potter, *Admiral Arleigh Burke* (New York: Random House, 1990), pp. 76–77, 83–84.

7. Roscoe, pp. 239–42.

The Northern Solomons— Bougainville

BOUGAINVILLE

Bougainville at the top of the Slot was the last major obstacle on the road to Rabaul. Some 150 miles long and thirty miles wide, covering about 4,000 square miles, it was another piece of extremely hostile territory. It is the largest of the Solomon Islands, violin-shaped, split down its back by a mountain range which included two active volcanoes. Except for a coastal plain at its south end, it is covered in dense jungle. Buka Island lay just off the north coast, effectively part of the larger island. The Shortlands and the Treasury Islands were also strategically a part of the main island.

In the almost two years that Japan had occupied Bougainville, it had turned the island complex into a considerable fortress. First it had established a seaplane base. Then it had built four airfields; a fifth strip was located on Ballale, an island a few miles to the south. Under construction at Kieta was another strip. The fortress was garrisoned by some 60,000 men, two-thirds Army.

Fully aware of the looming major battle, the Japanese had prepared for it. Among other things, they had made a determined effort to sweep the islands clear of Allied coastwatchers and residual Australian

Army elements. Those few who escaped these attentions had had to be evacuated by submarine in March.

Strategic Interest

Bougainville was by now of interest to the Allies for only one reason. CARTWHEEL's principal objective was still Rabaul, but now with a twist. Out of the August 1943 Combined Anglo-American Chiefs of Staff conference at Quebec had come a decision not to actually seize Rabaul, but rather only to neutralize and by-pass it, relying primarily on Allied air power to do it. Achieving this effectively meant having Allied forward airfields on Bougainville. On them the Allies would base the escort fighters for the heavy bombers coming up from the south in ever-increasing numbers to pound Rabaul. On them, too, the Allies would base the shorter-legged dive- and torpedo-bombers needed to sink Rabaul's ships and silence its guns.

In the Solomons, seizing Bougainville—which could not be neutralized and by-passed—would complete task two. In this event, Halsey decided not to seize even all of forbidding, heavily-defended Bougainville itself. He intended only to seize enough of an enclave to provide for those airfields that he needed. This meant holding indefinitely a perimeter around the enclave, but considering the price taking the whole island would exact, this Halsey was willing to accept.

Halsey's Third Fleet was for Bougainville to be supported again by COMAIRSOPAC's (Vice Admiral Aubrey W. Fitch's) shore- and tender-based air. Wilkinson's III Amphibious Force was to bring in and land Lieutenant General Vandegrift's I Marine Amphibious Corps. Wilkinson would be in tactical command of the landing itself until Major General Roy S. Geiger—relieving Vandegrift—established himself ashore as commander of ground forces. The whole was to be orchestrated from forward headquarters on the Canal.

CAPE TOROKINA

Halsey chose Cape Torokina—about seven miles square, easily defended—in Empress Augusta Bay, about halfway up Bougainville's southwest coast, as the initial objective. Strategically, it would by-pass Choiseul, the adjacent large island to the southeast, and the Shortlands. It would bring all of Bougainville's airfields within a radius of sixty-five miles and Rabaul itself within 215 miles—a range that Allied fighters could easily cover. It would also put behind the Allies the three main airfields in the south: Kahili, Kara, and Ballale.

Torokina was near enough to Rabaul to be a good base for fighters escorting bombers coming up at first from Munda headed north. It was separated from the larger enemy concentrations on the island by many miles of dense tropical rain forest. Thus the Allied troops could expect to have time to dig in—even to build fighter strips—before the enemy reacted in force.

Tactically, Torokina was held by a mere 1,000 troops. Once these had been denied access to the sea, their supplies could only come in over narrow jungle trails. Their supply problem would become acute. It was hoped that a series of small preliminary feints would help throw the enemy off balance.

Cape Torokina was the only point that offered any shelter for shipping on an otherwise unprotected coast open to the monsoons. But Torokina had its disadvantages, too. It still faced the breadth of the Solomon Sea, and was therefore open to the probability of heavy surf. U.S. knowledge of the terrain was scanty. Charts were sketchy and unreliable. U.S. fighter and eventually bomber strips could be dangerously swampy. But it was the best they had.[1]

PRELIMINARY MOVES

While MacArthur's planes struck Rabaul (New Britain) and Kavieng (New Ireland) from New Guinea, AIRSOLS moved up to Munda. From there, late in October, it pounded the enemy's Bougainville fields, all of them, including Buka and Bonis up north. Kahili—the strongest—was hit an average of four times a day.

The Japanese, knowing something big was coming but unable to work out where it would strike, decided they would build up Rabaul as their central air base. To the 200 or so planes of the IJN's land-based 11th Air Fleet stationed there—and still operational—the Combined

Fleet's Koga decided to add some 200 more, stripped again from his carriers. The next Allied advance was to be destroyed from the air.

The first Allied move—a necessary preliminary to the main event—was the seizure by New Zealand troops of the Treasury Islands on October 17. This was partly to distract the enemy, and partly to obtain support bases for the main event: a fighter strip, a radar station, and a small-boat base. This was GOODTIME. The enemy was taken by surprise. The tiny garrison resisted strongly, but the islands were under Allied control by November 6. A Marine parachute battalion roared into Choiseul by way of a further distraction at the same time. There they created as much of an uproar as they could before being pulled out. This was BLISSFUL, begun October 28.

In the Shortlands, the Allies were more elaborate. Their combat patrols deliberately left evidence of their visits. Their photo reconnaissance planes made leisurely, low-level flights almost daily, either followed by or following their bombers. The enemy fell for it, moving troops, artillery, and heavy equipment over from Bougainville, as was hoped. It was learned after the war that they firmly believed it was here the Allies would land. Compare all this with the preparations for WATCHTOWER, only fifteen months earlier. The Allies had learned a lot!

THE LANDING (OPERATION CHERRYBLOSSOM)

The landing at Torokina (CHERRYBLOSSOM) took place on November 1, as scheduled. Minesweepers led the way in. Escorts shelled the beaches. TBFs bombed and strafed for five minutes. As the air lifted its fire, Marines waded ashore. Half of the 300 immediate defenders died, the rest fled. The Allies lost seventy men. This first wave came from the Third Marine Division (MGen A. H. Turnage)— more than 14,000 men on twelve transports, escorted by eleven DDs and strong air cover. But conditions were worse than any previously met with. An unexpected strong onshore wind raised such high surf that eighty-six landing craft broached and were stranded, ruining much of their cargo and putting a strain on the rest of the boat pool. Moreover, many of the beaches were narrow, bordering closely on a vast swamp. These beaches became piled with equipment, food, ammunition, and fuel. One small enemy air raid during the landings was beaten off with no significant loss. Later in the day, a hundred enemy carrier types came in from Rabaul, but they too were beaten off. The transports withdrew at nightfall, most of their work done. Three of them returned the next morning to finish it.[2]

EMPRESS AUGUSTA BAY (NOVEMBER 2)

A strong enemy cruiser-destroyer force—two heavy and two light cruisers plus six destroyers—now came rushing in from the northwest to put an end to this affair. Four U.S. light cruisers and eight destroyers commanded by Admiral Merrill prepared to meet them. They were at the time down south at Vella Lavella, refuelling and taking a breather.

In the enemy force were heavy cruisers *Myoko* and *Haguro*, light cruisers *Sendai* and *Agano*. The heavies were in column in the center of the formation, with three DDs on either flank. The light two—small cruisers—really acted as destroyer-leaders, one for each of the two divisions into which the DDs were divided.

Merrill adopted a similar formation, but echeloned his columns back to his left rear. Burke's division (*Charles Ausburne, Dyson, Stanly, Claxton*) to the east, led. In center column were light cruisers *Montpelier* (flag), *Cleveland, Columbia,* and *Denver*—the main battle line. To the west came Commander B. L. Austin's four DDs, slightly behind. Merrill and Burke had long worked together. Austin was a newcomer, unused to Merrill's ways.

Merrill's plan was to position himself off Empress Augusta Bay, blocking the entrance. Once battle was joined, he intended to elbow the enemy west, fighting a long-range gun battle. But the DDs were to open the action with their own torpedo attacks; the cruisers were to hold their fire until the DDs had had their chance.

As soon as radar contact was made, Merrill set course due north. Burke's van DDs took off, racing northwest for a torpedo firing position. What followed were essentially three separate stories: Burke's, Merrill's, and Austin's. Action opened at 020246. Burke launched his torpedo attack, but without result. Merrill's cruisers made a simultaneous turn about, to reverse course. Austin was sent to hit the enemy's southern flank.

The enemy sighted Merrill's cruisers and turned southwest to roughly parallel them. As soon as Merrill learned of this, his cruisers opened fire. *Sendai* was sunk. *Hatzukaze* was sunk. Maneuvering in the dark at high speed, both sides suffered from a series of collisions. Merrill's cruisers were never able to nail the enemy heavies. After an hour's duel, at 0337 the enemy pulled out, fleeing northwest back toward Rabaul and air cover. Merrill pursued until dawn. Merrill then turned back, expecting heavy retaliation by air from Rabaul. He got it.[3]

EVALUATION

Just from the record presented here, it does seem that if the "line of battle" formation—one long mixed column—was to be retained in a fight, the DDs had to be turned loose. The instant they identified the enemy, DDs should have launched their torpedoes and reported, not report the contact and wait for orders. They then had to be allowed to maneuver as a unit, to develop their own subsequent opportunities to use their torpedoes or guns, or to just get out of the way. They should not be held within the cruisers' gun range. But aside from working with—running interference for—the cruisers, DDs by themselves constituted a potent threat.

One way or the other, it does seem that to ever become truly effective in night actions, the DDs first needed to be formed into semipermanent combat groups, as Deyo said. These groups needed to work up their operation plans. They needed to train together. The officers had to get to know each other. In narrow seas, the nighttime clashes were too sudden, too high speed, too intense for anything else.

The USN was obviously finally getting the hang of operations with cruiser-destroyer forces. Merrill's DDs were not kept close to the main battle line and held there within gun range. Instead, they were given freedom of action, well removed from the main body. They were used offensively, not defensively. Except for Moosbrugger at Vella Gulf, however, the Allies had yet to see them in truly independent squadron actions.

Merrill's victory was marked by a tremendous expenditure of ammunition. The USN had fired nearly forty-six hundred rounds of 6-inch alone, for a maximum twenty hits. The torpedoes put in their usual miserable performance. Out of fifty-two fired, only two torpedoes struck home, both on a crippled ship—maintenance, maybe, manufacture certainly.

KOGA REACTS

Admiral Koga in Truk had already decided on a serious reinforcement of his Rabaul surface forces, to match that of his air and to take some of the load off them. Grimly, he now sent his southern command a force of no fewer than seven heavy cruisers, a light cruiser, and four DDs. Added to what was still left in Rabaul, for Bougainville this spelled trouble.

Halsey now had no battleships, but he did have two carriers: fleet carrier *Saratoga*, fully repaired, and light carrier *Princeton*, formed into Task Force 38 under Rear Admiral Frederick C. Sherman. When news of Koga's reinforcements arrived, Sherman made a high speed run north and got in the first blow. Sherman's strike was a heavy one—ninety-seven planes. His CAP was provided by AIRSOLS from Baracoma. Weather was foul. AA fire was intense. Enemy pilots were good. Still, the Allies shot down twenty-five enemy fighters for five of their own. The Navy did so much damage to six enemy cruisers and two DDs that the next morning only one cruiser and a few destroyers were left in the harbor. The rest were pulled back to Truk, never to return. For the Allies, November 5 had been a red-letter day.

Nimitz in Pearl Harbor now lent Halsey two new fleet carriers—*Essex* and *Bunker Hill*—and new light carrier *Independence*, under Rear Admiral Alfred E. Montgomery. Montgomery was slated to reinforce Sherman for a second strike on Rabaul. On the eleventh, however, Sherman's strike was hampered by bad weather. Montgomery delivered nearly 200 aircraft over the port. They blew the stern off a heavy cruiser, sank one DD, and heavily damaged another. Montgomery's second strike was met going in by a well-over-a-hundred plane counterstrike, coming out at noon. The Allied strike was cancelled and a huge free-for-all blew up over the carriers. For three quarters of an hour, the ships, maneuvering violently, put up a curtain of AA fire. The Navy lost just eleven planes, the enemy perhaps twenty percent.[4]

Rabaul continued to send air raids over, but never in sufficient numbers to be much more than a nuisance. The main effect of these raids was yet more attrition of the IJN's carrier planes, pilots, and aircrew. More than two-thirds of the carrier aircraft sent to reinforce Rabaul, and half their pilots, had been lost, to little end. The 11th Air Fleet they had been sent to strengthen was no better off.

CAPE ST. GEORGE (NOVEMBER 25)

The sixth and last naval battle in this prolonged second phase of the now disproportionate struggle for the Solomons took place on the night of November 25, Thanksgiving 1943. Once again, it was a fight that developed as a result of an enemy attempt at reinforcement, this time with nine hundred men in three destroyer-transports, escorted by two large new enemy DDs. Some specialists would also be brought out.

About 250130, Captain Burke's five DDs began a patrol in the waters between Buka and New Ireland. Burke had his two divisions ranged in two-column echelon formation—*Charles Ausburne* in the lead, followed by *Dyson* and *Claxton*. *Converse* and *Spence* trailed on parallel course to port. Burke was to cut athwart the Buka-Rabaul nightly traffic lane.

The night was moonless, and overcast. There were sporadic rain squalls. Visibility was 3,000 yards. At 0141 *Dyson* made radar contact, a target 22,000 yards to the northeast. Burke headed his squadron for the enemy, moving his second division from left rear to right rear. Burke was bearing down on the two enemy men-of-war which were screening the three transports astern of them and to the east. These last duly appeared on the scopes. The enemy—without radar—was taken completely by surprise and forced to fight blindly in the dark.

Burke's standard operating procedure was followed. Burke's van DDs closed the range to 5,500 yards. Five torpedoes were fired by each van DD, fifteen in all. The leading two new enemy DDs—

Onami and *Makinami*—were sunk or left sinking, putting the three transports on their own. *Converse* and *Spence* were left to finish off the cripple while Burke's three pounded after the fleeing transports. Burke turned his guns on them. In the ensuing gun action, one of them—*Yugiri*—was also sunk. No U.S. ship was even hit, even though Burke chased the remaining two enemy DDs back almost to Simpson Harbor.[5] So after Moosbrugger's, Merrill's, and Burke's performances, it seems the Allies were finally learning how to fight the IJN at night.

SOLDIERING ON

Meanwhile, on Bougainville the Allies continued to reinforce and enlarge their beachhead. However, they failed to intercept two small Japanese reinforcements run in from Rabaul. One was landed close to Torokina and the other at the islands' far northern end.

The Japanese launched a major attack on the enlarged beachhead on November 25. The Marines handily beat them off. Geiger and his Marines were relieved on December 15. By Christmas 1943, the U.S. force ashore behind its fortified Bougainville perimeter consisted of an Army corps headquarters and two Army infantry divisions. On March 25, 1944, after one last futile attack which cost the Japanese 10,000 men, organized resistance in the Solomons ended. Twenty months from Savo.

Meanwhile, eight battalions of CBs and a New Zealand Army engineer unit had built first a modest fighter strip, then a much larger one, capable of taking heavy bombers. The Allies were now ready for Rabaul.

Air-Ground Support

Bougainville marked the beginning of close-air support in the sense we know it today. The capabilities of close support had hitherto not been utilized to the fullest possible extent. Air support was in fact not trusted by those it was to help.

Marine air-ground liaison parties ("forward air controllers") were again organized. But this time there was to be proper preparation for their use. One officer from the operations staff section of each rifle battalion and regiment was also oriented in supporting air's capabilities as well as its limitations, procedures for requesting such support, and air-ground communications methods. This worked. It provided the model for all future efforts.

On December 25, MacArthur, who already held Arawe on New Britain's southwest coast, landed the First Marine Division at Cape Gloucester on the island's northwest coast. In so doing, he cut off the only overland route to and from Rabaul.

RABAUL

Rabaul and its secondary base Kavieng had become for the enemy a useless liability. It had no longer any value as a naval base. It was no longer able to launch effective air strikes. It was nonetheless garrisoned by some 100,000 troops, well dug in, capable of a strong defense. Further, the geography was right for another by-pass. Controlling the eastern approach to Rabaul was Green Island. Dominating the northern approach to Kavieng was Emirau. Controlling the western approaches to both Rabaul and Kavieng was Manus. None was more than 220 miles distant from the Rabaul area. Admiral Halsey sold King on now by-passing Rabaul during a trip back to Washington from Noumea. Nimitz and MacArthur concurred during a meeting at Pearl. All three islands were easily taken. Rabaul's encirclement was now complete.

CARTWHEEL had not gone altogether as intended—specifically not in terms of either time schedule or intermediate objectives—but Rabaul was no longer a threat to anybody's plans. In all, some 100,000 troops were trapped in the Bismarcks. Some 30,000 more were caught on Bougainville and Choiseul. Control of these narrow seas was the Allies'. The South Pacific campaign was effectively over. Task three was never carried out.[6]

THE END

On June 15, 1944, Admiral Halsey turned over command of SOPAC to Vice Admiral John H. Newton, his longtime deputy at

Noumea, and left for Pearl Harbor. Halsey retained command of his Third Fleet, which on paper he took with him. All of his Third Fleet's ships, aircraft, and bases were actually turned over to MacArthur's Seventh Fleet, now commanded by Vice Admiral Kinkaid. MacArthur took them northwest along the New Guinea coast, toward Leyte.

Halsey led his new Third Fleet to further fame west across the far reaches of the Central Pacific. He and MacArthur met again at Leyte, in October 1944. Both ended up in Tokyo Bay in 1945, victors.

NOTES

1. William F. Halsey and J. Bryan III, *Admiral Halsey's Story* (New York: McGraw-Hill, 1947), pp. 173–75.

Samuel Eliot Morison, *The Two-Ocean War* (Boston: Little, Brown, 1963), pp. 285–86.

2. Halsey and Bryan, pp. 175–85, passim.

3. Theodore Roscoe, *United States Destroyer Operations in World War II* (Annapolis, MD: Naval Institute, 1953), pp. 243–47.

4. Halsey and Bryan, pp. 180–83.

5. Roscoe, pp. 264–67.

6. Halsey and Bryan, pp. 190–91.

10

Conclusion

When the USN entered the Solomons back in August 1942, it was a "blue water" high seas, big ship, big gun Mahanian navy par excellance. Its officers had been brought up on—and the Naval War College had exhaustively taught—World War I's Anglo-German Battle of Jutland. In its war plans it dreamed of fighting its way across the wide, empty Central Pacific to defeat the IJN in one great decisive battle somewhere in the neighborhood of the Philippines. It never dreamed that it would also have to slog up the narrow, constricted, jungle-lined, badly charted Solomons seas.

The rampaging main Pacific aircraft carrier war was in fact fought for command of the sea, primarily against a large enemy fleet heavy itself with carriers, out in the broad expanses of blue water. It was a war of long distances, free maneuver, and huge air strikes, as we all know. It always provided the distant and sometimes the close cover for the other war.

The other—amphibious—war was on the contrary fought in narrow seas and restricted waters, exploiting this cover. It was fought against a largely shore enemy, by a series of expeditionary forces. The Navy here only reluctantly provided carriers for support, battleships for shore bombardment, transports and landing ships and craft, minesweepers and escorts, and the Marines to seize and hold its advanced bases. Except for the "Leathernecks," there was little glory here.

Amphibious warfare was war tied to a fixed objective. It was centered on taking and holding a series of bases, limited in direction and distance each time by an inevitable compromise between the thrust of the campaign and the operational range of shore-based planes. Carrier support could fill in gaps here, but not for very long. The Solomons Campaign—the first—best demonstrates the usual challenges and limitations of such warfare.

THE CAMPAIGN

As early as February 1942, Admiral King in Main Navy was taking the position that Japan must not be permitted to consolidate its formidable gains. Limited offensives against the Japanese had to begin and bases secured for future advances. This was part of his offensive defense. Otherwise, Japan would certainly be capable of advancing from Rabaul in the Bismarck Archipelago southwest into New Guinea and southeast into Samoa and even New Caledonia. Australia might be too large a nut even for the Japanese to crack, but the Allies dared not risk this; they would require Australia for a major base as they recovered the Philippines and defeated Japan.

En route to becoming a competent "brown water" (riverine and estuarine) and "white water" (coastal) navy, the U.S. Navy had to learn, unlearn, and relearn many things. For this—except for the Marines— it was unready, both psychologically and materially, and paid for this.

Reality impacted the Navy quite early, in the Solomons. Carrier close support for the Solomons entry—the landing at and the seizure of the Tulagi area—was going to be sufficient as long as there was surprise. This sufficiency would erode with time. Shore- and tender-based air therefore had to play an unusually large role before, during, and after the presence of the carriers. They had range that the carrier-borne types did not have, but there were many functions— CAP and some kinds of strike—such air was not in a position to perform.

The carrier-borne air was in any event never happy about being tied down in a necessarily small area to close support of such an operation within range of enemy shore-based air. Under these conditions, it would be too easy for the enemy to find the carriers and then mobilize superior force against them. This worry jeopardized the whole operation at birth, and at one point left the amphibious force to fate.

U.S. carriers supported the Tulagi landings from positions just to the southwest of the Canal. But the carriers pulled out early, not even staying the full forty-eight hours to which they had committed in the plans. When they did come back—several weeks later—it was well to the east of the islands—to really blue water.

In any case, the early shortage of carriers led to primary reliance on shore-based air, CACTUS being only one example. Shore-based AIRSOLS played a major role in all events, both as an important objective for both sides, then as SOPAC's major offensive arm. In the final days, the only carriers it had came on loan. One result of this reliance on shore-based air was to limit the length of U.S. tactical jumps as they went up the islands to the reach of their fighter cover. They went from one airfield to the next. More carrier air would have given the Allies much greater flexibility during the whole affair, even working from east (or west) of the islands.

This air picture left the Allies with several continuing problems. The operational radius for the action of enemy single-engined planes was approximately 300 miles. That of similar U.S. planes—more sturdily built—was comfortably only 200. Any enemy base within 300 miles had to be considered a threat. U.S. bases, however, could not reach beyond 200. The answer, again, was carriers. For this sort of thing, even small ones could do. They might even be better.

Early in the Solomon days an operational pattern developed. Within range of CACTUS, in daylight, U.S. forces controlled the waters. The IJN controlled them at night. Whatever U.S. ships did, they had to be back either in a safe haven or out of IJN reach by nightfall. Whatever the IJN did, it had to be out of U.S. reach by daylight. Whenever either was caught out, they took serious risk of being sunk, the Allies by IJN surface ships, theirs by Allied air. So it was under cover of this darkness, then, that the IJN carried out its reinforcement and resupply efforts, using what the Allies took to calling the "Tokyo Express." This Express involved the sending of troop and supply ships—and escorts—down the Slot. After completing their primary task, the escorting ships—cruisers and DDs, at first—typically shelled the Marine perimeter, then roared back up the Slot. As the tide of the campaign shifted, the IJN was forced to use only DDs and destroyer-transports for this work.

The Allies did fully appreciate the importance of CACTUS right from the start. From it—once it was up and going—AIRSOLS soon controlled Solomon waters, at least by day. From it the Allies developed some of their determination to fight a primarily naval air war—and an amphibious one—rather than a major surface one. That remained true all the way up the islands.

The IJN never retook full control of Solomon waters once CACTUS was going. They would have had to retake it and use it themselves to help mop up Allied remnants throughout the Tulagi area. Only then could they have picked up on the original push south.

The USN lost two carriers off Guadalcanal—*Wasp* and *Hornet*. *Saratoga* was twice torpedoed by submarines and severely damaged. *Enterprise* was hit from the air three times and heavily damaged. The IJN lost only one carrier. But this does not tell the whole story. American pilots were chewing up the IJN's air arm. There do not seem to be any overall Japanese pilot loss figures, but they were huge. They were leaving the carriers—numerous of which remained—without experienced pilots to fly the planes.

Tokyo Expresses continued to run in one form or another—from Rabaul in the final days—until the very end. The Express kept Japanese forces ashore in the Solomons alive—sometimes barely so. It provided the enemy's baseline support. It contributed to the various buildups. The escorts soon, however, gave up shelling U.S. positions as they left. That became too costly and produced too little.

The Solomons saw the development of another, related operational pattern. The U.S. has identified six naval battles as having taken place around the Canal, and another six during the climb from there north. Most of these—all except the first and the last ones—had as a task providing cover to a major run of the Express. Whether the USN "won" or "lost" these battles, they often did not realize that another Express had successfully completed its run behind the cover.

The way to put an end to the Tokyo Express would have been for the USN not to learn just to survive in the Slot at night, but also how to work there. Then they would have had to position superior naval forces so as to impose a twenty-four-hour blockade to the north of the Canal, or New Georgia, or Bougainville, and keep them there. Since such was not initially possible—they had neither enough ships nor the right tactics—they began painfully to build that "Gator Navy" they should have had all along.

After the December battles no Japanese combattant larger than destroyer ever again appeared off Guadalcanal. That if nothing else signalled the end for them on the island.

In the end, U.S. production always enabled them to replace their losses with more, even better ships, something Japan could seldom do. Gradually, the Allies put the squeeze on the Express, even though they never did entirely cut it off. With better tactics, radar (something IJN DDs never got), VT fuzes, and the new 40-millimeter guns the Allies could hardly miss.

The fight for Guadalcanal's 2,500 square miles of jungle and mud cost the United States and its allies twenty-four naval vessels DD-sized and larger, totalling 126,000 tons. The IJN lost two battleships among a total of nineteen warships sunk, totaling 127,500 tons. Of the 36,000 Japanese who fought on or over the Canal (excluding shipboard personnel), 15,000 were missing or dead, 10,000 died of sickness, and 1,000 were captured. The U.S. committed a total of 60,000, of whom 1,600 were killed. Neither side ever computed its human losses at sea.

The Americans' most decisive victory in the Guadalcanal Campaign was in the air. The Zero was still the best fighter in the theater but was already outnumbered by Allied planes piloted by men who had learned either from experience or from other pilots how to contend with it. Pulling back and shortening their lines, the Japanese were still strong. But the Allies were rapidly getting stronger, flooding the area with their forces. New Georgia, Vella Lavella, and Bougainville followed, inexorably, or so it seemed. The Allies learned to by-pass geography too expensive to take and not really needed. They learned to fight at night in narrow seas.

In the Solomons' narrow waters, the Allies learned once again that there is always close, direct, and continuous interaction in such areas between fighting on land and at sea. Here, too, there was a littoral area—the coastal lands—which could be dominated from the sea, and inshore waters which could be dominated from the land. The former might include whole islands; the latter, entire sounds and gulfs, shore to shore. The relative importance of this interaction—the reach of one into the other—might vary, depending on the weapons and tactics used, and on the visibility at the time.

Finally, the Allies learned "island hopping," by-passing strongly-held Japanese islands that were not needed and that were seen as no threat, isolating them and letting them wither on the vine. Submarines later provided their only link with the outside.

Reading this list must make everything seem academic, but all was not beer and chips. The IJN's 24-inch Long Lance torpedoes were an extremely unpleasant surprise, leaving mental scars that the Allies never really got over. The Allies were never able to achieve full command of the Slot, or to put a stop to the Tokyo Express, early or late. Tokyo was repeatedly able to evacuate its last remaining troops without the Allies being aware of what was going on.

OPERATIONAL PATTERNS

In the Solomons, surface engagements sometimes lasted only minutes, the worst one (Savo) only eight. They were fought at point-blank range, as little as 3,000 yards. These battles were among the most furious sea battles ever fought. They were usually fought in narrow, treacherous waters utterly unsuited to the maneuvering of large ships, especially at night.

In the Solomons, surface naval battles reduced themselves to Japanese torpedoes versus American guns. Only late did we get the equipment and learn to fight them on even terms.

United States light cruisers—especially the 33-knot *Atlanta* class, carrying sixteen 5-inch dual purpose guns on 6,000-tons—ended up the Solomons' capital ships. But the Solomons turned out to be a destroyer war. Boat for boat, Japanese destroyers were better designed, manned and equipped than the Allies', at least until the *Fletcher*-class boats arrived.

U.S. PTs got a good work-out in the Slot every night. These were 80-foot Elco-type craft, essentially light motor torpedo boats. The Allies could have done with some of the British 115-foot heavy Vosper-type motor gun boats used with such effect in the English Channel and North Sea in many of the Solomons' night actions, backing up the PTs.

Until nearly the Solomons' last days, the Allies could not claim to have total air superiority. At best, they had only local control over their holdings, even as they kept pushing them north. They never could absolutely isolate the battlefield, even at the end. On the surface, then, everybody joined the fight.

In the Solomons, mines did not play the role they could have been expected to. Shallow, constricted waters mean mines, used both offensively and defensively. The enemy seems to have used none, the Allies relatively few. But both sides were prepared to sweep, and did. There were no mines at Jutland. In both cases, the corporate memory was too strong to be easily overcome. Allied mining—surface and air—was tactical, in support of other operations. It began right in August 1942, at Malaita, and ran sporadically right through until ended at Rabaul, in February 1944. Compared with those used in Europe, the numbers were trivial.

All in all, Japanese losses to Allied mines here probably totaled fifteen ships sunk, for some 24,100 tons, and eight ships damaged, for about 23,700 tons. The Allies, of course, lost none here to enemy mines, either surface-laid or air-dropped.

Both sides did use submarines in their attempts to isolate the immediate battle area. Neither succeeded. Only one major enemy naval vessel was sunk by Allied submarines here in all of 1942: heavy cruiser *Kako*, by S44. The following year there were no major kills here at all. There should have been more—and none in 1944. In 1942,

Japanese submarines cost the USN carrier *Wasp*, sunk, plus severe damage to *Saratoga* and battleship *North Carolina*. In 1943, assigned mostly other tasks, enemy submarines were withdrawn from offensive patroling. They sank no major Allied naval vessels that year—none in 1944, either. In both cases, the boats used were too big—1,500-2,000-ton fleet boats. The Slot was too shallow for them. In reasonable weather a hunting plane could visually locate a large submarine under as much as 125 feet of water. Smaller 500-600-ton boats would have done better. Also, in the USN's case, the torpedoes were substandard, as has been mentioned before.

When the USN exited the Solomons, Halsey's Third Fleet consisted of III Amphibious Force, with more combatant ships than most whole navies; I Marine Amphibious Corps; and AIRSOLS, larger than most air forces. Camp Crocodile and CACTUS housed the staffs, all getting quite expert.

The Bougainville (Torokina) operation—the Solomons' last—was a model of its kind. Skillfully carried out, Bougainville depended not just on weight of numbers but also on maneuver and deception. In executing this landing, Halsey called on CINCPAC only for carriers for air support and battleships for shore bombardment before and after the landing. Both of these he got. Rabaul, for which so many men had died, was in the end not taken. Rabaul had been isolated and rendered harmless. The Allies no longer needed it, so they let it wither and die on its own. Taking it would have been the toughest job of them all.

FRIENDLY FIRE

There is in the narrow seas a permanent tension, one at least not found to the same degree on the open sea. In the narrow seas there are really only the quick and the dead. As Captain Burke pointed out, the difference between a good officer and a bad (dead) one was about ten seconds—the time it took to estimate the situation, made a decision, and give an order. But then one runs into the problem of "friendly fire." IFF becomes a crucial matter, often reducing itself to visual checkout. By that time, one might be blown off his bridge. Not to get it right can mean sinking the wrong ship.

THE IJN

Three Japanese admirals—Nagumo at Pearl, Mikawa at Savo, and Kurita at Leyte—won startling major victories, but only incomplete ones. Nagumo aborted his third strike that planned to finish off the base. Mikawa quit before getting the transports off Red Beach, Kurita before getting those off Leyte. All three could have completed their tasks. None did. There might be something in Japanese naval culture which encourages such behavior.

SHIP DRIVERS AND INTELLIGENCE

The USN's Admiral Turner ably led his Solomons amphibious forces—except, I think, for his handling of intelligence at Savo. Could he have been repeating past behavior patterns? As pre-World War II chief of the War Plans Division at Main Navy, he had worked out for himself what he thought should be the Navy's posture in the Pacific. He then went so far as to quash any intelligence which undermined his position. He was always a one-man show. That day at Savo, apparently, indications that Mikawa was up to something kept coming in. But partially misled by bad reporting, Turner refused to credit Mikawa with the ability to attack him either with surface forces or that night. Exhaustion and bad temper combine badly.

WORLD WAR II TURNING POINT

There have in naval historical circles long been discussions about whether the Battle of the Coral Sea or the better-known Battle of Midway was World War II's Pacific turning point. Or were they both? A case can be made for either. I would now here put forward the idea that a third major turning point of the Pacific War has been recounted in these pages—Admiral Halsey's five-day naval battle of Guadalcanal.

The Battle of the Coral Sea ended up more or less a draw. Even just to have fought it to a draw under the handicaps the U.S. Navy had was indeed a kind of victory. Moresby was saved, yes. But it was a naval draw nonetheless, not a Mahanian decisive battle. On the other hand, the Battle of Midway was unquestionably an American victory—the

USN here traded one of its carriers for four of theirs. But at its end, the IJN was still the stronger fleet, and could still have won that decisive battle Tokyo was after.

At Coral Sea and Midway, the Allies succeeded in halting the Japanese advance. In the Solomons, the Allies not only stopped them, they began to push them back. Halsey listed all three as turning points.

The Naval Battle of Guadalcanal then has to be *the* turning point. Almost everything in CINCPAC was committed to the battle. If the IJN had committed all of the fleet—not just a part of it—and had beaten the Allies there, they would have had their decisive battle. This was their last real chance, but they let it pass. Even after Guadalcanal, Yamamoto still commanded forces roughly twice the size of the U.S. Navy. His Combined Fleet was rigorously trained, and in spite of the loss of five fleet carriers together with their seasoned pilots, he could muster six or so more. The remainder of Yamamoto's fleet was essentially intact and included *Yamato* and *Musashi* with their 18-inch guns. But it was now too late. The great outpouring of American naval power had begun. After Guadalcanal, Tokyo could indeed several times have lengthened the war—at Saipan or Leyte, for instance—but it could not have won it.

Several other writers at least agree with me on some version of the Naval Battle of Guadalcanal being the turning point. Among the Americans are Paul S. Dull, apparently, and Eric Hammel and Jack Coombe. Raizo Tanaka of the Express, Yoshiyuki Yokai, and Sokichi Takagi seem to agree also, although their agreement is not always phrased exactly this way. Masanori Ito agrees as well.

For the U.S. Navy in the Pacific, the Solomons Campaign was in many respects unique. It was to some degree an accident, most of the time fought on a shoestring, not a massive effort deliberately planned and carefully staffed. There, the Navy fought with too little and sometimes second-best or even defective equipment. It was inexperienced and in some ways ignorant, at least at first. There the Navy at one time threw cruisers against battleships (and won). Against all this background clutter, the Naval Battle of Guadalcanal just gets lost. In any case, Guadalcanal did not emphasize the points the U.S. Navy wished to make after the war. The two previous battles served it better.

The ships, planes, bases, leaders, and men that had made up the Third Fleet and were to be the core of the Seventh were a very different body from the ones that had landed at Tulagi, and had suffered Savo and other defeats. They had fought their way up the Solomons, and won. But more important for the Navy, from a hurried collection of half-trained men and too few ships it had not only acquired more and better to work with, but it had learned to use it, the hard way. For the Navy, the whole Solomons was a learning experience. For this, it had paid, in ships, planes, and blood. In the Solomons, the Americans were bloodied, shaking off peacetime attitudes and learning new skills. There they first tested a wartime breed of fighting leaders. There they developed the new equipment—PT-boats, for instance—and tactics necessary to war in a narrow sea. For the Navy's officers and men, this has to be considered an especially shining hour.

Appendix A: Ships and Craft

1. DESTROYERS

a. Coming after years of construction from British designs, and a transitional series (*Akikaze*-class) of their own, the Japanese *Fubuki*-class destroyers of the 1920s and 1930s represented the first modern IJN fleet DDs. From them stemmed all subsequent fleet destroyers. They were still around in 1942.

The *Fubukis* were a great improvement on previous designs. With a larger, better hull form, more and larger guns, 24-inch (not 21-inch) torpedoes, and new hydraulic ammunition hoists, the *Fubukis* mounted six 5-inch (no longer 4.7-inch) guns in twin turrets (3 x 2) and nine torpedo tubes in three protected batteries (3 x 3). Displacing 1,750 tons, they were capable of 38 knots. They carried a full set of reload torpedoes on board.

The even larger *Kagero*-class DDs of the 1930s and 1940s were as good as they came. They represented all that the IJN valued in a DD. Descended from the *Fubukis*, they were even better sea boats. Like the *Fubukis*, the *Kageros* mounted six 5-inch guns in three twin mounts, but these guns were now dual purpose (anti-surface and anti-aircraft) guns. There were now only two 24-inch torpedo batteries, but they were quadruple (2 x 4) shielded mounts. Again, there was a full set of reload torpedoes, but they were better placed. All this on 2,033 tons capable of 35 knots.

b. To counter these Japanese DDs, the USN's *Fletcher*-class were in 1942 the best the Allies had. They displaced 2,050 tons and could make 35 knots. Their main battery consisted of five 5-inch guns in single turrets (5 x 1), ten (5x2) 40-millimeter twin mounts, and ten (2x5) 21-inch torpedo tubes. The standard U.S. 5-inch/38 caliber and the 40-millimeter guns were both dual purpose. They were—for DDs—good sea boats.

Before them had come the *Benson-Livermores*. They displaced 1,630 tons and could make 37 knots. They were armed with four 5-inch guns in single mounts, two 40-millimeter twins, and ten 21-inch torpedo tubes.

Earlier had come the *Sims* and the *Cravens*. The *Cravens* displaced 1,500 tons and could make 36.5 knots. They were armed with four 5-inch guns in single mounts, four 1.1-inch AA guns, and sixteen 21-inch tubes.

Even if not included in the original fit, all U.S. DDs soon carried radar and sonar, and, of course, depth charges. As the war progressed, DDs lost some of their pre-war guns and torpedo tubes and many of their ship's boats, searchlights, and heavy masting in order to provide weight margin and space for the new electronics, AA guns, and other additional AA and ASW gear.

2. U.S. PT-BOATS

Elco 80s were wooden-hulled, gasoline-driven, 80-foot-long motor torpedo boats (see Drawing 1). Tuned up, they carried four 21-inch torpedoes at forty knots. They also carried a 37- or 40-millimeter gun, a 20-millimeter gun, and four (2 twin) .50 caliber machine guns. They mounted a radar, depth charges (no sonar), and a smoke generator. They carried their own kind of torpedo.

At first, their torpedoes were World War I-vintage Mark VIIIs. Designed then for destroyers, they carried a 300-pound warhead 10,000 yards at twenty-seven knots. They had to be fired from a tube. These torpedoes were replaced with Mark XIIIs. Designed for aircraft, they were smaller and lighter, carrying a 600-pound warhead at forty-five knots. They were side-launched, from a rack.

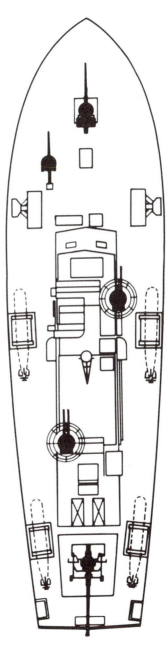
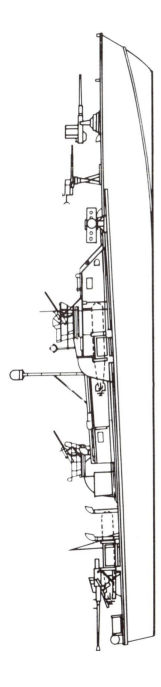

Drawing 1
PT-Boat

3. JAPANESE BARGES

The snub-nosed, self-propelled enemy barges generally came in two standard steel-hulled sizes—forty-six feet and fifty-six feet. The forty-six footer had a bow ramp, drew a draft of about three feet. It took seventy men on ship-to-shore and interisland passages, or ten tons of cargo, at about 8 knots. The sides of these craft were armored against light weapons fire, and they themselves carried twin 25-millimeter guns, or something similar. A forty-nine-foot wooden-hulled version saved on steel.

Appendix B: Equipment

1. AIRCRAFT

In the Solomons, the IJN's operational both carrier-borne and land-based fighter was the single-seat, single-engined Mitsubishi A6M1—the Zero. Known to us officially as the Zeke, it was armed with two 20-millimeter cannon and two .30-caliber machine guns, and was good for 340 miles an hour. As a fighter-bomber, it could carry two 130-pound bombs. It had a 31,000-foot service ceiling and a designed endurance of 1,166 miles. The Zero was extremely maneuverable and a fast climber, and dogfighting with it was to be avoided.

Also much seen in the Solomons was the IJN's land-based multi-place twin-engined bomber—the Mitsubishi G4M2—the Betty. Capable of delivering a payload of one torpedo or a ton of bombs, it could make 325 miles an hour and had a range of 2,262 miles. For defense, the Betty carried an assortment of five cannon and machine guns. Like the Zero, it lacked self-sealing fuel tanks and tended to burn when hit. Neither carried any armor.

The operational USN carrier-borne and Marine land-based fighter at the time of the Solomons was the single-seat single-engined Grumman F4F—the Wildcat. Armed with six .50-caliber machine guns, it was capable of 318 miles an hour. As a fighter-bomber, it could carry two 250-pound bombs. The Wildcat had a 34,800-foot service ceiling and a 925-mile range. Compared to the Zero, it had a slower climb and was markedly less maneuverable. However, it did carry a bullet-proof windshield, some armor behind the pilot, and self-sealing fuel tanks, all of which the Zero lacked.

The Wildcat was gradually supplemented by the then land-based single-seat Vought F4U Corsair. Armed with six .50-caliber machine guns, it could do 446 miles an hour. As a fighter-bomber it could carry two 1,000-pound bombs.

Other than these, the two-place single-engined Douglas SBD—the Dauntless—was our all-purpose work-horse. It scouted, with a range of over 1,000 miles. It level- and dive-bombed, carrying up to 1,600 pounds of bombs. Even with a top speed of only 230 miles an hour, it could in a pinch double as a fighter. It had two fixed forward-firing .50-caliber machine guns and one flexible twin .30 caliber in the rear cockpit. The Dauntless was a very rugged plane.

2. TORPEDOES (STANDARD)

The U.S. Mark X 21-inch torpedo was of World War I vintage. It carried a 500-pound warhead 3,500 yards at thirty-six knots, perhaps useful against merchantmen, but not against modern warships. The old S-class submarines were armed with this one.

The U.S. Mark XIV 21-inch torpedo was developed in 1931. It carried a 640-pound warhead 4,500 yards at forty-six knots. It had a thirty-one-knot setting which would give twice the range, but this was seldom used. Steam propelled, it had a quite visible wake.

The U.S. Mark VI exploder (detonator or pistol) was a double exploder, offering a choice of magnetic or contact detonation. Only the contact setting could be depended on, and then only if the target was hit square on.

The depth settings on U.S. torpedoes were inaccurate. They ran deep; a fact discovered only in combat. None of this had been corrected at the time of the Solomons. The USN just learned how to live with it.

The Japanese Long Lance 24-inch torpedo carried a 1,210-pound warhead 22,000 yards at forty-nine knots. Oxygen-driven, these torpedoes were practically wakeless. They carried twice the destructive power five times as far as the USN's did. They also had a thirty-six-knot setting which would double the range.

IJN DDs carried a full set of reloads. Reloading an IJN DD's torpedo battery required ten minutes.

Appendix C: Personalities

Ainsworth, Walden L.: cruiser-destroyer task group commander; rear admiral

Barbey, Daniel E.: amphibious force commander; rear admiral

Basilone, John: machine gun section leader; sergeant

Briscoe, Robert P.: destroyer leader; captain

Burke, Arleigh A.: destroyer leader; tactical thinker; captain

Callaghan, Daniel J.: cruiser-destroyer task group commander; rear admiral

Campbell, Colin: destroyer leader; captain

Crutchley, V.A.C.: cruiser-destroyer task group commander; rear admiral RN (RAN)

Deyo, Morton L.: CINCPAC staff; captain

Fitch, Aubrey W.: SOPAC shore-based air commander; rear/vice admiral

Fletcher, Frank J.: carrier task force commander; vice admiral

Gamble, Lester H.: PT commander; lieutenant (jg)

Geiger, Roy S.: Marine air commander, later Commanding General I Amphibious Corps; brigadier/major/lieutenant general

Ghormley, Robert L.: SOPAC commander, relieved by Halsey; vice admiral

Halsey, William F.: SOPAC commander, relieving Ghormley; vice admiral/admiral

King, Ernest J.: Chief of Naval Operations and C-in-C U.S. Fleet; admiral

Kinkaid, Thomas C.: carrier task group commander; rear/vice admiral

Koga, Mineichi: C-in-C IJN Combined Fleet, succeeding Yamamoto; admiral

Kurita, Takeo: commander IJN Center Force off Samar; vice admiral

Lee, Willis A.: battleship task group commander; rear admiral
MacArthur, Douglas: SOWESPAC commander; Army general
McCain, John S.: SOPAC shore-based air commander; rear admiral
McInerney, Francis X.: destroyer leader; commander
Merrill, Aaron S.: cruiser-destroyer task group commander; rear admiral
Mikawa, Gunichi: commander IJN Eighth Fleet in Rabaul; vice admiral
Miller, High B.: survivor, guerrilla; lieutenant
Mitscher, Marc A.: AIRSOLS commander, leader; rear admiral
Montgomery, Alfred E.: carrier task group commander; rear admiral
Moore, John R.: submarine commander; lieutenant commander
Moosbrugger, Frederick: destroyer leader, tactical thinker; commander/captain
Moran, Edward J.: PT flotilla commander; commodore
Munson, H. G.: submarine commander; lieutenant commander
Murray, George D.: carrier task group commander; rear admiral
Nagumo, Chuichi: IJN carrier force commander; vice admiral
Newton, John H.: deputy SOPAC commander; vice admiral
Nimitz, Chester W.: CINCPAC commander, in Pearl; admiral
Patch, Alexander M.: division/corps commander; Army major/lieutenant general
Robinson, Hugh M.: PT squadron commander; lieutenant
Scott, Norman: cruiser-destroyer task group commander; rear admiral
Searles, John M.: PT commander; lieutenant (jg)
Sherman, Forrest: carrier commander; captain
Sherman, Frederick C.: carrier task group commander; rear admiral
Tanaka, Raizo: IJN destroyer squadron commander; early leader of Tokyo Express; rear admiral
Thurber, Harry R.: SOPAC staff; captain
Turner, Richmond K.: amphibious force commander; rear admiral
Vandegrift, Alexander A.: First Marine Division commander, I Amphibious Corps commander, Commandant of the Marine Corps; major/lieutenant general
Van Voorhis, Bruce A.: Navy pilot; lieutenant commander
Walker, Frank R.: destroyer leader, captain
Wilkinson, Theodore S.: III Amphibious Force commander; rear admiral
Wright, Carleton H.: cruiser-destroyer task group commander; rear admiral
Yamamoto, Isoroku: C-in-C IJN Combined Fleet; shot down; admiral of the fleet.

Appendix D: Abbreviations, Acronyms, and Code Words

AAW	antiaircraft warfare
AIRSOLS	Allied shore-based air detachments, Solomons
ASW	antisubmarine warfare
Avenger	TBF (Grumman torpedo bomber)
"Black Cat"	night-flying PBY equipped with radar and light
BLISSFUL	code name for the Marine raid on Choiseul
CACTUS	code name for Henderson Field complex (Guadalcanal)
"the Canal"	Guadalcanal (slang)
CAP	combat air patrol, airborne fighter defense
CARTWHEEL	code name for the seizure of Rabaul (New Britain)
Catalina	PBY (Consolidated patrol bomber)
CBs	naval construction battalions
CHERRYBLOSSOM	code name for the landing at Torokina (Bougainville)
CIC	combat information center
C-in-C	Commander-in-Chief
CINCPAC	Commander-in-Chief, Pacific
CLEANSLATE	code name for the occupation of the Russells
Coastwatchers	clandestine Solomons observer corps
"the Corps"	the U.S. Marine Corps

Corsair	F4U (Chance-Vought fighter), land-based in Solomons
Dauntless	SBD (Douglas scout bomber), used for dive bombing
DD	destroyer (5-inch guns, torpedoes, no armor)
D-Day	execution day for operation; L-Day
DesSlot	Solomons ad hoc destroyer force
DM	destroyer-minelayer (modified old DD)
Elco	Electric Boat Company (Groton CT)
ELKTON	joint SOPAC-SOWESPAC code name for the seizure of New Georgia (and Vella Lavella) and other places
flag	flagship
"Gator Navy"	amphibious forces (slang)
GIs	the troops (literally, government issue)
GOODTIME	code name for the New Zealand occupation of the Treasuries
heavy cruiser	8-inch guns, light armor
Hudson	PBO (Lockheed patrol bomber)
IJN	Imperial Japanese Navy
Ironbottom Sound	the water between Guadalcanal and Tulagi
L-Day	landing day; D-Day
"Leathernecks"	U.S. Marines (slang)
light cruiser	6-inch guns, very light armor
Long Lance	Japanese 24-inch torpedo
Main Navy	U.S. Navy headquarters building, on Washington's Constitution Avenue
Orange	U.S. strategy to defeat Japan; the Pacific part of Rainbow 5
PSP	pierced steel matting for air strips
PT-boat	motor torpedo boat
RAAF	Royal Australian Air Force
radar	electronic surface and air detection and gunnery control devices

Rainbow 5	U.S. plan for the war against Japan (and Germany); see Orange
RAN	Royal Australian Navy
RN	(British) Royal Navy
RNZAF	Royal New Zealand Air Force
Seabees	see CBs
SHOESTRING	code name for the amphibious seizure of the Tulagi area, enlarged to include Guadalcanal
the Slot	the Solomons' sheltered inside passage
SOPAC	South Pacific command, at Noumea
SOWESPAC	Southwest Pacific command (MacArthur)
"tin cans"	destroyers (slang)
TOENAILS	code name for the Solomons side of ELKTON
Tokyo Express	the nightly troop and supply runs by Japanese destroyers down the Slot
USN	United States Navy
VHF	very high (line of sight) frequency radio
VT fuze	proximity fuze based on small radar
WATCHTOWER	code name for the seizure of the Tulagi area
"X"	Guadalcanal
"Y"	Tulagi
Zero	Mitsubishi A6 fighter

Bibliography

Agawa, Hiroyuki. *The Reluctant Admiral.* Tokyo: Kodansha International, 1979. Yamamoto and the IJN.

Barbey, Daniel E. *MacArthur's Amphibious Navy.* Annapolis, MD: Naval Institute, 1969. Seventh Fleet Amphibious Force operations 1943–1945.

Barnhart, Michael A. *Japan Prepares for Total War.* Ithaca, NY: Cornell, 1987. The search for economic security 1919–1941.

The Battle of Guadalcanal 11–15 November 1942. Washington, DC: Naval Historical Center, 1994. Reissued, declassified combat narrative.

The Battles of Cape Esperance 11 October 1942 and Santa Cruz Islands 26 October 1942. Washington, DC: Naval Historical Center, 1994. Reissued, declassified combat narrative.

The Battles of Savo Island 9 August 1942 and the Eastern Solomons 23–25 August 1942. Washington, DC: Naval Historical Center, 1994. Reissued, declassified combat narrative.

Blair, Clay, Jr. *Silent Victory.* New York: J. B. Lippincott, 1975. 2 vols. The U.S. submarine war against Japan.

Buell, Thomas B. *Master of Seapower.* Boston: Little, Brown, 1980. A biography of Admiral King.

Bulkley, Robert J., Jr. *At Close Quarters.* Washington, DC: Naval History Division, 1962. PT boats in the United States Navy.

Cook, Charles. *The Battle of Cape Esperance.* Annapolis, MD: Naval Institute, 1992. A good standard view.

Coombe, Jack D. *Derailing the Tokyo Express.* Harrisburg, PA: Stackpole, 1991. The naval battles for the Solomon Islands that sealed Japan's fate.

Dull, Paul S. *A Battle History of the Imperial Japanese Navy (1941–1945).* Annapolis, MD: Naval Institute, 1978. An authoritative text full of Japanese orders of battle.

Dyer, George Carroll. *The Amphibians Came to Conquer.* Washington, DC: Government Printing Office, 1971. 2 vols. A biography of Admiral Turner.

Evans, David C. *The Japanese Navy in World War II in the Words of Former Japanese Naval Officers.* Annapolis, MD: Naval Institute, 1986. Includes a contribution by Admiral Tanaka.

Fahey, James C. *The Ships and Aircraft of the United States Fleet.* New York: Ships and Aircraft, 1945. A standard reference. Victory edition.

Feldt, Eric A. *The Coast Watchers.* New York: Doubleday, 1979. He organized and ran them.

Halsey, William F., and J. Bryan III. *Admiral Halsey's Story.* New York: McGraw-Hill, 1947. A good command view; autobiography.

Hammel, Eric. *Guadalcanal: Decision at Sea.* New York: Crown, 1988. Third and final volume in a Guadalcanal series, covering the Naval Battle of Guadalcanal and its decisive impact.

Hara, Tameichi, Fred Saito, and Roger Pineau. *Japanese Destroyer Captain.* New York: Ballantine, 1961. He served in the Solomons. Autobiographical.

Holmes, W. J. *Double-Edged Secrets.* Annapolis, MD: Naval Institute, 1979. U.S. Naval Intelligence operations in the Pacific during World War II.

Howarth, Stephen. *Morning Glory.* London: Hamish Hamilton, 1983. The story of the IJN.

Hoyt, Edwin P. *Japan's War.* New York: McGraw-Hill, 1986. The war from the other side.

———. *Yamamoto, the Man Who Planned Pearl Harbor.* New York: McGraw-Hill, 1990. For background.

Ind, Allison. *Allied Intelligence Bureau.* New York: Curtis, 1958. MacArthur's intelligence coordinating authority.

Johnson, Ellis A., and David A. Katcher. *Mines Against Japan.* White Oak, MD: Naval Ordnance Laboratory, 1973. The ultimate reference on the mines.

King, Ernest J., with Walter M. Whitehill. *Fleet Admiral King.* New York: W. W. Norton, 1952. A naval record; autobiography.

Koburger, Charles W., Jr. *Narrow Seas, Small Navies, and Fat Merchantmen.* New York: Praeger, 1990. Naval Strategies for the 1990s, operating from the seas.

Ladd, J. D. *Assault From the Sea 1939–45.* London: David and Charles, 1976. Details on landing ships and craft.

The Landing in the Solomons 7–8 August 1942. Washington, DC: Naval Historical Center, 1994. Reissued, declassified narrative.

Lord, Walter. *Lonely Vigil.* New York: Viking Press, 1977. Coastwatchers in the Solomons.

Loxton, Bruce, with Chris Coulthard-Clark. *The Shame of Savo.* Annapolis, MD: Naval Institute, 1994. Anatomy of a naval disaster.

Miller, Edward S. *War Plan Orange.* Annapolis, MD: Naval Institute, 1991. U.S. strategy to defeat Japan 1897–1945.

Miller, John, Jr. *Cartwheel: the Reduction of Rabaul.* Washington, DC: Department of the Army, 1959. The ultimate objective.

Miller, Thomas G., Jr. *The Cactus Air Force.* New York: Harper & Row, 1969. The story of Henderson Field and its fliers.

Morison, Samuel Eliot. *History of United States Naval Operations in World War II.* Boston: Little, Brown, 1947 and after. vol. 5: *The Struggle for Guadalcanal.* vol. 6: *Breaking the Bismarcks Barrier.*

———. *The Two-Ocean War.* Boston: Little, Brown, 1963. The short history, with additional comments.

Okumiya, Masatake, and Jiro Horikoshi, with Martin Caidin. *Zero!* New York: Bantam, 1991. The ultimate source on the plane.

Potter, E. B. *Admiral Arleigh Burke.* New York: Random House, 1990. A biography.

———. *Bull Halsey.* Annapolis, MD: Naval Institute, 1986. A biography.

———. *Nimitz.* Annapolis, MD: Naval Institute, 1976. A biography.

Potter, John Dean. *Yamamoto.* New York: Viking Press, 1965. A biography.

Roscoe, Theodore. *United States Destroyer Operations In World War II.* Annapolis, MD: Naval Institute, 1953. Excellent source on the DDs.

Sherman, Frederick C. *Combat Command.* New York: Dutton, 1950. Autobiography using the Pacific carrier war as a backdrop.

Sherrod, Robert L. *History of Marine Corps Aviation in World War II.* Washington, DC: Combat Forces Press, 1952. Valuable reference.

Silverstone, Paul H. *U.S. Warships of World War II*. Annapolis, MD: Naval Institute, 1989. A standard reference.

Spector, Ronald H. *Eagle Against the Sun*. New York: Free Press, 1984. The American war with Japan. Good overall view.

Stafford, Edward P. *The Big E: The Story of the USS Enterprise*. New York: Random House, 1962. Lucky little *Enterprise* traces her luck.

Tanaka, Raizo. "The Struggle for Guadalcanal" in David C. Evans. *The Japanese Navy in World War II*. Mr. Tokyo Express speaks.

Taylor, Theodore. *The Magnificent Mitscher*. Annapolis, MD: Naval Institute, 1954. A biography.

Tillman, Barrett. *Avenger at War*. Annapolis, MD: Naval Institute, 1990. The TBF in World War II.

_____. *Corsair*. Annapolis, MD: Naval Institute, 1957. The F4U in World War II.

_____. *Wildcat*. Annapolis, MD: Naval Institute, 1990. The F4F in World War II.

Toland, John. *The Rising Sun*. New York: Random House, 1970. 2 vols. The fall of the Japanese empire 1936–1945.

Tregaskis, Richard. *Guadalcanal Diary*. New York: Popular Library, 1943. Foreword by General Vandegrift. Good on the ground combat. News reporter's stories.

Vandegrift, A. A. *Once A Marine*. New York: W. W. Norton, 1964. Autobiography.

Van der Vat, Dan. *The Pacific Campaign*. New York: Simon and Schuster, 1991. A recent summary.

Warner, Denis, and Peggy, with Sadao Seno. *Disaster in the Pacific*. Annapolis, MD: Naval Institute, 1992. New light on the Battle of Savo Island.

Watts, Anthony, and Brian G. Gordon. *The Imperial Japanese Navy*. New York: Doubleday, 1971. A basic source of IJN ship information and history.

Wolfert, Ira. *Battle for the Solomons*. Boston: Houghton Mifflin, 1943. News reporter's stories.

Index

Agano (light cruiser), 107

Ainsworth, Walden L. (rear admiral), 78, 84, 85, 86, 88–89

Air-ground support, 25, 90, 111–12

AIRSOLS, 68, 74, 82–83, 86, 105, 109

AIRSOPAC, 87, 104

Akagi (carrier), 4

Aoba (cruiser), 36, 54–55

Arawe, 112

Argonne (transport), 15

Army, 8, 52, 55, 58, 61, 68, 72–73, 83, 97, 111

Astoria (cruiser), 35, 37, 38

Atlanta (cruiser), 62

Australia (RAN cruiser), 36, 40

Avenger. *See* TBF

Bagley (destroyer), 35

Barakoma Bay, 97, 109

Barges (Japanese), 78, 94–95, 98–99

Bases, 14, 15–18, 23–24, 73

Betelgeuse (transport), 31

Bismarck Archipelago, 5, 9–10, 80, 112. *See also* Rabaul

Black Cat, 74, 101

BLISSFUL, 106

Blue (destroyer), 35, 37

Boat pools, 31, 106

Boise (cruiser), 54–55

Bougainville, 82, 86, 102, 103, 104, 112

Briscoe, Robert P. (captain), 84

B-17 (bomber), 27, 47, 86

Buchanan (destroyer), 61

Buin, 83, 86, 87

Bunker Hill (carrier), 109

Burke, Arleigh (captain), 89, 95, 99–100, 107, 110–11

By-passing, 96, 102, 112

CACTUS, 41–42, 43–44, 45, 52, 56, 58, 62, 63, 73, 75–76, 83

Callaghan, Daniel J. (rear admiral), 61, 62

Campbell, Colin (captain), 84

Canberra (RAN cruiser), 35, 37, 38

Cape Esperance, Battle of, 53–55

Cape Gloucester, 112

Cape St. George, Battle of, 110–11

Cape Torokina, 104–6

CARTWHEEL, 9–10, 80, 104, 112

Catalina. *See* PBY

CBs. *See* Construction battalions

Charles Ausburne (destroyer), 107, 110

CHERRYBLOSSOM, 106–7

Chevalier (destroyer), 101

Chicago (cruiser), 35, 38, 74

Chikuma (cruiser), 59

Chitose (seaplane tender), 44–46

Choiseul, 105, 106, 112

Chokai (cruiser), 29, 36, 37, 38

CINCPAC, 8, 14, 19, 53, 68, 76. *See also* Nimitz, Chester W. (admiral)

Claxton (destroyer), 107, 110

CLEANSLATE, 75–76

Cleveland (cruiser), 107

Coastwatchers, 10, 77–78, 103

Colombia (cruiser), 107

Combat information centers, 74

Combined Chiefs of Staff (CCS), 104

Combined Fleet, 42, 109

Communications, 37, 40, 45–46. *See also* VHF radio

Construction battalions, 31–32, 111

Converse (destroyer), 110–11

Craven (destroyer), 95

Crutchley, V.A.C. (RN/RAN rear admiral), 20, 31, 35–37, 39–40

DeHaven (destroyer), 74

Denver (cruiser), 107

DesSlot, 89

Destroyers, 69–70, 71–72, 76–77, 99–100, 108, 110–11

Deyo, Morton L. (captain), 68, 108

Duncan (destroyer), 55

Dunlap (destroyer), 95, 96

Dyson (destroyer), 107, 110

Eastern Solomons, Battle of, 44–46

Efate, 14, 73

Eighth Fleet, 27, 47, 109

11th Air Fleet, 61, 105, 110

ELKTON, 80, 87, 96

Emirau, 112

Empress Augusta Bay, Battle of, 107–8

Enterprise (carrier), 20, 24–25, 44–46, 58–59, 61, 63, 68

Espiritu Santo, 14, 22, 24, 73

Essex (carrier), 109

Farenholt (destroyer), 55

F4F (fighter), 43–44

Fighter direction centers, 24–25, 90–91

First Marine Division, 18, 68, 112

Fitch, Aubrey W. (vice admiral), 104

Fleet Air, Noumea, 73

Fletcher (destroyer), 71

Fletcher, Frank Jack (rear/vice admiral), 15, 19–20, 24, 30–31, 41, 44–46

Florida Island, 15, 16, 24

Forward air controllers, 90, 111–12

Fubuki (destroyer), 55

Furutaka (cruiser), 36

Geiger, Roy S. (brigadier/major general), 104, 111

George F. Elliott (transport), 29

Ghormley, Robert L. (vice admiral), 14–15, 18, 19–20, 30–31, 41, 57

GOODTIME, 106

Green Island, 112

Greenwich Island, 86

Gregory (destroyer transport), 48

Guadalcanal, Naval Battle of, 59–65

Guadalcanal/Tulagi, 5, 11, 14, 15–16, 22, 24, 26–27, 76. *See also* Tulagi

Gwin (destroyer), 89

Haguro (cruiser), 107

Halsey, William F. (vice admiral/admiral), 57–58, 60, 63, 65, 68, 75, 79–80, 82, 86, 87, 104, 109, 112–13

Haruna (battleship), 56

Hatzukaze (destroyer), 108

Helena (cruiser), 54, 88

Helm (destroyer), 35

Henderson Field. *See* CACTUS

Hiei (battleship), 62

Hiryu (carrier), 4

Hobart (RAN cruiser), 35

Honolulu (cruiser), 69, 70, 72

Horaniu, 98

Hornet (carrier), 19, 44–45, 52, 53, 58–59

Imperial Japanese Navy (IJN), 2, 4, 8, 13–14, 15, 16–17, 43, 46, 58, 60, 64–65, 73, 75, 76, 83, 87–88, 89, 110

Independence (light carrier), 109

Intelligence, 29–30, 36–37, 43, 60, 72

I3 (submarine), 94

Japan, 2–4

Jarvis (destroyer), 29

Jintsu (light cruiser), 44, 47–48, 88–89

Joint Chiefs of Staff (JCS), 9–10

Juneau (cruiser), 58

Kaga (carrier), 4

Kagero (destroyer), 48

Kahili, 83, 86, 105

Kako (cruiser), 36, 39

Kavieng. *See* Bismarck Archipelago; Rabaul

Kieta, 14, 22

King, Ernest J. (admiral), 8, 9–10, 14, 19, 21, 50, 112. *See also* Main Navy; Washington, D.C.

Kinkaid, Thomas C. (rear/vice admiral), 58–59, 61, 63, 113

Kinugasa (cruiser), 36, 63

Kirishima (battleship), 62, 64

Koga, Mineichi (admiral), 84, 106, 109

Koli Point, 26, 86

Kolombangara, 88, 96–97

Kolombangara, Battle of, 88–89

Kongo (battleship), 56

Koro, 20–21

Kula Gulf, Battle of, 87–88

Landing ships and craft, 91, 106.
     See also Barges
Lang (destroyer), 95
Leander (RNZN cruiser), 88
Lee, Willis A. (rear admiral), 61,
     63, 64
Little (destroyer transport), 48
Logistics, 17–18, 25–26, 27, 31–
     32, 41–42, 56, 91
Long Island (escort carrier), 41
Lunga Point, 16, 26, 52

MacArthur, Douglas (general), 8,
     9–10, 18, 19, 79–80, 82, 112,
     113. *See also* SOWESPAC
Mackinac (seaplane tender), 24
Main Navy, 8, 50
Makiguma (destroyer), 85
Makinami (destroyer), 111
Malaita, 24, 84
Manus, 112
Marines, 9, 14, 18, 20, 21, 25–
     26, 32, 41, 42, 48, 52, 68, 87,
     90, 97, 106, 111, 112
Maury (destroyer), 95
McCain, John S. (rear/vice admi-
     ral), 20, 23, 30, 73
McCawley (transport), 25, 31, 40,
     87
McFarland (seaplane tender),
     24
McInerney, Francis X. (com-
     mander), 84
Meade (destroyer), 64
Meiyo Maru (transport), 29
Melanesians, 10
Meredith (destroyer), 56
Merrill, Aaron S. (rear admiral),
     84, 86, 87, 107–8

Mikawa, G. (vice admiral),
     2719629, 35–37, 39
Minegumo (destroyer), 84
Mine warfare, 84–86, 87, 94–95
Minneapolis (cruiser), 69, 70, 72
Mitscher, Marc A. (rear admiral),
     73, 82–83, 87, 89–90
Montgomery, Alfred E. (rear ad-
     miral), 109
Montpelier (cruiser), 107
Moosbrugger, Frederick (com-
     mander), 95–96
Moran, Edward J. (commodore),
     94
Munda, 74, 78, 79, 80, 83, 87,
     90, 105
Murasame (destroyer), 84
Murray, George D. (rear admiral),
     58
Mutsuki (destroyer), 47
Myoko (cruiser), 107

Nagara (light cruiser), 62
Ndeni, 19, 24, 58
Neville (transport), 25
New Caledonia, 10, 14, 15, 17–
     18, 23. *See also* Noumea
New Georgia, 79–80, 86–87
New Hebrides, 9, 14, 23
New Orleans (cruiser), 69, 70,
     72
Newton, John H. (vice admiral),
     112
Nimitz, Chester W. (admiral), 8,
     9–10, 21, 53, 58, 68, 109,
     112. *See also* CINCPAC
Northampton (cruiser), 58, 69, 70,
     72

North Carolina (battleship), 8, 45, 52, 53
Noumea, 14, 15, 17–18, 58, 112–13. *See also* New Caledonia
Noyes, Leigh (rear admiral), 20, 24

O'Bannon (destroyer), 101
O'Brien (destroyer), 52
Onami (destroyer), 111
I Marine Amphibious Corps, 104

Pacific Fleet, 3, 4, 40, 57
Papua, 5, 9–10, 113
Patch, Alexander M. (major general), 72–73, 74, 75
Patterson (destroyer), 35, 38
PBY (seaplane), 17, 24, 48. *See also* Black Cat
Pearl Harbor, 2, 4, 22, 36, 112–13
Pensacola (cruiser), 58, 69, 70, 72
Philippines, 2, 5, 10, 40, 113
Portland (cruiser), 58
Princeton (light carrier), 109
PT-boats, 63, 87, 94–95
PT59, 94

Quincy (cruiser), 35, 37, 38

Rabaul, 5, 9–10, 16, 19, 22, 27, 47, 79, 80, 86, 87, 93, 104–5, 110, 112
Radar, 37, 49–50, 53, 54, 62, 71, 74, 76, 84, 88, 90, 96
Rainbow 5, 7, 40
Ralph Talbot (destroyer), 35, 37
Rekata, 14, 30
R4D (cargo plane), 41

Rigel (transport), 14
RO103, 87
Rupertus, William H. (brigadier general), 25
Russells, the, 75–76
Ryujo (light carrier), 44, 46

Salt Lake City (cruiser), 54–55
Samoa, 18, 23
San Diego (cruiser), 58
San Francisco (cruiser), 54–55, 61, 62
San Juan (cruiser), 35, 58
Santa Cruz Islands, Battle of, 58–59
Saratoga (carrier), 19, 20, 24–25, 44–45, 51, 53, 68, 109
Savo Island, Battle of, 35–39
SBD (scout/torpedo/dive bomber), 43
Scott, Norman (rear admiral), 53, 58, 60, 62
Second Marine Division, 68
Selfridge (destroyer), 101
Sendai (light cruiser), 107–8
Seventh Fleet, 113
S44 (submarine), 39
Sherman, Forrest (captain), 41
Sherman, Frederick C. (rear admiral), 109
SHOESTRING, 21–22
Shokaku (carrier), 4, 44, 59
Shortlands, the, 49, 87, 103, 105, 106
Solomon Islands, 5, 9–10, 10–11, 13–14
SOPAC, 13, 14–15, 17–18, 20, 37, 53, 57, 68, 75, 112. *See also* Ghormley, Robert L. (vice

*admiral); Halsey, William F.
(vice admiral/admiral)*
Soryu (carrier), 4
South Dakota (battleship), 58, 59,
61, 64
South Pacific Air Forces, 20, 23–
24. *See also* AIRSOPAC; Fleet
Air, Noumea
SOWESPAC, 9, 19, 37, 79–80,
82, 97. *See also* MacArthur,
Douglas (general)
Spence (destroyer), 110–11
Squadron, 2, 47–48, 69
Stack (destroyer), 95
Stanly (destroyer), 107
Sterett (destroyer), 95
S38 (submarine), 29, 36
Strategy, 2–3, 7–8, 9–10, 10–11,
13–14, 22, 52, 58, 65, 67, 73–
74, 93, 96–97, 104, 112
Strong (destroyer), 88, 93–94

Tactics, 26–27, 35–36, 49–50,
53–54, 55, 62, 63, 71, 87, 89,
94, 95–96, 107. *See also* De-
stroyers; Torpedoes
Takanami (destroyer), 71
Tanaka, Raizo (rear admiral), 44,
46, 47, 62, 63–64, 67–68, 70–
72
Tangier (seaplane tender), 17
Tassafaronga, Battle of, 70–72
TBF (torpedo/dive bomber), 86
Tenryu (light cruiser), 36
Teruzuki (destroyer), 94
III Amphibious Force, 104
Third Fleet, 57–58, 113
Third Marine Division, 106
Thurber, Harry R. (captain), 96

TOENAILS, 80, 86–87
Tokyo Express, 42, 47–48, 49,
53, 55, 67–68, 70, 75, 88, 89
Torpedoes, 52, 59, 69–70, 70–
72, 95–96, 99–100, 109
Treasury Islands, 103, 106
Truk, 19, 22, 42, 80, 93, 109
Tulagi, 9, 10, 14, 15, 16, 17–18,
19, 26–27, 73
Turnage, A. H. (major general),
106
Turner, Richmond Kelly (rear ad-
miral), 19–20, 24, 29–30, 36–
37, 52, 53, 60, 61, 87

United States, 2, 3, 7–8, 13
U.S. Navy (USN), 8, 46, 64–65,
76, 89. *See also* Destroyers;
Torpedoes

Vandegrift, Alexander A. (ma-
jor/lieutenant general), 18, 25,
31, 42, 67, 72–73, 104
Vella Gulf, Battle of, 95–96
Vella Lavella, 88, 96–98, 102
Vella Lavella, Battle of, 100–101
VHF radio, 21, 24, 46, 90
Vila, 74, 80, 83, 87, 96
Vincennes (cruiser), 35, 37, 38
Vireo (tug), 56

Walker, Frank R. (captain), 101
Washington (battleship), 53, 58,
61, 64
Washington, D.C., 7, 36, 57–58,
112. *See also* Combined Chiefs
of Staff (CCS); Joint Chiefs of
Staff (SCS); King, Ernest J. (admiral); Main Navy

Wasp (carrier), 8, 20, 24–25, 41, 44–45, 52, 53
WATCHTOWER, 13, 18, 19–20, 20–21, 106
Wildcat. *See* F4F (fighter)
Wilkinson, Theodore S. (rear admiral), 87, 89, 95, 96, 97, 104
Wilson (destroyer), 35
Woodlark Island, 82
Wright, Carleton H. (rear admiral), 68, 70–72

Yamamoto, Isoroku (fleet admiral), 42, 65, 67, 83–84
Yorktown (carrier), 15
Yubari (light cruiser), 36
Yugiri (destroyer), 111
Yugumo (destroyer), 101
Yunagi (destroyer), 36

Zeilin (transport), 61
Zero (IJN fighter), 44, 61
Zuiho (light carrier), 59
Zuikaku (carrier), 4, 44, 56

About the Author

CHARLES W. KOBURGER, JR., retired from the U.S. Coast Guard Reserve with the rank of Captain after twenty years of active duty. He is now an independent consultant in maritime affairs, specializing in Coast Guard-related tasks. He has been published many times on both sides of the Atlantic and has been translated into French.

Interpretations of Greek Mythology

INTERPRETATIONS OF GREEK MYTHOLOGY

Edited by Jan Bremmer

BARNES & NOBLE BOOKS
Totowa, New Jersey

© 1986 Jan N. Bremmer
First published in the USA 1986 by
Barnes & Noble Books
81 Adams Drive
Totowa. New Jersey. 07512
Printed in Great Britain

Library of Congress Cataloging-in-Publication Data

Interpretations of Greek mythology.

    Includes bibliographies and index.
    1. Mythology, Greek. I. Bremmer, Jan N.
II. Graf, Fritz.
BL782.I58 1987   292′.13   86-20638
ISBN 0-389-20679-2

Contents

List of Figures and Table

Abbreviations

Preface

1. What is a Greek Myth?   1
   Jan Bremmer

2. Oriental and Greek Mythology: The Meeting of Parallels   10
   Walter Burkert

3. Oedipus and the Greek Oedipus Complex   41
   Jan Bremmer

4. Wolves and Werewolves in Greek Thought   60
   Richard Buxton

5. Orpheus: A Poet Among Men   80
   Fritz Graf

6. Reflections, Echoes and Amorous Reciprocity:
   On Reading the Narcissus Story   107
   Ezio Pellizer

7. Greek Myth and Ritual: The Case of Kronos   121
   H. S. Versnel

8. Spartan Genealogies: The Mythological Representation
   of a Spatial Organisation   153
   Claude Calame

9. Myths of Early Athens   187
   Robert Parker

10. Myth as History: The Previous Owners of the
    Delphic Oracle   215
    Christiane Sourvinou-Inwood

11. Three Approaches to Greek Mythography   242
    Albert Henrichs

12. Greek Mythology: A Select Bibliography (1965 – 1986)   278
    Jan Bremmer

Notes on Contributors   284

Index   287

Figures and Table

Figures

2.1	Seal Impression from Nuzi: Death of Humbaba	30
2.2	Shield Strap from Olympia: Perseus and Gorgo	31
2.3	Seal from Cyprus: Hero Fighting Monster	31
2.4	Seal from Assur: Death of Humbaba	32
2.5	Clay Plaque from Gortyn: Death of Agamemnon	32
2.6	Seal from Tell Keisan: Death of Humbaba?	33
2.7	Seal from Nimrud: God Fighting the Snake	33
2.8	Corinthian Amphora: Perseus and the *kêtos*	34
8.1	The Aegean World	157
8.2	The Peloponnese and Central Greece	167
8.3	The Genealogy of the First Kings of Sparta	181

Table

11.1	Variants of the Kallisto Myth	256–257

Abbreviations

ABV	J. D. Beazley, *Attic Black-Figure Vase Painters* (Oxford, 1956)
Add	L. Burn and R. Glynn (eds), *Beazley Addenda. Additional References to ABV, ARV & Paralipomena* (Oxford, 1982)
AJA	*American Journal of Archaeology*
ANEP	J. B. Pritchard, *The Ancient Near East in Pictures Relating to the Old Testament* (Princeton, 1954 (Supplement 1968))
ANET	J. B. Pritchard (ed.) *Ancient Near Eastern Texts Relating to the Old Testament*, 3rd edn (Princeton, 1969)
ARV	J. D. Beazley, *Attic Red-Figure Vase-Painters*, 2nd edn (Oxford, 1963)
BCH	*Bulletin de Correspondance Hellénique*
BICS	*Bulletin of the Institute of Classical Studies at the University of London*
Burkert, *GR*	W. Burkert, *Greek Religion. Archaic and Classical* (Oxford, 1985)
—— *HN*	—— *Homo Necans. The Anthropology of Ancient Greek Sacrificial Ritual and Myth* (Berkeley, Los Angeles, London, 1983)
—— *OE*	—— *Die orientalisierende Epoche in der griechischen Religion und Literatur*, SB Heidelberger Akademie der Wissenschaften, Philos.-hist. K1. 1948, 1.
—— *S&H*	—— *Structure and History in Greek Mythology and History* (Berkeley, Los Angeles, London, 1979)
Calame, *Choeurs*	C. Calame, *Les Chœurs de jeunes filles en Grèce archaïque*, 2 vols (Rome, 1977)
CQ	*Classical Quarterly*
CR	*Classical Review*
Detienne, *Dionysos*	M. Detienne, *Dionysos mis à mort* (Paris, 1977)

—— *Invention*	—— *L'Invention de la mythologie* (Paris, 1981)
FGrH	F. Jacoby, *Die Fragmente der griechischen Historiker* (Berlin-Leiden, 1923–58)
GRBS	*Greek, Roman, and Byzantine Studies*
HSCP	*Harvard Studies in Classical Philology*
IG	*Inscriptiones Graecae*
JdI	*Jahrbuch des deutschen archäologischen Instituts*
JHS	*Journal of Hellenic Studies*
JNES	*Journal of Near Eastern Studies*
LIMC	*Lexicon Iconographicum Mythologiae Classicae* (Zurich, 1981–)
MH	*Museum Helveticum*
Para	J. D. Beazley, *Paralipomena. Additions to Attic Black-Figure Vase-Painters and to Attic Red-Figure Vase-Painters* (Oxford, 1971)
PCG	R. Kassel and C. Austin (eds), *Poetae Comici Graeci* (Berlin and New York, 1983–)
RE	*Realencyclopädie der klassischen Altertumswissenschaft*
SEG	*Supplementum epigraphicum Graecum*
SIG	W. Dittenberger, *Sylloge Inscriptionum Graecarum* 3rd edn (Leipzig, 1915–24)
SMSR	*Studi e materiali di storia delle religioni*
TGrF	*Tragicorum Graecorum Fragmenta*, vol. 1, ed. B. Snell (Göttingen, 1971); vol. 3, ed. S. Radt (1985); vol. 4, ed. S. Radt (1977)
ZPE	*Zeitschrift für Papyrologie und Epigraphik*

Preface

This collection of original studies offers new interpretations of some of the best known characters and themes of Greek mythology, reflecting the complexity and fascination of the Greek imagination. Following analyses of the concept of myth and the influence of the Orient on Greek mythology, the succeeding chapters shed new light on the threatening appearance of wolf and werewolf and on such familiar figures as Oedipus, Orpheus and Narcissus. The puzzling relationship of myth and ritual is illuminated by a discussion of the ambiguities in the traditions surrounding Kronos. Where does myth end and history begin? Studies of the first Spartan and Athenian kings demonstrate ways in which myth is manipulated to suit history, and an examination of the early stages of the Delphic oracle shows that some history is actually myth. Finally, an analysis of Greek mythography illustrates how myths were handed down in the Greek tradition before they became part and parcel of Western civilisation. The volume is concluded with a bibliography of the best mythological studies of recent decades. All chapters are based on the most recent insights and methods, and they display a great variety of approaches.

The volume would never have materialised without a chance meeting with Richard Stoneman, Senior Editor at Croom Helm. I am very grateful for his most pleasant co-operation in the preparation of this book. I also owe grateful thanks to Sarah Johnston and Ken Dowden, who were willing to shoulder the difficult task of revising most of the translations. Kees Kuiphof skilfully gave cartographical assistance.

Finally, a Dutch initiative in mythology would have greatly

surprised Friedrich Creuzer, one of the great students of Greek mythology in the nineteenth century. Having left Heidelberg in the summer of 1809 to take up a professorship at Leiden, he soon returned to Germany: for, as he put it, he could not conceive any mythological thoughts because the country was too flat. Holland still has no mountains, but interest in mythology abounds as we hope this book may show.

J.B.
Ede, Holland

Note

1. Cf. F. Creuzer, *Aus dem Leben eines alten Professors* (Leipzig and Darmstadt, 1848): "In Holland dann — feine Städte, hübsche Leute — aber ich konnte keinen mythologischen Gedanken fassen in dem flachen Lande." I owe this reference to Albert Henrichs.

1

What is a Greek Myth?

Jan Bremmer

What exactly is a Greek myth?[1] In the past, many solutions to this problem have been proposed, but in the course of time all have proved to be unsatisfactory.[2] The most recent analyses stress that myth belongs to the more general class of traditional tales. For example, Walter Burkert, the greatest living expert on Greek religion, has stated that 'myth is a traditional tale with secondary, partial reference to something of collective importance'.[3] This definition raises three important problems that we will discuss briefly in this introduction. First, how traditional is a Greek myth? Second, to what degree does Greek myth contain matter of collective importance? And finally, if myth is a traditional tale — what then is the difference between myth and other genres of traditional tales, such as the fairy-tale or the legend?

1. How Traditional is Greek Myth?

It is extremely difficult to determine the age of the average Greek myth. Many tales were recorded relatively late, and therefore we cannot ascertain the precise date of their origin. Yet Homer already refers to the Theban Cycle, the Argonauts and the deeds of Herakles. Moreover, there are a number of vignette-like passages in his poems in which he briefly mentions heroes such as Hippokoon, Phorbas and Anchises, all of whom are located in the Peloponnese and are also found in mainland traditions. Homer also makes fleeting reference to details that apparently have been derived from little-known sagas that range in setting from Crete

1

to Northern Thessaly, such as 'the grave of Aipytos where men like to fight hand to hand' (*Iliad* 2.604), Areithoos 'the club-bearer' (7.8f, 137f) or Amyntor who lived in a 'strong home' in Eleon (10.266). None of these persons comes from Ionia, Aeolia or the islands, so they most probably derive from sources dating back at least to the time before the Greeks emigrated to those areas at the end of the second millenium BC. Taking the mainland as our point of departure, we can also observe that the archaic poet Alcman (about 600 BC) mentions details about Odysseus and Circe that are different from those found in Homer but not necessarily of a later date. If, indeed, various figures originate in pre-emigration sources, then the existence of a Mycenaean layer in Greek mythology seems assured.[4]

Can we go back further? The great philologists of the last century discovered that Greek and Vedic poetry shared the formulas *kleos aphthiton*, or 'imperishable glory', and *klea andron*, or 'glories of men'. Further investigations have confirmed the existence of a common Indo-European poetic language; organisations of poets such as the Homeridai of Chios or the Kreophyloi of Samos would have been bearers of this poetic tradition.[5] Investigations into Indo-European mythological themes have been less successful. The whole fabric of Indo-European mythology, which Max Müller and his contemporaries erected in the course of the nineteenth century, had already collapsed by the end of that century. Yet some complexes stood the test of time. The myth of Helen, for example, has been shown to have close analogies in Vedic and Latvian mythology. In Sparta, Helen was worshipped as the goddess who supervised the life of girls between adolescence and motherhood. As the wedding also plays an important role in Vedic and Latvian traditions, the proto-myth of Helen was probably part of Indo-European wedding poetry.[6]

Can we go back even further? Burkert recently has studied Herakles' capture of cattle, which were hidden in a cave, from a shape-changing opponent. This capture, as he shows, is closely analogous to the Vedic Indra's fight against the demon Visvarupa, or 'of all shapes', who had also hidden his cows in a cave. But Burkert also showed that there are close analogies for these fights in the mythology of various hunting peoples of Siberia and the Arctic.[7]

Another ancient tradition lies behind the epic of the Trojan

War. Various leading figures, such as Achilles, display the characteristics of the ephebe, the Greek warrior at the brink of adulthood. Many details of Achilles' life correspond to such figures as CuChulainn, the exemplary ephebic warrior of Ulster; Nestor's youthful exploits are part of a similar initiatory tradition. Moreover, among a number of European peoples the storming of a (fake) castle was part of the young men's rituals. As Fritz Graf observes, the convergence of Greek and Irish tradition strongly suggests an Indo-European epic tradition closely connected with the young warrior's initiation. Myths associated with the central institutions of archaic societies, such as the wedding and the rites of puberty, or with matters of vital concern, such as the quest for animals (Herakles and Indra), have a much better chance of survival, indeed, than myths connected with more temporary institutions, such as the foundation of clans or temples. In the case of initiation, a poetic tradition is all the more probable because some Greek poets (still?) acted as initiators in the archaic age.[8] The close association of poets with initiation can also be found in *The Book of Dede Korkut*, a collection of tales set in the heroic age of the Oghuz Turks, who in the course of the ninth and tenth centuries emigrated from Siberia in the direction of Anatolia. Moreover, the tradition of the Trojan war finds a close parallel in Caucasian myths, in which a hero besieges a king who has offended his honour, and takes his castle through a ruse; the storming of a castle is also part of Caucasian folklore. Do we perhaps encounter here mythical themes of Eurasian pastoral peoples that reach back into time immemorial?[9]

On the other hand, myth was also often untraditional. The suitors of Penelope request the newest song (*Odyssey* 1.352), and archaic poets regularly stress their own originality.[10] In fact, many *mythoi* clearly are not very old. Hesiod derived part of his theogony from the Orient (cf. Burkert, this volume); the epic of the *Nostoi*, the homecoming of the Trojan heroes, presupposes Greek colonisation in Southern Italy; and the myth of Theseus' foundation of democracy illustrates the decline of the aristocracy's power in the late archaic age. The respective audiences of these *mythoi* must surely have recognised the novelty of these tales at the time of their first performances, even though they soon became incorporated into the traditional corpus of myths. Mythology, then, was an open-ended system. As has been pointed out recently, it is precisely

3

this improvisatory character of myth that guarantees its centrality in Greek religion. 'It is not bound to forms hardened and stiffened by canonical authority, but mobile, fluent and free to respond to a changing experience of the world.'[11] On the other hand, the divine authority of the archaic poet assured the truthfulness of the tale (cf. below). It was only in Hellenistic times that Callimachus (fr. 612) had to write: 'I sing nothing which is not attested'. When the poet had no more divine authority, tradition had to be invoked as the legitimising factor.

2. The Collective Importance of Myth

Having seen that myths can be tales from time immemorial but also contemporary inventions, we will now look at their place in Greek society. In the modern Western world, myths of the Greeks and other peoples are primarily *read*, but in the earliest Greek literature, the Homeric epic, *mythos* meant 'word, tale'.[12] The oldest *mythoi*, then, were tales recited in front of an audience. The fact of oral performance means that myth cannot be looked at in isolation; we must always consider by whom and to whom the tales were told. It is impossible to trace here in detail the development of the triad narrator – *mythos* – audience through the whole of Greek history; for our purpose it is sufficient to make a few observations about the main differences between the archaic age and later periods.

In Homer, the narrator of *mythoi* was the poet, the *aoidos*, who was society's bearer of tradition and its educator *par excellence*. Public performance obliged him to remain aware of his public's taste; unpopular new myths or unacceptable versions of old ones would be rejected by the public and, surely, not repeated in further performances. The poet's stature in society was reflected by his, in a certain sense, near-supernatural status. He and his songs were called 'divine' and he himself 'of the gods'. His epic poetry was believed to have been transmitted by the Muses who 'watch everything'. The divine origin of his poetry enabled him to invent new myths or change the content of the old ones; he could also freely change the poetic form — the original Indo-European eight-syllable line was developed into the hexameter.[13]

In the course of the archaic age, a whole complex of factors, such as colonisation, the growth of democracy, and the introduction of writing and money, dramatically changed the character of society. These developments also changed the status of the poet, the acceptance of myth, and the nature of the poet's audience. As Claude Calame has shown, the Muses played an increasingly subordinate role in archaic poetry. This declining position, as he persuasively suggests, reflected the poet's more secular role in society and growing consciousness of his own creativity. Moreover, the arrival of literacy enabled intellectuals to fix and scrutinise the tradition. The traditional *mythoi* now came under attack from philosophers and historians — authors who wrote in prose and who did not subject their opinions to the censure of the community in public performance. At first sight, the myths' audience remained the same, as the poets continued to perform in aristocratic circles, but their patrons were now in the process of losing part of their political power — a development that must also have had repercussions for the poet's position in society. These developments accelerated in the course of the classical period, although poets still continued to relate myths (tragedy!), and in the Hellenistic age the poet's function in society had largely been lost to philosophers and historians. The versions of myths that Callimachus and his friends wrote were no longer directed at society at large, but rather primarily at a small circle of literary friends. Post-Hellenistic travellers, such as Pausanias, still recorded the archaic myths connected with the temples they visited, but these tales now had lost completely their erstwhile relevance to the community.[14]

In one area, however, certain aspects of myth continued to prosper. The Greek colonisation of the East promoted feverish activity in the invention of mythical founders and genealogies, and in the explanation of strange names. In general, however, the new myths, which were mostly *bricolages* of the old, established ones, no longer were composed by poets but by historians, who wrote in prose and did not claim to be divinely inspired. The popularity of myth lasted well into the Roman Empire, but the *mythoi*, which once helped men to understand or order the world, now functioned primarily as a major part of a cultural tradition whose importance increased as Greek independence diminished. As various cities lost their political significance, it was their mythical past that could still furnish them with an identity and help them to distinguish themselves from other cities. Myth, then, meant rather

5

different things to the Greeks at different stages of their history.[15]

3. Myths and Other Traditional Tales

When we take the triad poet – *mythos* – audience as our point of departure, it becomes easier to see the difference between Greek myth and other genres of popular tales, such as the fairy-tale or the legend. Fairy-tales are told primarily in private and in prose; they are situated, furthermore, outside a specific time and place. Whereas Greek myth always details the place and origin of its heroes, fairy-tales content themselves with stating that 'once upon a time' a king was ruling — we never hear in which country or in which age. An individual fairy-tale therefore exists in isolation, while a Greek myth evokes further myths in which the same named heroes are involved; it is almost true that every Greek myth is ultimately connected in a chain of association with every other Greek myth. Moreover, fairy-tales are told not to order or explain the world, but to entertain their audience, although moralistic overtones were often introduced.

The English word 'legend' comprises two genres of tales that in German are distinguished as *Legende* and *Sage*. The *Legende* is primarily a hagiographical legend, a story in prose about a holy person whose life is held up to the community with the exhortation: 'go and do likewise'. These stories, then, clearly were invented or told by the church to influence the lives of the faithful. As such, they are restricted in scope and also are typical products of a more literary age — 'legend' comes from the Latin *legenda*, or 'things to be read'.

The *Sage* is a legend that explains buildings or stresses the boundaries between man and animals (cf. Buxton, this volume, Ch. 4); it accounts for extraordinary events and catastrophes; and it describes a world peopled by spirits and demons. For those who believed these legends, *Sagen* will have functioned very much like *mythoi* in archaic Greece. And just as *mythoi* helped to bolster the identity of the Greeks under the Roman Empire, *Sagen* acquired a political significance in the later nineteenth century when they were collected by German bourgeoisie in search of a common past.[16]

On the other hand, although these legends claim to be true,

there are no claims of divine inspiration; moreover, the stories normally are told in private and in prose; It has recently been persuasively suggested that the word *Sage* presupposes an archaic, perhaps even Indo-European, narrative prose tradition. Unlike at Rome, however, where the foundation myth of Romulus and Remus was apparently handed down in prose, in archaic Greece myths were the exclusive territory of poets. It is true that distinguished scholars, such as G. S. Kirk, have made use of the notion of the folktale to explain motifs of Greek myth, but it must be stressed that such tales simply are not attested in archaic Greece.[17]

What exactly is a Greek myth? We started this chapter with Burkert's definition of myth as 'a traditional tale with secondary, partial reference to something of collective importance'. This definition has proved to be valid for the whole period of Greek history. At the same time, however, we have seen that myths are not always traditional tales, nor is their collective importance the same during the whole of Greek history. Perhaps one could propose a slightly simpler definition: 'traditional tales relevant to society'. It is true that to us the appearance of gods and heroes is an essential part of Greek myth, but the supernatural presence is only to be expected when religion is embedded in society.[18] Western secularised societies have nearly abolished the supernatural, but they usually still have their favourite (historical) tales that serve as models of behaviour or are the expression of the country's ideals. It is their relevance to Greek society that makes the *mythoi* still fascinating today, for however different the Greeks were from us, they were also very much the same.[19]

Notes

1. The notes are confined to the most recent literature. I am in general much indebted to Fritz Graf, *Griechische Mythologie* (Munich and Zurich, 1985).

2. For a survey of the various explanations, see G. S. Kirk, *Myth: Its Meaning and Functions in Ancient Mythology and Other Cultures* (Berkeley, Los Angeles, London, 1970) 1–41; W. Burkert, 'Mythos und Mythologie', in *Propyläen Geschichte der Literatur*, I (Berlin, 1981) 11–35; Graf, *Mythologie*, 15–57.

3. Traditional tales: Kirk, *Myth*, 31–41 and *The Nature of Greek Myth* (Harmondsworth, 1974) 23–37; Burkert, *S&H*, 23; Graf, *Mythologie*, 7.

4. Pre-Homeric mythology: Graf, *Mythologie*, 58–68. Mycenaean layer: A. Hoekstra, 'Epic Verse before Homer', *Med. Ned. Ak. Wet., Afd. Letterk., N.R., 108* (1981) 54–66; note also A. Snodgrass, 'Poet and Painter in Eighth-Century

What is a Greek Myth?

Greece', *Proc. Cambr. Phil. Soc.*, *25* (1979) 118–30, esp. 122. Alcman: C. Calame (ed.), *Alcman* (Rome, 1983) 487, 496, 574, 612.

5. Formulas: see most recently E. D. Floyd, '*Kleos aphthiton*: An Indo-European Perspective on Early Greek Poetry', *Glotta*, *58* (1980) 133–57; G. Nagy, 'Another Look at *Kleos Aphthiton*', *Würzb. Jahrb.*, *7* (1981) 113–16; but see now M. Finkelberg, *CQ*, *36* (1986) 1–5. Poetical language: the standard study is R. Schmitt, *Dichter und Dichtersprache in indogermanischer Zeit* (Wiesbaden, 1967); see most recently W. Meid, *Dichter und Dichtkunst in indogermanischer Zeit* (Innsbruck, 1978); C. Watkins, 'Aspects of IE poetics', in E. Polomé (ed.), *The Indo-Europeans in the 4th and 3rd Millenia* (Ann Arbor, 1982) 104–20. Poetic organisations: W. Burkert, 'Die Leistung eines Kreophylos: Kreophyleer, Homeriden und die archaische Heraklesepik', *MH, 29* (1972) 74–85.

6. Helen: M. L. West, *Immortal Helen* (London, 1975); Calame, *Chœurs* I, 333–50 (Helen in Sparta).

7. Herakles: Burkert, *S&H*, 85f, who is overlooked by J. M. Blazquez Martinez, 'Gerion y otros mitos griegos en Occidente', *Gerion, 1* (1983) 21–38.

8. Initiation and Trojan War: Graf, *Mythologie*, 71–4. Ritual background of Trojan War: J. Bremmer, 'Heroes, Rituals and the Trojan War', *Studi Storico-Religiosi, 2* (1978) 5–38; F. Bader, 'Rhapsodies homeriques et irlandaises', in R. Bloch (ed.), *Recherches sur les religions de l'antiquité classique* (Paris and Geneva, 1980) 9–83. Poet as initiator: Calame, *Chœurs* I, 393–5; Graf, this volume Ch. 5, section 9; note also J. F. Nagy, *The Wisdom of the Outlaw. The Boyhood Deeds of Finn in Gaelic Narrative Tradition* (Berkeley, Los Angeles, London, 1985) Chs. 1 and 6, on Finn as poet and initiator.

9. Oghuz Turks: G. Lewis (ed.), *The Book of Dede Korkut* (Harmondsworth, 1974) 59–87. Caucasian parallels: W. J. Abaew, 'Le Cheval de Troie. Parallèles Caucasiens', *Annales ESC, 18* (1963) 1041–70; Bremmer, 'Heroes', 31 (storming castle). For other possible age-old traditions, see Burkert, *S&H*, 85, 95.

10. Originality of poet: Hom. *Od.* 1.351f; Alcman fr. 14 Page = 4 Calame; Pind. *Ol.* 3.4, 9.48f; W. J. Verdenius, 'The Principles of Greek Literary Criticism', *Mnem.* IV *36* (1983) 14–59, esp. 22f (with extensive bibliographies).

11. J. Gould, 'On Making Sense of Greek Religion', in P. Easterling and J. V. Muir (eds), *Greek Religion and Society* (Cambridge, 1985) 1–33, 219–21.

12. For the meaning of *mythos*, see C. Spicq, *Notes de lexicographie néo-testamentaire*, II (Fribourg, 1978) 576–8; Detienne, *Invention*; L. Brisson, *Platon, les mots et les mythes* (Paris, 1982).

13. Poet: H. Maehler, *Die Auffassung des Dichterberufs im frühen Griechentum bis zur Zeit Pindars* (Göttingen, 1963); B. Snell, *Dichtung und Gesellschaft* (Hamburg, 1965); Verdenius, 'Principles', 25–37. Divine origin: Hom. *Il.* 18.604; *Od.* 1.328, 8.498, 17.385 and 518f; Hes. *Th.* 94f; P. Murray, 'Poetic Inspiration in Early Greece', *JHS, 101* (1981) 87–100; Verdenius, 'Principles', 37–46. Poetic form: N. Berg, 'Parergon metricum: der Ursprung des griechischen Hexameters', *Münch. Stud. zur Sprachw.*, *37* (1978) 11–36.

14. Declining role of Muses: C. Calame, 'Entre oralité et écriture: Enonciation et énoncé dans la poésie grecque archaïque', *Semiotica, 43* (1983) 245–73. Critique of myth: Detienne, *Invention*, 123–54; J. Bremmer, 'Literacy and the Origins and Limitations of Greek Atheism', in J. den Boeft and A. Kessels (eds), *Actus: Studies in Honour of H. L. W. Nelson* (Utrecht, 1982) 43–55. The role of myth in Hellenistic poetry and post-Hellenistic authors is still in need of investigation; there are some good observations in P. Veyne, *Les Grecs ont-ils cru à leurs mythes?* (Paris, 1983).

15. Cf. P. Weiss, 'Lebendiger Mythos: Gründerheroen und städtische Gründungstraditionen im griechisch-römischen Osten', *Würzb. Jahrb.*, *10* (1984) 179–207.

16. Difference between myths and other traditional tales: see most recently L. Röhrich, 'Märchen-Mythos-Sage', in W. Siegmund (ed.), *Antiker Mythos in unseren Märchen* (Kassel, 1984) 11–35, 187–9; J. Scullion, '*Märchen, Sage, Legende*: Towards a clarification of some literary terms used by Old Testament scholars', *Vetus Test.*, *34* (1984) 321–36. Political significance of *Sagen*: R. Schenda, 'Maren von Deutschen Sagen. Bemerkungen zur Produktion von "Volkserzählungen" zwischen 1850 und 1870', *Geschichte und Gesellschaft, 9* (1983) 26–48.

17. Indo-European prose tradition: E. Risch, 'Homerisch *ennepo*, Lakonisch *epheneponti* und die alte Erzählprosa', *ZPE, 60* (1985) 1–9. Folk tales: Kirk, *Myth and Nature of Greek Myth*.

18. For the notion of embedded religion, see R. C. T. Parker, 'Greek Religion', in *The Oxford History of the Classical World* (Oxford, 1986) 254–74.

19. For information, comments and correction of the English I am indebted to Fritz Graf, Nicholas Horsfall, Sarah Johnston, André Lardinois, and Professor Rüdiger Schmitt.

2

Oriental and Greek Mythology: The Meeting of Parallels

Walter Burkert

1. Some General Reflections

Are there migrating myths? This question, which has often been asked, is a fascinating one, but it is not at all clear whether we should start searching for empirical evidence with which to answer it, or preclude it, from the outset, by definition. 'Parallels' have haunted the study of folklore from the start; theories of migration or of multiple, spontaneous generation still confront one another; Adolf Bastian advocated the concept of 'Elementargedanken',[1] Waldemar Liungmann proclaimed 'Traditionswanderungen Euphrat-Rhein'.[2] The fact that any diffusion of tales must have taken place largely through oral transmission, whereas only written sources are available for historical documentation, multiplies the problems. But it is the very concept of myth that engenders a special difficulty: although no readily available definition of myth has won general acknowledgement,[3] the consensus is that myth, compared with folktale in general, must have a special social and intellectual relevance to archaic societies. This requirement binds myth to particular cultural and ethnic entities, to traditional closed societies or groups. Some of the most successful modern interpretations of even Greek mythology are based on such an assumption, and concentrate on the closed circle of the unique Greek polis.[4] But the more illuminating and fulfilling the message of myth may appear in such surroundings, the less transferable, by definition, it will be. Leibnizian monads stand without windows through which to communicate with what might be outside. The most narrow definition of myth as 'the spoken part of

10

the ritual' generally is rejected nowadays, but the connection of myth with ritual remains an important fact, and the concept of 'charter myth' repeatedly proves useful. But indeed, on account of this, myth seems tied to historically unique organisations or even organisms; acceptance of this assumption would dispose of any idea of 'migrating myths' were it not for migrating societies: the Locrians in Italy worshipped their Ajax as they had in central Greece; the begging priests of the Anatolian Mother Goddess, the *metragyrtai*, brought ritual castration and the corresponding Attis myth to the Greek and Roman world.[5] But these are special cases.

Yet it is clear that Greek mythology spread widely throughout the Mediterranean, dominating in particular the imaginations of the Etruscans and Romans; to explain this diffusion as either a series of misunderstandings or a schoolchild's memorisation of literature, rather than as an example of living and 'genuine' myth, would be much too simple. But if it is granted that Greek myths 'migrated' to Italy, then not even Greek myth can be assumed to have arisen spontaneously from uncontaminated 'origins'; it arose within a society that formed itself in intense competition with older, Eastern civilisations.

Myth, in fact, is a multi-dimensional phenomenon, and although its function is most vital in closed archaic societies, it should be seen and investigated in all its various aspects. There are two main dimensions of myth, corresponding to the well-known linguistic distinction between the 'connotative' and 'denotative' functions of language:[6] there is a narrative structure that can be analysed as a syntagmatic chain of 'motifemes', and there is some reference, which often may be secondary and tentative, to phenomena of common reality that are thus articulated, expressed and communicated; this reference is most manifest in the use of proper names. In most mythical texts, both dimensions intertwine and influence one another; their dynamics, however, are quite different. The narrative structures are based on a very few general human or even pre-human programmes of action, and thus are quite easily understood and encoded in memory, to be reproduced, or re-created, even from incomplete records. This is the fascination of a tale to which we all are sensitive. One favourite tale type is the 'quest' — the subject of Vladimir Propp's *Morphology of the Folktale*. Its ubiquitous subtype is the 'combat tale'; other types include 'the girl's tragedy' and 'sacrifice and restitution'.[7]

The denotative 'application' on the other hand, which turns a tale to myth, is anything but general; it depends on particular situations, which may well be unique. Yet because tales are a means of communication, not private signs, particularisation is limited; there are no private myths. In fact, there are varying levels of generalisation in most human aspects of reality; certain societal configurations and problems will recur in similar forms in many places; the nature – culture antithesis, dominating the analysis of myths by Claude Lévi-Strauss,[8] is basic to mankind, and the particular theme of life-versus-death opens still wider horizons. Thus, some diffusion not only of tales but of myths, including definite 'applications', becomes possible after all. Even if 'genuine', living myth is rooted in a special habitat, it may well find fertile soil, to which it can easily adapt, in other places or times; it may even transform new surroundings, processing reality, as it were, by its special dynamics.

One should still pay attention to the distinction made by Alan Dundes, among others,[9] between 'motifemes' and motifs: although a tale, even a mythical tale, consists of a well-structured chain of 'motifemes', each of which has its necessary and immutable place, there are also single surface elements that are detachable and may 'jump' from one tale to another, especially if some original, 'salient' feature of one catches the imagination, like genes, as it were, 'jumping' between chromosomes. Thus, certain motifs recur throughout the world; or at any rate this is the impression conveyed by Stith Thompson's indispensable *Motif-Index*.[10] Whether historical diffusion has occurred even at the level of motifs is still a serious question. But it is a question that must be kept distinct from the problem of 'migrating myths', the concept of which implies the transfer of a narrative chain and thus also, usually, the transfer of 'application', or the message of the myth.

In the catch-phrase 'Oriental and Greek' the specialist still hears a ring of dilettantism; methodological circumspection encourages avoidance of the topic. Sheer accumulation of evidence, however, has begun to force the issue. Greek literary culture did not thrive in isolation, but rather in the shadow of older civilisations, assuming and then outgrowing what was ready at hand.[11] The term 'oriental' in itself is more than questionable; it is a label that all too clearly echoes the ethnocentric perspective of 'Westerners' and tends to obscure the fact that quite different civilisations existed more or less to the east, or the southeast, of Europe. There was the first rise of high culture, characterised by state organisation and literacy, in Mesopotamia and Egypt in the third millenium BC. Whereas Egypt is enclosed by natural boundaries, Mesopotamian influence began to spread towards both the Mediterranean and the Indus at quite an early date. During the second millenium there developed several adjacent civilisations each of an individual type, Europe taking a share of cultural pride with the rise of the Minoan – Mycenaean civilisation. This civilisation, unfortunately, has not produced any extant literary texts as yet and thus must still remain in the background as far as myth study is concerned. More fertile archives are provided by the continuing literature of Egypt and Mesopotamia, or come from Syrian Ugarit-Ras Shamra and from Anatolian Hattusa-Boğazköy. Bronze Age traditions end abruptly in both places, as in Greece, at about 1200 BC. After the 'Dark Ages' there emerge, in addition to some relics of Hittite tradition in Southern Anatolia, a lively and varied urban civilisation in Syria and Palestine, which can claim the decisive invention of the 'Phoenician' script, and also the 'miracle of Greece', which asserts its status through the poetry of Homer and Hesiod. This contribution was to endure, whereas, of the Syrian – Palestinian literature, only the Hebrew Bible was to survive later catastrophes.

What is left, thus, is a chance selection taken from much richer literatures and, presumably, oral cultures, which can be the basis for a comparison of 'oriental' and Greek mythology: Sumero-Akkadian and Egyptian sources are rich but geographically distant from those of Greece; Old Testament texts are of a very peculiar type. There remain the fragmentary tablets from Bronze Age Hattusa and Ugarit; the Phoenician and Aramaic literature from Iron Age Syria, which must have been closest to that of the Greeks, has vanished completely, as has the Phrygian and Lydian literature of Anatolia, if indeed it ever existed.

There are two main periods when cultural contacts between the East and Greece apparently were most intensive: the late Bronze Age (14/13th century BC) on the one hand (to Cyrus Gordon is due the concept of an 'Aegean Koine' for this period[12]) and the 8/7th century BC, when Phoenicians and Greeks were to penetrate the whole of the Mediterranean in a competitive effort. The latter has been called the 'orientalising period' by archaeologists; its historical background is the military expansion of Assyria that brought unity and devastation to Late Hittites, Syrians, Palestinians and Egyptians. That the later periods shall not concern us here should not detract from their importance; at that time, however, Greek civilisation had long reached its own form and was repelling all unassimilated 'barbarian' elements. The formative period of Greek civilisation, if it ever existed, must have belonged to the 'orientalising period'.

2. Ninurta and Herakles

Of all Greek mythological figures, Herakles is perhaps the most complicated and the most interesting. He is by far the most popular of Greek heroes, a fact reflected by the formidable mass of evidence. At the same time there is not one authoritative literary text to account for this character — in the way Homer's *Iliad* accounts for Achilles — but rather a plethora of passing references; furthermore, no single place gives him a home and background, but rather the whole Mediterranean provides a changing complex of stories connected to quite different local cults. Yet there is an identity marked by his name and by a canon of iconography that was established at an early date. The attempts to understand the origins and the development of the Herakles figure as a series of literary 'inventions' are bound to fail.[13]

The identity of Herakles consists in a series of exploits, *âthla*, which all are of the 'quest' type. Most of them have to do with animals; their canonical number is twelve. Herakles is a marginal figure, wearing a lion skin, wielding a club or a bow, leading an itinerant life. He has an intermediate status even with regard to gods, he is worshipped both as a dead hero and as an immortal god. Although invincible, he must submit to the command of a king of 'wide power', 'Eurystheus'. His father is Zeus, the ruling god of the pantheon.

Ever since the oriental evidence became available, striking Mesopotamian parallels to the Herakles figure have been noticed.[14] New texts and pictorial representations are still turning up and more surprises may lie ahead. One important Sumerian – Akkadian text, 'Ninurta and the Asakku', was finally published in 1983.[15]

The god Ninurta, 'Lord of the Earth', who became conflated

with Ningirsu, 'Lord of Girsu', at an early date,[16] is a valiant champion who fights monsters, proving victorious in each case. His renown — and this has become fully known only with the recent publication of the text — is based on a series of twelve 'labours': he overcame, killed, and brought to his city twelve fabulous monsters. They include a wild bull or bison, a stag, the Anzu-bird, a lion, 'terror of the gods', and above all a 'seven-headed serpent'; naturally this last attracted attention most of all since it had become known from texts and pictures. The series has been called 'the trophies of Ninurta'. An enumeration of twelve labours is also contained in King Gudea's description of the temple of Ningirsu at Lagash, known as Gudea's 'Cylinder A'.[17] An incomplete list occurs in another Sumerian–Akkadian literary composition, 'The Return of Ninurta to Nippur'.[18] None of the texts, so far, gives an elaborate narrative account of Ninurta/Ningirsu's 'trophies', they are just mentioned as if they were a well-known series. The epic texts may be somewhat later than King Gudea's reign, which is dated to *c.* 2140 BC, but clearly belong to the epoch of 'Sumerian renaissance' (22/21st century BC). Consider that, in addition to 'twelve labours', Ninurta is a son of Enlil, the storm god, the ruling god of the pantheon, that he is said to have 'brought' the trophies to his city,[19] that he is usually identified with the figure of a god with club, bow and animal's skin on Mesopotamian seals,[20] and the association with Herakles becomes inescapable. Levy and Frankfort, impressed by the seal picturing the fight with the seven-headed snake, have already stated that this must be a case of migration of myth from East to West (n 14); van Dijk is positive about the connection, too, although he prefers to hypothesise a 'common source' in pre-history.

As one looks more closely at details, however, the outlines of the myths become less distinctive, and peculiarities come to the foreground that make the 'parallels' less striking. It is not only that the 'trophies' are not quite the same in different texts (the same can be said for the labours of Herakles), but also that some of them remain quite obscure,[21] and even those readily understood include 'gypsum' and 'strong copper', demons difficult to imagine in confrontation with Herakles. What is more important is that the myths of Ninurta/Ningirsu are deeply enrooted in the world of Sumer, the cults and the temples. Gudea's Cylinder A assigns a place to all the twelve 'trophies' at the Ningirsu temple of Lagash, at 'a 'place of libations', i.e. a place integrated in the temple cult. 'Ninurta and the Asakku' tells how a demon of the 'Mountain' was overcome in order to make the mountains available for mining, and the 'fate' of 19 minerals fittingly concludes the narrative; it was Gudea who started the economic exploitation of the 'mountains'; his patron god therefore assumes the role of culture hero in this context. The poem, no doubt, was to be recited at a festival;[22] this function is clearer still in the case of 'Ninurta's Return to Nippur'. We are dealing with myths in the full sense, in their unique historical setting — which makes them unlikely candidates for 'migration'. Ninurta/Ningirsu turns out to be so very Sumerian that the resemblance to Herakles fades.

One might even become suspicious that orientalists, who are still based strongly in a classical background, sometimes find their evidence to be just slightly more Greek than would an untried eye. Van Dijk would allow the Sumerian 'stag with six heads' to correspond to both the Cerynthian hind and the Erymanthian boar — neither of which, incidentally, is know to have had more than one head — and wishes to add cows to the exploits of Ninurta.[23] More disquieting is the fact that Gilgamesh has been credited with a 'lion skin' in practically all translations available, whereas the crucial word in the Akkadian text may equally be read as 'dog skin', which seems to suit the occasion better: to put on this skin is an act of self-abasement in the context of mourning for Enkidu.[24]

To complicate matters further, there are other identifications for both Ninurta and Herakles in the dialogues of East and West: the Asakku monster in 'Ninurta and the Asakku' couples with a mountain, begetting a brood of formidable stones that frightens even the gods.[25] This seems parallel to the Hittite myth of Kumarbi begetting Ullikummi, the diorite monster destined to overthrow the gods.[26] If Kumarbi, in turn, is understood to correspond to Kronos, and Ullikummi to Typhon, then the champion and saviour of the gods, in line with Ninurta and the Hittite weather god, would be Zeus instead of Herakles. In fact, Ninurta, when fighting the Asakku, has all the equipment of a weather god, including the rainstorm and the thunderbolt. When, on the other hand, knowledge of the 'seven planets' was transmitted from Babylonia to the Greeks, probably in the fifth century, Ninurta's star was 'translated' as that of Kronos/Saturnus, whereas Marduk's star became that of Zeus/Jupiter, with Herakles taking no part.[27] On the other hand, there is the well-known identification of Herakles with Melqart of Tyre, which, although its basis remains unclear to us, was taken for granted for many centuries.[28] Was the basis primarily the gods' role in colonisation, or the fact that both were immortalised through fire? Another, much discussed syncretism occurred at Tarsus in Cilicia, where Santas/Sandon was understood to represent Herakles, again, as it seems, in the context of a fire ritual.[29] This syncretism in no way can be traced to Ninurta/Ningirsu. There is, moreover, an identification of Herakles with Nergal, the Mesopotamian god of the Netherworld,[30] whose iconography includes club and bow. It has been suggested that even Herakles' name can be derived from that of Erragal – Nergal,[31] but such suggestion rests on uncommonly slippery grounds.

Thus, the real problem is not a lack but rather a surplus of interrelations. Similarities within the myths and iconographies of a large group of divine figures native to several adjacent civilisations or language groups seem to be 'family resemblances', but there is not a single clear line that ties one element to another and to nothing else. There is no single 'Herakles myth' that could have been passed, like a sealed parcel, to new possessors at a certain time and place. Communication is broad but indistinct.

In fact, we are dealing here with the most general type of tale, the 'quest' and 'combat tale'. The snake or dragon is suited ideally to play the role of the adversary in this context,[32] as is the lion in more heroic variants. Even a widely significant number such as twelve could recur in different cultures independently. Any connection with the twelve signs of the zodiac, incidentally, should be discarded as far as the older period is concerned.[33]

And yet the parallels between Ninurta and Herakles seem deep and pervasive. Their quests, fulfilling the basic goal of 'get and bring', serve their communities by making the surroundings humanly manageable, by turning 'nature' into 'culture', be it by taming animals or by disclosing minerals. Both Herakles and Ninurta are culture heroes; a comparison of the two obviously aids in interpretation by placing this specific role of theirs in sharper relief.[34]

It is the leitmotiv of the 'dragon with seven heads' that

encourages one to assume more direct connections. Seven is a favourite number in Eastern Semitic civilisations. The seven-headed snake first makes its appearance in glyptic art[35] and also appears somewhat later in Sumerian literature. The Sumerian–Akkadian bilingual texts remained available until the fall of Niniveh; a list of Ninurta's trophies, including the seven-headed snake, entered into a ritual litany used in the temple cult of the first millenium.[36] The Sumerian designation *muš-sag-imin* is unequivocal and readily understood, as is the Akkadian translation, *ṣēru seba qaqqadašu*. There is clear evidence that the god slaying the seven-headed serpent entered West Semitic literature in the Bronze Age and survived there down to the first millenium; the champion is Baal at Ugarit, but the text describing the exploit recurs nearly word for word in Isaiah's praise of Jahwe.[37] The formula must have been preserved orally, as part of a ritual litany. This still does not tell us how, when and where this motif reached the Greek world. Herakles fighting the hydra appears as a drawing on Boeotian fibulae about 700 BC.[38] It is not possible to show iconographic dependency on an Eastern model in this case, but for the curious detail that a crab is connected with the scene, whereas crabs (or scorpions) appear on the earliest, pre-Sargonic representation.[39] It would be excessively sceptical to deny any connection with the East, where a broad and continuous tradition of the 'seven-headed snake' is established by the documents we have, but the contacts must have taken place at an inaccessible level of oral tales. The lion fight enters Greek iconography somewhat earlier and clearly derives from Eastern prototypes; but this is a separate tradition.[40]

The hypothesis of borrowing, however, does not explain why Greek mythology locates the dragon fight at Lerna, a place of springs where the dragon developed into a water snake, *hydra*, or the details of the crab's and Iolaus' participation in the combat, or why the lion was transferred to Nemea. Local, perhaps pre-existing Argive traditions may have been overlaid by oriental influence. It might be claimed that we are tracing only single motifs that 'jumped' between basically similar yet separate mythical conceptions. We remain completely in the dark as to the question whether a complete system of 'twelve labours' ever was transmitted. If such a list of Herakles' labours in Greece can be traced to Peisandros of Rhodos, i.e. before or about 600 BC, transmission of a complete set could be imagined. Frank Brommer, not a negligible expert, insists that the cycle is not attested unequivocally before 300 BC.[41] Most scholars, however, would be inclined to use the twelve metopes of the temple of Zeus at Olympia to establish a clear *terminus ante quem* for the cycle of twelve. Even so, the gaps in our documentation cannot be closed.

3. Cosmogonic Myth

Few events in Greek studies of this century can rival the impact Kumarbi created around 1950. There had been signals before, but it was Güterbock's *Kumarbi* of 1946, made widely known by Albin Lesky, among others,[42] that definitely drew the attention of Hellenists to the Hittites. At nearly the same time the epoch-making decipherment of Linear B engendered a general enthusiasm for the Bronze Age, and Boğazköy-Hattusa and Mycenae began to be viewed as partners, not to forget Bronze Age Troy.

The Hittite text that has been called 'Kingship in Heaven' offers parallels to Hesiod's *Theogony* so close in outline and details that even sceptics could hardly object to their connection. Both texts present a sequence of divine dynasties, each being overthrown by the next, until the ruling god of the pantheon, the weather god, finally assumes control. The god 'Heaven' himself, Anu/Uranos, is vanquished by means of castration, performed by Kumarbi in the Hittite version, Kronos in the Greek; the castrator is an intermediate figure, who rises to power only to lose it again. His speciality is swallowing what he cannot contain: Kumarbi swallows the 'manhood of Anu' and becomes pregnant with three gods, among them the weather god; Kronos swallows his own children, including the weather god Zeus. These chronologically parallel correspondences of extremely strange events leave no doubt that the texts are related intimately, the Hittite text being earlier by some 500 years. It is possible, of course, to stress the differences amidst the common features,[43] or in a Freudian vein to point to 'unconscious human desires' underlying both versions;[44] but that diffusion, nay, borrowing of myth did occur in this case has not been seriously denied.

The main problem that seemed to remain was whether such borrowing took place during the Bronze Age or later during the 'orientalising epoch', i.e. around the time of Hesiod. The degree of transformation and re-elaboration of oriental materials in both Hesiod and Homer and the splendour of the Mycenaean world together argue for an early transmission, but the trade and communication routes from the 'Late Hittites' and from Syria via Cyprus right to Hesiod's Euboea have attracted greater attention recently; evidently there were quite intensive contacts in the eighth century.[45] It is clear that the two theses — Bronze Age and Iron Age transmission — are not mutually exclusive; there may well have been early contacts and late reinforcements. The decision thus mainly depends on general presumptions about stability or mutability of an oral system of myth.

Questions become more complex, however, as it is realised that in this case, too, it is not enough to compare one Hittite text with one work of Hesiod in order to establish a one-way connection. As in the case of the Herakles themes, there exists quite a family of related texts that represent several civilisations and literatures; it becomes troublesome to identify definite channels in a complicated network. 'Kingship in Heaven' has a kind of sequel, 'The Song of Ullikummi':[46] Kumarbi, dethroned, takes his revenge by copulating with a rock and engendering the diorite monster that is to overthrow the gods. This story evidently corresponds to the Greek story of Typhoeus/Typhon, who challenges the reign of Zeus after the Titans' defeat. The connection is made certain by a detail of locality: the gods in 'Ullikumi' assemble on Mount Casius in Cilicia, and it is on this very mountain that Zeus fights with Typhon, according to Apollodorus.[47] The reference to a region where Hittite, Hurrite and Ugaritic influence meet could not be clearer.

Yet the Apollodorean version of the Typhon fight bears still stronger resemblance to another Hittite text, 'The Myth of Illuyankas',[48] in which a dragon fights the weather god. In both tales the weather god is defeated by his adversary in the first onslaught, and vital parts of his body are taken from him — heart and eyes in the Hittite text, sinews in Apollodorus — which must be recovered by a trick, in order that the weather god may resume battle and emerge victorious. Illuyankas is a 'snake', Typhoeus is endowed with snakeheads in Hesiod and has a snake's tail in Apollodorus and in sixth-century iconography.[49] Typhon, thus, could be called a conflation of Ullikummi and Illuyankas, although

20

this still would be simplistic. His name has been connected with the Semitic word 'North' — ṣapōn in Hebrew. There is the 'Mountain of the North', which, from Syria, again would be Mount Casius; there is a 'Baal of the North', *Baal Ṣapūna*.[50] In fact, Typhon has the character of a storm god himself. He is thus a complex figure that cannot be derived from one or two threads of a linear transmission. The complexity of mythical tradition even within the world of the Hittites is exemplified by a sudden reference in the 'Ullikummi' text to 'the olden copper knife with which they separated heaven and earth',[51] which reflects a version of the cosmic myth especially close to that of the Hesiodic Kronos, who cuts Heaven from Earth with a steel knife, but apparently different from that of Kumarbi, as found in the text 'Kingship in Heaven'.

Hittite and Ugaritic texts have restored the respectability of an account of Phoenician mythology that survives in an elaboration of imperial date, by Herennius Philon of Byblos.[52] Hesiodic touches in his account cannot be denied, but he has four generations of 'kings' in heaven, *Elioun* 'the Highest' preceding Uranos and thus corresponding to *Alalu* in 'Kingship in Heaven'. This is enough to establish the survival of Bronze Age cosmic mythology in Phoenician cities down to late antiquity, although probably neither in unitary nor unchangeable forms.

Hittite and Ugaritic civilisations communicated both directly and through a third civilisation, that of the Hurrites; the names Kumarbi and Ullikummi are Hurrite, and Hurrite influence is prominent in ritual as in mythology. But interconnections extend still further. Even before the Hittite discoveries, Francis Macdonald Cornford,[53] in the wake of the 'Myth and Ritual' movement, had recognised the remarkable structural resemblance of Hesiod's *Theogony* to the Babylonian epic of creation, *Enuma elish*;[54] a systematic investigation of the relationships, including those involving Kumarbi, was undertaken by Gerd Steiner. *Enuma elish*, too, includes a sequence of ruling gods among whom arise two major conflicts; a father god is laid to rest — although not 'Heaven' in this case, but Apsu, the 'Water of the Depths' — and the leading god of the pantheon — Marduk in the case of Babylonia — qualifies for the kingship through a fierce fight. *Enuma elish*, however, is only one of several Mesopotamian creation stories, and by no means the earliest. One important precedent, as it now turns out, is 'Ninurta and the Asakku'.[55] The

21

adversary in this text, coupling with the mountain and begetting stones, is an avatar, in turn, of Kumarbi and Ullikummi (n 26). We finally begin to hear a many-voiced interplay of Sumerian, Akkadian, Hittite and West Semitic texts, all of which seem to have some connection with Hesiod. It is impossible, however, to construct a convincing stemma of these relations; perhaps it would not even make sense to try. It is better to acknowledge the lively communication between these societies and to take into account the general background of the myths when interpreting the special adaptations found in the single texts that have survived by chance.

A remarkable addition to the Greek corpus has recently emerged: the Derveni papyrus preserves quotations from an early Orphic theogony, which can probably be dated to the sixth century BC.[56] This theogony includes generations of 'Kings' among the gods, corresponding closely to those in Hesiod, but also diverges in some remarkable ways. We find that the castration of Uranos by Kronos, who committed 'a great deed', is interpreted by the commentator as the separation of heaven and earth; later, however, Zeus is made to 'swallow the genitals' of the god 'who first had ejaculated the brilliance of the sky (*aithér*)'; this must be Uranos, the 'first king'.[57] Through this act Zeus somehow gets pregnant with all the other gods, the rivers, springs, and all other sorts of beings; they all 'grew in addition on him' (12.4), whereas he had become the only one, the *monogenés* (12.6). Surprisingly enough, this text thus preserves the most striking incident of the Kumarbi story: the swallowing of the genitals and the conception of mighty gods, including a river — the Tigris in the case of Kumarbi. It is also remarkable that the Orphic theogony has four generations of 'kings' among the gods,[58] as in the Hittite text and in Philon of Byblos, although the count has been shifted by the addition of Dionysos and the dropping of a king before Uranos. This may be connected with the fact that Zeus fills the role of Kumarbi. The Derveni text has many lacunae and interpretations will remain controversial; but it does prove, finally, that Oriental–Greek relations, at least in regard to cosmogony, were not confined to the single channel that led to Hesiod. There was much more around than we had imagined.

Cosmogonic myth, for us, has a special dignity and significance because it appears to foreshadow the philosophy that was to evolve with the Presocratics. This was already the perspective of Plato and Aristotle,[59] and it now appears that 'the origin of Greek philosophy from Hesiod to Parmenides' — to paraphrase a well-known title[60] — must be extended back to Sumerians, Babylonians and Hittites, not to mention the Egyptians.

There is a certain danger in this perspective, which might be called the teleological fallacy: instead of being judged in its own right, a phenomenon is judged by what was to take its place in later evolution. This is not to deny that the stories of procreation and combat that make up the narrative structure of mythical cosmogony show remarkable speculative energy and acquire a unique appeal by means of the repercussions of the vast and wondrous object to which they are applied. But at the same time, cosmogonical myths, just as other myths, have settings and functions defined and particularised by the time and place in which their archaic community of origin exists. In the Near East, cosmogony had special relationships to ritual. It was the discovery that *Enuma elish* was recited at the Babylonian New Year festival that triggered the 'Myth and Ritual' movement,[61] the exaggerations of which should not obscure the basic facts. Older compositions such as *Lugal-e* no less clearly refer to festivals; *Illuyankas* is explicitly called the cult legend for the Purulli festival of the Hittites.[62] Theodor Gaster may have gone too far in construing just one pattern of dramatic festival to which the myths should be related.[63] But it is evident that stories about the generations of gods and their final fight for power were understood to reflect and comment upon the establishment of power in the city, which was renewed periodically at the New Year festival. Ritual is the enactment of antitheses, from which the thesis of the present order — the status quo — differs; and myth tells about distant times when all the things we take for granted and consider self-evident or 'natural' were 'not yet' there: the past reflected by ritual presents alternatives, inchoate and perverse in contrast to what has been achieved. It is most remarkable that Greece, unlike other ancient societies, did not utilise these applications of cosmogonic myth in permanent institutions. The festival of Kronia,[64] fittingly placed before the New Year festival, could be compared, but it remained rather insignificant in the sequence of celebrations. Zeus' fights with the Titans and Typhon, as far as we can see, never directly entered ritual; they were used freely, however, in art and poetry, retaining a message of sovereignty against debased enemies; thus Typhōs is introduced in Pindar's first Pythian ode. Cosmogonic myth in the narrower sense equally remained free for rethinking by the Presocratic philosophers.

Yet cosmogonical myth had fulfilled still another requirement: it formed part of incantations for magical healing. Private superstition may seem a strange bedfellow with august ceremonies of the cities and with nascent philosophy. But cosmogony makes sense even there: as illness is an indication that something has gone wrong and is moving towards catastrophe, it is of vital importance to find a fresh start; the most thorough method is to create a world anew, acknowledging the dangerous forces preceding or still surrounding this *kosmos* but extolling the victorious power that guarantees life and lasting order. Thus, in Babylonian texts we find cosmogonies used as charms against a toothache or a headache, or for facilitating childbirth; practically all the literary texts can also be used as mythical precedences of magical action: to stop evil winds, to procure rain, to ward off pestilence. The people who performed such cures, whether we call them priests or magicians, were the intellectuals of their epoch, and they were often mobile groups that could successfully make a living in foreign lands. In classical Greece, itinerant priests who offered various cures accompanied by pertinent myths and rituals were known as 'Orphics'; it is all the more remarkable that Near Eastern myths can be found in Orphic tradition. Even the notorious Orphic myth of anthropogony, the rise of mankind from the soot of the Titans who had killed Dionysos, has its closest analogy in Mesopotamian myths about the origin of man from the blood of rebellious gods, slain in revenge.[65]

One 'conduit'[66] through which cosmogonic myth was transported from East to West may thus be identified with these itinerant magicians or charismatics. Yet detailed documentation is still not available, and we cannot fix either time or place in a precise way. There may have been other, contemporaneous channels of communication, operating at the various levels of folktale, intellectual curiosity, or even literature. How much our knowledge depends on chance has been shown once more by the Derveni find, a stroke of luck not likely to occur a second time.

4. Trails of Iconography

Although mythological research normally gropes in the dark for a realm of oral tradition that is not directly accessible, one form of evidence still springs to the eye; it is especially rich and influential just by its permanence, and its time and place of origin is usually identifiable: the pictorial tradition, iconography. Pictures or sculptures may survive for millenia; pictures easily jump language barriers. If myths are expressed in pictures, these play a fundamental role in the fixation, propagation and transmission of those myths: haven't most of us formed our concept of 'dragon' from the pictures we have seen, probably at an early age?

In fact it is neither natural nor necessary that pictures should refer to myths or tales. Judging from present evidence there were no representations of this kind in Mycenaean art.[67] Yet *Sagenbilder* make their appearance in Greek art about 700 BC and have played a prominent role ever since;[68] and there were precedents both in Mesopotamian and Egyptian art. Of course, our knowledge is largely dependent upon the physical properties of the materials used: some, such as textiles[69] or paintings on wooden tablets had hardly a chance of survival; there was just a slight chance for some of the most important, wall paintings and metal reliefs; stone sculptures are most durable, but least transportable; the richest corpus that remains is seals, especially the typical Mesopotamian cylinder seals and their impressions preserved in clay.[70] Painted ceramics were not used for pictures of this kind in the East.

Yet mythical picture books must be used with special care. Pictures are just signs, although we habitually give them some signification. This signification often may be some definite action, such as greeting, fighting, love-making, and this makes correspondence with a tale possible, as any narrative structure consists of a sequence of actions. Combat scenes, especially, can hardly be misunderstood. The sequence, nevertheless, cannot be contained in one picture; the production of a sequence of pictures to illustrate one tale is a rare and special development. It is equally impossible for a simple picture to give the kind of explicit reference that language affords by proper names. Thus on principle it is unclear whether a picture refers to an individual myth, made specific by the proper names contained in it, such as 'Herakles' or 'Achilles'. Again, to add names by writing, or to work out a specific canon of attributes to differentiate gods, heroes or saints is a rare and secondary development. Greeks have used these devices since the archaic age. Oriental art is less distinct. At the same time iconography develops its own canon, as pictures are copied from pictures: these are clear and demonstrable filiations, but totally at the level of *signifiant*, with little regard for signification and none at all for reference. Thus iconography clearly indicates connections even between different civilisations; yet as re-interpretations and misunderstandings may occur at any time, pictures cannot securely indicate the diffusion of a myth. Even the certainty that special compositions of mythological content have been transmitted is not yet a solution to the problem of 'travelling myths'.

One iconographic pattern of Mesopotamian art demands special attention because it is connected with the most prominent literary text of the East: *Gilgamesh and Enkidu slaying Humbaba*. It may be described as the symmetrical three-person combat scene: two champions are attacking from either side a wild man, represented *en face* in the middle, nearly collapsing on his knees in the 'Knielauf' position, which signifies an attempt at escape. This type makes its appearance in Old Babylonian times and continues to appear down to the Assyrian and neo-Babylonian epoch, spreading also to Iran, Southern Anatolia, Syria and Galilea.[71] There is no direct proof that the figures should be called Gilgamesh, Enkidu, and Humbaba, in accordance with *Gilgamesh* Tablet III to V; but because Humbaba is a man of the woods, and there is written evidence that Humbaba is represented by a frontal grim yet grinning face,[72] this identification of the 'wild man' at the centre of the composition with his mask-like face has usually been accepted for at least the bulk of the representations. It is almost the only mythical scene in Mesopotamian iconography that thus can be interpreted as referring to a literary text; normally glyptic art seems to be just heraldic, symbolic or ritualistic.

It has been pointed out more than once that in Greek art this scene became 'Perseus killing the Gorgo':[73] at the centre is the Gorgo, with the mask-like, grinning face of a 'wild' creature, in 'Knielauf' position; the champions — Perseus and Athena — stand on either side, taking hold of the monster. Even the detail that is so important for the Greek tale, that Perseus should turn his eyes away from the monster, has oriental precedents. In these, the champions are frequently differentiated, one wearing a long garment, the other a short one; for the Greeks, the fighter with the long skirt has become a female, Athena. The correspondence is compelling: the Greek artists must have seen oriental models of the type, presumably either in the form of seals or metal reliefs.

At the same time, it is clear that this transference of a mythical scene does not constitute a transmission of myth. There is not complete misunderstanding either, however: the signification of the 'combat scene', two fighters helping each other against a 'wild' creature, has been understood clearly. Yet the contexts do not mingle. The Humbaba fight belongs to the exploits of a cultural hero: Gilgamesh secures the access to the 'cedar forest' in order to procure timber for the city, a feat analogous to Ninurta's fighting the monster of the mountain. The tale of Perseus, on the other hand, has clear characteristics of an initiation myth: the hero travels to marginal areas to get his special weapon that commands death. The most striking detail, the hero turning his face away from the enemy, proves to be a creative misunderstanding: on the oriental prototype the hero is looking for a goddess who is about to pass him a weapon; Greek imagination has a monster instead with petrifying eyes. Details of the Gorgo type, incidentally, have their special iconographic ancestry; it cannot be derived fully from Humbaba.[74] The new creation, for the Greeks, is an iconographic sign without special ties to rituals or local groups, to be used freely in an 'apotropaic' sense on pediments, shields, or in other contexts, a terror to scare away mischief from temples or warriors.

There is a curious seal from Cyprus belonging to this context that deserves special mention.[75] It differs from the type in so far as it has only one champion. He is decidedly turning his face away from the monster, which he is seizing with his left hand while raising his weapon, a *harpe*, with his right. The monster, *en face* and in 'Knielauf', has Egyptianising locks and something like diffuse rays stretching out from its head — for Greeks, these would be the snakes surrounding the Gorgo's head — and the feet are huge bird's claws. This detail is securely rooted in Mesopotamian iconography, where Lamashtu and Pazuzu, dreaded demons, are represented in this way. Both, incidentally, have some further traits in common with the Gorgo (n 74). The picture was published at the beginning of this century in Roscher's *Lexikon der griechischen und römischen Mythologie* as being a clear illustration of the Perseus story; Pierre Amiet, on the other hand, has recently interpreted the seal in the context of Ugaritic mythology, without ever mentioning Perseus and the Greeks. It is unclear whether the seal came from a Phoenician or a Greek city of Cyprus; interpretation must probably remain a riddle. There were also other oriental or orientalising versions of the Perseus myth. At Tarsos he had some special connection with fish;[76] this may or may not be connected with the huge fish behind the champion on the Cypriot seal.

Perseus' ties to fish and the sea are still more prominent in another feat, the slaying of the *kêtos* and the liberation of Andromeda. This event was set at Ioppe/Jaffa,[77] and there is a Canaanite myth that seems to be the direct antecedent of the Greek tale: Astarte is offered to Jam, the god of the sea.[78] One Greek vase painting of Perseus, Andromeda, and the *kêtos* (all indicated by inscriptions), the oldest of its kind that is known so far, has some odd singularities: Perseus is fighting with stones, and Andromeda, unfettered, is helping him. These very details turn out to be directly dependent on an oriental prototype, represented especially by one seal of Nimrud that has often been reproduced:[79] a god is assaulting a monstrous snake and two minor figures are assisting him. The iconographic correspondence, especially as regards the stance of the champion and the monster's head, is overwhelming. Yet for Mesopotamians, this clearly was a god, engaged in cosmogonic struggle, Marduk fighting Tiamat, according to the current interpretation; on another, quite similar seal he is carrying lightning in his hands;[80] for the Greeks, this is another heroic adventure in a context of initiation. There is a curious misinterpretation involved: on the Assyrian seal, the six dots in the sky behind the champion represent a constellation, as paralleled on many seals of the kind (usually these are 'seven stars'); the Greek artist, in a more realistic vein, took them for stones and placed the pile on the ground securely between the champion's feet. We thus find a strange interplay of contacts and separation: the story, the setting and the picture are 'oriental', but the parcel is untied, the strings are separated and made to enter novel combinations so that the result is anything but a mechanical replica of its antecedents.

The three-person combat scene, however, produced another strange offspring in Greek art: one of the oldest representations of the death of Agamemnon killed by Klytaimnestra and Aigisthos evidently reproduces the pattern. This a clay plaque from Gortyn,[81] a place notorious, in any case, for its strong Eastern connections during the archaic period; the very technique of using terracotta moulds was developed in Crete from Phoenician practices. The two champions, differing in their dress, have become male and female, just as in the Perseus version; the victim is seen *en face*, as ever, pressed down from both sides. Yet the victim is made a king by the addition of throne and sceptre, which Aigisthos is seen to grab; and the tricky garment used to suffocate Agamemnon has been added. This is a deliberate composition, meant to illustrate a famous Greek tale, but the iconographic outlines have been borrowed from the oriental prototype; remodelling has not been a complete success. As to the contents, there appears to be no connection at all: Agamemnon is not a 'wild man'. Yet there may be unknown intermediates. It is striking that on some oriental exemplars, especially one that comes from the West Semitic region, Tell Keisan in Galilea,[82] there is a fourth person added to the three-figure scene, a smaller female raising her hands in a gesture of mourning. For the Greeks, this will be Electra. This would suggest that even in this case of creative misunderstanding, there was not just one chance event that has to account for the transformation, one artist in Gortyn stumbling on an oriental model while trying to illustrate the tale of Agamemnon, but multiple channels of communication.

This essay has been neither systematic nor aimed at completeness, entering, as it does, a field where much is still to be explored. It has been restricted to connections with Mesopotamia, while similar observations of equal importance could be made with regard to Egypt; suffice it to mention Amphitryon.[83] The examples adduced here may serve to establish some more general tenets, however: 'Oriental' and Greek mythology were close enough in time, place and character to communicate with each other. More than casual parallels are evident; sparks jumped from one to the other repeatedly. There are fundamental similarities, for instance in the quest of the culture heroes, be it Ninurta or Herakles; there was diffusion of motifs such as the lion fight or the seven-headed snake; more profound influence came about with the adoption of cosmogonic myth; there was also an impact of iconography especially in the orientalising epoch, which however left room for many creative re-interpretations. It is not, or not yet, possible to isolate specific occasions or single routes of transfer. One should rather acknowledge a complex network of communication, with single achievements standing out against a common background, while the 'origins' of myth are not to be sought in East or West, Bronze Age or Neolithic, but in a more common human ancestry.[84]

Figure 2.1: Seal Impression from Nuzi: Death of Humbaba. (See note 71, p. 39)

Figure 2.2: Shield Strap from Olympia: Perseus and Gorgo.
(See note 73, p. 39)

Figure 2.3: Seal from Cyprus: Hero Fighting Monster. (See note 75, p. 39)

Figure 2.4: Seal from Assur: Death of Humbaba. (See note 71, p. 39)

Figure 2.5: Clay Plaque from Gortyn: Death of Agamemnon. (See note 81, p. 40)

Figure 2.6: Seal from Tell Keisan: Death of Humbaba? (See note 82, p. 40)

Figure 2.7: Seal from Nimrud: God Fighting the Snake. (See note 79, p. 39f)

Figure 2.8: Corinthian Amphora: Perseus and the *kêtos*. (See note 79, p. 39f)

Notes

1. On the concept of 'Elementargedanke' by Philip Wilhelm Adolf Bastian, see *Enzyklopädie des Märchens* I (Berlin, 1977) 1324–7.

2. W. Liungmann, *Traditionswanderungen Euphrat-Rhein*, 2 vols (Helsinki, 1937/8).

3. See G. S. Kirk, *Myth, Its Meaning and Functions in Ancient and Other Cultures* (Berkeley, Los Angeles, 1970) 1–41; Burkert, *S&H*, 1–34; F. Graf, *Griechische Mythologie* (Munich and Zurich, 1985) 7–14.

4. See especially the publications of the 'school of Paris': e.g. J.-P. Vernant, *Mythe et société en Grèce ancienne* (Paris, 1974); J.-P. Vernant and P. Vidal-Naquet, *Mythe et tragédie en Grèce ancienne* (Paris, 1972); M. Detienne, *Les jardins d'Adonis* (Paris, 1972) and *Dionysos*.

5. Burkert, *S&H*, 102–5.

6. Ibid., 1–34.

7. V. Propp, *Morphology of the Folktale* (Bloomington, 1958; original edn, Leningrad, 1928); Burkert, *S&H*, 14–18.

8. C. Lévi-Strauss, *Mythologiques* I–IV (Paris, 1964–71); idem, 'La geste d'Asdiwal', in *Anthropologie structurale deux* (Paris, 1973) 175–233.

9. A. G. Dundes, *The Morphology of North American Indian Folktales* (Helsinki, 1964); idem, *Analytic Essays in Folklore* (The Hague, 1975) 61–72 (1st edn 1962).

10. S. Thomson, *Motif-Index of Folk-Literature* I–VI (Copenhagen, 1955–8).

11. See Burkert, *OE*.

12. C. H. Gordon, 'Homer and the Bible', *Hebrew Union Coll. Ann.*, *26* (1955) 43–108.

13. A recent attempt by F. Prinz in *RE* Suppl. 14 (1974) 137–96; the fullest

account of the literary evidence remains L. Preller, *Griechische Mythologie*, 4th edn, ed. C. Robert, vol. II (Berlin, 1921) 422–675; for the archaeological evidence, see F. Brommer, *Herakles*, 4th edn (Darmstadt, 1979); see also Burkert, *S&H*, Ch. IV.

14. See A. Jeremias in W. H. Roscher (ed.), *Ausführliches Lexikon der griechischen und römischen Mythologie* (henceforth cited as *RML*) vol. II (Leipzig, 1890–7) 821–3 with reference to earlier suggestions; B. Schweitzer, *Herakles* (Tübingen, 1922) 133–41; after the discovery of the Tell Asmar seals (see below, n 35), G. R. Levy, 'The oriental origin of Herakles', *JHS*, *54* (1934) 40–53; H. Frankfort, *Cylinder Seals* (London, 1939) 121f; see Burkert, *S&H* 80–83.

15. J. van Dijk, *LUGAL UD ME-LÁM-bi NIR-ǴAL, Le récit épique et didactique des travaux de Ninurta, du déluge et de la nouvelle création*, vol. I (Leiden, 1983). (The text is henceforth cited by the traditional incipit *Lugal-e*). A preliminary and sometimes misleading account had been given by S. N. Kramer, *Sumerian Mythology*, 2nd edn (New York, 1961) 78–92; see also T. Jacobsen, *The Treasures of Darkness* (New Haven, 1976) 129–31.

16. On Ningirsu and Ninurta see D. O. Edzard in H. W. Haussig (ed.), *Wörterbuch der Mythologie* I (Stuttgart, 1965) 111f, 114f; the twelve 'trophies' are enumerated in *Lugal-e* 129–33, cf. van Dijk 10–19.

17. Gudea A. XXV.24–XXVI.14; (outdated) transcription and translation in F. Thureau-Dangin, *Die sumerischen und akkadischen Königsinschriften* (Leipzig, 1907) 116–19; translation in A. Falkenstein, W.v. Soden, *Sumerische und Akkadische Hymnen und Gebete* (Zurich, 1953) 162f; new treatment in J. S. Cooper, 'The Return of Ninurta to Nippur', *Anal. Or.*, *52* (1978) 145f; only here the number 12 comes out. These beings are called 'heroes killed', XXVI.15 ('getötete Helden' Falkenstein; 'héros tués' van Dijk 10).

18. See now Cooper, 'The Return of Ninurta', traditional incipit: *An-gim dimma*. The 'trophies' occur in lines 32–40 and 54–62. A comparative analysis of the lists of 'trophies' is given by Cooper 141–54; further comments by van Dijk 10–19.

19. This detail is in the text of *An-gim*.

20. See below, note 24.

21. For six of them van Dijk gives only a transcription instead of a translation.

22. See van Dijk 7–9.

23. Van Dijk 11, 17, with explicit reference to the cows of Geryon.

24. *Gilgamesh* VII.iii.48 = VIII.iii.7 (where the relevant sign is partially destroyed); R. C. Thompson, *The Epic of Gilgamish* (Oxford, 1930) transcribes *maški kalbim* at the first, *maški labbim* at the second place (p. 45, 49); *labbim* also in W.v. Soden, *Akkadisches Handwörterbuch* 526 B, s.v. *labbu*. Sign no. 322 (Borger) can be read *kal* as well as *lab*. *Mašak kalbi* appears on a school tablet, *Materialien zum Sumerischen Lexikon*, vol. VII (ROME, 1959) 123, 20. For *kalbu*, 'dog', to denote 'humility', 'disparagement of oneself' see *Chicago Assyrian Dictionary*, vol. VIII (K) (Chicago, 1971) 72. The translations opt for 'lion': E. Ebeling in H. Gressmann (ed.), *Altorientalische Texte zum Alten Testament*, 2nd edn (Berlin, 1926) 165; A. Heidel, *The Gilgamesh Epic and Old Testament Parallels*, 2nd edn (Chicago, 1949) 59; *ANET*, 86; P. Labat, *Les Religions du Proche Orient* (Paris, 1970) 191, 197; A. Schott, *Das Gilgamesch-Epos*, neu herausgg. von W.v. Soden (Stuttgart, 1982) 67. The seals have many gods or heroes with club and bow. Very few seem to wear 'animal skins'. One figure with 'lion skin' in D. Collon, *Catalogue of the Western Asiatic Seals in the British Museum: Cylinder Seals*, vol. II (London, 1982) no. 213.

25. *Lugal-e* 26–45; van Dijk 55–7.

26. H. G. Güterbock, *Kumarbi* (Zurich, 1946); *The Song of Ullikummi* (New Haven, 1952); E. Laroche, *Catalogue des textes Hittites* (Paris, 1971) no. 345; *ANET* 120–5; see n 46.

27. References for 'Planet Ninurta' in F. Goessmann, Planetarium Babylonicum. *Summerisches Lexicon*, ed. A. Deimel, vol. IV 2 (Rome, 1950) 53; cf. 124.

28. Hdt. 2.43f; bilingual inscriptions, e.g. P. M. Fraser, *Ann. Br. Sch. Athens, 65* (1970) 31–6; *Tyrioi Herakleistai* on Hellenistic Delos, etc.; see R. Dussaud, 'Melqart', *Syria, 25* (1946/8) 205–30; U. Täckholm, 'Tarsis, Tartessos und die Säulen des Herakles', *Opuscula Romana, 5* (1965) 142–200, esp. 187–9. D. van Berchem, 'Sanctuaires d'Hercule-Melqart', *Syria, 44* (1967) 73–109, 307–38; C. Grottanelli, 'Melqart e Sid fra Egitto, Libia e Sardegna', *Riv. Studi Fenici, 1* (1973) 153–64. The inscription from Pyrgi brought testimony for the 'burial of the god' (see J. A. Soggin, 'La sepoltura della divinità', *Riv. Stud. Or., 45* (1970) 242–52) corresponding to the 'tomb' (Clem. Rom. *Rec.* 10.24.2) and the 'awakening' of Melqart (Menandros, *FGrH* 783 F 1) at Tyre; for a representation of the 'god in the flames' at Pyrgi see M. Verzàr in *Mél. Ec. Fr. Rome, 92* (1980) 62–78.

29. H. Goldman, 'Sandon and Herakles', *Hesperia*, Suppl. 8 (1949) 164–74; E. Laroche, 'Un syncrétisme gréco-anatolien: Sandas = Héraklès', in *Les Syncrétismes dans les religions grecque et romaine* (Paris, 1973) 103–14; S. Salvatori, 'Il dio Santa-Sandon: Uno sguardo ai testi', *Parola del Passato, 30* (1975) 401–9; on the numismatic evidence see P. Chuvin, *J. des Sav.* (1981) 319–26.

30. H. Seyrig, 'Antiquités Syriennes: Héraclès-Nergal', *Syria, 24* (1944/5) 62–80; W. Al-Salihi, 'Hercules-Nergal at Hatra', *Iraq, 33* (1971) 113–15.

31. M. K. Schretter, *Alter Orient und Hellas* (Innsbruck, 1974) 170f following a suggestion of K. Oberhuber. Erragal (Irragal) as a name for the god of the underworld occurs in *Atrahasis* II.vii.51 = *Gilgamesh* XI.101.

32. See Burkert, *S&H* 6; 14–16; 20.

33. Porph. *'Peri agalmatōn'* fr. 8, p. 13,3 Bidez; cf. O. Gruppe in *RE* Suppl. 3 (1911) 1104. Number 12 of the zodiacal signs has a complicated prehistory and is not established before the sixth century; see R. Böker in *RE* 10A (1972) 522–39 s.v. *Zodiakos*.

34. See Burkert, *S&H*, Ch. IV.

35. (1) Predynastic seal from Tell Asmar: *Oriental Institute Communications 17: Iraq Excavations 1932–1933* (Chicago, 1934) 54, fig. 50; G. R. Levy, *JHS, 54* (1934) 40; H. Frankfort, *Stratified Cylinder Seals from the Diyala Region* (Chicago, 1955) no. 497; Burkert, *S&H* 82; P. Amiet, *La Glyptique Mésopotamienne archaïque*, 2nd edn (Paris, 1980), no. 1393; (2) Predynastic shell plaque: *ANEP*, no. 671; Amiet, no. 1394; (3) Sargonic seal from Tell Asmar: *Or. Inst. Comm., 17*, 49, fig. 43; *JHS, 54*, pl. 2; Frankfort, *Strat. Cyl. Seals*, no. 478; R. M. Boehmer, *Die Entwicklung der Glyptik während der Akkad-Zeit* (Berlin, 1965), no. 292; *ANEP*, no. 691; Amiet, no. 1492; (4) Sumerian macehead in Copenhagen: H. Frankfort, *Anal. Or., 12* (1935) 105–8, fig. 1–4; O. Keel, *Wirkmächtige Siegeszeichen im Alten Testament* (Fribourg, 1974) fig. 40.

(1)–(3) are combat scenes; (4) has the snake above 'Imdugud' birds; (1) and (4) show coiled snakes, (2) and (3) four-footed dragons. From the back of the creature at (2) and (3) there rise vertical lines which have been intepreted as either 'tails' (Boehmer, 52) or 'flames' (Frankfort, *Or. Inst. Comm., 17*, 54; idem, *Cylinder Seals* (1939) 122); they recur in the Late Hittite relief from Malatya, showing gods fighting with the (one-headed?) snake, E. Akurgal, *Die Kunst der Hethiter* (Munich, 1961) fig. 104; *ANEP*, no. 670.

36. The 'Converse Tablet' ed. W. Lambert in *Near Eastern Studies in Honor of W. F. Albright* (Baltimore, 1971) 335–53; 336f; cf. Cooper, 'The Return of Ninurta', 147.

37. M. Dietrich, O. Loretz and J. Sanmartin, *Die keilalphabetischen Texte aus Ugarit* (Kevelaer, 1976) no. 1.5 I 27–30 (*ANET* p. 138); *Isaiah* 27,1; L. R. Fisher (ed.), *Ras Shamra Parallels* (Rome, 1972) I 33–6, no. 25.

38. K. Fittschen, *Untersuchungen zum Beginn der Sagendarstellungen bei den Griechen* (Berlin, 1969) 147f; Brommer, *Herakles*, 13, pl. 8; Burkert, *S&H* 78,2; 81. Two champions fighting a huge two-headed (?) snake appear on a white-painted plate from Cyprus, eleventh century: V. Karageorghis, *Comptes-rendus de l'Académie des Inscriptions et Belles Lettres* (1980) 28, fig. 7; there are no clear iconographic correlations to Eastern or Western types.

39. Burkert, *S&H* 80f with n 3.

40. Fittschen, *Untersuchungen* 84–8; Burkert, *OE* 22f.

41. For Peisandros, see G. L. Huxley, *Greek Epic Poetry from Eumelos to Panyassis* (London, 1969) 100–5. Brommer, *Herakles* 53–63; 82.

42. H. G. Güterbock, *Kumarbi, Mythen von churritischen Kronos* (Zurich, 1946) with the texts 'Kingship in Heaven' (Laroche, *Catalogue*, no. 344; *ANET* 120f) and 'Ullikummi' (see above, n 26). The discovery had been signalled by E. Forrer in *Mélanges F. Cumont* (Brussels, 1936) 687–713, cf. F. Dornseiff in *L'Antiquité classique*, 6 (1937) 231–58; A. Lesky, *Gesammelte Schriften* (Bern, 1966) 356–71 (1st edn, 1950); cf. A. Heubeck, 'Mythologische Vorstellungen des Alten Orients im archaischen Griechentum', *Gymnasium*, 62 (1955) 508–25; P. Walcot, *Hesiod and the Near East* (Cardiff, 1966); M. L. West, *Hesiod Theogony* (Oxford, 1966).

43. M. P. Nilsson, *Geschichte der griechischen Religion*, 3rd edn, vol. I (Munich, 1967) 515f. See also Kirk, *Myth*, 214–20; Burkert, *S&H* 20–2.

44. E. R. Dodds, *The Greeks and the Irrational* (Berkeley, 1951) 61.

45. Transmission via Late Hittites and/or Syria was Heubeck's thesis; cf. Burkert, *OE*, passim. Walcot, *Hesiod*, 127–9 and West, *Theogony*, 28f argued for transmission in the Mycenaean epoch. Survival of the Hittite Illuyankas myth into late Hittite times is usually inferred from the Malatya relief; see above, n 35.

46. See above n 26; on Caucasian parallels, W. Burkert, 'Von Ullikummi zum Kaukasus: Die Felsgeburt des Unholds', *Würzb. Jahrb. N.F.*, 5 (1979) 253–61.

47. *ANET* 123; Apollod. 1 (41) 6.3.7. The *Iliad* has Typhoeus *en Arimois* (2.783; cf. Hes. *Theog.* 304), which might be the first Greek reference to 'Aramaeans'. On Typhoeus in Hes. *Theog.* 820–80, see West, *Theogony*.

48. Laroche, *Catalogue*, no. 321; *ANET* 125f; cf. Burkert, *S&H* 7–10. An independent variant of the myth still recurs in Nonnos 1.154–62, cf. M. Rocchi, *Studi Micenei ed Egeo-Anatolici*, 21 (1980) 353–75.

49. Hes. *Theog.* 824–6; *speîrai* Apollod. 1 (42) 6.3.8; Chalcidian Hydria in Munich: K. Schefold, *Frühgriechische Sagenbilder* (Munich, 1964) pl. 66.

50. *Baal Ṣapuna* 'Lord of the North', is attested at Ugarit and in the treaty of Esarhaddon with Tyre (*ANET* 534); cf. *Exodus* 14.2; ṣ i.e. *dad* will appear as *t* in Aramaean, cf. *Ṣōr* (Ugaritic, Hebrew) = *Tyros*. See O. Eissfeldt, *Baal Zaphon, Zeus Kasios und der Durchzug der Israeliten durchs Meer* (Halle, 1932); E. Honigmann in *RE* 4A (1932) 1576f; F. Vian in *Eléments orientaux dans la religion grecque ancienne* (Paris, 1960) 26–8.

51. Ullikummi iii-c, *ANET* 125.

52. Text in *FGrH* 790; O. Eissfeldt repeatedly advocated the authenticity of the 'Sanchuniaton' tradition: *Ras Schamra und Sanchunjaton* (Halle, 1939) 75–95; idem, 'Taautos und Sanchunjaton', *Sitzungsber. Berlin* (1952), 1. The new commentary by A. I. Baumgarten, *The Phoenician History of Philo of Byblos* (Leiden, 1981) concludes that Philo is better explained in non-Ugaritic terms. See also J. Ebach, *Weltentstehung und Kulturentwicklung bei Philo von Byblos* (Stuttgart, 1979).

53. F. M. Cornford, *Principium Sapientiae* (Cambridge, 1952), esp. 'Cosmogonical Myth and Ritual', 225–38, and 'The Hymn to Marduk and the Hymn to Zeus', 239–49. This book was edited posthumously; the chapters had been written before the Kumarbi discovery; see E. R. Dodds's note, p. 249.

54. New edition of the cuneiform text: W. G. Lambert and S. B. Parker,

Enuma Eliš (Oxford, 1967); transcription of I–IV in G. Steiner, *Der Sukzessionsmythos in Hesiod's 'Theogonie' und ihren orientalischen Parallelen* (Diss., Hamburg, 1959); *ANET* 60–72; A. Heidel, *The Babylonian Genesis* (Chicago, 1942; 2nd edn 1951).

55. See van Dijk, 9f. Some other Babylonian creation stories are included in Heidel, *Babylonian Genesis*, 61–81. A further Sumerian text in J. van Dijk, 'Existe-t-il un "Poème de la Création" sumérien?', in *Cuneiform Studies in Honor of S. N. Kramer*, ed. B. L. Eichler (Neukirchen-Vluyn, 1976) 125–133.

56. The whole text has become available, though not in a final form, in *ZPE, 47* (1982). Seven columns had been edited by S. G. Kapsomenos, *Deltion, 19* (1964) 17–25; cf. W. Burkert, 'Orpheus und die Vorsokratiker', *Antike und Abendland, 14* (1968) 93–114. See now M. L. West, *The Orphic Poems* (Oxford, 1983) 68–115.

57. ὃς μεγ' ἔρεξεν 10.5; the author etymologises Kronos from κρούειν, as 'things being clashed together' were separated, and the sun was fixed in the middle between earth and sky, col. 10/11. αἰδοῖον κα[τ]έπινεν, ὃς αἰθέρα ἔχθορε πρῶτος 9.4. πρωτογόνου βασιλέως αἰδοίου 12.3. That ἐχθορεῖν is used as a transitive verb is clear from 10.1 ἐχθόρηι τὸν λαμπρότατόν τε [καὶ λ]ευκό[τ]ατον paraphrasing αἰθέρα ἔχθορε; cf. θρώσκων Aesch. fr. 15 Radt = 133 Mette. West, *Orphic Poems*, 85f, followed by J. S. Rusten, *HSCP, 89* (1985) 125f, takes αἰδοῖον as an adjective, combining ingeniously 4.5 with 9.4, and thus makes the Kumarbi motif disappear. This is to impute to the commentator a gross misunderstanding of the Greek text he had before his eyes in a complete copy; he twice makes δαίμονα [κυδρ]όν the object of ἔλαβεν (5.4; 4.8), not of κατέπινε. West (p. 86) also inserts Phanes Protogonos before Uranos, in accordance with the Orphic Rhapsodies, but without support in the Derveni text. 10.6 Οὐρανὸς Εὐφρονίδης, ὃς πρώτιστος βασίλευσεν must be identified with the πρωτόγονος βασιλεύς 12.3, or else Uranos would not be the 'first' king.

58. The four kingdoms appear in the crucial testimony for Orphic anthropogony, *Orphicorum Fragmenta* 220 Kern = Olympiod. *In Phaed.* p. 41f Westerink, in accordance with the Derveni evidence. See also *OE* 116f.

59. Plato refers to *Iliad* 14.201 = 302 in *Crat.* 402 ab, *Tht*, 152e, 180cd, as does Arist. *Met.* 983 b27. Eudemus fr. 150 Wehrli, preserved by Damaskios, *De primis principiis* I 319–21 Ruelle, made a systematic collection of cosmogonic myths.

60. O. Gigon, *Der Ursprung der griechischen Philosophie von Hesiod bis Parmenides* (Basle, 1945). For the continuity from mythical to Presocratic cosmogony see also U. Hölscher, 'Anaximander und der Anfang der Philosophie', in *Anfängliches Fragen* (Göttingen, 1968) 9–89 (Ist edn 1953).

61. S. H. Hooke, *Myth and Ritual* (Oxford, 1933). For the ritual of the Babylonian New Year's Festival, see *ANET* 331–4, with mentions of the recital of *Enuma elish*.

62. 'What follows is the cult legend of the Purulli Festival', *ANET* 125. For *Lugal-e*, see above, n 15.

63. T. H. Gaster, *Thespis. Ritual, Myth, and Drama in the Ancient Near East*, 2nd edn (Garden City, 1961).

64. L. Deubner, *Attische Feste* (Berlin, 1932) 152–5. Cf. Burkert, *GR*, 227–33; Versnel, this volume, Ch. 7.

65. See Burkert, *OE*, 115f.

66. The investigation of 'conduits' and 'multi-conduit-transmission' goes back to Linda Dégh, see Enzyklopädie des Märchens III (Berlin, 1981) 124–6.

67. See E. Vermeule and V. Karageorghis, *Mycenaean Pictorial Vase Painting* (Cambridge, 1982).

68. See Schefold, *Sagenbilder*; Fittschen, *Untersuchungen*.

69. K. S. Brown, *The Question of Near Eastern Textile Decoration of the Early First*

Millenium B.C. as a Source for Greek Vase Painting of the Orientalizing Style (Diss., University of Pennsylvania, 1980) thinks this influence has been rather overrated.

70. An indispensable older work is W. H. Ward, *The Seal Cylinders of Western Asia* (Washington, 1910); still useful is O. Weber, *Altorientalische Siegelbilder* (Leipzig, 1920); Frankfort, *Cylinder Seals*; A. Moortgat, *Vorderasiatische Rollsiegel* (Berlin, 1940; 2nd edn 1966). Recent interest has concentrated on the early epoch: Boehmer, *Entwicklung*; Amiet, *La Glyptique Mésopotamienne archaïque*; D. Collon, *Catalogue of the Western Asiatic Seals in the British Museum: Cylinder Seals* II (London, 1982); a good survey with bibliography: R. M. Boehmer in *Der alte Orient. Propyläen Kunstgeschichte* XIV, ed. W. Orthmann (Berlin, 1975) 336–63.

71. D. Opitz, 'Der Tod des Humbaba', *Archiv für Orientforschung*, 5 (1928/9) 207–13; P. Calmeyer, 'Reliefbronzen in babylonischem Stil', *Abh. Bay. Ak. der Wiss.*, N.F., 73 (1973) 44f; 165–9; C. Wilcke, *Reall. der Assyriologie* IV (Berlin, 1975) 530–5 s.v. *Huwawa*; E. Haevernick and P. Calmeyer, *Arch. Mitt. Iran, N.F.* 9 (1976) 15–18. For late Hittite reliefs at Tell Halaf, Karkemish, Karatepe, see H. Frankfort, *The Art and Architecture of the Ancient Orient* (London, 1963) pl. 159 C; H. J. Kantor, *JNES*, 21 (1962) 114f. The composition seems to be misunderstood or reinterpreted in Phoenician art, R. D. Barnett, *Iraq*, 2 (1935) 202f, but a fine example of the normal type is a bowl from Nimrud, ibid. 205 = Vian, *Eléments orientaux* (above, n 50) pl. IVb. For a seal from Galilea see below, n 82. See Figure 2.1, this volume: Seal impression from Nuzi, *Ann. Am. Sch. Oriental Res.*, 24 (1944/5) 60 and pl. 37, 728; *JNES*, 21 (1962) 115; Figure 2.4, this volume: Seal from Assur, Berlin 4215, eighth century BC: D. Opitz, *Arch. f. Orientforsch.*, 5 (1928/9) pl. XI 2; *AJA*, 38 (1934) 352; Moortgat, *Vorderas. Rollsiegel*, no. 608 (date: p. 67f); Calmeyer, 'Reliefbronzen', 166, fig. 124.

72. Wilcke, s.v. *Huwawa*, 534. See also V. K. Afanasyeva, 'Gilgameš and Enkidu in Glyptic Art and in the Epic', *Klio*, 53 (1970) 59–75.

73. C. Hopkins, 'Assyrian Elements in the Perseus-Gorgon-Story', *AJA*, 38 (1934) 341–58; B. Goldman, 'The Asiatic Ancestry of the Greek Gorgon', *Berytus*, 14 (1961) 1–23; H. J. Kantor, 'A Bronze Plaque with Relief Decoration from Tell Tainat', *JNES*, 21 (1962) 93–117; Burkert, *OE*, 81–4. Figure 2.2, this volume, is a shield strap from Olympia, E. Kunze, *Olympische Forschungen* II (Berlin, 1950) pl. 57; Kantor 115.

74. T. G. Karayorga, *Gorgeie Kephale* (Athens, 1970); J. Floren, *Studien zur Typologie des Gorgoneion* (Munich, 1977); Burkert, *OE*, 81–4, also for relations to Lamashtu and Pazuzu.

75. M. Ohnefalsch-Richter, *Kypros, the Bible, and Homer* (London, 1893) pl. 31, 16 cf. p. 208; A. de Ridder, *BCH*, 22 (1898) 452 fig. 4; *RML* III (1902–9) 2032, art. 'Perseus'; Ward, *Cylinder Seals*, no. 643c p. 211f; Weber, *Siegelbilder*, no. 269; *AJA*, 38 (1934) 351; *Berytus*, 14 (1961) 22; P. Amiet, *Orientalia*, 45 (1976) 27 with reference to Ugaritic mythology (26); Burkert, *OE* 83, 22; see Figure 2.3, this volume. B. Brentjes, *Alte Siegelkunst des Vordenen Orients* (Leipzig, 1983) 165, 203, has a new drawing, the inventory number VA 2145, and the information — contrary to Ohnefalsch-Richter — 'in Bagdad gekauft'. He simply calls the picture 'Greek'.

76. See Burkert, *HN* 209f.

77. Strabon 16 p. 759; Konon *FGrH* 26 F 1, 40; Ios. *Bell. Iud.* 3.420; Paus. 4.35.9. Andomeda's father Cepheus is son of Belos as early as Hdt. 7.61; Eur. fr. 881.

78. The 'Astarte Papyrus', a heavily mutilated Egyptian text with Canaanite names, *ANET* 17f.

79. See Figure 2.7, this volume: Neo-Assyrian Seal, 'Williams Cylinder' (Pierpont Morgan Collection no. 688, New York): Ward, *Seal Cylinders* 201f, no.

578; A. Jeremias, *Handbuch der altorientalischen Geisteskultur*, 2nd edn (Berlin, 1929) 431, fig. 239a. Weber, *Altor. Siegelbilder*, no. 347; Kramer, *Sumerian Mythology* pl. XIX 2; M. L. West, *Early Greek Philosophy and the Orient* (Oxford, 1971) pl. IIa; P. Amiet, *Syria*, *42* (1965) 245. For the interpretation 'Marduk fighting Tiamat' see Ward 201f; he also states that the six 'stones' seem to be derived iconographically from the seven dots = seven stars often represented on seals. Figure 2.8, this volume: Late Corinthian Amphora, Berlin; *RML* III 2047; Schefold, *Sagenbilder* pl. 45; *LIMC* 'Andromeda' no. 1 (where the singularities mentioned in the text are set forth).

    80. Ward. no. 579; Weber no. 348; Kramer pl. XIX 1.

    81. *LIMC* 'Agamemnon', no. 91, from Gortyn (Mus. Iraklion) , 675/50 BC; Schefold, *Sagenbilder* pl. 33; M. I. Davies, *BCH*, *93* (1969) 228, fig. 9–10. See Figure 2.5, this volume. Davies especially deals with a Cretan seal (about 700 BC; *LIMC*, Agamemnon no. 94); this has only two persons and thus does not belong directly to the type treated here.

    82. O. Keel, in J. Briend and J. B. Humbert (eds), *Tell Keisan (1971–76), une cité phénicienne en Galilée* (Fribourg, 1980) 276f, pl. 89,17; 136,17. See Figure 2.6, this volume. Cf. the Assyrian Seal, Ward, *Seal Cylinders*, 211, fig. 642; Hopkins, 'Assyrian Elements', 354, fig. 12.

    83. The begetting of the Pharao by Amun is represented in Egyptian temples by a pictorial cycle, first at Der-el-Bahri (Hatchepsut, 1488–1467) and Luxor (Amenophis III, 1397–1360); see H. Brunner, *Die Geburt des Gottkönigs* (Wiesbaden, 1964). J. Assmann, 'Die Zeugung des Sohns', in J. Assmann, W. Burkert and F. Stolz, *Funktionen und Leistungen des Mythos* (Fribourg, 1982) 13–61; that the Amphitryon story is derived from there, with the detail that Toth = Hermes should accompany Amun = Zeus on his amorous ways, has been stated repeatedly: A. Wiedemann, *Herodots zweites Buch* (Leipzig, 1890) 268; Brunner 214; W. Burkert, *MH*, *22* (1965) 168f; S. Morenz, 'Die Geburt des ägyptischen Gottkönigs', *Forschungen und Fortschritte*, *40* (1966) 366–71; R. Merkelbach, *Die Quellen des Alexanderromans*, 2nd edn (Munich, 1977) 77–82. The decisive motif, the god assuming the shape of the king, does not appear in the oldest Greek sources, *Od*, 11.266–8. and Hes. fr. 195 = *Aspis* 1–56, but may be presupposed on the chest of Kypselos (Zeus as a 'man wearing a chiton': Paus. 5.18.3); see also Pherekydes *FGrH* 3 F 13; Charon *FGrH* 262 F 2.

    84. My thanks to Sarah Johnston for correcting the English style of this essay — responsibility for its final form, though, remains with me — and to Cornelius Burkert for his drawings.

3

Oedipus and the Greek Oedipus Complex

Jan Bremmer

Oedipus is one of the few figures of Greek mythology whose name is still a household word. His fate has inspired playwrights, librettists, film-makers,[1] and attracted the attention of Freud and Lévi-Strauss, the founding fathers of psychoanalysis and structuralist anthropology respectively (cf. below). In spite of the enormous interest, a satisfactory interpretation of the myth has still not been arrived at. The following inquiry does not pretend to present the last word about Oedipus, but it hopes to show that historical, sociological and structuralist approaches can all cast light on one and the same myth — and sometimes have to be employed simultaneously. Only an eclectic analysis makes the best use of the riches of the mythological tradition.

The Oedipus myth has been discussed in various ways. Older scholars tried above all to recover the myth's earliest stages. They compared its various versions in epic, tragedy and later Greek mythography, and in this way they were able to demonstrate that in the course of time important changes had occurred. For example, originally Delphi was absent from the story, and Oedipus remarried after his wife's death. Only in classical times did the poets' interest shift from the family to the individual; in archaic Greece an *Antigone* was unthinkable.[2]

The most recent, structuralist approach has proceeded regardless of these chronological considerations. In a noteworthy analysis, Claude Lévi-Strauss compared the relationship between Kadmos and his sister Europa to Antigone's attitude to Polynices' corpse, and concluded that these incidents have as a common feature the overrating of blood relations. In addition, he drew far-reaching conclusions from the physical defects which are suggested, according to him, by the names of Oedipus, 'Swollen foot', his father Laios, 'Left-sided', and his grandfather Labdacus, 'Lame'. However, it has to be objected that Antigone is only a post-Homeric arrival in the Oedipus myth, and the name Laios (*Láïos*) does not derive from the Greek word *laiós*, 'left'. Historical and linguistic knowledge remains indispensable, even in a structuralist approach. Lévi-Strauss's procedure is of course perfectly understandable from his experience with the non-literate peoples of Latin America; it is usually impossible to distinguish between historical layers in his own chosen area. In Greek mythology, on the contrary, such a distinction is often possible, and a chronological determination of the various motifs must therefore always be attempted.[3]

Although I shall incorporate the chronological perspectives of the older scholars and shall make use of structuralist methods, I shall be more indebted to scholars who followed a rather different approach, namely the great Russian folklorist Propp and the Belgian Marie Delcourt.[4] Both scholars analysed the myth by studying the meaning of all of its individual motifs. They thought they could detect an initiatory pattern in the myth, but failed to integrate Oedipus' incest convincingly into this solution. Yet in principle their approach seems sound — only by studying all the individual motifs against the background of a unifying pattern can a myth as a whole be properly evaluated. However, the popularity of the Oedipus theme means that the scope of the inquiry has to be delimited. Following Lévi-Strauss's methodological guideline that a myth should be studied with reference to its own ethnographical context,[5] I shall analyse the Oedipus myth as much as possible within the context of the archaic and classical age. In practice, this means that the sources can be restricted to those versions which were known to the tragedians of the fifth century;[6] versions which have become rationalised or adapted to the more bourgeois climate of Hellenistic times need not be taken into consideration.[7] This chapter, then, will concentrate on two aspects of the myth. First, successive episodes of Oedipus' life will be looked at, with particular reference to the parricide and incest, and secondly, an attempt will be made to locate the Greek Oedipus complex in a specific historical setting.

1. Oedipus

How did it all begin? In the fifth century, various versions of the myth's early history were current. In Aeschylus' *Seven against Thebes* the Delphic oracle warns the Theban king Laios that he will only save the city if he dies childless. In Sophocles' *Oedipus Rex* the oracle proclaims that the newborn son will kill his father, but in Euripides' *Phoenissae* the oracle takes place before Oedipus' birth. This variation can hardly be due to chance. The very beginning of the myth was an area where the poets could freely exercise their ingenuity without altering the traditional plot of the myth. Both oracle and prophecy will not have been introduced into the myth before the eighth century, since that was when Delphi first rose to fame and the Greek polis came into existence. The oracle probably replaced a seer: a poet could hardly get Oedipus away from Thebes and ignorant of his true parentage without a prophecy (however given). Even if there is an answer to this problem for the pre-history of the myth, for the classical period the presence of the oracle is most important because it introduces such motifs as human v. divine intelligence, vain attempts to escape from oracles, limitations of human understanding and fate — motifs which evidently fascinated the classical audience.[8]

In order to forestall the outcome of the oracle, King Laios had Oedipus exposed. The myth indicates two locations of the exposure which are not as different as they might appear at first sight. According to the first version, Oedipus was exposed on Mt Cithaeron and found by a shepherd from Sicyon. The tradition of Oedipus' discovery near Thebes by a Sicyonian shepherd is an interesting glimpse into the sparsely documented activities of Greek herdsmen. Undoubtedly, his presence is a nice example of transhumance — the system by which herds graze in the mountains in the summer, and in the valleys during the winter. A detailed exposition of the myth may well have elaborated the difficulties experienced by the shepherds in bringing the foundling home![9] According to the second version, Oedipus was put in a chest and thrown into the sea. Fortunately, he was rescued by the queen of Corinth (or Sicyon) who was doing her laundry at the seashore. Washing clothes may not seem a very royal activity, but in the *Odyssey* Nausicaa too departs on a washing expedition; the motif will predate the Classical Age when the enclosure of women was too strict to allow such activities.[10]

Both versions employ common mythological motifs. Paris was exposed on Mt Ida and rescued by a shepherd, and Perseus was exposed at sea in a chest. Whereas older scholars felt the need to determine the priority of one of the two versions, the structuralist will observe that sea and mountains are both in opposition to the fertile land around the polis. Evil beings and polluted objects were carried to the mountains or cast into the sea, and a Greek curse tersely says: 'into the mountains or into the sea'. Both areas, then, contain the same message: the child was exposed on a spot from which no escape was possible.[11]

Oedipus was not the only foundling to survive. We need only think of other famous persons such as Sargon, Cyrus, Perseus, Romulus and Remus, and Pope Gregory in order to realise that this motif is very widespread.[12] All these foundlings have in common that they grow up to become important wordly or spiritual leaders. Various scholars have suggested that the exposure reflects a ritual theme such as the rites of initiation, or, as in the case of Oedipus, the punishment for parricide (i.e. to be drowned in a bag).[13] None of these explanations is really convincing. It is more natural to see in the exposure a narrative ploy: the important position of the hero in later life within the community is thrown into greater relief by his earlier removal from that community.[14] Given its knowledge of the exposure motif in the case of Perseus and other heroes, a Greek audience unfamiliar with the myth probably will have interpreted Oedipus' exposure in an analogous way until it dawned upon them that in this particular case the exposure prepared the way for terrible things to come.

When Oedipus was exposed, his feet were mutilated. Vladimir Propp (above, note 4) has pointed out that in many legends the foundling is symbolically killed. This could also be the explanation for Oedipus' mutilation — the wounded feet meant a *de facto* death. On the other hand, there is something odd about this motif. After all, Oedipus was a baby: how could anyone have expected that he would run away? The role of the mutilation is actually secondary in the myth. It does not occur in those versions where Oedipus is exposed at sea, nor does Sophocles let his hero limp in the *Oedipus Rex*.[15] And yet, this subsidiary motif has exercised an enormous influence on modern interpretations. According to their various orientations, scholars have explained it as a sign of

44

autochthony, a defect of communication, the reverse of good king-ship or the overcoming of fear of castration.[16] All these explana-tions misjudge the typical Greek way of playing with names. Popular etymologies always confirm the values already ascribed to the bearer of a name; they do not produce these values. In other words, the etymological interpretation is always secondary, and cannot be used as the main key in decoding the myth.[17]

After the shepherds had found Oedipus, they brought him to the court of King Polybus. The king's name is fixed in all versions of the tradition, but the name of his wife varies; she is called Merope, Periboia, Medusa or Antiochis. Evidently, changing women's names was one of the poetic means of giving a story a new look.[18] Even though the royal couple pretended that Oedipus was their own son, his education at another court can hardly be separated from fosterage, the initiatory custom according to which Greek and other Indo-European aristocratic children were raised at a court or family different from their own. This once widespread custom lasted until the later Middle Ages, and in England became transformed into the institution of the public school.[19] The exposure myths could easily incorporate initiatory motifs, since boys usually had to spend some time away from home during their rites of puberty; Cyrus' and Romulus and Remus' growing up among their contemporaries also reflects Persian and Roman rites of initiation. It was normal for the young aristocrat to return home when he had grown up in order to pass through the final puberty rites. Similarly, Oedipus left the court when he had reached adulthood.[20]

We need not analyse the reasons why Oedipus left his foster parents, or why Laios left Thebes in order to consult the Delphic oracle. Motivations were typically a territory where poets could use their imagination. It is far more interesting to inquire why Oedipus killed his father at a triple crossroads. Carl Robert spent much effort on localising the scene of the crime, and even pub-lished photographs of it,[21] but it seems more important to observe that the Greeks considered a triple crossroads an ominous spot. It was the place where ghostly Hecate was worshipped, where Plato wants corpses of parricides to be stoned, and where in Late Antiquity the poet Nonnus still has women commit murders.[22] Evidently, mythopoeic imgination did not chose its scenery at random but deliberately.

After the murder of his father, Oedipus continued his journey to Thebes where he solved the Sphinx's riddle. A full text of the riddle only emerges in the fourth century:

> There walks on land a creature of two feet, of four feet, and of three; it has one voice, but sole among animals that grow on land or in the sea, it can change its nature; nay, when it walks propped on most feet, then is the speed of its limbs less than it has ever been before.

Versions of the riddle have been collected in other parts of the world, but the Greek version, unlike that of other peoples, never mentions the various stages of life as morning, afternoon and evening.[23] The earliest sources locate the monster in the mountains where it usually kills Theban youths; later sources dramatise the situation by mentioning the ecclesia or acropolis of Thebes.[24] Monsters naturally belong in the wild, but it may seem curious that in literature and iconography the Sphinx is virtually always represented as a girl, although a vase with an onanising Sphinx does exist. The monster's female sex fits in well with the Greek tendency to represent monsters as female, in particular as girls and/or old women, as is illustrated by the cases of the Medusa, Gorgo, Chimaera, Lamia, the Sirens, Erinyes, Scylla and Charybdis. Whereas modern fiction likes to represent the ultimate danger as coming from outer space, male Greek imagination always thought of the opposite sex.[25]

It has recently been argued that the episode with the Sphinx is a later addition to the Oedipus story, since there is no unanimity regarding the sender — Hera, Ares and Dionysos are mentioned; moreover, the episode is absent from similar folktales. This argument is unacceptable. First, Hesiod (*Th.* 326) knows of the Sphinx as a threat to the Thebans, and parts of the riddle's text already appear on a newly published sixth-century vase; allusions to it are to be found in early fifth-century literature. This chronological evidence would in itself dispose of the claim that the Sphinx is a later addition. Secondly, motivation is variable in poetic tradition, as we saw before. Thirdly, the comparison with other folktales forces the Sphinx episode into the shackles of a primeval version which is non-existent in the historical tradition but has to be reconstructed from much later versions. There is no reason, then, to exclude the Sphinx episode from the original myth.[26]

By freeing the Thebans from the Sphinx, Oedipus acquired the throne and the hand of the queen. The *Odyssey* version of the Oedipus myth, the oldest version that exists, stresses the role of Epikaste (Jocaste) in this marriage: 'she who had married her son' (11.273). Similarly, the suitors of Penelope were waiting to see whom she would choose to marry. These myths presuppose a matrimonial system in which gaining the hand of the queen-widow implies occupation of the throne. The same system could be found elsewhere. Herodotus relates the gripping story of Gyges and the wife of the Lydian king Candaules; another Lydian king was also succeeded by a subordinate who married the adulterous queen. In Persia, the Magus Smerdis married Cambyses' widow Atossa, who was incorporated into Darius' harem after Smerdis' death, and — a very late example — in the eleventh century, the Scandinavian Knut married the widow of Ethelred, the defeated English king.[27]

If Oedipus' wedding had been the end of the myth, the result of the analysis would have been obvious. In the 1930s, Louis Gernet had already compared Oedipus' confrontation with the Sphinx with ordeals of other heroes such as Theseus, Iamos and Pelops, and interpreted these tests as an 'initiation royale'. The pioneer of the study of Greek initiatory rites, Jeanmaire, also recognised in this part of the myth 'le thème d'avènement', but at the same time he wondered about the link with incest and parricide. Could these latter two motifs really be connected with the theme of initiation?[28]

There can be no doubt, in fact, that parricide can be brought into the orbit of puberty rites, as is illustrated by the Theseus myth. Scholars have long recognised that the Attic version of the myth reflects an initiatory scenario: the prince who is educated away from home defeats the monstrous Minotaur and returns home to become king. In the case of Theseus, the king is not straightforwardly murdered, but his suicide is caused by Theseus forgetting to change the sails. In other words, in this particular case myth has mitigated parricide. In its undiluted form, the crime occurs in a Bororo myth. A boy named Geriguiguiatugo raped his mother and was therefore abandoned by his father. After the performance of a series of hunting feats, he returned, provided his tribe with fire and killed his father. The rape of his mother symbolises separation from the world of women. The killing of his father expresses a 'social principle of universal validity: "for society to go on, sons must destroy (replace) their fathers"'. Walter Burkert has wisely pointed to the initiatory pattern of this Bororo myth. Lévi-Strauss, on the other hand, mentions the connection of the myth with initiation but fails to note its importance for the interpretation of the very myth which constitutes the starting point of his analysis of South American mythology.[29]

We can systematise these myths as follows:

Oedipus	Theseus	Geriguiguiatugo
fosterage	fosterage	
parricide	conquest of monster	hunting feats
conquest of monster	'parricide'	parricide
king	king	culture hero

Up to this point, these myths display a comparable structure: a young man performs an impressive feat, defeats a monster, kills his father (or is the cause of his death) and becomes king (or culture hero). The order of motifs 2 and 3 is different in the case of Oedipus and Theseus, but this difference does not seem to be of any particular interest. Propp attached great value to the fixed order of the motifs in a given folktale, but his point of view is hardly supported by Greek myths and their plots.[30] Yet, however comparable these myths are up till this point, the problem remains of how Oedipus' incest can be fitted into this scheme. Is an interpretation which takes ritual as the starting point of the myth perhaps more satisfactory?

Around the beginning of this century an explanation of the myth was looked for in Oedipus' connection with Demeter at the level of cult. It was typical of historians of Greek religion that they tried to regain firm ground by concentrating on ritual instead of myth after the excesses of Max Müller and Usener. And indeed, a local historian Lysimachos mentions a cult of Oedipus and his grave in the sanctuary of Demeter in Boeotian Eteonos. Carl Robert, recently followed by Burkert, saw in this cult the origin of Oedipus' marriage, since Demeter was the Greek mother *par excellence*. However, the burial in Demeter's sanctuary does not make Oedipus a son of the goddess. Moreover, the assumption implies that at a very early stage the Boeotians of Eteonos already worshipped an unknown hero who had nothing to do with Oedipus, and who, for unknown reasons, was transferred to Thebes by an unknown poet; in addition, this solution leaves the link with parricide totally unexplained. It seems rather less complicated to assume that the cult at Eteonos originated in epic tradition like so many other heroic cults.[31]

Solutions via initiation or via ritual prove to be unsatisfactory: an investigation into the striking combination of parricide and incest may perhaps be more rewarding. We start with a closer look at parricide. Modern Western society has become differentiated to such a degree that few people are dependent on their fathers for their future; neither are fathers very dependent on their children any more for care in their old age. Consequently, parricide does not play a major role in the modern imagination. It is therefore well to remember that in ancient Greece sons were totally dependent on their fathers for their later status, and that parents looked to their children as a kind of pension. The great stress Greeks laid on honouring parents is a clear indication of a situation in which an underlying tension between fathers and sons must always have existed.[32] An ever-present possibility, parricide was considered to be one of the most appalling of crimes. One of the signs of the rule of Hate, as envisaged by Empedocles, is the murder of the father, followed by the consumption of his flesh. Imputation of parricide was one of the 'unspeakable things' which could well result in legal action; even the word 'parricide' was only mentioned with reluctance, if at all.[33]

Incest was equally appalling, even though the Greeks did not have a specific word to denote the practice; nor did they condemn sexual relationships between relatives to the same degree as has been usual in the modern Western world. Marriages between uncle/aunt and niece/nephew were relatively current in both the archaic and classical period. Marriages of first cousins and those between half-brothers and half-sisters were also not uncommon.[34] Those between brothers and sisters seem to have been just beyond the limits of the admissible, although Carians, Egyptians and the Ptolemies permitted them.[35] The *Odyssey* can still describe the marriage of Aeolus' children without comment, even though it is located on an island outside normal civilisation. In Hesiod's *Theogony*, brother/sister marriages among the gods are evidently not considered to be a problem, but such marriages occur in most mythologies of the world without any apparent condemnation. In the classical period, imputation of incest with a sister belongs to the normal vocabulary of legal and political abuse, but these accusations never seem to have led to a formal trial. In the early Hellenistic period, Philetas still mentions a marriage of Aeolus' children without any penalty or punishment. In the same period, Hermesianax relates the story of Leucippus falling in love with his sister. Although his mother condoned the affair, it had terrible consequences. When the sister's fiancé denounced the couple to their father, the old man tried to catch the couple *in flagrante delicto*. In the turmoil that followed the daughter was inadvertently killed by the father, who in turn was killed by the son, also inadvertently. Even in this Greek soap opera, love between brother and sister is condoned by the mother, although the parricide indicates rejection by the poet.[36] The same disapproval appears in Euripides who lets Aeolus put his incestuous daughter to death. Ovid even pictures her fate in the cruellest of terms — it was apparently a relationship which only gradually became totally inadmissible.[37]

Not so sex between parents and children. In Orphic mythology, Zeus' rape of his mother Rhea/Demeter results in the birth of a daughter, Persephone, with two faces, four eyes and horns: the mother is so shocked that she leaves her baby. The same poetry has Zeus mating with Persephone in the shape of a snake. However, the background of these idiosyncratic beliefs is still very much under-researched; it seems therefore too early to draw conclusions from them. The imputation of sex between father and daughter or mother and son was part of normal political and legal abuse. We can hardly be surprised, though, that discussions of real cases are lacking — even today these matters are usually clouded in a veil of secrecy. At the imaginative level, however, various examples of such relationships can be found. Having tasted his own children, Thyestes later inadvertently slept with his daughter and in this way begat Aigisthos, the murderer of Agamemnon. In a probably Hellenistic tale, the chief of the Pelasgians, Piasos raped his daughter Larissa, who in retribution managed to drown her father in a barrel of wine. In another tale, Harpalyke of Argos was raped by her father Klymenos. Subsequently, she killed her youngest brother (or her son) and served him up to her father during a public banquet. The gods changed her into a bird and her father committed suicide.[38]

In these stories, incest leads to parricide or cannibalism, whereas parricide can lead to incest (Oedipus) or cannibalism (rule of Hate). This cannot be chance. For the Greeks, incest, parricide and cannibalism were the great taboos which marked off the civilised from the rest of the world. Transgressions in these particular areas were the crimes ascribed to the *tyrannos*, the one person who had placed himself outside normal society. These were also the transgressions propagated by the Cynics in their opposition to the ruling norms of the polis. Cannibalism, incest and killing old people were also crimes which the Greeks ascribed to surrounding peoples in order to stress the superiority of their own civilisation. They were not unique in this attitude, though.[39] Cannibalism and incest were also standard accusations levelled by Europeans against inhabitants of countries discovered in the early modern age; indeed, these imputations seem to occur all over the world.[40]

We can now see that there is a strong moralistic flavour about these stories, since the monstrosity of the transgression is commented upon by letting the protagonist commit a further monstrosity. Whoever commits incest is prone to become a parricide or cannibal as well. Or, whoever commits parricide will become incestuous and consume human flesh. The corollary must be that Oedipus' incest is not a pre-Freudian reflection on his relationship with his mother but a comment on his parricide. The lack of any profound interest in his mother is confirmed by the variety of her names: epic poetry calls her Epikaste, tragedy Jocaste.[41]

There are two more aspects to be considered. First, those who break the great taboos sometimes experience an abnormal end, as two further examples may illustrate. A late archaic poet related how Odysseus' son by Circe, Telegonus, unknowingly killed his father. Subsequently he married Penelope, and his brother Telemachos, in a way his double, married Circe. Both sons, then, married the wife of their father who was not their own mother — a 'soft' version, so to speak, of the myths we have been discussing. After the wedding all the protagonists were immediately removed to the Isles of the Blessed. The heroisation shows that people who commit crimes like parricide or incest acquire a status beyond normal humans, although they can also become infra-human. The Hellenistic poet Boios told a story about Aegypus, a Thessalian boy who inadvertently slept with his mother, Boulis. In this case the 'culprits' were changed into birds. One last example. The death of Oedipus in Kolonos as related by Sophocles is a typical Athenian *Lokallegende* which arose in the fifth century when a number of heroes, such as Admetus, Adrastus and Orestes, were annexed by Athens. However, as the previous examples show, the Athenian heroisation of Oedipus was the actualisation of a possibility inherent in the myth, although the tradition of his tomb and his heroic status could conceivably antedate fifth-century Athenian tradition. The monstrosity of the acts is further illustrated by the fact that poets can hardly imagine that any person would *deliberately* kill his father or sleep with his mother. In most cases, the deeds are committed inadvertently or as the punishment of a god.[42]

After the incest was discovered, Jocaste hanged herself: permanent incestuous relationships were unthinkable. This way of death was typical for female suicides. Weapons were the realm of men, and women seem to have respected their monopoly. Oedipus remarried, and again the names of his wife vary. It is hard for us to understand that a poet could let Oedipus remarry, but the wedding may well have been a poet's solution to the question 'What happened next?' In a way, the myth was finished after the discovery of the incest but an audience always wants more. So what can a poet do other than go on with what always happens? The earliest stages of the Indo-European languages did not have a word for 'widower'. This absence undoubtedly reflected a social reality: to be a widower was not a permanent male status. So Oedipus had to remarry. Similarly, Jason gave funeral games after his murder of Pelias, and Orestes provided a funeral banquet after killing the murderer of his father. Although we are told that Oedipus suffered greatly, he remained king, most likely died in battle and received a normal funeral; his blindness is probably mentioned first in the *Oedipodeia*, an epic poem of the seventh (?) century. Does this mean that the Homeric age rated parricide a very serious crime, but still less serious than later centuries? Or are the strife and death of his sons also part of the terrible consequences of Oedipus' parricide? There is something unsatisfactory about his end.[43]

Having looked at the successive periods of Oedipus' life, we can finally consider the problem of the myth's origin. Where was the myth told first? As Burkert (see n 2) observes, its place of origin is highly uncertain. The family of Oedipus is not well established at Thebes at all, since there are no indissoluble ties with local institutions and cults. The composition of the myth illustrates this lack of dependence on any one specific local ritual. The Oedipus myth is clearly a *bricolage* from various mythical motifs: the exposure, the coming of age of a prince, and the combination of parricide and incest. As we have seen, these motifs can occur separately in a variety of myths, but they have been combined to particularly startling effect in the Oedipus myth which an early poet located in Thebes for reasons unknown to us.

Despite the uncertainty about the myth's origin we would like to close this study with a suggestion regarding its meaning and place of recitation in the early archaic age. In the classical period, Oedipus' life had become part of the tragic chain of events of Labdacus' doomed house, but his life is still considered in its own right in the oldest version of his myth (*Odyssey* 11.271–80). Oedipus' father was the king of Thebes, and Oedipus himself, as the *Odyssey* notes, 'continued to rule' after his mother's suicide — thus sovereignty is singled out as his most important quality. Like many other archaic myths, the myth of Oedipus is concerned with the succession to the throne.[44]

In this case, however, the myth relates the story of a *perverted* succession — the incest being the narrative expression of society's disapproval of parricide: Oedipus is a model of how not to succeed to the throne. In the classical period the aspect of succession no longer appealed to the poets, but in the early archaic age this aspect must have been highly relevant. Considering the importance attached to sovereignty, it is not impossible that at one time the myth was told to princes during their puberty rites. By growing up, princes form a threat to their fathers whose throne they will one day have to occupy. In a way, the Oedipus myth can be read as a warning to the younger generation: 'You have grown up but you must continue to respect your fathers.' There is something Freudian about this myth.

2. A Greek Oedipus Complex?

Freud proposed a different solution. Having observed that neurotic children may be in love with their mother and want to kill their father, he stated that the same feelings, although less clear and less intense, can be found in normal children; the Oedipus myth supported this observation. The thesis has rightly been combated by Vernant who pointed out that his foster mother would have had to be the focus of Oedipus' feelings, not Jocaste.[45] It is nevertheless striking that we do find a kind of Oedipus complex in classical Greece. In the *Oedipus Rex*, Jocaste says to Oedipus: 'Many mortals have slept with their mother in their dreams.' Plato mentions similar dreams, and in a chapter of his *Dreambook* which reads like a Greek Kinsey report, Artemidorus gives a detailed exposition of them.[46] Is it purely by chance that we first start to hear about these dreams in the fifth century? Probably not. In the early archaic age upper-class mothers — the only ones about whom we have any information — will have had limited contact with their sons, since at an early age these were removed from home for fosterage or other types of initiatory education. Moreover, women had a relatively varied social life in which up to a certain extent they could freely mix with males. In the course of that age drastic changes took place. Except in certain Dorian communities, the customary rites of initiation gradually disappeared, and husbands started to separate their women from the presence of other men; a not so splendid isolation became the rule.[47]

These changes must have had a considerable impact on the mother-son relationship. We may compare developments in modern Greek villages. Since the tractors have removed working women from the fields, women are leading a much more restricted life at home. The pampering of their sons has now become one of the foci of their life. The same development will have taken place in classical Greece. The women of the upper classes had to stay at home, and they were not even allowed to dine with their husbands when other men were present. Raising the children now became one of their main activities. In Plato's *Laws*, the Athenian stranger mentions that the children are under the care of their nurses and mothers until they come into the hands of teacher and *paidagogoi*. The Obsequious Man of Theophrastus even has to ask his host to let the host's children join them for dinner. The consequent close contact between sisters and brothers enables Electra to say to Orestes: 'nor did the household raise you: I was your nurse'. We do not know exactly how long a boy remained under his mother's wing, but during the events leading up to the liberation of Thebes from the Spartan domination in 379, a Theban brought his fifteen-year old son along to a banquet organised by one of the pro-Spartan collaborators. The boy came from the women's quarters.[48]

It was these changes in women's lives, I suggest, which gave rise to dreams of sleeping with the mother. Similarly, we cannot fail to note that Freud's observations took place after drastic changes in most women's lives, since in the course of the nineteenth century the social contacts open to women once again became restricted in the upper classes. It seems likely that this development, coupled with the rise of the nuclear family as we know it today, generated the social environment which produced the feelings observed by Freud.[49] Even the Oedipus complex has a history.[50]

Notes

1. Cf. L. Edmunds, *Oedipus. The Ancient Legend and Its Later Analogues* (Baltimore and London, 1985) 3-6 (with earlier bibliography); add C. Ossola, 'Edipo e ragioni di Stato', *Lett. It.*, *39* (1982) 482-505; H. Schmitz, 'Oedipus bei Dürrenmatt', *Gymnasium*, *92* (1985) 199-208. Edmunds's study is very informative regarding the later analogues but less satisfactory in its treatment of the Greek myth; see my review in *JHS*, *106* (1986).
2. See the balanced appraisal by E. L. de Kock, 'The Sophoklean Oidipus and Its Antecedents', *Acta Class.*, *4* (1961) 7-28 (with earlier bibliography) and *Acta Class.*, *5* (1962) 15-37; see also W. Pötscher, 'Die Oidipus-Gestalt', *Eranos*, *71* (1973) 12-44; T. Stephanopulos, *Umgestaltung des Mythos durch Euripides* (Athens, 1980) 99ff; W. Burkert, 'Seven against Thebes: an Oral Tradition between Babylonian Magic and Greek Literature', in *I poemi epici rapsodici non omerici e la tradizione orale* (Padua, 1981) 29-48; J. -P. Vernant, 'Oedipe', in Y. Bonnefoy, *Dictionnaire des Mythologies* II (Paris, 1981) 190-2; R. C. T. Parker, *Miasma* (Oxford, 1983) 385f.
3. C. Lévi-Strauss, *Structural Anthropology* I (Harmondsworth, 1972) 213-18, 1st edn (1955). *Contra*: E. Leach, *Lévi-Strauss* (London, 1970) 62ff; Detienne, *Dionysos*, 19f.
4. M. Delcourt, *Oedipe ou la légende du conquérant*, 2nd edn (Paris, 1981); V. J. Propp, 'Edip v svete folklora', *Učenye zapiski Leningradskogo gosudarstvennogo universiteta*, Ser. fil. *72* (1944) fasc. 9, 138-75 = V. J. Propp, *Edipo alla luce del folclore* (Turin, 1975) 85-137 = L. Edmunds and A. Dundes (eds), *Oedipus: A Folklore Casebook* (New York, 1983) 76-121.
5. C. Lévi-Strauss, *Anthropologie structurale* II (Paris, 1973) 175-233.
6. I will only give the older sources. For an exhaustive study, see C. Robert, *Oedipus*, 2 vols (Berlin, 1915) and *Die griechische Heldensage* I (Berlin, 1921) 876-902, and Edmunds, *Oedipus*, 6-17; add the reference to Oedipus' incest in Ibycus (Page, *Suppl. Lyr. Gr.*, 222); P. J. Parsons, *ZPE*, *26* (1977) 7-36 and J. M. Bremer, *Lampas*, *13* (1980) 355-71 on Stesichorus' version of the Oedipus myth.
7. I follow here C. Sourvinou-Inwood, *Theseus as Son and Stepson* (London, 1979) 65 n 68, who has introduced the notion of the 'original pattern' of the myth, that is to say 'all versions formed while the mentality which operated on the creation of the myth was still alive and operative, so that the myth was understood and reshaped in its own terms'.
8. Cf. J. Fontenrose, *The Delphic Oracle* (Berkeley and Los Angeles, 1978) 55ff, 96-100.

9. Exposure on Cithaeron: Soph. *OT*; Eur. *Phoen.* 25; Sen. *Phoen.* 31–3; Nic. Dam. *FGrH* 90 F 8; Apollod. 3.5.7; J. Rudhardt, 'Oedipe et les chevaux', *MH*, *40* (1983) 131–9. Shepherds: C. Segal, *Tragedy and Civilisation: An Interpretation of Sophocles* (Cambridge, Mass., 1981) 31; M. C. Amouretti, 'L'Iconographie du berger' in *Iconographie et histoire des mentalités* (Paris, 1979) 155–67. Transhumance: St Georgoudi, *Rev. Et. Gr.*, *87* (1974) 167–9.

10. Washing queen: *Corp. Vas. Ant.* France 23: Louvre 15, pl. 10; Hyg. *fab.* 66. Nausicaa: Hom. *Od.* 6.90–5. Other washing women: *Od.* 15.406; Eur. *Hipp.* 121ff; Nonnus *D.* 3.90–3.

11. Paris: R. A. Coles, *A New Oxyrhynchus Papyrus: The Hypothesis of Euripides' Alexandros* (London, 1974); *P. Oxy.* 3650. Perseus' exposure: M. Werre-de Haas, *Aeschylus' Dictyulci* (Diss., Leiden, 1961) 5–10; J. H. Oakley, 'Danae and Perseus on Seriphos', *AJA*, *86* (1982) 111–15. Polluted objects: Parker, *Miasma*, 210; Curse: H. S. Versnel, *Studi Storico-Religiosi*, *1* (1978) 41f.

12. Cf. G. Binder, *Die Aussetzung des Königskindes: Kyros und Romulus* (Meisenheim, 1964); idem, in K. Ranke (ed.), *Enzyklopädie des Märchens* I (Berlin and New York, 1977) 1048–66; B. Lewis, *The Sargon Legend* (Cambridge, Mass., 1980).

13. See especially Delcourt, *Oedipe*, 1–65.

14. On the exposure motif see also J. Bremmer and N. Horsfall, *Studies in Roman Myth and Mythography* (London, 1986), Ch. 3 (by Bremmer).

15. Mutilation of feet: Soph. *OT* 1026; Eur. *Phoen.* 28–31; Androtion *FGrH* 324 F 62; Peisandros *FGrH* 16 F 10; Apollod. 3.5.7. Marginal role: P. G. Maxwell-Stuart, *Maia*, *27* (1975) 37–43. Sophocles: O. Taplin, *Entr. Hardt.*, *29* (1982) 155f.

16. Cf. Lévi-Strauss, *Structural Anthropology* II; J. -P. Vernant, 'From Oedipus to Periander', *Arethusa*, *15* (1982) 19–38; D. Anzieu *et al.*, *Psychanalyse et culture grecque* (Paris, 1980) 9–52; note also the critique of Lévi-Strauss and Vernant by H. Lloyd-Jones, 'Psychoanalysis and the Study of the Ancient World', in P. Horden (ed.), *Freud and the Humanities* (London, 1985) 152–80, esp. 166–71.

17. Cf. E. Risch, *Kleine Schriften* (Berlin and New York, 1981) 294–313; C. Calame, 'Le nom d'Oedipe', in *Edipo. Il teatro Greco e la cultura europea* (Rome, 1986) and 'L'antroponimo greco come enunciato narrativo: appunti linguistici e semiotici', in *Mondo classico. Percorsi possibili* (Ravenna, 1985) 27–37.

18. There are many examples of changing names of females in Pherecydes *FGrH* 3; note also the various names of Orpheus' wife (Graf, this volume, Ch. 5, section 1), and of Oedipus' mother and his second wife (below); see also Henrichs, this volume, Ch. 11, section 2, on names in myth.

19. Fosterage: Bremmer and Horsfall, *Studies*, Ch. 4 (by Bremmer). Public school: N. Orme, *From Childhood to Chivalry: the Education of the English Kings and Aristocracy 1066–1530* (London, 1984) 44–80.

20. Cyrus: G. Widengren, *Der Feudalismus im alten Iran* (Cologne, 1969) 64–95. Romulus and Remus: Bremmer (above, note 14). Return home: Schol. *Od.* 11.271.

21. Killing: Soph. *OT* 806–7, 810–13; Eur. *Phoen.* 44; Nic. Dam. *FGrH* 90 F 8; Apollod. 3.5.7; cf. Robert, *Oedipus* I, 86f.

22. Hecate: Sophocles F 535.4 Radt; Ar. *Plut.* 594–7; Apollod. *FGrH* 244 F 110a; Chariclides *PCG* IV F 1 with Kassel and Austin ad loc.; Parker, *Miasma*, 30. Plato: *Leg.* 873c. Nonnus: *D* 9.40, 47.484.

23. Text of riddle: Asclepiades *FGrH* 12 F 7a (tr. L. Edmunds); cf. A. Lesky, *Gesammelte Schriften* (Munich, 1966) 318–26; H. Lloyd-Jones, in R. Dawe *et al.* (eds), *Dionysiaca* (Cambridge, 1978) 60f. Other versions: Frazer on Apollod. 3.5.8.

24. Sphinx: A. Lesky, *RE* II 3 (1929) 1703–25; J. -P. Moret, *Oedipe, la Sphinx et*

les Thébains, 2 vols (Rome, 1984). Location Sphinx: Moret, *Oedipe* I, 69–75. Ecclesia: Asclepiades *FGrH* 12 F 7b. Acropolis: Apollod. 3.5.8.

25. Sphinx a girl: Pindar fr. 177d; Soph. *OT* 1199; Eur. *Phoen*. 48, 806, 1042; Moret, *Oedipe* I, 51f (who stresses the Sphinx's resemblance to the Pythia). Onanising Spinx: Moret, *Oedipe* I, 144–6. Monsters female: J. Gould, *JHS, 100* (1980) 55f; J. Bremmer, 'La donna anziana', in G. Arrigoni (ed.), *Le donne in Grecia* (Rome and Bari, 1985) 275–98, esp. 291.

26. *Contra*: L. Edmunds, *The Sphinx in the Oedipus Legend* (Königstein, 1981); note also the critique by C. Callanan, *Fabula, 23* (1982) 316–18; R. Parker, *CR, 34* (1984) 336. Vase: Moret, *Oedipe* I, 39f. Allusions: West on Hes. *Op*. 533.

27. Lydia: Hdt. 1.713; Nic. Dam. *FGrH* 90 F 44. Atossa: Hdt. 3.68, 88. Knut: D. Whitelock *et al*. (eds), *The Anglo-Saxon Chronicle*, 2nd edn (London, 1965) C 1017.

28. L. Gernet and A. Boulanger, *Le Génie grec dans la religion*, 2nd edn (Paris, 1970) 77f; H. Jeanmaire, *Rev. Phil*., *21* (1947) 167; Delcourt, *Oedipe*, and Propp 'Edip', also suggested a connection with initiation.

29. Theseus and initiation: H. Jeanmaire, *Couroi et courètes* (Lille, 1939) 243–5, 338–63; F. Graf, *MH, 36* (1979) 13–19. Interpretation of parricide: Sourvinou-Inwood, *Theseus*, 15, quoting Leach, *Lévi-Strauss*, 80. Bororo myth: Burkert, *S&H*, 14; C. Lévi-Strauss, *The Raw and the Cooked* (London, 1970) 35–48.

30. For a critique of Propp, 'Edip', see A. Taylor, 'The Biographical Pattern in Traditional Narrative', *J. Folkl. Inst.*, *1* (1964) 114–29.

31. Eteonos: Lysimachos *FGrH* 382 F 2, cf. Robert, *Oedipus* I, 44; Burkert, 'Mythos und Mythologie', in *Propyläen Geschichte der Literatur* I (Berlin, 1981) 11–35, esp. 19. L. Farnell, *Greek Hero Cults and Ideas of Immortality* (Oxford, 1921) 334 had already noted: 'His [Oedipus'] cult is extraneous and cannot be dated to a very early period.' L. Edmunds, 'The Cults and the Legend of Oedipus', *HSCP, 85* (1981) 221–38, is not convincing.

32. Honouring parents: K. J. Dover, *Greek Popular Morality in the Time of Plato and Aristotle* (Oxford, 1974) 273–5. Father/son relationship: S. Bertman (ed.), *The Conflict of Generations in Ancient Greece and Rome* (Amsterdam, 1976); A. Maffi, 'Padri e figli fra diritto positivo e diritto imaginario nella Grecia classica', in E. Pellizer and N. Zorzetti (eds), *La paura dei padri nella società antica e medievale* (Rome and Bari, 1983) 3–27.

33. Parricide: Parker, *Miasma*, 124. Hate: Empedokles B 137 Diels/Kranz. Unspeakable: D. Clay, 'Unspeakable Words in Greek Tragedy', *Am. J. Phil*., *103* (1982) 277–98.

34. Uncle/aunt and niece/nephew: Bremmer, *ZPE, 50* (1983) 175 n 13, 181 n 43. First cousins: W. Thompson, 'The Marriage of First Cousins in Athenian Society', *Phoenix, 21* (1967) 273–82. Half-brothers/sisters: W. Lacey, *The Family in Classical Greece* (London, 1968) 106; A. R. W. Harrison, *The Law of Athens* I (Oxford, 1968) 22f.

35. Carians: S. Hornblower, *Mausolus* (Oxford, 1982) 358–63. Ptolemies and Egyptians: K. Hopkins, 'Brother-Sister Marriage in Roman Egypt', *Comp. Stud. in Soc. and Hist*., *22* (1980) 303–54. It is noteworthy that incest between brothers and sisters is not mentioned in the Egyptian, late Hellenistic (cf. L. Koenen, *ZPE, 54* (1984) 9–13 and in *Studia Hellenistica, 27* (Leuven, 1983) 174–89) *Potter's Oracle*, although in later apocalyptic literature sex between siblings frequently is a sign of the end of the world; cf. K. Berger, *Die griechische Daniel-Diegese* (Leiden, 1976) 89f.

36. Aeolus: *Od*. 10.5–12; cf. P. Vidal-Naquet, *Le Chasseur noir*, 2nd edn (Paris, 1983) 53. Imputations: H. Mattingly, *The University of Leeds Review, 14* (1971) 284 (Ostracon mentioning Cimon), cf. Parker, *Miasma*, 98; Lys. 14.28 (Alcibiades). Philetas: Parthen. 2. Leucippus: Parth. 5; cf. E. Pellizer, *Favole d'identità — favole di*

paura (Rome, 1982) 66–9. For all the mythological stories, see J. Rudhardt, 'De l'inceste dans la mythologie grecque', *Revue franç. de psychanal.*, *46* (1982) 731–63, esp. 733–9, to whom I am deeply indebted; add E. Rohde, *Der griechische Roman und seine Vorläufer*, 3rd edn (Leipzig, 1914) 448.

37. Aeolus: Euripides *Aeolus* (Nauck, *Tr. Graec. Fragm.*, p. 365f); cf. Arist. *Nub.* 1371f, *Ran.* 1081; Plato *Leg.* 838c; Ov. *Her.* 11.3–130.

38. Orphic mythology: M. L. West, *The Orphic Poems* (Oxford, 1983) 93ff. Abuse: Hipponax fr. 20 Degani (= 12 West); Lysias fr. 30; Isaeus 5.39. Pelopeia: Radt on Sophocles *Thyestes* (p. 239f). Larissa: Parthen. 28; Nic. Damasc. *FGrH* 90 F 19; Strabo 13.621c; Schol. Ap. Rhod. 1.1063; Eustath. 357.43f. Harpalyke: Euphorion fr. 26; Parthen. 13; Hyg. *Fab.* 206, 242, 246, 253; Nonnos *D* 12.70–5; Schol. *Il.* 14.291; Rohde, *Der griechische Roman*, loc. cit.

39. Cannibalism, incest and parricide as the great crimes: Detienne, *Dionysos*, 154; A. Moreau, 'A propos d'Oedipe: la liaison entre trois crimes — parricide, inceste et cannibalisme', in S. Saïd *et al.*, *Etudes de littérature ancienne* (Paris, 1979) 97–127; Parker, *Miasma*, 326. *Tyrannos*: Detienne, *Dionysos*, 144; Vernant (above), n 16), 33f. Cynics: Vidal-Naquet, *Chasseur*, 368; Parker, loc. cit. Stock accusations: A. Henrichs, *Entr. Hardt.*, *27* (1981) 233f (cannibalism); J. Bremmer, *The Early Greek Concept of the Soul* (Princeton, 1983) 103f (killing old people); B. H. Stricker, 'Camephis', *Med. Nederl. Ak. Wet.*, Afd. Letterk., N.R. 38, 3 (1975) with an exhaustive, if uncritical, collection of references to incest in the ancient world (I owe this reference to Theo Korteweg).

40. Cf. W. Arens, *The Man-Eating Myth* (New York, 1979) who wrongly denies the existence of cannibalism altogether, cf. P. Vidal-Naquet, *Les juifs, la mémoire et le present* (Paris, 1981) 197ff; A. Pagden, *The Fall of Natural Man* (Cambridge, 1982) 80–90.

41. Epikaste: Hom. *Od.* 11.271; Apollod. 3.5.7. Jocaste: Soph. *OT* 632, 950; Eur. *Phoen.* 12, 289, etc.

42. Telegonus: Proclus apud Kinkel, *Ep. Gr. Fr.* 57f; Apollod. *Epit.* 7.36 with Frazer ad loc. Boios: Anton. Lib. 5. Athens: A. Brelich, *Gli eroi greci* (Rome, 1958) 40. Athenian cult of Oedipus: A. Henrichs, 'The "Sobriety" of Oedipus: Sophocles *OC* 100 Misunderstood', *HSCP*, *87* (1983) 87–100; Vidal-Naquet in J.-P. Vernant and P. Vidal-Naquet, *Mythe et tragédie en Grèce ancienne*, II (Paris, 1986) 199f.

43. Hanging Jocaste: *Od.* 11.277f; Soph. *OT* 1263f, *Ant.* 53f, cf. N. Loraux, 'Le corps étranglé', in Y. Thomas (ed.), *Du châtiment dans la cité* (Rome, 1984) 195–218 and *Façons tragiques de tuer une femme* (Paris, 1985). Names of wives: *Oidipodeia* apud Paus. 9.5.11; Pherecydes *FGrH* 3 F 95; Peisandros *FGrH* 16 F 10; Onasias apud Paus. 9.5.11; Schol. *Il.* 4.376. On the problem of Oedipus' wives and children see also the forthcoming commentary on his new edition of the epic fragments which Dr Malcolm Davies kindly let me read. I regret that I was only able to read his illuminating commentary at too late a stage in the preparation of this chapter. Widower: P. Koschaker, *Zs. f. ausl. u. intern. Privatrecht*, Sonderheft zu Bd. 11 (1937) 118. Death and funeral: *Il.* 23.679; Hes. fr. 192; Soph. *Ant.* 53f. Blindness: Burkert, 'Seven against Thebes', 30 (Oedipus' blindness in the *Oedipodeia*): R. G. A. Buxton, 'Blindness and Limits: Sophokles and the Logic of Myth', *JHS*, *100* (1980) 22–37; D. Bouvier and P. Moreau, 'Phinée ou le père aveugle et la marâtre aveuglante', *Rev. Belge Phil. Hist.*, *61* (1983) 5–19.

44. Cf. Gernet and Boulanger, *Le Génie grec*, 76f on the archaic myths concerning the succession to the throne.

45. S. Freud, *Die Traumdeutung* (Vienna, 1900) 180ff (= *Standard Edn* IV, 258, 261–4). *Contra*: Vernant, 'Oedipe sans complexe', in J.-P. Vernant and P. Vidal-Naquet, *Mythe et tragédie en Grèce ancienne* (Paris, 1972) 75–98. It seems, though,

that Vernant does not always do Freud full justice, cf. F. Schuh, *Hephaistos*, 5/6 (1983/4) 265–7; Lloyd-Jones, 'Psychoanalysis', 164f.

46. Soph. *OT* 981f; Plato *Rep.* 571c; Artemidorus 1.79; cf. Pack (Teubner edition) ad loc. and S. Price, 'The future of dreams: from Freud to Artemidorus', *Past & Present* (1986); E. R. Dodds, *The Greeks and the Irrational* (Berkeley and Los Angeles, 1951) 47, 61f.

47. Women: G. Wickert-Micknat, *Die Frau* = Archaeologia Homerica III R (Göttingen, 1982). Fosterage: see note 19. Initiation: Brelich, *Gli eroi greci*, 124–8.

48. Modern Greece: M.-E. Handman, *La Violence et la ruse. Hommes et femmes dans un village grec* (Aix-en-Provence, 1983) 121f, 141–4. Raising children: Plato *Leg.* 7.808e; Theophr. *Char.* 5.5; Soph. *El.* 1143–8; Plut. *Pel.* 9.5, *Mor.* 595b. For this part of my argument I am totally indebted to M. Golden, *Aspects of Childhood in Classical Athens* (Diss., Toronto, 1981) 268–71, to whom the reader is referred for a more detailed discussion of these passages.

49. L. Stone, *The New Republic*, 8 July 1985, p. 30: 'Clinical Freudianism, with its stress on penis envy, early incestuous experiences (real or imagined), and the Oedipus complex, looks increasingly like the product of a Victorian, central European, middle-class, male chauvinist society. Some of its major hypotheses may well not apply to other times and other places.'

50. For information, comments and correction of the English I would like to thank Richard Buxton, Claude Calame, Albert Henrichs, André Lardinois, Alasdair MacDonald and Robert Parker. I owe a special debt to J.-M. Moret for the generous and timely gift of his splendid *Oedipe*.

4

Wolves and Werewolves in Greek Thought

Richard Buxton

One of the most promising developments in the recent study of myth has been the emphasis placed on the 'logic of the concrete'. This phrase, borrowed from Lévi-Strauss's investigation of *la pensée sauvage*,[1] refers to the tendency of 'primitive' forms of classification — as deployed, for instance, in myths and rituals — to be articulated in terms of empirical categories (raw/cooked, wild/tame, in the bush/in the village, etc.) and tangible things in the real world (honey, oak-trees, gold, etc.). In the present paper I take the example of one thing in the world — the wolf — to show how this sort of thinking operated in ancient Greece. In section 1. I examine a variety of contexts in which wolves appear. My aim is to demonstrate how the complex reality of the wolf tended to be pared down in the tradition to a small number of characteristics which were 'good to think with',[2] and how even writers of a 'scientific' type were influenced by features of the wolf as depicted in myth. In section 2. I use the specific example of the werewolf to indicate how Greek wolves were 'good to think with' in one particular myth-and-ritual complex; and I make some more general points about ways in which myth and ritual can be seen to complement and yet to contrast with each other.

1. Greek Wolves, Real and Imagined

Before mankind's systematic attempts to exterminate it, the grey wolf (*canis lupus*) was a tremendously widespread predator.[3] In North America it was found coast to coast; in the Old World it

60

extended from Britain south to Spain and Portugal, east across Europe to Russia, China and Japan. In the New World grey wolves are now virtually extinct except in Alaska: extensive use of strychnine in the nineteenth century, and a decline in the population of the wolf's prey (especially caribou), have contributed towards the decline. A comparable though less drastic sequence of events has occurred in Europe. By 1800 wolves were extinct in the British Isles.[4] According to a major investigation published in 1975 by the International Union for the Conservation of Nature and Natural Resources,[5] wolves are now extinct in France, Belgium, the Netherlands, Denmark, East and West Germany, Switzerland, Austria and Hungary; virtually extinct in Finland, Norway and Sweden; and endangered in Portugal, Spain, Italy, Bulgaria, Czechoslovakia, Poland and the USSR. To judge by figures for wolf kills, the population of wolves in Greece is fairly stable. Kills stand at about 600–700 per year, the bulk of them being in Macedonia, but some also in Epirus, Thessaly and Thrace. Unfortunately no reliable inference can be made about the size of the whole wolf population of Greece on the basis of figures for kills.

The animal responsible for the decline of the wolf is man. Why this human hostility to the wolf? Normally wolves prey on large, hoofed beasts — the ungulates: caribou, bison, antelope, deer, moose, elk. When these are scarce the wolf turns to smaller mammals such as mice and rabbits, or to man's domesticated herds. It is the fact that since the Neolithic period man has raised stock which has brought him into conflict with the wolf.

It is no surprise, then, that in classical antiquity we find numerous references to the wolf as a cruel, predatory enemy. Plutarch (*Sol.* 23.3) reports that 'the Athenians were from of old great enemies of wolves, since their country was better for pasturage than for growing crops'. So Solon introduced a law that 'the man who brings in a wolf is paid five drachmas; for a wolf-cub, one drachma'.[6] (According to Demetrios of Phaleron, five drachmas was the price of an ox, one drachma that of a sheep.) Wolves were proverbial for cruelty; hence Orestes' words about his own and his sister's implacability: 'like a raw-minded wolf, our disposition, which we get from our mother, cannot be appeased' (Aesch. *Cho.* 421–2). Already in Homer the wolf is seen as deadly and bloodthirsty, as in the famous simile about the Myrmidons (*Il.* 16.156ff).

In representing wolves as cruel adversaries of man Greek thought was simply reflecting the stark fact of the competition between the two species. But other qualities ascribed by Greek tradition to wolves begin to take us away from a direct transcription of 'reality'. It will be convenient to concentrate on the two most prominent qualities: wolves co-operate; and they belong outside.

The perception of wolves as co-operative does far more than simply reflect the existence of wolf-packs. In a range of historical periods and in many different types of source, from the technical to the poetical to the anecdotal, the point is developed and elaborated. Xenophon (*Hipparch.* 4.19 – 20) describes how, in attacking a convoy, some drive off the guard while others seize the plunder. An epigram in the Palatine Anthology tells of a traveller who jumped into the Nile to escape wolves: 'but they continued the chase through the water, each holding on by its teeth to another's tail. A long bridge of wolves was formed over the stream, and the self-taught stratagem of the swimming beasts caught the man' (9.252).[7] Aelian too describes how wolves co-operate at a kill (*NA* 8.14), and he also has the tail story: when wolves cross a river 'they fasten their teeth in one another's tails . . . and swim across without harm or danger' (*NA* 3.6). There is alas no reliably recorded evidence of wolf behaviour of this kind — the wolf is in its own right a particularly powerful swimmer.[8] The important thing is that wolves were *perceived* as acting co-operatively.

The tradition of lupine co-operation is a long one. The grammarian Timotheos of Gaza (5/6th century AD) observes in his *On Animals*[9] that, when two wolves coincide at a kill, 'the shares are equal'.[10] Once more it is instructive to consider the situation at an actual kill. In Greece today — and it is unlikely that things were very different in antiquity — large kills are rare, so the issue of sharing does not arise. (You don't share a mouse.) When a large kill is made, the cubs will usually be allowed in first, and thereafter there is a definite *non*-equality: dominant animals (i.e. those highest in the 'pecking' order) get first go, and so on down the line. But what is true is that there is a structured aspect to a kill, so that the notion of co-operation has a basis in actual behaviour. Myth 'clarifies' an asymmetrical order into equality.

It is a small step from the idea that wolves treat each other as equals to the idea that wolves are all alike; and this step was also taken in Greek belief. Thus we find in Aesop (343 Perry) a story about a battle between the dogs and the wolves. The dog general was unwilling to engage the enemy because they (the wolves) were all alike, while the dogs — some being Cretan, some Molossian, some Thracian, not to mention the variations in colour — were all different. Once more the underlying notion is that the wolves will prove successful by virtue of being able to co-operate more closely than their adversaries.

Like the co-operative wolf, the wolf as outsider has a grounding in observable reality. Not only do wolves in general roam in areas which seem to humans to be outside the confines of human territory, but the *lone* wolf — having dropped out of or been expelled from a pack as a result of wounding in a fight or infirmity, and thus being a kind of outsider even amongst a community of outsiders — is a recognised part of wolf ecology, known to antiquity as to us (e.g. Aristot. *HA* 594a30). However, as with co-operation, the point is developed so that the wolf becomes a powerful image for the man apart from other men. In his poem about a person in exile Alkaios writes as follows: 'I live a life in the wilds, longing to hear the agora . . . I am in exile, living on the boundary . . . here I settled alone as a *lykaimiais*' (Lobel/Page 130.16 – 25). The last word is a puzzle, and the interpretation 'a wolf-thicket man' is far from certain.[11] But for an association with exile, wildness and solitariness a compound of *lykos*, 'wolf', is highly appropriate.[12] There is a similar logic in Pausanias' aetiology for the shrine of Apollo Lykios at Argos, according to which, when Danaos arrived as an outsider in Argos, he found a wolf killing the leader of a herd of cattle. 'It occurred to the Argives that Gelanor' — Danaos' rival for the throne — 'was like the bull, and Danaos like the wolf; for as the wolf will not live with men, so Danaos up to that time had not lived with them [i.e. the Argives]' — because he had come from Egypt (2.19.3 – 4).[13] Another mythical exile who had to do with wolves was Athamas (Apollod. 1.9.2). Having killed his son through Hera's madness and been banished from Boeotia, he was told by an oracle to dwell where he should be entertained by wild beasts. This he duly did when he found wolves 'distributing amongst themselves portions of sheep'. Here a human settlement replaces sharing-between-wolves. Thus on the one hand wolves prefigure human society: to share is to be part of a community. On the other hand they contrast with it as barbarity contrasts with civilisation: what they are sharing, after all, is raw meat. The Athamas story neatly embraces both the principal features of the mythical wolf in Greece: as co-operator, it illuminates the human condition by similarity; as outsider, it illuminates it by contrast.[14]

So far my account has been synchronic, and has drawn together material from a variety of sources without differentiation on grounds of date or context. To what extent do we need to modify that approach in view of the evidence?

We may start with the matter of historical development. The most recent scholarly treatment of the wolf in ancient Greece, that by C. Mainoldi, puts forward the argument that Greek perception of the wolf underwent one major change over time: from being 'le modèle de l'animal fort' in the Homeric poems, the wolf subsequently became marginalised as an emblem of savagery and, above all, of *dolos*, trickery.[15] The post-Homeric association between the wolf and *dolos* is indeed certain: in *Pythian* 2 Pindar expresses the wish: 'May I love my friend; but against my enemy I shall make a secret attack, like a wolf, treading now here now there on my crooked paths' (83–5); a Platonic letter describes a false or tricky friendship as *lykophilia* (318e); Aelian knows how wolves can make up for a lack of strength by feigning a frontal attack, darting aside and leaping on the back of the victim (*NA* 5.19); and perhaps the wolf's best *dolos* is his similarity to a dog, as stated in Plato's *Sophist* (231a).[16] However, not only in the Euripidean *Rhesus* but also in the *Iliad* does the spy Dolon wear a wolfskin during his cunning night exploit (*Il.* 10.334; Eur. *Rhes.* 204ff);[17] and it is hardly coincidence that Odysseus' grandfather, who had been given by Hermes outstanding skill 'in theft and in oath' — the latter on the principle that whoever has power over bonds has power also to break them — is in the *Odyssey* named as Auto*lykos* (19.394ff). In short, the idea that trickery is a later development in the Greek image of the wolf seems to me unjustified. Not only that: in my view *no* development in that image can be isolated and located chronologically until we reach the zoological studies of Aristotle.

Differentiation by context, on the other hand, is possible and revealing. In Homeric epic the emphasis (with the exception of the Dolon episode) is on wolves as a collectivity, fierce in the fight and so suitable for comparison to warriors. In the field of political philosophy Plato characteristically uses the violent aspect of the wolf to think about tyranny.[18] In fable the wolf appears frequently, often with emphasis on its cunning, and often too being presented in contrast with the dog.[19] In such contexts, and in others — for instance the passages from *Choephoroi* and *Pythian* 2 cited earlier — the wolf is used as a means for expressing something about human behaviour. But there is another sort of context which illustrates even more strikingly just how pervasive were the patterns of thought embedded in myth. I refer to works which were explicitly about animals, and which we might variously ascribe to the categories 'folklore' and 'zoology'. As we shall see, the distinction is not unproblematic.

We may begin with a report by Plutarch:

> Antipater in his book *On Animals* asserts that wolves give birth at the time when trees that bear nuts or acorns shed their flowers: when they eat these, their wombs are opened. But if there is no supply of these flowers, their offspring die within them and cannot see the light. Moreover those parts of the world that are not fertile in nut-trees or oak-trees are not troubled by wolves. (*Qu. Nat.* 38)

This is a fine example of how Greek thought could combine a traditional pattern of ideas with shrewd empirical observation. Our first reaction is perhaps to find a 'logic of myth' behind Antipater's account, since there was in at least one region an acknowledged religious link between acorns and wolves: Arcadia. Arcadians are perceived as acorn-eaters, hence as pre-civilised;[20] Arcadians are also worshippers of Zeus Lykaios, in whose cult both wolves and oak-trees figure (see below); wolves are outside civilisation, and so are associated with acorn-eaters, who are before it. But there is sound zoology here too. Wolves do indeed share a habitat with nut- and oak-trees. Good years for nuts and acorns mean plentiful supplies of the small animals eaten by wolves, and this plenty means in turn that wolves produce large litters. But when food is scarce, there is in foxes and rabbits a higher proportion of aborted foetuses than in times of plenty, and it is likely that the same is true for wolves. Antipater's assertion thus provides evidence for a remarkable coincidence between traditional and empirical modes of thought.

We might expect *a priori* that if any ancient authority is going to privilege the empirical against the traditional, it will be Aristotle. And in some cases we do indeed find him carefully recording data which subsequent zoological research has corroborated: 'poly-dactylous quadrupeds (such as the dog, lion, wolf, fox and jackal) all bring forth their young blind, and the eyelid does not separate until some time after birth'; 'the penis is bony in the fox, wolf, marten and weasel'. More rarely, statements of a straight-forwardly zoological kind are simply wrong, e.g. 'the neck is flexible and has a number of vertebrae in all animals except the wolf and the lion, in which the neck consists of one bone only'.[21] In fact all mammals have seven bones in the neck; but, interestingly, some wolves suffer from severe arthritis of the spine, and it is possible that Aristotle's information resulted from observation of an animal so afflicted — it is on general grounds not improbable that infirm wolves offered greater opportunity for close scrutiny than healthy ones.

In addition to findings of the sort just mentioned, though, Aristotle has other things to say about the wolf; and here the mythical representation of the animal becomes visible once more. At one point he describes it as *gennaios* (thorough-bred), *agrios* (wild) and *epiboulos* (scheming) (*Hist. An.* 488b17). At another the direction of the enquiry seems to be affected by the threatening and predatory figure cut by the wolf in popular belief, when he tackles the matter of wolves eating people. But the specific contri-bution made by Aristotle to this (apparently) endlessly intriguing issue — he asserts that only *lone* wolves eat men, not wolves in packs (*Hist. An.* 594a30) — is zoologically plausible: the lone wolf, which by definition lacks the support of the pack, is likely to have restricted access to prey, and so might in extremity have to resort to human meat.[22] In fact, even where Aristotle's zoological researches are explicitly influenced by the mythical tradition, what is remarkable is the coolness of his judgement:

An account is given of the she-wolf's parturition which comes very near the fabulous [*pros muthon*], viz. that there are just twelve days in the year during which all wolves bring forth their young. The reason for this, they say, is found in a fable, which alleges that it took twelve days to bring Leto from the land of the Hyperboreans to Delos, during which time she had the appear-ance of a she-wolf because she was afraid of Hera. Whether twelve days really was the time or not has not yet been definitely established by observation; that is merely what is asserted. (*Hist. An.* 580a14)

It may be added that the situation is identical today: we know nothing about the exact birth-periods of European wolves; but it is zoologically certain that there will be a restricted period for birth, and *it is unlikely that this will be more than 2–3 weeks.* As with Antipater's assertion mentioned above, the coincidence between myth and empirical observation is notable; and so too is the ability of Aristotle to set himself apart from the tradition and to reflect critically upon it.

A few conclusions may be drawn from the material presented in this section. (1) Sometimes Greek perception of the wolf directly reflects the facts of human and lupine existence: humans compete with wolves for food, so wolves appear in myth as cruel foes. (2) In other respects traditional thought works on reality by selective emphasis and 'clarification': wolves share a kill *equally*; they are *all alike.* (3) The tradition is not uniform: in different contexts different aspects of the wolf are stressed, though within the broadly similar image shared by all. (4) Aristotelian zoology represents a marked contrast to the mythical tradition. But the distinction between folklore and zoology is not rigid: we find excellent zoology in anecdote, and mythological patterns and concerns in zoology.

2. The Werewolf of Arcadia

Having tried to give a general overview of the place of the wolf in Greek thought, I turn now to one particular aspect of the subject: the cult and myth of the Arcadian werewolf. This complex of religious practice and belief constitutes the single most striking instance of the wolf as 'good to think with' surviving from ancient Greece.

We begin with a point of terminology. It seems sensible to distinguish between werewolfism and lycanthropy. The former may be defined as the belief that people are able to turn into wolves; the latter denotes a psychotic disorder according to which one believes that one has oneself turned into a wolf.[23] Compared with the enormous number of werewolf and lycanthropy cases recorded for medieval Europe,[24] evidence for such phenomena in antiquity is rare. (We are of course at liberty to wonder how representative our sample is, but all we can do is to operate with what information we have.) Instances of lycanthropy are few and late, but Markellos of Side significantly reports that sufferers experienced their symptoms at night (in February) and in cemeteries, i.e. in a context removed both temporally and spatially from that of normal life — we recall that the Petronian werewolf metamorphosed by moonlight and on a road beside some grave-markers.[25] Stories of ancient werewolf belief are again scarce, although there is this time a certain amount of material from Greece. Once more we should note the typical geographical remoteness, as with the Neuri, adjacent to the Scythians in Herodotos' narrative: 'The Scythians, and the Greeks settled in Scythia, say that once a year every one of the Neuri is turned into a wolf, and after remaining so for a few days returns again to his former shape' (Hdt. 4.105). That the Neuri are located by Herodotos next to the Androphagi is wholly logical: in accordance with a pattern of thought common in Greece and in a vast number of other cultures, marginal peoples are perceived as behaving in ways inverse to those favoured by the 'central' people.[26] Whether the story about the Neuri is entirely a product of this sort of inverse projection, or whether an actual ritual lies behind it, is impossible to decide; but the existence of an initiatory *rite de passage* is perfectly plausible, either on the assumption that the participants literally adopted wolf-disguise,[27] or on the view that one who temporarily withdraws 'outside' is metaphorically wolfish.

The Neuri were outside, but the Arcadians were before — in fact, before the moon, *proselenoi*;[28] and Arcadia was the location of the werewolf cult best known to us from the Greek world. Even today Mount Lykaion has a remote and slightly eerie beauty; how much more eerie in antiquity since, so it was said, a rite of cannibalism was practised there. Pausanias refuses to discuss it (8.38.7); but Plato speaks of a rite in which human innards are mixed with parts of other animals, and the person who tastes the human must turn into a wolf (*Rep.* 565d). One does not need to go all the way with Arens' ultra-sceptical approach to anthropophagy[29] to be doubtful about at least *some* reports of institutionalised cannibalism: as Servius puts it, 'in sacred rites that which is simulated is accepted as reality' (on *Aen.* 2.116). When Kourouniotis dug the site at the beginning of this century he found no human bones,[30] and, as Walter Burkert has pointed out, only a very few people are going to know exactly what is in the casserole — the rest is suggestion.[31] But more profitable than speculation about the precise contents of the cauldron is some consideration of the symbolism and social context of the ritual. And here we do get a clue from Pausanias, who reports:

> They say that ever since the time of Lykaon a man was always turned into a wolf at the sacrifice to Lykaian Zeus — but not for his whole life; because if he kept off human flesh when he was a wolf, he turned back into a man after nine years; if he tasted human flesh, he stayed a wild beast for ever. (8.2.6)

The wolf stands for one who by his behaviour has set himself beyond humanity: so much is clear. But why did the Greeks enact this ceremony of ritual exclusion? Before we can attempt an answer we must consider a ritual which sounds remarkably similar to the Lykaion ceremony. Pliny the Elder reports that, according to the Arcadians, a member of the family of Anthos was chosen by lot, left all his clothes on an oak-tree, swam across a pool, went away 'into a deserted area', and turned into a wolf. After nine years, provided he had eaten no human meat, he swam back across the pool, took up his clothes, and resumed human shape (*NH* 8.81). A similar version is given by Augustine (citing Varro), though he refers more vaguely to 'the Arcadians' instead of to a specific family (*Civ. Dei* 18.17). Two questions present themselves: (1) How do we interpret the ritual described by Pliny? (2) How does it relate to the ceremony mentioned by Pausanias and Plato?

(1) Pliny's ritual centres on two symbolic gestures: stripping, and crossing water. Both mark the transition from inside to outside, human to animal. Stripping is associated with animal metamorphosis both in antiquity and later. Pamphile and Lucius in *The Golden Ass* strip before their metamorphoses take place (3.21,24). The werewolf in Petronius removes his clothes before changing shape; and the crucial importance of the clothes for the transition is indicated by the fact that the werewolf 'fixes' them by urinating around them, after which they turn to stone (62). Numerous medieval werewolf legends confirm the role of clothes as

boundary-marker, as in Marie de France's lay *Bisclavret*. A Breton lord changes into a wolf three days a week; before doing so he removes his clothes, without which he is deprived of the means of transition back to humanity. His wife and her lover steal his clothes, but eventually the lord is able to recover them, and with them his human form.[32]

Water is another boundary between the human and wolfish states. Once more there are medieval parallels: in 1580 Jean Bodin recorded a story, set in Livonia, in which crossing water is a prelude to metamorphosis (of twelve days' duration) into wolfish form.[33] One all-too-common reductionist tactic is to link such phenomena to the fact that rabies — a supposed 'origin' of werewolf belief — is characterised by hydrophobia: water thus quite literally marks a barrier between man and werewolf (= rabies victim).[34] But such a realist approach gets us nowhere in our attempt to understand the symbolic role of the supposed 'symptom' in its ritual context.[35] More plausibly one might regard the Arcadian pool in a wholly content-free way as simply a boundary between inside and outside; but that would be to ignore the place of water in general, and bathing in particular, in Greek cult.[36] Washing or bathing in water from a spring is an element in several important Greek *rites de passage*. After death the corpse was stripped, washed and dressed in new robes as a prelude to being 'carried out'; before making the transition back to normal life the mourners would themselves bathe. After a birth, mother and child would bathe as a part of the return to normality. Bride and groom bathed before the marriage ceremony. Washing, and sometimes bathing and changing of clothes, was required before the performance of prayer or sacrifice, and preceded other forms of access to the sacred such as prophecy, incubation, and initiation into the mysteries.[37] Thus crossing the boundary between sacred and non-sacred space, and between sacred and non-sacred periods of time, is regularly accompanied by bathing. In one way the relevance of this to Pliny's Arcadian ritual is clear enough, since entering and leaving a sacred space is clearly part of the symbolic drama. But if the ritual as a whole is a *rite de passage*, then bathing becomes that much more appropriate.[38]

In recent years a good deal of attention has been directed towards rituals of transition in ancient Greece. In particular there have been investigations into the presence of initiation rituals — or survivals of them — in archaic and later Greek culture.[39] Fruitful though much of this work has proved, there has been an occasional tendency to exaggerate the explanatory value of initiation. It may therefore be worth spelling out that some rituals — consulting an oracle, for instance — were self-evidently not initiatory, while others — such as the ceremonies surrounding birth, marriage and death — certainly shared with initiation rituals the pattern of separation/marginalisation/reintegration but were equally certainly not initiatory in the way that, say, the *ephebeia* was. Yet in spite of those reservations it seems to me likely that the ritual described by Pliny was indeed initiatory; at least, the evidence we have is compatible with such a hypothesis. A man — probably, as we shall see, a young man — underwent a rite of separation, left society and became temporarily a non-person, subsequently returned and, after a rite of reintegration, rejoined the community, presumably with a different (? adult) status. The negative imagery (wolf; in the wilds) characterising the liminal period is just what we should expect, given the anthropological parallels.[40] One aspect of the symbolism is particularly interesting: abstention from human meat. The 'wolf' must retain one link with humanity if his eventual return is to be possible.

(2) There are obvious similarities with the Lykaion ritual: the avoidance of human meat, the metamorphosis into a wolf, the period of nine years. At the very least Pausanias and Pliny were reporting rituals which shared some of the same symbols. But were they relating different aspects of the *same* ritual?[41] Perhaps the most persuasive account is that of Burkert, according to whom the Plinian version reflects a watered-down, 'civilised' form of the ritual which became confined to a single conservative family.[42] On this view we should imagine an earlier situation in archaic Greece in which a whole age-group of young men were initiated into Arcadian adult society. Before they became fully-fledged citizens they were obliged to undergo a period of separation from society as 'wolves', i.e. outsiders. When they reached the age of full social adulthood they became true descendants of Arkas, 'The Bear' — Pausanias conveniently tells us that Arcadian warriors wore the skins of two animals, the wolf and the bear (4.11.3). Supporting the initiation hypothesis is the story (recorded by Pausanias, Pliny and Augustine)[43] of an Arcadian who returned after a nine-year

lupine absence to win the Olympic boxing event: it was surely a *young* man who went into the wilds.

The only problem with this interpretation seems to me the nine years. We could of course take it as merely symbolic of 'a period of time', and leave the matter at that.[44] But if we take it at face value, and if we see the ritual as applying, at least originally, to a whole age-group of young men, then we have to give a reasonable answer to the question, 'What were they *doing* for nine years?' — nine years of 'das Leben als "Wölfe" in der Wildnis'.[45] It is not quite the same as withdrawing to the young men's huts for a spell of a couple of months before rejoining the tribe.[46] If we want to regard the Lykaion ritual as being originally an initiation ceremony for an entire age-group then we have to be sceptical about those nine years, at least until they are explained in a way which makes sense in relation to the real life of a historical Arcadian community.[47] In any case it is unwise to be too dogmatic about what happened on Mount Lykaion. We know, for instance, of a ritual there connected with making rain;[48] we know also that the opposition sunlight/shadow was important;[49] and it is difficult, and probably misleading, to try to incorporate all this material into a single ritual complex. But if we retain the idea of an initiatory rite of passage we have at least a very plausible hypothesis for understanding the logic of the central werewolf ceremony.

We have not yet finished with Mount Lykaion, for associated with it there was a myth. The most dramatically exciting account of Lykaon is in Ovid's *Metamorphoses* Book 1, but the most suggestive from the mythological point of view is in Pausanias (8.1–2). According to his version, Lykaon's father was Pelasgos, the first man who lived in Arcadia. Pelasgos introduced certain aspects of civilisation: shelters against the elements and clothing made from sheepskins. Moreover he stopped his subjects eating leaves, grass and roots, and introduced them instead to acorns. Lykaon continued the civilising process by founding a city and instituting games in honour of Zeus. At that time, because of their justice and piety, men ate at the same table as the gods. But Lykaon carried out the sacrifice of a child on Zeus' altar on Mount Lykaion; as a consequence he was turned into a wolf.

One way of coming to grips with the Greek myths is to identify recurrent themes, and so to observe what Greeks felt to be important. A major theme in the Lykaon myth is the importance of maintaining proper relationships with the gods, and the dangers of not so doing. Countless other myths make a similar point: punishment follows all kinds of transgression against the gods, from failure to honour them (Hippolytos, Pentheus) to ill-advised rivalry (Arachne, Marsyas) to figurative or real violation (Aktaion, Teiresias, Ixion). More specifically, the Lykaon myth narrates the consequences of abusing hospitality, and here it resembles the story of Tantalos, another who was host to the gods at a cannibalistic feast. But Lykaon is a bringer of culture as well as a criminal, and the whole narrative in Pausanias is from another point of view the story of the origins of civilisation in Arcadia: after relating what Pelasgos and Lykaon did he tells us that one of Lykaon's descendants, Arkas, will invent agriculture, bread-making and weaving (8.4.1). However, the myth also makes clear that humanity's cultural progress is not unalloyed: part and parcel of the human condition as we know it is that we no longer eat with the gods.

There is a close analogy with Hesiod's account of what happened at Mekone, where Prometheus' attempted deception of Zeus resulted in a definitive end to the commensality of men and gods (*Theog.* 535ff). But the difference is as striking as the similarity: in the Lykaon story the rupture between men and gods is far more drastic. This becomes evident if we look at some of the variants — another fruitful way of uncovering the logic of myth. According to Apollodoros Lykaon's *sons* are the guilty ones, and they (except the youngest) and their father are thunderbolted (3.8); while Hyginus speaks of Lykaon turning into a wolf and his sons being thunderbolted (176). The implications of the equivalence between thunderbolting and metamorphosis into a wolf have been drawn by Borgeaud.[50] In the case of thunderbolting, Zeus' power is completely manifested (cf. the fate of Semele); in the case of metamorphosis, the guilty party is not simply banished from Zeus' table, he is banished into animality. Coupling the two versions we arrive at a doubly radical break between men and god: men recede below humanity, god's divinity is unanswerably affirmed. Only in future generations will human/divine relations be on a firmer footing — at a more respectful distance.

Another significant theme is the metamorphosis itself.[51] Not only is Lykaon like a wolf, he *is*, permanently, a wolf. Here again is an enormously common pattern in Greek myth: a departure from the norm — often a transgression — is fixed for ever by a change into a non-human state, frequently one (as with Lykaon) appropriate to the nature of the transgression or abnormality.[52] Furthermore the fact that in the Lykaon myth (as usual in Greek metamorphoses) it is a god who effects the alteration is worth bearing in mind if the analogy between classical and medieval werewolves threatens to become too insistent. In both cultures to be a wolf signifies that one has forfeited humanity and is obliged to lead an 'outside' existence. But the medieval werewolf, perceived as being able to change his shape from the God-given human form with which he started, is typically represented as having that power thanks to demonic assistance. The conceptual background to medieval werewolfism is Christianity.[53]

Any Greek myth should be responsive to an enquiry into its themes. But some myths, thanks to the accidents of survival and the character of the stories themselves, may take on added significance when seen in juxtaposition with a ritual. This is undeniably the case with the myth in question here, which exists in a virtually symbiotic relationship with the werewolf ceremony of Mount Lykaion. On the one hand the myth 'confirms' the ritual, giving it greater resonance. Each time a man leaves the sanctuary to become a wolf, that man in a sense *is* Lykaon: in virtue of the conclusive banishment originally experienced by Lykaon, the exclusion dramatised in the ritual is that much more intense (or so we may surmise — the emotions involved in a ritual are hard enough to assess in a contemporary context, let alone in one sketchily known from antiquity). On the other hand myth and ritual are *contrasting* symbolic languages, the one tending to make explicit and absolute that which the other leaves implicit and temporary. Thus the metamorphosis of Lykaon is permanent, while the exclusion dramatised in the ritual is temporary and reversible. One may note the parallel with the scapegoat: in myth the designated individual is killed; in ritual merely expelled.[54]

A Modern Postscript

At certain points in this paper I have discussed the far from simple relationship obtaining between traditions about and empirical observation of the wolf in Greek antiquity. My invoking of modern zoology as a control on some of the ancient data may have created an impression that nowadays we have an accurate and tradition-free picture of the wolf. It is true that in this century the science of ethology has made quite extraordinary strides; and studies of wolf behaviour are no exception to this generalisation.[55] But knowledge of such matters is very thinly diffused. In the industrialised West, at any rate, the wolf is present largely as a residual folklore image. And in the mind as in terms of actual population it seems to be on the decline: in urban folklore, as the motorway has replaced the forest as the location of danger, so the phantom hitchhiker threatens to oust the werewolf.[56] But the continuing popularity of werewolf films and literature[57] perhaps suggests that this beast remains good to think with, since it calls into question the boundary between human and 'bestial'. Even ordinary wolves still cause public and media terror if they get out of place. Above all there remains a fascination — the lupine equivalent of the debate over cannibalism — with the question, 'Do wolves make unprovoked attacks on human beings?'[58] The evidence seems in fact to be that, while *rabid* wolves will indeed run amok and bite at random, normally wolves are too terrified of man to attack even when hungry. It is of course hard to substantiate this, since it is often impossible to decide whether any given report, particularly if it is not contemporary, involves a rabid or a non-rabid wolf; and, to add to the confusion, feral dogs can easily be mistaken for wolves.[59] In any case, such cool evaluations of the evidence seem flimsy when confronted with a powerful folklore image. Whether that image will diminish or grow when all the real wolves have been exterminated is beyond even guesswork.[60]

Notes

1. C. Lévi-Strauss, *The Savage Mind* (Eng. tr., London, 1966).
2. On the pedigree of this expression see G. E. R. Lloyd, *Science, Folklore and Ideology* (Cambridge, 1983) 8, n 7.
3. For general discussions see L. D. Mech, *The Wolf: The Ecology and Behavior of an Endangered Species* (New York, 1970) and E. Zimen, *The Wolf: His Place in the Natural World* (Eng. tr., London, 1981).
4. Cf. A. Dent, *Lost Beasts of Britain* (London, 1974) 99–134.
5. *Wolves*, ed. D. H. Pimlott (Morges, 1975).
6. Rewards offered in late eighteenth-century France are set out in A. Molinier and N. Molinier-Meyer, 'Environnement et histoire: les loups et l'homme en

France', *Rev. d'hist. mod. et contemp.*, *28* (1981) 225–45, at 228; this is the only serious attempt known to me which offers a historical ecology of the wolf in a particular region. Bounties of £5 per head in Cromwellian Ireland: C. Fitzgibbon, *Red Hand: The Ulster Colony* (London, 1971) 37.

7. Here and several times elsewhere I have followed or adapted the Loeb translation.

8. For advice on all matters of wolf biology and behaviour mentioned in this article I am indebted to Dr S. Harris of the Department of Zoology at Bristol University.

9. M. Haupt, 'Excerpta ex Timothei Gazaei libris de animalibus', *Hermes, 3* (1869) 8, lines 27–9.

10. See M. Detienne and J. Svenbro, 'Les loups au festin ou la cité impossible', in M. Detienne and J.-P. Vernant, *La Cuisine du sacrifice en pays grec* (Paris, 1979) 215–37, on the parallel with 'isonomic' distribution between hoplites.

11. See D. L. Page, *Sappho and Alcaeus* (Oxford, 1955) 205–6.

12. Connection between wolf and outlaw: Harry A. Senn, *Were-wolf and Vampire in Romania* (New York, 1982) 16, and J. Bremmer, 'The *suodales* of Poplios Valesios', *ZPE, 47* (1982) 133–47, at 141, n 35 (bibliog.).

13. On this passage see C. Mainoldi, *L'Image du loup et du chien dans la Grèce ancienne d'Homère à Platon* (Paris, 1984) 25–6. (Mainoldi's study is careful and extremely interesting.) Apollo Lyk(e)ios: F. Graf, *Nordionische Kulte* (Rome, 1985) 220–6.

14. We may recall that the origins of Rome were perceived as lying with a renegade band of young men, led by the foster-children of the she-wolf — outsiders in co-operation; cf. A. Alföldi, *Die Struktur des voretruskischen Römerstaates* (Heidelberg, 1974), esp. 119–33.

15. Mainoldi, *L'Image*, 97–103, 127.

16. Wolves and dogs similar: cf. also Diod. Sic. 1.88.6. But the perceived relation between the two is complex and ambiguous. Although dog can be seen to stand to wolf as tame to wild, the tameness of dogs is problematic. On the one hand, they protect human civilisation by warding off wild beasts, and are domesticated to the extent of being regularly eaten (cf. N.-G. Gejvall, *Lerna*, vol. 1, *The Fauna* (Princeton, 1969) 14–18). On the other hand, dogs are potential killers and may threaten man (n.b. Aktaion). On dogs see H. H. Scholz, *Der Hund in der griechisch-römischen Magie und Religion* (Berlin, 1937); R. H. A. Merlen, *De Canibus: Dog and Hound in Antiquity* (London, 1971); N. J. Zaganiaris, 'Le chien dans la mythologie et la littérature gréco-latines', *Platon, 32* (1980) 52–87; Mainoldi, *L'Image.* N.b. also T. Ziolkowski, *Varieties of Literary Thematics* (Princeton, 1983) Ch. 3 ('Talking dogs: the caninization of literature'); and, for a brilliant analysis of a medieval cult and legend, J.-C. Schmitt, *The Holy Greyhound* (Eng. tr., Cambridge, 1983).

17. Dolon the wolf: L. Gernet, *The Anthropology of Ancient Greece* (Eng. tr., Baltimore, 1981) 125–39; F. Lissarrague, 'Iconographie de Dolon le loup', *Rev. Arch.* (1980) 3–30. The attempt by Mainoldi, *L'Image*, 20, to explain away the wolf/trickery link in the Doloneia is unconvincing.

18. E.g. *Rep.* 416a, 565e–66a; *Phaedo* 82a. Cf. Mainoldi, *L'Image*, 187–200, and D. Lanza, *Il tiranno e il suo pubblico* (Turin, 1977) 65–7.

19. List of references given by Mainoldi, *L'Image*, 209–10, n 12.

20. Cf. P. Borgeaud, *Recherches sur le dieu Pan* (Rome, 1979) 30–2.

21. Aristotelian references: *Gen. An.* 742a8 (eyelid); *Hist. An.* 500b23 (penis); *Part. An.* 686a21 (neck); translations adapted from Loeb.

22. But see postscript.

23. Lycanthropy is not unknown to modern psychiatry, although it is very rare:

see H. A. Rosenstock and K. R. Vincent, 'A case of lycanthropy', *Am. Journ. Psychiatry*, *134*:10 (Oct. 1977) 1147–9.

24. G. Ronay, *The Dracula Myth* (London, 1972) 15, gives a figure of 30,000 cases of lycanthropy investigated by the Roman Church between 1520 and the mid-seventeenth century. On werewolf belief in early modern Europe see L. Harf-Lancner, 'La métamorphose illusoire: des théories chrétiennes de la métamorphose aux images médiévales du loup-garou', *Annales ESC*, *40* (1985) 208–26. M. Summers, *The Werewolf* (London, 1933), may still be consulted, though with great circumspection.

25. Galen, *On Melancholy*, ed. Kühn, XIX, 719; text of Markellos in W. H. Roscher, 'Das von der "Kynanthropie" handelnde Fragment des Marcellus von Side', *Abh. der Königl. Sächs. Ges. Wiss.*, phil.-hist. Cl., 17 (Leipzig, 1897) 79–81. Ancient lycanthropy: G. Piccaluga, *Lykaon: un tema mitico* (Rome, 1968) 60ff; M. Ullmann, 'Der Werwolf. Ein griechisches Sagenmotiv in arabischer Verkleidung', *Wiener Zs. f. die Kunde des Morgenlandes*, *68* (1976) 171–84; Burkert, *HN*, 89 with n 28. Burkert rightly states that lycanthropy is culturally determined, but his view that it 'no longer plays a role in modern psychiatry' needs rephrasing as 'a *significant* role'; cf. my n 23. Petronius: *Satyr.* 61–2.

26. Cf. T. E. J. Wiedemann, 'Between men and beasts: barbarians in Ammianus Marcellinus', in *Past Perspectives*, ed. I. S. Moxon, J. D. Smart and A. J. Woodman (Cambridge, 1986) 189–201. On the 'other' in Herodotos see F. Hartog, *Le Miroir d'Hérodote* (Paris, 1980); on perceived cultural differences between 'same' and 'other' see T. Todorov, *La Conquête de l'Amérique* (Paris, 1982).

27. Cf. K. Meuli, *Gesammelte Schriften* (Basle, 1975), vol. 1, 160.

28. See Borgeaud, *Recherches*, 19–23.

29. W. Arens, *The Man-Eating Myth* (New York, 1979).

30. *Eph. Arch.* (1904) 153–214, at 169. More on the excavation at *Eph. Arch.* (1905) 161–78; *Praktika* (1909) 185–200.

31. Burkert, *HN*, 90.

32. Bisclavret: S. Battaglia, 'Il mito del licantropo nel *Bisclavret* di Maria di Francia' in his *La coscienza letteraria del medioevo* (Naples, 1965) 361–89; M. Bambeck, 'Das Werwolfmotiv im *Bisclavret*', *Zeitschr. f. Roman. Philol.*, *89* (1973) 123–47; F. Suard, '*Bisclauret* [*sic*] et les contes du loup-garou: essai d'interprétation', in *Mélanges . . . offerts à Ch. Foulon*, vol. II (Liège, 1980) 267–76.

33. *De la démonomanie des sorciers* (Paris, 1580) 99.

34. For the werewolf-rabies equation see Ch. 12 of I. Woodward's lurid book *The Werewolf Delusion* (New York, 1979).

35. Equally beside the point is the attempt to explain the religious phenomenon of werewolfism by reference to iron-deficiency porphyria (*New Scientist*, 28 Oct. 1982, 244–5). One may compare C. Ginzburg, *The Night Battles* (Eng. tr., London, 1983) 18, on the need to explain the beliefs of the Friulian *benandanti* 'on the basis of the history of popular religiosity not on that of pharmacology or psychiatry'.

36. See M. Ninck, *Die Bedeutung des Wassers im Kult und Leben der Alten*, *Philologus* Supplbd. 14.2 (Leipzig, 1921) 148ff, for the role of water in mythical metamorphoses.

37. Death: R. Ginouvès, *Balaneutikè* (Paris, 1962) 239–64; R. Parker, *Miasma* (Oxford, 1983) 35–6. Birth: Ginouvès 235–8; Parker, 50–1. Marriage: Ginouvès, 265–82. Prayer, sacrifice: Ginouvès, 311–18. Prophecy, incubation: Ginouvès, 327–73. Mysteries: Ginouvès, 375–404.

38. There is a striking parallel with the rite of adult baptism in the early Church. Many fonts had three steps leading down from one side and three steps leading up out of the other side: the initiate thus crossed the font. (See. A.

Khatchatrian, *Les Baptistères paléochrétiens* (Paris, 1962) nos. 83, 136, 194, 270 and
371.) The going down into the font was regarded as equivalent to Christ being
placed in the tomb, and the going up out of it was interpreted in terms of resurrec-
tion (e.g. Ambrose *de Sacr.* 3.1.2; cf. J. G. Davies, *The Architectural Setting of Baptism*
(London, 1962) 22–3).

39. The major anthropological influence is A. van Gennep, *Les Rites de passage*
(Paris, 1909), with important amplification by V. Turner, *The Forest of Symbols*
(Ithaca, 1967) 93–111. On Greece see H. Jeanmaire, *Couroi et Courètes* (Lille,
1939); A. Brelich, *Paides e Parthenoi* (Rome, 1969); J. Bremmer, 'Heroes, rituals
and the Trojan War', *Studi Storico-Rel.*, *2* (1978) 5–38; Burkert, *GR*, 260–4.

40. See Turner, *Forest*, esp. 96.

41. For the different views see Mainoldi, *L'Image*, 31, n 11.

42. Burkert, *HN*, 88.

43. Paus. 6.8.2; Pliny 8.82; Aug. *Civ. Dei* 18.17.

44. Seven years as wolf: Giraldus Cambrensis, *Topographia Hibernica* 2.19; one
year: *The Mabinogion*, tr. J. Gantz (Harmondsworth, 1976) 105. Nine years as a
transitional period: Felix's *Life of Saint Guthlac*, ed. B. Colgrave (Cambridge, 1956)
Ch. 18. Compare also Homeric 'for nine days . . . but on the tenth . . .': *Lex. des
frühgr. Epos s.v. ennea, ennemar*; N. J. Richardson, *The Homeric Hymn to Demeter*
(Oxford, 1974) 165–6.

45. Burkert, orig. edn of *Homo Necans* (Berlin, 1972) 105.

46. See B. Sergent, *L'Homosexualité dans la mythologie grecque* (Paris, 1984) 51–2,
on two months as a common period for initiatory withdrawal.

47. Cf. J. Z. Smith, *Imagining Religion* (Chicago, 1982) 60–1, on the need not to
abandon 'our sense of incredulity, our estimate of plausibility', in such matters.

48. Paus. 8.38.4. Piccaluga, *Lykaon*, interprets the entire cult activity on
Lykaion in terms of drought/water: the first item in her subject index is 'acqua:
passim'. But her desire to unify the heterogeneous data is over-zealous.

49. According to Pausanias (8.38.6) no person could enter the precinct of Zeus
Lykaios on normal, i.e. non-sacred occasions. If anyone, man or beast, did enter,
he cast no shadow — in other words, ceased to be alive. (A variant also recorded by
Pausanias makes this explicit: a person entering dies within a year.) Polybius
(16.12.7) and Plutarch (*Qu. Gr.* 39) confirm the shadow story. Evidently it marks
in an emphatic way the inside-sanctuary/outside-sanctuary boundary. But is there
more to it than that? In front of the altar of Zeus there were two pillars 'towards the
rising sun', with gilded eagles upon them (Paus. 8.38.7). The detail is enigmatic
and, given the state of our knowledge, the sunlight, like the rain, must remain
peripheral to our reading of the werewolf rite.

50. Borgeaud, *Recherches*, 45–7.

51. On this see in general the Budé edition of Antoninus Liberalis,
Metamorphoses, by M. Papathomopoulos (Paris, 1968), and G. K. Galinsky, *Ovid's
'Metamorphoses'* (Oxford, 1975).

52. Some examples in *JHS*, *100* (1980), 30–5.

53. Augustine (*Civ. Dei* 18.18) ascribes all metamorphoses to demons, who have
no power of creation but who change *in appearance* things created by God. On philo-
sophical disputes about the status of metamorphosis in medieval times see Ch. 2 of
Summers *The Werewolf*; and cf. G. Ortalli, 'Natura, storia e mitografia del lupo nel
Medioevo', *La Cultura*, *11* (1973) 257–311, at 286f.

54. Cf. J. Bremmer, 'Scapegoat rituals in ancient Greece', *HSCP*, *87* (1983)
299–320, at 315–18.

55. Cf. works referred to in notes 3 and 5.

56. See J. H. Brunvand, *The Vanishing Hitchhiker* (New York, 1981).

57. See T. Gerhardt, 'Der Werwolf im Groschenroman', *Kieler Blätter zur*

Volkskunde, 9 (1977) 41–54.

58. Respectable scholars take the matter up eagerly. Eduard Fraenkel, *Horace* (Oxford, 1957), put in a stop-press footnote: 'I can now add that during the exceptional cold spell of February 1956 a postman was attacked and eaten by wolves . . . in the immediate neighbourhood of Horace's farm' (186, n 3). Peter Levi repeats the *topos* in the Penguin translation of Pausanias (Harmondsworth, 1971) 324, n 115.

59. Molinier and Molinier-Meyer, *Environnement et histoire*, analyse 45 attacks by wolves on humans between 1797 and 1817 in six French *départements*. Their guarded conclusion is that non-rabid wolves would attack children, especially those looking after flocks. Less often, adults were attacked; and, according to these authors, the attackers were not always rabid. But all adults fatally wounded or 'partiellement dévorés' were victims of rabid wolves. The authors estimate statistically that the rabid wolf is twenty times more dangerous than the non-rabid wolf.

60. Versions of this paper have been read at Ioannina, Bristol, Oxford, Swansea and at an annual meeting of the Classical Association at Nottingham. I am indebted to the many colleagues who offered advice and criticism on each of these occasions. I am also most grateful for help received from don Renato De Vido, Professor J. G. Davies, and the editor of this volume.

5

Orpheus: A Poet Among Men

Fritz Graf

The myth of Orpheus, in the form in which it entered European consciousness, is quite young: it was Virgil (*Georg.* 4,453–525) and Ovid (*Met.* 10,1–11.84) who narrated it in its canonical form. Their accounts look organic enough. Orpheus lost his wife, Eurydice, at the time of their wedding; grief-stricken, he went down to Hades, overcame all hostile powers through the power of his song, but failed in the end: turning too soon to see his wife, he lost her for good. In reaction, he fled human companionship, especially that of women, and his mournful singing attracted wild beasts, trees and rocks. Finally maenads attacked him, tore his body to pieces and threw it into a river; miraculously preserved, his head kept on swimming and singing on the waves.

A look at the earlier testimonies and the mythographers, how-ever, shows that this narrative is a composite of four different themes:[1] the story of how Orpheus lost his wife and tried to fetch her back; how his music attracted animals, trees, and even rocks; how he died at the hands of the maenads or of Thracian women, and what happened to his severed head. These four themes account for nearly all the myths we know about Orpheus: a fifth major theme, one not integrated into the vulgate but, to antici-pate, attested at the earliest date, is the story of how Orpheus accompanied the Argonauts on their adventurous trip.

The task of understanding the figure of Orpheus — a Thracian singer and lyre-player, son of a Muse and a shadowy king or the god Apollo himself — is not an easy one, in consequence of the inadequacy of our sources. It has, nevertheless, been undertaken many times and with widely divergent results.[2] This essay will, once again, attack the same problem. And though sketchy in some parts, it hopes to present a well-known mythological figure in a partly new light.

1.

The moving story of Orpheus' frustrated love goes back, as is universally agreed, to a Hellenistic source.[3] There is much less agreement about earlier forms of this myth. Did it always end unhappily, or was there a version where Orpheus succeeded in his quest? The evidence seems, at first, somewhat ambiguous.

The first allusion to an unsuccessful ending is in Plato's *Symposium* (179 DE), in a rather surprising form. The gods, Plato makes Phaedrus say, deceived Orpheus by not giving him his wife but only showing him an apparition, *phasma*, of her, as a punishment for his cowardice: had he not been a coward, he would have died to follow her, as Alcestis had done who died out of love for her husband. This variation certainly is Plato's — but he varies the canonical form with its unhappy ending.

The evidence before Plato is less clear. The first reference to the myth occurs in Euripides' *Alcestis*, performed in 438 BC. Alcestis, who chose to die instead of her husband Admetus, takes her farewell; in a long speech, Admetus expresses his grief and promises to love her for ever — and if he had the power of Orpheus, he would go down to entice Persephone and her husband to give him back his wife, and neither Cerberus nor Charon could keep him back 'before I would bring back thy life to the light' (357–62). The words are ambiguous, and it does not necessarily follow that Orpheus had been successful. One might even argue that Admetus hopes to have more success than his famous predecessor, whom Cerberus and Charon had kept back.[4] Nor does a successful ending follow from a passage in Isocrates' *Busiris* (8) where the rhetor compares Busiris 'who killed the living before their time' to Orpheus 'who brought back the dead from Hades': what matters is the clever contrast, and Isocrates at all events overstates his case, since he makes Orpheus bring back the dead, *tous tethneotas*. It is not difficult to see that he did not mention the outcome in order to avoid endangering his recherché comparison.

A similar ambiguity surrounds the two references in Hellenistic poetry. Hermesianax (around 300 BC) ends his account of how Orpheus went to Hades for his wife with the words: 'Thus singing, he persuaded the great Lords that Argiope [as Hermesianax calls the wife] might take the spirit of fragile life' (fr. 7 Powell). The outcome is open, and since the poet narrates the myth in praise of another poet's love, as a mythical precedent of his own love and poetry, he needs must leave it open — especially if the myth had ended in failure. In the anonymous *Epitaph for the poet Bion*, its author wishes to be able to go down to Hades, like Orpheus, like Odysseus, like Herakles, and to sing before Kore (121–32): he is certain that his song will move the Mistress of the Dead — especially since she is Sicilian, as is his bucolic song. Again, it is the powerful song that matters; the poet might hope to be more successful than Orpheus — after all, his song is nearer and dearer to Persephone than Orpheus' had been.

There is, finally, the famous relief from the later fifth century which comes, presumably, from the altar of the Twelve Gods on the Athenian Agora. It represents Hermes, Orpheus and his wife. As to the exact interpretation, archaeologists are divided into those who see a 'tragical note', i.e. the final parting of the lovers, and those who do not. For our discussion it is therefore not very helpful.[5]

There is, then, no unambiguous testimony to a happy ending of Orpheus' quest. What is more, it seems clear that at least the writers (I venture no opinion about the unknown sculptor) were not so much interested in the outcome as in the story — that Orpheus went out of love, in his living body, down to Hades, and overcame all the dangers there, thanks to his powerful music. It is a myth about a master-musician and, at least in Hellenistic time, a poet's poet, a mythical prefiguration of the poet. Even Plato, in his emphasis on the katabasis in life, which he devalued when compared to suicide, shows this point of view. His formulation — 'the gods only showed him a *phasma* of her' — is, then, a perfectly understandable abbreviation of the finale we know from Virgil and Ovid.

2.

We may, therefore, assume that the myth has had a relatively uniform pattern from its first attestation in 438 BC. As to its age and its possible earlier appearance, we simply lack information. Nevertheless, scholars attributed to it a hoary antiquity. It was reckoned to be 'the most significant . . . element that can be compared to shamanic ideology and technique'.[6] The problem, though, is somewhat more complex than this.[7]

It is not in dispute that among the most important tasks a shaman has to perform is the ritually enacted journey to the beyond to get information or to fetch back a soul; he does this on behalf of his community. He is helped by his drum, without which he would be helpless, and by his spirit, both of which he had acquired during his period of initiation. The myth of Orpheus thus could be viewed as reflecting shamanistic ritual — there are even shamans who use a stringed instrument instead of a drum.[8] The changes — that Orpheus is a master-musician, not a healing priest, and that he acts out of his private love — are understandable as adaptations to the level of classical Greek culture.

Complications come with a whole body of stories aptly labelled 'The Orpheus Tradition', most of them from North American Indians, some from the Pacific rims of Asia and from Polynesia.[9] In these stories, a man (rarely a woman) goes to the world of the dead to fetch back a near relative — wife, husband, lover, brother or sister. He/she overcomes the difficulties of this alien world, is helped by its inhabitants and rulers and is given back his beloved — under conditions, though, which may resemble those of the Greek myth (not to look back or not to touch the beloved on the way up) or may concern their life afterwards (never to strike her, among other things). In most cases, these conditions are broken (this is, after all, their narrative function), and the quest fails.

The attestations of these stories present some formidable problems of origin and diffusion. Their closeness on both sides of the Pacific makes it likely that they originated from one source, presumably in Asia; in any event, the story must have existed long before the last Indian crossed the Bering Strait sometime between 10,000 and 2,500 BC, when we find the oldest Esquimo cultures in these parts: the Esquimoes show no traces of this story.[10] As for its origin, the closeness to shamanistic experience has often been stressed, and Åke Hultkrantz suggested that its nucleus was the record of an actual shamanistic séance — although in very few cases, and never in America, is the Orpheus-figure a shaman, and he never succeeds through his musical ability.[11] One might thus doubt Hultkrantz's hypothesis; still, the similarity of the stories, not least their common difference from actual shamanistic ritual, is proof that the diffusionist theory is right. If this is so, and if the story goes back some millenia, then some doubts may be cast on the relevance of its shamanistic origin for the understanding of the Greek myth: it might have become detached from its ritual origin long ago and have travelled through the populations between Pacific Asia and the Mediterranean in the mouths of many generations of story-tellers. To the Greeks at least, it did not point to shamanism, but explored the power of music which could bridge the gap between mortality and immortality, albeit not to the extent of resuscitating the dead. Nobody in Greek mythology — not Herakles and Odysseus with their heroic *arete*, not even Asclepios with his *sophia* as a healer — was permitted this ultimate power which would have touched upon the very borderline between the human and the divine condition in a much more fundamental and devastating way than simply the descent into Hades by a living man.

3.

The second theme — Orpheus enchanting animals, trees and rocks with his song — is attested somewhat earlier. Simonides in a fragment of one of his odes is the first to formulate it for us; then follow Aeschylus and Euripides.[12] Again, it is an image of poetry and music surpassing the boundaries of human existence, this time the boundary between man and the rest of the creation. As Greek man defines his status as *brotos* compared to the *ambrotoi*, the undying gods, so does he towards animals: full humanity, according to Greek anthropology, was gained by overcoming the animal-like condition, *theriodes bios*.[13]

For this story again, shamanistic roots have been claimed. In the Finnish poem *Kalevala*, the singer, blacksmith, and magician Väinämöinnen attracts the animals by his marvellous song (*canto* 41), and parallels are found in North European poetry as well as in epics in Northern Eurasia, India, or China. A ritual background is possible: the magical attraction of animals through music before the hunt, one of the tasks of the shaman.[14] But again, the problem is not that easy. The extant testimonies, at least those from poetry, show the pride and self-definition of the singers reflected in the mythical image of the marvellous singer; there are, furthermore, possible Near Eastern parallels as well.[15] Again, the shamanistic background recedes to a point where it is virtually of no consequence for understanding the Greek myth, and again possible ways of transmission other than direct contact with a shamanistic culture are at least conceivable.

4.

The next theme is the death of Orpheus. Two main traditions are preserved: in one, Orpheus is killed by ordinary Thracian women, in the other by maenads, mythological beings. The Romans, Virgil and Ovid, blend the traditions, making the maenads Thracian women — *Ciconum matres* (*Georg.* 4.520) or *nurus* (*Met.* 11.8), 'mothers (viz. daughters) of the Ciconians'; Thrace, to them, is a country with mythical dimensions. A third tradition is local, and has Orpheus killed by lightning: it goes back, as I. M. Linforth convincingly argued, to pro-Thracian myth-making at the beginning of the Peloponnesian War.[16] The maenads are attested earlier: Aeschylus in his *Bassarai* is the first to introduce them.[17] The motivations for their attack vary, but it is always, in some way or other, the wrath of Dionysos which sends them (except in Virgil and Ovid who motivate from purely human reasons). The Aeschylean account is preserved in the remnants of Eratosthenes' narration of how the lyre became a constellation. It had been invented by Hermes and handed over to Apollo (this story is known since the Homeric Hymn to Hermes), then to Orpheus; after the latter's violent death, Zeus set it among the stars. Eratosthenes gave as motivation (in Martin West's reconstruction) that Orpheus in his journey to the Beyond had a revelation which made him convert from Dionysos to Helios: Dionysos, thus rebuked, took his revenge. Hyginus in his *Astronomica* (2.7) offers a different reason: when singing in praise of the gods before Pluto and Persephone, Orpheus forgot Dionysos — this is a common motif, most prominent in the myth of the Calydonian Hunt, when Oeneus forgot to sacrifice to Artemis, who sent the boar to punish him.[18] The other motivation is singular, but convincing: after the journey in the dark, Helios' power might be better appreciated. It could have been Aeschylus' own invention.

There are more reasons given in our sources for the attack of the Thracian women, but there is nevertheless one common theme. The motivations given by Plato (*Symp.* 179 D: the gods punished Orpheus for his cowardice) and Isocrates (*Busir.* 38f: the gods punished him because he told shocking stories about them) may be set firmly aside as idiosyncrasies of their respective authors; a further explanation offered by Hyginus (*Astron.* 2.7: Aphrodite, disappointed of the love of Adonis, made all the women mad with love for Orpheus and they pulled him to pieces when they tried to get hold of him) looks rather like a bad joke based on a well-known myth. The other explanations agree in the fact that the women resented Orpheus because he kept away from them — either he stayed away from human beings completely (Virgil) or he assembled only the men around him or he even introduced homoerotic love.[19] Attic red-figured vases from the 480s onwards always depict the attack by Thracian women, and never by maenads; vases of the same period show him singing among the men only — but in one case armed women lurk in the background.[20] This, then, is the vulgate version: Orpheus died at the hands of Thracian women because they were angered about his aloofness. The vases show that this vulgate preceded Aeschylus in time: he already knew a story where Orpheus came to grief in Thrace, at the hands of women. He also knew about a special relationship between Orpheus and Dionysos. The only such connection we know of is attested later: Orpheus is the poet of the Bacchic mysteries; explicitly stated in a host of later texts, this is alluded to in the still somewhat enigmatic bone-tablets from Olbia, dated to the latter half of the fifth century.[21] The *Bassarai* brings this theme up to the 470s or 460s; a few vases attest it for the middle of the century (n 20). Orpheus is not only a powerful poet, then; his poetry is, at an early stage, connected with Bacchic mystery-cults.

5.

Orpheus is also always a Thracian. Three localisations are mentioned. A *physikos Herakleides*, not necessarily Heraclides Ponticus,

Aristotle's pupil, connects him with the interior of Thrace, around Mt Haemus: here, according to Heraclides, in a sanctuary of Dionysos there were tablets (*sanides*) with Orpheus' magical recipes.[22] The geographer Pomponius Mela (2.17) adds that Orpheus had initiated the maenads in the same region. More texts connect him with the coast of Southern Thrace, around Mt Pangaeum. Aeschylus in the *Bassarai* made the mountain the place where the maenads attacked and killed the singer (see n 17). Several authors call him a Ciconian: it is a purely poetical localisation, deriving from Homer's knowledge of this tribe.[23] Another tribe Orpheus is connected with are the Odryseans: they became prominent in the years between 450 and 330, when Teres and his son Sitalces founded the Thracian empire which was, during the Peloponnesian War, an ally of Athens. It was presumably during this period when this localisation of Orpheus originated.[24]

But neither the interior nor coastal Thrace could show a grave of Orpheus, despite his presumed death on Mt Pangaeum.[25] A grave, or rather two graves, are attested in a third region: Pieria, to the northeast of Mt Olympus. The region is, in historical times, Macedonian, but Thucydides and Strabo preserve the tradition of an earlier, expelled Thracian population. Archaeology confirms this change in population and dates it to the early archaic age.[26]

The central site for Orpheus is Leibethra, on the foothills of Mt Olympus. The town possessed a statue (*xoanon*) of Orpheus, carved out of cypress wood: it had sweated when Alexander set out on his campaign, to foreshadow the sweat Alexander's exploits would cause historians and poets.[27] The town also had a sanctuary of Orpheus where he received Olympian sacrifices and which women were forbidden to enter. Conon, who collected the story at the beginning of the Christian era, adds the aetiological myth (*FGrH* 26 F 1,45). On certain days, Orpheus assembled the warriors of Macedonia and Thrace[28] in a building well equipped for initiations (*teletai*); when celebrating these rituals, they had to leave their weapons outside. The women resented being excluded. Perhaps also, Conon adds, they resented the fact that Orpheus was not interested in their love. The weapons outside the building gave them their chance: one day, they took them up, entered the building, killed whoever opposed them, tore Orpheus to pieces and threw the limbs into the sea. Inevitably, a plague ensued. The oracle which the Leibethreans consulted ordered them to bury

Orpheus' head. A fisherman caught it at the mouth of the river Meles, untouched by death and sea-water. It was buried under a great monument, and a sanctuary and cult developed.

The sources of Conon are notoriously difficult to trace; our account is no exception.[29] Not everything in it is clear. Leibethra is well away from the sea; how then could the limbs be thrown into it? The river Meles, which washed the head out into the sea, is another puzzle: it cannot be the well-known river near Smyrna but must be a local stream, unattested elsewhere.[30] The importance given to the head is also somewhat incongruous: there are other stories about Orpheus' head, but there its role is more functional: it either gives oracles or causes exceptional musical ability (see below). Still, there is no good reason to suspect that Conon's narrative is fraudulent — and, as will be shown presently, its underlying assumptions are corroborated from elsewhere. It thus attests a cult of Orpheus and an aetiological story involving secret rituals of Orpheus for the local warriors.

A more complex account of Orpheus in Pieria is given by Pausanias (9.30.4–12). He starts by sketching the vulgate mythology of Orpheus, with a longer account of his death: he was killed by Thracian women who were angry because he had taken their menfolk away and roamed with them all over the country. The women only dared attack them when all were drunk, and they killed Orpheus. This is the reason why the Thracian warriors have to intoxicate themselves when they go fighting. This, of course, is just a slight rationalisation of a very archaic fighting technique, the 'Kampfwut' — an ecstasy or trance which the warriors reach by various means before the battle and which enables them to perform spectacular feats. It is attested for many archaic Indo-European societies, among them the Germans, the Celts, the Iranians and, later, Iranian Assassins. The important thing is that these ecstatic warriors always form secret societies (most prominently the Assassins): Orpheus roaming the country with a huge band of presumably well-armed men looks like the mythical image of such a society.[31]

Thus far, Pausanias does not give a precise localisation. But when he comes to the grave of Orpheus, he does: the grave monument, a column with an urn on top containing the bones of Orpheus, can be seen at the very place where the women killed him, close to the town of Dium, at the river Helicon or Baphyras, shortly before it vanishes underground. The reason for this disappearance is again the murder of Orpheus: when the women wished to clean themselves in the stream, it simply vanished. It might be that this is no more than Pausanias' own attempt to connect the myth he told of Orpheus' death with the monument near Dium — but, at any rate, he knows of a grave at this place. This leaves Leibethra out: in Pausanias' time it had ceased to exist.[32] A friend in Larisa had told him why. The Leibethreans had received an oracle that a sow (*hys*) would destroy their city if the sun could see the bones of Orpheus; understandably enough, they didn't worry much about this. But one day, a shepherd slumbered at the base of Orpheus' monument, and the buried hero made him play so sweetly that a crowd of shepherds was attracted: in their eagerness to be as close to the music as possible, they toppled and broke the urn. Thus, the sun could see the bones. The following night a rivulet, the Hys, swollen because of heavy rains, overflowed and destroyed the town. It never was rebuilt, and the people of Dium brought the monument into their town.

This story is clearly an alternative explanation for the monument at Dium. That it was fetched from Leibethra is incompatible with the idea that it still marks the very spot where Orpheus died. Neither does the story square with Conon's description of a *temenos* and a monument under which Orpheus' head was buried; but Pausanias is talking about something which no longer existed in his time, and his friend projected the monument of Dium into that of Leibethra. The whole story is an invention with a clear bias against Leibethra, the most prominent place in Orpheus' mythology. Much earlier, Strabo had heard another story at Dium. The Thracian (Ciconian) Orpheus spent his time in the village of Pimpleia near Dium, acquired many followers through his music, prophecies and rituals, and became a political power, till some of those whom he had scorned (*hypidomenous*) killed him (7 fr. 18). This looks like the transposition of the usual story into another frame, that of political power play and intrigue. Dium, at any rate, had its own tradition as well.

There is more to this story. It is surprisingly close to the account of how the Pythagoreans (or, as other sources unhistorically relate, Pythagoras himself) came to a violent end in Croton. Pythagoras, as much priestly figure as philosopher, collected many followers, and the group gained political power, until their opponents set fire to their meeting place and killed many of them.[33] Strabo's story about Orpheus seems dependent on the Pythagorean one which is attested from the late fourth century and preserves historical knowledge about the end of Pythagorean politics in Croton.

There are other connections between Pythagoras and Pierian Orpheus. The pseudepigraphical Doric *Hieros Logos* of Pythagoras, written in late Hellenistic time somewhere in southern Italy, opens with the story of how Pythagoras had gone to Leibethra to be be initiated (*orgistheis*) and had learned from the initiator (*telestas*) Aglaophamus this same Sacred Tale (*Hieros Logos*) about the gods. It went back to Orpheus who had learned it from the Muse, his mother, on Mt Pangaeum.[34] The geography is slightly blurred: the author telescopes Pierian Leibethra and the Thracian Mt Pangaeum; he is not the only one to do so, and in general the Doric Pseudopythagorica seem somewhat hazy about the Greek East.[35] The important thing is that again Leibethra is to the fore: here Aglaophamus initiated, as Orpheus had before him; this tradition was then handed over to Pythagoras. Given this, it is not impossible that the story of the Pythagoreans influenced the Orpheus legend. It might even have been the same milieu of the southern Italian Pythagoreans who had developed the Pseudo-pythagorica which was also responsible for the story in Strabo. There is one slight but revealing difference. In the Pythagorean story, the enemies are political opponents; in the story about Orpheus, they are men whom Orpheus had 'overlooked': this detail must come from the vulgate tradition, where Orpheus had 'overlooked' the women, his murderesses.

Thus, two places in Pieria preserved monuments of Orpheus. If the place where a hero has his grave is really his place of origin,[36] Orpheus is no Thracian, but a Pierian. It is, of course, just possible that both Leibethra and Dium took over the Panhellenic myth of Orpheus and created cults and monuments at a time when local patriotism wished to glorify the past, and when they also wished to have a hero known all over Greece. It is strange, though, that in these legends we meet an Orpheus somewhat different from the singer we have encountered up to now: a leader and initiator among warriors, celebrating secret rituals in a *telesterion* or roaming over the countryside — in short, a priestly leader of a men's society. That should preserve traces of a local, indigenous tradition.

6.

But there is more. The story of how Orpheus built his *telesterion* and assembled the men has a parallel in the famous story Herodotos (4.94–6) tells about Zalmoxis, the Thracian slave of Pythagoras.[37] Zalmoxis, upon returning to his native tribe, built a men's house (*andreōn*), assembled the eminent men of the tribe, feasted and taught them that eternal life was in store for them after their death. To prove his point, he disappeared into an underground chamber he had secretly built. The tribesmen mourned him as dead — but after three years he returned alive.

The story points in two directions. On one side is Thracian religion. Usually, Zalmoxis is considered a divinity who acted as a divine initiator in a secret cult.[38] But it had a political side as well, alluded to already in the Herodotean account — that he invited the most prominent men of the tribe (*tōn astōn tous prōtous*). Other sources say that he had been councillor to the Thracian king before becoming a god (Strabo 7.3.5 p. 298, after Posidonius) and that he was a lawgiver among Thracians (Diod. 1.94.2): his mysteries were no marginal eschatological cult, but had to do with the centre of power, and the priests who performed them were considered his successors and at the same time royal councillors — most prominent being Decaenus, the high priest in the reign of king Burebistas (Strabo, loc. cit.). The institution is reminiscent of the role the warriors' secret society developed into in the Iranian kingdom, where the initiated warriors became the closest followers and vassals of the king; the former secret society retained the political and military power of the kingdom.[39] An ancient etymology for Zalmoxis' name points the same way. It derives the name from *zalmos*, 'bear's hide', because as a baby Zalmoxis was enveloped in such a hide — but the *berserkir*, 'Bärenhäuter', is a Nordic ecstatic warrior clad in a bear's skin.[40]

On the other side is the Pythagorean connection, well known and often discussed.[41] Herodotos attributes the stratagem of Zalmoxis to the fact that he had learnt such wisdom from Pythagoras. A very similar account of a trick Pythagoras performed is told by Hermippus (fr. 20 Wehrli). W. Burkert concluded from it that Pythagoras had the aspect of a 'hierophant in the cult of Demeter',[42] that is, again, of an initiator. The Pythagorean society was not only a political club, but also a cult association with Pythagoras as its head.

Orpheus, as we met him at Leibethra and Dium, is akin to both Zalmoxis and Pythagoras. But the Herodotean account of Zalmoxis cannot be reduced to Greek fancy along the lines of the legend of Pythagoras, as Herodotos already implies for reasons of chronology (4.96), because there is independent and concurring evidence for a Thracian divinity Zalmoxis. Similarly, the legend of Orpheus cannot be reduced to simple invention after the model of Pythagoras. It seems rather that Pieria preserved (although transformed) institutions and rituals of a warriors' society, and that Orpheus was connected with it as the heroic or divine initiator. We cannot know whether the origins of these institutions were Thracian or Macedonian.[43] One might even venture a further guess. Homosexuality can belong to this sort of background, especially to its initiation rituals: Orpheus' introducing homosexuality to Thrace might preserve older traditions than we had thought.[44]

There is another trace of this same background. Ephorus (*FGrH* 70 F 104) tells that Orpheus had learnt his initiations and mysteries from the Idaean Dactyls on Samothrace, who were sorcerers and initiators. This group, centred around a Great Goddess, also reflects the structure of a secret society.[45] The art of Orpheus, it seems, was at least not incompatible with this.

7.

Except in the account of Conon, the legends about the head of Orpheus are centred around one place, the island of Lesbos. Myrsilus, the island's historian, locates its grave near Antissa: it is the reason why the nightingales of Antissa sing much more sweetly than those elsewhere (*FGrH* 477 F 2). Other authors make it the reason for the spectacular musical ability of the Lesbians, without giving an exact location of the grave.[46]

Three later texts are more circumstantial. According to Lucian (*Adv. Indoct.* 109–11), the head was buried in Lesbos, 'there, where now their Baccheion is'. Problems remain: it is clear neither which temple of Dionysos is meant (though H.-G. Buchholz suspects the one at Antissa[47]), nor what the exact relationship was between god and hero. In the *Life of Apollonius of Tyana* (4.14),

92

Philostratus tells how his hero visited the oracle of Orpheus' head on Lesbos. It had been closed long ago by Apollo himself, but if we are to believe Philostratus, the site was still visible. In the *Heroicus* (28.8–12), the same writer cites two oracles of Orpheus, uttered by his head 'in a hollow of the earth' (*en koilēi tēs gēs*), perhaps a cave. Both oracles are fictitious: one is uttered at the time of the Trojan War, the other is given to Cyrus of Persia. If we combine these data, we should locate the oracle in the Baccheion of Antissa, or rather, since Antissa was destroyed in about 167 BC and its inhabitants transferred to Methymna (Livy 43.31.14 and Pliny *Nat.* 5.139), in a temple in that city: both Lucian and Philostratus are writing well after the disappearance of Antissa. Methymna had a famous cult of Dionysos Phallen whose strange statue was carried around during his festival; it consisted of not much more than a head and perhaps a phallus.[48] Fishermen had once fished it out of the sea. The two legends are very close, the one perhaps modelled on the other; yet, the Orpheus myth is not devoid of meaning. There exists a whole body of legends about how an object was brought from the sea. It was always rather strange, and it always caused a cult with certain peculiar features to be instituted — in one case, a legend from Ostia, an oracle of Hercules.[49] At the same time, these strange arrivals inaugurate something new, not yet existing. The other story, how the head of Orpheus brought about the musical ability of the Lesbians, would thus conform as well.[50]

The literary texts range from the early third century BC to the early third century AD. Somewhat earlier is a group of pictorial representations. A red-figured hydria in the Basel museum, from the 440s, shows the head somewhere lower down; to the left and slightly higher up is a bearded male with a wreath and two spears, bending towards the head. The rest of the picture is filled with Muses. The identity of the man is unknown, but he seems to be the finder of the head.[51]

Not very much later are two other red-figured vases. A hydria in Dunedin shows Orpheus' head confronted by Apollo and, again, surrounded by two females, the Muses. The head on the ground and Apollo seem to be conversing.[52] A cup in Cambridge again has the god confronting the head. This time Apollo stands to the right, stretching out his right arm over the head, which again is lying on the ground, towards a youth sitting to the left. The head addresses the young man who busily writes down its utterances.

On the back there are again two Muses.[53] The same dictation scene is found on two Etruscan mirrors from the fourth century, with the exception that instead of Apollo and the Muses a crowd of divinities stands around. One mirror, in the Siena museum, has the name VPFE, i.e. Orpheus, beneath the head.[54]

The Cambridge cup has been understood as the scene where Apollo stops the oracle.[55] Taken together with the three related representations, this seems rather unlikely: nowhere else is there resistance either from a god or from the Muses. It is equally easy to understand the Cambridge scene as showing how Apollo orders the youth to take notes. Notes of what?

Texts of Orpheus written down on tablets are mentioned at about the same time the Cambridge cup was painted. In his *Alcestis*, Euripides speaks of the tablets (*sanides*) on which the voice of Orpheus (*Orpheia gērys*) has written down medicines as strong as those which Apollo had given to the sons of Asclepius (966–71) — but not even they can bring the dead back to life. The 'voice of Orpheus writing down': it is a strange expression, even for a choral lyric, and the idea of dictation is not far off. The tablets, then, contain magical recipes for healing. This is not very far from oracles: oracles are, among other things, concerned with the healing of illness, both private and epidemic. Apollo is the healer as well as the oracle-giver; Asclepius heals through dream-oracles; another great healing-hero is the seer Amphiaraus.

There is more. In some passages in the Greek magical papyri, the performer of a magical ritual has to keep a writing tablet ready and to write down whatever the god reveals during the ritual or in a dream provoked through the ritual: what is thus written down is a *pharmakon*, a recipe, or an oracle.[56] The magician busily writing down what the god or demon dictates comes very close to the vase paintings. Furthermore, there exist numerous gem-stones with the representation of a dictating head and a scribbling youth, all from Italy, all amulets, dated to the third century BC. Furtwängler connected them with the myth of Orpheus. Today, archaeologists prefer to see the Etruscan demon Tages revealing the *disciplina Etrusca*. But since the mirrors show that the myth of Orpheus' head was well known in Etruria in the fourth century, and the iconography of the gems is not far from that of the vases and mirrors, Orpheus might still be somewhere in the background — a magical Orpheus, that is, procuring amulets.[57]

Euripides calls the tablets Thracian, and his scholiast cites the
enigmatic Herakleides regarding a sanctuary in the interior of
Thrace where such tablets could be seen (see n 22). This may go
too far. But at any rate magical spells of Orpheus (which Euripides
knows as well in *Cyclops* 646 – 8) have not much to do with the
legend of Orpheus' head on Lesbos. It would be advisable to
separate the images from the texts. On Attic pottery, it seems
somewhat easier to see the representation of a myth explaining
well-known magical recipes, than of a local Lesbian legend in a
form unattested before the high Empire: Myrsilus and Phanocles,
the Hellenistic sources, present it in quite a different form. That
leaves only the Basel hydria unaccounted for. Its iconography does
not fit into the rest of the series and could point to the Lesbian
version or have another meaning, yet to be found.[58]

Again, these legends have been connected with shamanism:
there are shamanistic stories of prophesying heads.[59] But such
stories are spread more widely than the narrow area of shamanism, and there are even Greek examples without any further
possible shamanistic trait. Again, the evidence for an Orpheus
myth with a shamanistic background is ambiguous, at best.
Orpheus the magician and oracle-giver, the *mantis* (seer) as
Philochorus of Athens calls him (*FGrH* 328 F 76), could as well
originate in the rites and ideologies of men's secret societies: the
Dactyls, the initiators of Orpheus (note 45), are well versed in
magic, the members of Iranian secret societies were thought to be
magicians as well, and the Germanic Wotan/Odin, who presides
over initiations and ecstatic warriors' societies and whose name is
connected with 'wuot', fighting ecstasy, is also a sorcerer.[60]

8.

There is one theme left, Orpheus the Argonaut. Two comprehensive but rather late accounts exist, one in Diodorus Siculus, going
back to the mythographer Dionysius Scytobrachion in the third
century BC, the other of Apollonius of Rhodes at about the same
time.[61] In Apollonius' lengthy epic, Orpheus is represented as a
miraculous singer whose art charms animals and all nature. It had
been the wise centaur Chiron who advised Jason to take Orpheus
among the crew: he was the only one to overcome the perilous

songs of the Sirens. Aboard ship, he was principally the *keleustes* who beat the rhythm to the oarsmen; he was also the bard who sang during symposia, festivals, even the wedding of Jason and Medea. His prayer also dealt very effectively with the Hesperids (4.1409ff), his advice makes the Argonauts initiate themselves into the Samothracian mysteries (1.915ff), erect an altar to Apollo after an apparition (2.669ff), and offer the Apolline tripod to Triton in order to overcome the dangers of Lake Tritonis (4.154–9). He is, however, no *mantis*; the official seers are Mopsos and Idmon. Orpheus, once again, is mainly a mighty singer. When he sings a theogony and hymns to the gods, this reflects existing poetry under his name; both a theogony and hymns are known to the commentator in the Derveni papyrus in the later fourth century.[62]

Dionysius is more rationalising and excludes most fairy-tales and miracles, as befits a follower of Euhemerus. The supernatural powers Orpheus possesses are his as a gift of the Samothracian gods whose only initiate aboard ship he is (Diod. 4.43.1). By virtue of this distinction, he stills the storms through his prayer to them (4.43) and gains the favour of the sea-god Glaucus (4.48.5–7).

Earlier evidence is scanty. In the earlier fourth century, the historian Herodotos knows that it was Chiron who sent Orpheus, because of the Sirens (*FGrH* 31 F 43a). This episode might even be attested much earlier. On an Attic black-figured vase in Heidelberg (580–570) a singer is depicted, standing between two Sirens: he has been called Orpheus.[63] It cannot be totally excluded that on this Orientalising frieze, the juxtaposition of two Sirens and a singer has no deeper meaning. Still, the image is isolated, and the interpretation tempting.

Euripides in his *Hypsipyle*, the story of the Lemnian princess and mistress of Jason, mentioned Orpheus among the Argonauts; his name occurs twice among the extant fragments. He was the *keleustes* of the Argo, as in Apollonius; after the death of Jason, he cared for his two sons by Hypsipyle, and educated Euenus in music and his brother in arms.[64] Again, Orpheus is only the musician, though a valiant one. Pindar, in his fourth Pythian ode of 467 BC, gives the list of the Argonauts (*v.* 170ff). Besides Orpheus, sent by Apollo, there are Herakles and the Dioscuri, sons of Zeus, Poseidon's sons Euphemus and Periclymenus, Echion, sons of Hermes, Zetes and Kalais, the Boreads, and finally Mopsos, the *mantis*.[65] Orpheus is the 'lyre-player, father of songs, well-praised Orpheus' — again not much more than a poet's poet. The earliest certain representation, a metope from the Sicyonian treasure-house at Delphi, is a surprise: besides Orpheus (his name inscribed), there stands on the prow of the Argo another singer, whose name is illegible.[66] Whatever his name, the fact that at this time there were two singers aboard the Argo is confusing.

Orpheus, as far as the sources go, is a member of the group because of his one special skill, music, as Tiphys is included because of his skill with the helm, and Mopsos as the seer. The skill of Orpheus, though, has one special goal: to overcome the Sirens' song. The Siren adventure belongs to the oldest stratum of the epos, as Karl Meuli showed, antedating the text of the *Odyssey*.[67] It would thus be a fair guess that Orpheus had been introduced already very early, together with the Sirens (this was the opinion of Meuli), were it not that the second singer on the Sicyonian metope makes such a conclusion appear somewhat hasty. But even if Orpheus was a later addition to the story, eclipsing his predecessor, the unknown singer on the metope, he was included specifically as a singer.

This is at variance with — again — the shamanistic theory. To those who hold it, the voyage of the Argo is a shaman's voyage into the Beyond, with Orpheus as the leading shaman.[68] This is untenable. Neither is Orpheus the leader of the band, not even the spiritual leader, not is the trip of Jason and his crew a shaman's voyage. The parallels point in another direction.

It is well known that the list of the Argonauts varies from author to author. Like other stories of this sort, notably the Calydonian Hunt, it offered itself as a focus for different traditions. There is, however, a common denominator among the participants. They are young, adolescents rather than adults — *neoi, kouroi, ēitheoi*, as Apollonius often says. The very few older men among them have an interesting position. One, Iphiclus, is the maternal uncle of Jason; another, an Iphiclus again, is the maternal uncle of Meleager.[69] In many archaic societies, Greece not excluded, the maternal uncle is quite important. He has to initiate the nephew, as do the sons of Autolycus, the brothers of Odysseus' mother, the young Odysseus.[70] Apollonius also says that many of the participants were sent by their fathers, and Pindar uses similar phraseology: this might be an old feature of the myth and points to the interest the fathers felt in the participation of their sons.[71] Jason himself has characteristics of an adolescent during initiation, as Angelo Brelich showed with regard to the curious detail of his wearing only one sandal.[72] But Jason and his crew are not just a band of initiates. They are the prince and his fellow-initiates. The picture is reminiscent of the custom Ephorus (*FGrH* 70 F 149) records from aristocratic Crete: the young nobleman, during his initiation in the wilderness, is accompanied by an older man, his lover, and a group of friends from the same age-group.[73] The erotic element is not wholly absent from the Argonauts either: among them, there are Herakles and Hylas, lover and beloved (Ap. Rhod. 1.131) or, as another version has it, the Lapith Polyphemus and Hylas (Euphorio fr. 76); even though these variations cannot belong to a very old stratum of the story, they fit into the common background. The boundary line between such a group and a group of warriors is very narrow, if they stand together long enough, as the Argonauts certainly do. And behind Autolycus at least, the werewolf, and the Arcadian Ancaeus who is wearing a bear's hide, appear again the Nordic ecstatic warriors who formed similar bands.[74]

From another, even more speculative side, a similar result appears. Meuli connected the myth of the Argonauts with a familiar fairy-tale pattern, called after the Grimm brothers 'Die kunstreichen Brüder'. A young hero performs difficult and dangerous tasks to gain a princess or a treasure or both, and he is helped by a group of specialists, often brothers — one runs swifter than the wind (compare the Boreads among the Argonauts), another sees miraculously far (Lynceus), and so on; Orpheus and Tiphys could fit into the pattern. Meuli derived this tale from an even more archaic one, the 'Helfermärchen', where the hero is helped not by human specialists but by animals. The structural connection is convincing, the evolutionary paradigm might be more open to doubt. More important, though, Vladimir Propp derived the 'Helfermärchen' from the scenario of initiation rituals. One might do the same for the structurally equivalent human version, and thus for the myth of the Argonauts.[75]

Not a shamanistic background, then, lies behind this myth, but that of archaic initiatory rituals — more specifically, the initiation of aristocratic warriors. This background is at least as widespread as the shamanistic one, and it is preserved at the time of Ephorus among the backward Cretans. Just where Orpheus comes in, is less clear. As one of the specialists, his role could be very old, as Meuli thought. But it is equally well conceivable that he was added later, at the latest in the seventh century BC. It is tempting to connect his inclusion in an initation myth with the role he had in Leibethra, if only he were more central in the myths of the Argonauts. As it stands, his outstanding musical ability is explanation enough for the inclusion.

9.

Who, then, is Orpheus?

To the Greeks, he primarily was the most gifted musician and singer, potent enough to overcome the Sirens and the Lords of the Netherworld, to transcend the boundaries of humanity in charming animals, trees and rocks, to inaugurate the musical ability of the Lesbians, and of their nightingales. He was considered an author of theological poetry, and as early as Aeschylus he was connected with the cult of Dionysos. This connection must stem from the fact that he wrote texts for these mystery cults (later, other cults attracted him as well). Additionally, he or rather his head was the author of powerful spells — poetry and sorcery are not all that far apart.[76]

Deeper down in time and structure, there might be some elements common to shamanistic narrations. But none is so marked that it presupposes direct contact with a shamanistic culture; all could have travelled as stories without rituals over countries and centuries. Much more prominent are elements which belong to an initiatory society of warriors, a phenomenon well attested among the Indo-Europeans and still lingering just beneath the surface of some archaic Greek institutions.[77] The Leibethrean cult, if we are to believe Conon, was among them. This might be another reason for his association with the secret societies of Bacchic mysteries.[78]

Nothing looks very Thracian. Why, then, is Orpheus a Thracian?[79] The answer can only be tentative and sketchy. Orpheus, first of all, is not the only mythological singer who is regarded as a foreigner. Thamyris is a Thracian too, as is Musaeus (though he was perhaps formed after Orpheus); even the Muses come from Thracian Pieria. Olen, whose hymns Delos remembered, was considered a Lycian. Only Linos was a Greek from

Thebes, it seems, though a son of the Muse Urania; the origin of the shadowy Pamphos is unknown.[80] Did all the more prominent mythical singers originate in non-Greek mythology?

The question, asked this way, starts from a wrong assumption. When a figure in Greek mythology is given a foreign origin, this does not necessarily mean that he was, at a certain point of Greek history or rather pre-history, introduced from outside into the system of Greek mythology. In the first place, it means that this figure was felt as foreign, strange to this system, at least in archaic and classical times, when most myths gained their definite forms. There are, of course, figures who really did originate outside Greece — Cybele for example, the Phrygian, or perhaps Hecate, the Carian: but their origin was remembered because it corresponded always to an essential strangeness of these divinities and their cults — the ecstatic frenzy of the Metroic rites, the dog-sacrifice or the connection with sorcery and the dead in the case of Hecate.[81] Other figures might or might not have originated in a foreign mythology — take Ares the Thracian or Dionysos, who was said to have come from Asia Minor or Thrace: both are already present in the Mycenaean pantheon, and it is impossible to prove or disprove whether they were introduced from outside or not. But it is highly unlikely that such an introduction would have been remembered through the Dark Ages: in historical times, they were experienced as strangers, their cults retained strange features — Ares, the divinity of the bloody and cruel aspect of war which is kept well outside of the order of the polis; Dionysos, the god who sends ecstatic madness which disrupts the ordered life of the polis.[82]

The reality Orpheus and his fellow-singers belongs to is *mousiké*, music and poetry. Seen in this perspective, their foreignness must point to an otherness not quite congruent with the daily life of the polis which archaic Greeks felt in relation to poetry and music, and to poets as well. There are some indications of this, on different levels. There is, of course, Plato who puts poetic inspiration under the general heading of *mania*, madness (*Phaedrus* 245 A). But inspiration, as Penelope Murray showed, does not necessarily have such an ecstatic character; in a less violent form it is already present in the archaic age. The poet has a special relationship with his inspiring divinities, the Muses, which at the same time sets him apart from his fellow-men. Already Demodocus and Phemius in the *Odyssey* claim this relationship (8.44, 22.347–9); Hesiod and Archilochus had been personally initiated by the Muses.[83] Homer himself, the arch-poet, was blind: this is a symbol of otherness current in other contexts as well, no incidental biographical detail.[84] Poets, in the archaic age, aspired to a special social standing because of their *sophia*, wisdom, as did other extraordinary figures.[85] Poetry and music, finally, belong to special, sacralised occasions. The poets of old were mainly poets of religious hymns (Orpheus, Olen, Musaeus): religious poetry is sung during sacrifices, ritually marked off from daily life — see, for example, the paean sung by the Achaean youths to propitiate Apollo's wrath early in the *Iliad*: after the hecatomb and the communal meal, 'all day long, the young men of the Achaeans propitiated the god with dance and song (*molpê*), singing the beautiful paean' (1.472f). And outside the religious occasions proper, the prominent place for poetry was the symposion, another occasion marked off as sacralised by introductory and closing rituals.[86]

No need, then, to look for a special reason for Orpheus' Thracianness. Neither his association with Dionysos or with other mystery-cults caused it, nor is there any reason to read his myth only in a historising way, as previous generations of scholars did. Rather, his fame as a poet made him — or kept him, if he really was a hero or god of the Pierian Thracians — a Thracian: it is, we recall, just this role as a poet which we met in all his myths. As to the background of secret societies we found in his Pierian myth, we cannot be absolutely certain whether this is a projection of his role in Bacchic societies or rather preserves traces of a ritual origin of Orpheus. But since Conon's account preserves genuine-looking ritual information, since the details in Pausanias fit in, at least in a general way, with what Conon says, since Bacchic societies are nowhere in Greece all-male groups but rather female associations,[87] and since, finally, according to some scholars the poets of archaic Greece show features which make them come close to initiators,[88] it seems plausible to credit Orpheus with a genuine ritual background in such secret societies.[89]

Notes

1. The sources are collected in O. Kern (ed.), *Orphicorum Fragmenta* (Berlin, 1922) *Pars prior: Testimonia potiora*. The main mythographical accounts are Apollod. 1.14; Hyg. *Astr.* 2.7; Conon, *FGrH* 26 F 1,45; a remarkable synopsis of all the material is K. Ziegler, *RE* 18 (1939) 1268 – 80; the early testimonies are discussed at great length in I. M. Linforth, *The Arts of Orpheus* (Berkeley, 1941).

2. To give a sample: Orpheus a divinity of the Netherworld: E. Maass, *Orpheus* (Munich, 1895), still repeated by M. Guarducci, *Epigraphica*, *36* (1974) 29. A Frazerian priest-king: L. R. Farnell, *The Cults of the Greek States*, vol. 5 (Oxford, 1909) 105f. The sacred fox, totem animal of a fox tribe: S. Reinach, *Mythes, cultes et religions*, vol. 2 (Paris, 1910) 107 – 10. An old 'Jahresgott' whose song symbolises the joys of summer (a very Nordic feeling), whose death, the winter: C. Robert, in his edition of L. Preller, *Griechische Mythologie*, vol. 2 (Berlin, 1920) 400. A historical personality, a Greek missionary among the wild Thracians: W. K. C. Guthrie, *Orpheus and Greek religion* (Cambridge, 1st edn 1935; 2nd edn 1952) 56. A shaman who had lived in Mycenaean Boeotia: R. Böhme, *Orpheus. Das Alter des Kitharöden* (Bern, 1970) 192 – 254. A Bronze Age Thracian known in Greece before the Archaic Age: M. Durante, *Sulla preistoria della tradizione poetica greca*, vol. 1 (Rome, 1971) 157 – 9. A 'mythical shaman or prototype of shamans': E. R. Dodds, *The Greeks and the Irrational* (Berkeley, 1951) 147 — the most fashionable idea nowadays, see notes 6f.

3. The most influential study is still C. M. Bowra, *CQ* 46 (1952) 113 – 26, who thinks that the unhappy ending is the invention of Virgil's Hellenistic source. E. R. Robbins, in J. Warden (ed.), *Orpheus, The Metamorphoses of a Myth* (Toronto, 1982) 15f, duly repeats this.

4. Linforth, *Arts of Orpheus*, 16f, considers it the only reference to a happy ending.

5. Ample bibliography in W. H. Schuchhardt, *Das Orpheusrelief* (Stuttgart, 1964); see esp. H. A. Thompson, *Hesperia*, *21* (1952) 47 – 82; E. B. Harrison, ibid. 33 (1964) 76 – 82; M. O. Lee, ibid. 401 – 4; E. Langlotz in *Festgabe Johannes Straub* (Bonn, 1977), 91 – 112.

6. The first to connect Orpheus and shamanism was Karl Meuli in an introduction to the translation of the *Kalevala* (Basle, 1940); see his *Gesammelte Schriften* (Basle, 1975) 697. Much more influential became E. R. Dodds, *The Greeks and the Irrational*; after him, M. Eliade, *Shamanism. Archaic Technique of Ecstasy* (London, 1964) 391; then R. Böhme with his adventurous thesis, *Orpheus*, and most recently M. L. West, *The Orphic Poems* (Oxford, 1983) 3 – 7 (henceforth cited as West, *OP*).

7. The problem has become urgent because contemporary anthropologists, after a period of rather loose terminology, are bringing back the concept of shamanism to a narrow functional survey; see, for a short survey, J. N. Bremmer, *The Early Greek Concept of the Soul* (Princeton, 1983) 25 – 48, esp. 48, n 95.

8. See M. Eliade, *Shamanism*, 168 – 80 (drum); D. Schröder, in C. A. Schmitz (ed.), *Religionsethnologie* (Frankfort, 1964) 312 – 4 (spirits): H. Fromm, *Das Kalewala. Kommentar* (Munich, 1967) 259 (string instruments).

9. The standard monograph is Åke Hultkrantz, *The North American Indian Orpheus Tradition* (Stockholm, 1957); for more see D. Page, *Folktales in Homer's Odyssey* (Cambridge, 1973), 15 – 18; G. R. Swanson, *Ethnology*, *15* (1976) 115 – 23.

10. For a summary, see H.-G. Bandi, *Urgeschichte der Eskimos* (Stuttgart, 1965), esp. 138 – 42. The absence of the Orpheus Tradition is all the more striking since both shamanism and eschatological accounts are well attested in Esquimo cultures; see, e.g., H. Barüske (ed.), *Eskimo-Märchen* (Düsseldorf and Cologne, 1969) nos. 8 – 14.

11. A story about Manchu shamans in Å. Hultkrantz, *North American Indian*, 192; the origin in an actual séance, ibid. 220 – 9.

12. Simonid. fr. 567 Page; Aesch. *Ag.* 1629 – 31; Eur. *Bacch.* 650 and *Iph. Aul.* 1211 – 4. The motif became powerful in later antiquity, see R. Eisler, *Orphisch-dionysische Mysteriengedanken in der christlichen Antike* (Vorträge Warburg, 1922 – 3) 3 – 32; E. Irwin, in Warden, *Orpheus*, 51 – 62.

13. For a summary see W. K. C. Guthrie, *A History of Greek Philosophy*, vol. 3 (Cambridge, 1969) 60 – 3.

14. Väinämöinen and Orpheus: Meuli, *Schriften*, 697; the ritual background, ibid. 693; the literary parallels in Fromm, *Das Kalewala*, 256 – 9.

15. B. Kötting, in *Mullus. Festschrift Theodor Klauser* (Münster, 1964) 211 (pictorial representations).

16. Alcidam. *Ulix.* 24 cites an epigram about Orpheus' death by lightning; the same story with verbal reminiscences in another epigram in Diog. Laert. *prooem.* 1.4 and *Ant. Pal.* 7.617 which goes back to Lobon of Argus fr. 508 *Suppl. Hell.*; a prose account in Paus. 9.30.5. The interpretation in Linforth, *Arts of Orpheus*, 15f, with reference to his earlier study, *Tr. Am. Phil. Ass.*, *63* (1931) 5 – 11.

17. Aesch. fr. 82 Mette (cf. p. 138f Radt); an ample discussion in M. L. West, *BICS*, *30* (1983) 64 – 7.

18. The sources in West, *BICS*, *30* (1983) 66f.

19. Orpheus assembling the men: Conon, *FGrH* 26 F 1,45; Paus. 9.30.5; introducing homoerotic love, Phanocles fr. 1 Powell; Ov. *Met.* 10.83 – 5; Hyg. *Astr.* 2.7.

20. F. M. Schöller, *Darstellungen des Orpheus in der Antike* (Diss., Freiburg, 1969) 55 – 69; E. R. Panyagua, *Helmantica*, *23* (1972) 90 – 111; see also F. Brommer, *Vasenlisten zur griechischen Heldensage*, 3rd edn (Marburg, 1973) 504 – 7. One vase, *ARV* 1042, *inf.* 2 introduces Dionysos as well, see West, *BICS*, *30* (1983) 81 note 18; several vases from the mid-fifth cent. add a satyr to Orpheus' audience, Schöller 53 (influence from the stage?).

21. See West, *OP* 17 – 19, with the necessary references.

22. Schol. Eur. *Alc.* 968. Cobet had conjectured Herakleitos; Wehrli keeps the text out of his fragments of Heraclides Ponticus.

23. The Cicones in Hom. *Il.*, 2,846.17.73; connected with Orpheus, Ps.-Aristot. fr. 641,48; Verg. *Georg.* 4,520; Ov. *Met.* 11,4 (but *Edonidae* ibid. 69); Suid. O 655.

24. King of Macedonians and Odrysians: Conon, *FGrH* 26 F 1,45; Odrysian: Suid. O 656; West, *BICS*, *30* (1983) 81, n 16, puts the connection too late.

25. The only testimony as to a grave in Ciconian territory is Ps.-Aristot. loc. cit., an epigram whose wording comes close to the one of Lobon and which Diog. Laert. gives to the grave at Dium (see n 16); the third epigram, the epitaph in Alcidamas, gives no localisation.

26. The testimonies for Pieria in *Orphicorum Fragmenta* T 38 – 41, first although vague attestation is Eur. *Bacch.* 560. The expulsion of the Thracians in Thuc. 2.99 and Strabo 10.2.71, p. 471; for Thracian towns more to the North, see Hecataeus *FGrH* 1 F 146; for the archaeological record, N. G. L. Hammond, *A History of Macedonia*, vol. 1 (Oxford, 1972) 416 – 18.

27. Plut. *Alex.* 14.9.671 F; Arrian. *Anab.* 1.11.2; more in *Orphicorum Fragmenta* T 144.

28. Obviously a compromise between the mythical tradition and Conon's own historical and geographical knowledge.

29. See *FGrH* ad loc.; Henrichs, this volume, Ch. 11, section 1.

30. See N. G. L. Hammond, *Macedonia*, 129, n 4. Guthrie, *Orpheus*, 35 opts for the Smyrnaean river and makes unfounded conclusions.

31. For a survey see G. Widengren, *Der Feudalismus im alten Iran* (Köln and Opladen, 1969) 45–63; A. Alföldi, *Die Struktur des voretruskischen Römerstaates* (Heidelburg, 1974) 33–7. Add the Assassins from Marco Polo, *Il Milione*, ed. D. Ponchiroli (Turin, 1974) Ch. 31, 32–4; for the Celts also H. G. Wackernagel, *Altes Volkstum in der Schweiz* (Basle, 1956) 124–6.

32. The archaeological record for Leibethra contains only archaic and hellenistic finds; Hammond, *Macedonia*, 136 (if the site really is Leibethra).

33. Principal source is Aristoxenus fr. 18 Wehrli; see K. von Fritz, *RE* 24 (1963) 211–18; W. Burkert, *Lore and Science* (Cambridge, Mass., 1972) 115–18.

34. Iamb. *Vit. Pyth.* 146 = H. Thesleff, *The Pythagorean Texts of the Hellenistic Period* (Åbo, 1965) 164.

35. For the Italian pseudopythagorica see H. Thesleff, *An Introduction to the Pythagorean Writings of the Hellenistic Period* (Åbo, 1961) esp. 99–101 and 104f; geographical confusion also in Himer. *Or.* 46,3 Colonna; *Piere̅ Bistonis* in Ap. Rhod. 1.34 is a poetical way of saying Thracian Pieria.

36. For the grave as the centre of heroic worship see already E. Rohde, *Psyche* (2nd edn Freiburg, 1898) vol. 1, 159–66; F. Pfister, *Der Reliquienkult im Altertum*, vol. 2 (Giessen, 1912) 510f. The maxim has, of course, no value for pan-Hellenic heroes, especially those of epic poetry: it is all the more regrettable that we cannot know whether Orpheus was already part of the oldest stratum of the Argonautica; see below, note 67.

37. For Zalmoxis, see A. D. Nock, *CR, 40* (1926) 184–6; J. Coman, *Bull. Inst. Arch. Belge, 10* (1950) 177–84; F. Pfister, in *Studies D. M. Robinson* (St Louis, 1953) vol. 2, 1112–23; M. Eliade, *Zalmoxis. The Vanishing God* (Chicago and London, 1972) 21–75; Burkert, *Lore and Science*, 156f; A. Pandrea, *Balkan Studies, 22* (1981) 226–46; for an analysis of Hdt. 4.94–6 see F. Hartog, *Le Miroir d'Hérodote* (Paris, 1980), 102–26.

38. Hellanicus *FGrH* 4 73, in a passage otherwise heavily dependent on Herodotus, states *expressis verbis* that 'he taught secret rites (*teletas katedeixen*) to the Thracian Getae'. See especially M. Eliade, *Zalmoxis*, who is very careful to separate Zalmoxis and shamanism.

39. See Widengren, *Der Feudalismus*, especially 9–43; Alföldi, *Römerstaates*, 34–7; from a different perspective, R. Merkelbach, *Mithras* (Königstein, 1984) 23–30.

40. Alföldi, *Römerstaates*, 46f; O. Höfler, in O. Beck *et al.* (eds), *Reallexikon der germanischen Altertumskunde*, vol. 2 (Berlin and New York, 1976) 298–304.

41. Especially by W. Burkert and F. Hartog, see above, note 37.

42. Burkert, *Lore and Science*, 119 (the citation), 159 (Hermippus).

43. The role of Artemis Tauropolus in the Macedonian army rests on these same institutions, see F. Graf, *Nordionische Kulte* (Rome, 1985) 413–17; a Thracian all-male symposium, connected with Dionysiac iconography, is represented on a gold cup of King Cotys (reigned 383–360); see *Gold der Thraker* (Mainz, 1979) 144–6, no. 292 (I owe this reference to W. Burkert).

44. The initiatory aspect of homosexuality is discussed by J. N. Bremmer, *Arethusa, 13* (1980) 279–98; cf. H. Patzer, *Die griechische Knabenliebe* (Wiesbaden, 1982).

45. See Burkert, *GR* 280–3.

46. Phanocles fr. 1 Powell; Aristid. *Or.* 24.55 Keil; a similar story, but for Pierian nightingales, in Paus. 9.30.6.

47. H.-G. Buchholz, *Methymna* (Mainz, 1975) 203, 209f.

48. Paus. 10.19.3; Euseb. *Praep. Ev.* 5.36.1–3. See M. P. Nilsson, *Griechische Feste* (Leipzig, 1906) 282f; Burkert, *HN* 202f.

49. Discussion in Graf, *Nordionische Kulte*, 300–3.

50. Burkert, *HN* 201f.

51. M. Schmidt, *Ant. Kunst, 15* (1972) 128–37 (a very thorough discussion of all relevant documents).

52. *ARV* 1174. Bibliographies in Schöller, *Darstellungen*, 69; Schmidt, ibid. 130.

53. *ARV* 1401,1. Bibliographies in Schöller, ibid. 69; Schmidt, ibid. 130.

54. Bibliographies, Schöller, ibid. 98, notes 10 (Siena) and 13 (Paris), see Schmidt, ibid. 134.

55. C. Robert, *JdI, 32* (1917) 146f. It became the *opinio communis*, see e.g. Guthrie, *Orpheus*, 36, despite some objections, the most important from Schmidt, ibid. 131, who separates the vases from the texts.

56. *Pap. Graec. Mag.* VIII 90, XIII 91.646.

57. A. Furtwängler, *Die antiken Gemmen* (Leipzig and Berlin, 1900) vol. 3, 254–52; *contra* R. Herbig, *JdI, 49/50* (1944–5) 113f; reasonable objections, Schmidt, ibid. 133f.

58. M. Schmidt, ibid. 132f, thinks the finder was the poet Terpander; it is a guess. She also thinks that the head was in a cave where one had to descend with the help of ropes, which would recall Philostr. *Heroic.* 28; but the finder does not have ropes, but two spears, as far as I can see.

59. Dodds, *The Greeks*, 147; Eliade, *Shamanism*, 391; the protest in J. N. Bremmer, *Early Greek Concept*, 46f, with ample parallels; some more in C. G. Jung, *Gesammelte Werke*, vol. 11 (Zurich, 1963) 262–8.

60. Iran: G. Widengren, *Der Hochgottglaube im alten Iran* (Uppsala and Leipzig, 1939) 324f; Odin: J. de Vries, *Altgermanische Religionsgeschichte*, vol. 1, 2nd edn (Berlin, 1956) 499–502 (initiations); vol. 2, 2nd edn (Berlin, 1957) 73f (magician), 94–100 (men's societies).

61. Diod. 4.40–56 = J. Rusten, *Dionysius Scytobrachion* (Opladen 1982) 144–68; Ap. Rhod. 1.23–32 and *passim*; see K. Ziegler, *RE* 18 (1939) 1255–7.

62. P. Derv. in the preliminary edn *ZPE, 74* (1982); hymns are mentioned col. 18,11; a theogony is cited throughout.

63. H. Groppengiesser, *Arch. Anz.* (1977) 582–610.

64. Eur. *Hypsipyle* fr. 1, col. III 8–14 and fr. 64, col. II 98–102 Bond. The Euenus story is an aition for the Attic genos of the Euenidai.

65. The epithet *euainetos* reminds one of the epithet used by Ibycus fr. 306 Page, *onomaklytos*: lack of other distinctions of Orpheus, or a common epic tradition? *Onomaklytos* would fit into a hexameter. See also n 71.

66. *Fouilles de Delphes*, vol. IV:1 (Paris, 1909) 27–30 (description); vol. IV (plates) (Paris, 1926) *plate* 4.

67. Meuli, *Schriften*, 593–676, a slightly abbreviated version of his doctoral dissertation *Odyssee und Argonautika* (Basle, 1921); for Orpheus, see ibid. 567.

68. E. Robbins, in Warden, *Orpheus*, 7f.

69. Jason's uncle, Ap. Rhod. 1.45; Meleager's, 1.201; he is accompanied also by his father's brother, 1.191.

70. For Greece, J. N. Bremmer, *ZPE, 50* (1983) 173–86; for a wider background, idem, *Journal of Indo-European Studies, 4* (1976) 65–78; for the initiatory background of the Odysseus and Meleager stories, N. Rubin and W. Sale, *Arethusa, 16* (1983) 137–71.

71. For another possible hint of earlier traditions see above, note 65.

72. A. Brelich, *La Nouvelle Clio, 7/9* (1955/57) 496ff, see also his *Gli eroi greci* (Rome, 1958) 220.

73. The classical account is H. Jeanmaire, *Couroi et Courètes* (Lille, 1939), Ch. 6; cf. J. N. Bremmer, *Arethusa, 13* (1980) 279–98.

74. Autolycus as a werewolf: Burkert, *HN* 120; Buxton, this volume, Ch. 4; Ancaeus and bears, K. Meuli, *Schriften*, 601f. (without, however, connecting him with the berserks); see J. N. Bremmer, *ZPE, 47* (1982) 146f.

75. Meuli, *Schriften*, 593–610; V. Propp, *Istoričeski korni volšebnoj skazki*,

Orpheus: A Poet Among Men

(Leningrad, 1946). (Italian edn, Turin 1972; French edn, Paris 1983; Spanish edn, Madrid 1984.)

76. Bacchic cults since the Olbia tablet, see above note 19; the literary sources, explicit since Diod. 1.96.4–6, in *Orphicorum Fragmenta* T 94–101 (Damagetus *Ant. Pal.* 7,9 would be earlier, but its authenticity is dubious). Eleusis since Ar. *Ran.* 1044 (F. Graf, *Eleusis und die orphische Dichtung Athens* (Berlin, 1974) 22–39; objections: Detienne, *Dionysos* 169f; West, *OP* 23f). For the archaic unity of poet, seer and magician, N. K. Chadwick, *Poetry and Prophecy* (Cambridge, 1942); according to J. Vendryès, *La Religion des Celtes* (Paris, 1948) 302, the Celtic term for seer, *ofydd*, derives from the name of Ovid; see also E. Bickel, *Rhein. Mus.*, *94* (1951) 257ff.

77. As M. P. Nilsson tried to show long ago for the Homeric kingship, *Sitzungsberichte Berlin* (1927) 23–40 = *Opuscula Selecta*, vol. 2 (Lund, 1952) 871–97.

78. For a Thracian representation connecting an all-male group and Dionysiac iconography, see above, note 43.

79. Although the vases depict Orpheus first as a Greek and only after about 450 as a Thracian, and although Pausanias was surprised at the Greek costume of Orpheus on the painting Polygnotus had executed in the 460s at Delphi (10.30.6), this does not mean that around 450 Orpheus changed nationality. Rather, the Greeks became more interested in the peculiarities of barbarians at about that time and wished to differentiate them better from themselves.

80. For the evidence see West, *OP* 39–61 (singers) and L. R. Farnell, *The Cults of the Greek States*, vol. 5 (Oxford, 1909) 434–7 (Muses).

81. Cybele: M. J. Vermaseren, *Cybele and Attis* (London, 1977) 13–37; Hecate: T. Kraus, *Hekate* (Heidelberg, 1960); for both see also Graf, *Nordionische Kulte*, 107–15, 257–9.

82. Ares: a Thracian divinity, M. P. Nilsson, *Geschichte der griechischen Religion*, 3rd edn, vol. 1 (Munich, 1967) 517; C. Danoff, in *Kl. Pauly, 5* (1975) 779–81 (import from Thrace in Mycenaean times): the Mycenaean material, M. Gérard-Rousseau, *Les Mentions religieuses dans les tablettes mycéniennes* (Rome, 1968) 38f, more in Burkert, *GR*, 57. Dionysos: the Forschungsgeschichte, P. McGinty, *Interpretation and Dionysos* (The Hague, 1978); A. Henrichs, *HSCP, 88* (1984) 205–40; the role of Dionysos in Greece, A. Henrichs, in *Jewish and Christian Self-Definition* (London, 1982) vol. 3, 137–60.

83. Hesiod *Th.* 26–43; Archilochus *SEG* 15,517, col. II 22–40; inspiration in Archaic Greece, P. Murray, *JHS, 101* (1981) 87–100.

84. Blindness and seers, W. R. Halliday, *Greek Divination* (London, 1913) 77–9; and outsiders, Paus. 7.5.7; see also R. Buxton, *JHS, 100* (1980) 22–37.

85. Poets: H. Maehler, *Die Auffassung des Dichterberufs im frühen Griechentum* (Göttingen 1963); J. Svenbro, *La Parole et le marbre. Aux origines de la poétique grecque* (Lund, 1976); B. Gentili, *Poesia e pubblico nella Grecia antica* (Rome, 1984) 203–31; other 'wise men': M. Detienne, *Les Maîtres de vérité dans la Grèce archaïque*, 2nd edn (Paris, 1973).

86. There is no detailed study of the ritual aspect of the symposium; see meanwhile P. Von der Mühll, *Ausgewählte kleine Schriften* (Basle, 1976) 489.

87. A. Henrichs, in *Mnemai. Classical Studies . . . Karl K. Hulley* (Chico, Calif., 1984) 69–91 corrects earlier misconceptions.

88. See Bremmer, this volume, Ch. 1, note 8.

89. I thank J. N. Bremmer, N. Horsfall and my Zurich colleague H.-U. Maag for valuable help and information.

6

Reflections, Echoes and Amorous Reciprocity:
On Reading the Narcissus Story

Ezio Pellizer

Translated by Diana Crampton

n¹ Conon, Diegeseis 24

There is in the region of Boeotia a town called Thespiae, not far
from Mt Helicon, where the child Narcissus was born. He was
very beautiful, but also disdainful of Eros and of those who
loved him. Whereas his other lovers eventually stopped loving
him, Ameinias persevered, constantly pleading with him. And,
because Narcissus gave him no hope, and indeed sent him the
gift of a sword, the said Ameinias stabbed himself at the youth's
door, not without first invoking the vengeance of the god. So
Narcissus, contemplating his own reflection in a spring, and
contemplating his own beauty reflected in the water, absurdly
fell in love with himself. In the end, Narcissus, in despair,
admitted he had suffered a just punishment for the wounds
inflicted on the loving Ameinias, and killed himself. From then
on, the Thespians decided to honour and venerate the god Eros
even more, not only with public sacrifices, but also with private
cults. The people of the town think that the Narcissus flower
first grew in that place where the blood of Narcissus was spilt.

n² Pausanias 1.30.1

The altar within the city called the altar of Anteros they say was
dedicated by resident aliens, because the Athenian Meles,
spurning the love of Timagoras, a resident alien, bade him
ascend to the highest point of the rock and cast himself down.

107

Now Timagoras took no account of his life, and was ready to gratify the youth in any of his requests, so he went and cast himself down. When Meles saw that Timagoras was dead, he suffered such pangs of remorse that he threw himself from the same rock and died. From this time, the resident aliens worshipped as Anteros the avenging spirit of Timagoras.

(tr. by W. H. S. Jones (Loeb))

n³ *Pausanias 9.31.7–8*

(a) In the territory of the Thespians is a place called Donacon (*Reed-bed*). Here is the spring of Narcissus. They say that Narcissus looked into this water, and not understanding that he saw his own reflection, unconsciously fell in love with himself, and died of love at the spring. But it is utter stupidity to imagine that a man old enough to fall in love was incapable of distinguishing a man from a man's reflection.

(b) There is another story about Narcissus, less popular indeed than the other, but not without some support. It is said that Narcissus had a twin sister; they were exactly alike in appearance, their hair was the same, they wore similar clothes, and went hunting together. The story goes on that Narcissus fell in love with his sister, and when the girl died, would go to the spring, knowing that it was his reflection that he saw, but in spite of this knowledge finding some relief for his love in imagining that he saw, not his own reflection, but the likeness of his sister. The flower narcissus grew, in my opinion, before this, if we are to judge by the verses of Pamphos.

(tr. by W. H. S. Jones (Loeb))

n⁴ *Vatican Mythographer II.180*

The nymph Alcyope created Narcissus from the river called Cephisus; the soothsayer Teiresias foretold that he would be fortunate if he did not place too much faith in his beauty. The daughter of Iuno, Echo, fell in love with him, and, unable to win his love, followed him although he fled from her, repeating the last sounds of his words, and thus died of love. We have only her voice, for she was turned into stone and hidden in the mountains. This happened at the instigation of Iuno, because Echo often delayed her with her verbosity, so thát she was not able to surprise Jupiter as he chased nymphs through the mountains. It is also said that because of her deformity she was hidden in the mountains so that she could not be seen, but only heard. Regarding the said Narcissus, for the extreme disdain and cruelty shown to Echo, he was made to fall in love with himself by Nemesis, that is, the Fate who punishes the disdainful, so that he was consumed by no lesser flame. So he fell exhausted from the hunt by a fountain, and as he drank the water, he saw his own image, and believing it to be that of another, he fell in love, and was so consumed by his desire that he died. From his remains grew the flower that is called the narcissus by the nymphs called the Naiades, who cried for the sad fate of their brother.

1.

Conon's story (n^1), as is customary, begins with a general utterance, functioning to situate the narrative events in a particular space (Thebes, Boeotia, etc.); there then follows a description of the character and qualities of one of the persons who will be involved in the events. In this case, we find Narcissus, extraordinarily beautiful and at an ephebic age, yet disdainful and intractable in his amorous adventures. It is implicit that our subject (S1) swims against the social, or rather the underlying psychological current, which is safeguarded by the god who presides over amorous encounters (Eros); in other words a young man of extraordinary beauty generally should not be averse to the attentions of his lovers, as such an attitude constitutes a violation of the amorous *dike* sanctioned by the god himself.[1]

The following segment introduces a second subject (Ameinias, S2) who, in contrast to the other *erastai* (lovers), soon becomes bored with courting the ungrateful *ephebe* in vain, and persists, with great constancy, in his desire for Narcissus. We may describe quite simply a second general utterance, whereby S2 is in disjunction with his object (Narcissus), then there is a modal utterance, because Ameinias *wants* to obtain the conjunction with his object, but in this story his desire is not realised. Furthermore, we find ourselves confronted with a second complex object, which in this case is a modal object: S2's desire turns both on a simple transformation of state (that is the conjunction with the object from which he finds himself divided) and a modal transformation, as Narcissus in turn is required to desire (or, rather, to want to do). In Ameinias' intentions and desires we have a conjunction, that is, the appropriation of an object, as well as a persuasive action: all set in motion by Eros, the heavenly figure of passionate love, who seems to constitute the addresser (implicitly or explicitly) characteristic of this type of story, and who in n^1 in particular, appears as the addresser of the final sanction, as we shall see below. Ameinias in love, then, desires to achieve a persuasive act, a transfer of the modality of wanting on to Narcissus; such a transfer aims to make the object of his desire *do*. In other words, it is a programme of seduction, which in our story is not realised.

The third segment is a performance, which at first appears extremely simple, consisting in the transfer of an object (the sword) from Narcissus to Ameinias, S1 having the function of addresser, S2 of addressee. Yet it is easy to see from the qualities of this transferred object (a weapon, an instrument of separation and death) that after having been interpreted by the addressee (according to some competence that is not made clear here) as an obligation (an invitation, an injunction, that is, a persuasive act), it sets in motion the following utterance, that is, the auto-attribution of death by Ameinias. A persuasive action thereby is accomplished by Narcissus, who pushes his lover to perform a suicide programme — the lover, however, not failing to invoke the wildest maledictions against the young man before dying. Apart from being defined as a negative sanction against Narcissus' actions, this disillusioned lover's curse is also an illocutionary act of request to the deity, to sanction what has happened and to execute a further narrative programme, one of punishment and vendetta. The transformations set in motion by the deity are shown in the following two segments: the first consists in the realisation — at least partially — of the narrative programme, unsuccessful for Ameinias, to perform the transfer of the modal object (the wanting, or even better, a particular and complex form of wanting, that is, amorous desire) on to Narcissus. But because such a desire this time focuses on Narcissus himself (S1), we once again find a reflexive act, in which S1 attributes the modal object to himself. In the changed judgement of Narcissus, who is sorry not to have returned Ameinias' love, there is, then, a new sanction, and hence a second transformation, symmetrical to that manifested in the second narrative programme and consisting in the fact that Narcissus also kills himself. So we have a third reflexive act, in which someone attributes the object — in his case, death — to himself once more.

In conclusion: one unrealised and three complete narrative programmes draw into relief the very simple narrative structure of this story, which is articulated in the modality of impassioned wanting, and presents in characteristic fashion a specific recurrence: the addresser and addressee coincide three times, or at least the same working subject is the object of the action performed by itself. This redundancy, or better, this manifest recurrence, times three, has in the economy of the story the effect of showing the complex seme of /reflexivity/. In other words, a vast constellation of reflexive actions seems to be derived from the negation of reciprocity in amorous relations.

Although the names of the characters are changed, and the geographical location is different, story n^2 (Pausanias) appears to be constructed according to a practically identical narrative structure: it varies only in some elements of detail, as a simple analysis of those segments constitutive to both stories may show.[2] Furthermore, the story of Timagoras' unhappy love for the young Meles provides us with an interesting definition — both onomastic and morphological, as well as figurative — of the second contextual seme pertaining to these stories, as we shall see below: the winged figure of the god Anteros (brother of Eros,[3] and represented as his counter and mirror image), a punishing demon (*daimon alastor*) of unreciprocated love, it must be admitted, is a most effective incarnation of the seme of /reciprocity/.

2.

We can see how these diverse figures, at the level of discursive structures, are semantically invested in the stories of unhappy love we have examined, and how they are articulated according to semantic isotopies amenable to a consistent reading of all the possible variations. Let us begin with the mirror. Narcissus' falling in love with himself is provoked by the contemplation of his own beauty reflected in a spring, which serves as a mirror. Thus, the mirror image that reproduces oneself to oneself appears, a *visual* metaphor of reflexivity and of the double, of the coincidence of the other with oneself. In other words, Narcissus' mirror functions as a sort of hyper-mask in which the *I* and the *he* coincide, quasi-metaphor of the third person being compressed into the first person.[4] Other interesting isotopies may be found in other stories relating to the theme of Narcissus, if we wish to account for its entire system of transformations and variations. Take for instance, the events in the following *logos* by Pausanias (n[3b]), where the story of Narcissus is subjected to a rationalisation procedure (which is rather ingenuous but diffuse from the sixth century BC until about the beginning of the last century), that attempts to present myths as more plausible.[5] Pausanias (or his source) perceives that the most intolerable and scandalous element of the story is that a young man should be so stupid as to fall in love with the reflection of his own image without realising it. He therefore proposes a different version, evidently aimed at attenuating such an absurdity. In fact, a passionate love for a twin sister occurs in the new story, hence the love is simply an incestuous love. His sister, then, is described as totally identical (*es hapan homoion to eidos*), which accentuates the fact that this is an intentional search for identity: 'they dressed in similar clothes, they wore their hair in the same way'. Here, then, appears /gemellarity/, which evidently functions as genetic identity, corresponding to a physical difference, which in this case is one of gender. Here too, a form of 'specularity' is repeated in the moment of searching for similarity in the love object, which may tend towards total identity with oneself; one attempts to short-circuit transitivity on to the other, and thereby to deny the difference in a sort of compression of the reciprocal into the reflexive. The mirror (reflection of the spring) here is relegated to the lower level of *aide-mémoire*, of small consolation for the loss of the loved object, but it must be said that in this love between twins, 'specularity' and reflexivity are definitely present.[6] Both the identical clothes and the identical hairstyle attempt to elide the sexual differences between male and female; the denial of any form of difference is notable. Furthermore, even Eros and Anteros are brothers (although not twins); they are complementary, to the extent that the growth of one is impossible without the presence and reciprocal growth of the other, as recounted by Themistius.[7]

3.

Echo, the wood nymph (I chose, somewhat randomly, the story found in *Vatican Mythographer* II.180). Version n^4 is by far the best known throughout the European cultural tradition, thanks to Ovid, to Latin and medieval mythographers and to Boccaccio. It also spread during the Renaissance (Natalis Comes, etc.) to influence the painting, the music and the literature of subsequent centuries. This story is constructed in such a way as to draw clearly into relief the coherence and homogeneity of the 'Narcissus story' in its entire system of variations, and it permits us to see how narrative mechanisms function, generating different versions of the stories, centring on a definite character — or, if you like, to see how the transformations of a theme are organised diachronically, over a long period of time. In version n^4, the figure of Ameinias, the unfortunate *erastes*, does not exist any more; hence the element of the homosexual relationship disappears. The person who plays the actantial role corresponding to that of the unhappy lover (Ameinias or Timagoras in n^1 or n^2), going more or less along the same 'figurative path' (*parcours figuratif*), is now a nymph, of the female sex (remember the appearance of the sister in n^{3b}), called, as everyone knows, Echo. In this nymph's name and virtues, it is almost too easy to see her distinctive characteristics, that is to say, /vocality/ and, moreover, /reflexivity/. In other words, the unhappy nymph in love, described by Ovid (by verbal games that today may appear to be in bad taste[8]) as a voice without a presence, and who identically repeats the last syllables presented to her, is none other than 'specular' vocality. This reflected vocality thereby pertains, at this level of common isotopy, to preceding stories, to which, however (even in its transformations, and indeed thanks to them), it adds only the seme of /vocality/.

It therefore seems possible to conclude that a story, subjected to variations in its enunciative modality (or simply narrated in a different cultural context) can generate, in itself, several of its own variants, simply by amplifying, along a homogeneous axis, the choice of relevant semantic traits. This must be exactly what happened in our case, because Echo's story seems indeed to be constructed successively (by the work of a hellenistic Alexandrian poet from which may derive Ovid's story, or by Ovid himself), and apparently was inspired by a preceding tale about Narcissus in which there was no trace of vocal reflexivity, but in which appeared the optic reflexivity of the mirror. The complex seme of /reflexivity/, in a certain sense, may have generated this variant, simply transmuting the optic on to the vocal axis. As we have seen, something similar occurred in the Pausanias version (n^{3b}), where 'specularity' and 'love of the same', attempting to 'rationalise' the absurdity of the myth, together produced the figure of the twin sister.

4.

A powerful name: Plato. If we now look through the vast amount of material offered us by the *imaginaire* of ancient Greece, searching for a figure that symmetrically unifies the traits of complementarities, of the double pressed into one, of reciprocity that compresses itself into unity, of a sort of 'specularity' where the mirror seems to join itself to the reflected image (rather like the child who moves towards the mirror to the point of touching it, pressing his or her nose to it), we note that this figure indeed exists, even if it is an effort to imagine it; the result, once visualised, may be decidedly monstrous. The figure we seek is described in Plato, *Symposium* 180 *et seq.*, in the famous story of Aristophanes about the origin of love. Once, Aristophanes says, men had roundish bodies, with four hands and four legs, two sexual parts, two faces attached to one head, and four ears. There were three genders, male, female, and *androgynos*, gender being determined according to whether these strange beings had two male sexual parts, two female sexual parts, or one male and one female part. And because these individuals, who were so complete in themselves, were too self-confident and somewhat truculent, Zeus had to cut them in half. He then pulled the skin over the wound, tying it up at the point that is now the navel, and begged Apollo to twist the head so that it faced in the same direction as the cut. Finally, because these halves had some problems copulating — as one might imagine — Zeus also caused the sexual parts to be displaced to the front. From then on, these halves looked for each other, attempting to join themselves together again, desperately looking for their lost unity and original identity.

The platonic myth of the *androgynos* is too well known to require repetition of all its details. In any case, one must recognise that this famous figurative representation of a coincidence of the reciprocal in the reflexive reveals itself as highly pertinent to the entire system of meaning that we have tried to reconstruct in the preceding stories. Moreover, it provides an extremely vivid picture of how it is possible, via the figures of the *imaginaire*, to reconcile somehow the unity, the identity, the totality of the individual with complementariness, 'specularity', or duplicity — with, in a word, 'otherness'.[9]

An apparently clearly articulated underlying system can be perceived through this series of vivid representations, whether they are narrative or not. This system seems to be constructed according to a form of logic. We can see delineated, for example, in the very linguistic formulation of the narrative discourse, the specific function of some grammatical categories — for example the function of the reflexive pronoun *heautos*, or the reciprocal adjective *allelous*, which is formed by doubling *allos*, 'twice other', and has no nominative. These grammatical forms are, not surprisingly, repeated several times, not only in the story of the *androgynos*, but also in the other stories examined. Furthermore, we can see how the figurative — or narrative — exploration of passionate attitudes (love, passion *par excellence*) renders operative various possibilities of *rapprochement* and juxtaposition of the two principal verbal diatheses, the active — which the ancient Indian grammarians called *parasmaipadam*, 'word for an other' — and the medium — called *atmanepadam*, 'word for itself' — whereas the passive diathesis is secondary, simply the active seen from the point of view of the object. Finally, a general overview of this system of narrative representations shows, it seems to me, the articulation of some logical categories, and reveals the opposition /identity/ v. /otherness/, which may be represented schematically by a Greimasian *carré*, in which also are organised the *contradictoires* (/non-identity/ v. /non-otherness/ in the axis of the *sub-contraires*):

115

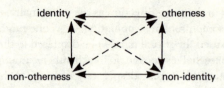

If general reflection on passionate love seems above all to draw into relief the problem of reconciling oppositions of the two contraries — that is, of defining the possible relations between the experience of the self and the recognition of the other — it is possible also to situate along the inferior axis (called that of the sub-contraries) some hypothetical and imaginary possibilities of different types of intermediate orientations. Such possibilities include the figure of the twin sister, who is not identical to Narcissus although she is of the same blood and similar to him, and also the figure of the *androgynos*, from whom it is possible to construct a monstrous image (which is neither the identical nor the other), simply by exploiting the possibilities intrinsic to the notion of symmetry. We should note that each of the two parts of the *androgynos* is called by Plato *symbolon*; certainly not in the actual sense of the word, but in the original (etymological) meaning of 'one part of a whole, divided into two, which may be made to coincide by putting it together (*sym-ballo*) with the other half', as is possible with the two parts of a coin, or with pieces of a stick broken in two.

5.

The narrative theme explored here has taken us a long way and could take us even further. I have endeavoured to show some of the rules of the game that generate these representations, articulating their narrative manifestations, in an attempt to conclude whether it is possible to identify some form of logic at the basis of such rules. It is possible to conclude tentatively that, through the figurative and discursive exploration of the categories dealing with passion and lack of reciprocity, indifference, desperation, reflexive love followed again by more despair and remorse, etc., that is, dealing with a series of euphoric, aphoric and dysphoric states and actions, these stories attempt to express a vast reflection that focuses on the definition of the self and the other, on reflexivity, complementariness and amorous reciprocity. And it is precisely passionate love that seems to function as the privileged operator of those transformations that reveal the meaning — or at least one meaning — shared by all these stories: the definition of the correct orientation of passionate attitudes in interpersonal relationships. This, then, is the 'moral of the story', whereby the winged figure of the *daimon* Anteros, together with that of the unhappy *androgynos* seems, on its own, to be the most effective metaphoric image.

In conclusion, I would like to examine another short passage from Plato, from the *Phaedrus*, another dialogue mainly dedicated to examining the passion of love (255 c–e). Here Plato unites, in a rather impressive manner, a large number of the figurative elements that we have found scattered here and there in the course of our inquiry, principally using a metaphorical system, the similarities of which to that system revealed by the examination of the Narcissus stories are too strong to be mere coincidence or 'free invention' of the Athenian philosopher. Having ascertained that amorous desire is like a *rheuma*, or current that flows from the loved object, Plato adds that this current of beauty, like a breath or an echo (*hoion pneuma e tis ekho*) reflected from a smooth and solid surface, bounces back to the point of origin, returning to the loved one through the eyes, in a look. He then continues 'and like someone who has contracted an eye disease from someone else, he cannot explain how, but without realising it, sees himself in the loved one, *as in a mirror* [*hosper en katoptroi*]'. And when the lover is far away, the loved one, now also in love in turn, 'desires and is desired, bearing *anteros* as the reflected image of *eros*', that is, he perceives the effects of passionate love in terms of 'specular' reciprocity.

Plato is, without doubt, principally interested in defining the *other* by means of studying the effects love produces on the self, whereas the preceding accounts attempt rather to demonstrate the disastrous effects of refusing reciprocity, which produces a closure in the narcissistic circle of the self. One realises, however, that in this impressive passage of Plato's, the reappearance of the figure of *anteros*, of amorous reciprocity, of the self who merges with the other and then returns to the self, of this finding-once-more with this bounce-back the image of the echo and the mirror, serves as a summary, as an inventory of the elements that constitute the system of meaning on which is based the theme of Narcissus in all its variations and narrative manifestations. We can now follow it through a long tradition, leading from Conon to Pausanias, from Ovid through the medieval mythographers and Boccaccio to Natalis Comes, from Calderòn to Scarlatti, and hence (why not?) to Sigmund Freud and his followers. The deep structures on which this has been articulated, however, were already present in the mind of the philosopher who not infrequently amused himself by telling certain 'myths' that were no longer myths, but rather intentionally symbolic systems, elaborated in the space of very rich and organised thought, just as they had been present in the *imaginaire* that generated these stories in an unspecified and unspecifiable epoch, certainly before the time of Plato himself.

After having followed the tortuous events of these stories — or rather, having attempted to explain their mechanisms — I still have the impression that the history of many narrative themes that have attained greater fame in our culture, and therefore a consistent part of the history of literature itself, are perhaps (to paraphrase J. L. Borges) no more than 'the history of differing intonations of some metaphors'.[10]

Notes

1. This rule has been illustrated well by Bruno Gentili, 'Il "letto insaziato" di Medea e il tema dell'*adikia* a livello amoroso nei lirici (Saffo, Teognide) e nella Medea di Euripide', *Studi Class. Or., 21* (1972) 60–72; p. 63: 'If respect for *dike necessarily* demands that the lover should in his turn be loved in an indissoluble chain of faithfulness and reciprocal loyalty, violation of this rule (*adikia*) in turn *necessarily* constitutes a sin which must be expiated' (emphasis in text); p. 64: '. . . sooner or later whoever rejects the love of the lover will pay the price for his own *adikia*'. On the use of the couplet *dike/adikia* in the language of love, see also Maria G. Bonanno, 'Osservazioni sul tema della "giusta" reciprocità amorosa da Saffo ai comici', *Quad. Urb. Cult. Class., 16* (1973) 110–20, M. Vetta, 'La "giovinezza giusta" di Trasibulo: Pind. *Pyth.* VI 48', *Quad. Urb. Cult. Class.*, n.s., *2* (1979) 87–90, and my 'La donna del mare. La *dike* amorosa "assente" nel giambo di Semonide sopra le donne, vv. 27–42', also in *Quad. Urb. Cult. Class.*, n.s., *3* (1979) 29–36. On the forms of *eros* in Greece see also my *Favole d'identità — Favole di paura* (Rome, 1982), and the very useful volume edited by C. Calame, *L'amore in Grecia* (Rome-Bari, 1983).

2. For an introduction to the analytical method used in this article, see J. Courtés, *Sémiotique narrative et discoursive* (Paris, 1976): Groupe d'Entrevernes (various authors), *Analyse sémiotique des textes* (Lyons, 1979); A. J. Greimas, *Du sens II. Essays sémiotiques* (Paris, 1983).

3. The rather facile psychoanalytic approach of D. Braunschweig and M. Fain, *Eros et Antéros. Réflections psychanalytiques sur la sexualité* (Paris, 1971) 139–158, to the function of these two *daimones* does not seem very useful. An enigmatic *Antéros* may be found in the singular sonnet of Gerard de Nerval's *Chimères*; see the fine analysis by J. Geninasca, *Analyse structurale des Chimères de Nerval* (Neuchatel, 1971) 38 and 223–36. On the ephebic *eros* in mythical stories, cf. B. Sergent, *L'Homosexualité dans la mythologie grecque* (Paris, 1984) 97–123, 210, which provides a rich bibliography on this theme; also the little-known study by C. Diano, 'L'eros greco', in *Saggezza e poetiche degli antichi* (Vicenza, 1968) 167–83 = *Ulisse, 18* (1953) 698 *et seq.*

4. See the interesting reflections of L. Marin, 'Masque et portrait: sur l'opérateur "masque" dans quelques textes du XVIIème siècle français', in *Atti del Convegno internazionale 'Nel senso della maschera: Au sense du masque',* Montecatini, 15–17 October 1981, forthcoming. For mirror effects in painting, cf. Caterina Limentani Virdis, *Il quadro e il suo doppio. Effetti di specularità narrativa nella pittura fiamminga e olandese* (Modena, 1981) (brought to my attention by Oddone Longo) and in general J. Baltrušaitis, *Le miroir: révelations, science-fiction et fallacies* (Paris, 1979). On the mirror and mask in Greek mythology and culture, the reflections by J.-P. Vernant in the *Annuaire du Collège de France 1979–80. Résumé des cours et travaux*, 453–66, have, as always, been most stimulating for me.

5. For Pausanias' attitude to myth see P. Veyne, *Les Grecs ont-ils cru à leurs mythes?* (Paris, 1983) 105–12 and *passim*.

6. The bonds of reciprocity and 'specularity' that are formed in the psychology of two twins (in this case both male) are remarkably perceived and described in the novel by Michel Tournier, *Les Météores* (Paris, 1975).

7. Cf. Themist. *Orat.* 24, 305 a–b: 'O Aphrodite, your true son Eros may perhaps have been born alone, but certainly he could not grow up alone; it is necessary for you also to have Anteros, if you wish that Eros may grow. And these two brothers will be of the same nature: they will each cause the growth of the other. And *looking at each other* they will also blossom, but they will diminish, if one (or the other) is left alone.'

8. For example, Ovid. *Met.* 3.386–7:

'Huc coeamus!' ait, nullique libentius umquam
responsura sono 'coeamus!' rettulit Echo, . . .

('Here let us meet,' he cries. Echo, never to answer another sound more gladly, cries: 'Let us meet' . . .). There is a *double-entendre* in the verbe *coire*, meaning 'to meet, come together' and also 'to copulate'. On these playful echo effects in Ovid see G. Rosati, *Narciso e Pigmalione* (Florence, 1984) 29–30; a shorter version of Ch. I, 'Narciso o l'illusione letteraria' appeared as 'Narciso o l'illusione dissolta' in *Maia, 28* (1976) 83–108.

9. I shall limit myself to citing the study by L. Brisson, 'Bisexualité et médiation en Grèce ancienne', *Nouv. rev. psychoanal., 7* (1973) 27–48. The entire volume, on the theme *Bisexualité et différence des sexes*, is of great interest for the study of these problems.

10. A general bibliography on Narcissus would be inappropriately long; many references may be found in the notes in Rosati, *Narcissus*, and P. Hadot, 'Le mythe de Narcisse et son interprétation par Plotin', *Nouv. rev. psychanal., 13* (1976) 81–108. The entire volume is dedicated to the Narcissus theme and its mythical, literary, artistic and psychological aspects. See however the notable study by Louise Vinge, *The Narcissus Theme in Western Literature up to the Early 19th Century* (Lund, 1967).

I wish to offer grateful acknowledgements to Bruno Gentili, Claude Calame and

Reflections, Echoes and Amorous Reciprocity

Catherine and Jacques Geninasca, who patiently read an early draft of these reflections and who offered to me, as always, helpful suggestions and wise counsels.

7

Greek Myth and Ritual:
The Case of Kronos

H. S. Versnel

'Myth, in my terminology, is the counterpart of ritual: myth implies ritual, ritual implies myth, they are one and the same'; thus E. Leach takes his stand in a discussion that can have no end.[1] At the beginning of that discussion stands myth, identified as 'mistaken explanation' of ritual, to use Frazer's famous phrase. An inverse relationship has been postulated by the myth-and-ritual school of Hooke and his followers: myth as the scenario for ritual. A third possible explanation for the link between the two was offered by Jane Harrison: 'They probably arose together. Ritual is the utterance of an emotion, a thing felt in *action*, myth in words or thoughts. They arise *pari passu*.' One recognises expressions of this view in several more recent anthropological studies. On the other hand, in his fundamental critical work, G. S. Kirk argues that any monolithic theory regarding myth and ritual should be rejected: all three forms of interrelation do indeed occur, but it must be remembered as well that there are many more rites without myths and myths without rites than there are related rites and myths.

Kirk does have a point, of course, but that does not mean the end of the myth and ritual investigation. If 'myth and ritual do not correspond in details of content but in structure and atmosphere',[2] it is worthwhile investigating whether there are indeed any examples at all of a myth and rite operating *pari passu* as 'symbolic processes for dealing with the same type of situation in the same affective mode' (Cl. Kluckhohn). W. Burkert has done so in recent years with regard to Greece, in his analysis of myth and ritual complexes, specifically the Arrhephoria festival and the myth of the Lemnian women. Although even Kirk has been convinced by Burkert's arguments that in these complexes myths and rites indeed are more or less parallel representations of a certain affective atmosphere surrounding the turn of the year, it cannot be denied that in both complexes strong aetiological components are present, too; if the myth does not explain details of the ritual, it does, at any rate, translate them into words and images.

It is my belief that there was in Greece a myth and ritual complex — also related to the transition from the old year to the new — in which myth and rite have indeed been formed *pari passu*, possibly even more clearly than in the cases just mentioned, and have developed as parallel expressions — interrelating ones, true enough, but interrelating in such a subtle and at the same time complicated manner that here at least the rite cannot be taken as example for the myth, nor the myth as scenario for the rite. I am referring to the myth and ritual complex of Kronos and the Kronia.[3]

1. Kronos: the Myth

The oldest version of the myth of Kronos is also the most complete. Apart from minor additions and variations — in themselves often quite significant — the myth as Hesiod tells it in the *Theogony* has not changed essentially in the course of time.[4] A short summary:

Like Iapetus, Themis, Rhea and so on, Kronos belongs to the race of the Titans, children of Uranos and Ge, the first generation of gods. Kronos hated his father, who had banished his children to the depths of the earth. At their mother's lamentations, only Kronos among the Titans was prepared to take action against his father, and with his sickle he cut ('mowed') (181) off Uranos' genitalia. From the resulting drops of blood sprang the Erinys, the giants and the nymphs. Out of the froth (= the semen) of the genitalia, which had fallen into the sea, Aphrodite was born. Next, Kronos and his sister/spouse, Rhea produced children, including the first generation of Olympians, the family of gods currently in power: Hestia, Demeter, Hera, Poseidon, Hades, and lastly Zeus. Kronos, fearing that one of them would overthrow him (462) 'gulped down' all his children immediately after their births (*katepine*: 459, 467, 473, 497). Rhea, however, brought her last child, Zeus, into the world on Crete, where he grew up hidden in a cave without his father's knowledge. Instead of the baby, Rhea had fed Kronos a stone wrapped in swaddling clothes. Once he had grown up, Zeus forced Kronos to regurgitate the other children; first came the stone, which has been displayed in Delphi ever since (cf. Sourvinou-Inwood, this volume, Ch. 10, Appendix). After this liberation he freed Kronos' brothers, the Cyclopes, who had been chained in the Underworld by their father, Uranos (501); in return for their rescue, the Cyclopes gave Zeus his thunderbolt. The hundred-handed giants also were freed (652, 659) from their subterranean prison at the edge of the world (621/2), where they had been held in heavy irons (618), in order to assist Zeus and the other Olympians in their battle against the Titans. An interpolated passage (*Th.* 687 – 712) does, indeed, say that Zeus destroyed the Titans with his thunderbolt, but the authentic text ascribes the victory to the hundred-handed giants, who drove the Titans deep under the earth and bound them in strong chains (718). It is true that this part does not say explicitly that Kronos suffered the same fate, but a later passage, in which the monster Typhoeus (who according to the scholiast on *Il.* 2.783 is a son of Kronos) waylays Zeus, includes an interpolated line (851): 'The Titans, in Tartarus, keeping Kronos company.'

In *Works and Days* 168, it is mentioned that Zeus settled the heroes after their deaths along the edges of the earth, where they lead carefree and happy lives on the Islands of the Blessed, where the spelt-giving soil yields a rich harvest three times a year. An interpolated verse (169) then continues: 'far from the immortals. Among them Kronos is king', and in a subsequent interpolated passage it is stated: 'his bonds the father of men and gods had broken'. Although not Hesiodic, this version must have been known as early as the archaic era.[5] Pindar is familiar with it (*Ol.* 2.70 v.).

Since the publication of the Hurrian-Hittite Kumarbi myth in 1945[6] scholars have agreed all but unanimously that Hesiod indirectly must have derived important parts of the Kronos myth from this much older tale. For here Kumarbi castrates his father Anu by biting off his genitalia and becomes pregnant by them with three (or five) children, among whom is the god of the storms, comparable to Zeus. Kumarbi regurgitates all the children except the god of the storms, who emerges by a more or less 'natural' route and dethrones his father. His father makes a final attempt at resistance with the assistance of a monster born from his semen (Ullikummi), but to no avail.

The striking resemblance between the two tales has led even to the hypothesis, notably argued by W. Burkert,[7] that the derivation of the *Theogony* myth from an oriental tradition could not have taken place until the eighth or seventh century, as this was the period in which 'orientalisation' had a much greater impact on the Greek world than scholars previously have been inclined to believe. Parts of the motif are found as early as the *Iliad*: Kronos is the father of Zeus, Hades and Poseidon (15.187) and of Hera (5.721; cf. 4.59). He resides at 'the limits of the earth and of the sea', where Iapetus is, too. This place is identified with the depths of Tartarus, which 'lies around it' (8.477–80) a subterranean abode to which Zeus has expelled his father and where he remains among the 'subterranean gods' (14.274; cf. 15.225).

Later versions add new elements. In Apollodorus 1.1ff, the Kouretes have a secure position as Zeus' protectors. It is by means of an emetic that Kronos is made to vomit; furthermore, he also has fathered the hybrid Cheiron (1.2.4). Apollodorus does not enlarge on Kronos' whereabouts after his defeat, although it is this aspect in particular that traditionally was enriched elsewhere with stereotyped features, and which right down to Roman times gave rise to variation and amplification. This tendency also began with Hesiod.

So far the picture has been largely negative, a picture that already in antiquity met with resistance: parricide, infanticide — even cannibalism[8] — rebellion in a ruthless struggle for power, a complete absence of moral standards, and lawlessness: all these elements were spotted and — sometimes — condemned.[9] Kronos' stock epithet *ankulometes* — possibly meaning 'with the curved sickle' originally[10] — was generally interpreted as 'with crooked tricks' or 'devious', a negative description; his actions were part of the unbridled excesses of a distant past, his punishment seemed just, his time was over. Apparently the oriental myth was associated with a god, possibly of pre-Greek signature, who no longer functioned as an active and intervening god.

Yet all this is only one side of the matter. There is another, which is the diametrical opposite of this negative picture. Kronos is king, or to express it more strongly 'Kronos is *the* king'.[11] The title *basileus* (king) is stereotypical from Hesiod until late antiquity. Strikingly, Julian, *Conviv.* 317 D, still makes a distinction between Kronos and Zeus: 'O, King Kronos and Father Zeus'. Kronos is even presented as the one who introduced the principle of kingship. Hesiod (*Th.* 486) calls him 'the first king' and as late as Byzantine times an author says: 'Kronos introduced kingship.' That nothing negative is implied by the term *basileus* is apparent from another epithet: *megas* (great), with which he is qualified in the *Iliad*, as well as by Hesiod.[12] On the contrary, Kronos' kingdom, which usually is visualised as existing on earth, was a realm of peace, justice and prosperity. Pindar so strongly associated such benefits with human kingship that he calls the abode whither the pious travel after death, a king's 'tower' (*Ol.* 2.125vv).[13] Such references bring us to the topic of the famous *Saturnia regna* or 'life at the time of Kronos', as the Athenians called the happy period under Pisistratos (Aristotle *Athenaion Politeia* 17.5), the Golden Age at the beginning of time, now irrevocably in the past. This image, too, is familiar even to Hesiod. In his description of the races of men, which perhaps also was derived from oriental myth and seems to have been a tradition unknown to Homer, he says everything began with the Golden Race (*Works and Days* 109–26): people lived like gods, without worry, exertion or suffering. They were not bothered by old age: their limbs were eternally young and they revelled happily (115). Death came like sleep. The earth yielded fruit of its own accord, abundantly and plentifully, and people lived contentedly in the midst of peace and profusion. After their disappearance from the face of the earth they became good *daimones*, guardians of mortals and bestowers of wealth (126). This marks the beginning of a rich tradition of utopianism and 'wishing-time'[14] with which Kronos is closely associated; this, too, since Hesiod, for according to him the people of the Golden Race lived when Kronos was king in Heaven (*Works and Days* 111). The tradition of making this utopian time Kronos' era can be followed from the *Alkmaeonis*, via Empedocles and the *Inachos* of Sophocles (alone among tragedies); the theme widens in Old Comedy, as is shown especially in Athenaeus 6.267E ff. In Old Comedy the motif of abundance, of a 'land of Cockaigne' receives particular attention; there are descriptions of primeval eras, of Pluto's underworld, and of the far-away land of the

Persians, who generally were notorious for their excess and luxury.[15]

In connection with this motif and partly as a reaction to it as well, there arose in the fourth century a remarkable alternative, possibly under the influence of Antisthenes. According to Plato, Kronos' realm is not one of superabundance. On the contrary, it is a realm of simplicity, indeed, of the simplicity of animals. Here bliss is defined ethically and justice is the code-word; this theme blossomed in Latin literature, particularly under the influence of Cynics and the like, as rejection and condemnation of the decadent luxury of real life.[16] This rejection led to the development of a peculiar ambiguity in the appreciation of, and accordingly in the 'setting' of the 'natural, wild existence'. When the natural, wild existence was portrayed as unbridled and inhuman, it was placed before the realm of Kronos/Saturnus, which brought moral standards, justice and civilisation. Alternatively the era of Kronos/Saturnus itself was the wild life, but then 'wild' had the sense of the simple, natural, but not bestial — a life without the complexities of civilisation.

As the geographic horizon expanded, Kronos moved ever further to the West,[17] where he was identified with similar deities, such as Saturnus. Eventually we find him on a utopian island west of Britannia, where he is represented as either asleep or in chains. On the other hand he was also placed to the East in Phrygia, asleep again.[18] In structural terms, a god sleeping and a god wearing chains are identical:[19] both gods are 'out of action'.

This highly selective survey offers a remarkably ambiguous, even contradictory, picture. Kronos is, on one hand, the god of an inhumanly cruel era without ethical standards; on the other he is the king of a Golden Age of abundance, happiness and justice. He is the loser who has been exiled, chained and enslaved, but also the great king *par excellence*, who has been liberated and rules supreme. His realm is thought to have existed either before historical times, or after time, i.e. in death. It was sometimes situated on the earth, sometimes deep down in the earth, sometimes at the edge of the world. It is possible to construct the following table of oppositions:

	Negative	Positive
Kronos as a person:	father-mutilator child-murderer cannibal tyrant	wise, great king

His rule:	lawlessness
	lack of moral standards
	unstable hierarchy
	struggle for power,
	   rebellion
		ideal situation
		materially: abundance
		land of Cockaigne
		no slavery
		ideologically: natural
		   order and justice
		peace
		simplicity

His present situation:	locked up, chained enslaved asleep: powerless	liberated or escaped a great king of blessed people

In addition the following oppositions beyond the categories of positive and negative can be set forth:

Place or time of Utopia:	**in illo tempore**
	irrevocably past
	
	out of reach
		still existing but not in
		   'this world':
		either in the hereafter
		   (for chosen people)
		or in far away outer
		     regions (e.g. the
		     West)
		**within reach, in a
		special sense**

Such a violent opposition within one and the same divine ambiance calls for an explanation. Explanations have been proposed, of course. They generally boil down to a denial of the seriousness of the contradictions. The difficulty of accepting such explanations, however, becomes clear from a review of the cult and the rites surrounding the god, in which exactly the same ambiguity exists.

2. Kronos: the Rite

'Kronos scheint im Kult keinen festen Platz zu haben, er is ein Schatten': thus Nilsson, unconsciously varying a statement by von Wilamowitz: 'Er ist eben ein Gott ausser Diensten, abgetan wie die rohe Urzeit.'[20]

    The evidence fully bears out the correctness of these statements.

A really old cult is attested only in Olympia, where Kronos' priests are called *hoi basilai* — a possible, but not certain, correlate of Kronos' kingship (*basileus*). We know of only one temple in Athens built by Pisistratos for Kronos and Rhea. The only known temple statue is the one of Lebadeia, belonging to the Trophonios sanctuary. In Athens, on the 15th of Elaphebolion (± April), Kronos was given a cake having twelve little globules on it. These few facts outline the cultic tableau:[21] a few further pieces of ritual data will be given below. Realising, on the other hand, that 'Kronion', as a month name as well as a city name[22] — the latter especially in Sicily — is quite common, one cannot but come to the conclusion that, in earlier times, Kronos must indeed have had a cultic significance that he later lost, perhaps after being ousted by a newly introduced generation of gods. The result is, to quote Nilsson (ibid.) once again: 'Er ist mythologisch, nicht kultisch.' This is, as I hope to show, a correct conclusion, having, however, implications reaching much further than was suspected by Nilsson, who was interested primarily in gods tangible in cult. The following short description of a number of rituals associated with Kronos does not contradict this conclusion, but rather, as will become clear, confirms it.

Kronia were celebrated on Rhodes on the sixth of Metageitnion (text: Pedageitnion). Porphyry (*On Abstinence* 2.54) tells of humans being sacrificed to Kronos during that festival.[23] Later, a condemned criminal was kept alive until the Kronia, and then taken outside the gates to Aristobule's statue, given wine to drink and slaughtered. From the date it has been concluded that this typical example of a scapegoat ritual springs from the Artemis cult and became associated with Kronos only later. This may quite well be true, although it is dangerous to build a case on a chance temporal coincidence. Important, however, is the fact that elsewhere as well, Kronos is associated specifically with bloody and cruel human sacrifices; the ancient attitude is summarised by Sophocles (*Andr.* fr. 126 Radt) as follows: 'Of old there is a custom among barbarians to sacrifice humans to Kronos.' Clearly this is about barbarians, as are other testimonia. Best known are the Phoenician–Punic human sacrifices, which are supposed to have been introduced by a former king, El/Kronos.[24] The Carthaginian god in whose huge bronze statue children were burnt to death also was identified with Kronos/Saturnus.[25] It was said that in Italy and

Sardinia, too, humans had been sacrificed to Saturnus[26] — probably just as legendary a fact as Istros' (*FGrH* 334 F 48) remark about Crete that the Kouretes in ancient times sacrificed children to Kronos, or the later reports by Christian authors about human sacrifices in Greece itself.

Surveying all these data, one is not surprised that in places Kronos stands as a *signum* for human sacrifice, bloody offering and even cannibalism. Side by side with the above-mentioned text by Sophocles stands, for instance, Euhemerus' view (Ennius *Euhemerus* 9.5) that Kronos and Rhea and the other people living then used to eat human flesh.

A more negative and gruesome picture hardly can be imagined. Therefore, the appearance of another, again utterly contrasting one is all the more striking. According to Empedocles, and in Pythagorean circles generally, Kronos is the very symbol of unbloody sacrifice.[27] The Athenian cake sacrifice is a good illustration of this,[28] and Athenaeus 3,110B informs us that by way of offering the Alexandrians used to put loaves of bread in Kronos' temple, from which everybody was allowed to eat. This peaceful and joyous aspect crops up in an almost hyperbolic form in the Attic celebration of the Kronia.[29] Apart from a short mention by Demosthenes 24.26, with mention of the date (12 Hekatombaion = ± August), we have two somewhat more detailed reports.

Plutarch *Moralia* 1098B: 'So too, when slaves hold the Kronia feast or go about celebrating the country Dionysia, you could not endure the jubilation and din.'
Macrobius *Saturnalia* 1.10.22:

Philochorus [*FGrH* 328 F 97] says that Cecrops was the first to build, in Attica, an altar to Saturn and Ops, worshiping these deities as Jupiter and Earth, and to ordain that, when crops and fruits had been garnered, heads of households everywhere should eat thereof in company with the slaves with whom they had borne the toil of cultivating the land, for it was well pleasing to the god that honour should be paid to the slaves in consideration of their labour. And that is why we follow the practice of a foreign land and offer sacrifice to Saturn with the head uncovered. (tr. P. V. Davies).

The former text merely says that slaves/servants had a festival with a banquet, during which they enjoyed themselves mightily, and which — in Plutarch's time at least — was celebrated in Attica at any rate.[30] The latter testimonium is more explicit.

Finally, the Roman poet Accius (*Ann.* fr. 3 M, Bae.; *Fr. poet. lat.* Morel p. 34) adds that most Greeks, but the Athenians in particular, celebrated this festival: 'in all fields and towns they feast upon banquets elatedly and everyone waits upon his own servants. From this had been adopted as well our own custom of servants and masters eating together in one and the same place.'

Some scholars have contended that Accius projected the attested Roman custom of masters waiting upon their slaves at the Saturnalia, to the Greek Kronia, about which we know only that masters and slaves dined together. However, there is no ground for such scepticism. First, our other sources are much too scanty. Secondly, when masters regale their servants, this implies naturally some sort of reversal of normal functions, whether this is ritually demonstrated or not. A number of closely related 'Saturnalian' festivals in Greece show that freedom of slaves could indeed take various forms. In Troizen, for instance, the slaves were for one day allowed to play knuckle-bones with the citizens, and the masters treated the servants to a meal, possibly during a Poseidon festival. During the Thessalian festival of the Peloria, dedicated to Zeus Peloros, strangers were offered a banquet, prisoners freed of their fetters; slaves lay down at dinner and were waited upon by their masters, with full freedom of speech. At Hermes festivals on Crete, too, the slaves stuffed themselves and the masters served. Ephoros (*FGrH* 70 F 29) even knows of a festival in Kydonia on Crete where the serfs, the Klarotes, could lord it in the city while the citizens stayed outside. The slaves were also allowed to whip the citizens, probably those who had recklessly remained in the city or re-entered it. In connection with this, Bömer[31] has drawn attention to a formerly neglected datum, to wit, that on a specific day of the Spartan Hyakinthia 'the citizens treated all their acquaintances and their own slaves to a meal'. The Hermes Charidotes festival on Samos, during which stealing and robbing were permitted, presents a slightly different situation, because the specific master-slave relationship was not involved. More examples could be given, but these suffice.

Before summarising our findings about the ritual, there must be one more word about iconography.[32] Except on coins, representations of Kronos with uncovered head are very rare for the older period. The usual type of statue is of a seated Zeus-like god, his head leaning on a hand. The back of the head is almost always covered by a fold of the robe. This type occurs as early as the fifth century BC, and is found quite frequently until late in the Roman period. Even the ancients could only guess at the meaning of this headgear, which was unusual in Greece: 'Some claim his head is covered because the beginning of time is unknown' — such is the guess of the Vatican Mythographer III.1.5, alluding to the identification of Kronos/Chronos. Modern scholars have considered grief as a possible reason — sadness at his downfall and oppression — or the secrecy of his plans. No unanimous conclusion has been reached, however. We are told several times that the feet of the Roman statue of Saturnus were shackled (or wrapped in woollen bandages) and that on his holiday the statue was freed of its chains.[33] Apollodorus of Athens (*FGrH* 224 F 118) states that this was also a Greek custom with regard to the Kronos statue, although Macrobius, who quotes him, incorrectly dates this festival in December. Some modern scholars, including Jacoby,[34] interpret this statement as referring to Roman customs that this author of the second century BC supposedly knew of. In my opinion it is at least equally probable that he was familiar with such a custom from his own Greek surroundings, perhaps in particular from Alexandria, where he lived and from where our knowledge of other new elements comes as well. A Kronos/Saturnus in chains is, for that matter, a topos in the later magical papyri.[35]

This survey of cultic and ritual aspects has brought us to the conclusion that Kronos is just as ambiguous a figure in ritual as in myth. For ritual, too, we can draw up a diagram of opposing positive and negative elements.

	Negative	Positive
Type of sacrifice:	pre-eminently bloody	bloodless sacrifices, cakes, loaves of bread
Atmosphere of Kronos rite:	frightening ritual of homicide, infanticide: *extreme tension*	exulted celebrations with unlimited freedom and abundance: *extreme relaxation*
Iconography	head covered (= ?) in shackles all year long	freed from shackles on holiday

(the last possibly, but not conclusively, Greek)

131

3. Kronos: the Contradiction

It has become clear that oppositions within the myth of Kronos have close correspondences in ritual. On one hand, there is a complex of failing standards and lawlessness, patricide and infanticide, cannibalism, rebellion and enslavement: *Kronos ankulometes*. On the other hand, there is the complex of peace and natural well-being, material abundance and ethical justice, the breaking of chains: *Kronos megas*.

Either of the two complexes is in itself quite familiar: the negative one shows the characteristics typical of chaos, which, as we will see, in many cultures has been visualised as a primordial era before the introduction of human culture, but which in certain situations can return to the real world for a short while.[36] The positive complex presents the usual image of Utopia where — not always, but often — a natural abundance eliminates social tensions and suppressions, sometimes eliminates even the existing hierarchy. The bewildering thing about Kronos is that, in his surroundings, these extreme oppositions are united in one greater unit — without, however, being reconciled. This has naturally not escaped scholars' attention. 'Diese Vorstellungen sind unvereinbar,' von Wilamowitz wrote in 1929; 'Ce Cronos, père de Zeus . . . est un personnage divin fort ambigu,' Vidal-Naquet wrote fifty years later.[37]

That the ancients also observed the contradictions — consciously or unconsciously — is apparent from a great number of details. The stock epithet *ankulometes* is usually interpreted as meaning 'plotting crooked, devious things', but side by side with this it is also explained as 'sensibly deliberating on crooked matters'.[38] The opposition between bloody and bloodless sacrifices also leads to contradictions: Athenaeus' report of the Alexandrians' sacrificing loaves of bread to Kronos violently clashes with Macrobius' information (*Sat.* 1.7.14 vv) that it was the Alexandrians in particular who made bloody sacrifices to their Kronos (and Serapis), in a typically Greek manner. Comparable to this is the fact that in the Athenian inscription mentioned above the unbloody sacrifice of a round cake to Kronos is immediately followed by a sacrifice of a piece of pastry in the shape of an ox (unbloody, but referring to bloody matters).[39] Cheiron's status ever since Pherecydes[40] as the son of Kronos, is in my opinion,

132

based on this ambiguity: Cheiron, too, is a creature midway between human and animal, having elements of the wild, bestial and uncontrolled (especially when connected with the centaurs as a group) and also having elements of culture and justice: Cheiron teaches the art of healing and other arts, and already in Homer is called 'the most righteous of the centaurs' (*Il.* 11.832).

In antiquity, too, people noticed the paradox and sometimes tried to get rid of it, for instance by condemning and ignoring Kronos' negative aspects. Modern scholars dislike contradictions even more, perhaps. One of the commonest modern mechanisms for explaining contradictions is to call them anomalies that developed accidentally, either under the influence of foreign cultures or as a result of the gradual clustering within Greece of initially quite unrelated traditions. Furthermore, an internal evolution and deformation is also possible. Pohlenz, for instance, searches for a solution to his problem: 'das goldene Zeitalter . . . passt schlecht genug zu dem Frevler Kronos', in a merging of different traditions: the mythical one involving an evil Kronos supposedly was combined later with the merry agricultural festival that was assumedly specifically Attic. Marót — '*Kronos ankulometes* auch sonst scharf von *Kronos megas* zu trennen' — even perceives two completely independent original Kronos figures, namely, a cosmogonic and a vegetative dying and rising god.[41] The discovery of the Kumarbi poem, of course, provided the 'oriental excuse': this horrid tale allegedly had nothing to do with the original Kronos and simply was ascribed to him later on. Many more such 'solutions' have been proposed. Gods, myths and rites are — and on this issue I would not leave any doubt — products of age-long traditions showing development, deformations, assimilations and amalgamations. The multi-faceted Apollo is one example;[42] an opposition within one name, Zeus Olympios and Zeus Meilichios, another. Nevertheless, the analysis of such historical processes offers a solution of very restricted relevance only. For assimilation and identification do not occur arbitrarily; there must have been affinities or similarities encouraging the process: why was Kronos the one to be identified with Kumarbi? Undoubtedly not merely because he was a fading god, who suffered no damage from this nasty imputation. In other words, the question should not concern primarily the *how*, but the *why*. More relevant is, however, the following: even if a diversity in the origins of various elements can be shown, the most important problem remains: the explanation of the fact that the Greeks since Hesiod — in whose works the opposition, as we have seen, is already fully present — not only tolerated the clashing components of the Kronos figure for centuries, but apparently deliberately enlarged them: we find specifications about Kronos as god of the human sacrifice in the same period in which Kronos was given additional significance as the god of Cockaigne in comedy and as gentle king of a realm of peace in philosophy. Any explanation is in this case only entitled to that name if it accepts the *coincidentia oppositorum* as a structural datum and makes it the core of the problem.

Matters are complicated by the fact that there is no unanimity about the development of the isolated complexes either. Golden Age and Attic Kronia evidently belong together as far as atmosphere is concerned. But how did they come together? The explanations of the older studies, practically without exception, presuppose a development. The myth came first, then the ritual, says von Wilamowitz: 'Die Menschen wollen für einen Tag das selige Leben führen, wie es im goldenen Zeitalter unter Kronos gewesen war.' No, the ritualists riposte, 'antike Feste entstehen nicht auf diese Weise' (Deubner, as well as Nilsson, Ziehen, Jacoby, Bömer and others), and Ed. Meyer explains that the image of the Golden Age arose precisely from this type of festival.[43] The festival itself, it was unanimously decided, belongs to a widespread genre that entitles oppressed people, servants or slaves, to one single day of relaxation, for reasons of humanity for instance.[44] At any rate it is certainly not connected only with the harvest, and therefore it could be associated with various gods.

The very same 'which was first' question applies to the negative aspects of the myth and ritual. According to Gruppe, the myth of the child-devourer was fabricated after the example of the ritual child and human sacrifices; Pohlenz, on the other hand, sees things exactly the other way round: because the myth was familiar, Kronos came to be associated with all kinds of human sacrifices.[45] Indeed the only Greek human sacrifice, viz. the one on Rhodes, originally belonged to Artemis.

All these views involve a fundamental assumption of the interrelatedness of myth and rite, but none of them even approaches a meaningful interpretation of the Kronos complex as a whole. The only theory from this period (the early twentieth century) that does aspire emphatically after that goal has one drawback: it is untenable. Frazer[46] has integrated the whole of the Kronos myth and ritual complex in his comprehensive theory of the dying and rising god/king of the year: Kronos is a vegetative dying and rising god. His festival therefore must be considered a celebration surrounding the turn of the year; the human sacrifices are explained as a substitute for regicide. Under this theory the dark and the bright aspects are integrated in one comprehensive picture. Frazer is, however, a fallen colossus and although elements of his general theory have certainly remained of value, Andrew Lang's attack[47] on the Kronos theory in particular is irrefutably final. The Kronia are not evidently harvest festivals in all cases, Kronos' sickle does not necessarily make him a vegetation god, merry slaves' feasts are not connected only with Kronos, etc., etc. The golden bough is broken, and yet Frazer was the first to take the contradiction seriously and to try to integrate it in a holistic explanation. Without Frazer, the following passage by Karl Meuli,[48] who actually uses a different model of interpretation, would not have been conceivable: 'Bei den gefesselten Göttern zeigt sich der Zusammenhang von Leben und Tod, von Glück und Grauen; sie sind böse und gefährlich, darum bindet man sie mit Ketten fest; und sie sind wenn ihnen die Fesseln gelöst sind, gnädig und gütig und schenken den Menschen das Glück.' Here too is a serious approach to the contradiction, but it departs from another point: the festival of unchained gods and men. For 'Immer gilt für die Menschen, was für ihre Götter gilt; beim Fest sind auch sie gelöst und vom Zwang des Alltags befreit.' Whereas the myth and ritual complex of the dying and rising vegetation was Frazer's frame of reference, Meuli concentrates on the link with death. We will not follow him in this view any more than we followed Frazer. Death symbolism does play a part, but is not the centre of interpretation. The complex of chaining and being unchained, rather, will be the starting point for our interpretation of the *coincidentia oppositorum*, and, behind it, of the connection between Kronos' myth and ritual.

4. The Festival of Reversal

The Kronia belong to the 'Saturnalia-like' festivals, as has often been stated. As in the case of carnival or one of its medieval equivalents, 'la fête des fous', social and hierarchical roles are reversed: the fool is king and rules at will. Under his rule, humans turn into animals, women play men's roles; children command their teachers, slaves their masters. We find freedom for women at other Greek festivals; at the Kronia and related festivals it is the slaves who are free. They sometimes are literally unfettered, then treated to a banquet, often even waited upon by their masters. There is freedom of speech, in Rome even the freedom of putting the masters on trial; also in Rome, slaves take the whip to freemen, or, something more peaceful but no less unusual, play knuckle-bones with them. Drinking wine is sometimes explicitly permitted; this is quite contrary to conventions, for slaves do not drink wine, or at best drink it only in scanty measure.

Two aspects are combined here: on one hand the reversal of roles, on the other the elation caused by the collective abundance of food and drink, summarised by Macrobius *Saturnalia* 1.7.26: *tota servis licentia permittitur*. In modern literature, this kind of festival is known under different names: 'periods of licence' (Frazer), 'rituals of rebellion' (Gluckman), 'rituals of conflict' (Norbeck), 'legitimate rebellion' (Weidkuhn), side by side with German terms such as 'legale Anarchien', 'Ventilsitten' or 'Ausnahmezeiten'.[49] The emphasis on the legitimate deviance is linked to the type of functionalistic explanation attached to it. For a short time, oppressed social groups are given an opportunity to release pent-up aggression in a game of reversed roles; thus the possible dangers of a real revolution are neutralised. This is in fact the 'no-nonsense' interpretation of Nilsson and Bömer, and this function of the festival has sometimes been recognised as such by the participants themselves; for instance an ex-slave typified it in 1855 as a 'safety-valve to carry off the explosive elements'.[50] Nowadays more emphasis is laid on the demonstrative and symbolic aspects: via ritual, the conflict is made clear in an enlarged but symbolic form, and the real conflict is encapsulated. 'The supreme ruse of power is to allow itself to be contested ritually in order to consolidate itself more effectively' (G. Balandier).[51]

This explanation, useful though it may be, does not cover the total range of the phenomena. At least equal attention should be paid to the legitimising effect. The established order is confirmed by the absurdity of the world turned topsy-turvy. A precursor in this view was Gluckman,[52] according to whom these rites 'give expression, in a reversed form, to the normal rightness of a particular kind of social order'. Their main function is to attain 'cohesion in the wider society'. Of course, both functions can reinforce each other, but they are still distinguishable: neutralising potential aggression is not identical to legitimating the social *status quo* by means of the absurd. Or as B. Sutton Smith[53] says about 'playing': 'We may be disorderly in games either because we have an overdose of order *or* because we have something to learn through being disorderly.'

In point of fact, both aspects often exist side by side in different forms: the dissociative one acted out in the conflict of role reversal, the integrating and legitimising one present not only in the role-playing but also demonstratively so in the *collective* and *egalitarian* experience of the festival as image of abundance. Whereas earlier interpreters of the carnival laid special emphasis on the 'safety-valve effect', recent scholars pay attention to the solidarising and legitimising functions too.[54] Reversal rituals may function in very different contexts[55] and are by no means restricted to agricultural rituals (Frazer) or death symbolism (Meuli). The religious anchorage is quite variable too, i.e. there is not necessarily a connection with any one specific reversal god. Indeed, gods need not be involved at all.

The theories mentioned above deal with categories of social and socio-psychological processes, a level at which legitimation and solidarising take place via general consensus about the rightness of the established order. This is the field in which generations of sociologists since Durkheim have operated, and the field in which, in their opinion, religion was a function too. Many of them, however, including convinced functionalists, have withdrawn from this extreme point of view: 'the functional explanation of religion does not explain religion, rather it explains a dimension of society' — thus M. E. Spiro, and P. Berger,[56] too, has once more brought our attention to 'substantive versus functional definitions of religion.' 'All societies are constructions in the face of chaos. The constant possibility of anomic terror is actualized whenever legitimations obscuring the precariousness are threatened or collapse,' Berger and Luckman[57] write, and in such situations, or more regularly in ceremonially created periods of crisis — literally: separation between two eras, situations, periods — a 'deep legitimacy' is required, referring to a mythical reality outside ours, 'the other reality', lying outside history and space, an eternal truth that existed before time but still exists behind it and behind our reality, and occasionally mingles with ours in 'periods of exception'.[58]

Seen from this perspective, the reversal ritual offers another, deeper meaning. Although not linked to any particular type of festival or sector of social life, as I have said, reversal rituals are found predominately in the ceremonies accompanying a critical passage in the agricultural or social year, moments of stagnation and rupture at which chaos threatens, e.g. initiation, festivals of the dead, and in particular the eating or offering of the first fruits of the harvest or the first wine as a recurrent, or the accession of a new ruler as an incidental, incision in the progress of time. One or more such events may develop into one or more regular New Year celebrations,[59] in which various elements are united into a fixed pattern. Eliade and Lanternari[60] in particular have given a complete description of this 'grande festa'. It is essential that the caesura between old and new is experienced as a disruption of social life, a vacuum that is filled by a temporary return of the mythical primordial era from before Creation or before the birth of the present culture.[61] This invariably happens in images of chaos, dissociation, dissolution of order, a topsy-turvy world, e.g. a temporary abolition of kingship and laws. There are orgies in the sense of drinking bouts as well as in the sexual sense, ritual fights between two groups, return and welcome of the dead. *Rites de séparation* may precede (purification, expulsion of the *pharmakos* (scapegoat), bloody sacrifices, extinguishing of fire), *rites d'aggrégation* follow: the wearing of new clothing, lighting of fire, renewal of kingship, the 'fixing of the fate' for the coming year. The chaos that is acted out ritually is often anchored mythically in primeval chaos, for instance in the image of the struggle between creator-god and chaos-monster, or of deluge and consequent re-creation. This primal chaos manifests itself as a temporary elimination of all contours, a return to a state undefined by bounds and moral standards, expressing itself in the creation of monsters and monstrosities; a period of total freedom (= total lawlessness as well as total abundance).[62] This lends to the festival an atmosphere of utter ambivalence: sadness, anxiety, despair because of the catastrophe of the disrupted order; elation, joy and hope because of the liberation from chafing bonds, and the pleasant experience of temporary abundance. Thus the reversed world of society in crisis is an image of the cosmic chaos of mythical times. Both modern approaches to the reversal festival, the functionalist one and the cosmic-religious one, will contribute to an interpretation of the contradictions of the Kronos myth and ritual complex.

5. The *licentia* of the Kronia and Related Festivals

5.1 *The Paradox of the Impossible Harmony*

Like the period of licence in anthropology, the Kronia (and similar festivals) have two aspects. The first one is the 'orgiastic' aspect of the shared experience of merry-making and abundance in an atmosphere of dissolution of hierarchy, which includes a component of strong cohesion and solidarity.[63] Not only the slave, but everyone experiences the liberation as temporary relaxation based on equality. Here, therefore, *harmony* prevails. This harmony, however, was experienced as unpleasantly ambiguous as we learn from two closely related literary representations of 'Der Traum von der grossen Harmonie':[64] comedy and Utopia.

Just like the Saturnalian festival, comedy is pre-eminently a solidarising medium.[65] Collective laughter is cohesive and marks the boundaries of the cognitive and affective territory of a group.[66] In Old Comedy, the representation of the land of Cockaigne, generally as image of the golden primeval era, occasionally as a vision of the future, is a standard theme. In this imagery, the earth bears fruit of its own accord and the food offers itself ready cooked.[67] Quite frequently this *automaton* implies the superfluity of labour and consequently of slaves, in Aristophanes' *Birds* 760–5 in passing, in Krates' *Wild animals (PCG* IV F 16 Kassel/Austin) as the central theme of a discussion. This image also is found in philosophers such as Empedocles (B128 Diels/Kranz) and Plato, *Republic* 271 D-272 B.[68] In complete freedom there was complete equality and complete abundance. In King Kronos' time 'people even gambled with loaves of bread' (Kratinos *PCG* IV F 176 Kassel/Austin), and Telekleides *Amphictyones* fr. 1 Kock, describes a country where there were indeed slaves, who, however, did not work (!) but 'played at dice with pigs' vulvae and other delicacies'. That is utter freedom, but it is actually too good to be true.

139

Frequently, therefore, a few uncomfortable afterthoughts are found in the same context.

Pherecydes fr. 10 Kock describes a slaveless society, but also makes it perfectly clear that in consequence the women have to work their fingers to the bone in order to get the work done, and the fields are neglected so that people starve (idem fr. 13). In Herodotos 6.137,[69]Hekataeus for the same reason makes the slaveless primeval situation end negatively via the labour of women and children. And in his utopian scheme for women, Aristophanes grants everybody equal property, but does not manage this without the labour of slaves. In other words: abundance, equality and abolition of slavery are all very well, but only for a short time, in an imaginary world. In such a chaos, reality would disintegrate.

Herodotos 3.18 relates an Ethiopian custom of laying 'a table of Helios': at night boiled meat is taken to a meadow and during the day everybody is allowed to eat it. The natives, however, say that it is the earth itself that time and again produces this food. Here again the *automaton*/luxury motif is found in combination with the notion of equality. The sacrificial loaves in the temple of Kronos in Alexandria, which everybody was allowed to eat, come to mind. Such images bring us to the concept of Utopia, which also is related to the Saturnalia.[70] Here, too, elements of the *automaton* and easy living prevail: they are found as early as Homer's land of the Phaeacians, in the tales of the Hyperboreans, of Iamboulos' Sun Islands and of Euhemerus' Panchaia. In the latter two, slavery is absent. But these are Utopias of a fairy-tale nature ('utopia d'evasione'), which by definition lie at the edge of or over the edge of the world, the *eschatiai*, an all but unreachable land, and at the same time a 'land of no return', like Elysium after death. But as soon as the political or social Utopia takes on a model function as 'utopia di ricostruzione'[71] and consequently is not absolutely inconceivable (Hippodamos, Plato, Aristotle), labour is indispensable and slavery a matter of course. In the Messianic Utopian vistas accompanying the accession of Roman emperors[72] we also find in great detail all the themes of abundance and *isonomia*, the annulment of debts and disappearance of poverty — all this sometimes summarised as a liberation from chains — but there is no question of a liberation of slaves. What is possible in the fairy-tale is undesirable in real life, it is even threatening. Lucian (*Saturn.* 33) says that equality is most pleasant at table, but that

Kronos grants this equality only during holidays (ibid. 30).

Such aspects of the Kronia point out a marked ambivalence in the Greek concept of harmony: the ideal of freedom and abundance is unstable, it cannot last, because it carries the seed of real social anomie and anarchy. It is a dangerous game, just as was the dice-playing allowed to the slaves: on this day the relationships are open, the dice are thrown and there is the possibility that it is not the master but the slave who will win. This is equality no longer, it is the world turned upside down.

5.2 *The Paradox of the Festive Conflict*

The second socially functional aspect of the Kronia and related festivals is that of the reversal of roles. There is no harmony here; on the contrary there is intensified and formalised *conflict*: the hierarchy is turned the other way round. Cockaigne and the world reversed very frequently go hand in hand. *Adunata* often herald the coming of the Golden Age.[73] But the radical shifting of boundaries in role reversal offers not only greater boisterousness but also deeper disturbance: here, anarchy has a truly subversive character. Once again, comparisons with comedy and Utopia are enlightening.

The freedom of slaves in Old Comedy never implies their dominance. Aristophanes experiments to the very limit with reversal between the sexes, but he is extremely reticent on the topic of reversal between slaves and citizens. Slaves do not even assist in the revolution of women: 'De pouvoir servile, il n'est pas et il ne peut pas être question.'[74] The reason is evident: even as a comic scene, this image would meet with resistance: slave rebellion was a structurally feared phenomenon, and by no means an imaginary one.

One can even less expect, therefore, to find rule by slaves in Utopia. It is possible to imagine a reversed world, often transformed in images from the animal world in which the weak gain the victory, for instance in the chiliastic expectance of salvation, but slaves ruling society is a notion that can enter the heads only of slaves. As a matter of fact, Eunous, the leader of a slave revolt in Sicily, does call himself king and has his former masters wait upon him; the Circumcelliones have their carts pulled by their former lords.[75] This might have been *their* idea, but it certainly was not *the* idea. It is precisely the task of ritual, drama and wish-dream to

141

canalise and neutralise any excessive inclinations in this direction. The reversal of roles is supposed to legitimise its opposite, not itself.

Ritual is more direct than literary representation. It is understandable that ritual reversal, however necessary as a 'holiday' of limited duration, includes a strongly threatening component. Images of reversal may, as has been said, precede or accompany the Golden Age, but they also, and often, precede or accompany apocalyptic catastrophe. In strong contrast to the Messianic images of reversal during the early imperial era, the text of Tertullian *Apologeticum* 20: 'humble ones are raised, high ones are brought down' serves as an announcement not of the realm of bliss but of a period of chaos and catastrophe: 'justice becomes a rarity . . . the natural shapes are replaced by monsters', exactly as in Egyptian prophecies and elsewhere.[76] Reversal, therefore, may point in two directions: to total freedom = abundance, and to total freedom = lawlessness, chaos. One of the implications is that rites of rebellion carry the seeds of real revolution. Aeneas Tacticus 22.17 states that festivals are the most frequent occasions of revolution in the state,[77] and that goes *a fortiori* for those festivals that carry an element of ritual rebellion, as is illustrated by the rich tradition of carnival and revolution in particular.[78]

In both aspects of the socially legitimate *licentia*, the harmonious and the conflictive, we observe a violent contradiction: on one hand they aim at relaxation by means of laughter, elation and abundance, on the other they refer to the impossible and the undesirable: chaos, revolution, and, in close alliance with these, murder and manslaughter, lawlessness, the disintegration of society. What is a social ambiguity here, has been made the structual theme in the cosmic-mythical model.

6. Kronos as King of Primeval Chaos

Like other cultures, Athens had several New Year festivals. One of these, the Anthesteria festival,[79] shows an all but complete set of characteristics of the 'grande festa': the opening of the wine-jars (*primitiae* situation), *licentia* in the form of ridicule and abuse, collective wine-drinking in which children and slaves were allowed to share, a sacred wedding of the king. In addition to these joyous aspects there are threatening elements: the arrival of Kares or

Keres, primeval inhabitants or ghosts of the dead who are given a warm welcome and subsequently wished away, banquets for the dead, the temporary closing down of the temples in an atmosphere of doom. In all respects, clearly, there is a temporary return of chaos in its two aspects, mythically represented in the commemoration of deluge and re-creation. The official New Year's Day, however, fell in midsummer, in the month of Hekatombaion, formerly called Kronion. Two veritable New Year festivals, the Synoikia and the Panathenaea, are preceded by two festivals that have the typical structure of the incision festival, marking the period 'in between': the Skira and the Kronia.[80] The Skira on 12 Skirophorion shows the following characteristics: an *apopompe* of the priests and the primeval king out of the city — in the myth the king is killed; women, at liberty to call meetings, take over men's roles; boisterous fun and playing at dice; a sacrifice of an ox, which is called *disertis verbis bouphonia*, 'murder'. A complex, therefore, in which joy and gloom unite in role reversals and the abolition of the normal social relationships.

These festivals are not connected with Kronos, but the Kronia festival in which, as we have seen, role reversal and *licentia* dominate, and which falls between Skira and the New Year festivals, is emphatically dedicated to Kronos, in the month that originally bore his name. In light of the cosmic-religious interpretation of the festivals surrounding the turn of the year, several of our earlier observations suddenly take on an understandable and structural meaning. 'Kronos ist mythologisch, nicht kultisch', Nilsson said. He is more right than he realised; indeed, this statement touches the heart of the matter. During the festivals mentioned — although this is not known of the Kronia — one of the expressions of stagnation of the 'normal' existence is the closing down of the temples: the contact with the gods currently ruling is broken, the pre-Olympian era returns temporarily. It is precisely Kronos' mythical character as god of a primordial time that explains his presence in the un-cultic vacuum between the times. He is primeval chaos in person, in its dual aspect of freedom as a joy and freedom as a threat. Lacking fixed boundaries, there is a high 'entropy'. The unstable equilibrium may be upset any time. Ritually, this is expressed by, among other things, the freedom to play dice and gamble; in this chaos between times, fate still must be determined: the 'fixing of the fate' in Babylon is an annual re-creation, in Italy Fortuna Primigenia reigns when Jupiter is still *puer*.[81] Everything is still unsettled, as is the question of who will be boss: slave or master. In Greece, too, this era before history or this time between the times, is characterised by 'abnormal' creatures which do not fall in natural categories: Kronos' era is the period of giants, creatures with a hundred hands, monsters and Cyclopes. The Thessalian Peloria festival — a typical reversal festival — refers to mythical giants from the primeval era.[82] As 'masks' they may return temporarily in the period of crisis between the times. In fact this is a variation of the return of the dead, who also belong to another time and another reality: the world of the dead, too, is 'upside down'[83] and shows the ambivalence of 'dämonische Bedrohung oder die eschatologische Verheissung' (B. Gladigow).[84] In the matter of the Kares or Keres the two images, primeval creatures and the dead, seem to intermingle.

Kronos is the god in chains: already in Hesiod the terms 'binding' and 'fettering' are typically connected with his myth. His statue is 'chained', perhaps already in the Hellenistic period, certainly in Rome. Kronos does exist, but only in mythical times: before the present reality (during the primeval era), or after it (death), or at the outermost edges of this reality (the *eschatiai*). He is either a prisoner or asleep. Without being able to go into details I interpret his representations with covered head as follows: as always in the Greek–Roman world, covering or wrapping up the head indicates that the person concerned is (temporarily) withdrawn from the present reality, is in (or in contact with) 'the other reality'.[85] This is the essence of Kronos. His era, however, returns once more in the chaos of the year festival: he is unchained, he wakes up or he is revived and again assumes kingship for a limited period: the return of the *basileus*, a term and a concept that for Greek and certainly for Athenian ears carries the primordial connotation of the beginning of time,[86] as elsewhere, too, the return of the wish-time is closely connected with the figure of a king (the return of the 'sleeping' king, slave risings, Eunous, etc., *Saturnalium princeps*, *rex*; Prins Carnaval). His rule refers to the dual freedom of unlimited abundance and abolition of the established hierarchy on one hand, and of the absence of law and standards, and of rebellion, on the other. All this is expressed by the mythical and ritual images that we have described in the first part of this study, the utopian images of abundance and *euphoria* and the dystopical ones of the absence of moral standards, inhumanity and rebellion.

7. Conclusions

Our conclusions can be expressed concisely, because they are in fact obvious from the foregoing. We have asked how we can explain the violent contradictions in Kronos' myth and ritual if we do not content ourselves with the unsatisfactory emergency-solutions that resort to the fortuities of derivation, acculturation and evolution. Our solution, to which, indeed, others have given the first impulses,[87] is that the contradiction between the joyous and the frightening aspects of the Kronos complex is a structural characteristic of the god and his religious context. The explanation of this lies in his function as god of the periods of reversal and chaos. We have found that there are ambiguities on two levels. In the functionalistic view, the legitimate anarchy nears the limits of the permissible. The collective culinary orgy as well as, *a fortiori*, the reversed hierarchy contains the seeds of the socially impossible and undesirable. The oxymoron of euphoria and panic reaches a paroxysm in the Rhodian Kronia: the victim is given wine to drink and then murdered. In the cosmic-religious view, on the other hand, abundance and role reversal appear to be images of the renewed experience of primeval chaos that is Utopia and dystopia at once: the relaxation of the banquets of the Golden Age under Kronos in one and the same image as the 'sardonic' tension of Kronos' Thyestian repasts.[88] This means that on both levels the contradiction is a structural characteristic of Kronos' myth and ritual and that, therefore, attempts to soften the contradiction or 'render it harmless' via an exclusive appeal to historical development are not only superfluous but unjustified.

Our main question concerned the relationship between myth and ritual. How are we to see this relationship in the case at hand and to what extent is mutual dependence present here? W. B. Kristensen wrote long ago: 'Saturnus was a slave himself.'[89] He was berated for his folly and praised for his courage.[90] The brachylogy of this phrasing must lead inevitably to misunderstandings. None the less it refers directly to the question we have asked ourselves. Is the mythical 'unchaining' of Kronos a projection of the slave's freedom at festivals such as the Kronia? Or, on the other hand, was the myth of the Golden Age the example for the relaxation of the Kronia festivals? Furthermore, how are we, then, to interpret the dependence of the dark and cruel aspects of myth and rite: was human sacrifice the example of or an imitation of Kronos' mythical atrocities?

It will be clear by now that there can be no question of such a one-sided dependence of myth and rite, in any direction. By no means do I deny that the myth and ritual complex we have described is a crystallised product of processes to which many influences — non-Greek as well as Greek — have contributed and whose details escape us. But the tenets of anthropology and comparative religion enable us to design a hypothesis about the fundamental connection between the mythical and ritual components underlying this process of assimilation and evolution.

Our starting point is the statement that Kronos, for whatever reason, disappeared from active cult and became a 'mythical' god, and that this god *consequently* was considered to be a representative of the mythical era before history proper, which began with Zeus and the Olympians. Given this essential point, this kernel was open to connections with two chains of association, in principle independent but psychologically closely related, with regard to the mythical character of this primeval era and the ritual experiencing of the same atmosphere at some points of stagnation during the year. Both these associations are characterised by the phrase 'absence of order'. Mythically, the primeval era is represented in many cultures as chaos of two types: a positive, Utopian one and a negative one — the catastrophic annihilation of human values. Equally, the absence of order is expressed ritually on all sides by feasts of abundance on one hand and reversal of roles on the other. Here, 'abnormality' may lead to associations with murder in the form of human sacrifice. Both myth and rite 'say' the same thing: the Utopian *cannot*, the dystopian *must not* exist 'in reality'. In myth, this is expressed by the projection of these images on the *eschatiai* of time and space, Kronos' mythical territory. In ritual it is expressed by realising the impossible for just a few hours and thus underlining its exceptional character: the relaxation and reversal are indeed subservient to society's well-functioning, but as images of either the impossible or the undesirable and therefore as exceptions. Whereas such festivals are understood widely as a temporary return of chaos — and show by their nature every characteristic of it — in Greece it was natural to associate them with Kronos' mythical era, which was thought to return for one day.

All this justifies the conclusion that we do have in this complex, indeed, an example of correspondence between myth and rite in 'structure and atmosphere', and in such a way that both 'symbolic processes deal with the same type of experience in the same affective mode', and this *'pari passu'*, according to the postulates referred to in our introductory section.

Notes

1. In treating this subject I have had to restrict myself most severely. With regard to what is said here in the Introduction I must refer to my detailed review of the myth-and-ritual discussion in *Lampas, 17* (1984) 194 – 246, which is at present being edited for a book in English on 'Ambiguities in Greek and Roman Religion'. There, too, the sources of the quotations will be found; at the time I had not seen C. Calame's 'Le processus symbolique', *Doc. de travail. Centro Intern. Semiot. Lingu., 128/9* (1983). Furthermore I have confined myself in this article to essentials and kept the body of notes, especially, as concise as possible. An originally planned addition in the form of a discussion of the Roman Saturnalian festival also had to be omitted entirely for reasons of space.

2. Thus the recent formulation by F. Graf, *ZPE, 55* (1984) 254.

3. Materials and discussions in: M. Mayer, 'Kronos', in *Roscher Lexikon* II, 1 (1897) 1452 – 573; M. Pohlenz, 'Kronos und die Titanen', *Neue Jahrb., 19* (1916) 549 – 94; idem, 'Kronos' in *RE* XI (1921) 1982 – 2018. Recent literature in W. Fauth, 'Kronos', in *Kleine Pauly* 3 (1979) 355 – 64. These authors are cited henceforth by name and year only.

4. A structuralist analysis of the Hesiodic myth: M. Detienne and J.-P. Vernant, *Les ruses de l'intelligence. La mètis des Grecs* (Paris, 1974) 62 – 103.

5. See M. L. West, *Hesiod. Works and Days* (Oxford 1978); W. J. Verdenius, *A Commentary on Hesiod Works and Days, vv 1 – 382* (Leiden, 1985) ad loc.

6. The texts in *ANET* 120 – 6. A short and recent treatment with extensive bibliography: Burkert, *S&H*, 18 – 22.

7. W. Burkert, 'Oriental Myth and Literature in the Iliad', in R. Hägg (ed.), *The Greek Renaissance of the Eighth Century B.C. Tradition and Innovation* (Stockholm, 1983) 51 – 6; Burkert, *OE*.

8. Even allowing for the differentiation in categories of cannibalism as suggested by Detienne, *Dionysos*, 136.

9. E.g. Plato, *Resp.* 2,377E – 378D; *Eutyphro* 5E – 6A; Cicero, *ND* 2,24,63ff.

10. See: *Lexikon des frühgriechischen Epos,* s.v.; Chantraine, *Dictionnaire étymologique de la langue grecque,* s.v.

11. Thus: J. E. Harrison, *Themis*, 2nd edn (Cambridge, 1927) 495; 'Kronos immer *basileus* genannt': M. P. Nilsson, *Geschichte der griechischen Religion* I, 3rd edn (Munich, 1967) 511 n 4. In Hesiod: *Th:* 462,476,486,491; *Erga* 111,169ff. More references in Pohlenz (1916) 558 and (1921) 1988; Mayer (1897) 1458; on the

regime of Kronos, 'das ja immer eine Königsherrschaft ist': B. Gatz, *Weltalter, goldene Zeit und sinnverwandte Vorstellungen* (Hildesheim, 1967) 134 and register A3a; A4b.

12. *Il.* 5.271; 14.192 and 243; Hes. *Th.* 168,459,473,495.

13. Cf. L. Gernet and A. Boulanger, *Le Génie grec dans la religion*, 2nd edn (Paris, 1970) 89.

14. The two most accessible surveys: A. O. Lovejoy and G. Boas, *Primitivism and Related Ideas in Antiquity* (Baltimore, 1935) 23–102; Gatz, *Weltalter*.

15. On these motifs see Gatz, *Weltalter*, 114ff and the literature cited below, note 67.

16. H. Hommel, 'Das hellenische Ideal vom einfachen Leben', *Studium Generale, 11* (1958) 742ff; R. Visscher, *Das einfache Leben. Wort und Motivgeschichtliche Untersuchungen zu einem aktuellen Thema* (Göttingen, 1965).

17. See Pohlenz (1921) 1998ff.

18. Kronos was often assimilated with divinities of Asia Minor: K. Meuli, *Gesammelte Schriften* II (Basle and Stuttgart, 1975) 1076; L. Robert, *Hellenica, 7* (1949) 50–4.

19. W. B. Kristensen, 'De antieke opvatting van dienstbaarheid', *Med. Kon. Ak. Wet.* (1934) = idem, *Verzamelde bijdragen tot kennis der antieke godsdiensten* (Amsterdam, 1947) 215; I. Scheftelowitz, 'Das Schlingen und Netzmotiv', *Rel. Vers. Vorarb., 12* (1912) 8. On the other hand 'Wecken und Lösen sind verschiedene Bilder für denselben religiösen Gedanken': Meuli, *Gesammelte Schriften* II, 1076.

20. Nilsson, *Griechischen Religion*, 511; U. v. Wilamowitz, 'Kronos und die Titanen', *Sitzber. Berlin* (1929) 38 = Wilamowitz, *Kleine Schriften*, 2nd edn, V,2 (Berlin, 1971) 157–83.

21. For full references and more details on the cult see: Pohlenz (1921) 1982–6. On the *popanon*: L. Deubner, *Attische Feste* (Berlin, 1932) 154.

22. Collected by Pohlenz (1921) 1984f; Nilsson, *Griechischen Religion*, 512; Wilamowitz, 'Kronos', 36; *RE*, s.v. *Kronion*.

23. It is irrelevant to my investigation whether this is indeed a historical human sacrifice or, more likely, a legendary sacrifice framed on the theme of the cruel myth, such as the case treated by A. Henrichs, 'Human Sacrifice in Greek Religion', in *Le Sacrifice dans l'antiquité* (Entretiens Hardt *27*, Geneva, 1981) esp. 222 n 6.

24. E.g. Philo of Byblos *ap.* Porph. *De abst.* 2.56; Euseb. *Praep. ev.* 1.38 d, 40 c; *Or. pro Const.* 13.

25. The *locus classicus*: Diod. 20,14,6. See M. Le Glay, *Saturne Africain* (Paris, 1966).

26. E.g. Dion. Hal. 1.38.2; Diod. 5.66.5; Demon in Schol. Hom. *Od.* 20.302; Suda, s.v. Σαρδάνιος γέλως on which see M. Pohlenz, *Berl. Phil. Wochenschr.* (1916) 949. Cf. D. Arnould, 'Mourir de rire dans 'l'Odyssée': les rapports avec le rire sardonique et le rire dément', *BAGB* (1985) 177–86.

27. See Pohlenz (1916) 553; (1921) 2009f for references.

28. On sacrificial cakes and bloodless sacrifices see A. Henrichs, 'The Eumenides and Wineless Libations in the Derveni Papyrus', in *Atti del XVII Congresso Int. di Papirologia*, II (Naples, 1984), 255–68, esp. 257–61.

29. This festival and related ceremonies of the 'Saturnalian' type both in Greece and Rome have been discussed many times. The most important discussions are: M. P. Nilsson, *Griechische Feste* (Berlin, 1906) 35–40, 393; F. Bömer, 'Untersuchungen über die Religion der Sklaven in Griechenland und Rom', III, *Abh. Ak. Mainz, Geistes- und Sozialw. Kl.* (1961) 415–37; H. Kenner, *Das Phänomen der verkehrten Welt in der griechisch-römischen Antike* (Klagenfurt, 1970) 87–95. I have not seen Ph. Bourboulis, *Ancient Festivals of the Saturnalian Type* (Thessalonica,

1964). A short summary: Burkert, *GR* 231f. On the Attic Kronia in particular: Deubner, *Attische Feste*, 152–5. In a recent informative article on 'Poseidon's Festival at the Winter Solstice', *CQ, 34* (1984) 1–16, 'N. Robertson curiously underestimates the fundamental meaning of role reversal both in festivals of Poseidon and in general.

30. Some scholars argue that the masters have retired from the festival by this late period (Nilsson *RE* 11 (1921) 1975f; Bömer, 'Die Religion der Sklaven', 417), or, even more ingeniously, 'Probably the masters only appeared for the first course or two . . .' (H. W. Parke, *Festivals of the Athenians* (London, 1977) 30), but it is equally possible that only the most conspicuous features have found a place in the reports.

31. Bömer, 'Die Religion der Sklaven', 179: Polykrates *ap.* Athen. 4,139 C ff (*FGrH* 588 F 1). All other references may be found in the literature cited above, n 29.

32. See the extensive discussions in Mayer (1897) 1549–73; Pohlenz (1921) 2014ff.

33. Macrob. *Sat.* 1.8.5; Min. Fel. 22.5; Stat. *Silv.* 1.6.4 (and commentary by Vollmer); Arnob. 4.24. Cf. Bömer, 'Religion der Sklaven', 425. On fettered gods in general see: G. A. Lobeck, *Aglaophamus* (Königsbergen, 1829) 275; Meuli, *Gesammelte Schriften* II, 1035–81; M. Delcourt, *Héphaistos ou la légende du magicien* (Paris, 1957) 18ff; 65ff.

34. *FGrH* Comm. 244 F 118, followed by Meuli, *Gesammelte Schriften* II, 1039 n 9.

35 A. Dieterich, *Abraxas* (Leipzig, 1891) 76ff.

36. On the symbolism of chaos see literature cited by H. S. Versnel, 'Destruction, *Devotio* and Despair in a Situation of Anomy: The Mourning for Germanicus in Triple Perspective', in G. Piccaluga (ed.) *Perennitas* (Rome, 1980) 591 n 209 and 594 n 216; M. Eliade, *Traité d'histoire des religions*, 2nd edn (Paris, 1964) Chs XI and XII, *passim*. Cf. below, note 76.

37. Wilamowitz, 'Kronos', 36; P. Vidal-Naquet, *Le Chasseur noir*, 2nd edn (Paris, 1983) 363.

38. References in note 10 above.

39. Deubner, *Attische Feste*, 154f; K. Marót, 'Kronos und die Titanen', *SMSR, 8* (1932) 48–82; 189–213, esp. 67 n 2.

40. Pherecydes in schol. Apoll. Rhod. 1.554; 2.1235; Pind. *Pyth.* 3.1ff; 4.115; *Nem.* 3.47; Apollod. 1.9; Verg. *Georg.* 3.92. Pan, too, is the son of Kronos in one tradition: Ph. Borgeaud, *Recherches sur le dieu Pan* (Rome 1979) 66f.

41. Pohlenz (1921) 2006; K. Marót, 'Kronos', 58 and 213.

42. See H. S. Versnel, 'Apollo and Mars one hundred years after Roscher', *Visible Religion, 4* (1986) 134–72.

43. Wilamowitz, 'Kronos', 37; Nilsson, *Griechischen Religion*, 514; other references in Bömer, 'Religion der Sklaven', 420 n 2; E. Meyer, *Kleine Schriften* II, 39ff.

44. Nilsson, *Griechischen Religion*, 36; Bömer, 'Religion der Sklaven', 422.

45. Pohlenz (1921) 1998, where other references can be found.

46. J. G. Frazer, *The Golden Bough* 3rd edn, III, 9ff; VI, 351ff; IX (Aftermath) 290ff.

47. A. Lang, *Magic and Religion* (London, 1901) 82ff. For (critical) views on Frazer in general see Versnel (above, note 1) 234 n 15 and 239 n 82.

48. Meuli, *Gesammelte Schriften* II, 1034f.

49. For more literature on rites of reversal see Versnel, 'Destruction', 582ff; idem (above, note 1) 241 n 99; 242 n 115.

50. F. Douglass, *My Bondage and my Freedom* (New York, 1855) 253ff and the

comments by E. Genovese, *Roll, Jordan, Roll* (New York, 1974) 577ff, both cited by J. N. Bremmer, 'Myth and Ritual in Ancient Rome: the Nonae Capratinae' in J. N. Bremmer and N. M. Horsfall, *Studies in Roman Myth and Mythography* (London, 1986). A. C. Zijderveld, *Reality through a Looking-glass* (London, 1982) demonstrates the same awareness in medieval carnival-clubs.

51. G. Balandier, *Political Anthropology* (Harmondsworth, 1972) 41. Cf. I. M. Lewis, *Social Anthropology in Perspective* (Harmondsworth, 1976) 142, with interesting parallels of modern 'feasts of fools'. Similar views on chiliastic movements: A. F. C. Wallace, *Religion: An Anthropological View* (New York, 1966); W. E. Mühlmann, *Nativismus und Chiliasmus. Studien zur Psychologie, Soziologie und historischer Kasuistik der Umsturzbewegungen* (Berlin, 1961).

52. M. Gluckman, *Custom and Conflict in Africa* (Oxford, 1959) 109 – 36 from which I quote; idem, *Order and Rebellion in Tribal Africa* (London, 1963) 110 – 36. His first remarks: *An Analysis of the Sociological Theories of B. Malinowski* (Oxford, 1949) 16.

53. B. Sutton Smith, 'Games of Order and Disorder' as quoted by V. W. Turner in B. A. Babcock (ed.), *The Reversible World* (Ithaca and London, 1978) 294.

54. Safety-valve: e.g. in P. Burke, *Popular Culture in Early Modern Europe* (London, 1978) 202ff; N. Z. Davies, *Society and Culture in Early Modern France* (London, 1975) 122ff. The aspect of legitimation: *inter al.* in Zijderveld, *Reality* and H. Pleij, *Het gilde van de Blauwe Schuit. Literatuur, volksfeest en burgermoraal in de late middeleeuwen*, 2nd edn (Amsterdam, 1983) 63, 87, 241f; N. Schindler, 'Karneval, Kirche und die verkehrte Welt', *Jahrb. f. Volkskunde*, NF *7* (1984) 9 – 57. For some specific cases see: A. H. Galt, 'Carnival on the Island of Pantellaria', *Ethnology, 12* (1973) 325 – 39; D. Gilmore, 'Carnaval in Fuenmayor: Class Conflict and Social Cohesion in an Andalusian Town', *Journ. Anthrop. Res.*, *32* (1975) 331 – 49; L. Barletta, *Il carnevale del 1764 a Napoli. Protesta e integrazione in uno spazio urbano* (Naples, 1981).

55. This was demonstrated by E. Norbeck, 'African Rituals of Conflict', *Amer. Anthrop.*, *65* (1963) 1254 – 79 with a mild criticism of Gluckman.

56. P. L. Berger, 'Some Second Thoughts on Substantive versus Functional Definitions of Religion', *Journ. Scient. Study Rel.*, *13* (1974) 125 – 33.

57. P. L. Berger and T. Luckman, *The Social Construction of Reality* (New York, 1971) 121.

58. These concepts are being used by P. Weidkuhn, 'The Quest for Legitimate Rebellion. Towards a Structuralist Theory of Rituals of Reversal', *Religion, 7* (1977) 167 – 88, who finds his inspiration in Eliade.

59. Several New Year festivals in one year: M. P. Nilsson, *Primitive Time-reckoning* (Lund, 1920) 270.

60. M. Eliade, *Le mythe de l'éternel retour. Archétypes et répétition* (Paris, 1949) Ch. II, pp. 83ff; idem, *Traité d'histoire des religions*, 2nd edn (Paris, 1964) 326 – 43; V. Lanternari, *La grande festa. Storio del Capodanno nelle civiltà primitive*, 2nd edn (Bari, 1976).

61. The death of a king may provoke the very same associations and imagery: Versnel, 'Destruction' on mourning, chaos and anomy.

62. On chaos as 'l'absolue liberté' and the ambiguity of the sentiments involved, see Eliade, *Traité*, 76 and *passim*.

63. On the cohesive force of the Greek festivals see: F. Dunand, 'Sens et fonction de la fête dans la Grèce hellénistique. Les cérémonies en l'honneur d'Artemis Leucophryène', *Dial Hist. Anc.*, *4* (1978) 201 – 18.

64. The German title of the translated version of J. Servier, *Histoire de l'utopie* (Munich, 1971).

65. The relationship was already noticed by F. M. Cornford, *The Origin of Attic*

Comedy (London, 1914); on the social function of Greek comedy see, e.g., J.-C. Carrière, *Le Carnaval et la politique. Une introduction à la comédie grecque* (Paris, 1979); for Rome see E. Segal, *Roman Laughter*, 2nd edn (Cambridge, Mass., 1970).

66. Cf. A. C. Zijderveld, 'The Sociology of Humour and Laughter', *Current Sociology, 31* (1983) 1–103, esp. 47.

67. On the *truphè* motif see: H. Langerbeck, 'Die Vorstellung von Schlaraffenland in der alten attischen Komödie', *Zeitschr. f. Volksk., 59* (1963) 192–204; W. Fauth, 'Kulinarisches und Utopisches in der griechischen Komödie', *Wiener Stud., 7* (1973) 39–62. On the *automaton* motif: Gatz, *Weltalter*, 118 and register B I,1; H. J. de Jonge, 'BOTPYC BOHCEI', in M. J. Vermaseren (ed.), *Studies in Hellenistic Religions* (Leiden, 1979) 37–49. On absence of slavery: R. von Pöhlmann, *Geschichte der sozialen Frage und des Sozialismus in der antiken Welt*, 3rd edn (Munich, 1925); J. Pečirka, 'Aristophanes' Ekklesiazusen und die Utopien in der Krise der Polis', *Wiss. Zeitschr. Humboldt Univ. zu Berlin, Gesellsch.-Sprachw. Reihe, 12* (1963) 215ff; Vidal-Naquet, *Le Chasseur noir*, 230ff.

68. Theopompus *FGrH* 115 F 215 says that in Arcadia masters and slaves were sitting at the same tables and sharing the same food and drink.

69. On this passage as a conjunction of utopia and elysium: L. Gernet, 'La cité future et le pays des morts' in idem, *Anthropologie de la Grèce antique* (Paris, 1968) 139; Vidal-Naquet, *Le Chasseur noir*, 363.

70. A survey in J. Ferguson, *Utopias of the Classical World* (London 1975). On easy living, e.g. A. Giannini, 'Mito e utopia nella letteratura greca prima di Platone', *Rend. Ist. Lomb., 101* (1967) 109ff. On the Phaeacians: Vidal-Naquet, *Le Chasseur noir*, 60ff; on the Hellenistic utopias see the literature cited by M. Zumschlinge, *Euhemeros. Staats-theoretische und Staats-utopische Motive* (Diss., Bonn, 1976). On absence of slavery in utopias: J. Vogt, 'Slavery in Greek Utopias' in: idem, *Ancient Slavery and the Ideal of Man* (Cambridge, Mass., 1975) 26–38, esp. 29ff; Gatz, *Weltalter*, 127 and register B4c.

71. The terms are introduced by Giannini, *Mito e utopia*.

72. See the references to epigraphical sources: Versnel, 'Destruction', 551ff. The literary sources in Gatz, *Weltalter*, 131ff. Releasing of fetters e.g. in Philo, *Legatio ad Gaium* 146. This is a general image of the coming of the millenium: W. A. Meeks, *The First Urban Christians. The Social World of the Apostle Paul* (New Haven and London, 1983) 184f.

73. Kenner, *Das Phänomen*, 70 gives examples and literature in n 214; S. Luria 'Die Ersten werden die Letzten sein', *Klio, 22* (1929) 405–31 regards these as two stages of an historical process, which is quite unnecessary.

74. Vidal-Naquet, *Le Chasseur noir*, 226 and 267–88; cf. N. Loraux, *Les Enfants d'Athéna* (Paris, 1981) 157–96; J. C. Carrière, *Le Carnaval*; L. Bertelli, 'L'utopia sulla scena: Aristofane e la parodia della città', *Civiltà class. e crist., 4* (1983) 215–63. E. David, *Aristophanes and Athenian Society of the Early Fourth Century BC* (Leiden, 1984) rightly contrasts this with the general criticism of social misuses.

75. On the messianistic side of Eunous' revolt see P. Green, 'The First Sicilian Slave War', *Past and Present, 22* (1962) 87–93. On the Circumcellions: Versnel, 'Destruction', 552 and P. G. G. M. Schulten, *De Circumcellionen. Een sociaal-religieuze beweging in de late oudheid* (Diss., Leiden, 1984).

76. On these very interesting Egyptian prophecies see, e.g., S. Luria, 'Die Ersten'; J. Bergman, 'Introductory Remarks on Apocalypticism in Egypt', and J. Assman, 'Königsdogma und Heilserwartung. Politische und kultische Chaos-beschreibungen in Aegyptischen Texten', both in: D. Hellholm, *Apocalypticism in the Mediterranean World and the Near East* (Tübingen, 1983) 51–60 and 345–78.

77. Some instances: Xen. *Hell.* 4.4.2–4; Aen. Tact. 17.3; Diod. 13.104.5. Festivals are also ideal opportunities for sudden attack. L. A. Losada, *The Fifth*

Column in the Peloponnesian War (Leiden, 1972) 101; 111f.

78. On carnival and revolution see the literature cited by J. N. Bremmer, *The Early Greek Concept of the Soul* (Princeton, 1983) 118 n 133.

79. On the Anthesteria see the discussion and literature in Bremmer, ibid., 108–20.

80. A very good survey of this range of feasts in Burkert, *GR*, 227–34.

81. See the pertinent observations by A. Brelich, 'Osservazioni sulle "esclusioni rituali"', *SMSR*, *22* (1949/50) 16ff.

82. Thus Nilsson, *Griechische Feste*, 37. The *Pelores* are unconvincingly interpreted as the (great) dead by Meuli, *Gesammelte Schriften* II. Cf. Bremmer, op. cit., 123. Even less can I accept that 'the name *Peloria* is most naturally taken as designating the tables heaped with food': Robertson, 'Poseidon's Festival', 8.

83. J. Z. Smith, *Map is not Territory* (Leiden, 1978) 141–71.

84. B. Gladigow, 'Jenseitsvorstellungen und Kulturkritik', *Zeitschr. Religions- und Geistesgesch.*, *26* (1974) 308.

85. H. Freyer, *Caput velare* (Diss., Tübingen, 1963) is quite unsatisfactory in this respect.

86. See, e.g., R. Drews, *Basileus. The Evidence for Kingship in Geometric Greece* (New Haven and London, 1983) 7–9.

87. I mention here only: Meuli, *Gesammelte Schriften* II and 'Der Ursprung der Fastnacht', ibid. I, 283–99; A. Brelich, 'Osservazioni' and idem, *Tre variazioni romane sul tema delle origini*, 2nd edn (Rome, 1976) 83–95; Burkert, *GR*, 198: 'Kronos, the god of the first age, of reversal, and possibly of the last age', and 232: 'and so at his festival there is a reversion to that ideal former age, but a reversion that of course cannot last'.

88. *Katepine* — not only in Hes. *Theog.* (above, section 1; Burkert, this volume, Ch. 2, section 3) but also in Plato *Eutyphro* 6A and Apollod. 1.1.5 — is the very expression of this gluttony run wild.

89. Kristensen (above, note 19) 15.

90. 'einfach absurd': Bömer, 'Religion der Sklaven', 425; 'un lavoro geniale per impostazione e per alcuni intuizioni': Brelich, 'Osservazioni' 16 n 3.

8

Spartan Genealogies:
The Mythological Representation
of a Spatial Organisation

Claude Calame

Translated by A. Habib

1. The Comparative Perspective: Anthroponym as Spatial Symbol

From the archaic period onwards, the Greek taste for genealogies is striking: there are genealogies of gods (Hesiod), of heroes (Hekataios), of legendary kings whether related in epic (Eumelos at Corinth) or heading the chronographical sequence defined by the archon list (Athens).[1] This proliferation of genealogical activity is in no way surprising: its double function of measuring historical time whilst linking the present of the city to its legendary past is well known. Sparta is no exception, even if for us moderns there survive only late traces of this interest, in Pausanias and in the 'Library' attributed to Apollodorus. But as early as the seventh century BC we find in Tyrtaios echoes of a royal genealogy linking the rulers of Sparta with the legendary Herakleidai. And is it not precisely to this type of genealogy that the lectures given by the sophist Hippias at Sparta, described by Plato, owed their outstanding success?[2]

We shall turn later to the historical and literary problem of dating the Spartan royal genealogy. First let us read a passage that Pausanias significantly puts at the beginning of his description of Laconia:[3]

After the figures of Hermes we reach Laconia on the west.

153

According to the tradition of the Lacedaemonians themselves, Lelex, an aboriginal, was the first king in this land, after whom his subjects were named Leleges. Lelex had a son Myles, and a younger one Polykaon. Polykaon retired into exile, the place of this retirement and its reason I will set forth elsewhere. On the death of Myles his son Eurotas succeeded to the throne. He led down to the sea by means of a trench the stagnant water on the plain, and when it had flowed away, as what was left formed a river-stream, he named it Eurotas. Having no male issue, he left the kingdom to Lakedaimon, whose mother was Taygete, after whom the mountain was named, while according to report his father was none other than Zeus. Lakedaimon was wedded to Sparte, a daughter of Eurotas. When he came to the throne, he first changed the names of the land and its inhabitants, calling them after himself, and next he founded and named after his wife a city, which even down to our day has been called Sparta. Amyklas, too, son of Lakedaimon, wished to leave some memorial behind him, and built a town in Laconia. Hyakinthos, the youngest and most beautiful of his sons, died before his father, and his tomb is in Amyklai below the image of Apollo. On the death of Amyklas the empire came to Argalos, the eldest of his sons, and afterwards, when Argalos died, to Kynortas. Kynortas had a son Oibalos. He took a wife from Argos, Gorgophone, the daughter of Perseus, and begat a son Tyndareus, with whom Hippokoon disputed about the kingship, claiming the throne on the ground of being the elder. With the aid of Ikarios and his partisans he far surpassed Tyndareus in power, and forced him to retire in fear; the Lacedaemonians say that he went to Pellana, but a Messenian legend about him is that he fled to Aphareus in Messenia, Aphareus being the son of Perieres and the brother of Tyndareus on his mother's side. The story goes on to say that he settled at Thalamai in Messenia, and that his children were born to him when he was living there. Subsequently Tyndareus was brought back by Herakles and recovered his throne. His sons too became kings, as did Menelaos the son of Atreus and son-in-law of Tyndareus, and Orestes the husband of Hermione the daughter of Menelaos. On the return of the Herakleidai in the reign of Teisamenos, son of Orestes, both districts, Messene and Argos, had kings put over them; Argos had Temenos and Messene Kresphontes. In

Lacedaemon, as the sons of Aristodemos were twins, there arose two royal houses; for they say that the Pythian priestess approved.

Anyone sensitive to the discursive representation of space notices immediately the coincidence, in the first generation of the Spartan kings, between anthroponyms and toponyms: Eurotas, Taygete, Sparta, Lakedaimon, Amyklas are at the same time royal actors and specific local sites. To recount the sequence of matrimonial alliances and royal births is a strange way to stake out territorial space and to constitute political geography.

Yet the same process is met again in a more complex form at Greece's antipodes. The Iatmul, recently visited on the banks of the river Sepik in Papua-New Guinea, are in the habit of competing in long oral contests, with each clan's mythology as the stake. Why devote to a mythology so important a part of heated political debates bearing on men's families? The fact is that the mythological debate is essentially a matter of long lists of proper names; and every name is related to a living member of the Iatmul community as well as to an ancestral figure, a mythological tale, a physical or biological phenomenon, but above all to a location in the Iatmul's real or mythological geography.[4] It is a way of classifying the living, a way of tying them to the clan's history and to the universal physical organisation, a way, in fine, of representing space — in terms of course of social space with its corollary, economic order. This is how the Iatmul can debate a clan-estate problem by comparing lists of anthroponyms attributed to the mythical figures of the clans in question. If one disregards the strict genealogical organisation which Papuans on the banks of the Sepik set aside in favour of a series of substitutions on the paradigmatic axis, the parallel with ancient Sparta is positively striking.

Ideally we would gather other parallels that would enable us to reach an abstraction on a reality of a structural order; but lack of space precludes taking the comparison any further. At least it has the merit of showing the fruitfulness of the comparative perspective in explaining the religious phenomena of antiquity. Although Spartans are no Papuans, there is at Palimbei, as there was at Sparta, a sequence of anthroponyms designating legendary figures which notably enunciates a social space and a social organisation. If the Papuan parallel points at least to the general function of setting up a series of mythological names, one may go on to ask why the Spartan anthroponymic sequence assumes the form of a genealogy. The question here is no longer that of the social role played by mythic discourse, but of the narrative function of its discursive and textual presentation. So it is no longer comparatism that is called for, but narrative analysis — even when the genealogical form, compared with the pattern that narratology has attempted to formulate, displays singular and even bewildering features.

Since genealogical narrative as seen from the narrative standpoint is essentially made of state-enunciates, and since the attribution of a series of predicate qualities to the semiotic subject concerned belongs to this category of enunciates, our analysis here will be particularly focused on the values each actor, introduced by the genealogy, is invested with — all the more so since in fact Greek authors draw readily from the meaning of proper names a confirmation of the qualities ascribed to the actors in the state-enunciates of the same narrative.[5]

2. Spartan Genealogy and its Spatial Development

2.1 Lelex and the Leleges: Autochthonous Generation

As in Athens, the first Spartan king was an autochthon. This primordial qualification fixes in Laconian soil the roots of a being whose name refers nevertheless to a multitude of sites in continental Greece as well as in Ionia. An aboriginal population called Leleges is in fact attested in regions as diverse as Aitolia, Akarnania or Lokris in western Greece; Boeotia, Megara, or Thessaly in central Greece; even in Miletos and various places in the Troad. From a historical point of view, this diffusion of the Leleges appears to be part of the legendary tradition as soon as it can be observed in literary texts. In the *Iliad*, the Leleges are closely related to the Trojans since it sites them at Pedasos in the Troad and states that Laothoe, Priam's concubine, is the daughter of their king. Hesiod makes Lokros, one of the founders of Lokris, the ruler over the Leleges. And Alkaios mentions that the city of Antandros, an Aeolian town not far from the Trojan Mt Ida, is the foremost city of the Leleges.[6] Besides Sparta, it is only according to the tradition of Leukas that the eponymous ruler of

Figure 8.1: The Aegean World

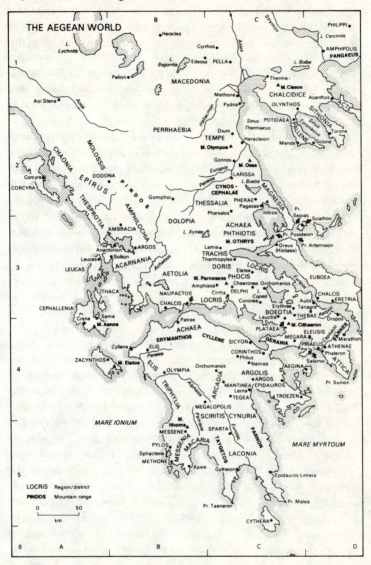

this omnipresent tribe of Leleges is considered as an autochthon. Elsewhere, at Megara for instance, Lelex appears bearing the features of a stranger, Poseidon's son, who, arriving from Egypt, took over the succession to the royal power after the Megarids adopted the Dorians' mores and language.[7]

Whether they are descended from a king or born on their soil or from a ruler exiled from Egypt, or whether on the contrary they have their origin in Caria (as Herodotos seems to suggest) and are even Carian slaves, the Leleges represent in any case one of those aboriginal tribes, like the Pelasgians or the Carians themselves, to which the Greeks attributed the earliest occupation of their own territory. Among these early tribes mentioned by the Greek narratives of the foundations of cities, modern historians have of course looked for the trail of a pre-Hellenic ethic substratum and reconstituted a no less hypothetical historic process of population settlement in Greece. By these means they have attempted to confer a historic value on the migratory movements, of which aborigines are often the protagonists. The decipherment of Linear B and the setting back from the eighth century BC to the fourteenth century BC of the period when the Greek language was first in use has fortunately dealt a definitive blow to such historical speculations.[8]

Inevitably in the research into the origin of the Leleges there remain some conjectures regarding the etymology of the name they bear. Most likely, as with 'bar-barians', reduplication in the name of the Leleges indicates they spoke a language which was alien to Greek ears.[9] In the various legends portraying them, the Hellenic successors of the Lelegian dynasts are generally occupied giving new names to cities founded by aboriginal tribes: this is a probable way for the imagination of legend to mark the passage from non-Greek to Greek. It seems that in the series of proper names which the Iatmul use for justifying their clan claims, the morphology of the first name in each list — unlike the other names, which are without exception *redende Namen* — does not lead to a directly decipherable signification: only from the second 'generation' does the anthroponym designate through its signifier and its morphology the qualities of the individual it is naming.[10]

Oscillating between autochthony and its opposite, territorial exteriority, the Lelegian ruler embodies in any case the otherness that will allow the assertion of identity. Hence his initial, aboriginal, position. As with every tale, genealogy begins its narrative process with a lack-situation, and the only 'action' in the Spartan genealogical narrative ascribed to King Lelex corresponds to his giving his subjects his own name, a name that in all probability signifies otherness. But this initial lack, through its autochthonous rooting and above all through the process of generation, contains in itself the elements of the semantic universe that is to be asserted. It is a way, as in the first phases of the Hesiodic theogony, of assuming and figuring the transition from an undifferentiated state to a first, semantically marked, existence.[11] And it will be noticed, significantly, that two traditions parallel to that of Pausanias give a wife to Lelex. Therefore differentiation does not occur through parthenogenesis, but is immediately constituted by the masculine/feminine duality. When embodied by a naiad or nymph, this feminine belongs also moreover to the outside and non-civilised field.[12]

2.2 Myles: the Space of Cereal Cultivation

In Pausanias' tradition, Lelex ends up by being the cause of differentiation, through the process of generation. Genealogical narrative attributes two sons and one daughter to Sparta's first sovereign. The eldest, Myles, carries in his very name a trace of the action legend ascribes to him. Myles was in fact considered the first man to have invented the mill (*mule*) since he is the first to grind (*alesai*) corn in a place named Alesiai which was between the site of the future Sparta and Mt Taygetos. With this etymological double-play, genealogy does not limit itself to the slicing of a first space into Leleges territory, hitherto not defined: it binds that space together with one of the features constituting the very foundation of the Greek representation of civilisation — with ground corn, symbol of agricultural activity and, to put it more accurately, of cereal cultivation as opposed to hunting and pastoral activity.[13] So there is no surprise in discovering in the space, where Myles lays the economic and material foundation of Spartan civilisation, a sanctuary to Lakedaimon, the ruler who will give his name to this land.

With Lelex's other children the Lelegian territory will undergo, from this central point marked by the civilisation of ground corn, some remarkable spatial extensions. First, in Messenia: there is no room for Polykaon, the second son, to take his place next to his brother, Lelex's successor. He retires into exile beyond Mt

Taygetos and marries, in what is to be Messenia, the daughter of Triopas of Argos, Messene. To ensure the conquest of the land that bears her name and before she gives it a capital city, Andania, Messene calls to her aid the Argives and also the Spartans. It is therefore due to the intervention of a feminine figure that the civic definition and identity of the Messenian territory are established, while a male contingent from Argos puts a military seal on that conquest and men from Sparta ensure the political power sequence. The coincidence on the one hand with the feminine and masculine, and on the other, with the Argive ancestry and the Spartan sovereignty, will leave its mark. For Messene the Argive and Polykaon the Spartan will lay the foundations of a sanctuary to Zeus on Mt Ithome in the geographic centre of the Messenian territory.[14] We must recall here that Triopas, like Lelex, is one of those characters who, related to numerous migratory moves, finds himself placed at the start of several royal genealogies, in particular in Thessaly where he is linked with the Lapiths, if not at Rhodes and in Caria where he follows the Leleges' route in reverse.[15] Triopas has also an important part to play, even negatively, in establishing Demeter's cult. It is not excluded either that through his daughter he brought to Messenia the cereal cultivation values indispensable to this territory's economic development, territory coveted by the Spartans for its agricultural wealth.

But future Sparta, through the genealogical narrative, extends also from its agricultural centre as defined by the miller-king Myles towards the east: Therapne gets its name from that of Lelex's daughter.[16] There is no reason to believe that it is by chance that the legend conjures up at the genealogical beginning of Sparta the probable place of residence and the actual place of the cult of the 'Mycenaean' sovereigns, Menelaos and Helen, and that of the Dioskouroi, Helen's twin brothers. This does not mean that the genealogical narrative, which we shall date to the start of the classical period, keeps intact the memory of events going back to the thirteenth century BC; but at Sparta, as in so many other Greek cities, it is a Mycenaean site which, as early as the archaic period, will serve as a setting for the cult devoted to the protagonists turned heroes of the Trojan War. Archaeological discoveries reveal that if the site of Sparta itself was probably not occupied before the protogeometric era (from the tenth century BC), on the other hand

Therapne is with Amyklai the richest Mycenaean site in that region.[17] This non-occupation of Sparta proves the vacuity of any use of genealogy as a document for its early history. On the other hand, a genealogical representation dating from the classical period could not fail to site a place so important in cult and legend at that time in relation to the centre. This is a point we shall make more than once: the genealogical narrative retells history in the perspective of the political situation in Sparta at the start of the fifth century BC.

2.3 Eurotas: Extension of the Cultivated Space

Let us now return to the centre and to the direct agnatic descent from Myles, initiator of Spartan cereal cultivation. It is Myles' son, Eurotas, who succeeds his father.[18] Genealogical tradition ascribes to this third king of Sparta the clearing and draining of the Laconian plains and the canal dug to let the then stagnant waters flow towards the sea. It became the river bearing his name. A late text adds that the clearing of the land that became the valley of the Eurotas took place after the Flood, that is to say, according to the Spartan chronology, before the intervention of Lelex, himself linked with the time of the Flood.[19] If this relative dating of a civilised intervention is chronologically speaking not absolutely consistent, it nevertheless harmonises with the series of cultural actions of the first rulers of legendary Greece. In any case, this cleansing by Eurotas represents a second extension of Laconian space and simultaneously an expansion of civilisation: not only Alesiai but the whole plain of the Eurotas is given over to agriculture. From then on the Eurotas is a river of civilisation.[20]

And doubtless it is not mere coincidence that the Spartans later associated in a single sanctuary to Hera the commemoration of Eurotas overflowing onto the arable soil and that of the sacrifice offered to Aphrodite-Hera by mothers who saw their daughters join in the state of matrimony. It is well known that in Greece in the representation of civilisation, cereal cultivation is used in particular as a metaphor for marriage: Eurotas, domesticated, ensures the productivity of the entire plain it has created; the mother who bends her daughter under the matrimonial yoke guarantees the continuity of the Spartan families.[21]

161

2.4 Lakedaimon and Sparte: the Political Centre

Eurotas, however, in another respect confronts us with a blockage in the process of the agnatic legitimacy, since he has no male issue.[22] So he gives his daughter Sparte in marriage to one of the other great hero-founders of Laconia, Lakedaimon, the son of Zeus and of the nymph Taygete. Whatever the reason for substituting a uterine lineage for the agnatic lineage, it tallies with a basic reorganisation of Laconian space: first, by defining a political centre and including this centre in a well-demarcated territory. This inclusion is figuratively represented as an enclosure of the female by the male: Sparta is 'embraced' by Lakedaimon.

The son of Zeus and Taygete actually starts by giving the land and its inhabitants his own name; then he lays the foundation of a city and gives it his wife's name. Lakedaimon's country, Lakedaimonia, now possesses its capital city, founded by a man and not a woman, as was the case for Andania in Messenia. In this toponymic definition, genealogy, though capable of reconstructing a story, is also trying to rationalise a linguistic usage already somewhat fluctuating. Although for the ancients as for the moderns Sparta designates hardly anything else but the city of this name, Lakedaimon refers to the city and also to the region of which it is the capital, thus covering the sense given to the geographical term Laconia. Whilst giving coherence to the use of names, which had been normal since the time of Homer, the genealogical narrative at the same time removes their aboriginal name from the natives to endow them with a definite identity of a political order: the inhabitants of the Eurotas plain are no longer babbling Leleges, but Lakedaimonians, that is free men given the freedom of the city in the state of Lakedaimon. In antiquity, the name Lakedaimonians always and officially refers to a political entity and not to an ethnic one.[23] Through the founding acts of Lakedaimon's predecessors runs an *isotopia* of an agricultural order; those of Lakedaimon define a civic perspective. It is evident also that Lakedaimon's relationship with Zeus links his image with the civic state. Sparta's new king is therefore the son of the king of the gods, the keeper of the world-order.[24] This divine descent puts him on an equal footing with Zeus' other sons who are generally culture heroes and/or city founders: Minos, founder and king of Knossos: Arkas, eponymous hero of the Arcadians; Zethos and Amphion, builders of Thebes; Epaphos, maker of many cities; and several other names could be cited. More often than not these various heroes have for their mother a nymph seduced by a Zeus generally metamorphosed. Lakedaimon is therefore no exception. The privileged relationship that Sparta's founder enjoys with the king of the gods is moreover confirmed by the existence in Sparta of the royal cult performed in honour of Zeus Lakedaimon (Herodotos 6.56.1); the epiclesis tends to identify the son with the father. Lakedaimon is in any case king by divine right.

Lakedaimon is also master of spatial delimitations by means of names. Just as he honours his wife, who has transferred to him the political power of the Leleges, by naming the newly founded capital after her, so he honours his mother, Atlas' nymph-daughter that Zeus seduced, and gives her name to the highest mountain range in the land.[25] To the definition of Spartan territory and its political centre, Sparta, is added the identification of a boundary, in fact the limit *par excellence*. The Taygetos range clearly divides Sparta from Messenia, its higher peaks reaching over 2,400 m. The fact that it coincides with a nymph's image does not permit Mt Taygetos simply to act as a topographical limit: it embodies also marginal values that the image of the mother does not represent so strongly in Greece as that of the nymph. The famous throne of Amyklai shows the young Taygete abducted by Zeus. Consequently the nymph, a maiden, is forced to submit to male violence, outside wedlock. The legend adds that the *parthenos* harassed by the god's attentions is granted the help of the virgin Artemis and changed into a doe. This metamorphosis places the nymph twice over under the jurisdiction of the goddess of the extra-civilised field: maiden and doe, she ends up by becoming its incarnation in a mountainous and wild country. Pindar already had cited the doe with the golden antlers consecrated by Taygete to Orthosia, Sparta's Artemis.[26] Lakedaimon's wife, through her name and the legitimacy of the royal power she hands down, had inscribed the space defined by the new king of Sparta in the political field; his mother, on the other hand, all round this civilised territory, stands for the liminal field of the wild.

One must take note that other versions of the legend of Eurotas ascribe other daughters than Sparte to the river-king. The most significant version goes back, if not to Pindar, certainly to Sosibios, a Laconian historian of the Hellenistic period; here Eurotas is not Sparte's father, but Pitane's: this gives its origin to one of the *obai*, the districts of classical Sparta. This is another way of inscribing into Eurotas' issue Laconia's political centre while it adds perhaps to the Spartan genealogical narrative a look in the direction of Arcadia and Elis. Evadne, the daughter born to Pitane through her union with Poseidon, will become the mother of Iamos who, after having been fed on honey by the snakes of the Alpheios will found the oracle of the Iamids at Olympia. A parallel version gives to Eurotas a daughter named Mekionike; from her union, also with Poseidon, she will start the line of descendants who will become the founders and colonisers of Thera and Kyrene, Laconian sites in origin.[27] So it is here that the space of the process of the Spartan colonisation is staked out and inscribed in genealogy. A separate study could be devoted to this new direction followed by the genealogical narrative.

2.5 Amyklai: Enlargement of the Political Territory and of its Centre

As a result of the brief matrilinear interruption in an otherwise entirely patrilinear genealogy presented by the union of Lakedaimon and Sparte, sole heiress of Eurotas' power, Laconia's political centre and the divine origin of the royal power has been defined; and in addition boundaries have been set *vis-à-vis* the wild, the domain of Artemis. Amyklas' accession to the throne, as a son of Lakedaimon and Sparte, signifies the return to an agnatic lineage. This return coincides with a complementary definition of the political centre. For Amyklas is founder of a town that will take his name. As with Therapne, we learn from archaeology that Amyklai was an important site during the Mycenaean period, and at the beginning of the archaic period became the most important of the city's cult places. In the course of the eighth century BC it was added to the four *obai* constituting the city of Sparta, being integrated in this way with the political centre.[28] So if it is with Therapne, Lelex's daughter, that the place of worship dedicated to 'Homeric' heroes enters into the space defined by the genealogical narrative, it is with Amyklas, the son of Lakedaimon and Sparte, that the inclusion of the Mycenaean site is brought about both on the political level and that of heroic cult. The political aspect of this narrative is shown in the foundation of a town; the cultic aspect is embodied in the figure of one of Amyklas' sons, Hyakinthos, the athlete ephebe killed inadvertently by his lover Apollo. Both were honoured when one of the greatest festivals of ancient Sparta took place: included in the celebration of the final phase of the initiation that Spartan youths, boys and girls, underwent, the Hyakinthia was a festival that gathered together at Amyklai every social group forming the political community.[29]

Before we come to the next generation, we should not pass over Eurydike, daughter of Lakedaimon and Sparte. Her exogamic marriage to Akrisios, king of Argos, extends Spartan space in the direction of the Argolid. More precisely, this union makes Spartan genealogy coincide with its Argive equivalent. For Akrisios like Proitos is a grandson to Lynkeus, himself a nephew of Danaos, the famous culture hero of the Danaoi of the Argolid who succeeded to the kingdom of the descendants of Argos, founder of the city of that name. The union of the Argive Akrisios with the Spartan Eurydike brought about the birth of Danae, mother of Perseus, the famous slayer of the Gorgo.[30]

The evidence given on the extent of Spartan territorial and political claims by the genealogy's marriage alliance with one of the first kings of Argos receives striking confirmation in Sparta on both the spatial and cultic levels. For in the centre of the city there was a temple dedicated to the protectress divinity of Argos, Hera Argeia — a temple erected by no other than Eurydike, daughter of Lakedaimon.[31] But the marriage relationship that represents and lays down the Spartan claims on Argive space has a very different character from the Messenian case. From the Spartan perspective, the marriage of Polykaon and Messene was uxorilocal but patrilinear; that of Eurydike and Akrisios is virilocal but matrilinear. We shall see that this inversion reflects a precise political and historical situation in the relationship of Sparta with its neighbours and in the territorial organisation of the whole Peloponnese.

2.6 The Sons of Amyklas: Confirmation of the Centre and Opening towards the Exterior

The legendary founder of Amyklai obviously does not remain celibate: he marries Diomede, who through her father Lapithes, founder of the *genos* of the Lapiths, links the house of the Spartan kings with the Thessalian genealogy.[32] She provides Amyklas with a good number of male descendants, but the quantity seems to have as a corollary a relative feebleness of characterisation. Hyakinthos is certainly the most original of Amyklas' and Diomede's three sons; it is with him that Amyklai's inclusion on the cultic level is achieved. But Hyakinthos is not Amyklas' eldest son: at his death he is succeeded by Argalos, also known as Harpalos, who even if he dies young has a son from whom Agenor, then Patreus, eponymous hero and founder of Patras in Achaia, will be descended. From now on the kings of Spartan origin that the genealogy establishes in the land of the Achaians extend over practically the whole of the Peloponnese the clanic representation of the Spartans' spatial pretensions.[33] Sparta's official genealogy, however, seems rapidly to forget about Argalos, substituting on the Lacedaemonian throne Amyklas' second son, Kynortas. All one knows of this equally ephemeral king is the tomb the Spartans built for him, which in Pausanias' time still stood in the centre of the city next to the funeral monument of Castor the Tyndarid. Nevertheless it is to be noticed that both Argalos' and Kynortas' names can be connected with the various names given to the *obai*, the 'villages' that formed the city of Sparta.[34] As their father did before them, Amyklas' sons seem to have become eponymous heroes of the spatial and political constituents of the centre.

2.7 Oibalos: Reassertion of the Argos–Sparta–Messenia Triangle

With Kynortas' descendants, the genealogy, after representing the development and semantic definition of a territory by means of the hitherto concluded unions, is in a way going to 'dynamise' this first construction. This 'dynamisation' inside the space so far defined begins with the marriage of Kynortas' son Oibalos with Perseus' daughter Gorgophone, i.e. the marriage of the king of Sparta with his cross-related grand-daughter! The striking fact in this marriage is not so much the union with a collateral relation than, within the context of the *rapprochement* of Sparta with Argos, the union with a woman who has been married before and had children from her first marriage. For, according to Pausanias (2.21.7), Gorgophone's marriage was to Perieres, the son of Aiolos. And she would become the first woman to have been married twice.

The spatial consequences of this double union are truly significant. According to legend, the line of the first Messenian king, Polykaon, was extinct after the fifth generation. And it is actually the Thessalian Perieres who will be asked to take the throne of Messenia. After its first foundation — as will be recalled — by the

Figure 8.2: The Peloponnese and Central Greece

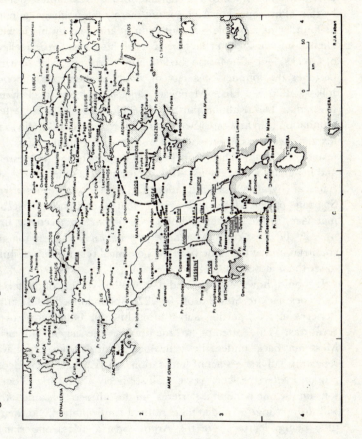

Argive Messene with the help of her Spartan and Lelegian husband Polykaon, Messenia undergoes a second act of foundation through the intervention of the Thessalian Perieres who takes as his first wife Gorgophone, also an Argive. It is beyond question that this taking of power constitutes a new act of foundation, for it is evidenced as much by the character of Perieres' father Aiolos as by that of his sons. For Aiolos is not merely the Aeolians' ancestor as founder of a people — a function guaranteed by his forbears Deukalion and Hellen (the hero that left his name to the Hellenes or Greeks) — but he is also the father of seven sons, each of whom becomes the founder of a city or state: Orchomenos, Corinth, Iolkos, Phocis, Elis, Magnesia and finally, with Perieres, Messenia. The tradition portraying Aiolos' and his sons' acts of foundation is in any case ancient: traces are found in Boiotia in the texts of Hesiod as in Sparta itself in a fragment of Alcman.[35] The installation of the Thessalian Perieres on the throne of Messenia and his union with Perseus' Argive daughter result in the decisive removal (by an act of foundation) of the land of Messenia from Spartan power. It will be seen that Gorgophone's second marriage, to the Spartan Oibalos, will prepare indirectly at first, by way of cross-cousins, a new *rapprochement* between the two countries and at the same time the polemical relationship destined to set them at odds.

It should, however, be stated that another version of the legend that goes back to Stesichoros (fr. 227; Apollodoros 3.10.3), turns Perieres into a Spartan, substituting him for Oibalos as son of Kynortas. This attempt to manipulate the legend to bring Messenia back under the genealogical jurisdiction of Sparta, repeating Polykaon's act of foundation, is nevertheless doomed to remain ineffective. For, as we shall see later, attributing Oibalos' sons on the one hand and Perieres' on the other to the same father will do nothing to hinder their mutual confrontation. So for the time being, let us leave the Argos–Sparta–Messenia triangle being broken up through the intervention of Aeolian exteriority.

Returning now to the first version of the legend, there are a few signs that allow us to see in the figure of Oibalos a founder like his Messenian counterpart Perieres. The Spartans had built a heroon, to Amyklas' grandson, linked by its topographical position with the sanctuary of Poseidon Genethlios, the guardian of the *gene*, the clans constituting the first Spartan citizens. Further, since Hesiod,

168

Tyndareus, the most famous of all Oibalos' sons, has the patronym *Oibalides*; this name will be taken up again, in the plural, by an inscription on Thera to designate the ancient aristocratic families of Sparta who claimed through this onomastic expedient descent from Oibalos.[36] So here we have, opposing each other, Perieres, second (Aeolian) founder of Messenia, and Oibalos, who begins a new dynasty after the political and religious recentring of Sparta, notably embodied in the figure of Amyklas.

2.8 The Children of Gorgophone: Deviances and Polemics

2.8.1. The Messenian Branch. Perieres has two sons. The eldest, Aphareus, promptly gives Messenia a new capital. The former capital, Andania, where Perieres still lives, will continue to be the place of one of the most important Greek mystery cults after Eleusis. On the other hand, he marries none other than Arene, daughter of Oibalos. He gives the town he has just founded the name of his young wife, just as Polykaon named Messenia after his wife Messene.[37] Thus Messenia's bonds with Sparta are newly tied through a woman and no longer through a man, as was the case in the second generation with Polykaon. Moreover, where Gorgophone was the first woman to marry twice, Arene and Aphareus have the same mother: so their union represents a second violation of the norm of unique, exogamic marriage.

Furthermore, Aphareus receives at Arene in Messenia his second-cousin Neleus, like him a grandson of Aiolos. He then proceeds to divide his kingdom and gives his parallel second-cousin, expelled from Iolkos by his twin brother Pelias, the western, maritime part of Messenia, of which Pylos becomes the capital. Another version of the legend makes Pylos a foundation independent from Messenia, due to the Leleges that came from the Megarid; it is then later conquered by Neleus and not made over by the Messenian king. But the point is nevertheless that one must see written in the genealogy a most important partition of the Messenian territory and the definition of a coastal region which, once abandoned, will never be economically as important for the Spartans as the central plain.[38]

One can add to this territorial division, asserting a second time the Aeolian, not Spartan, connections of Messenia, the welcome that Aphareus gives to the figure representing Neleus' Athenian counterpart, Lykos, the son of Pandion, expelled from Athens by his brother Aigeus. Lykos will be concerned with reactivating the mysteries of Andania on the pattern of those of Eleusis.[39] The territory of Messenia, after a Spartan attempt at control, again looks northwards, in the direction of Thessaly and Attica.

2.8.2 The Spartan Branch. On the Spartan side, one can witness the same contradictory concomitance of the work of refounding the city with abnormal and polemical relationships between the representatives of political power. Gorgophone gives Oibalos three sons who will be in conflict the moment the problem of their father's succession arises. Tyndareus, the rightful heir *qua* eldest, takes power, but Hippokoon, on the pretext that he himself is the eldest, forms an alliance with Ikarios, the youngest son, to contest the legitimacy of Tyndareus' power. The latter sees himself forced to surrender the throne to his brothers. He takes refuge at Pellana not far from the source of the Eurotas, or, according to a different version, in Messenia with his half-brother Perieres, or again with King Thestios at Pleuron in Aitolia. The scholiast on Euripides' *Orestes* sums up best the spatial aspect of these various versions and shows that Tyndareus' refuge corresponds to the *eschata*, the most remote parts of Sparta. This is confirmed by Plutarch when he states that the frontier of the land of Sparta was not far from Pellana. One notes incidentally that the various versions of this famous legend of Tyndareus' exile have seen to it that the illegitimacy of his brother Hippokoon's action is based on his having a different mother than Gorgophone and being consequently a bastard.[40]

2.9 The Tyndarids: Centripetal Polemics

The recovery of power starting from the boundaries of Spartan territory involves the confrontation of Tyndareus' sons with those of Hippokoon. This narrative sequence in the genealogy compels us to anticipate in order to examine the generation following that of Tyndareus, an anticipation all the more necessary since tradition not only gives Hippokoon twelve, even twenty sons, but adds to Tyndareus' sons the prestigious Dioskouroi, receivers of cultic honour *par excellence* as the divine incarnation of the *neos*, the young athlete who after his initiation gains the status of soldier-citizen.[41] Our analysis will be centred on the genealogical aspect of the many qualities attributed to the Tyndarids and on the spatial representation that derives from it. Castor and Pollux are, then, the sons of

Tyndareus and Leda, the daughter of Thestios the Aitolian with whom the Spartan king sought refuge after the *coup* of his brother Hippokoon. But the Dioskouroi are *Dios kouroi*, 'sons of Zeus', from the earliest tradition that shows these twin heroes in both their human and their divine ancestry.[42] This double filiation is again, as with Lakedaimon, going to place the responsibility for the recapture of power on Zeus. The Dioskouroi will in fact be the agents by the support they give to their human father Tyndareus.

But this reassertion of the legitimate power in Sparta also takes on a spatial aspect since the intervention of the Dioskouroi begins from the boundaries of the Spartan territory where their father is exiled. When their paternity is attributed to Zeus, the Dioskouroi are born on Mt Taygetos. But when legend makes them Tyndareus' sons, they are born on Pephnos, a small island on the frontier between Messenia and Lakonia. From Pephnos, Hermes takes them to that other frontier territory, Pellana. Finally, the genealogical text on which the present analysis is based locates the birth of the Dioskouroi at Thalamai, a Laconian village not far from Pephnos.[43]

The various versions of the legend of Tyndareus' exile and the birth of the Dioskouroi impart a centrifugal movement we have not seen so far to the Spartan genealogical structure. But this movement from the centre towards the margins of the territory is meant — as we have said — better to prepare a new establishment of the centre. A sudden change in the semio-narrative structures underlying the genealogy narrative will correspond precisely to this first separation. Spartan genealogy has been presented so far as a cumulation of state-enunciates; in the form of matrimonial alliances, these enunciates have progressively defined the limits of Spartan territory as well as openings towards the exterior, marking out space in a way befitting good neighbours. Born from the interior, in the very centre of this space, the rivalry which suddenly opposes some of Oibalos' sons to others introduces a polemical relationship expresssed narratively by the appearance of an anti-subject and also by an action ('Hippokoon banishes Tyndareus'). Spatially, the irruption of confrontation into the narrative is conveyed by the centrifugal movement described above.

2.9.1 The Battle against the Hippokoontids. The 'lack-situation' brought about by Tyndareus' unjust exile will be reversed by the intervention of his sons against those of Hippokoon: the narrative equilibrium, broken by the polemic relationship, must be regained. We cannot here go into all the details of an account that would take us far beyond Laconia's frontiers, but it must be mentioned that the legend sets all the weight of the restoration of the equilibrium on Herakles' shoulders. For it is to the famous culture hero, the son of Zeus and the Mycenaean Alkmene, that genealogy, transformed into narrative, ascribes Tyndareus' restoration to the throne of Sparta. This restoration of order and legitimacy in Sparta figures in a series of Herakles' interventions in various cities of the Peloponnese. The hero's fight beside the Tyndarids and their father to regain power usurped by Hippokoon and defended by his own sons is narratively motivated by the help the latter are bringing to Neleus. Neleus and his sons dared to stand against Herakles' intervention at Pylos, and in his battle against the Neleids the hero spares only Nestor, the future king of the city. Let us leave aside the probable reduplication, after his intervention at Pylos, of Herakles' fight at Sparta against the Hippokoontids and the other motivations that the legend mentions, in order to stress the fact that already in the seventh century BC Alcman had put the myth of Herakles' battle with the Hippokoontids in the mouth of one of the *choroi* of young girls for whom he composed the *Partheneia*, and had doubtless made the Hippokoontids rivals in love of the Dioskouroi. The problem of the succession to the throne of Sparta combines again with the question of marriage alliance. As in the previous stages of the genealogy, the taking over of a political space is a matter of the implantation and integration of womanhood.[44]

2.9.2 The Fight against the Apharetids. The polemical relationship is not solely set up in the interior; it becomes also the new mode for asserting power outside of the territory that the genealogy demarcates. The fight of Herakles and the Tyndarids against the Hippokoontids has taken us from the father's generation to that of the sons, even if the outcome restores the power of the father, Tyndareus. After Hippokoon's sons, it is the sons of Aphareus, king of Messenia, whom, according to legend, the Dioskouroi must meet next, though the episode admittedly is not integrated in the genealogical text. Besides Aphareus, Perieres has a second son called Leukippos. Aphareus, through his union with Arene, daughter of Oibalos, has two sons, Idas and Lynkeus. Leukippos has two daughters, Hilaeira and Phoibe, better known as the Leukippidai. Leukippos' daughters, while still virgins, will soon find themselves at the centre of the rivalry in love which opposes Castor and Pollux, sons of the Spartan Tyndareus (their cross-related cousins) and Idas and Lynkeus, sons of the Messenian Aphareus (their parallel cousins).

The legend, which goes back to the *Kypria* and is alluded to by Pindar, has several versions. In spite of their inevitable variations, each is centred on an infringement of social rules: an attempt at endogamic union (the Apharetids are about to marry their parallel cousins, the Leukippidai); subversion of the rules of hospitality (Aphareus' sons, guests of the Tyndarids, make a mockery of their hosts); abduction, disregarding the rules of offering a gift in compensation (according to the Apharetids, the Tyndarids abduct the Leukippidai without giving a dowry to the maidens' father); plundering on the economic level (the Dioskouroi seize the plough-oxen of the Apharetids); contravention of the rules of combat for hoplites (Aphareus' sons attack Pollux by throwing a stone from their own father's tomb at him); forsaking the dying (the Apharetids die alone, says Pindar). But for the articulation of the plot, one always finds at the centre of the legend the matrimonial union of the Leukippidai with the Dioskouroi, the sons of Tyndareus.[45]

It is once more through the device of marriage alliance that the political control of Sparta over Messenia is represented. With the marriage of Leukippos' daughters with Tyndareus' sons and the physical disappearance of their Messenian suitors, legend denies to Perieres' family any male issue and consequently any claim to the throne of Messenia. Once again, as on the occasion of Perieres' accession, the throne of Messenia is left without a legitimate heir. But here the gap in the legitimate line of descent of Messenia occurs through acts of war, or rather by means of a series of violent and deviant actions bearing the character, in the Greek represen-tation of age-classes, of the activity of the neo-initiate about to become a citizen-soldier. Reversing the rules of adult behaviour, as the Greeks do in their imagery of adolescence, these actions go as far as to assimilate Aphareus' sons to savage monsters sharing the primeval and violent nature of the Titans. The narrative consequence is that Sparta no longer controls Messenia through the means of matrimonial unions: Messenia submits completely through an agonal battle that takes on the deviant aspects of primordiality. Some support for this can be found in the fact that when presently the Herakleidai intervene in the Peloponnese, Nestor at Pylos is the sole representative of Messenia.

2.9.3 Helen and her Inheritance. The re-institutionalisation of Spartan power is begun by Tyndareus in the 'dynamisation' of relationships between the protagonists of the genealogy and continues with a narrative in a polemical key. That this is a matter of a stage in the reassertion of royal power is proved by the double intervention of Zeus, who was already present in the first definition of Laconia's political centre by Lakedaimon. Zeus, divine father of the Dioskouroi, steps in at Pollux's side to strike Idas with a thunderbolt as once he struck his rivals the Titans with lightning in the Titanomachia.[46] Zeus again is divine father to Helen, heiress to the throne of Sparta after her brother's disappearance. Castor, the mortal, is killed in the fight against the Apharetids; Pollux, Zeus' protégé, is made immortal by his divine father. Old Tyndareus then summons Menelaos, Helen's husband, to succeed him on the Spartan throne.[47] In spite of the legend's variations concerning a succession troubled particularly by the Trojan war, it is in fact Menelaos and Helen who are ruling over Laconia when Telemachos, in his search for his father, stays at the court of Sparta. So there has been a real matrimonial exchange between the rulers of the Argolid and those of Sparta: Klytemnestra, Tyndareus' elder daughter, is married to Agamemnon who rules over Argos and Mycenae; and Menelaos, his younger brother, marries Klytemnestra's sister, thus inheriting Sparta's monarchic power and becoming Tyndareus' successor. The marriage of Menelaos with Helen is therefore uxorilocal and, as with Sparte, it is by matrilinearity that power is transmitted by Tyndareus' successor; but Sparta's new king is no longer a Laconian like Lakedaimon, Taygete's son.[48] For the first time in the genealogy, autochthonous lineage seems to lose its grip on power.

2.10 Hermione and Orestes: the Death Knell of Endogamy

The conjugal exchange between Sparta and Argos takes a second form in the following generation when Hermione, the only daughter of Menelaos, is married to Orestes, the son of

Agamemnon and Klytemnestra.[49] In this way Orestes becomes heir to the Argive power as well as the Spartan; but this concentration, coinciding with an alliance between doubly parallel cousins, is by definition doomed to failure. From the Spartan standpoint, this doubly endogamic alliance puts an end to any patrilinear and virilocal legitimacy centred on Sparta. Legend in any case has Orestes die not in Sparta, but in Arcadia!

2.11 *The Herakleidai: Definitive Establishment of Power at Sparta*

Unlike the second institutional operation of the genealogy that resulted in asserting through Sparte and Lakedaimon's marriage the political aspect of a spatial centre, the third of these operations, a narrative development of polemics and of the semantic figure of warfare, is fundamentally negative as regards Sparta. Even Helen, heiress to the throne after her brothers' disappearance, flees to Troy. Moreover, the transmission of power by means of matrilinear and uxorilocal succession does not create any recentring of power as was the case with Sparta. It is not surprising therefore that Teisamenos, the only son of the cousins Hermione and Orestes, fails to restore the situation. His deviant heredity has no other result than to prepare the return of the Herakleidai and their installation on the Spartan throne and on that of other regions of the Peloponnese that he later held.[50] The result of this warlike intervention is a new partition of the Peloponnese, a repeat of the Spartan genealogy's original division, and the installation of definitive dynasties: to Temenos, the Argolid; to Kresphontes, Messenia; and Laconia goes to the two sons of the third brother, Aristodemos. Eurysthenes and Prokles thus become the initiators of the Spartan double kingship of Agiads and Eurypontids.[51]

Legend seems immediately to write Sparta's supremacy into the narrative of the intervention of the Herakleidai: it is only by guile that Kresphontes manages to get Messenia; the legitimacy of his power is thus immediately questioned. On the other hand, Herodotos himself tells us that according to the Spartans the twins who began their double royal dynasty were born to Aristodemos by a woman named Argia. Through this conjugal device, the Heraklid dynasty, as Herodotos adds, not only goes back to Herakles, but can also claim descent on the Argive side from Perseus and his grandfather Akrisios.[52] So the establishment of Heraklid power in the Peloponnese marks a new beginning whilst taking up and reasserting the spatial schema that was built in the first stages of the genealogy.

3. Birth of a Genealogy: the Historical Context

If the genealogical narrative is looked at as a reasoned representation of a space, it poses a number of questions of an historical type to anyone who examines it. I stated earlier that I prefer to leave to others the thorny problem of an eventual relationship between the actions and actors of the genealogy and hypothetical historical events enacted by real protagonists. Without denying the possibility of relationships of this type, it must be recognised that archaeology at least shows that Sparta did not physically exist at the time when, about the fifteenth century BC, a relative chronology would place the intervention of Lelex and his descendants. As for Therapne and Amyklai, Mycenaean sites very active in the thirteenth century BC, we saw that in the course of the eighth century the institution of heroic cults gave them a new function, marginal in relation to the civic role Sparta began to assume, but essential for the founding ideology of the archaic city and the ritual observances that gave it physical expression.[53] The gap between the scenario of the genealogical narrative and any kind of historic 'reality', however, can only discourage an attempt to see in the first a reflection of the second.

On the other hand, one is justified in asking if the legend as representation, in particular as ideological representation, is not a 'narrativisation' of a precise state of the territory's political divisions in a given historical situation. This situation would then coincide with the moment when the genealogy was formed and its elements would refer to the situation of the enunciation. Yet to inquire about the conditions of the enunciation and about the dating of the narrative comes down first to posing the rather complex problem of the sources of Pausanias and in particular his third book, devoted to Laconia.[54] If there is no possibility of determining the exact source of the genealogy opening Book 3, there are nevertheless some scattered indications drawing our attention towards sixth-century epic poets, in particular Kinaithon of Sparta, author of epic genealogies quoted by Pausanias for the descendants of Orestes, and Asios of Samos, cited in connection with Leda's ancestry.[55] One can add to these indications allusions to some of the genealogy's protagonists in fragments of Spartan poets of the end of the seventh century: Tyrtaios, who praises Zeus' gift of Sparta to the Herakleidai, and of course Alcman, relating the legend of the combat of the Dioskouroi with the sons of Hippokoon and probably also with the Apharetids.[56] But it is clearly impossible to recover and reconstruct from the mosaic of isolated fragments the linear development of the genealogy whose framework Pausanias gives us.

The last resort — to be handled with care lest one falls into the trap of an hermeneutic circle — is the correspondences between the definitive spatial image presented by the genealogy and the historical point when the territory is similarly divided. In the genealogical narrative, then, asserted at the time of each re-institutionalisation and confirmed by the division of the Peloponnese amongst the Herakleidai, one finds the Argos – Sparta – Messenia triangle, with Sparta as apex. This image can only have taken shape after the final submission of Messenia during the seventh century and loses all reality after its liberation in 370. At the same time, it is an image that also very likely takes into account two fundamental political events: the Spartans' appropriation of Orestes when the hero's bones are brought back from Arcadia to Sparta in the middle of the sixth century, and the neutralisation of the Argolid after the successive incursions of the Spartans in the Thyreatid (544) and at Sepeia in 495/4.[57] Sparta's policy of expansion towards the Argolid, which takes the ideological form of the annexation of the Achaean genealogy to write it into the aboriginal genealogy, has left several traces, in particular in Herodotos' works. Even well into the fifth century, the historian echoes the Spartan attempts since the mid-sixth century to achieve hegemony over the Peloponnese, and their efforts at justification through the alleged Achaean ancestry of their rulers.[58] One may therefore entertain the idea that the genealogical narrative we have analysed found its canonical form and consequently its enunciative setting during the period of the consolidation of the Spartan hegemony over the main part of the Peloponnese, during the second half of the sixth century and the first quarter of the fifth.

4. The Genealogical Narrative as a Symbolic Process

The ideological function of the Spartan genealogy is to represent, within precise historical conditions of the expansion of the city, not only a space with its given political limits and social values, but also the manner in which the spatial situation was gradually brought about. This has been stated repeatedly. But why use the form of genealogy?

First, probably, because, through the narrative process of cumulation instead of confrontation, it allows a linear (diachronic) development to lead into a static (synchronic) representation. So if Spartan genealogy does assume correctly the ideological function assigned to it, one may ask for example if it does not bear the imprint of the ideology of the three Indo-European functions. Answers to this question have been attempted not unsuccessfully in relation to the Spartan double kingship (reduplication of the first function) and, rather less successfully, regarding the tripartition of the Peloponnese between the Herakleidai.[59] Since the intervention of Herakles' descendants represents the outcome of the genealogy, why should its development up to this new starting point not bear equally the imprint of the ideology of these three functions?

Such is certainly the case within the genealogy for the act constitutive of the space of Messenia: the mark of political and religious power is seen in the institution, by the first rulers of Messenia, Messene and Polykaon, of the cult of Zeus; the warrior function enters with the support of Argive and Spartan soldiers in the occupation of the territory of the future Messenia; the activity of agricultural production is alluded to in the conflict between Demeter and Triopas, Messene's father.

But it is probably also the case with the process of the constitution of Sparta and Laconia as developed by the genealogical narrative overall. The three-functional ideology can be seen in a division of the ten royal generations preceding the Herakleidai into three groups following each other in the narrative temporality of the genealogy. From Lelex to Eurotas via Myles, the *isotopia* which runs through these rulers' founding acts articulates above all the values attached to the earth and to cereal cultivation: the narrative begins, then, by actualising the function of production. Starting with Sparte and her husband Lakedaimon, son of Zeus, continuing

178

with Amyklas, the founder of Amyklai, and then his son Hyakinthos at the start of the Amyklaian festival in honour of Apollo, it is obvious that the political and religious function is taking shape. Next, Oibalos assumes a position of intermediary between norm and deviance, between a narrative that is static and one that is truly polemical, and also intermediary between affirming the initial spatial triangle and challenging it. This failed re-institutionalisation is the act of the three following generations (Tyndareus, Dioskouroi and Helen, Orestes), and the agonal fights in which they are the protagonists clearly actualise the military function. Thus, thanks to the genealogical form, diachrony and synchrony come to coincide in a probable manifestation of the Indo-European ideology of the three functions.

But beyond the Indo-European imprint and the coincidence between static or on the contrary linear and genetic structure, the genealogy allows one above all to give shape to the transition from a degree zero to a state of differentiation. It is then able to take provisionally the turn of traditional narrative which always presupposes duality in the opposition in action of subject and anti-subject or, if one admits the existence of the level of fundamental syntax and semantics, the relationships of contrariety and contradiction that the semiotic square of Greimas' theory articulates.[60] Seen from this perspective the development of the Spartan genealogy is entirely significant, especially in its spatial manifestation. In the first two stages of its development (territorial demarcation assuring Sparta's economic foundations, determination of the political centre and boundaries of its territory), the text makes full use of the narrative possibilities specific to genealogy with the attribution of original characteristics which every new birth and every matrimonial conjunction establishes by means of state-enunciates. The territory constituted in the genealogy thus grows spatially as well as qualitatively, without essential reversals, through the form of the various actors that every new state-enunciate sets up.

In the end, everything happens as though the constant actor who in traditional narrative assures the unity of the narration had been replaced by space, since it is territorial unity that assures the narrative coherence of the genealogy over the succession of its actors. Moreover, the generation of the territory and its representatives originating in a unique autochthonous ancestor enables the narrative in a way to put the genealogy into perspective and to establish Sparta definitively as the centre of focus. Lelex's position thus refers to the situation of the enunciator of the genealogy.[61] But no sooner is the centre defined with its territory and boundaries within the Argos–Sparta–Messenia triangle than confrontation arises. Then, from the double marriage of the Argive Gorgophone, the tensions between the three poles come to light; through the expedient of simple conjugal unions covering the state-enunciates actualised up to this stage, genealogy becomes 'narrativised' and is the site of a polemical action. There seems to be no other way of re-establishing the narrative equilibrium than through the marriage of Hermione and Orestes, with the unique power instituted by this union on the confronting parties; but this is only how it appears, since the alliance in fact bears in its doubly endogamic character the very reasons of its inanity. Hence the return of the Herakleidai and the reaffirmation of the spatial configuration to which the first two stages of the genealogical process had already led.

So the royal genealogy constitutes a real principle of explanation and of figurative manifestation for the transition from the one to the multiple and to the differentiated. Yet generation also passes through matrimonial union and it is due to conjugal union that womanhood becomes integrated into the political centre. This womanhood is in general a representation of exteriority, whether defined in relation to the adult man's civilisation (Lelex's wife is a nymph or a naiad; Taygete, Lakedaimon's mother, is a virgin and a nymph); or whether she signifies otherness in relation to political territory (Messene is Argive, as is Gorgophone, Oibalos' wife; Diomede, Amyklas' wife, is Thessalian; Leda, Tyndareus' wife is Aitolian). Womanhood fixes its roots not so much in the non-civilised as in the exterior, in the Other. But because of these roots and because of conjugal union, the passage from the exterior to the interior takes place within womanhood. The marginality often attributed to the Greek image of woman has, then, a conditional value;[62] her presence is only acknowledged as a means for the political adult identity to take shape. Zeus' illegal and savage union with the maiden Taygete is transformed in the succeeding generation into the eminently political marriage of their son Lakedaimon with Sparte, thus rushing to the rescue of the Spartan patrilinear legitimacy in dire need of a male heir.

Furthermore, the conjugal union, sign of the wedded couple's

Figure 8.3: The Genealogy of the First Kings of Sparta

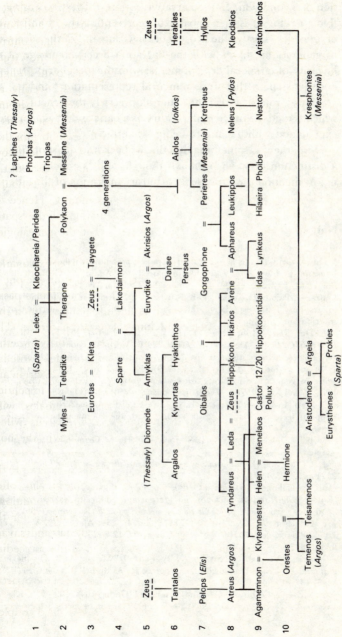

passage to adult social status, corresponds narratively to the sanction of a condition. In the narrative within which it acts as narrative operator, it is then capable of representing the establishment of an order. Lastly, the process of begetting and of the succession of generations shares with the narration a certain image of the linearity of temporal developments, with this peculiarity, that for once it is space that finds temporal representation, and not the other way round. Was it not after all precisely the genetic pattern which served the nineteenth century as a basis and image for every explanation with a claim to being 'scientific'?

Here, then, is something that throws back into question too neat a distinction between 'rational' thought and 'symbolic' thought, not to mention the supposedly arbitrary operation of the latter![63]

Notes

* This contribution is a version of a paper presented at the Universities of Lausanne and Urbino. I would like to thank J. -M. Adam, A. -C. Berthoud, Ph. Borgeaud, J. Bremmer, M. Del Ninno, M. Detienne, B. Gentili, M. Haus, D. Lanza, G. Paioni, H. Pernet, J.-B. Racine, and C. Reichler for their most helpful suggestions. I am especially grateful to A. Habib for his translation of this contribution into English.

1. Hes. *Theog.* 116ff; Hecat. *FGrH* 1 F 3ff; Eumel. *FGrH* 451 T 1, F 1ff; *Marm. Par. FGrH* 239 (cf. Dem. Phal. *FGrH* 228 F 1). On theogonic and (historical) genealogies see now, respectively, M. L. West, *Hesiod. Theogony* (Oxford, 1966) 1–16 and F. Jacoby, *Atthis* (Oxford, 1949) 134–40, 219–23. On the genealogical genre in general see F. Graf, *Griechische Mythologie* (Munich and Zurich, 1985) 117–37 and M. L. West, *The Hesiodic Catalogue of Women* (Oxford, 1985) 11–18.

2. Tyrt. fr. 2.12–15 West = 1a.12–15 Gentili/Prato; see also below, note 56. Hippias' lectures: Plato *Hi. Ma.* 285de, with the commentary by Detienne, *Invention*, 163–7.

3. Paus. 3.1.1–5, tr. W. H. S. Jones and H. A. Ormerod (Loeb), spelling adapted.

4. Cf. M. Stanek, *Sozialordnung und Mythik in Palimbei = Basler Beitr. z. Ethnol.*, 23 (Basle, 1983) 174–82.

5. See Calame, 'Le Nom d'Oedipe', in *Edipo, il teatro greco e la cultura europea* (Rome, 1986) and 'L'antroponimo greco come enunciato narrativo: appunti linguistici e semiotici', in *Mondo classico. Percorsi possibili* (Ravenna, 1985) 27–37.

6. Cf. Hom. *Il.* XX.92–6, XXI.86f.; Hes. fr. 234; Alc. fr. 337 Voigt; Hdt. 1.171; Pherekydes *FGrH* 3 F 155; F. Geyer, *RE* 12.2 (1925) 1890–3; W. Kroll, ibid., 1893.

7. Aristot. fr. 546 (= Strabo 7.7.2); Paus. 1.39.6 and 44.3. On the many foundations of cities by autochthonous heroes see A. Brelich, *Gli eroi Greci* (Rome, 1958) 137–9.

8. See, e.g., G. Busolt, *Griechische Geschichte* I (Gotha, 1893) 182–5. F. Kiechle, *Lakonien und Sparta* (Munich, 1963) 20–9 commits the same methodological error,

although to a lesser extent.

9. Strabo 7.7.2 connects the name with the verb *(sul)lego* 'to speak'. On modern etymologies of *Leleges*, see P. Kretschmer, 'Die Leleger und die ostmediterrane Urbevölkerung', *Glotta*, *32* (1952) 161–204, who connects the name with the root *läg* meaning 'man' ('Mensch'); see also H. Frisk, *Griechisches etymologisches Wörterbuch* II (Heidelberg, 1970) 103; Burkert, *S&H*, 132. On the onomatopoeic value of the term *barbaros* as referring only to the acoustic perception of a foreign language, see Hdt. 2.57.

10. Stanek, *Sozialordnung*, 177.

11. Cf. Hes. *Theog.* 116–37; Alcm. fr. 5.2 Page (= 81 Calame) with my commentary in *Alcman* (Rome, 1983) 444–54.

12. Cf. Apollod. 3.10.3 (Lelex's wife is the naiad Kleochareia); schol. Eur. *Or.* 626 calls Lelex's wife Peridea (not Peridike, as Schwartz suggests on the basis of a single manuscript); see also J. Andrée-Hanslik, *RE* 19.1 (1937) 720.

13. Paus. 3.20.2, cf. Theophr. fr. 2 Pötscher, M. Detienne, *Les Jardins d'Adonis* (Paris, 1972) 194–217, and M. Detienne and J.-P. Vernant, *La Cuisine du sacrifice en pays grec* (Paris, 1979) 58–63.

14. Paus. 3.1.1, 4.1.1f, 4.3.9. The artificial creation of an archaic capital by the Messenians in their attempts at rewriting history after the liberation of their area in the fourth century hampers in exact localisation of Andania; cf. F. Kiechle, *Messenische Studien* (Kallmünz, 1957) 78–81 and below, note 37. It is noteworthy that Paus. 4.31.11 describes a temple decorated with pictures of the Messenian kings beginning with Aphareus.

15. Call *Cer.* 24–30; Diod. Sic. 5.61.2, cf. E. Wüst, *RE* 7 A (1939) 168–74.

16. Paus. 3.19.9; see also schol. Eur. *Or.* 626.

17. It seems impossible to identify Helen and Menelaos' 'Mycenaean' Sparta (Hom. *Od.* 4.1, 10) with Therapne; cf. P. Cartledge, *Sparta and Lakonia* (London, 1979) 44f, 75–93, 337–9. On the Mycenaean occupation of Therapne and the Menelaion, see H. W. Catling, 'New Excavations at the Menelaion, Sparta', in U. Jantzen, *Neue Forschungen in griechischen Heiligtümern* (Tübingen, 1976) 77–90. The studies by C. Bérard and A. Snodgrass, in G. Gnoli and J.-P. Vernant (eds), *La Mort, les morts dans les sociétés anciennes* (Cambridge and Paris, 1982) 89–105 and 107–19, respectively, discuss the foundation of heroic cults on ancient Mycenaean sites.

18. Schol. Eur. *Or.* 626 call Myles' wife Teledike and not Kleochareia, as Schwartz wrongly conjectures, forgetting that according to a different version Kleochareia is Lelex's wife (cf. above, note 12).

19. Schol. Eur. *Or.* 626; cf. Hes. fr. 234. Deukalion and the Flood: Apollod. 1.7.2; *Marm. Par. FGrH* 239, A 4. On the uncivilised aspects of the personified river before it becomes the Eurotas, see the legend in Ps. Plut. *Fluv.* 17.1, which reverses the genealogical order by making Eurotas son of the nymph Taygete and Lakedaimon (cf. below, note 25).

20. Schol. Eur. *Or.* 626 attribute to Myles a daughter Pedias (the manuscripts offer the readings *paidian, kepedian* and *kepaidian*), but Apollod. 3.14.5 makes Pedias (whose name he considers to be a derivative in *-ad-*) the daughter of the Lacedaemonian Mynes, a name which naturally has to be corrected in Myles (with the genitive *Mylou* rather than *Myletos*). Pedias married the successor of Kekrops to the throne of Attica, Kranaos, whom Apollodorus connects with the time of Deukalion and the Flood.

21. Paus. 3.13.8f; on the connection between marriage and cereal agriculture see J.-P. Vernant, *Mythe et société en Grèce ancienne* (Paris, 1974) 146–51.

22. For the terminology used, see C. Lévi-Strauss, *Les Structures élémentaires de la parenté* (Paris, 1949) 153–87 and S. Tornay, 'L'Etude de la parenté', in J. Copans

et al., *L'Anthropologie. Science des sociétés primitives?* (Paris, 1971) 49–111.

23. Cf. F. Bölte, *RE* 3 A.2 (1929) 1267–94 (on the denotations of the names *Lakedaimon* and *Sparte*) and ibid., 1280–92 (Lacedaemonians).

24. Cf. Burkert, *GR*, 200–7.

25. See also Apollod. 3.10.3; schol. Eur. *Or.* 626. Ps. Plut. *Fluv.* 17.3 relates that Taygete, having been raped by Zeus, committed suicide from grief; this suicide took place at Mt Amyklaion, since called Taygetos.

26. Paus. 3.18.10; Pind. *Ol.* 3.30 with the scholia *ad loc.* On Artemis and Taygete see also Hom. *Od.* 6.103; Eur. *Hel.* 381–4.

27. Pind. *Ol.* 3.30 and schol. ad loc. = Sosib. *FGrH* 595 F 21; schol. Pind. *Pyth.* 4.15. On the five *obai* which constitute the city of Sparta see, e.g., A. Toynbee, *Some Problems of Greek History* (Oxford, 1969) 260–5; on Euphemos, Poseidon's son, see F. Chamoux, *Cyrène sous la monarchie des Battiades* (Paris, 1953) 83–9.

28. See Paus. 3.1.3; Apollod. 3.10.3; Steph. Byz. s.v. *Amyklai*. On Amyklai's history see most recently Cartledge, *Sparta*, 65–8, 106–8.

29. Apollod. 3.10.3. On the archaeological proofs of Mycenaean Amyklai and its continuous inhabitation into the archaic age, see E. Buschor and M.v. Massow, 'Vom Amyklaion', *Ath. Mitt.*, *52* (1927) 1–85; Cartledge, *Sparta*, 30–101; J. T. Hooker, *The Ancient Spartans* (London and Toronto, 1980) 25–46. On the Hyacinthia in Amyklai see Calame, *Chœurs* I, 305–23; Hooker, *Spartans*, 60–6. Note also that the rhetor Aristides *Or.* 11.79 mentions Apollo as honouring Amyklas, Narcissus and Hyakinthos.

30. See especially Pherecyd. *FGrH* 3 F 10; Apollod. 2.2.1–2; Paus. 3.13.8. On the role of Egyptian Danaos in the Argolid and of Lynkeus, the son of his brother Aigyptos, see G. A. Megas, 'Die Sage von Danaos und den Danaiden', *Hermes*, *68* (1933) 415–28 and Detienne, *Dionysos*, 37–40.

31. Paus. 3.13.8; cf. H. Hitzig and H. Bluemmer, *Pausaniae Graeciae descriptio*, vol. I.2 (Leipzig, 1899) 782.

32. Apollod. 3.10.3; Schol. Nic. *Ther.* 902 make Diomede into a nymph. On Lapithes see Diod. Sic. 4.69.1–5, 5.61.3; Steph. Byz. s.v. *Lapithe*.

33. Paus. 7.18.5; cf. Hitzig and Bluemmer, *Pausaniae Graeciae descriptio*, 811; Hsch. s.v. *Agigaios*.

34. Paus. 3.13.1. Aristid. Mil. *FGrH* 444 F 1 makes Leukippos into Amyklas' son, which makes Koronis, Asklepios' mother by Apollo, Amyklas' grand-daughter — a new way of associating Sparta's king with Apollo (cf. n 29). If Kynortas' name is to be associated with the well-known name of the *oba* Kynosoura, Argalos' name cannot but be associated with the *oba Arkalon* which is known from one fifth-century inscription only (*IG* V.1.722, 4 = *SEG* 11.475a, 4); cf. A. J. Beattie, 'An Early Laconian *Lex Sacra*', *CQ*, *45* (1951) 46–58; Kiechle, *Lakonien*, 123–5.

35. Paus. 4.2.2, 4; Apollod. 1.9.5, 2.4.5. On Aiolos' offspring, see Hes. fr. 10; Apollod. 1.7.3. Perieres was known in Sparta at least from the seventh century onwards; cf. Alcm. fr. 78 Page = 202 Calame.

36. Paus. 3.15.10; cf. S. Wide, *Lakonische Kulte* (Leipzig, 1893) 45–7; Hes. fr. 199.8; *IG* XII.3.869, 6; see also E. Wüst, *RE* 17.2 (1932) 2092–5.

37. Paus. 4.3.7, 4.1.5, 4.2.4. Arene's location is even more uncertain than that of Andania, which is situated north of Mt Ithome in the northern part of the Messenian plain; cf. M. N. Valmin, *Etudes topographiques sur la Messénie ancienne* (Lund, 1930) 89–125, 140f.

38. Paus. 4.2.5f; see already Hom. *Od.* 11.235–59. On the various versions of Neleus' legend see M.-C. van der Kolf, *RE* 16.2 (1935) 2269–80. On the history of Pylos and Methoner see Kiechle, *Messenische Studien*, 31–3, 65–71.

39. On Lykos see Soph. F 24.2 Radt; Paus. 4.1.5. This is perhaps a very young

tradition, cf. W. A. Oldfather, *RE* 13.2 (1927) 2399–401.

40. Cf. schol. Hom. *Il.* 2.581; schol. Eur. *Or.* 457. Pellana lies on the eastern slopes of the Taygetos, not far from the sources of the Eurotas, cf. Strabo 8.4.4 and 7.5; Pellana is also Lykurgos' refuge (Pol. 4.81.7). On Tyndareus' flight to Pellana see also Paus. 3.21.2; on his flight to Thestios see Apollod. 3.10.5; Strabo 10.2.24, which perhaps derives from the epic poem the *Alcmaeonis* (cf.fr. 5 Kinkel). Cf. also Apollod. 3.10.4f which makes Ikarios into Tyndareus' companion.

41. Hippokoontidai: J. Zwicker, *RE* 8.2 (1913) 1774–6; Henrichs, this volume, Ch. 11, section 2. On the Spartan cults of the Hippokoontidai and Dioskouroi see Wide, *Lakonische Kulte*, 304–25; Calame, *Chœurs* I, 332f, 347f and II, 54f.

42. Castor and Pollux as sons of Tyndareus: Hom. *Od.* 11.298–305; sons of Zeus: Hes. fr. 24. Double ascendance: *H. Hom.* 17.2, 33.1f; Alc. fr. 2, 10(b) Page = 2, 82a Calame (in Sparta itself at the end of the seventh century); see also E. Bethe, *RE* 5 (1905) 1112f.

43. *H. Hom.* 17.3, 33.4; Paus. 3.36.2 (deriving from Alcm. fr. 23 Page = 211 Calame); Paus. 3.1.4.

44. Hom. *Il.* 5.396f and 11.689–761 already mentions Herakles' intervention in Pylos; Sosibios *FGrH* 595 F 13 the one in Sparta, which is already mentioned by Alcm. fr. 1 Page = 3 Calame. For a detailed discussion, with all sources, see Calame, *Chœurs* II, 52–9.

45. On the rivalry between the Apharetidai and Tyndaridai concerning the Leukippidai, who were the incarnation of the newly initiated girls ready for marriage, see the detailed discussion in Calame, *Chœurs* I, 326–33.

46. Pind. *Nem.* 10.71f; cf. Calame, 'Les figures grecques du gigantesque', *Communications*, *42* (1985) 147–72.

47. Divine origin of Helen: Hom. *Il.* 3.199, 488; *Od.* 4.184, 23.218, etc. Leda as mother of Helen and the Dioskouroi: S. Eitrem, *RE* 12.1 (1924) 1116–25. Death of the Dioskouroi: *Cypr.* fr. 5 and 9 Kinkel; Apollod. 3.11.2. Contest for Helen's hand: Stes. fr. 190 Page; Eur. *Iph. Aul.* 58; Isocr. *Hel.* 10,40; Apollod. 3.10.8. Note that only Paus. 3.1.5 (rather vague in this respect) lets the Tyndaridai themselves rule for a time.

48. Stes. fr. 216 Page even moves Agamemnon's palace from Mykenae to Sparta (cf. also Sim. fr. 549 Page). Pindar *Pyth.* 11.32 situates the palace at Amyklai, in this way re-establishing virilocality. The uxorilocal and matrilinear character of Helen's wedding with Menelaos has nothing to do with matriarchy, as is suggested by S. Pomeroy, *Goddesses, Whores, Wives, and Slaves* (New York, 1975) 22f.

49. Orestes in Sparta: Pind. *Pyth.* 9.24, 27 and *Nem.* 11.44; Paus. 2.18.6, 3.16.7. Hom. *Il.* 3.175 already knows Hermione as the only daughter of Helen and Menelaos, but in the *Odyssey* (4.4–17) she marries Achilles' son, Neoptolemos. Eur. *Or.* 1653–9 (note also *Andr.* 966–76) combines both versions of the legend. At least Sophocles (*TGrF* 3, p. 192 Radt = Eust. *Od.* 1479.10–12)) already mentions Orestes' marriage with Hermione.

50. On Teisamenos and his eviction by the Herakleidai, see the summary of Sophocles' *Hermione* (quoted n 49); Paus. 2.18.7f, 2.38.1, 7.1.7; Apollod. 2.8.2–3; Pol. 2.41.4; Strabo 8.7.1, etc.

51. Cf. C. Robert, *Die griechische Heldensage* I (Berlin, 1920) 656–64, 671–75; C. Brillante, *La leggenda eroica e la civiltà micenea* (Rome, 1981) 149–82 (from a historical perspective).

52. Kresphontes: Isocr. 6.22; Plat. *Leg.* 692b; Apollod. 2.8.4. Aristodemos and Argia: Hdt. 6.52f, 7.204, 8.131, cf. G. L. Huxley, 'Herodotos on Myth and Politics in Early Sparta', *Proc. Roy. Irish Ac.*, *101* (1983) 1–16, and P. Carlier, *La Royauté en Grèce avant Alexandre* (Strasbourg, 1984) 375ff.

53. Cf. Calame, *Chœurs* I, 305–23 and 341–50 on the political significance of both Helen and Menelaos' cult at Therapne and of the Hyakinthia festival celebrated at Amyklai; see also Brillante, *La leggenda eroica*, 87–145.

54. Cf. O. Regenbogen, *RE* Suppl. 8 (1956) 1019–24; L. Beschi and D. Musti, *Pausania. Guida della Grecia I. L'Attica* (Milan, 1982) XXIV-XXXV. Pausanias' book 4 on Messenia in general derives its information from the histories written after the liberation of Messenia in the fourth century (Rhianos and Myron); cf. L. Pearson, 'The Pseudo-History of Messenia and its Authors', *Historia*, *11* (1962) 397–426.

55. Paus. 2.18.6 (= Cinaeth. fr. 4 Kinkel), 3.13.8 (= Asius fr. 6 Kinkel = test. 7 Gentili/Prato). On these two indirect citations and the possible dates of these two poets, see G. L. Huxley, *Greek Epic Poetry* (London, 1969) 40, 80f, 94–6. When introducing the Spartan genealogical narrative, Pausanias (3.1.1) simply speaks of an (oral?) Lakedaemonian tradition.

56. Tyrt. fr. 2.2–15 West = 1a.12–15 Gentili/Prato; Alcm. fr. 1.1–11 Page = 3.1–11 Calame and 7 P = 19 C; see also Alcm. fr. 2 P = 2 C; on the legendary tradition which connects the Spartan king list with the Herakleidai see Cartledge, *Sparta*, 53, 341–6.

57. On the double conquest of Messenia and the various military interventions of Sparta against Argos see, especially, G. L. Huxley, *Early Sparta* (London, 1962) 56–9, 68f, 83f; Cartledge, *Sparta*, *passim*; Hooker, *Spartans*, 106–14, 145–57.

58. Cf. Huxley, 'Herodotos on Myth', 5–16; on the origin of the Peloponnesian League see A. H. M. Jones, *Sparta* (Oxford, 1968) 44–7.

59. B. Sergent, 'La représentation spartiate de la royauté', *Rev. Hist. Rel.*, *189* (1976) 3–52 and 'Le partage du Péloponnèse entre les Héraclides', *Rev. Hist. Rel.*, *190* (1977) 121–36 and *191* (1978) 3–25.

60. Cf. A. J. Greimas and J. Courtès, *Sémiotique. Dictionnaire raisonné de la théorie du langage* (Paris, 1979) 29–33, 157–60, 380f; J. -C. Coquet, 'L'Ecole de Paris', in J. -C. Coquet (ed.), *Sémiotique. L'Ecole de Paris* (Paris, 1982) 5–64, esp. 48–52.

61. Cf. M. -J. Borel *et al.*, *Essai de logique naturelle* (Bern, 1983) 53–70 on the *processus de 'schématisation'*.

62. Cf. L. Gallo, 'La donna greca e la marginalità', *Quad. Urb. Cult. Class.*, *47* (1984) 7–51.

63. See Calame, 'Le processus symbolique', *Document de travail du Centro Internazionale di Semiotica e di Linguistica* (Urbino, 1983) 128–9.

9

Myths of Early Athens

Robert Parker

*In memory of T. C. W. Stinton**

In glamour and ancient renown, Athenian mythology can scarcely
compete with several other regional mythologies of Greece. Few
Athenian heroes appear in early sources, and perhaps the only
ancient Attic *geste* of the first quality was that of Theseus with the
Minotaur. Attic mythology has none the less a distinctive interest
for the mythographer, for several reasons. Rare though Attic
stories may be in Homer or Hesiod, in Apollodorus and Ovid they
abound. In the fifth and fourth centuries Athens and Athenians
increasingly dominated literary and artistic culture, while there
emerged in Atthidography a distinctive literary genre specifically
concerned with the country's antiquities, including its mythology.
As a result many existing local stories were dignified with a place
in high art and literature, and not a few others were told for the
first time. Thus the development of Attic mythology is a notable
instance of the 'invention of tradition'.[1] Most of these stories have
public and sometimes political themes. While the myth of
Oedipus, say, is only coincidentally Theban, the Attic myths are
almost all intrinsically Attic, in that the city's origins and institutions form their subject. Only two cycles treat that most characteristic theme of Greek mythology as a whole, the tensions and
traumas of domestic life.[2] Attic mythology is therefore a distinctively 'political mythology',[3] through which the Athenians forged
a sense of their identity as a people. The quite extraordinary
development that the figure of Theseus underwent in the fifth
century is a glittering example of an 'invention of tradition' which
was also the forging of a 'political myth'.[4]

A final attraction of Attic mythology is the opportunity it offers of observing a set of myths in a specific social and historical context. A myth is an item of shared cultural property, and has no intrinsic or essential meaning. Even if one could find what Mr Casaubon[5] and so many others have sought, a 'Key to (all) Mythologies', it would only turn to reveal an empty room. To speak of a myth's 'meaning' is legitimate only as a shorthand way of referring to the sum of the qualities that cause people to listen to it with interest and remember it. And that is all that the interpreter needs to or can explain, the source of a myth's appeal for a particular society at a particular time. (This is not, of course, to deny that a myth may continue to appeal to many different societies for broadly the same reasons.) Myths ought therefore to be approached through a study of 'hearer/viewer response' and 'reception', if we may borrow and adapt these terms of contemporary literary theory.[6] Of course, we can almost never in the ancient world study the 'reception' of a myth with proper precision, and often we are reduced to guessing about possible responses from a mere summary of the plot. But the Attic myths are an unusually favourable case, because rich and diverse contemporary evidence is often available, from vase painting and sculpture as well as from literature.

In myths as in organisms, the capacity for change seems to be almost a condition of life. One of the striking characteristics of Greek mythology as a whole is the way in which it retained that life-giving mutability long after the introduction of writing.[7] Of the approaches to mythology that are familiar today, the one that seems most old-fashioned is in some respects the most soundly based theoretically: for the painstaking historical analysis of the variants and development of a myth does justice to this power of change, as well as being a kind of study of 'reception'. The weakness of that method, which received its classic expression in the work of Carl Robert,[8] was the lurking presumption that in mythology as in textual criticism the point of studying the variants is to get back to the uncorrupted original, where meaning resides. But it is obviously unsatisfactory to 'explain' the myth of Oedipus by reference to a (as it happens, hypothetical) ritual origin, an origin unknown to the millions of people who have heard the myth with fascination. There is perhaps no helpful discrimination to be drawn in terms of 'authenticity' between different variants of a myth or stages in its development, or between 'real myth' and

188

'literary myths' or the like. Certainly, very drastic alterations do take place in the character of the mythological tradition. Important variables include the social context in which myths are reproduced, the literary or artistic form in which they are embodied, the principles by which they are organised, the toleration of supernatural elements within them, the competition that they undergo from accounts of the past based on different principles, the esteem in which they are held, and, simply but crucially, the extent to which they are widely familiar. But it is always the same river that flows through this changing landscape. There are developments in the tradition but no breaks; no point can be located where myth ceases, as it were, to be itself.[9] Even the extensive effort by fourth-century writers to systematise and rationalise received mythology, which was doubtless the most significant single reshaping of the tradition, did not lack antecedents;[10] and in attempting to preserve the myths as history rather than jettison them as fable these writers perpetuated one of mythology's ancient functions, that of providing an account of the past. Perhaps we should consider the history of mythology not as a decline from myth into non-myth but as a succession of periods or styles, developing out of one another, as in art. That metaphor, however, does not remove but emphasises the need to distinguish between the products of different periods.

The period chosen for this essay is the second half of the fifth century, for which the evidence is most abundant. The stories will be presented according to their rough chronology in mythological time. It is unlikely, though, that many Athenians at this date thought of them in this way. Many people doubtless knew something of the order of the kings, but the important point about most of the stories was surely not their place in a chronological sequence. Who even now can say offhand whether Demeter or Dionysos arrived in Attica first? (There is an answer to that question; but one puzzles in vain whether the rape of Cephalus came before or after that of Orithyia.) The systematisation of the tradition was the work of the Atthidographers, beginning with Hellanicus at the end of the fifth century. They introduced new kings to the king-list,[11] to make the chronology of Attic myth match better with that of Greece as a whole, and must have been obliged to assign every floating story to a specific reign. In the fifth century there were already one or two works that grouped Attic myths together,[12] but probably most Athenians learnt them not in that form, as a cycle, but one by one as they were portrayed in particular works of art or poems or told in relation to particular cults or shrines. What really mattered chronologically about the myths was that they described events of the 'generation of heroes' (Hdt. 3.122) and not of men.

Not every Athenian myth can be discussed in the space available. Since the later traditions, largely dominated by Theseus, have been much and well studied of late, we will concentrate on the earlier ones, those that fall in mythological time before the death of Erechtheus. The Eleusinian myth of Demeter's arrival and the largely apolitical myth of Cephalus and Procris are deliberately excluded; other omissions will probably be accidental.[13] With these preliminaries completed, Athenian history can commence.[14]

It begins, one might say, with the birth of Athena.[15] She was one of several Olympians whose birth was miraculous; this was a mark of their high destiny as well as a symptom of the unsettled conditions of a young world. She was born, without a mother, from Zeus' head; she leapt forth, fully mature in all but size and heavily armed, to the wonder and terror of the attendant gods. That much is common to virtually all the descriptions and representations of the birth. There is evidently a connection between Athena's strange origin and her strange nature. The goddess who 'loves din and war and battle' (Hes. *Theog.* 926) has wholly escaped from feminine influence and is in the most literal sense a 'father's child' (Aesch. *Eum.* 738; cf. Pearson on Soph. fr. 564). The weakness of infancy, when even men are womanly, is not for her; and there is a metallic brilliance about her epiphany appropriate to one who never lurked in 'the darkness of the womb' (Aesch. *Eum.* 665). As a female who 'sided with the male in everything (short of accepting marriage)' (Aesch. *Eum.* 737), the friendly helper of male heroes, she was the ideal patroness for patriarchal Athens. At the same time, her origin from the most dignified part, indeed almost the 'self' of Zeus, explains her unique and for Athenians most welcome closeness to the lord of the universe (e.g. Aesch. *Eum.* 826–8, 997–1102).[16] In many vase paintings, Hephaestus has helped the birth by cleaving Zeus' head with an axe (cf. Pind. *Ol.* 7.35–8) and is shown hurrying away, alarmed no doubt by the exuberant creature who has emerged. It was right that one god of crafts should assist at the birth of another, and the Athenians, for whom the association of Athena and Hephaestus was particularly important, evidently relished the motif.[17]

It is not clear whether certain more elaborate accounts, which set the birth in a broader mythological context, were well known at Athens. For Hesiod, it was associated with a threat to Zeus' newly established sovereignty, and with the power of *metis*, wiliness, 'cunning intelligence'. Metis (personified), Zeus' first wife, was to have borne first Athena, then a son mightier than its father. Zeus therefore swallowed her; Athena emerged from his head, the son remained unborn (Hes. *Theog.* 886–900; cf. 'Hes.' fr. 343).[18] The myth explained the unique resourcefulness of Zeus, who had assimilated Metis, and of Athena, whose mother she was. It also confirmed that there were to be no more revolutions in heaven. *Metis* was now under control, shared with the loving daughter, the father's child, but not with an independent threatening son. A further elaboration (already partially present in Hesiod *Theog.* 927–9; cf. fr. 343.1) made the birth part of a contest in asexual generation between Zeus and the jealous Hera. This ended in decisive humiliation for the woman, since Zeus without Hera could produce splendid Athena, Hera without Zeus merely crippled Hephaestus and the monster Typhoeus (*Hom. H. Ap.* 305–55). The respective role of the two parents in generation was long to be controversial in Greek thought, and the myth reads like a comic anticipation of Aristotle's doctrine that the child's form derives from the father, the mother providing merely the less honourable matter.[19] Thus Athena's lack of a mother became less a way of describing her unique nature than of making a point about the relation of the sexes. We do not know how many Athenians drew this conclusion from the myth, but Aeschylus' Apollo certainly does, in a famous passage in *Eumenides* (658–66).[20]

As it happens, there is more artistic than literary evidence for the myth's popularity at Athens, and so the nuances of its reception there remain uncertain. From about 570–530 it was a favourite subject for vase painters. It then declined in popularity and had almost disappeared by 460, but remained such a central Athenian myth that it could not be omitted from the Parthenon: in a somewhat rationalised iconography, with Athena standing beside Zeus rather than emerging from his head, it occupied the important east pediment.[21] The association between Athena and

Zeus was probably the most important single source of the myth's appeal for the Athenians. It meant that they too had contact along a chain of patronage with the ruler of the world. As we shall see, 'dearness to the gods' (*theophilia*) is a central concern of many of these myths,[22] and 'dearness to Zeus' is of course its most desirable form.

Athena took an active part in the War of the Gods and Giants, another Panhellenic myth that had been so thoroughly assimilated by the Athenians that it must be included here.[23] There are indeed hints of specific Athenian variants or offshoots,[24] among them one that cast Theseus' cousins the Pallantids as giants, but there is no doubt that the dominant version even in Athens was the Panhellenic one. The battle was portrayed on countless vases (from about 565), on the pediment of the sixth-century temple of Athena, and, in the Parthenon, both on the metopes and inside the shield of Pheidias' cult-statue. Above all, it was the traditional decoration of perhaps the most important symbolic object of Athenian religion, the robe offered to Athena every four years at the greater Panathenaea. The central significance of the myth must have been the same for the Athenians as for the Greeks at large. It told how Zeus had been confirmed in his sovereignty, how therefore the present world-order had been made secure, by a display of tempered force against enemies who were the embodiment of *hybris*, lawless violence. Unlike the earlier war against the Titans (with which, though, it had become confused by the time of Euripides), this was a collective act of all the Olympians, and one undertaken in defence of the existing order and not in rebellion against it. Such a myth of the establishment of divine and cosmic order was fit emblem for the Panathenaea, the great festival of social unity and order.[25]

There was particular significance for Athenians in the glorious part played by their own warrior-goddess, second only to that of Zeus himself. It established that she was, for all time to come, Athena Victory (Eur. *Ion* 1528–9). Though won in war, this title was equally appropriate to her as patroness of the sporting competitions of the Panathenaea: for Victory in whatever sphere derived from the same golden goddess. Perhaps in the fifth century victory over the giants came to be seen as a prefiguration of the Greeks' famous victories over the barbarians. That symbolism is certainly found in the hellenistic period; and already in the first

Pythian Ode of 470 (15–28, 71–5) Pindar pointedly juxtaposes
Typhoeus, a Giant-like figure, with barbarian enemies. (It was
even possible to deploy the imagery against other Greeks, if we
accept that the hybristic giants of Pindar's eighth *Pythian* embody a
victims' view of Athenian imperialism.)[26] At all events, Athena's
triumph over Enceladus, laboriously woven on her robe every four
years by the Athenian women, helped to guarantee the strength of
their menfolk's spears.

From gods we turn to men. Whatever certain antiquarians
might say, the general belief among Athenians was that their first
king had been Cecrops.[27] Cecrops had no parents, but had
emerged from the earth itself. No myth described the circumstances of this strange birth, but the most familiar fact about
Cecrops was that he bore the mark of it in his 'double form': above
the waist he was a man, below a curling snake (e.g. Eur. *Ion*
1163–4; Ar. *Vesp.* 438). Having emerged from the earth, he still in
part resembled the creature that slips to and fro between the upper
and lower worlds.

The next Attic king Erichthonius/Erechtheus was also earth-
born, and vase painters often show Cecrops as a witness of his successor's birth.[28] The juxtaposition suggests that the two legends
should be taken together, as a pair. Cecrops in these scenes always
has his semi-serpentine form, whereas the baby is fully human.
The effect of this contrasted juxtaposition of the two earth-born
kings is twofold: on the one hand it emphasises the idea of autochthony, since the Athenian royal line proves to be earth-born twice
over, while on the other differentiation and progress are revealed,
with Cecrops representing an intermediate stage between wholly
earthy and wholly human.[29] Upon Cecrops are unloaded all the
sinister connotations of pre-human birth.

The birth of Erichthonius/Erechtheus is one of the earliest-
attested Athenian legends. It is mentioned in a passage in the
Catalogue of Ships in the *Iliad* which will surely go back at least to
the sixth century, even if it is an 'Attic interpolation'.[30] The
passage speaks of

> great-spirited Erechtheus, whom once Athena
> daughter of Zeus reared, but the grain-giving soil bore him,
> and Athena set him down in Athens, in her rich temple
> (2.547–9).

The future king is born from the ground, but taken at once by a goddess into her care. This central idea is illustrated on the fifth-century vases: a goddess emerges from the ground and hands to the waiting Athena a baby, which stretches eagerly to meet its new nurse. By the end of the sixth century the child had been given a father, Hephaestus, who is sometimes shown attending the birth. Hephaestus had been seeking to rape Athena but the virgin evaded him, his seed fell on the ground, and from it sprung Erichthonius/ Erechtheus.[31] This story of amorous mischance suited the mythological Hephaestus, constantly subject to ludicrous indignities, but the substantial point of the invention was surely to put the proto-Athenian under the joint patronage of Athena and Hephaestus.

Erichthonius/Erechtheus has sometimes been identified as an instance of a figure characteristic of Minoan-Mycenaean religion, the 'divine child' growing up in the care of foster-nurses. But, however things may have been in early times, post-Mycenaean Greeks must surely have felt a difference between, say, baby Zeus, a god in exile, and baby Erechtheus, a child of the earth protected by a powerful goddess. All the Athenians accessible to us seem to have understood the birth of Erichthonius/Erechtheus as a myth of national origins. There was no separate tradition about the Athenians at large: the two earth-born kings are mythical representatives of the whole Athenian people in their claim to autochthony. Indeed in poetry (particularly) the Athenians were sometimes spoken of as actual descendants of their first kings, as 'Cecropids' or 'Erechtheids'.[32]

What then did this myth of national origins say? It put the proto-Athenian in the closest possible relation with Athena, while respecting her virginity; in its developed form it introduced Athena's regular associate Hephaestus as a kind of father for the child. Thus the Athenians were 'children of blessed gods' (Eur. *Med.* 825), living in 'a land most dear to the gods' (Aesch. *Eum.* 869). There was no more important guarantee of prosperity than this.[33] As 'children of Hephaestus' the Athenians were marked, intriguingly, as a technological people (Aesch. *Eum.* 13). One wonders whether that conception was more popular outside Attica or within it, and whether in Athens it was as dear to the knights, say, as to the potters.[34]

The myth also, of course, endorses the Athenians' claim to the prized 'autochthony'. Indeed it shows a lawyer's cunning in insisting that the Athenians are 'born from the earth', while reserving their title as 'children of blessed gods'. In ordinary language 'autochthonous' meant little more than 'native' as opposed to 'immigrant': the myth interprets the idea of 'nativeness' with drastic if logical literalism, as physical birth from the native soil. The Athenians were probably correct in believing that they had occupied the same territory for longer than most of the Greek states around them. From this historical reality they created what every state requires, a myth to make its citizens glad that they were born in that state and no other. The ideal of autochthony was a form of collective snobbery. Athenians *en masse* were invited to despise other states (Dorians above all) just as an aristocrat might despise a metic. Athenians were, so to speak, the only authentic citizens of Greece, all other groups being mere immigrants, a motley rabble tainted with foreign blood.[35] No patriotic orator could neglect the theme, and many new twists were discovered: only the Athenians had a truly filial relation to their native land; they were juster than other Greeks, because they held their land by birthright and not seizure; they were even born egalitarians, being all sprung from the same earth.[36]

These hyper-patriotic interpretations are first attested in the 420s (Hdt. 7.161.3; Eur. *Erechtheus* fr. 50.6–13), at a time when anti-Dorian sentiment was no doubt particularly strong because of the Peloponnesian war (cf. Thuc. 6.77.1, with K. J. Dover's note). They are applied, then and later, to the general notion of Athenian autochthony, not to the particular myths of Cecrops and Erichthonius. We cannot strictly prove that these latter had originally been understood in the same way; they might in theory have been merely myths of origin, answering the question 'where do Athenians come from?', rather than myths of an origin superior to that other states. An increase in patriotic emphasis there no doubt was, in the heyday of the funeral orations; in all probability, though, some association between autochthony and 'true birth' (cf. Ar. *Vesp.* 1076) had always been present.

Erichthonius/Erechtheus' childhood did not pass off without incident. Athena hid the child in a chest with a snake or snakes to guard him, and gave the chest to the daughters of Cecrops, Pandrosus, Aglaurus and Herse, to keep, with instructions not to open it. But they did, and, terrified by the sight of the snakes, they hurled themselves from the Acropolis, where they lived, to their death on the rocks below (Eur. *Ion* 21–4, 271–4). Most accounts add that one daughter, normally Pandrosus, remained obedient to Athena and escaped her sisters' fate.[37] As has long been recognised, this myth very probably has its origin in ritual performed by the Arrephoroi, young girls in the service of Athena who lived on the Acropolis for a period, at the end of which they made a ritual descent (perhaps from the Acropolis) carrying sacred objects, the nature of which they were forbidden to know.[38] But since the story, a popular one with vase painters (Eur. *Ion* 271), had clearly escaped from the narrow sacral context, we need to consider the source of its more general appeal.

It is based upon two popular narrative motifs, the 'disobeyed command' and 'good and bad sisters'. Into this frame it fits characters who were of intrinsic interest to Athenians: Aglaurus and Pandrosus (though not Herse) were prominent figures in cult, and, like so many heroes of Athens' earliest myths, had precincts on or near the Acropolis. Indeed the story to some extent explains familiar topographical facts, since the survivor Pandrosus had her precinct on the heights of the Acropolis, while that of Aglaurus who leapt to her death was on the slopes below it.[39] Even more interesting than the sisters perhaps was the snake associated with the young Erichthonius/Erechtheus: for the most famous inhabitant of the Acropolis was the sacred snake that lived, very suitably, in the precinct of Erichthonius/Erechtheus, and was believed to guard the city (Hdt. 8.41) just as its mythical predecessor had guarded the wonder-child. Is it coincidence that a recently discovered vase which portrays this myth introduces the figure of *Soteria*, 'safety, salvation'? Possibly the myth evoked indirectly quite powerful feelings about the safety of the city.[40] And whether or not this public association was present, it certainly established a link between Erichthonius/Erechtheus, the exemplary proto-Athenian, the nursling of Athena, and any Athenian woman's own child: for Athenian women put gold amulets in the form of snakes around their own babies, 'observing the custom of their forefathers and of earth-born Erichthonius' (Eur. *Ion* 20–6, 1427–9).

Apollodorus introduces a detail absent from other accounts. Athena was rearing Erichthonius in secret from the gods because she hoped to make him immortal; and that, it seems, was why she hid him in a box and entrusted him to the Cecropids (*Bibl.* 3.14.6). Presumably the girls' meddling spoilt the goddess's plans. This is a motif more familiar from the *Homeric Hymn to Demeter*, where Demeter's attempt to immortalise the Eleusinian prince Demophon fails through human weakness (226–74). It perhaps better suits the Eleusinian context, since the story of immortality (inevitably) lost seems there to prepare for a second best, the institution of Mysteries that help mortals to secure a better lot in the afterlife (*Hymn* 270–4, 470–82). In relation to the bright hope of early Athens, by contrast, the tragic note jars. It may none the less have been heard by some; there is no way of telling when the assimilation of Erichthonius to Demophon may have first occurred.[41]

In one respect, there was something unsatisfactory about the myth even in its familiar form. In cult Aglaurus was patroness of the ephebes, the city's future warriors, and yet the myth showed her first disobedient, then panic-stricken. The anomaly was removed in a probably fourth-century version by a characteristic procedure of adaptation and conflation.[42] In this account Aglaurus did indeed hurl herself to her death from the Acropolis — but in response to an oracle declaring that the war against Eleusis would only end when an Athenian sacrificed himself for the city. The motif of a saving sacrificial death is obviously borrowed from the older Athenian legends of the daughters of Leos and Erechtheus; with the help of it, the patroness of the ephebes became a true model for them to follow.

As the most prominent female Athenians of the earliest times, the daughters of Cecrops were credited with descendants.[43] In particular, one of them, variously identified, was seduced by Hermes and gave birth to Keryx, founding father of the Eleusinian family of the Kerykes. This simple and appropriate aetiological tradition is doubtless ancient, but there is as yet no trace in classical sources of the complex story of greed, erotic intrigue and jealousy that was later spun out of it.[44]

About the doings of Cecrops himself there is little to be said. When in the fourth century the Atthidographers constructed a systematic account of the growth of civilisation in Attica, he became a key figure who introduced the first basic institutions of a way of life removed from barbarism. He brought the Attic people together into the first twelve townships and established the earliest Athenian rituals, those that were conducted in the innocent ancient way without blood sacrifice and that honoured the old gods who ruled before Zeus. Cecrops is seen, as it were, as Kronos to

Erichthonius/Erechtheus' Zeus, and his reign takes on certain tinges of the golden age. He was eventually credited with the foundation of many institutions, including that of marriage. A kind of mythographic imagination was, certainly, still at work in shaping the image of Cecrops as a 'culture hero'; but there is no trace of this conception in the fifth century, and even in the fourth century perhaps not before Philochorus.[45]

In the early tradition the one great event of his reign was the contest of Athena and Poseidon for Attica. This was the subject of the west pediment of the Parthenon,[46] and very appropriately, since two familiar sights of the Acropolis were the central items of evidence in the gods' dispute. Poseidon asserted his claim to the land by striking the rock with his trident and bringing forth a salt spring, the famous 'sea' of the Erechtheum; Athena planted the first of all olive-trees, that which still grew in the fifth century in the Pandroseum. One picture of the scene even emphasises these local associations by introducing the sacred snake of the Erechtheum.[47] For want of an early narrative account, several details are obscure. Cecrops was certainly involved in the dispute, either as actual judge, appointed 'because of his virtue', or as a witness, the judges being the twelve gods.[48] In late versions the land was to belong to the god who could offer the greater benefits to Attica. Accordingly, they caused their respective symbols, the olive-tree and the 'sea' (or a horse), to spring from the ground during the actual trial. It looks as if in the classical legend the issue was merely one of priority.[49] Immediately on arrival in Attica, Poseidon brought forth the sea, and Athena planted the olive, as ways of staking their respective claims to the land. A quarrel ensued, during which Poseidon possibly threatened the sacred olive with his trident, and Zeus possibly hurled a thunderbolt to separate the disputants.[50] In the ensuing trial, both gods appealed to the tokens as 'evidence' of their prior claim (Hdt. 8.55). Athena prevailed, strangely to our ears, because she had called Cecrops to witness her act of planting, while Poseidon who had in fact arrived first lacked witnesses (Apollod. *Bibl.* 3.14.1).[51] Enraged at the verdict, Poseidon began to flood the Thriasian plain, until ordered by Zeus to desist (Apollod.; Hyg. *Fab.* 164).[52]

Several features of this myth are clear. It explains Athena's primacy in the city's pantheon, brings drama to the familiar monuments of the Acropolis, and depicts the origin of one of

Attica's most characteristic products and most venerable religious symbols:[53] for, whatever the goddess's exact motives may have been, it was a great moment when Athena 'revealed the first shoot of the grey olive, a heavenly crown and a glory for bright Athens' (Eur. *Tro.* 802; cf. *Ion* 1433). If an attack on the olive-tree by Poseidon was indeed stayed by the thunderbolt, that would be a further most apposite detail, since Athenians apparently believed that Zeus wielded his thunderbolt in defence of the sacred olives of Attica (Soph. *OC* 705 with schol.). And this is pre-eminently another myth that illustrates Athens' dearness to the gods. 'All men should praise our land . . . first and above all because it is dear to the gods. The quarrel and trial of the gods who disputed for it bear witness to what I say. Ought not a land which gods commended to be praised by all mortals?' (Pl. *Menex.* 237c–d). It was a high tribute, too, to Cecrops' qualities that he was permitted to judge between the gods (Xen. *Mem.* iii.5.10).

But the myth perhaps has another and less comfortable aspect. It is one of a group of myths that describe the disputes of gods for particular territories. In these stories, the victor is the city's chief god, while the loser is always Poseidon, except in Sicily where it is Hephaestus.[54] The loser too is commonly worshipped by the community in question, but he is not just their second most important god. Poseidon is the most fearsome of the Olympians, the sender of storms and earthquakes, and Hephaestus in Sicily had his home in the volcano Etna. There is an implicit connection between the terrifying powers of the god, and his anger at defeat; the myth explains the uncomfortable presence within the state of a dangerous god. In Attica, as we have already noted, the resentful Poseidon threatened floods, while in Argos he took an opposite revenge and left the great plain waterless (Paus. 2.15.5). This Poseidon is the malevolent god of the *Odyssey*; there too, of course, he is opposed to Athena.

It has recently been suggested that our myth was first invented in or near the 470s, as a way of acknowledging mythologically through the figure of Poseidon the new importance of sea-power in Athenian life.[55] That suggestion fits ill with the analysis just given, which was based on the broader type to which the Attic myth belongs; for angry Poseidon might be more likely to thwart than to favour Athenian endeavours at sea. That consideration, though, is decisive only for those who put their faith in the fixed meaning of a myth, rather than in its historically varying meanings. The Athenians could have adopted the old mythical pattern but chosen to stress within it Poseidon's interest in Attica rather than his lasting resentment. Certainly, we find later in Plutarch and Aristides the conception of a sporting Poseidon who bears no grudge for defeat (Plut. *Quaest. Conv.* 741a; Aristid. *Panath.* 41 Lenz-Behr). Poseidon could have been appeased and brought round to favour Athens much like the Eumenides of Aeschylus. This is a case where we must practise the art of not knowing. The evidence is just not available that would have shown how the Athenians responded to Poseidon's role in the myth.[56] The related problem of the myth's date of introduction is similarly insoluble.

Cecrops' only son Erysichthon 'died childless', apparently before his father (Apollod. *Bibl.* 3.14.2). He was remembered as little more than a name, and as (presumably) eponym of the historical Athenian *genos* of the Erysichthonidai. The few traditions about him almost all relate to Delos, and were probably for the most part invented by the propagandist Phanodemus in the fourth century, to prove the antiquity of Athens' interest in that island.[57] Erysichthon being dead, Erichthonius/Erechtheus probably succeeded Cecrops. (In the fourth-century king-lists, two shadowy kings intruded between them, Cranaus and Amphictyon. Both had been known as names in the fifth century, but there is no indication that they already had a fixed place in the royal genealogy.)[58] There was no tradition either about the old king's death or about his successor's title to the throne. Such lacunae are wholly characteristic of this early Attic mythology, which had never been put into order in a continuous poetic narrative but existed in fragments associated with particular monuments and cults. Indeed, for Plato, Cecrops, Erechtheus, Erichthonius and Erysichthon are all figures 'whose names have been preserved without their deeds' (*Criti.* 110a). Of Erichthonius/Erechtheus in particular one might say that '*magni stat nominis umbra*'. His pre-eminent role in early Athenian cult is clear from Homer (*Il.* 2.547–51; *Od.* 7.81), and he continued to have great genealogical importance,[59] but in the fifth century only one heroic deed was recorded of him. Before mentioning that, though, we must touch on the issue of his double name.

In sources of the fifth century and earlier, Erechtheus is much the commoner form. Erichthonius is not securely attested until about 440/30. According to a tradition first found at the same time, they were distinct figures, Erichthonius being the father or grandfather of Erechtheus.[60] Their deeds too are to some extent distinguished: Erichthonius is never credited with Erechtheus' war against Eleusis, or with his children, while it is he and not Erechtheus who in fourth-century sources founds the Panathenaea. But one crucial myth is shared between the two. In Homer the earth-born nursling of Athena is Erechtheus (*Il.* 2.547–8); on vase paintings, in *Ion* (267–70) and in most later sources Erichthonius supplants him, though the older tradition still lingers on in Herodotus (8.55). It has often been inferred that Erechtheus and Erichthonius were simply alternative forms of the same name, and that the single figure with two names came to be divided into two figures. The actual development was perhaps more complex,[61] but it certainly seems to be true that we are dealing with joint-heirs to a single mythological inheritance. Erichthonius has no substantial myths of his own, but borrows and usurps from Erechtheus. Erechtheus indeed is forced to yield up his childhood to the older man. This is, of course, another indication of the fragmentation of these traditions, which work with isolated incidents rather than a continuous conception of a whole heroic career.

Erichthonius' only independent action was to found the Panathenaea, and to make certain inventions associated with the festival. These are fourth-century traditions, and must derive from Erichthonius' by then canonical status as nursling of the goddess whom the great festival honoured.[62] Erechtheus' great exploit was the war against Eumolpus and his Eleusinian or Thracian allies. It was to become the first of what one might call the 'four labours of the Athenians'. This canon was established by the speakers of the public funeral orations that were so distinctive a vehicle of Athenian ideology from about the middle of the fifth century. From the wide existing range of Athenian myths, some of them concerned with individual and domestic life, they selected four that could be reshaped as paradigms of a distinctively Athenian blend of righteousness and valour in the communal enterprise of warfare. Two of the chosen myths celebrated the Athenian heroism that had always in the last resort proved sufficient to repel the threatening incursions of barbarians. Two presented Athens as the common refuge of the oppressed, the state that had both the will and the power to stand up for sacred rights. Characteristically, it was a new social institution, the public funeral, that stimulated this new development in mythology.[63]

Our first knowledge of the myth comes, appropriately, from Euripides' *Erechtheus*, a work deeply imbued with the patriotic values of the funeral speeches. It was almost certainly produced while work was at progress on the new Erechtheum, the foundation myth of which it told. Eumolpus was the son of Poseidon and of Chione, a Thracian princess who, at least in later tradition, was born of an Athenian mother. After many adventures, he led an army of Thracians into Attica to help the Eleusinians in a war against Athens. He hoped to install his father Poseidon on the Acropolis in place of Athena, and so reverse the unjust outcome of the famous dispute. Erechtheus consulted Delphi, and was told that victory would be his if he sacrificed one of his daughters before the battle. With the consent of his wife Praxithea he did this, and two further daughters sacrificed themselves voluntarily. Erechtheus duly killed Eumolpus and expelled the Thracians, but at the moment of victory vengeful Poseidon slew him in turn, or persuaded Zeus to do so. On Athena's orders Erechtheus is now worshipped in a fine temple on the Acropolis, bearing the name 'Erechtheus-Poseidon', 'because of him who killed him'. His daughters too receive cult at the place of their death, particularly when invasion threatens, while Praxithea was chosen by the goddess herself to become the first priestess of Athena Polias. And a descendant of Eumolpus in perhaps the fifth generation, again called Eumolpus, founded the Mysteries at Eleusis. Such in outline seems to have been the plot of Euripides' play.[64] The prologue was probably spoken by Poseidon, the exodos by Athena, so that as in *Hippolytus* the two competing gods ringed the human action of the play.

We have, then, a story of a threatening barbarian invasion that could only be checked by a king's willingness to subordinate his dearest personal interests to the public good. (In later allusions it is the king's attitude rather than that of his wife or hapless daughters that is stressed.) A leader's daughter-sacrifice had been an abomination for Aeschylus, but the theme is here suffused in a warm patriotic glow, and the horror is mitigated as often in Euripides by the victims' ready submission to their fate.[65] There was, of course, an example in all this for every citizen. On the divine level the war was a re-enactment of the old quarrel between

Athena and Poseidon, in yet more threatening terms; for the ever-dangerous god was now aligned with a barbarian horde. In the event Athens remained a Greek and not a barbarian city, Athens and not Poseidonia; and from this victory emerged a whole series of the city's cults, including several of the most celebrated. The play showed the religious order of the city created or confirmed by the patriotism of the citizens.

How much of this complex of motifs antedated Euripides? There are no certain earlier allusions; but passing references in almost contemporary works that are unlikely to be dependent on *Erechtheus* suggest that several features of Euripides' myth — the Eleusinian war, the maiden sacrifice, the destruction of Erechtheus through Poseidon — were already familiar.[66] One feature that is not attested before Euripides is Eumolpus' Thracian origin. It is thoroughly unexpected, since Eumolpus is evidently the eponym of the Eleusinian priestly *genos* of the Eumolpids, and duly appears as a respectable Eleusinian prince in the *Homeric Hymn to Demeter* (154). His descent from Poseidon, too, well suits an Eleusinian, since the god was worshipped there under the title 'father' (Paus. 1.38.6). Euripides' version retains the association with Eleusis, but reserves the foundation of the Mysteries for a second Eumolpus five generations later; by then, no doubt, the Thracian blood would have been diluted to an acceptable level.[67] There has clearly been an innovation here at some date; but it is hard to believe that Euripides had no semblance of authority for changing a war against Eleusinians into a war against Thracians, and so transforming one of the most honoured religious families of all Greece into descendants of a barbarian war-lord. It was probably the prestige at Eleusis of Thracian Orpheus that first made Eumolpus into a Thracian,[68] that Orpheus who himself came to be seen as founder of the Mysteries. But Thrace in Athenian mythology had a double significance. It was the home of Orpheus and thus a source of religious revelation, but it was also the first fully barbarian land abutting the Greek mainland. Eumolpus probably became a Thracian because of the first set of associations, only to be transformed by the patriotic tradition into the scapegrace embodiment of the second. There is some evidence that perhaps points to an earlier independent tradition of a war between Erechtheus and the Thracians.[69] If one existed, it will have eased the transformation of an Atheno–Eleusinian into an Atheno–Thracian conflict. At all events, the fourth-century tradition had almost forgotten that this war had anything to do with Eleusis, and remembered it only as the prototype of the Persian wars, the first incursion of barbarian arms into Greece (e.g. Dem. 60.8).

Probably, therefore, the earlier myth used similar motifs in describing a conflict between Athens and Eleusis. (How far the process of transformation had gone before Euripides we cannot say.) Since Poseidon was a prominent Eleusinian god, the divine conflict would have been appropriate in this version too. It used to be thought that the myth in this form reflected an actual historical conflict; but the archaeological support for that view has collapsed, with the demonstration that the supposedly 'archaic' defensive wall between Athens and Eleusis belongs to the fourth century.[70] There is no independent evidence to suggest that Eleusis was incorporated into the Athenian state later than other of the 'cities' of Attica, or with any more difficulty. The area in which the relation of Eleusis to Athens was unique was, of course, that of religion. The myth emphasises this special relationship by a technique of contrast (since the war led to peace). Pausanias' account perhaps suggests the spirit, at least, of the original denouement: 'They settled the war on the terms that the Eleusinians should be subject to the Athenians in other respects but should conduct the ceremonies themselves.' (1.38.3). The myth of the war was also no doubt very closely associated with the several rituals that involved processions from Athens to Eleusis (or vice versa), or places *en route*; most particularly, at the Skirophoria, the priest of Poseidon/Erechtheus and the priestess of Athena Polias, in this context a most significant combination, walked out westwards to Skiron, the spot where according to one tradition the decisive battle occurred.[71] The old myth probably dramatised such local (though by no means trivial) themes and concerns; but the struggle between neighbouring Attic communities that it portrayed could be seen as disreputable, and it had to give way to the great saga of the barbarian repelled.

Erechtheus had several further daughters. One was Orithyia, the bride of Boreas the North Wind. Whether the bearer of such a name ('she who races in the mountains'?)[72] had always been a royal princess must be doubtful, but that is how the only myth we know portrays her. Orithyia was not the only girl to have been swept away by a storm (cf. Hom. *Od.* 20.66–78), and at one level the myth expresses the frightening power of a force of nature. But Boreas was a god as well as a wind, and it also illustrates the 'rough favour' (Aesch. *Ag.* 182–3) of the Olympians in their dealings with mortals. The rape of mortal by god has two aspects. On the one hand it is a frightening and irresistible incursion, a seigneurial act of power; but it is also a contact of rare intimacy between the two worlds, which gives the victim's family and community almost unique claims upon the condescending god. This is a theme upon which, in a different context, Euripides plays poignantly in one of his loveliest choral odes (*Troades* 820–58). Appropriately, therefore, the rape often takes place amid an assemblage of early Attic heroes; Cecrops and his three daughters as well as Erechtheus are all present and named, in defiance of chronology, on an amphora by the Orithyia painter, and Athena, too, often watches the scene without obvious disapproval. Boreas was rough and alien enough (witness the vase paintings), but he knew how to be grateful, as the help he gave against the Mede in 492 and again in 480 well showed, when the Athenians accepted the advice of an oracle (Hdt. 7.189) to 'call on their son-in-law' for aid. (The Athenians at large are conceived, revealingly, as sharing in relationships contracted by Erechtheus). This display of divine gratitude in a crisis was the source of the myth's great popularity in the fifth century. The many vase paintings, the monumental sculptures, the play by Aeschylus, the new temple of Orithyia by the Ilissus all served to remind the Athenians of how they overcame the Mede through the help of friends in high places.[73] When they decorated their temple of Apollo on Delos with two scenes of Athenians raped by immortals, they were proclaiming to the world the gods' great love for Athens.[74]

Orithyia's marriage was not without issue; and some of her children, Zetes and Calais and Cleopatra, wife of Phineus, were to achieve fame in the mythological world. Through them Attica acquired a rather distant connection with the glamorous Argonautic expedition. The origin of this association is uncertain, but it was certainly known to Sophocles: the chorus in *Antigone* ponder the melancholy fate that befell Cleopatra, daughter of a god and grand-daughter of an Athenian though she was (966–87).[75]

Another daughter of Erechtheus made an influential marriage in the early time, when mankind had only existed for three generations and was still being divided into its racial groups. We encounter here a central concern of Greek political mythology, the genealogical relations of peoples. In this case, a controversy about the origins and thus the obligations of the Ionians is fought out through the person of the hero Ion. A recently published fragment of the Hesiodic *Catalogue*[76] has confirmed that the following stemma is ancient:

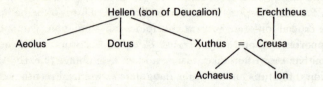

So juxtaposed, Ion and Achaeus are evidently patrons of Achaea in the northwest Peloponnese, which was recognised by the nine Ionian cities of Asia Minor as their homeland and according to tradition had once been called Ionia (Diod. Sic. 15.49.1). Numerous sources duly associate the heroes with this region, from Herodotus (7.94) onwards. But Athens too claimed to be 'the most ancient land of Ionia' (Solon fr. 4a.2 West), and her status as such is recognised in the choice of an Athenian mother (a daughter of Erechtheus, naturally) for Ion. Pseudo-Hesiod's genealogy is perhaps a compromise between two beliefs or claims about the site of the true primeval Ionia. Certainly Ion himself is connected by Herodotos with Athens (8.44) as well as with Achaea, and is repeatedly forced to migrate physically from the one place to the other in more elaborate later accounts.[77]

Thus Athenians of the fifth century inherited a tradition which associated Ion with Athens, but a little precariously, through his mother only. It was therefore a problem to explain how he had achieved such prominence at Athens that the four Attic tribes were named after his sons (Hdt. 5.66; Eur. *Ion* 1575–81), as in terms of mythological genealogy they necessarily were: for these tribe names were also found in Ionia proper, and so were a prime part of that heritage of Ion which was transmitted through Athens to the broader Ionic world.[78] The best that could be done was to say that Ion was summoned to serve as 'general' in a dangerous war (Erechtheus' against the Thracians, when it is identified), and owed his influence to military success.[79] An exception had of course to be made here, in Ion's favour, to the normal mythological rule that kings are their own generals. It was perhaps Euripides in *Ion* who first adopted the radical solution of eliminating the boy's foreign father in favour of Apollo.[80] As Ion was now of pure Athenian blood (with a dash of ichor), he became a fit heir to the throne of Erechtheus (*Ion* 1573–4). Euripides duly installs him there,[81] in defiance of tradition, and without explaining how the throne passed back from Ion's line to Erechtheus' normal successor, Pandion. Athens' relations with her Ionian allies were at this date crucial for her very survival (cf. *Ion* 1584–5), and it was not inopportune to place the Ionians' ancestor at the very centre of primitive Athenian society.[82] Nor will Athenians have resented the notion that after conceiving Ion by a god, Creusa went on to bear Dorus and Achaeus to a mortal (*Ion* 1589–94): Ion's uncle Dorus was thus reduced to his younger half-brother, born of inferior and, to boot, half-Athenian stock. But Euripides' innovation (if such indeed it was) was too bold to be taken up by the subsequent tradition, and Ion remained a general and an immigrant. And this was, perhaps, not an inappropriate expression of the Athenians' own sense of their Ionian identity. An Athenian was of course an Ionian, and at certain times it was important to insist on the point; but in general being an Ionian was very much secondary to the central business of being an Athenian.

Erechtheus was succeeded by . . . . But we must leave the Athenians as Bacchylides portrays them in his eighteenth ode, Waiting for Theseus.[83]

Notes

*Christiane Sourvinou-Inwood and I join in paying tribute to a fine scholar and mythographer, whose generosity towards other scholars in time and ideas always seemed to have no limits.

1. Cf. E. Hobsbawm and T. Ranger (eds), *The Invention of Tradition* (Cambridge, 1983). The gradual emergence in literature of Attic myths is surveyed by E. Ermatinger, *Die attische Autochthonensage bis auf Euripides* (Berlin, 1897) 1–36.
   2. Cephalus and Procris; Procne, Philomela and Tereus.
   3. Cf. H. Tudor, *Political Myth* (London, 1972).
   4. See, e.g., W. R. Connor, 'Theseus in Classical Athens', in A. G. Ward *et al.*, *The Quest for Theseus* (London, 1970) 143–74; F. Graf, *Griechische Mythologie* (Munich and Zurich, 1985) 130–5.
   5. In George Eliot's novel *Middlemarch*.
   6. See, e.g., T. Eagleton, *Literary Theory* (Oxford, 1983) Ch. 2.
   7. Cf. Detienne, *Invention*, Ch. 2.

8. Culminating in the venerable *Die griechische Heldensage* (Berlin, 1920–6).

9. On the continuing vitality of the myths see P. Veyne, *Les Grecs ont-ils cru à leurs mythes?* (Paris, 1983), *passim*; on the developments, Bremmer, this volume, Ch. 1, section 2.

10. There was extensive systematisation, of a kind, in the Hesiodic *Catalogue* cf. the 7th/6th century: cf. M. L. West, *The Hesiodic Catalogue of Women* (Oxford, 1985) 31–50; while large tracts of heroic epic lacked 'incredible events' (*apista*) of the kind certain fourth-century writers sought to eliminate.

11. See U. Kron, *Die zehn attischen Phylenheroen* (Berlin, 1976) 106, for references to studies, above all by F. Jacoby, on this complex topic.

12. West, *Hesiodic Catalogue*, 103–9, argues for an extensive Attic section in that work (and for Attic origin, 168–71); and there were numerous Attic myths in the mythographic work of the Athenian Pherecydes, of perhaps the second quarter of the fifth century (*FGrH* 3: see F 2, 34, 53, 84, 116, 120, 144–55), though we do not know how they were arranged.

13. Ares' trial at the Areopagus is left out, though it falls in the period covered, because it needs to be discussed along with the other aetia for Attic courts, which do not. Cf. Hellanicus, *FGrH* 323a F 1, with Jacoby.

14. There is a brilliant sketch of Athenian mythology by N. Loraux, s.v. 'Cité grecque' in Y. Bonnefoy (ed.), *Dictionnaire des mythologies et des religions des societés traditionnelles et du monde antique* (Paris, 1981) 203–9; to this I am much indebted. For comprehensive accounts one must go back to J. E. Harrison and M. de G. Verrall, *Mythology and Monuments of Ancient Athens* (London, 1890) i–clvi, and Robert, *Heldensage*, 135–74, 676–756, though much of the ground is covered in Kron's excellent *Phylenheroen*. E. Kearns, *Some Studies in the Significance of Attic Hero-cult in the Archaic and Classical Periods* (Diss., Oxford 1983: forthcoming), contains a chapter on 'Heroic Mythology'. The myths of the Acropolis are briefly surveyed in R. J. Hopper, *The Acropolis* (London, 1971) Ch. 2; on political aspects see M. P. Nilsson, *Cults, Myths, Oracles and Politics in Ancient Greece* (Lund, 1951) 49–64.

15. For bibliography see M. L. West's note on Hes. *Theog.* 886–900; E. H. Loeb, *Die Geburt der Götter in der griechischen Kunst* (Jerusalem, 1979) 197 n 8; add Burkert, *GR*, 142–3; H. Cassimatis in *LIMC* II.I. s.v. *Athena*, 985–90 (citing the sources), 1021–3; K. Schefold, *Götter und Heldensagen der Griechen in der spätarchaischen Kunst* (Munich, 1978) 12–20; idem, *Die Göttersage in der klassischen und hellenistischen Kunst* (Munich, 1981) 19–23; F. T. v. Straten, *Lampas*, *17* (1984) 162–83.

16. Athena as friendly helper: see P. Friedrich, *The Meaning of Aphrodite* (Chicago, 1978) 83; *LIMC* II.I s.v. *Athena*, 1026f. Head as 'self': see R. B. Onians, *The Origins of European Thought* (Cambridge, 1951) 96–102; J. Bremmer, *The Early Greek Concept of the Soul* (Princeton, 1983) 16f. Athena and Zeus: cf. C. J. Herington, in G. T. W. Hooker (ed.), *Parthenos and Parthenon* (*Greece and Rome* suppl., 1963) 61–73; N. Loraux, *Les Enfants d'Athéna* (Paris, 1981), 141–5.

17. Though they did not invent it: see, e.g., numbers 361–2 of the catalogue in *LIMC* s.v. *Athena*.

18. Cf. M. Detienne and J. -P. Vernant, *Cunning Intelligence in Greek Culture and Society*, tr. J. Lloyd (Hassocks, 1978) Ch. 4; and on asexual generation M. Detienne, *Traverses* 5–6 (1976) 75–81.

19. Cf. G. E. R. Lloyd, *Science, Folklore and Ideology* (Cambridge, 1983) 86–105.

20. Cf. the superiority claimed for Aphrodite Ouranios as being 'motherless' and 'having no share of the female' in Pl. *Symp.* 180d–181d.

21. See especially F. Brommer, 'Die Geburt der Athena', *Jahrb. römisch-germ. Zentralmus. Mainz, 8* (1961), 66–83.

22. On this concept cf. F. Dirlmeier, *Philologus, 90* (1935) 57–77, 176–93; A. W. H. Adkins, *JHS, 92* (1972) 11–17; J. Griffin, *Homer on Life and Death* (Oxford, 1980) 85–8.

23. See F. Vian, *La Guerre des géants* (Paris, 1952); P. Demargne in *LIMC* II.I. s.v. *Athena,* 990–2. No early connected account survives: for the literary allusions see Vian, 2 n 2.

24. E.g. Soph. fr. 24.6–8 (Pallantids), Arist. fr. 637 (Panathenaea commemorate Asterios): cf. M. Mayer, *Die Giganten und Titanen in der antiken Sage und Kunst* (Berlin, 1887) 182–93; Vian, *Guerre,* 261–4, 272–7.

25. Panathenaic robe: Eur. *Hec.* 466–74, *IT* 222–4, Vian, *Guerre,* 251. Its symbolic importance: e.g. Ar. *Eq.* 566. *Hybris* punished: e.g. Bacch. 15.62–3, Pind. *Pyth.* 8.12–18. Panathenaea: Vian, *Guerre,* 259. Vian argues, 246–53, that the Gigantomachy was evoked or imitated at several stages in the ritual of the Panathenaea: Nilsson in his review, *Gnomon, 25* (1953) 5–9, is (perhaps unduly) sceptical.

26. Victory: cf. F. W. Hamdorf, *Griechische Kultpersonifikationen der vorhellenistischen Zeit* (Mainz, 1964) 58–62. Symbolism in Hellenistic period: see, e.g., Paus. 1.25.2, Callim. *Del.* 174. For the classical period Vian, *Guerre,* 288 is sceptical, E. Thomas, *Mythos und Geschichte* (Cologne, 1976) 40ff, receptive. On Pind. *Pyth.* 8.12–18 see most recently M. W. Dickie in D. E. Gerber (ed.), *Studies in Honour of Leonard Woodbury* (Chico, Calif., 1984) 83–109, who disputes the political reading.

27. See, e.g., Thuc. 2.15.1. On the shadowy kings before Cecrops see Jacoby on Philochorus, *FGrH* 328 F 92; on Cecrops, Kron, *Phylenheroen,* 84–103.

28. See Kron, *Phylenheroen,* 90–2, 55–67; on representations of the birth see too C. Bérard, *Anodoi* (Rome, 1974) 34–8; Loeb, *Geburt der Götter,* 165–81. In literature: Eur. *Ion* 20–6, 267–74, 999–1005, 1427–9.

29. So Loraux, *Enfants d'Athéna,* 39.

30. Cf. Kron, *Phylenheroen,* 32–7. The passage is accepted as genuine, without discussion on this point, by G. S. Kirk in his commentary (Cambridge, 1985) ad loc.

31. So, e.g., Apollod. *Bibl.* 3.14.6, where see Frazer's note. The derivation of Erichthonius' name from wool, *erion,* and earth, *chthon,* is apparently not attested before the third century. Sixth century: on the Amyclaean throne, Paus. 3.18.13 (though cf. the caveat of N. Robertson, *HSCP, 87* (1983) 287–8).

32. Divine-child: so J. D. Mikalson, *Am. J. Phil.,* 97 (1976) 141–53. National origins: see above all N. Loraux, 'L'autochtonie: une topique athenienne', in her *Enfants d'Athéna,* 35–73 (from *Annales,* 1979). I am less convinced by her further argument (in 'Le nom athenien', ibid. 119–53) that the prominence in the myth of Athena, the motherless child, means that this myth too emphasises 'la dominance de la part paternelle' (146). 'Cecropids': see Robert, *Heldensage,* 138 n 7, and lexica to Sophocles and Euripides s.v. *Erechtheidai.* Descent is claimed explicitly, beyond what the patronymic implies, in, e.g., Soph. *Aj.* 202, and in passages referring to the Athenians' divine ancestors, cf. Eur. *Med.* 825 with Page's note.

33. Cf. note 22 above.

34. Cf. the interesting speculations of H. Jeanmaire on the influence of artisans on myth-making, *Rev. Arch.,* 48 (1956) 27–39. On the close relations in Athenian cult between Athena and Hephaestus see the references of Loraux, *Enfants d'Athéna,* 135f, and cf. n 17 above; Loraux emphasises, p. 132, that the Athenians seem to have played down their descent from Hephaestus, which is explicitly mentioned only in Aesch. *Eum.* 13.

35. See the texts cited in R. Stupperich, *Staatsbegräbnis und Privatgrabmal im klassischen Athen* (Diss. Münster, 1977) ii, 33, n 4 to p. 42; and cf. Loraux, 'Cité grecque' (note 14 above). It is not clear whether the famous Attic/Ionic cicada

brooches were a 'symbol of autochthony' (the cicada too being earth-born) for their wearers, as they certainly were for commentators later in antiquity (cf. A. B. Cook, *Zeus*, iii, Cambridge, 1940, 250 n 8): cf. R. L. Hunter's commentary (Cambridge, 1983) on Eubulus fr. 10, the only relevant classical allusion (also discussed by R. B. Egan, *CQ*, *79* (1985) 523–5).

36. Dem. 60.4; Lys. 2.17; Pl. *Menex.* 239a. In a different context, special *obligations* to a mother are emphasised: Eur. *Heracl.* 826–7, Pl. *Resp.* 414d–e.

37. So, e.g., Paus. 1.18.2, Apollod. *Bibl.* 3.14.6. A different tradition in Amelesagoras, *FGrH* 330 F 1 (cf. Jacoby ad loc. for related texts). See in general U. Kron in *LIMC* I.I. s.v. *Aglauros, Herse, Pandrosos*, 283–98.

38. Paus. 1.27.3; cf. W. Burkert, *Hermes*, *94* (1966) 1–25; E. Simon, *Festivals of Attica* (Wisconsin, 1983) 39–46; N. Robertson, *HSCP*, *87* (1983) 241–88, the last dissenting from the modern consensus that the descent was from the Acropolis.

39. Pandrosus: Paus. 1.27.2. Aglaurus: G. S. Dontas, *Hesperia*, *52* (1983) 48–63. Pfeiffer argues (on Callim. fr. 238.11) that Euphorion (fr. 9.4 Powell) located the leap on the southwest side of the acropolis, some way therefore from the Aglaurion, which as we now know was on the east; but it is unclear what Euphorion meant by *Glaukopion* (perhaps the Acropolis itself). Cecrops and, of course, Erechtheus also had Acropolis precincts.

40. The snake: see J. G. Frazer on Apollod. *Bibl.* 3.14.6 (though note that Erichthonius/Erechtheus is not himself anguiform in early sources). On snakes and children see Burkert, *Hermes* (1966), 15 n 4, and for the 'guardian' snake Soph. *Phil.* 1328. The vase (a pyxis of the late fifth century): *Archaeological Reports* 1984–5, 9; cf. N. Robertson's theory, *HSCP* (1983), esp. 259, 276, that the Arrephoria related to a talisman of Athens' safety. The vase is said to offer the form Eruchthonios: probably a slip, but one thinks of *eruo-chthon*, 'save-land' (a sense argued for Erysichthon by N. Robertson, *Am. J. Phil.*, *105* (1984) 388).

41. On their relation see N. J. Richardson, *The Homeric Hymn to Demeter* (Oxford, 1974), 234–5.

42. Schol. Dem. 19. 303 = Philochorus *FGrH* 328 F 105; cf. R. Merkelbach, *ZPE*, *9* (1972) 277–83. The alteration creates acute chronological difficulties (cf. Jacoby, ad loc.), which make it uncertain how much of the scholion derives from Philochorus.

43. Aglaurus was mother by Ares of Alcippe, Hellanicus *FGrH* 323a F 1, Apollod. *Bibl.* 3.14.2; the tradition derives from her close association with Ares via the ephebes. Apollod. *Bibl.* 3.14.3 unusually makes Cephalus a child of Hermes and Herse. In their main legend, of course, both girls die as virgins.

44. See Androtion *FGrH* 324 F 1, with Jacoby, and for possible representations in fifth-century art, Kron in *LIMC* I.I. 297. Complex story: first in Callimachus, see A. Henrichs, *Cronache Ercolanesi*, *13* (1983) 33–43.

45. See on all this Philochorus, *FGrH* 328 F 94–8, with Jacoby; S. Eitrem in *RE* 11 (1922) 123; A. Brelich, *Gli eroi greci* (Rome, 1958) 172; S. Pembroke, *Journal of the Warburg and Courtauld Institutes*, *30* (1967) 30–1 (on marriage). Before Philochorus I know only Xen. *Mem.* 3.5.10 (vague), and ?Clearchus fr. 63 Wehrli (but how much is really Clearchus?); but cf. U. Kron in *LIMC* I.I, 297, on her no. 29 (speculative).

46. Cf. E. Simon in *Tainia, Festschrift R. Hampe* (Mainz, 1980) 239–55; J. Binder in *Studies Presented to Sterling Dow* (*GRBS* Monographs 10, 1984) 15–22.

47. The Leningrad hydria, *LIMC* II.I, 996, no. 453. Or is this the witness Cecrops (cf. Callim. fr. 260.26)?

48. As judge: ?Parthenon pediment; Xen. *Mem.* 3.5.10; Callim. fr. 194.66–8; rejected variant in Apollod. *Bibl.* 3.14.1; as witness, Callim. fr. 260.25–6, Apollod. loc cit.

49. So first C. Robert, *Hermes, 69* (1881) 60–87; cf. L. Preller and C. Robert, *Griechische Mythologie* 4th edn (Berlin, 1887) 203 n 1 for his subsequent controversy with E. Petersen, and now J. Binder in *Dow Studies*. The key texts in support of Robert are Hdt. 8.55, Isocr. *Panath.* 193, Apollod. *Bibl.* 3.14.1, and schol. Ael. Arist. vol. 3 Dindorf, 58.25–7.

50. Cf. respectively Robert, *Hermes* (1881) 65–6; Simon, in *Tainia*, 245–8, the latter supported by a recent find said to show a thunderbolt between Athena and Poseidon; cf. R. Lindner, *JdI, 97* (1982) 385 n 250. Neither point is found in literary sources, and Poseidon's gesture on the Leningrad hydria (above, note 47) is not necessarily one of attack. But Poseidon's son Halirrhothius certainly attacked the sacred olives in resentment at the verdict (schol. Ar. *Nub.* 1005).

51. Of course, a version with Cecrops as judge rather than witness might have contained different grounds for the verdict. Robert suggests a simple preference on Cecrops' part for Athena. In Hesych. s.v. *Dios thakoi*, Athena wins by promising Zeus, one of the judges, special privileges on the Acropolis.

52. Anger of Poseidon also in the delightful but undatable version of Varro *ap.* Augustin. *De Civ. D.* 18.9 (cf. schol. Ael. Aristid. vol. 3 Dindorf, 60.5–12): the Athenians *en masse* are the jury; the women, who are enfranchised at this date, all vote for Athena; angry Poseidon deprives them of the vote, decrees that no child shall be known by his mother's name, and forbids the women to be called 'Athenaeae' (i.e. citizens). Cf. Loraux, *Enfants d'Athéna*, 121f.

53. Cf. M. Detienne, *Rev. Hist. Rel.*, *178* (1970) 5–11, reprinted in M. I. Finley (ed.), *Problèmes de la terre en Grèce ancienne* (Paris, 1973) 293–7.

54. For Poseidon see Plut. *Qu. Conv.* 741a (and the Loeb notes, ad loc.), where some five instances are cited; E. Wüst in *RE* 22 (1953) 460–1. For Hephaestus see Simonides 552; cf. *RE* 8 (1913) 322–3. For criticism of historical interpretations of these Poseidon myths see Pembroke, *Journal of the Warburg and Courtauld Institutes*, *30* (1967), 25–6.

55. J. Binder, in *Dow Studies*, 15–22, developing a suggestion of L. H. Jeffery that the Acropolis cult of Erechtheus only became a cult of Poseidon-Erechtheus at about that time. On the latter point, is such a transmutation of a venerable cult plausible at this date? Would not the Athenians have preferred another way of introducing Poseidon to the Acropolis, rather than the archaic-sounding assimilation? And what justified the assimilation? (Christiane Sourvinou-Inwood, in conversation.) As for the myth, its antiquity was already doubted by Harrison, *Mythology and Monuments*, xxvi, who noted its absence from earlier art; it first appears on the Parthenon and in Hdt. 8.55, and is implied in Eur. *Erechtheus* (see below, note 64).

56. But note that he remains an enemy in Eur. *Erechtheus* (below), and his son Halirrhothius is in Attic myth an anarchic figure (cf. *RE* 7, 1912, 2268–70).

57. Cf. Phanodemus, *FGrH* 325 F 2, with Jacoby's commentary. For the interest of the Erysichthonidae in Delos (source of Phanodemus' conception, or a consequence?), see N. Robertson, *Am. J. Phil.*, *105* (1984) 385–7. For Erysichthon as judge in the trial of Athena and Poseidon, see Apollod. *Bibl.* 3.14.1; on possible representations in art see Kron, *Phylenheroen*, 69, 93, 97. The eponym of the Erysichthonidae was originally perhaps another Erysichthon, the hungry father of Mestra, revealed as an Athenian by Hes. fr. 43a 2–69, esp. 66–9: cf. Robertson, op. cit. 388–95.

58. Aesch. *Eum.* 1011, cf. Robert, *Heldensage*, 150; Paus. 1.14.3 = Choerilus *TGrF* 2 F 1. On these kings see Apollod. *Bibl.* 3.14.5–6; but Isocr. *Panath.* 126 still has Erichthonius succeed directly to Cecrops.

59. Cf. West, *Hesiodic Catalogue*, 106–7, 133.

60. Erichthonius is first certainly so named, apparently, on the kylix of the

Codrus painter, *c.* 440/30, Berlin (West) F 2537, Beazley, *ARV* 1268, 2, Kron, *Phylenheroen*, 250, E 5. The same vase also names a distinct Erechtheus; for their relationship see Eur. *Ion* 267–8 (where the exact sense of *progonos patēr*, is, perhaps deliberately, unclear.) Earlier references to Erichthonius are either not verbatim (*Danais* fr. 2 Kinkel, Pindar fr. 253), or may refer to someone else (Sophocles fr. 242.1). The fullest discussion is by Ermatinger, *Autochthonensage*, 37–62; cf. Kron, *Phylenheroen*, 37–9.

61. Single figure: so, e.g., Burkert, *Hermes* 1966, 24 n 2; cf. Kron, *Phylenheroen*, 38 n 129. Assimilation followed by re-division of two distinct figures with similar names is perhaps more plausible.

62. First in Hellanicus, *FGrH* 323a F 2; cf. Burkert, *Hermes* (1966), 23 n 1, and for possible earlier representations Kron, *Phylenheroen*, 75f. Originally perhaps Erechtheus founded the festival.

63. Cf. Stupperich, *Staatsbegräbnis*, 42–8; N. Loraux, *L'Invention d'Athènes* (Paris, 1981) 133–56; W. Blake Tyrrell, *Amazons* (Baltimore and London, 1984) 13–19, 114–17. The other labours were the repulse of the Amazon invasion, and the wars in support of the Heraklidae and the relatives of the Seven against Thebes.

64. See C. Austin, *Nova Fragmenta Euripidea* (Berlin, 1968) 22–40, H. J. Mette, *Lustrum, 23–4* (1981–2) 117–24. *Erechtheus* is conventionally dated to *c.* 421 on the basis of Plut. *Nic.* 9.7, a shaky foundation (as Dr C. B. R. Pelling kindly confirms; cf. *JHS*, *100* (1980) 127–40, esp. 127–9). The dating from Plutarch is challenged by M. Cropp and G. Fick, *Resolutions and Chronology in Euripides* (*BICS* Supplement 43, 1985) 79f; they favour 421–410. Chione's Athenian mother: Orithyia (Apollod. 3.15.2), which means that Eumolpus' opponent Erechtheus is his own great-grandfather. From this incongruity Ermatinger, *Autochthonensage*, 83, concludes that the association Orithyia-Chione must be post-Euripidean, R. M. Simms, *GRBS*, *24* (1983) 197–208 less plausibly that Eumolpus originally fought not Erechtheus but Theseus. But perhaps in relation to the Orithyia–Chione–Eumolpus stemma Orithyia was primarily envisaged as an 'Athenian princess in Thrace' rather than a 'daughter of Erechtheus', so that the incongruity was not felt. Eumolpus' early adventures: Apollod. 3.15.4. Some of this is Euripidean (cf. fr. 39 Austin, with Richardson on *Hymn. Hom. Dem.* 154), but was there scope in a prologue for the whole of Apollodorus' elaborate account? (*pace* Robert, *Heldensage*, 171).

65. Cf. J. Schmitt, *Freiwilliger Opfertod bei Euripides* (Berlin, 1921), and on maiden sacrifice Burkert, *HN*, 58–72. Later allusions: see Austin, *Nova Fragmenta Euripidea*, 22–3.

66. War: Thuc. 2.15 (and cf. the bronze perhaps by Myron, Paus. 1.27.4, cf. 9.30.1, Robert, *Heldensage*, 141 n 3). Maiden-sacrifice and death of Erechtheus: Eur. *Ion* 277–82. On the pre-existence of these traditions see Ermatinger, *Autochthonensage*, 75–89. In Eur. *Erechth.* and elsewhere (Dem. 60.27, Philochorus *FGrH* 328 F 12) the daughters of Erechtheus are identified with the (Parthenoi) Hyacinthides, who received cult at 'Hyacinth hill' probably west of Athens (cf. Phanodemus *FGrH* 325 F 4 with Jacoby, *RE* 9, 1916, 2–3); but in Apollod. *Bibl.* 3. 15.8 the Hyacinthids are sacrificed to stay famine and plague caused by Minos' curse. Evidently the floating motif of maiden-sacrifice was liable to become attached to any cult-group of maidens, and various attempts could then be made to associate them with a particular war or crisis. The motif could also of course attach itself to a particular king and so to his (hitherto non-existent) daughters; since such daughters would not receive cult, there was then a pressure to assimilate them to a cult-group. Euripides' further assimilation of Erechtheids to Hyades (schol. Arat. 172, fr. 65.107 Austin) is unexplained.

67. Cf. the discussions cited in Schol. Soph. *OC* 1053; F. Jacoby, *Das Marmor Parium* (Berlin, 1904) 72–5.

68. So F. Hiller v. Gärtringen, *De Graecorum fabulis ad Thracas pertinentibus* (Berlin, 1886) 33; J. Töpffer, *Attische Genealogie* (Berlin, 1889) 37. Orpheus as founder of the Mysteries: first in (Eur.) *Rhes.* 943f, cf. F. Graf, *Eleusis und die orphische Dichtung Athens* (Berlin, 1974) 23–39; Graf, this volume, Ch. 5, section 9. A terminus *post quem* for Eumolpus' change cannot be established: it is not decisive (given the possibility that divergent versions can co-exist) that he is still Greek and peaceable on the well-known skyphos of the Macron painter (Brit. Mus. E 140, Beazley, *ARV* 459.3) and probably in Pindar fr. 346 (cf. H. Lloyd-Jones, *Maia, 19* (1967) 206–229: this could in theory be Eumolpus junior.) On Eumolpus in art see L. Weidauer, *Arch. Anz.* (1985) 195–210.

69. Paus. 1.5.2, 27.4, 38.3, as interpreted by Töpffer, *Attische Genealogie*, 40–4: cf. Jacoby, commentary on *FGrH* 328 F 13, p. 284 and (sceptical, not unreasonably) Ermatinger, *Autochthonensage*, 79–84.

70. See R. A. Padgug, *GRBS, 13* (1972) 135–50.

71. Cf. Burkert, *HN*, 143–9.

72. Cf. E. Frank in *RE* 18 (1942) 951.

73. On all this see E. Simon, *Antike und Abendland, 13* (1967) 101–26; on the artistic evidence also Schefold, *Göttersage* (1981), 318–22, with his references. The myth first appears, in a surprising non-Attic context, on the chest of Cypselus, if Pausanias' controversial identification (5.19.1) is correct. Otherwise it emerges in Attica *c*. 490.

74. On this temple see J. S. Boersma, *Athenian Building Policy from 561/0 to 405/4 B.C.* (Groningen, 1970) 171.

75. On Orithyia's further daughter Chione see above, note 64.

76. P. Turner 1 = Hesiod fr. 10a 20–23, ed. Solmsen-Merkelbach-West, *Fragmenta Hesiodea*, 2nd edn (Oxford, 1983) 227. On Ion I have found most useful E. Meyer, *Forschungen zur Alten Geschichte*, 1 (Halle, 1892) 127–50, esp. 144–50; Robert, *Heldensage*, 145–9; see too Ermatinger, *Autochthonensage*, 112–42; U.v. Wilamowitz, edition of Eur. *Ion* (Berlin, 1926) 1–10; and on the myths relating to the colonisation of Ionia as a whole (including those of Codrus and the Neleids), F. Prinz, *Gründungsmythen und Sagenchronologie* (Munich, 1979) 314–76.

77. Strabo 8.7.1, Paus. 7.1, etc.; cf. Robert, *Heldensage*, 147 n 1. This is probably Ephoran tradition. The co-existence of Athenian and Achaean claims about the colonisation is clear from Hdt. 1.145–6.

78. See, e.g., C. Hignett, *A History of the Athenian Constitution* (Oxford, 1952) 50–5.

79. Hdt. 8.44; Eur. *Ion* 59–64 (the motif is transferred to Xuthus); Thuc. 1.3.2 (unnamed); Arist. *Ath. Pol.* 3.2 and fr. 1; Philochorus 328 *FGrH* F 13 and the (?)Ephoran tradition (above, note 77). He was already associated with the Eleusinian campaign in Eur. *Erechtheus*, if fr. 53 is addressed to him (cf. Austin, *Nova Fragmenta Euripidea*, ad loc.). It is not clear in early sources whether Ion has been summoned from Achaea or e.g., Marathon, where according to later accounts (?deriving from cult; cf. *IG* I (3rd edn) 255 A 13 with Jameson's note) Xuthus had settled (Strabo 8.7.1; Eur. *Melanippe Sapiens*, Prologue, 9–11 p. 26 v. Arnim, perhaps implies Attic residence).

80. *Ion, passim*. Robert argues that this is a Euripidean invention; others (Meyer, Ermatinger, Wilamowitz, above, note 76) emphasise Pl. *Euthyd*. 302c–d, where it is said that Apollo is worshipped as *Patrōos* at Athens 'because of the begetting of Ion'. Perhaps then Euripides' innovation was merely to introduce a local tradition into literature. But Plato might be following Euripides (other sources for Apollo's parenthood, the testimonia to Aristotle fr. 1, are dependent in

their turn on Plato). Apollo's epithet is explicable without reference to Ion. Of Sophocles' *Ion* we know nothing.

81. Possibly also in *Erechtheus*: see above, note 79.

82. For propagation (?) of the cult of Ion in the empire note the Samian *horoi* of precincts of 'Ion from Athens', J. P. Barron, *JHS*, *84* (1964) 37; cf. R. Meiggs, *The Athenian Empire* (Oxford, 1972) 298. But one should not suppose that Ionians necessarily resisted the notion of their kinship with the Athenians: contrast, e.g., Thuc. 1.95.1. For Ion's cults in Attica see *IG* I (3rd edn) 383. 147–9, Paus. 1.31.3; there was another Attic Ion, too, Paus. 6.22.7. Ion scarcely appears in art, but for a possible illustration of Euripides' play see M. Schmidt in A. Cambitoglou (ed.), *Studies in Honour of Arthur Dale Trendall* (Sydney, 1979) 163–4.

83. I am very grateful to the editor of this volume for his encouragement, patience and helpful criticism.

10

Myth as History:
The Previous Owners of the
Delphic Oracle*

Christiane Sourvinou-Inwood
In memory of T. C. W. Stinton

Many Greek myths express important perceptions of the society that generated them and contain insights which are (or can be reinterpreted so as to become) significant for our own age; thus they can be said to be 'true' even today. But they are not 'true' narrative accounts of past events (though they present themselves in that guise) and they should not be taken at face value and assumed to contain descriptions of past realities — as they sometimes are. The myth I am discussing here (which claims that Apollo did not found the Delphic oracle but took it over from an earlier goddess) has often been assumed to contain true information about the oracle's early history. Moreover, this historical reading of the myth has functioned as an (implicit) perceptual filter shaping many scholars' interpretation of reality, that is, of the surviving information pertaining to the oracle's early history. My purpose is to show that the Previous Owners myth does not reflect cultic history but expresses certain important perceptions about the Delphic Apollo, the oracle and the cosmos. First I will deconstruct the argument in favour of the historicity of the myth and show that it depends on a series of hidden, mutually supporting, *a priori*, and sometimes demonstrably wrong, assumptions and that it is fallacious. In the second part I will analyse the myth and show that, while it cannot be cultic history, it makes perfect sense as a myth, articulating perceptions also known to us from other sources.

A variety of deities are named as Previous Owners in the different variants, but all versions include Gaia or Themis, or both.[1] Many scholars[2] believe that this story reflects a memory of a time in which Gaia and/or Themis were the oracular divinities at

Delphi, dispossessed by Apollo — who did not evict them altogether but allowed them to maintain a cult of secondary importance in the Delphic sanctuary. As we shall see,[3] the only 'evidence' for the view that these goddesses had preceded Apollo as oracular deities at Delphi is the existence of the myth — which can only be considered to be 'evidence' if it is assumed that the most reasonable interpretation of such a myth is that it reflects historical reality. This is an unwarranted — and fallacious — *a priori* assumption which, I shall show, lies at the core of the orthodox discourse's hidden circularity; it is the product of an implicit, rationalising, euhemeristic reading of myth, which, once explicitly set out, would be supported by few. For myths are not translations of events into mythological language, which scholars can translate back into history. The myths of resistance to Dionysos' cult, for example, are not, as some had imagined, reflections of a historical conflict; they articulate, and are articulated by, religious realities such as ritual tensions and symbolic oppositions.[4] Since myths are structured by, and express, the (religious, social and intellectual) realities and mental representations of the societies that produced or recast them,[5] any echoes of cultic history that may have gone into the making of a particular myth are radically reshaped and adapted, by a process of *bricolage*, to fit the 'needs', the 'spaces', created by the mythological schemata structuring that myth, which express, and are shaped by, those realities and representations.[6] Thus, the hypothesis that our myth is a reversible translation of history is invalidated. In any case, even if we cannot conclusively *prove* the fallaciousness of the assumption that the most reasonable interpretation of our myth is that it reflects historical reality, since that assumption is *a priori*, and thus culturally determined (by a rationalising mode of thought which privileges 'positivist' interpretations), and since it cannot be shown to be right, it must not be allowed to form the hidden centre of a discourse the validity of which depends on that assumption's validity. Given that alternative interpretations of the emergence and significance of the myth are possible — not to say more convincing — it is illegitimate to assume the myth's historicity and base the validity of the whole case on that. In fact, the myth's pattern of appearance offers a serious objection to the historical interpretation. For the two earliest accounts of the early history of the oracle, in the *Homeric Hymn to Apollo*[7] and Alkaios' *Hymn to Apollo*,[8] contradict the

Previous Owners myth and present Apollo as the founder and first owner of the Delphic oracle.[9] Thus, the presumption must be — especially since the two hymns originated in different religious environments, and the Pythian part of the Homeric hymn reflected the Delphic priesthood's theology — that 'Apollo's foundation of the oracle' was the early cultic myth on the oracle's origins, and that the Previous Owners story was invented at a later stage — unless some contrary evidence can be adduced, which, we shall see, it cannot. The data, when investigated in their own right, cannot support the historicity of the myth. They can only appear to support it when, in the context of attempts to validate that historicity, they are structured and questioned by means of conceptual schemata dependent on the very hypothesis that is being tested — a circular procedure leading to corrupted, and thus wrong, conclusions.

To eliminate bias, these data must be investigated through a neutral methodology which excludes prior assumptions. One strategy conducive to neutrality is to investigate each of the relevant grids of evidence (archaeological, cultic, mythological) separately and independently, to keep the deconstructive and the mythological analyses separate, and to compare the results of these independent investigations only at a later stage. This will prevent the common fallacy of combining elements from different grids, taken out of their proper context, to make up an apparently coherent case which is in fact radically flawed by hidden circularity. In addition, the proposed strategy allows cross-checks between grids, which can provide controls and, if appropriate, confirmations. A rigorous methodology also demands that the data should be studied in the context of the wider nexuses to which each particular set belongs (e.g. Mycenaean firgurines, or divine succession myths); for only this context can help determine their meanings in the particular case that concerns us — and so protect the investigation from *a priori* bias.

A fundamental plank of the case for our myth's historicity is the alleged Mycenaean cult of Gaia. The gist of my argument is that, though there may have been a Mycenaean shrine at Delphi, its possible existence is irrelevant to the myth's historicity. For it is only if we assume that the myth creates an *a priori* case for the existence of a Gaia cult — an assumption which our investigation purports to examine — that Gaia can be considered at all in connection with the Mycenaean cult; thus the relevance of the latter to the former rests on a circular argument. But even if we grant that special pleading as a working hypothesis, the notion that the supposed Mycenaean cult provides support for the myth's historicity has to rely on a further series of unwarranted assumptions — and in the end it proves untenable. There had probably been a Mycenaean shrine at Delphi, perhaps at Marmaria, at the later sanctuary of Athena Pronaia,[10] but not on the site of the temple of Apollo.[11] Since we know nothing about the deity or deities worshipped at this hypothetical Mycenaean shrine, the claim that it must have been an oracular shrine of Gaia is without foundation, wild. The female figurines (n 10) may have come from a shrine, but they do not show that that shrine's divinity was female. For almost all Mycenaean figurines are female; we do not know whom they represent.[12] But even if we knew that the chief deity of the hypothetical Mycenaean shrine had been a goddess, we would still know nothing about her. There is certainly no reason for thinking she was Gaia; for, we know from the Linear B tablets, the Mycenaeans had a genuinely polytheistic religion, with a hierarchically articulated pantheon[13] — in which, incidentally, Gaia is not attested. Thus the notion that the hypothetical Mycenaean cult at Delphi can support the view that Gaia's cult had preceded Apollo's is based on a circular argument; for Gaia can only be considered as a possibility at all if we begin with the assumption that the myth creates a presumption that Gaia's cult preceded Apollo's, and then look for evidence that can be made to support it. On that (hidden) assumption of historicity depends another, which in turn implicitly supports the first: the assumption that, since the myth tells us that Gaia preceded Apollo at Delphi, this must be presumed to be correct unless conclusively disproved. Given that only very rarely can anything be conclusively proved or disproved in early Greek religion, the fact that something as elusive as proving that a particular deity was not worshipped at a particular hypothetical Mycenaean shrine cannot be achieved has, obviously, no evidential value. And yet the orthodox discourse assumes implicitly that, failing conclusive proof against it, the view that Gaia preceded Apollo at Dephi stands.[14] Since, we saw, the assumption at the centre of this argument (the myth's presumption of historicity) is fallacious, and in fact the myth's pattern of appearance suggests that it does not reflect historical reality, the whole case pertaining to the alleged Mycenaean cult of Gaia at Delphi and its relevance to our myth is clearly circular and resting on fallacies. The view that it is erroneous is strengthened by further arguments.

There is no cult activity at either Marmaria or the site of the temple of Apollo between the Mycenaean period and the late ninth century;[15] this absence of continuity argues strongly against the view that the hypothetical shrine of Mycenaean Delphi can be connected with the Previous Owners myth. For the only thing that could (conceivably) have survived through the centuries in those circumstances is the mere memory of an earlier cult. Thus, the cultic discontinuity invalidates another nexus of arguments for the historical interpretation of the myth, the notion (which, we shall see, is also discredited on other grounds) that various elements in the cult of the Delphic Apollo are hang-overs from Gaia's. For if all that had survived from the hypothetical Mycenaean cult had been the memory that it had existed, Apollo's cult could not have inherited any cultic elements from it. Moreover, in so far as it is possible to assess scarce and dumb data of this kind, the evidence cannot support the notion that Gaia was the mistress of a Mycenaean oracle. We do not know whether Mycenaean oracles had existed, and if they had, what their diagnostic features would be. However, what we can see is that at Delphi, such Mycenaean elements as are capable of a religious interpretation are not of a type (or quantity) to suggest the presence of a cult-place in any way important or exceptional, anything other than an ordinary Mycenaean shrine. Given that the Pronaia deposit had been put together by seventh-century Greeks, who may, perhaps, be presumed to have selected the most impressive and unusual finds, and — to judge by the presence of the pottery — also a representative sample, I submit that this observation has more value than the usual *argumentum ex silentio*.

Now some more specific hypotheses connecting the hypothetical Mycenaean cult with the Previous Owners myth. Roux argues that, since Athena had been a Mycenaean goddess there is no reason to think that it was not she who had been worshipped at Marmaria in Mycenaean times.[16] There are serious objections to this argument. First, *a-ta-na po-ti-ni-ja* does not mean, as Roux thinks, 'auguste Athena' but 'potnia (Mistress) of Atana (probably a toponym)'.[17] Second,[18] it is illegitimate — especially since *a-ta-na po-ti-ni-ja* may suggest a geographically circumscribed deity — to conclude that Athena had been worshipped at Mycenaean Marmaria because many centuries later, and after a break in cult use, Athena's sanctuary was situated on the site where the Mycenaean shrine may have stood. Third, Athena is not a Previous Owner in the myth but, both in cult and myth, a collaborator and friend of Apollo.[19] Consequently, even if we assume that there had been a Mycenaean cult of Athena at Marmaria, and further that the memory of it had lingered through the Dark Ages despite the break, the myth of the Previous Owners would still not be reflecting that cult. Thus this would be an argument against interpreting the myth of the Previous Owners in terms of a relationship between the cult of Apollo and the supposed Mycenaean cult. In Béquignon's view,[20] a Mycenaean Gaia shrine at Marmaria was replaced by Apollo's sanctuary. But even leaving aside all the objections to the historical interpretation, if (as this view presupposes) the memory of the cult had been preserved through the Dark Ages, the archaic sanctuary would have been dedicated to Gaia, not Athena. For Cassola[21] divine names are not important, they allude to a female chthonic deity whose heir was Athena. But, we saw, there is no evidence whatsoever that the Mycenaean cult involved a female deity, let alone that she was chthonic. Two interdependent (implicit) assumptions sustain Cassola's argument — and all variations of this hypothesis. First, that the most plausible interpretation of the Previous Owners myth is that it reflected cultic reality. Second — implicitly supporting the first — an underlying evolutionary model which, though discredited as a serious account of the development of Greek religion, nevertheless still unconsciously informs many discourses: the model according to which Greek religion progressed from dark, chthonic (and female) deities to light and celestial ones[22] — derived from, and sustained through, the misinterpretation of classical Greek symbolic articulations (mistaken for reflections of past events) in this and other myths. These underlying assumptions make the historical interpretation of the Previous Owners myth seem eminently logical, for it conforms with the expectations which it helped form.

Now Poseidon: it has been claimed that, since he is a Mycenaean god and husband of Gaia, his cult at Delphi must go back to the Mycenaean period; and that this provides an additional argument for the early Gaia cult, and thus the historicity of our myth,[23] one version of which (Paus. 10.5.6) says that Gaia and Poseidon had shared the oracle before Apollo. However, Gaia's Mycenaean existence, we saw, is phantomatic, and we do not know whether Poseidon had been worshipped in Mycenaean Delphi. Furthermore, the notion that Poseidon's name designates him as 'husband of the Earth' is very far from certain;[24] nor is there any mythological support for the notion that he was the Earth's husband.[25] In addition, Poseidon's consort in Mycenaean cult is *Po-si-da-e-ja* (PY Tn 316.4);[26] if the evidence of the Pylos tablets is to be used, as it is by Roux for Poseidon's importance in Mycenaean religion (see n 23), it should not be used selectively, and Posidaeja must not be ignored in favour of a phantomatic union with Gaia (who is unattested in the Mycenaean period), a union whose claim to existence at any period is highly dubious. Thus we are left, once again, with a myth which, we shall see, makes perfect sense in its own mythological terms.

There is no evidence for a cult of Gaia and/or Themis at Delphi before the first half of the fifth century[27] — a period when its emergence should be seen as a response to the myth.[28] The case for an earlier cult of Gaia at Delphi runs as follows. We know from a fourth-century inscription and Plutarch's description that Gaia had a shrine south of the temple of Apollo.[29] After the temple's destruction at 548, its terrace was extended and a polygonal retaining wall built;[30] in the process several buildings were destroyed. Because the later shrine of Gaia was in this region, it is assumed by some that the area had belonged to Gaia before the rearrangement; on that view, the extension of the terrace of Apollo's temple encroached on Gaia's temenos and marked the god's final triumph.[31] However, the assumption that the spatial organisation of the Delphic sanctuary did not change between the early sixth and the fourth centuries, a period during which drastic rearrangements of space have indisputably taken place, is extremely implausible — and again depends on the *a priori* conviction that, given the myth's existence, Gaia's cult must be old. For it is illegitimate to assume, in the case of a continuously growing and developing sanctuary, that the fact that a deity was worshipped in one place in the fourth century entails that she had been worshipped in the same place in the early sixth, especially since we do not know whether or not she had been worshipped in that sanctuary at all in that early period — indeed this is what we are trying to find out. The earliest evidence for a Gaia cult probably belongs to the Kastalia area.[32]

Among the buildings buried under the new terrace is number xxviii,[33] about the function of which we know nothing. Its southwest angle is built against a rock, and at the foot of the rock there is a small spring. Because of its association with the rock, and especially with the spring, it has been suggested that xxviii was a building with some religious function rather than a treasury. This is probably right. But there is no justification for calling it a 'temple of Gaia'. This identification depends entirely on two preconceived — and fallacious — assumptions: first, that there must have been an early cult of Gaia because the myth says so; and second, that springs are associated with Gaia because in the context of certain modern perceptions of Apollo (which ignore his complexity and ambivalence and the development of his divine personality), the Apollo-springs association appears illogical, while the Gaia-springs one seems 'natural'.[34] Thus the data are forced into perverse explanatory patterns and linked by circular arguments, to produce interpretations which only appear convincing when viewed through the perceptual filters of the culturally determined expectations which generated them. The following facts show that the Gaia interpretation of building xxviii rests on a fallacious basis and is highly implausible. First, springs and water are connected with Apollo in his oracular function also in other important oracles, Didyma, Claros and Ptoion.[35] Second, at Delphi, in the period that concerns us, *c.* 600, there were two fountains associated with the temple of Apollo, fountain 24 and a spring behind the opisthodomos.[36] It is thus perverse to assume (on no evidence) that spring 16[37] had a different significance and association, and decide that it belonged to Gaia, and then identify building xxviii as the temple of Gaia *because* it is associated with this spring. Third, xxviii's entrance is at its north side, that is, it opens up towards the temple of Apollo. It thus related spatially to the temple, which suggests that it was associated with the cult of Apollo and not with a different, rival, cult.

Moreover, even if — despite what the evidence suggests — there had been a cult of Gaia earlier than the fifth century, and earlier than the myth, this would not be evidence for the view that Gaia preceded Apollo as mistress of the oracle. For, since Delphi was an established Apolline oracle in the eighth century (see e.g. *Od.* 8.79–81), soon after the beginning of cult-activity in the sanctuary, there is no place for Gaia as mistress of the oracle from the late ninth century onwards. Consequently, since Gaia did not have an oracular cult at Delphi before that date, even if her cult had begun before the myth's creation, it would not be evidence for the myth's historicity. Myth and cult interact, myths using existing cultic and theological material to weave their tales through *bricolage*. If a Gaia cult had preceded the myth, this would only entail that the chronological order of myth and cult, the two articulations of symbolic reality, would be the reverse of the one I envisage here; it would not be evidence for the material existence of this symbolic reality, that is, for the myth's historicity.

The third part of the case in favour of Gaia's ownership of the oracle consists in the claim that some cultic elements — the chasm and pneuma, the laurel, the omphalos, and the altar of Poseidon, Gaia's husband — are incompatible with Apollo's personality and thus a legacy from Gaia's chthonic oracle.[38] Some scholars claim that the Pythia's sex and the inspirational element in the divination also make better sense as a legacy from a chthonic goddess.[39] These arguments are wrong. First, the long gap in the cult-use of the relevant sites and in archaeologically detectable cult activities precludes any continuity in oracular or other cult practices of the kind presupposed by them. Second, the notion of divine personality on which the above theory is based is fallacious. For it ignores the (empirically demonstrable) complexity and ambivalence of divine personalities and the fact that they develop in the course of time, and are defined through their relationships with the other deities of the pantheon to which they belong, and with the worshipping group and its (changing) needs.[40] Thus, the notion that the elements under consideration are 'un-Apolline' is simply a culturally determined judgement, the result of the fact that we have been looking at Apollo's personality and the oracle's early history through a series of distorting mirrors: partly through the perceptual filter of the classical Delphic Apollo's persona, which had developed in response to, and interaction with, the needs which the god had been called upon to fulfil in the Greek world — and is not a good guide to the god's early profile; and partly through the filters created by our own constructs about his early history, which are based on culturally determined assumptions about, for example, what constitutes a logical connection between divine functions.[41] The study of these elements' cultic history shows that they are not a legacy from Gaia's cult. Poseidon's marriage to Gaia, we saw, is almost certainly a mirage. The laurel is closely and widely associated with Apollo from an early date, and not simply as a result of Delphic influence; in some cults this important aspect of the god's persona is crystallised in his epithet Daphnephorus, Apollo defined as the carrier of the laurel — connected with the laurel from Tempe which had a central part in Delphic myth and ritual.[42]

The chasm with the vapours is a Hellenistic invention, though some, probably small, symbolic, opening of the ground with a stomion is perhaps suggested by Aesch. *Cho.* 806–7.[43] Such a small (artificial) opening in the earth would relate the temple's space (which belongs to the human world and to culture) with the inside of the earth with its 'other worldly' symbolic connotations, and thus help put the prophesying Pythia in symbolic contact with the 'other world', situate her between this and the 'other' world, in an appropriate symbolic position for receiving prophetic inspiration from the god. In the classical period at least, the opening was not a vehicle of prophecy, nor was it connected with the myth of the discovery of the prophetic chasm, presented as the source of inspiration. For there are no classical references to such a role, and no sign representing, or signalling the presence of, the opening of the ground in the representation of the prophesying Themis (sitting on a tripod and holding a laurel-branch) on the cup Berlin 2538 (*ARV* 1269.5; *Para* 471; *Add* 177). More importantly, the notion that the 'chasm' was the source of inspiration presupposes the localisation of the consultation at one, unmovable, spot; recent research has led Amandry to doubt the established view that the fourth-century temple had been built over the repaired foundations of its predecessor, and to think that it may have been moved to the north of the earlier temple;[44] this would imply that the opening in the earth — assuming that it had existed at that time — was not a particular, special, prophetic chasm located at a particular spot in the adyton; and this fits my interpretation that this opening had simply a symbolic meaning — which was later reinterpreted. As for the Pythia, Apollo had a female seer also at Didyma, and he was associated with inspired divination also at other oracles; the (well-established) relationship between ecstatic

224

prophetess and god appears to have Near Eastern antecedents.[45] Thus there can be no support for the view that the Pythia's sex and the inspirational element of her prophecy are incompatible with Apollo and must be Gaia's legacy.

The omphalos[46] resembles closely in both shape and associations a particular type of oval stone (an actual example has recently been found) represented on some Minoan glyptic scenes, in which *an oval stone as a cultic object*, decorated with *fillets*, is associated with *eagle-type birds* and a *young male god* characterised by the *bow*. These scenes, together with some others, depict parts of a particular ritual which I examine elsewhere.[47] In my view, the young god involved in this ritual (after undergoing syncretism and change) contributed significantly to the Cretan component of the historical Apollo's personality. The omphalos, I believe, is one of the elements which Apollo's Cretan component contributed to the Delphic Apollo's persona; the Cretan component entered the Delphic cult (perhaps together with the title Delphinios), probably in the late eighth century, when there were contacts between Crete and Delphi,[48] and the growing Delphic cult and its god were developing in response to the needs they were fulfilling with increasing success, and crystallising into the main lines of the shape they were to have from then on. The stone's meanings in the Minoan ritual have similarities with, and may be the ultimate origin of (after reinterpretation and adaptation to fit a different cult nexus), some of the Delphic omphalos's meanings and associations: the eagles in one of its myths, and its funerary conno-tations — for that Minoan ritual involves death and renewal; it is also connected with hunting, and according to Burkert the omphalos pertains to the hunting ritual horizon, the category of ritual restoration.[49] Be that as it may, as Nilsson noted,[50] Apollo is the god most closely associated with cults involving stones in Greek religion; thus in any case the stone is anything but un-Apolline, and the notion that it is a legacy from Gaia is wrong.[51]

Now the mythological analysis. The myth's earliest-known variants belong to the fifth century. In Aesch. *Eum.* 1–8 the trans-fer of the oracle's ownership from Gaia to Themis to Phoebe to Apollo is friendly. In Pindar fr. 55 it is a violent event: Apollo seized the oracle by force, hence Gaia wanted him cast into Tartaros. In Eur. *Or.* 163–5 the Delphic tripod is referred to as Themis' tripod. (See the cup (of *c.* 440) with Themis sitting on the tripod; *ARV* 1269.5; *Para* 471; *Add* 177). In Eur. *Iphigenia in Tauris*, 1242–82 Apollo takes over the oracle from Themis by violence and faces Gaia's hostility. In Pind. fr. 55 we are only given the bare structure of the myth. No other figure, apart from Gaia and Apollo, seems to be involved.[52] At this time, the Delphic Apollo is, above all, the (celestial, male) god who establishes order, a lawgiver, guide and purifier. Gaia[53] is a primordial female deity, involved with death, deceitful and threatening, dangerous, representing a stage in cosmic history in which vengeance and not regulated civilised law obtained. She has given birth to various creatures, pestering gods and men. She is also a positive nurturing figure, but when contrasted to Apollo, as in this succession-by-conflict schema, she drifts towards the negative pole. The theme 'Apollo replaces another deity as master of the oracle', common to all variants of our myth, is a version of the mythological schema 'divine succession', which is shaped by, and articulates, social, religious and intellectual realities and collective representations.[54] In the most potent of the established divine schemata, the Hesiodic *Theogony*, as in our myth, a god of the younger generation replaces an older deity. Like the primordial goddesses in the *Theogony*, Gaia is integrated into the new order in a subordinate position. Thus, the Pindaric myth is a sovereignty myth[55] in which the establishment of order is preceded by disorder and followed by the integration of the primordial powers in the new order. Gaia's revenge, also found in the *Theogony*, depends on the fact that she represents a cosmic era in which vengeance, and not regulated civilised law, obtained. The Gaia–Apollo relationship has several meanings in this myth.[56] First, through the defeat of the female primordial goddess by Apollo the lawgiver and establisher of order, the triumph of law and order and the Delphic oracle's contribution to it are articulated. Second, this relationship expresses the two deities' complementarity. Gaia's chthonic — including her prophetic — powers are harnessed in the service of Apollo; this is the meaning of the mytheme, and the corresponding cultic reality, 'Gaia's cult continues in a subordinate place at Delphi.' The Gaia–Apollo relationship also articulates certain perceptions pertaining to prophecy which we shall discuss below.

This myth is structured by, and expresses, the perception that at Delphi the chthonic, dangerous and disorderly aspects of the cosmos have been defeated by, and subordinated to, the celestial guide and lawgiver. Apollo's oracle has tamed the darker side of the cosmos — both at the theological (Gaia's defeat) and at the human level: it gives men divine guidance through which they can cope with that dark side of the cosmos. A comparable perception is expressed in the motif 'killing the baneful dragon' in 'Apollo's foundation of the oracle' in the *Homeric Hymn to Apollo*.[57] The motif 'god or hero kills a chthonic monster' is connected with a foundation also in other myths.[58] It represents the establishment of order and the elimination of disorder, evil and danger to humanity, symbolised by a chthonic monster, a representation of raw nature at its most frightening and savage. Thus the dragon-killing in the *Homeric Hymn* expresses in symbolic terms the significance of the oracle's foundation: Apollo founded it in order to guide mankind, to give laws and establish order. Consequently, the mythological representation 'Apollo defeats the chthonic monster and integrates some of its aspects in his cult',[59] contained in the Previous Owners myth, appears in connection with Apollo's oracle already in the *Homeric Hymn*. Moreover, in that hymn, through the dragoness's association with Typhoeus, the last challenger to Zeus's power, the disorder and chaos preceding the oracle's foundation which she represented are symbolically equated with the conditions preceding, and opposed to, the establishment of Zeus' rule. Thus Apollo's killing of the dragon and founding of the Delphic oracle are represented as corresponding symbolically to the establishment of Zeus' reign. The dragon-killing is also a 'replay' of that struggle and victory, which ensured that Zeus' order will be served by the oracle.

The Previous Owners myth contains the same symbolic equivalence between Apollo's oracle and Zeus' rule. This equation is earlier than the *Homeric Hymn*. For the mytheme 'Zeus set up the sema of his assumption of sovereignty at Delphi' (Appendix) established a direct association between Delphi and Zeus' triumph over the old order; this was underpinned and strengthened by, and perhaps elaborated under the impetus of, Delphi's central role in promoting order in the Greek world, with Zeus as its ultimate guarantor. It is probably in the context of this elaboration that the 'dragon-killing' motif of the foundation legends was adapted so as to connect the monster with Zeus' enemies. Because it was a monster, it was connected with another monster among Zeus' enemies, Typhoeus; because it was associated with raw nature and, like all challengers to Zeus' rule and their allies, thought of in

227

terms of the earlier gods, it was partly modelled on Gaia, presented as a savage transformation of Gaia: a dangerous death-bringing female monster and (like Gaia) a kourotrophos — of the plague Typhoeus (*Hom. H. Ap.* 353–5). In the Previous Owners myth the earlier order is represented by the older goddesses themselves, so the 'dragon-killing' motif was reinterpreted: the dragon — modelled on the motif 'serpent/dragon as guardian of a spring/sanctuary'[60] — became the guardian of Gaia's oracle, thus making explicit the symbolic equivalence 'Apollo kills the dragon' ≡ 'Apollo takes over the oracle from Gaia by force'; for the violent takeover is focused on the killing of the oracle's guardian dragon.[61] While in the *Homeric Hymn*, Apollo creates order out of chaos, in the Gaia myth he establishes a higher type of order, which supersedes that of the primordial goddess. Its symbolic equivalence with the order of Zeus' reign articulates the view that the Delphic oracle has a central role in establishing that order among men.

The fact that the myth 'Gaia as a Previous Owner' contains formal elaborations of motifs and notions which appear in a simpler (and wilder) form in the *Homeric Hymn*'s dragon-killing, and is itself a more elaborate, acculturated, version of that myth, offers support for the presumption, enunciated earlier on, that the Previous Owners myth was later than 'Apollo's foundation of the oracle'.

In Euripides' *IT*, 1234–83 Apollo took over Themis' oracle after killing the dragon who guarded it; to avenge her daughter, Gaia sent prophetic night dreams which made Apollo's oracle redundant; Zeus, whose help Apollo sought, removed the night dreams' truthfulness and restored men's confidence in Apollo's prophecies. The revenge and the Apollo–Gaia conflict are also found in Pindar; in *IT* the oracle's owner is Themis, who, though a primordial goddess and Gaia's daughter, is associated with Zeus' order[62] and with Apollo — in myth (*Hom. H. Ap.* 123–5) and personality. Themis, then, was a symbolically mediating figure between Apollo and Gaia. In one variant the oracle passes from Gaia to Themis to Apollo.[63] Its transfer from Gaia to Themis is a transfer from a primordial and often savage goddess to one associated with order and justice; that from Themis to Apollo a transfer to the male (and thus symbolically superior) lawgiving and civilising god of the new order. When contrasted to Apollo,

Themis drifts towards her primordial female, older goddess aspect;[64] thus Apollo's ownership is symbolically correlative with the establishment of Zeus' rule.

Given the symbolic correlation between Apollo's Delphi and Zeus' rule (seen already in the *Homeric Hymn*), Gaia's possession of Delphi after Zeus became sovereign was symbolically unsatisfactory (at that point Apollo had not been born, and so could not step in). Thus, when the oracle acquired a pre-Apolline past, the myth created a 'space' for an intermediate figure, defined by the traits (a) 'older goddess somehow associated with Gaia' (for the structuring schema was 'Apollo replaces and older goddess', and its established form involved Gaia), and (b) 'figure associated with values pertaining to Zeus' order'. This space corresponds to Themis' persona, and, in my view, it is in this context that she became a Previous Owner of the Delphic oracle.[65] This variant stresses the oracle's close association with Apollo and Zeus, and its high claims to justice and order, and thus also its important role in establishing them. In some ways, 'Themis' ownership' can be seen as an elaboration of the formulation in Alcaeus' hymn '*prophēteu-[s]onta dikēn kai themin*', which describes Apollo's mission to Delphi and expresses the same perceptions of the role of the Delphic Apollo and his oracle. Given the model of a violent takeover leading to a higher order in Hesiod's *Theogony*, the violent transfer schema was one potential articulator of Apollo's takeover of Themis' oracle (cf. Apollod. 1.4.1). But the pull was towards the friendly transfer, with the conflict gravitating towards Themis' mother, Gaia. Themis and Apollo were positively related. The myth's structure creates a contrast between them — at the same time as it brings out their similarities; but the value of the Apollo–Themis relationship in this myth is also determined through their relationship as a pair to the pair Gaia–Apollo which is their alternative. When related to the Gaia–Apollo pair, the relationship between Themis and Apollo drifts towards the friendly pole, with Gaia–Apollo occupying the hostile one, as in *IT*.

In the *IT* version another set of relationships also comes into play: the pair Gaia–Themis is implicitly compared with, and presented as inferior to, the pair Zeus–Apollo. Zeus is the sovereign, thus his offspring, Apollo, wins. This is one of the myth's meanings. Gaia was a guarantor of the old order, but she is subordinate to Zeus, the guarantor of the new, higher, order, and of Apollo's prophecies. The (intertwined) representations 'male is superior to female', and 'the father – son relationship is superior to the mother – daughter one' structure, and are articulated in, this myth. To understand fully the myth's meanings we must consider its dramatic context. It is part of a song praising Apollo at a crucial moment in the action, thus presaging a happy ending, since it suggests that Orestes' doubts were mistaken and Apollo's guidance was right (see especially v. 1254). Within the song, the Previous Owners myth foreshadows that ending most potently. For it says that Apollo's prophecy is guaranteed by Zeus, which is equivalent to saying that Apollo's prophecy to Orestes was right, that they will be saved. The violent takeover of the oracle in the myth, which led to the establishment of a superior cult, foreshadows — and thus symbolically characterises, and will in its turn be characterised by — the end of the play: the violent takeover of an especially holy statue and the establishment of a new, superior, civilised, cult — of Artemis Tauropolos presented as an acculturated version of the Tauric cult.[66] Prophecy is an important theme in *IT*, as in the Previous Owners myth. It is mysterious and in some ways frightening — as well as order-creating and helpful; it is also uncertain and vulnerable to misinterpretation. In *IT* these negative characteristics gravitate to Gaia's prophecy, which is defeated in the myth and also proved fallacious within the play — for Iphigeneia misunderstood her prophetic dream (which only told part of the truth); they are also limited, and offer no guidance.[67] In the myth the prophetic dreams sent by Gaia are negatively characterised: they are born of malice, they come unbidden (and are thus not controllable), and they are associated, through language and content, with darkness and night. Thus, in both myth and play, the dark side of prophecy drifts to Gaia, and this allows Apollo's prophecy to emerge as wholly positive. Prophecy's dark side has been articulated, but, because it was attributed to the defeated and superseded Gaia, it has not contaminated Apollo's oracle; on the contrary, that oracle has contributed to the dark prophecy's defeat, and is thus presented as its opposite, strengthened by its failure.

This variant, then, was also shaped by, and expressed, a belief in progress — in the cosmos, and in prophecy, the instrument of communication between men and gods. It reaffirms the Delphic oracle's reliability as guide, and emphasises the association with Zeus and his order, which supersede the darker and more dangerous aspects of the cosmos, as of prophecy. It is a tale of reassurance, faith in progress in the divine order and in the possibility of divine guidance for humanity — through the Delphic oracle. In the play also the reliability of the Delphic Apollo's prophecy — after it had been repeatedly questioned (78–103; 573–5; 711–15; 723) — is proved; it offered guidance, salvation and happiness beyond Orestes' expectations and led to the foundation of a new cult beneficial for all time. This focal dramatic strand of the play is condensed, and foreshadowed, in the Previous Owners myth in 1234–83.

According to Aesch. *Eum.* 1–8, Gaia gave the Delphic oracle to Themis, succeeded with her consent by Phoebe, who gave it to her grandson Apollo on his birth. That this friendly transfer foreshadows the play's conclusion has been noted by others, as has the passage's relationship with Hesiod's *Theogony*.[68] Since in the early fifth century the established schema for the replacement of a primordial deity by a younger god was the violent transfer of the *Theogony*'s succession myth — through which Apollo replaced Gaia — the friendly transfer variant was perhaps created — in the context of the play's needs and aims — by Aeschylus. This would explain why there is, uniquely in his version, an extra mediating figure, Phoebe, whose close kinship with Apollo allows a friendly power-transfer from an older goddess to a younger god, through the schema 'gift on a special occasion' (compare, e.g., Diod. v.2.3). Phoebe is also a representation — in this play where male-female family relationships are an important issue — of a positive relationship between Apollo and the maternal side of his family — perhaps a symbolic counterweight to Orestes' matricide and Apollo's role in it and in its aftermath. The Aeschylean myth's meanings are a more ethical, 'civilised' version of the violent variants, ascribing a higher ethical tone to the oracle (and its god) — again represented as instrumental in establishing order, and symbolically homologous to Zeus' reign of justice.

One Ephoros fragment (*FGrH* 70 F 31b) tells us that Apollo and Themis founded the oracle together, to guide and civilise humanity, another (F 150) that Apollo obtained Delphi from Poseidon in exchange for Tainaron. The relationship between the two is unclear (cf. *FGrH* IIC, 49). They could be harmonised if

Apollo had obtained Delphi as a region (with or without a sanctuary) from Poseidon, and then founded the oracle with Themis. This joint foundation is a transformation of the mytheme 'Apollo succeeds Themis', stressing the two deities' similarity and complementarity. In one story (Paus. 10.5.6) Poseidon had owned the oracle jointly with Gaia, who gave her share to Themis, who gave it to Apollo, to whom Poseidon ceded his in return for Kalaureia. In both versions Apollo obtains Delphi from Poseidon through gift-exchange. Since it characterised Zeus' rule in the *Theogony*,[69] gift-exchange was the most fitting mode of succession in changes of ownership between 'younger gods', especially when, as here, it is differentiated from ownership changes involving symbolically charged generational differences. Pausanias (10.24.4) explains the presence of Poseidon's altar in the temple through his Previous Ownership of the oracle, thus showing that one function of the myth was to explain Poseidon's role in Delphic cult[70] and articulate his relationship to Apollo. The presence of certain significant physical elements and phenomena which belonged to Poseidon's sphere, springs, rocks and earthquakes, may also have been seen as tokens of that god's claim on the locality. Apollo and Poseidon are antithetical: Apollo belongs to the symbolic pole of culture, Poseidon to that of wild nature;[71] in the Delphic oracle — the myth says and the cult shows — Poseidon and his values are subordinate to Apollo and the Apolline. Poseidon and Gaia are semantically related; their relationship to each other is comparable to that between Apollo and Themis. As a pair co-operating at Delphi, they are opposed to (and the myth of their partnership may have been inspired by) the pair co-operating in the cult of the present: Apollo and Athena, both symbolically opposed to Poseidon[72] — and Gaia. Thus, these variants represent the Delphic oracle as a civilising centre, in which the 'wilder' deities — and what they represented — were subordinated to Apollo the lawgiver and civiliser. Clearly, the Previous Owners myth, once established, became the vehicle for articulating relationships between Apollo and the other Delphic deities, especially those symbolically antithetical to the order and civilisation represented by Apollo; thus, different variants of the Previous Owners myth, expressing different variations of the meaning 'from savage to civilised', were created by filling the 'wild Previous Owner' slot with different deities.[73]

The mytheme 'Gaia herself prophesied at her oracle', (Paus. 10.5.6) and the representation of Themis prophesying on the tripod, connect the Pythia with these two goddesses, ascribe this divination rite to them. This is correlative with, and so articulates and explains, a tension between on the one hand the prophetic ritual's order-creating function and Apollo the civilising god of order, and on the other a divination rite involving disorder (the Pythia's ecstatic state),[74] a mysterious access to the divine will, a temporary and partial blurring of the limits between mankind and the gods. Like Gaia, the Pythia is an ambivalent female figure who oversteps the normal limits; this, the myth implies, is because she is a legacy from Gaia, but now she operates under the control of Apollo the god of order, who has tamed the previously disordered — and fearsome — divination rite.

Thus, all variants of the Previous Owners myth are shaped by, and express, positive representations of the Delphic oracle and its god, and of the role and nature of prophecy, and also perceptions pertaining to the ritual and to relationships between deities — and through them also to the Greek conception of the cosmos. The Previous Owners myth, then, which does not fit the facts of, and therefore cannot be explained as, cultic history, makes perfect sense as a myth, expresses, and is structured by, significant Greek collective representations. In this sense, this myth is 'true'.[75]

Appendix: The Omphalos — Some Further Remarks

An important transformation of the Minoan ritual nexus 'oval stone, eagle-hawk and young god' in Delphic cult is the nexus 'omphalos, eagles and Zeus'[76] in the story that the omphalos marks the centre of the world, which was determined by Zeus, who released two eagles, one from the East and one from the West, who met at Delphi (cf. Pind. fr. 54). Here the god connected with the omphalos is Zeus; it is therefore interesting that the Minoan god involved in that ritual nexus had contributed — or rather, his later transformations did — to the creation of Zeus' (especially the young Zeus') persona[77] as well as Apollo's. Thus the fact that the Minoan god connected with the stone contributed to the creation of both Apollo and the young Zeus is reflected in the omphalos's association in the Delphic cult of the historical period with both Apollo (the sanctuary's presiding deity in whose adyton the omphalos stood) and Zeus — through the myth of Zeus' eagles.[78]

Zeus is also associated with another sacred stone at Delphi, which, in my view, is another transformation of the Minoan god's stone: the stone swallowed by Kronos which Zeus set up at Delphi as a sema (Hes. *Th.* 498–500) when he became the world's sovereign.[79] In my view, this mytheme arose in connection with the stone which (on my hypothesis) entered the Delphic cult as part of Apollo's Cretan component, through the interaction between four elements. First, the Minoan stone's association with the god who had contributed to the young Zeus' persona — which included the myths surrounding his birth and upbringing in Crete;[80] for this brought that stone within the orbit of the mythological nexus of Zeus' birth and its sequel. Indeed, in my view, the motif 'stone swallowed by Kronos instead of Zeus' — which is the second element that went into the making of the mytheme we are considering — was probably itself a mythological transformation of the ritual association between the stone and the Minoan god who contributed to the creation of the young Zeus' persona; for in both cases (in the Minoan ritual and in the Greek myth) there is a symbolic equivalence between the god's symbolic death and a stone. The third element is the fact that Apollo prophesied at Delphi under Zeus' supreme authority, which entailed an association between Delphi and the sovereign god. Finally, Delphi's identity as a major Panhellenic sanctuary created the symbolic space in which Zeus' victory could be connected with Delphi, made Delphi a plausible setting for the sema of Zeus' victory.

All interpretations of the omphalos can be made sense of if we understand it to be one transformation of the Minoan stone (the mythico-ritual nexus of which was reinterpreted so as to fit the Delphic cultic context), with Zeus' sema being another such transformation. The centre of the world interpretation and the myth of Zeus' eagles can be seen as an elaboration — in interaction with the (reworked) Minoan stone's associations with eagles — of the mytheme 'Zeus set up the sema marking his sovereignty at Delphi', which gave a cosmic dimension to the notion of a sanctuary as in some sense a centre of the world[81] — an enlargement underpinned at another level by Delphi's central place in archaic Greece. In any case, in this (centre-eagles) story the omphalos is also a sema of Zeus, also connected with his sovereignty of the world — which in the myth he is mapping. The two stones, then, are semantically very close, and this supports the view that they are related transformations of one earlier cult object. The omphalos's funerary interpretations[82] resulted from the interaction between the Minoan stone's funerary connections[83] and the funerary 'spaces' of Delphic myth and cult — which involved Dionysos and the Python. On this view, the Minoan stone gave rise to different cult objects, associated with different mythemes and rituals, through the interaction between, on the one hand, the mythemes and ritualemes associated with that stone when it entered Delphic cult, and on the other the 'spaces' in Delphic cult and myth — as they were developing in response to the needs which the oracle and its god fulfilled in archaic Greece. Through fission and conflation these transformations were apparently distributed between two physical objects: the omphalos in the adyton and Zeus' sema.

Notes

* I am very grateful to Professor C. Rolley for discussing this paper with me at great length. Professor H. W. Parke was kind enough to discuss Gaia with me, despite our disagreement.

1. The myth: Aesch. *Eu.* 1–8; Pind. fr. 55; Eur. *IT* 1234–83; Eur. *Or.* 163–5; Ephorus *FGrH* 70 F 31B, F 150; Aristonoos, *Paean to Apollo* (M. G. Collin, *Fouilles de Delphes III. Epigraphie* vol. ii (Paris, 1909–13)) no. 191, iii; Paus. 10.5.6–7, 24.4; Diod. 16.26; Plut. *Pyth. orac.* 402C–E; Schol. Eur. *Or.* 164; Photius, *Lex.* s.v. *themisteuein*; Pind. *Pyth.* Hypoth. a; Apollod. 1.4.1; Menander, *Rhet. Gr.* ed. Spengel, iii, pp. 441–2; Theopompus *FGrH* 115 F 80; Orph. *H.* 79; Hygin. *Fab.* 111; Lucan 5.79–81; Ovid. *Met.* 1.320–1; 4.643. Cf. also Plut. *Def. orac.* 414A–B.

2. See, e.g., H. W. Parke and D. E. W. Wormell, *The Delphic Oracle*, vol. i, *The History* (Oxford, 1956) 6–13; H. Gallet de Santerre, *Délos primitive et archaïque* (Paris, 1958) 150–1; M. Delcourt, *L'oracle de Delphes* (Paris, 1955) 28–32; R. Martin and H. Metzger, *La Religion grecque* (Vendôme, 1976) 15, 28–33; Y. Béquignon, 'De quelques usurpations d'Apollon en Grèce centrale d'après des recherches récentes', *Rev. Arch.* (1949) 62–8; G. Roux, *Delphes. Son oracle et ses dieux* (Paris, 1976) 21–34; H.-V. Herrmann, *Omphalos* (Münster, 1959) 100–16; H.-V. Herrmann, 'Zur Bedeutung des delphischen Dreifusses', *Boreas*, 5 (1982) 54–66; B. C. Dietrich, 'Reflections on the origins of the oracular Apollo', *BICS*, 25 (1978) 5. Sceptical/against: M. P. Nilsson, *Geschichte der griechischen Religion* I, 3rd edn (Munich, 1967) 171–2; C. Rolley, *Fouilles de Delphes V.3. Les trépieds à cuve clouée* (Paris, 1977) 137–8; J. Fontenrose, *The Delphic Oracle* (Berkeley, Los Angeles, London, 1978) 1; 4; P. Amandry, *La Mantique apollinienne à Delphes. Essai sur le fonctionnement de l'oracle* (Paris, 1950) 214.

3. And as Fontenrose, *Oracle*, 1, noted.

4. Discussion and bibliography: Burkert, *HN*, 177–8.

5. See, e.g., M. Detienne, *Dionysos Slain* (Baltimore and London, 1979) 14–6; N. Loraux, 'La Grèce hors d'elle', *L'homme*, *20* (1980) 108–10.

6. See, e.g., for Delphi: C. Sourvinou-Inwood, 'The Myth of the First Temples at Delphi', *CQ, 29* (1979) 231–51; F. Graf, *Griechische Mythologie* (Munich and Zurich, 1985) 106–7.

7. The bibliography is vast; most recently: R. Janko, *Homer, Hesiod and the Hymns. Diachronic Development in Epic Diction* (Cambridge, 1982) 99–132; W. G. Thalmann, *Conventions of Form and Thought in Early Greek Epic Poetry* (Baltimore and London, 1984) 64–73.

8. On which: D. L. Page, *Sappho and Alcaeus* (Oxford, 1955) 246–50.

9. Apollo is the first owner also in Paus. 10.5.7–8 which gives two versions of Apollo's 'foundation of the oracle': (a) it was founded for Apollo by Hyperboreans, (b) shepherds discovered it — an alternative to Diod. xvi.26 (chasm taken to be Gaia's oracle). The goat element is probably earlier than the Previous Owners myth. (Cf. below, note 47 and cf. also Apollo's pastoral function.) Paus. 10.5.7 shows that the goats were not perceived as inextricably bound with Gaia's ownership.

10. A deposit of Mycenaean objects (pottery, a few objects of metal, stone and glass paste, and about 175 female terracotta figurines and one animal figurine) was found in the archaic sanctuary of Athena Pronaia (R. Demangel, *Fouilles de Delphes II. Topographie et architecture. Le sanctuaire d'Athéna Pronaia* (Paris, 1926) 5–36); this is a seventh-century deposit, probably buried during the construction of the temple (cf. L. Lerat in 'Chronique des fouilles en 1956', *BCH, 81* (1957) 708–10), and made up of the 'holy' Mycenaean objects found by the locals while building and ploughing (cf. C. Rolley, 'Les grands sanctuaires panhelléniques', in R. Hägg (ed.) *The Greek Renaissance of the Eighth Century B.C.: Tradition and Innovation* (Stockholm, 1983) 113).

11. See Amandry, *Mantique*, 205–7; Rolley, *Trépieds*, 136–7; see also Martin and Metzger, *Religion*, 30–1. On the finds: L. Lerat, 'Fouilles de Delphes (1934–1935)', *Rev. Arch.* 1938, 187–207. The presence of rhyta does not entail a cult-place. Rhyta appear in domestic, funerary and cultic contexts; on the mainland most come from graves, a few from domestic contexts; in Minoan Crete large groups of rhyta are found in repositories of cult implements, but in Mycenaean shrines rhyta are rare (R. B. Koehl, 'The Functions of Aegean Bronze Age Rhyta', in R. Hägg and N. Marinatos (eds), *Sanctuaries and Cults in the Aegean Bronze Age* (Stockholm, 1981) 179–88). P. G. Themelis, *Annuario*, n.s. *45* (1983) vol. iii, 248–50 claims to have identified some Mycenaean capitals which he assumes to have come from a Mycenaean colonnaded room with a cultic function. The argument relies on unwarranted, mutually supporting assumptions. Even if the objects are (a) capitals (which is doubtful) and (b) Mycenaean, they cannot support Themelis' claims.

12. So when Herrmann (*Omphalos*, 100; 'Bedeutung', 54) states that Gaia's 'Idole' were found, he is completely misrepresenting and distorting the facts. Perhaps the archaic Greeks assumed that these female figurines pertained to a female deity, and so deposited them in Athena's sanctuary; but this says nothing about their Mycenaean significance. On Mycenaean figurines and their function most recently: E. B. French, 'Mycenaean figures and figurines, their typology and function', in Hägg and Marinatos (eds), *Sanctuaries*, 173–8; E. B. French, in C. Renfrew, *The Archaeology of Cult. The Sanctuary at Phylakopi* (London, 1985) 209–80.

13. A. Brelich, 'Religione micena: osservazioni metodologiche', *Atti e Memorie del primo Congresso Internazionale de Micenologia* (Rome, 1968) 924–7. So vague

notions such as 'the Great goddess of old Aegean religion' who lived on in Delphic tradition under the names of Gaia and Themis (Herrmann, *Omphalos*, 100) are entirely out of place.

14. This, for example, is the underlying implication in Roux, *Delphes*, 26.

15. See Rolley, *Trépieds*, 135–8, 142–3; Rolley, 'Sanctuaires', 109–14.

16. Roux, *Delphes*, 23. He takes Gaia to have been worshipped in the later sanctuary of Apollo.

17. On *a-ta-na po-ti-ni-ja*: M. Gérard-Rousseau, *Les mentions religieuses dans les tablettes mycéniennes* (Rome, 1968) 44–5; J. Chadwick, *The Mycenaean World* (Cambridge, 1976) 88–9; Burkert, *GR*, 44, 364 n 17, 139, 403 n 3.

18. See also Rolley, *Trépieds*, 136.

19. As Roux, *Delphes*, 25 admits.

20. Béquignon, 'Usurpations', 66–7. He thinks Mycenaean Gaia also had a small shrine at the site of the later Apollo sanctuary.

21. F. Cassola, *Inni Omerici* (Verona, 1975) 89. Cf. also Herrmann, *Omphalos*, 100.

22. See, e.g., Gallet de Santerre, *Délos*, 136; 150.

23. See Roux, *Delphes*, 25, 29–30.

24. Burkert, *GR*, 136; against the etymological argument also Chadwick, *Mycenaean World*, 86–7.

25. Burkert, *GR*, 136–8.

26. Cf. Gérard-Rousseau, *Mentions*, 184–5; Chadwick, *Mycenaean World*, 94–5.

27. The date of the statue bases; on the latter: P. de la Coste-Messelière and R. Flacelière, 'Une Statue de la Terre à Delphes', *BCH*, *54* (1930) 283–95; Amandry, *Mantique*, 208 n 3.

28. Metzger and Martin, *Religion*, 30, 33 acknowledge that there is no archaeological evidence to support the priority of Gaia's oracle.

29. Plut. *Pyth. orac.* 402 C–D; E. Bourguet, *Fouilles de Delphes III.V. Epigraphie. Les comptes du IVe siècle* (Paris, 1932) 25 col. III, A, 3–4; on Gaia's sanctuary: Bourguet, op. cit., 129 n 1; J. Pouilloux, *Fouilles de Delphes II. Topographie et architecture. La région nord du sanctuaire* (Paris, 1960) 96; M. F. Courby, *Fouilles de Delphes II. Topographie et architecture. La Terrace du temple* (Paris, 1927) 183–4.

30. Concise history of the site: P. de la Coste-Messelière, 'Topographie delphique', *BCH*, *93* (1969) 730–58. On this point cf. also P. Amandry, 'Chronique delphique (1970–1981)', *BCH*, *105* (1981) 677–9.

31. Cf., e.g., Courby, *Terrace*, 201; P. de la Coste-Messelière, *Au Musée de Delphes* (Paris, 1936) 69–72; *contra*: Amandry, *Mantique*, 210 n 2.

32. Some have argued that the bases had been moved there from a different location (cf. short discussion with bibliography: Amandry, *Mantique*, 208 n 3).

33. On this building: de la Coste-Messelière, 'Topographie', 734.

34. Cf. Martin and Metzger, *Religion*, 14–5; 28.

35. On Didyma, Claros and Ptoion, see Martin and Metzger, *Religion*, 35, 43–53, 53–60; Burkert, *GR*, 115; B. Fehr, 'Zur Geschichte des Apollonheiligtums von Didyma', *Marb. Winckelm. Progr.* 1971/2, 14–59; G. Gruben, 'Das archaische Didymaion', *JdI*, *78* (1963) 78–177; E. Touloupa, 'The sanctuaries of Mount Ptoion in Boeotia', in E. Melas (ed.), *Temples and Sanctuaries of Ancient Greece* (London, 1973) 117–23. At Didyma a laurel + spring combination as at Delphi. The hypothesis (see, e.g., Martin and Metzger, *Religion*, 44) that these Apolline oracles' associations with springs are a legacy of earlier Gaia cults replaced by Apollo, for which there is no evidence whatsoever, is another example of the fallacy just discussed.

36. De la Coste-Messelière, 'Topographie', 736.

37. On which: De la Coste-Messelière, ibid. 736–7.

38. Roux, *Delphes*, 25, 28–33, 116; Delcourt, *Oracle*, 31, 32, 144; Parke and Wormell, *Oracle*, 6–7; Herrmann, *Omphalos*, 100–16; J. E. Harrison, 'Delphika', *JHS*, *19* (1899) 205–51; B. C. Dietrich, *The Origins of Greek Religion* (Berlin, 1974) 308–9. For Martin and Metzger (*Religion*, 14–5, 28) the 'natural elements, water, tree, animals, chasm', were originally attached to Gaia. On·springs: see above; on animals: notes 9 and 47; and cf. Apollo's connection with wolves and deer.

39. Parke and Wormell, *Oracle*, 10, 12–13; Herrmann, *Omphalos*, 101 n 303.

40. See C. Sourvinou-Inwood, 'Persephone and Aphrodite at Locri: a model for personality definitions in Greek religion', *JHS*, *98* (1978) 101–21; and cf. J. -P. Vernant, *Mythe et société en Grèce ancienne* (Paris, 1974) 105–10; M. Detienne and J. -P. Vernant, *Les Ruses de l'intelligence* (Paris, 1974) 176.

41. On this: L. Gernet and A. Boulanger, *Le Génie grec dans la religion* (Paris, 1932, repr. 1970) 221–31; see above, note 40.

42. See Sourvinou-Inwood, 'First Temples' 233–6.

43. If it refers to Delphi, and not, as the scholium (on 806) claims, to Hades. On the chasm: Amandry, *Mantique*, 214ff; E. R. Dodds, *The Greeks and the Irrational* (Berkeley, Los Angeles, 1951) 73–4, 91–2 n 66; Martin and Metzger, *Religion*, 34–8; Fontenrose, *Oracle*, 197–203; Parke and Wormell, *Oracle*, 19–24; Roux, *Delphes*, 110–7; Burkert, *HN*, 122–3; S. Price, 'Delphi and divination', in P. E. Easterling and J. V. Muir (eds), *Greek Religion and Society* (Cambridge, 1985) 139–40.

44. Amandry, 'Chronique', 687–9; see also J.-F. Bommelaer, 'La construction du temple classique de Delphes', *BCH*, *107* (1983) 193. Against the view (which implies that prophesying is tied up with one spot) that the sekos was rebuilt first, because of the special needs imposed by the cult: Bommelaer *op.cit.*, 192–215.

45. See Burkert, *GR*, 115, 116–7. Dietrich, 'Reflections', 5, speaks of contamination between chthonic and Apolline oracles; but this is a simple assumption, based, moreover, on an *a priori* — and mistaken — construct: it depends on the existence of Bronze Age chthonic oracles, which itself depends on the historical interpretation of the Previous Owners myth and similar legends.

46. On the omphalos: Herrmann, *Omphalos*; Nilsson, *Griechischen Religion*, 204 and n 6; E. Richards-Mantzoulinou, 'Melissa Potnia', *Ath. Ann. Arch.*, *12* (1979) 72–92; and esp. Burkert, *HN*, 126–7. A list of representations of omphaloi: M. Blech, *Studien zum Kranz bei den Griechen* (Berlin and New York, 1982) 442.

47. In *Reading Dumb Images. A Study in Minoan Iconography and Religion* (forthcoming). Actual stone found: Renfrew, *Phylakopi*, 102; pl. 7. Scenes: stone + bird (eagle-hawk: not naturalistic, but a conflation combining the characteristics of both birds); Sellopoulo ring: *Ann. Br. School Ath.*, *69* (1974) pl. 37; Kalyvia ring: *Corpus der minoischen und mykenischen Siegel (CMS)* II.3 no. 114, in which the stone appears to be decorated with fillets; fillets also on the object in a fresco fragment which may, as Evans suggested, be an oval stone: Sir Arthur Evans, *The Palace of Minos* (London, 1921–35) vol. II.2, 839, fig. 555 and p. 840. Stone (with pithos and plant) and young male god with bow: ring AM 1919.56: C. Sourvinou (-Inwood), 'On the Authenticity of the Ashmolean Ring 1919.56', *Kadmos*, *10* (1971) 60–9, pl. I; the ring's authenticity is now accepted: see, e.g., I. Pini, 'Echt oder falsch? — Einige Fälle', *CMS Beiheft 1. Studien zur minoischen und helladischen Glyptik* (Berlin, 1981) 147. I am arguing (in the forthcoming book, on the basis of autopsy, microscopic examination of a cast and the study of many parallels) that the object in the god's other hand is a wild goat's horn. In my view, Apollo's association with goats (cf. Delos keraton (Callim. *Hymn to Apollo* 60–4), and the goats in Delphic myth) originated in Minoan Crete, but this is not the place to discuss this question. The Minoan god is also closely associated with a tree in the ritual involving the stone (cf. Sellopoulo and Kalyvia rings) — not a laurel, but a

fig-tree (the laurel pertains to the Dorian–NW Greek component of Apollo. On Apollo's components see Burkert, *GR*, 144–5). These remarks are based on the conclusions of my study of the Minoan ritual, itself based on internal Minoan evidence alone, to the complete exclusion of historical Greek data.

48. Rolley, 'Sanctuaires', 110–1; Rolley, *Trépieds*, 145ff. On Apollo Delphinios: F. Graf, 'Apollon Delphinios', *MH*, *36* (1979) 1–22.

49. Burkert, *HN*, 126–7. For more on the omphalos see above, Appendix.

50. Nilsson, *Griechischen Religion*, 204 and see 202.

51. For Herrmann, 'Bedeutung', *passim*, the tripod originated in the Mycenaean figurines' high-backed three-legged throne/chair, whose occupant he identifies as the Mother Goddess worshipped at Mycenaean Delphi, in myth Gaia–Themis, whom he associates with the Pythia sitting on the tripod. Apart from the implausibility of the identification of the tripod with the high-backed Mycenaean 'throne', Herrmann's reliance on the circular 'Mycenaean Gaia at Delphi' hypothesis invalidates his case. Amandry's suggestion (*Rev. Et. Gr.*, *97* (1984) xx–xxi. (I owe this reference to Professor C. Rolley)) that the Pythia's prophetic tripod (which, he says, had not been seen by the ancient writers and artists who spoke of, or represented it) may have been not a proper tripod but something related to the three-legged Mycenaean throne (survival of a tradition or preservation of a relic) is, in my view, wrong: (1) Though the Pythia was probably not in view when prophesying, we cannot know that the part of the adyton in which her tripod stood was not visible at other times. (2) There is no reason to suppose that the description of the instruments of divination would be kept secret, since the consultation procedure was spoken of freely. (3) The Delphian priesthood certainly did know what the prophetic tripod looked like, and it is highly implausible that they would have allowed its misrepresentation on, e.g., coins (e.g Delphic Amphictyony coinage: C. M. Kraay, *Archaic and Classical Greek Coins* (London, 1976) 122, pl. 22 no. 414: Apollo, omphalos and laurel, and with them, and thus part of the cult (which identifies it as the prophetic tripod) a normal tripod). (On the Delphic tripod: Burkert, *HN*, 121–5; Parke and Wormell, *Oracle*, 24–6; Roux, *Delphes*, 119–23; F. Willemsen, 'Der delphische Dreifuss', *JdI*, *70* (1955) 85–104.)

52. If Themis was an owner of the oracle in Pi. *P.* 11.9–10, which is unlikely (the case against: H. Vos, *Themis* (Assen, 1956) 62–3 with bibl.), the two versions could be harmonised if in fr. 55 Gaia was, as in Eur. *IT*, avenging Themis. The Gaia–Apollo conflict also in Theopompos *FGrH* 115 F 80.

53. On Gaia: M. B. Arthur, 'Cultural Strategies in Hesiod's Theogony: Law, family, society', *Arethusa*, *15* (1982) 64, 65, 66, 70–1, 76; Nilsson, *Griechischen Religion*, 456–61; L. R. Farnell, *The Cults of the Greek States*, vol. 3 (Oxford, 1907) 1–28, 307–11; L. Deubner, *Attische Feste*, 3rd edn (Vienna, 1969) 26–7.

54. See J.-P. Vernant, *Religion grecque, religions antiques* (Paris, 1976) 23.

55. On Zeus' conquest of sovereignty: Detienne and Vernant, *Ruses*, 61–124.

56. Cf. Vernant, *Religion grecque*, 25–6 on Hermes-Hestia.

57. See Burkert, *HN*, 121; Thalmann, *Conventions*, 72; J. Fontenrose, *Python* (Berkeley, Los Angeles, London, 1959) 13–22, 77–93.

58. J. Trümf, 'Stadtgründung und Drachenkampf', *Hermes*, *86* (1958) 129–57; F. Vian, *Les Origines de Thèbes. Cadmos et les Spartes* (Paris, 1963) 94–113.

59. The monster's rotting corpse gave Delphi the name Pytho and Apollo the epithet Pythian (*Hom. H. Ap.* 372–4). (Compare Eur. *Ion* 989–1119).

60. Bodson, *Animal*, 70 and n 89. (In the *Hom. H. Ap.* the dragoness was associated with a spring (300)). In Eur. *IT* the monster is male and Gaia's son.

61. In Menander Rhetor and in Pind. *Pyth.* Hypoth. a, the dragon does not guard the oracle; in the latter it usurps it and in the former it devastates the

countryside and keeps pilgrims away. (Cf. Plut. *Def. orac.* 414A–B).

62. Hes. *Th.* 901–2. On Themis: Vos, *Themis*, 39–78; F. W. Hamdorf, *Griechische Kultpersonifikationen der vorhellenistischen Zeit* (Mainz, 1964) 50–1, 108–10; Burkert, *GR*, 185–6; E. B. Harrison, 'The Shoulder-Cord of Themis', in U. Höckmann and A. Krug (eds), *Festschrift für Frank Brommer* (Mainz, 1977) 156–60; H. Lloyd-Jones, *The Justice of Zeus* (Berkeley, Los Angeles, London, 1971) 166–7 n 23; Nilsson, *Griechischen Religion*, 171–2; W. Pötscher, 'Moira, Themis und Timè im homerischen Denken', *Wien. Stud.*, *73* (1960) 31–5. On the primordial goddesses' integration in Zeus' order: Detienne and Vernant, *Ruses*, 102; Arthur, 'Strategies', 65. In my view, Ge-Themis is a later syncretism; Themis was not identified with Gaia in fifth-century religion; Aesch. *PV.* 211–13 is surely a theological statement similar to Heraclitus' (B15 Diels/Kranz) Hades–Dionysos identification. Perhaps it was inspired — given the mantic context — by our myth, under the impulse of the dramtic context: Themis is Prometheus' mother in *PV* (18, 874). Her identification with Gaia may depend on Prometheus' ambiguous generational affiliation (Detienne and Vernant, *Ruses*, 81–2. Affiliated to the Titans in 206–20, while as a Titans' son he should be of Zeus' generation) which it helps to blur.

63. Schol. Eur. *Or.* 164; cf. Paus. 10.5.6. Cf. also Aristonoos' paean iii; Photius, *Lex.* s.v. *themisteuein.*

64. A comparable drift in Kronos' relationships with Uranos and Zeus: Detienne and Vernant, *Ruses*, 101.

65. The connection of *themistes* (on *themistes*: Lloyd-Jones, *Justice*, 6–7, 84) and *themisteuō* (on *themisteuō*: Vos, *Themis*, 20–1) with prophecy enhanced her appropriateness as owner. (Cf. Diod. 5.67.4). But the original meaning of *themistes* was not, as has been claimed, 'oracular pronouncements' (see Vos, *Themis*, 17–22. Themis not oracular before the fifth century: Vos, *Themis*, 62–5; Hamdorf, *Kultpersonifikationen*, 51). In Delphic cult Gaia was more important than Themis.

66. In the play the transition from savage to civilised is effected through a movement from a barbarian land to Attica, in the myth through a movement in time and divine generations.

67. In strict logic, since Zeus removed the prophetic dreams' truthfulness, Iphigeneia's dream would be different from those sent by Gaia in 1262ff. But in symbolic logic they are the same; thus Iphigeneia believes in, and acts on, her dream.

68. F. I. Zeitlin, 'The dynamics of misogyny: myth and myth-making in the Oresteia', *Arethusa*, *11* (1978) 163–4; J. H. Finley, *Pindar and Aeschylus* (Cambridge, Mass., 1955) 277; D. S. Robertson, 'The Delphian Succession in the Opening of the Eumenides', *CR* (1941), 69–70. Cf. also P. Vidal-Naquet, 'Chasse et sacrifice dans l'Orestie d'Eschyle', in J.-P. Vernant and P. Vidal-Naquet, *Mythe et Tragédie en Grèce ancienne*, 2nd edn (Paris, 1981) 154–5.

69. Arthur, 'Strategies', 64.

70. G. Daux, 'Le Poteidanion de Delphes', *BCH*, *92* (1968) 540–9; Pouilloux, *La région nord*, 92–8.

71. Cf. Burkert, *HN*, 134; Parker, this volume, Ch. 9.

72. Cf. Burkert, *GR*, 139.

73. Cf. Plut. *Plyth. orac.* 402C–D: the Muses Gaia's paredroi at the oracle. (On the Delphic Muses: C. B. Kritzas, 'Muses delphiques à Argos', *BCH*, Suppl. vi (1981) 195–209; their dark side: ibid. 209 n 93.) In Pind. *Pyth.* a the oracle was owned by Nyx, then Themis, then Apollo, with a separate line of succession for the tripod: first Dionysos prophesied on it, then Python took it over and was killed by Apollo — probably reflecting the tradition that the tripod held

the remains of Dionysos or Python (cf. Burkert, *HN*, 123–5, also on the Apollo–Dionysos relationship at Delphi), reshaped through the Previous Owners schema which was a vehicle for articulating Apollo's relationships with other Delphic deities. Gaia's replacement by Nyx confirms that it was the slot 'primordial, antithetical to Apollo goddess' that was important. Nyx is more negative than Gaia, so the contrast was greater.

74. See also Burkert, *HN*, 130.

75. After this paper was completed, M. L. West's 'Hesiod's Titans' appeared in *JHS*, *105* (1985) 174–5; his thesis is based on the assumption of the myth's historicity against which I have argued here, and on a reversal of the usually accepted relationship between Aesch. *Eu.* 1–8 and Hes. *Th.*

76. Another such transformation may underlie Apollo's close association with a particular type of hawk, the kirkos. (On Apollo and birds: L. Bodson, *HIERA ZOIA. Contribution à l'étude de la place de l'animal dans la religion grecque ancienne* (Brussels, 1978) 94–8, my 'First Temples', 239 with bibliography.)

77. The Minoan young god is already syncretised as Dictaean Zeus (*di-kata-jo di-we*) in the Linear B tablets of Knossos (KN Fp 1.2). I discuss this syncretism elsewhere (cf. note 47). (Gérard-Rousseau, *Mentions*, 61 is wrong in thinking that the reading *di-we* is uncertain: see J. Chadwick, J. T. Killen and J. -P. Olivier (eds), *The Knossos Tablets*, 4th edn (Cambridge, 1971) 182; cf. also J. -P. Olivier, L. Godart, C. Seydel, C. Sourvinou, *Index Généraux du linéaire B* (Rome, 1973) s.v. *di-we* (p. 50).

78. A third god whose persona contained transformed elements of the young Minoan god is the god who became the dying Dionysos, and whom we may call, for convenience's sake, Dionysos/Zagreus. Thus it cannot be excluded that (the dying) Dionysos' association with the Delphic omphalos which is said to be his grave in Tatian, *Adv. Graec.* 8 may be another transformation of the association between the stone and the gods to whose persona the (transformations of the) Minoan god had contributed, especially since, as we saw (cf. text), the funerary connections of the omphalos correspond to similar connotations of the stone in the Minoan ritual.

79. Unworked wool was placed on it (Paus. 10.24.6), as on the omphalos. A. Frickenhaus, 'Heilige Stätten in Delphi', *Ath. Mit.*, *35* (1910) 271–2 saw this stone as the omphalos' 'Vorbild'.

80. On which cf. R. F. Willetts, *Cretan Cults and Festivals* (London, 1962) 199–220.

81. See on this Burkert, *HN*, 127, who notes that the image of the navel expressed anthropomorphically the concept 'centre of the world'.

82. Python's or Dionysos' tomb (references in Parke and Wormell, *Oracle*, 14 n 17).

83. See text above.

11
Three Approaches to Greek Mythography

Albert Henrichs

Apollodorus of Athens (*c.* 150 BC), one of the most knowledgeable authorities on Greek mythology in the Hellenistic period, searched the remotest corners of Greek literature for significant myths that would highlight the characteristics of individual gods and heroes. One day he came across an obscure epic poem called *Meropis*, which described in vivid detail how Athena killed and flayed the monstrous giant Asteros on the island of Kos and put on his impenetrable skin as a protective cloak. His curiosity aroused by the 'peculiar mythical content' (*to idiōma tēs historias*), he took copious notes which he eventually incorporated in his monumental survey of Greek religious beliefs entitled *On the Gods*. A century later the Epicurean philosopher Philodemus excerpted Apollodorus' work, or an existing compilation of it, and included a reference to the *Meropis* and to Athena's primitive dress in his scathing attack on Greek mythology and on the anthropomorphic conception of divinity that underlies it. Athena's Koan adventure does not surface again in the literature of later periods, even though the mythological material gathered by the Epicureans was widely used by the Christian apologists for equally polemical purposes.[1]

This memorable episode from the life of a leading Alexandrian scholar illustrates the concept as well as the practice of Greek mythography at least as effectively as any of the existing accounts of the major mythographers and their works.[2] The process by which the literary treatment of a given myth was channelled into the mainstream of mythography was repeated on innumerable occasions, most of which will have lacked the excitement that

Apollodorus must have felt when he discovered the *Meropis*. Once a myth became fixed in the literary tradition, it would either survive indefinitely along with the poem, play or other work of literature in which it was recorded, or it would eventually perish together with that record, unless some interested scholar saved it for posterity by including it in a collection of various myths. Such collectors of myths, who wrote down the mythical stories in plain prose, are called mythographers, and their collective product is mythography, a handmaiden of mythology.

The beginnings of Greek mythography go back to the genealogists (*FGrH* 1 – 14) and local historians (e.g. the Atthidographers, *FGrH* 323a – 334) of the fifth and fourth centuries BC. Asclepiades of Tragilus, a pupil of Isocrates, compared the myths of Attic tragedy with earlier treatments.[3] But the main mythographical collections date from the Hellenistic or early imperial period (*c.* 250 BC to AD 150) and fall into two broad categories. One approach was to collect relevant myths as background material for the explanation of major authors such as Homer, Pindar, the tragedians, and the Hellenistic poets. The ancient scholia to Pindar, Euripides, Theocritus, Apollonius of Rhodes and Lykophron are particularly rich sources of mythographical information.[4] The most remarkable corpus of myths in this category, both for its importance and its inaccessibility, are the mythographical scholia to the *Iliad* and *Odyssey*, which contain several hundred 'mythical narratives' (*historiai*). This vast collection of myths, collectively known as the Mythographus Homericus since 1892, circulated as a separate book in antiquity (at least from the first to the fifth century), but it has never been published as a single entity in modern times.[5] The second category comprises independent collections of myths organised around a uniform theme, such as the star-myths ascribed to Eratosthenes (below, section 3), the love stories collected by Parthenius, or the transformation myths (*metamorphōseis*) of Antoninus Liberalis. Outstanding in this category as the principal post-Hellenistic handbook of Greek myths is the *Library* ascribed to Apollodorus (first or second century AD), which is arranged genealogically by mythical families and which served as the model for many modern collections of Greek myths.[6]

The best introduction to the nature of Greek mythography is one that examines specific problems of authorship, dating, composition or source criticism that are typically encountered by those interested in a given mythographical work (section 1, on Conon), a major mythographical component (section 2, on mythological catalogues), or a particular myth (section 3, on the Kallisto myth). In dealing with these topics I have tried throughout to emphasise the great importance of Greek art and of new papyrus finds for the proper evaluation of the mythographical tradition.

1. An 'Obscure' Collection of Myths: Conon's *Diegeseis*

Conon's corpus of fifty 'Stories' (*Diegeseis*) ranks as the most interesting and at the same time the most neglected of the smaller mythographical collections. Our knowledge of the author derives entirely from his work. He must have been active during the reign of Augustus, since he dedicated his collection to another man of letters, King Archelaus Philopator, or Philopatris, of Cappadocia (36 BC – AD 17), in the same way in which Parthenius dedicated his collection of love stories to Cornelius Gallus. But whereas Parthenius' work survived in what appears to be its original form, Conon's did not, with the exception of three dozen lines on a papyrus fragment. The extant summary is the work of Photius, who excerpted the *Diegeseis* from the same mythographical manuscript in which he also read the *Library* of Apollodorus.[7] Conon's Atticising style and apparent charm as a storyteller suffered immeasurable damage in the process of abbreviation. Yet the narrative content of the collection appears to be intact, even though Photius reproduced the individual stories with less than uniform fidelity. Preserved for posterity by Photius, Conon is once again in danger of falling into oblivion. The Teubner edition promised by Edgar Martini for the *Mythographi Graeci* never appeared. It did not do Conon much good that Felix Jacoby included him half-heartedly in the first volume of his *Die Fragmente der griechischen Historiker* (by far the weakest in the series), where he does not belong and where few readers find him. The only published commentary is in Latin and dates from the very infancy of modern mythography. Written by C. G. Heyne's pupil Johann Arnold Kanne (1773 – 1824), it appeared in 1798, at a time when Heyne himself was preparing the second edition of his monumental exegetical notes on Apollodorus.[8] As long as no adequate commentary is available, Conon remains in the closet. No wonder that one finds him described today as 'an extremely obscure Hellenistic mythographer'.[9]

Conon is obscure not because he is particularly difficult to understand but because the miscellaneous nature of his collection makes it difficult to consult. He is the only Greek mythographer who adopted neither a uniform theme nor a recognisable principle of organisation for his work. Myths which describe the founding of cities or the institution of local cults or which explain the distant origins of geographical names and popular proverbs alternate with love stories involving mythical or historical characters, with novelistic or paraenetic tales, and with stories about incredible events. His collection is a microcosm of Hellenistic mythography in that it represents the types of myths most favoured by the leading scholar-poets and antiquarians of the preceding centuries, who collected and disseminated them. He records more than fifteen foundation myths (*ktiseis*), for which he had the same preference as Callimachus or Apollonius of Rhodes.[10] His interest in the aetiology of out-of-the-way cults matches that of Callimachus in the *Aitia*.[11] Although he was not as fond of mythical love stories as Parthenius or Ovid, he shares with them several memorable portrayals of pathetic love, all of which were inspired by Hellenistic models.[12] Since many Greek proverbs are incomprehensible without exact knowledge of the mythical figures and events to which they allude, the provinces of mythography and paroemiography occasionally overlap, as they do in the case of the two proverbs explained by Conon.[13] Also included in his collection are three reports of incidents contrary to the laws of nature. No modern reader would classify these stories as mythological, but they illustrate the facility with which certain stories passed from paradoxography to mythography, two narrative traditions that interacted freely throughout antiquity.[14] The extreme rationalism with which Conon glosses over the more fantastic aspects of some of his myths is reminiscent of similar explanations in Palaephatus (who may have written in the early Hellenistic period) and Dionysius Scytobrachion (third century BC).[15] Once or twice Conon makes use of the novella and the 'hidden message' (*ainos*), in an archaising vein which takes us beyond the Hellenistic period and back to the narrative modes of Herodotus and Ionian story-telling in general.[16] Conspicuous by their absence, however, are myths about gods. The Olympians are peripheral in Conon. He often makes them intervene in human affairs through oracles, dreams and punitive actions, but they remain at best recipients of cult, or mere ancestors of mortal heroes, who are the principal denizens of Conon's mythical world. Gods take second place, and are never as prominent as, for instance, Artemis in the Kallisto myth (below, section 3).

Despite their rich diversity, Conon's fifty 'stories' are with few exceptions distinctly local myths and legends (*Lokalsagen*), many of which lie completely outside the mainstream of Greek mythology. It is this regional orientation, unparalleled except in Pausanias, which gives Conon's collection its unmistakable flavour and which makes him an invaluable source of local lore. But some areas of the Greek world are better represented than others. While the central and southern parts of Greece are largely ignored, the three regions which receive the most attention are, in order of frequency, the eastern Mediterranean with Asia Minor; northern Greece, especially Thrace; and Magna Graecia, including Sicily, as well as Rome. On the whole, Conon's geographical horizons reflect the overall constellation of political power at the time of Archelaus, who ruled over parts of central Anatolia as one of Rome's vassals. But the unusual emphasis on myths located in Thrace requires a more specific explanation. Conon apparently made extensive use of the work of a local Chalcidic historian, Hegesippus of Mekyberna (*c.* 300 BC), whose history of Pallene (*Palleniaka*, *FGrH* 391 F 1–5) was presumably also available to Parthenius.[17] Unlike Apollodorus of Athens or, on a lesser scale, the author of the *Library*, Conon unfortunately never quotes the books which he consulted. His failure to do so has distracted attention from his own work by engaging scholars in a largely futile quest for his real or alleged sources. Poor Conon emerged from their scrutiny as a master compiler (ironically, a negative self-image of nineteenth-century scholarship) who ransacked one or several hypothetical 'mythological compendia' for obscure myths, ostensibly with no other purpose in mind than to enable a future generation of even more erudite men to reconstruct the lost sources from which he had drawn his knowledge. Thanks to such exclusive preoccupation with source criticism, the actual content of Conon's collection has never been fully explored and assessed, let alone exhausted.[18] What is needed is a comprehensive analysis of each of the fifty pieces, which should pay equal attention to source criticism (where some progress can be expected), narrative technique (more promising now that a true specimen of his writing has emerged), mythology, religion and social history. In each of these areas, Conon is likely to make some contribution.

A few samples, almost picked at random, must suffice as appetisers. For modern mythographers Conon offers not only numerous variants of known myths, but at least three myths that are found nowhere else: the foundation of Olynthos; the origin of the cult of Apollo Gypaieus (otherwise unattested) at Ephesus; and the aetiological myth of the transition of the control over the Didymean oracle of Apollo from Branchos to the Euangelidai.[19] In matters of cult, Conon provides valuable details about the ritual abuse (aischrology) customarily exchanged between male and female worshippers of Apollo Aiglatas/Asgelatas on the tiny island of Anaphe.[20] And finally, without Conon social historians would never know the full story of the famous homosexual courtship to which the author of the *Eudemian Ethics* (fourth century BC) alludes. It is about a Cretan named Promachos who undergoes numerous and dangerous tasks (*athla*) to please the boy Leukokomas with whom he is in love, only to find himself rejected. When the disappointed lover ostentatiously courts a rival, the boy kills himself.[21] Conon's version of the story is particularly instructive. Even the names of the two men are significant of their respective status: adulthood versus adolescence. This is not a myth in the full sense, but many Greek myths convey exactly the same message.

Conon is only one example of the many unfinished tasks in the field of Greek mythography that are still waiting for their heroes. Some of the others will be more difficult, if also more important: a full-fledged commentary on the *Library* of Apollodorus, not in the manner of Frazer's delightful farrago of unorganised parallel passages and old-fashioned armchair anthropology, but a more informed approach that reflects the relationship of the *Library* to the rest of the mythographical tradition and to the primary poetic sources; a complete edition, based on the MSS as well as the papyri, of the Mythographus Homericus; and, not an enviable task, an edition and source analysis of all the mythological Greek scholia on Gregory of Nazianzus by the so-called Pseudo-Nonnus.[22] If some of these tools had been available to me, the research for the following sections would have been easier.

2. Some Mythographical Components: Names and Catalogues

Greek myth focuses on the individual hero, whose status depends as much on his ancestry as on his ability to deal successfully with other heroes. Most mythical accounts, whether they are found in poetry, prose texts or vase painting, concentrate on heroic families and on the numerous modes of interaction between their members. Whenever heroes come together for some action, they are identified by their names, their lineage and their provenance. It follows that the names and genealogies of the countless heroes and heroines of Greek mythology are a main component of Greek mythography, much in the same way in which prosopography and chronology constitute the backbone of historiography. But the names of mythical figures were considerably more susceptible to transformation as they passed from one account into the next than were the names of historical persons. Regional versions of the same myth, for instance, would often offer new or different names, not to mention the desire for innovation on the part of bards, poets or local narrators. Even after a myth had entered the literary tradition, established names could still undergo serious deformations in the course of long centuries of written transmission. But it was the minor figures and less familiar names that were most vulnerable. It is not surprising, therefore, that the nomenclature of mythical figures tended to be in a state of flux. These fluctuations merit close attention. Just as variant readings and certain types of errors are important criteria for a proper assessment of manuscripts and for tracing their affiliations, the incidence of mythological names and their treatment in a given mythographical text often determine its value as a source and make it easier to define its place in relation to other sources. The following examples, which are very selective, illustrate some of the ways in which individual names and especially whole catalogues of names affect our understanding of the mythographical tradition.

The Hesiodic *Catalogue of Women* is a genealogical poem of the sixth century BC which depends so heavily on the prosopography of heroic families that hexameters composed of two, three and even four names are not at all unusual. In its complete form the *Catalogue* must once have constituted the largest non-Homeric repertoire of mythological names inherited from the archaic period. Even in the fragmentary state in which we read it today it contains invaluable information on heroic nomenclature. Its reconstruction from papyrus fragments and scattered quotations marks the most conspicuous contribution to the study of Greek mythography in recent decades.[23] Because of its systematic arrangement by mythical families, the *Catalogue* has done more than any other epic poem to shape the mythographical tradition of later periods. Its genealogies and lists of names are frequently echoed in the *Library* of Apollodorus. In more modest numbers names derived from the *Catalogue* have occasionally come to light in rather remote corners of the mythographical landscape. The five daughters of Doros, whose names once appeared in Book I of the *Catalogue* as unlikely mothers of the mountain nymphs, Satyrs and Kouretes, have re-emerged in a Vienna papyrus which lists various mythical families and their progeny.[24] An even more revealing instance of Hesiodic influence on later mythography is the dictionary of metamorphoses on a Michigan papyrus of the imperial period.[25] It describes the transformations of mythical figures whose names begin with the first letter of the alphabet. Three of its five extant accounts (*historiai*) are attributed to Hesiod. The source for the entries on Aktaion and Alkyone, daughter of Aiolos, is explicitly identified as the Hesiodic *Catalogue*. In all three cases the source attributions which are appended to the actual transformation stories repeat traditional formulas, 'as Hesiod recounts (*historei*)' or 'as Hesiod says in the *Catalogue of Women*'. Similar attributions occur frequently in the Mythographus Homericus as well as in most of the transformation myths collected by Parthenius and Antoninus Liberalis. But the papyrus dictionary is unique in that it combines attributions of the standard type with mythological accounts arranged in alphabetical order according to the names of their protagonists.

The Hesiodic *Catalogue* is not the only epic poem which is no longer extant but whose influence can still be traced in later mythography. Mythological names derived from epic sources more elusive than the *Catalogue* sometimes find their way into various kinds of mythographical papyri, where they are not always easy to recognise, especially if they are unusual or not otherwise attested. Such is the case with the Koan giant Asteros, who was rescued from oblivion by Apollodorus of Athens, as we saw earlier.[26] When the Cologne papyrus containing quotations from the *Meropis* was published in 1976, it was believed that Asteros' name as well as the title of the poem were absent from the rest of the mythographical tradition. But eventually both names were discovered in a poorly preserved passage of Philodemus, *On Piety*, which had long been misunderstood.[27] These names proved to be an important link between two major works of Hellenistic mythography. Scholars had always assumed that Apollodorus' monumental work *On the Gods* was the ultimate source for the mythological information found in Philodemus. The shared names, which occur nowhere else, are the first direct confirmation of their assumption.

Less spectacular but still unexplained is a series of mythological names on a Cornell papyrus which lists the parentage of Rhadamanthys ('son of Zeus and Europe'), Musaios ('son of Antiophemos'), Eumolpos ('son of Musaios') and Trophonios ('son of Apollo').[28] All of these genealogies have been known for a long time from various other sources.[29] The real interest of the papyrus lies in the preceding lines 2–5, which are poorly edited and require further study. There can be no doubt, however, that the lines in question offer several alternative genealogies of Triptolemos. The following translation reflects my tentative restoration of the Greek text: 'As for Triptolemos, [some (consider him) the son of] Keleos, [others] the son of [D]ysaules and B[r]auro, still others the son of Earth (Ge) and Heaven (Uranos).' The first geneaology is the standard Athenian version; the second is partially echoed elsewhere; the third, which is by far the most interesting, confirms a neglected variant reading in the *Library* of Apollodorus.[30] More importantly, the third genealogy also recalls the equally sublime descent ('I am the child of Earth and starry Heaven') claimed by the many initiates who commissioned the inscribed gold leaves which were found in tombs of southern Italy, Thessaly and Crete.[31] The editors of the Cornell papyrus provide no commentary on any of the names. Why were these particular names lumped together? Triptolemos, Musaios and Eumolpos are evidently Eleusinian, and so are several of their genealogies.[32] Rhadamanthys is associated with Greek beliefs about afterlife and fits well in an Eleusinian ambience, but the presence of Trophonios is not so easily explained.[33] Dysaules also points to Eleusis, where he and his wife Baubo appear as early as the fourth century BC as local autochthons said to have given hospitable reception to Demeter in the distant past.[34] The epic form of Antiphemos' name, i.e. Antiophemos, derives from the particular kind of Eleusinian poetry which circulated under the names of Musaios and Orpheus and which was still available to Pausanias.[35] It is obvious that the names and genealogies offered by the papyrus are no random collection, let alone a mere school text or writing exercise, as its editors suggested. This catalogue of Eleusinian names is considerably more valuable. It affords a rare prosopograpical glimpse of a particular local mythology which was once so popular in Eleusinian circles but which perished in later antiquity.

Before we can proceed to more conventional catalogues of mythographical names, we must first consider some complications which have to do with homonyms and variant names and which often arise in this connection. Different persons of the same name are as abundant in Greek mythology as they are in real life. Prose writers no less than poets add the father's name or use other means of identification to distinguish namesakes. Apollonius of Rhodes and Hyginus, to name only these two, go out of their way to differentiate between Argonauts of the same name.[36] But homonyms that were handed down without any specification could easily turn into a source of confusion, especially if unresolved questions of mythical chronology made matters worse, as in the case of the alleged homonyms Telamon and Chalkodon discussed by Pausanias.[37] He concludes his discussion with a sensible remark which suggests the dimensions of the problem: 'Obscure persons who share the same names (*homōnymoi*) with more illustrious men tend to be as common in all ages as they are in my own time.'

Variant names for one and the same person are usually easier to deal with than homonyms. In most cases they amount to nothing more than minor variations of the same name, such as Euryte/Eureite[38] or the alternation between Antiphemos and Antiophemos noted above. Occasionally the two forms are farther apart, as in Amphidamas/Iphidamas[39] for the son of Busiris, Dorykleus/Dorkeus[40] for one of the sons of Hippokoon or Epikaste/Jocaste[41] for Oedipus' wife and for the mother of Trophonios. But full-fledged alternate names, such as Iphigeneia/Iphianassa/Iphimede[42] for the daughter sacrificed by Agamemnon, are usually found in early stages of the mythological tradition, where they often raise questions that are difficult or impossible to answer.

The number of possible variables rises sharply when individual names are strung together to form long lists of up to fifty names.

Most instructive for our purposes are catalogues which exist in multiple versions and can be traced from epic poetry or archaic art down to the mythographers of the imperial period. Many catalogues fit this description, but only three or four merit our attention. One of them is the catalogue of the participants in the Calydonian boar hunt. The event is described in the *Iliad* (9.529–99), but the heroes remain nameless, with the exception of Meleagros, the leader of the hunt. The earliest catalogue of the Calydonian hunters is found in art rather than literature. The François vase (*c.* 570 BC) names twenty hunters, eight of whom reappear in various literary accounts of the hunt. The name of Pelias' son Akastos, however, recurs only on an Attic black-figure dinos (*c.* 580 BC) and, amazingly, in Ovid's *Metamorphoses*.[43] The continuity which links Ovid to the François vase would be less striking if we could be sure that Akastos was mentioned in Euripides' *Meleagros*. But alas, the better part of the play's messenger speech, in which the names of the hunters were recorded, is lost, and Akastos is not among the four surviving names.[44] Another hunter, Antaios/Ankaios, is the boar's principal victim on the François vase and on a contemporary Attic dinos in Berne as well as in Bacchylides and the mythographical tradition.[45] Such consistency reduces the distance between visual representations and written versions of the same myth and provides an immediate verbal rapport between some of the earliest mythological scenes in Greek art and the mythography of later periods.

But the continuity would be interrupted just as often, and old names were replaced by new ones. An interesting example of broken continuity in the transmission of mythological catalogues has to do with the funeral games of Pelias. Virtually ignored in extant Greek literature, these games have left only the barest trace in Greek mythography. Apollodorus mentions them in passing, but gives no details.[46] But identical lists of the heroes who had been victorious on this occasion can be found in Hyginus and in two papyri from the imperial period which command attention in connection with the thorny problem of Hyginus' Greek sources.[47] All three lists are of relatively late date and do not agree at all with the names of the victors and their various disciplines which Pausanias saw on the chest of Kypselos, a rare relic from the archaic period.[48] Pausanias read the names of five charioteers, two of which recur on Side B of the archaic Corinthian vase known as the Amphiaraos krater.[49] But the names of the remaining charioteers differ on the two vases, and the two shared names are absent from the later literary lists, which follow a separate tradition. In this case the continuity seems to have ended not long after the archaic period. What is more, a considerable degree of variation must be allowed even for the earliest versions of this catalogue, as the comparison of the two vases has shown.

Relatively short lists of genealogically related names are common in Greek mythology, but they frequently suffer abridgement when merged with more comprehensive catalogues. Various texts which list the sons of Hippokoon (Hippokoontids) or the sons of Thestios (Thestiadai) are revealing in this regard. Both groups are mentioned in connection with the Calydonian boar hunt, and some of their members double as Argonauts. The treatment of their names by poets and mythographers is far from uniform. Unlike the Hippokoontids, the Thestiadai are as often mentioned *en bloc*, 'the sons of Thestios', as they are by their individual names, depending on the preference of the author and on the context in which their names occur.[50] Authors mentioning the Thestiadai as part of a long catalogue of Calydonian hunters usually prefer the brevity of the generic name, whereas the individual names prevail in texts that are primarily interested in family history.[51] All told more than fifteen different names are attested. They tend to occur in certain fixed groupings which seem to reflect distinct traditions. Klytios and Prokaon are grouped together in the earliest texts, as are Kometes and Prothoos.[52] Later sources, however, ignore both pairs. Plexippos and Toxeus form another pair, which cannot be traced back beyond the Hellenistic period.[53] As usual, the fullest catalogues can be found in three of the later sources. They quote from four to seven names each, only three of which are identical in all three lists.[54] The ultimate origin of these lists must be sought in early epic treatments of the Meleagros myth.[55] For once the Hesiodic *Catalogue* can be ruled out as a source. The extant fragments suggest that the sons of Thestios must have been passed over in favour of his daughters.[56] All things considered, the names of the Thestiadai illustrate the unpredictable alternation of long and short lists of related names in our primary sources, an alternation which is still echoed in the mythographical tradition.

The Thestiadai are securely placed in the earliest non-Homeric accounts of the Calydonian hunt. The case is altogether different for the Hippokoontids, whose participation is not attested before Ovid and Hyginus.[57] Their combined testimony points to one or more distant Hellenistic sources which included the Hippokoontids in a catalogue of Calydonian hunters.[58] But the sons of Hippokoon are better known as victims of Herakles, who killed as many as ten or twelve of them when he restored Hippokoon's brother Tyndareus to the kingdom of Lakedaimon.[59] The fight against Herakles was their last hurrah, and it is in connection with their defeat and death at his hands that seventeen of their names, including several variant names, are mentioned.[60] Of the five names which survive in Alcman, our earliest source, only three recur in the two lists of much later date that are preserved in the mythographical tradition.[61] One of those shared names, Sebros, still appears in its original dialect form in the prose account of Pausanias. It is tempting to conclude that this picture reflects the gradual conflation of at least two separate traditions: a local Spartan catalogue of the Hippokoontids which is still available in Alcman's *Partheneion*, and another more 'Panhellenic' catalogue which may have been derived from genealogical poetry of the Hesiodic type.

The close study of mythological names and their transition from the poetic into the mythographical tradition is admittedly tedious. Modern unease over the tedium of the various catalogues itemising the names of Aktaion's dogs provides a measure of the distance which separates epic decorum and the mark it left on ancient mythography from our own aesthetic sensibilities.[62] At the same time such catalogues continue to be of interest as valuable heuristic tools which make it easier to see how specific mythological data derived from poetical accounts of the archaic or classical period were affected once they entered the mainstream of Greek mythography.

3. Applied Mythography: The Kallisto Myth

Although mythical names and genealogies deserve their share of scholarly attention, they are no longer the be-all and end-all of modern interest in Greek mythology. In the nineteenth century, however, there were periods when 'mythologists' of the calibre of Friedrich Gottlieb Welcker (1784–1868) and Hermann Usener

(1834–1905) regarded the etymological interpretation of mythical names as the magical key that would unlock the hidden secrets of many myths, and when it was equally fashionable for eminent scholars of a different persuasion, including Karl Otfried Müller (1797–1840) and Ulrich von Wilamowitz-Moellendorff (1848–1931), to concentrate their efforts on heroic families and to treat heroic myth as if it were tantamount to a historical record, full of more or less factual reminiscences of the distant past.[63] Nowadays the various etymologies of divine and heroic names which were once so hotly debated are all but forgotten, and myth is widely recognised as an autonomous mode of Greek thought and self-expression, distinct from historical memory and largely independent from it, even though myth often served as a substitute for history. Since the turn of the century the former preoccupation with isolated facets of Greek mythology has given way to a growing interest in myths as coherent narratives whose ritual and social significance transcends the literary context in which a given myth has been transmitted. In recent decades the foremost analysts of Greek myths have approached each mythical narrative as a cohesive and organised whole composed of constitutive elements which contribute to its overall structure and which are designed to bring out its inherent meaning. For all their differences, the dominant schools have much in common. 'Ritualists' like Walter Burkert tend to emphasise the social relevance of cult-oriented myths; 'structuralists' like Jean-Pierre Vernant read mythical texts as social documents that mirror the external and internal organisation of an entire society; and 'narratologists' who follow in the footsteps of Vladimir J. Propp (1895–1970) analyse the recurrent components of mythical narratives in terms of their sequential function.[64] What underlies their different approaches is a shared concern for the whole of the mythical narrative in relation to its constituent parts, and a willingness to pay equal attention to both. This new orientation has advanced our understanding of numerous Greek myths. But like any other method, it also has its pitfalls. Its practitioners do not always seem to realise that it is impossible to determine the overall structure of a particular myth, let alone its presumed meaning, without acquiring first as complete and clear an understanding of its transmission in antiquity as possible. This is where mythography comes in. Given the present tendency to explore each conceivable facet of a given myth and to wring every

Table 11.1: Variants of the Kallisto Myth

Sources → Story Pattern ↓	I Eratosthenic *Catasterisms*, Ursa Major = Hesiod fr. 163	II Eratosthenic *Catasterisms*, Ursa Major = Amphis fr. 47	III Eratosthenic *Catasterisms*, Ursa Major = Hesiod fr. 163
1. Kallisto's occupation	virgin huntress in Artemis' train	= I	= I
2. Zeus' appearance during union with Kallisto	his own (implied)	Artemis'	= I
3. Divine agent of animal transformation	Artemis	as in I	= I
4. Explanation for transformation	punishment for loss of virginity (cf. IV 6b)	punishment for blaming loss of virginity on Artemis	= I
5. Timing of transformation	after union with Zeus but *before* birth of Arkas	immediately before pregnancy or after giving birth	= I
6. Kallisto's death	= III	= III	Kallisto as bear *almost* shot by her son Arkas
7. Her ultimate fate	= III	= III	placed among the stars by Zeus

Sources → Story Pattern ↓	IV Apollod. 3.100–101	V schol. D(A) *Il.* 18.487 = Callimachus fr. 632	VI Paus. 8.3.6–7	VII Ovid (a) *Met.* 2.401–530 (b) *Fast.* 2.153–192
1. Kallisto's occupation	as in I	–	–	as in I
2. Zeus' appearance during union with Kallisto	(a) as in II (b) Apollo's	as in I (implied)	as in I (implied)	(a) as in II (b) —
3. Divine agent of animal transformation	Zeus	Hera	as in V	as in V
4. Explanation for transformation	Zeus' attempt to deceive Hera	Hera's jealousy and vengeance (implied)	as in V (implied)	as in V (explicit)
5. Timing of transformation	as in I	–	as in I	*after* birth of Arkas
6. Kallisto's death	Kallisto as bear shot by Artemis (a) at Hera's request (as in V–VI) (b) as punishment for lost virginity (cf. I 4)	as in IV (a)	as in IV (a)	as in III
7. Her ultimate fate	as in III	as in III	as in III	as in III

last ounce of possible relevance from it, one would expect students of Greek myths to use the available mythographical sources with the same discrimination which they apply to Homer, Pindar, the tragedians, Callimachus or Ovid, and to examine the attestation, authenticity and approximate date of any piece of mythographical information that might be relevant to their interpretation. This, however, is not the case, and sheer ignorance of the whole range of ancient mythography has never been more rampant than it is today. Not everybody interested in Greek myth and religion can be expected to pursue the study of Greek mythography for its own sake. But all analysts and interpreters of Greek myths must be prepared to scrutinise their assumptions in the light of the mythographical tradition before general conclusions about the structure and meaning of any myth are in order.

This is the kind of source-critical scrutiny which I propose to call 'applied mythography'. Of those myths which have received such close attention more than once, the story of Kallisto is particularly revealing. No single standard version of it existed in antiquity, but the recurrent elements of the myth which constitute its story pattern according to the principal versions (IV – VI) can be summarised as follows (see Table 11.1, vertical readings):

A virgin nymph and fellow huntress of Artemis, Kallisto was seduced by Zeus. While pregnant she was transformed into a bear. After she had given birth to Arkas, she was shot to death by Artemis and placed among the stars by Zeus.

This summary leaves room for all kinds of elaborations and variations. Full-fledged versions of the Kallisto myth which tell her entire story from her innocent service of Artemis to her rape, animal transformation, death and ultimate catasterism are confined to the mythographical tradition (I – V) and to two relatively late storytellers, Ovid (VII) and Pausanias (VI), who drew upon various branches of this tradition for their portrayals of Kallisto (see Figure 11.1, horizontal readings). Without exception, the extant versions date from the imperial period, but they reproduce earlier treatments of the myth which range in date from the late archaic to the early Hellenistic period and which are either reported anonymously (IV, VI, VII) or ascribed to specific authors like 'Hesiod' (I = III), the middle comedy poet Amphis

258

(II), and Callimachus (V). But the appeal to earlier authorities is deceptive. Source ascriptions found in the mythographical tradition are always suspect until proven accurate. In the absence of independent confirmation, which is usually unavailable, it is often impossible to decide whether the alleged authority is the source of the whole story or merely of one or two particular details, or even worse, whether that source may have told a different version of the same myth. The Kallisto myth is a conspicuous case in point. Because of the wide chronological distribution of its principal sources and the number of its variants, not to mention the serious difficulties which they raise, this myth has been a favorite battleground for modern 'mythographers', who have concentrated most of their efforts on the mechanical reconstruction of lost versions, those of 'Hesiod' and Callimachus in particular, without reaching much agreement.[65]

At the centre of the ongoing discussion lies a conglomerate of different versions of the story of Kallisto and Arkas which are recorded in various Greek and Latin collections of constellation myths under the two neighbouring constellations of Ursa Major and Arktophylax (Boötes).[66] The Greek constellation myths are mainly found in MSS of Aratus, where they occur in two forms, either as a separate anonymous collection (Catast.) or interspersed with the scholia to Aratus proper (schol. Arat.). The mythical 'tales' (*historiai*) of the Mythographus Homericus provide an exact parallel for this type of transmission. The Latin collections are represented by the *Astronomy* of Hyginus (*Astr.*), the so-called Aratus Latinus (Arat. Lat.), and the scholia to Germanicus' Latin adaptation of Aratus (schol. Germ.). Most of these texts were published synoptically by Carl Robert in 1878 and Ernst Maass in 1898.[67] But additional Greek sources have come to light in the meantime, and their importance is such that a new edition of the complete catasterismographic dossier is needed. It is essential to know that these texts fall into two fairly distinct groups. The principal sources (Group A) offer a fuller text than the rest, which suffered considerable abbreviation during the later imperial period. The abbreviated texts (Group B) omit, among other things, not only the Amphis version of the Kallisto myth (II) under Ursa Major but also the problematic reference to 'Hesiod' (fr. 163, right-hand column) under Arktophylax. Both groups are descended from a common ancestor, a Hellenistic collection of

constellation myths which is no longer extant. Group B is represented by a collection of epitomised catasteristic myths known as
the Epitome (Catast. Epit.), as well as by the majority of the schol.
Arat. MSS. Group A consists mainly of the three Latin collections
mentioned above, all of which include the Amphis version in one
form or another. In addition, however, there is a second collection
of Greek constellation myths which offers fewer myths but a more
complete text than Catast. Epit. and which belongs also to Group
A. This collection of excerpts (Catast. Exc.) includes the
Arktophylax myth with the reference to 'Hesiod' but unfortunately omits Ursa Major.[68] Although Robert knew the Amphis
version only from the Latin texts, he did not hesitate to assign it to
the original Greek collection.[69] He was right, but it was not until
1974 that the Amphis version was first published in its Greek form
from two rather untypical MSS of the schol. Arat., both of which
contain constellation myths that show close affinities with the
Greek as well as the Latin representatives of Group A.[70]

The complex transmission of the various forms of the Kallisto
myth in the catasterismographic tradition must be the starting
point for any attempt to reconstruct the pre-Hellenistic versions of
the myth and to interpret their meaning. The earliest known
versions, apart from the puzzling account in Euripides' *Helen* 375ff
where Kallisto's animal transformation seems to *precede* her mating
with Zeus, are exactly those which the Greek ancestor of the extant
collections of constellation myths ascribed to 'Hesiod' (under Ursa
Major) and Amphis. The same ancestor contained numerous
other references to early or rare authors and their works, including
the *Naxiaka* of Aglaosthenes (*FGrH* 499 F 1–3), the *Herakles* of
Antisthenes (fr. 24A Caizzi), the *Elegies Concerning Eros* of Artemidorus (*Suppl. Hell.* fr. 214 Lloyd-Jones/Parsons), the *Nemesis* of
Cratinus (*PCG*, vol. IV, p. 179), the *On Justice* and the *Erotikos* of
Heraclides Ponticus (frs. 51 and 66 Wehrli), an unknown work by
Myrsilus of Methymna (*FGrH* 477 F 15), the *Herakleia* of Panyassis
(frs. 3 and 10 Kinkel or Matthews) and of Peisander (fr. 1 Kinkel),
and finally, the *pièce de résistance*, the *Cretica* ascribed to Epimenides
(3 B 23–5 Diels/Kranz).[71] The nature and range of these quotations suggest strongly that the compilation was made in the early
Hellenistic period by a well-read Alexandrian scholar who is often
identified with Eratosthenes of Cyrene (third century BC) for
reasons which are understandable but far from compelling.[72]

Whatever his name, our compiler had access to at least two, possibly three different versions of the Kallisto myth, out of which he made one continuous account (I–III).[73] The Amphis version (II) was sandwiched as a mere variant between the Hesiodic version (I) and the catasterism proper (III). This peculiar arrangement has been a stumbling block for modern scholars who would like to know whether Kallisto's catasterism belongs to the Hesiodic version, to Amphis (highly unlikely), or to both, or whether it was taken from a third source.[74] In the absence of more explicit evidence, it is not at all certain that the catasterism was already known to 'Hesiod' (i.e. that it is pre-Hellenistic), nor is it safe to conclude from the dubious reference to Callimachus in version V that Kallisto's transportation into the skies was treated by him in detail, let alone that he invented it.[75] Regardless of its date, the catasterism is the most extraneous aspect of the myth. It has long been recognised that the story of Kallisto's offence and punishment must have existed prior to its connection with the constellation.[76] The original story pattern will have comprised, at the very least, the two elements which appear consistently in the written sources, the loss of virginity and the bear transformation. The catasterism, on the other hand, is an accretion of a well-known type which adds nothing of substance.

As told by the catasterismographers, the circumstances of the catasterism are extremely far-fetched and designed to explain the apparent pursuit of Ursa Major by Arktophylax in the sky. Some time after her transformation Kallisto was hunted by Arkas and took refuge in the sacred precinct (*abaton*) of Zeus Lykaios. When the Arcadians prepared to kill them both, Zeus intervened and turned them into stars. Ovid (VI), who had access to a Greek collection of constellation myths similar to the ancestor of the extant *Catasterisms*, naturally made the most of the near-fatal confrontation between mother and son.[77] To complicate matters even further, Kallisto's ultimate fate is related twice in most branches of the catasterismographic tradition. In the second account (under Arktophylax) the catasterism of Kallisto and Arktos has been artificially combined with the notorious cannibalism committed by her father Lykaon. The victim is Arkas, who is restored to life by Zeus so that he can hunt his mother the bear. This curious combination of the Lykaon and Kallisto myths, which is unattested elsewhere, is hardly more than mythographical patchwork, designed to bring together under a single rubric everything that was known about the family of Lykaon.[78] In this connection the name of 'Hesiod' is mentioned again, evidently as a source for Lykaon's crime and not as an authority for the combined stories.[79] M. L. West believes, with K. O. Müller, Robert and Sale, that the complex of myths concerning Lykaon, Kallisto and Arkas appeared twice in 'Hesiod', in the *Catalogue* as well as the *Astronomy*.[80] It is impossible to assign the extant Hesiodic versions of the Kallisto myth to one work or the other with any confidence. It is equally impossible, therefore, to determine to what extent these two treatments overlapped or differed. Merkelbach and West assigned versions I *and* III as well as the Lykaon/Kallisto myth reported under Arktophylax to the *Catalogue* (fr. 163) rather than the *Astronomy*. But West now seems to think that the catasterismographers followed the *Astronomy*. If so, we know absolutely nothing about the Kallisto of the *Catalogue*, except that she was 'one of the nymphs' (Apollod. 3.100) and therefore presumably not the daughter of Lykaon. Faced with such insurmountable difficulties, students of the Kallisto myth who take the concept of applied mythography seriously will have to think twice before they reconstruct 'the original myth' from the elusive Hesiodic versions.[81]

Even though the myth can be traced back to 'Hesiod' in the late archaic period, it does not fully emerge from obscurity until we come to Amphis in the first half of the fourth century. It is hardly necessary to dwell on the Amphis version, which gave a decidedly humorous twist to the myth. According to Amphis, Zeus disguised himself as Artemis when he seduced Kallisto, who later blamed the virgin goddess for the pregnancy for which Zeus was responsible. One would like to know more. Is it at all conceivable, even in comedy, that Zeus managed to conceal his true identity during the actual rape, or is it more likely that Kallisto recognised her aggressor but maliciously chose to accuse Artemis of something that was so contrary to the goddess's own nature? In Ovid's clever imitation (VIIa) the truth surely comes out *in flagrante delicto*, as was to be expected. But then Ovid's Kallisto does not put the blame on Artemis. Apart from its adaptation by Ovid, Amphis' comic parody is of marginal interest for the study of the myth in its more serious form.[82]

The three remaining versions (IV-VI) have much in common and derive from the same mythographical source, either the

Mythographus Homericus or the hypothetical 'Hellenistic handbook' (above, I). Invariably Kallisto is possessed by Zeus, changed into a bear by Zeus or Hera (*not* by Artemis), shot by Artemis at Hera's request, and put among the stars. It is widely held that the common source reproduced the Kallisto myth as told by some Hellenistic poet, which is plausible in the light of Ovid's imitation (VII), and that this poet was Callimachus, which is less plausible.[83] Pausanias (VI) and the Homeric scholiast (V) differ in length but not in substance, except for the rescue of Kallisto's unborn child, which is reported differently in versions IV and VI but omitted by the scholiast. In his usual manner, Apollodorus (IV) clutters his account with several variants, but he fails to tell us where he found them. He alone reports (IV 2b) that Zeus disguised himself as Apollo when he approached Kallisto. Given her constitutional aversion to male company, it is difficult to see how she would have let any man come within sight of her, even Artemis' brother. Still, a Hellenistic poet (not necessarily the same as the one mentioned before) might have thought otherwise, but he would have been more reluctant to attribute the paternity of Arkas to Apollo than Reinhold Franz, who announced the marriage of Kallisto and Apollo in 1890. This genealogical construction, which is based on Tzetzes' misreading of Apollodorus, has been revived in recent years and even used as evidence for the religious history of Arcadia.[84]

The most striking feature of versions IV – VII is the intervention of Hera. The motif of Zeus' deceived and jealous wife is more firmly rooted in the myths of Semele and Io, whence it was transferred to the Kallisto myth. In all three cases, Ovid (VII) outdid his predecessors in exploiting the psychological potential inherent in the triangle of husband, wife and mistress. Once Hera appeared on the scene, the role of Artemis had to be drastically diminished. Instead of being the divine protagonist, she now became Hera's creature. Her implacable wrath, which is so prominent in versions I – II, was either suppressed altogether (V – VI) or reduced to a mere mythographical variant (IV). Only Ovid has it both ways, as often, and manipulates Artemis' anger to set the stage for a massive display of Hera's jealousy. The prominent place assigned to Hera in the 'Alexandrian' version of the Kallisto myth makes for excellent poetry, but it leaves the original substance of the myth greatly impoverished. The conceptual connection between the virgin goddess, the loss of virginity, and the bear transformation of the new mother has been blurred almost beyond recognition. What had once been a unique and exemplary story of a maiden's dramatic transition to motherhood emerges from the Hellenistic reinterpretation as a conventional, if one-sided, love affair complicated by the marital dispute between Zeus and Hera.

Given the relatively late date of the available sources, it is impossible to reconstruct 'the original myth' of Kallisto with absolute certainty. But the concept of applied mythography, once followed through, makes it much easier to determine the narrative function and, if possible, the origin of each variant and to separate the consistent elements of the myth, which form its permanent core (to the extent that we are ever likely to know it), from more incidental features which owe their existence to literary convention or individual taste. Our mythographical analysis has shown that the following variables can be safely detached from the main story pattern: the disguise used by Zeus to deceive Kallisto (II 2, IV 2ab, VII 2a); the explanation for Artemis' wrath as found in Amphis (II 4); the jealousy of Hera (V–VII 4), and her active role in both the animal transformation (V–VII 3) and eventual death (IV–VI 6a) of Kallisto; and finally, Zeus rather than Hera as the agent of the bear metamorphosis (IV 3–4), a variation which implies Hera's jealousy and foreshadows her revenge.[85] The catasterism (III–VII), however, which forms the conclusion of the myth in all but the two earliest versions (I–II), is inseparable from the Hellenistic conception of Kallisto's ultimate fate. Yet it too must be set aside, as we have seen, as an accretion, the kind of stellar coda which this myth shares with all the other constellation myths. Once these embellishments have been removed, the substance of the myth remains. Apart from Zeus, who acts as a mere catalyst, the essential components have to do exclusively with Kallisto and Artemis. Their relationship is described as a series of three interconnected events, all of which affect Kallisto more directly than Artemis: the loss of virginity, the bear transformation, and the violent death. These three elements have been the main concern of modern interpreters for the past 160 years. Although their conclusions differ substantially, they all put the emphasis, in one way or another, on the transition from virginity to motherhood; on the significance of the bear (*arktos*), either as a 'sacred animal' or as a theriomorphic symbol of a particular biological or social status; and thirdly, on the conceptual link between the loss of virginity, animal transformation, and death. Today social interpretations prevail, and Kallisto is widely seen as the mythical model for the initiation of female adolescents into their adult roles, by analogy with the Attic 'bear-ritual' (*arkteia*), during which groups of prepubescent girls would 'play the bear' (*arkteuein*) in various sanctuaries of Artemis. Unattested in the ancient sources, the connection between the *arkteia* and the Kallisto myth, though hypothetical, rests on close structural similarities.[86] The case has been strengthened by the recent discovery of an Attic vase which shows Artemis shooting an arrow on one side and a mature woman and a younger man both wearing bear-masks on the other side.[87] This vase has the same shape as the numerous vases with representations of the ritual 'bear-girls' (*arktoi*) that were found in temples of Artemis throughout Attica. If the masquerade had both a ritual purpose and a mythical reference, it is tempting to connect it with the Kallisto myth and to assume that her bear transformation was re-enacted in the context of the *arkteia*. The woman would represent Kallisto, the bear-mother, and the young man would impersonate Arkas, the eponymous 'bear-man'.

While the mythographical approach cannot contribute directly to the process of extrapolating the meaning or function of a given myth from its narrative content, it can and must serve as a safeguard against interpretations which are based on distorted conclusions drawn from incomplete evidence. The lack of consensus concerning the death of Kallisto illustrates this point. Most interpreters assume that Kallisto's animal transformation functions as a prelude to her execution by Artemis. If Kallisto's death does indeed constitute the climax of this myth, it must by definition belong to the earliest-known versions. For this reason its occurrence in 'Hesiod' is often taken for granted, and rightly so, even though there is no direct proof.[88] Against this it has been argued that the form of the myth 'in which she was both changed [into a bear] *and* shot was late', and what is more, that her death at the hands of Artemis is, strictly speaking, incompatible with her transformation into a bear by the same goddess.[89] The first objection, raised by Sale, begs the question as long as Kallisto's ultimate fate in the pre-Hellenistic versions of the myth remains unknown. Those who wish to argue, as Franz and Sale did, that in 'the

Arcadian version' (a modern construct) Kallisto retained her human form while being shot by Artemis take recourse to two types of Arcadian coins from the fourth century BC which show Artemis shooting (obverse) and a purely human Kallisto transfixed by an arrow and accompanied by Arkas (reverse).[90] The absence of animal features may merely reflect dislike of a theriomorphic Kallisto on the part of this particular artist.[91] The degree to which representations of Kallisto in art were indeed affected by personal taste is well illustrated by four Apulian vases and vase fragments which are roughly contemporary with the Arcadian coins.[92] On three of the vases, Kallisto is shown in the process of being transformed into a bear, whereas the fourth vase shows her without animal features.[93] Unlike the die-makers, however, the vase painters tended to separate the motherhood of Kallisto from her death. Arkas appears on at least three of the four vases (one of the two fragments, Boston MFA 13.206 = *LIMC* Artemis 1388, is too small to judge), whereas Artemis is visible on only one vase, definitely absent on another, and not in evidence on the two fragments. Taken as a whole, then, the iconographical repertoire is too ambiguous to serve as a reliable substitute for lost versions of the myth. To answer the second objection, it should be sufficient to point out that no written form of the myth exists in which the bear transformation does not precede Kallisto's death. In addition, there is the parallel myth of Aktaion, whom Artemis transforms into a stag before he is killed by his own dogs, occasionally with the assistance of Artemis and her arrows, as on the Boston bell krater (*c.* 470 BC) from which the Pan painter derives his name.[94] Far from being a duplication of effort or, in narrative terms, a conflation of two variant modes of punishment, the combination of animal transformation and violent death confirms the persistent influence of hunting rituals on the religious mentality of the Greeks during the formative phase of their myth-making.[95]

Although the death of Kallisto is firmly established in the mainstream of the mythographical tradition, it is prevented for sentimental reasons in the catasteristic version (III, imitated by VII), in which Kallisto's son Arkas has taken the place of Artemis as the hunter who pursues the human bear, his own mother. It follows that the combination of death and catasterism in versions IV – VI is a secondary development, even though Orion too died before he was transformed into a constellation.[96] The remarkable prevention of Kallisto's death in the Alexandrian collection of catasterisms is clearly a special case which does not support the view that the bear transformation is structurally detachable from the actual killing. In the final analysis, the combined mythographical and iconographical evidence, though fragmentary and inconsistent, seems to bear out those scholars who have always insisted on a close connection between Kallisto's bear transformation and her death as a bear.

The preceding studies, however limited in scope, illustrate three different but connected aspects of Greek mythography: the nature of the relevant sources, the heuristic value of mythographical names, and, as the ultimate goal, the concept of applied mythography, which is instrumental in establishing the essential elements of a given myth. Large areas of the history of Greek mythography are still unexplored, and several important collections of myths lie ignored. Modern interpreters of Greek myths must constantly re-examine and strengthen the old foundations. If not, they build castles in the air.

Notes

1. P. Köln III 126 = H. Lloyd-Jones and P. Parsons, *Supplementum Hellenisticum* (Berlin and New York, 1983) no. 903A. Cf. Lloyd-Jones, 'The Meropis (*SH* 903A)', *Atti del XVII Congresso Internazionale di Papirologia*, I (Naples, 1984) 141–50; A. Henrichs, 'Philodems De Pietate als mythographische Quelle', *Cronache Ercolanesi*, 5 (1975) 5–38; below, note 27.
2. Cf. C. Wendel, 'Mythographie', *RE* 16.2 (1935) 1352–74; U. v. Wilamowitz, 'Die griechische Heldensage I–II', *Kleine Schriften*, V 2 (Berlin, 1937) 54–126; R. Häussler, 'Grundzüge antiker Mythographie', in W. Killy (ed.), *Mythographie der frühen Neuzeit. Ihre Anwendung in den Künsten*, Wolfenbütteler Forschungen, 27 (Wiesbaden, 1984) 1–23 (with useful bibliography).
3. *FGrH* 12. Asclepiades' *Tragodoumena* is a distant ancestor of the anonymous plot summaries (*hypotheseis*) for the major tragedians which have come to light on papyrus and which are an important source for the mythology of the classical period. See now P. Oxy. 52.3650–3; R. Kassel, 'Hypothesis', in W. J. Aerts *et al.* (eds), *Scholia. Studia D. Holwerda oblata* (Groningen, 1985) 53–9.
4. C. Wendel, 'Überlieferung und Entstehung der Theokrit-Scholien', *Abh. Kön. Ges. Wiss. Göttingen*, Phil.-hist. Kl., N. F. 17.2 (Berlin, 1920) esp. 90–102.
5. Cf. most recently F. Montanari, 'Revisione di *PBerol.* 13282. Le *historiae fabulares* omeriche su papiro', in *Atti del XVII Congresso Internazionale di Papirologia*, II (Naples, 1984) 229–42; B. Kramer and D. Hagedorn, *Griechische Papyri der Staats- und Universitätsbibliothek Hamburg*, Papyrologische Texte und Abhandlungen, 31 (Bonn, 1984) 25–34 (with full bibliography).
6. Edited by R. Wagner as volume I of the *Mythographi Graeci* (2nd edn, Leipzig, 1926). The most useful mythographical commentary presently available

is not to be found in J. G. Frazer's famous but disorganised notes attached to his Loeb edition (2 vols, London, 1921), but in the translations of K. Aldrich (Lawrence, Kansas, 1975) and M. Simpson (Amherst, Mass., 1976). The author of the *Library* (henceforth Apollod.) is not the same as his Hellenistic namesake, Apollodorus of Athens; cf. A. Diller, 'The Text of the Bibliotheca of Pseudo-Apollodorus', *Tr. Am. Phil. Ass.*, *66* (1935) 296–313. On the *Library* see E. Schwartz, 'Apollodorus', *RE* 1.2 (1894) 2875–86, repr. in *Griechische Geschichtsschreiber* (Leipzig, 1957) 207–23; Wilamowitz, *Kleine Schriften*, V 2, 68–76, 149–56.

7. Photius, *Bibl.* cod. 186, published with French translation by R. Henry, *Photius, Bibliothèque*, III (Paris, 1962) 8–39, whose notes merely summarise Hoefer (below); F. Jacoby used Martini's collations for his 1923 edition in *FGrH* 26 F 1 (with less than a page of commentary). Henry's edition provides the fullest information on the text of the two principal MSS but ignores important emendations, which Jacoby reports. P. Oxy. 52.3648 (second century AD), edited by M. A. Harder in 1984, preserves a much fuller version of substantial portions of *Dieg.* 46–7 than Photius. The papyrus is evidently part of a professional copy of the original work, whose style is exactly as Photius described it: charming and periodic but occasionally a little convoluted (*FGrH* 26 T 1). Cf. U. Hoefer, *Konon. Text und Quellenuntersuchung* (Greifswald, 1890) 30–113 (a comprehensive but highly speculative source-critical study of all but three of the fifty stories); Martini, *RE* 11.2 (1922) 1335–8 (mainly on Conon's style and sources, along the lines suggested by Hoefer). The title *Diegeseis* (i.e. *narrationes*) was also applied in antiquity to prose summaries of poetic works such as Homer's *Odyssey* and Callimachus' collected poems; see R. Pfeiffer, *A History of Classical Scholarship*, I (Oxford, 1968) 195.

8. *Cononis narrationes L. Ex Photii Bibliotheca edidit et adnotationibus illustravit Io. Arnoldus Kanne. Praefixa est epistola ad Heynium. Adiectum Chr. G. Heynii spicilegium observationum in Cononem* (Göttingen, 1798) 59–167 (Kanne's commentary) and 168–82 (Heyne's notes). Kanne's model was Heyne's own *Apollodori Atheniensis Bibliothecae libri tres* (Göttingen, 1782–3, in two volumes; 2nd edn 1803, rep. Hildesheim 1972; only the text of the second edition was reprinted, not the more than 400 pages of exegetical notes and indices). Kanne was a voluminous writer whose far-fetched oriental etymologies of Greek mythological names were notorious, cf. A. Henrichs, 'Welckers Götterlehre', in W. M. Calder III *et al.* (eds), *Friedrich Gottlieb Welcker. Werk und Wirkung* (Stuttgart, 1986) 179–229, at n 11.

9. P. Vidal-Naquet, 'The Black Hunter and the Origin of the Athenian Ephebeia', in R. L. Gordon (ed.), *Myth, Religion and Society* (Cambridge and Paris, 1981) 147–62, at 150 (= P. Vidal-Naquet, *Le Chasseur noir*, 2nd edn (Paris, 1983) 156), in a discussion of the myth of Xanthos and Melanthos, the aetiological explanation of the Apaturia, for which Conon (*Dieg.* 39) is our earliest direct source.

10. *Dieg.* 2–4, 8, 12–14, 19, 21, 28–9, 36–7, 41, 46–7 (cf. P. Oxy. 3648), 48. Cf. P. M. Fraser, *Ptolemaic Alexandria*, I (Oxford, 1972), 513f; F. Prinz, *Gründungsmythen und Sagenchronologie* (Munich, 1979).

11. *Dieg.* 6 (oracle of Clarian Apollo; cf. Apollod. Epit. 6.2–4); 11 (Lindian sacrifice; cf. Callim. *Ait.* frs 7.20 and 22–3; Apollod. 2.118); 15 (cult of Demeter at Pheneos, Arcadia; cf. Paus. 8.15.4); 17 (local cult of Herakles in Thessaly); 19 (Linos song and Argive festival called Arnis, with dog sacrifices; cf. Callim. *Ait.* frs 26–31; according to the *Diegesis* in P. Oxy. 20.2263 = *FGrH* 305 F 8bis, Callimachus' source was the history of Argos by Agios/Dercylus; see Wilamowitz, *Kleine Schriften*, V 2, 108–13, and R. Pfeiffer, *Callimachus*, II (Oxford 1951) 107f); 20 (Thracian hero cult); 24 (Narcissus and cult of Eros in Thespiai; cf. Paus.

9.31.7; B. Manuwald, 'Narcissus bei Konon und Ovid', *Hermes*, *103* (1975) 349–72; Pellizer, this volume, Ch. 6); 30 (sacred sheep of Helios in Apollonia, Illyria; cf. Hdt. 9.93f); 33 (cult of Leukothea in Miletus and oracle of Didymean Apollo; cf. Callim. fr. 229); 35 (cult of Apollo Gypaieus at Ephesus, otherwise unknown); 44 (oracle of Didymean Apollo); 45 (= O. Kern, *Orphicorum fragmenta* (Berlin, 1922) *testim.* 115; the fullest Greek account of the death of Orpheus, at Leibethra, Pieria, and his subsequent cult there, from which women were excluded, Graf, this volume, Ch. 5, section 5; on the sacrifices to Orpheus, not mentioned elsewhere, see J. Harrison, *Prolegomena to the Study of Greek Religion*, 3rd edn (Cambridge, 1922) 467–9); 49 (cult of Apollo Aigletēs on Anaphe, founded by the returning Argonauts; cf. Callim. *Ait.* frs 7.19 and 21; Ap. Rhod. 4.1694ff; Apollod. 1.139; below, note 20). Conon appears to have used local histories rather than Callimachus, in which case his information on Greek religion is particularly valuable.

12. Byblis and Kaunos: *Dieg.* 2; Parth. *Erot. Path.* 11; Ovid *Met.* 9.454–665; Ant. Lib. *Met.* 30; cf. F. Bömer, *P. Ovidius Naso. Metamorphosen Buch VIII–IX* (Heidelberg, 1977) 411f. Pallene and Kleitos: *Dieg.* 10; Parth. 6 = Hegesippus *FGrH* 391 F 2 (below, note 17). Oinone and Paris: *Dieg.* 23; Parth. 4; Ovid *Her.* 5; cf. Apollod. 3.154f.

13. *Dieg.* 28 ('Tennes' axe'; Paus. 10.14.3f gives the same combination of myth and proverb as Conon), 34 ('Diomedean pressure'). Cf. E. Leutsch and F. G. Schneidewin, *Corpus Paroemiographorum Graecorum*, vol. I (Göttingen, 1839) Index 499 and 517, vol. II (1851) Index 800 and 827; Hesych. D. 1881, T 473; O. Crusius, 'Paroemiographica. Textgeschichtliches, zur alten Dichtung und Religion', *SB Kön. Bay. Ak. Wiss.*, Phil.-hist. Kl. 1910, 4. Abh.; W. Bühler, *Zenobii Athoi Proverbia*, vol. 4 (Göttingen, 1982).

14. *Dieg.* 5 (a cicada assists a cithara-player; cf. Timaeus *FGrH* 566 F 43); 22 (a snake saves its master; cf. Ael. *Var. Hist.* 13.46); 43 (the lava of Mt Aetna spares two pious sons; see W. Theiler, *Poseidonios. Die Fragmente*, 2 (Berlin and New York, 1982) 53 on F 42). Cf. A. Giannini, *Paradoxographorum Graecorum reliquiae* (Milan, 1966); Callim. fr. 407 (a collection of regional *paradoxa*, preserved by Antigonus of Carystus, a younger contemporary of Callimachus).

15. *Dieg.* 1 (Midas' gold and long ears); 37 (the earthborn Spartoi of Thebes); 40 (Andromeda's sea-monster was a ship named Ketos whose crew was rigid with fear of Perseus, whence the myth of Gorgo's petrifying head; cf. Paleaph. 37). See J. S. Rusten, *Dionysius Scytobrachion*, Papyrologica Coloniensia, 10 (Opladen, 1982) esp. 93ff; Palaephatus *Peri Apiston* has been edited by N. Festa, *Mythographi Graeci*, III 2 (Leipzig, 1902).

16. *Dieg.* 38 (about a banker who tries in vain to cheat a friend out of his deposit; cf. Hdt. 6.86); 42 (Stesichorus' *ainos* about the power of the tyrant; cf. Philistus *FGrH* 556 F 6; Aristotle *Rhet.* 2.20, 1393b9ff).

17. On Conon's Thracian connection see Jacoby on *FGrH* 391; R. B. Egan, 'Aeneas at Aineia and Vergil's *Aeneid*', *Pacific Coast Philology*, *9* (1974) 37–47. Hoefer, *Konon*, 53–68 assigned eight of Conon's Thracian stories to Hegesippus, including the love story of Pallene and Kleitos also told by Parthenius (above, note 12). In the single MS of Parthenius, two sources are given for this story, Hegesippus' *Palleniaka* (*FGrH* 391 F 2) as well as Theagenes (774 F 17), author of *Makedonika*. The source ascriptions in Parthenius, like similar *Quellenangaben* in other mythographers such as the Mythographus Homericus (above, note 5), are not necessarily reliable. In the case of Parthenius, however, they are unusually specific, and most scholars accept them as accurate references to texts in which the myth in question was discussed, whether Parthenius actually used them as sources or not. Cf. C. Wendel, *Gnomon*, *8* (1932) 148–54; V. Bartoletti, *RFIC*, *76* (1948) 34f; R. Kassel, *Rhein. Mus.*, *117* (1974) 191.

18. Unless this has been done in the unpublished dissertation by R. B. Egan, 'The Diegeseis of Konon', University of Southern California (Los Angeles, 1971, *Diss. Abstr.* 32 (1971) 939A), which is said to include text, translation and commentary.

19. *Dieg.* 4 (the eponymous hero of Olynthos killed by a lion); 35 and 44 (above, note 11; the rival *genos* of the Euangelidai does not seem to occur outside Conon).

20. *Dieg.* 49, with the parallels noted above, note 11. Cf. H. Fluck, *Skurille Riten in griechischen Kulten*, Diss. Freiburg (Endingen, 1931) 59–62; J. S. Rusten, *HSCP*, *81* (1977) 157–61; Burkert, *OE*, 76f (but see the critique by G. Neumann, *Zs.f. vergl. Sprachforschung*, *98* (1985) 306).

21. *Dieg.* 16. Cf. Strabo 10.4.12 from Theophrastus, *Peri Erotos* (where the *erastēs* is called Euxynthetos, as in Plut. *Amat.* 20, 766D); Eth. Eud. 3.1, 1229a21 (where the *erastēs* is a nameless but 'fabled' [*mythologoumenos*] man from Crete; no details are given). K. J. Dover, *Greek Homosexuality* (Oxford, 1978) 51 mistakenly places Conon's story 'in late antiquity' and underestimates its interest.

22. Only various partial editions exist, including F. Creuzer's of 1817. Cf. S. Brock, *The Syriac Version of the Pseudo-Nonnos Mythological Scholia* (Cambridge, 1971). Brock's superior edition also gives the Greek text of some of the scholia.

23. M. L. West, *The Hesiodic Catalogue of Women. Its Nature, Structure and Origins* (Oxford, 1985).

24. P. Vindob. Gr. inv. 26727 lines 5–8, edited by P. J. Sijpesteijn and K. A. Worp, *Chronique d'Egypte* 97–8 (1974) 317–24. Doros' descendants are described in P. Turner 1 = Hesiod fr. 10a.1–19; cf. West, *Hesiodic Catalogue*, 59.

25. P. Mich. inv. 1447, edited by T. Renner, *HSCP*, *82* (1978) 277–93, with important commentary. The three Hesiodic fragments have been reprinted by Merkelbach and West in the OCT Hesiod (2nd edn, Oxford, 1983, pp. 231f, frs 10(d), 188A and 217A). Cf. West, *Hesiodic Catalogue*, 60f (Aiolos' daughters), 88 (Aktaion, whose inclusion in the *Catalogue* as the suitor of Semele was unknown before the publication of the Michigan papyrus), and 99 (Arethousa, the third Hesiodic entry in the dictionary).

26. See above, note 1.

27. A. Henrichs, 'Ein Meropiszitat in Philodems *De Pietate*', *Cronache Ercolanesi*, 7 (1977) 124–5. The lines of the Philodemus passage which precede the reference to Asteros and the *Meropis* continue to qualify as a fragment of the *Great Ehoiai*, but the printed version (Hes. fr. 363A) needs revision in light of the new readings.

28. P. Cornell 55 (Pack[2] 2646), published by W. L. Westermann and C. L. Kraemer, Jr, *Greek Papyri in the Library of Cornell University* (New York, 1926) 246. The Cornell papyri are now housed in the Michigan collection at Ann Arbor. Professor L. Koenen was kind enough to examine the papyrus for me.

29. For the genealogies of Musaios and Eumolpus see A. Henrichs, 'Zur Genealogie des Musaios', *ZPE*, *58* (1985) 1–8 (where references to the Cornell papyrus should be added in notes 6 and 9). Rhadamanthys, son of Zeus and Europe: *Il.* 14.321f, in an enumeration of Zeus' liaisons with mortal women which reflects the tradition of the Hesiodic *Catalogue*. Trophonios, son of Apollo: Philodemus, *On Piety* (P. Herc. 243 III 27f, published by A. Henrichs, *Gr. Rom. Byz. Stud.*, *13* (1972) 86ff and W. Luppe, *Cronache Ercolanesi*, *14* (1984) 118ff), a genealogy ultimately derived from the *Catalogue* via Apollodorus of Athens; Paus. 9.37.5; Philostr. *VA* 8.19; schol. Ar. *Nu.* 506; cf. Charax *FGrH* 103 F 5.

30. Paus. 1.14.3 reports four genealogies for Triptolemos: (1) son of Keleos according to the Athenians; cf. the Parian Marble *FGrH* 239 A 12; (2) son of Okeanos and Ge according to Musaios (2 B 10 Diels/Kranz = Orph. fr. 51 Kern); cf. Apollod. 1.32 = Pherecydes *FGrH* 3 F 53, where several MSS offer Uranos side by side with Okeanos as variant names for Triptolemos' father; (3) son of Dysaules

according to Orpheus (= Orph. fr. 51 Kern); (4) son of Raros and of Amphiktyon's daughter according to Choerilus (*TGrF* 2 F 1). Recent editors of Apollod. 1.32 either reject (Wagner) or ignore (Frazer) the variant *Ouranou*, which explains why it has been overlooked (below, note 31). The Cornell papyrus supports *Ouranou*. If dated correctly in the 'early first century (A.D.)' by its editors, the text of the papyrus (*Ouranou*) could claim greater antiquity, and perhaps more authority, than the readings presented by the *Library* (*Ouranou/Okeanou*) or Pausanias (*Okeanou*).

31. Cf. R. Janko, 'Forgetfulness in the Golden Tablets of Memory', *CQ, 33* (1985) 89–100, esp. 95 (where the various hexametrical versions of the genealogy are conveniently collected and discussed). As far as I can see, the striking coincidence between the claim of the initiates on the gold tablets and the genealogy of Triptolemos as reported in the Cornell papyrus and in the alternate text of Apollod. 1.32 has not been noticed in the vast literature on the subject. Uranos and Ge appear in several Orphic theogonies as the first couple (cf. M. L. West, *The Orphic Poems* (Oxford, 1983) 71 and 235), whereas the pair Okeanos/Ge seems to be unparalleled.

32. For an exhaustive discussion see F. Graf, *Eleusis und die orphische Dichtung Athens in vorhellenistischer Zeit* (Berlin and New York, 1974). Graf too ignored the Cornell papyrus and its genealogies, several of which accord well with his general thesis.

33. Graf, *Eleusis*, 121–6 on Rhadamanthys and Triptolemos as judges of the dead. The Boeotian Trophonios looks like an intruder in this Eleusinian company, but he too could have been drawn into the circle of Orpheus or Musaios before the Hellenistic period and without the knowledge of Pausanias, who is our principal source on Trophonios (9.39.5–14). Demeter surnamed Europe was known at Lebadeia as Trophonios' nurse (Paus. 9.39.5). If this connection is old, it could have facilitated the induction of Trophonios into Eleusinian literature.

34. Graf, *Eleusis*, 158–181; cf. M. Olender, 'Aspects de Baubô', *Rev. Hist. Rel.*, *202* (1985) 3–55, esp. 13f and 28–30. Dysaules and Baubo are husband and wife in Asclepiades *FGrH* 12 F 4 (cf. Palaephatus *FGrH* 44 F 1). Their relationship is perhaps implied by Clement of Alexandria *Protr.* 2.20.2 (= Orph. fr. 52 Kern), where Baubo, Dysaules and Triptolemos appear as a connected series of names in a list of Eleusinian autochthons. B[r]auro in the Cornell papyrus is probably a mistake for Baubo, which may have been caused by confusion with Brauron in Attica, famous for its cult of Artemis. The only attested bearer of the name Brauro is the wife of the Edonian king Pittakos (Thuc. 4.107.3). If Thracian, however, the new name of Dysaules' wife could be interpreted as further evidence of Thracian ancestors in Eleusinian genealogies; cf. Orpheus, Musaios and Eumolpos (Jan Bremmer).

35. The epic spelling Antiophemos in Paus. 10.5.6 and 10.12.11 (in both cases as father of Musaios) and more appropriately in *Orph. Arg.* 310 recalls Herodotus 7.153.1, where Antiphemos the founder of Gela (cf. Paus. 8.46.2) appears as Antiophemos in all MSS.

36. For instance Iphiklos, son of Phylakos (A.R. 1.45–8, Hyg. *Fab.* 14.2) versus Iphiklos the Thestiad (A.R. 1.201, Hyg. *Fab.* 14.17). Cf. O. Jessen, *Prolegomena in catalogum Argonautarum* (Diss. Berlin, 1889); C. Robert, 'Der Argonautenkatalog in Hygins Fabelbuch', *Nachr. Kön. Ges. Wiss. Göttingen*, Phil.-hist. Kl. (1918) 4, 469–500; M. W. Haslam on P. Oxy. 53.3702 fr. 2.

37. Paus. 8.15.6–7.
38. Apollod. 1.63 and Hes. fr. 10a.49.
39. Apollod. 2.117 and Pherecydes *FGrH* 3 F 17.
40. Apollod. 3.124 and Paus. 3.15.1.

41. Apollod. 3.48; schol. Tzetzes Ar. *Nu.* 506; cf. Bremmer, this volume, Ch. 3, on variations in women's names.

42. Schol. D. *Il.* 9.145; Hes. fr. 23a.17; *Cypria* fr. 14 Bethe = fr. 15 Allen.

43. *ABV*, 23; Ovid *Met.* 8.306. Even the longest catalogues (Apollod. 1.67; Hyg. *Fab.* 173) omit this name. Cf. Bömer, *Metamorphosen Buch VIII–IX*, 108–9; A. Stewart, 'Stesichoros and the François Vase', in W. G. Moon (ed.), *Ancient Greek Art and Iconography* (Madison, Wisconsin, 1983) 53–74, esp. 63 (with bibliography); G. Daltrop, *Die Kalydonische Jagd in der Antike* (Hamburg and Berlin, 1966) 15–21, with plates 2 and 4; A. Surber, *Die Meleagersage. Eine historisch-vergleichende Untersuchung zur Bestimmung der Quellen von Ovidi met. VIII. 270–546* (Diss. Zurich, 1880) 97–106. Akastos, one of the Argonauts (Paus. 1.18.1), also arranged the funeral games for his father Pelias (on the Amphiaraos krater, below, note 49; Hyg. *Fab.* 273.10).

44. Eur. fr. 530 Nauck[2].

45. Beme, private collection (R. Blatter, *Ant. Kunst, 5*, 1962, 45–7); Bacch. 5.117; Bömer on Ovid *Met.* 8.315; G. Arrigoni in *Scripta Philoga*, 1 (Milan, 1977) 19–20. Antaios (François vase), which is usually taken as a misspelling of Ankaios, could be a genuine variant name.

46. Apollod. 3.106 and 3.164.

47. Hyg. *Fab.* 273.10–11; P. Strasb. W. G. 332 (Pack[2] 2452), edited by J. Schwartz, 'Une source papyrologique d'Hygin le mythographe', *Studi in onore di Aristide Calderini e Roberto Paribeni*, II (Milan, 1957) 151–6, revised by S. Daris, *Aegyptus*, *39* (1959) 18–21. The other papyrus will be published by Dr M. A. Harder in a future volume of the *Oxyrhynchus Papyri*. It contains a series of mythographical catalogues comparable to those in the Strasbourg papyrus (in which a catalogue of the Muses and their liaisons precedes the victors at the funeral games for Pelias) and to the *Indices* in Hyg. *Fab.* 221ff. Schwartz suggested that the Strasbourg papyrus preserves the original *Greek* text of Hyginus. The Oxyrhynchus papyrus disproves the theory of a Greek Hyginus, while it reinforces the assumption of one or more Greek sources for the *Indices* in Hyginus. P. Med. Inv. 123 (below, note 62) is also related to the *Indices*.

48. Paus. 5.17.9–10. Cf. Stesich. fr. 1–3 (178–80) Page.

49. The two charioteers are Admetos and Euphemos. For the Amphiaraos krater (lost, formerly Berlin F 1655) see F. Hauser in A. Furtwängler and K. Reichhold, *Griechische Vasenmalerei*, vol. III (Munich, 1932) 7, with plates 121–2, and D. A. Amyx, 'Archaic Vase-Painting vis-à-vis "Free" Painting at Corinth', in Moon (ed.) *Ancient Greek Art and Iconography*, 37–52, with plate 3.2b.

50. Surber, *Meleagersage*, 94–6; add Stesich. fr. 45 (222) Page, Bacch. 5.93ff and 25.1ff.

51. Eur. fr. 534.6ff. Nauck[2] (generic name); Ovid *Met.* 8.304 *duo Thestiadae* (identified as Plexippus and Toxeus 8.440f; below, note 53); Apollod. 1.62 (individual names), 1.68, 71–3 (generic name). Stesich. fr. 45, Paus. 8.45.6 and Hyg. *Fab.* 173 (below, note 57), who mention several 'sons of Thestios' by name, have it both ways.

52. The first pair appears in Stesich. fr. 45 and Bacch. 25.29 (formerly Pindar fr. 343 Snell), whence schol. T *Il.* 9.567; for the second pair see Paus. 8.45.6 (in a description of sculptures by Skopas, from the early fourth century BC). The representation of Calydonian hunters in pairs was a feature of archaic art.

53. Schol. A. R. 1.199/201b; Ovid *Met.* 8.440f. Other sources mention Plexippos alone (Antiphon *TGrF* 55 F 1b) or in combination with Calydonian hunters other than Toxeus (Hyg. *Fab.* 173; below, note 54).

54. Eurypylos, Iphiklos the Argonaut (above, note 36), and Plexippos. Cf. Apollod. 1.62, schol. D(A) *Il.* 9.567 and P. Vindob. Gr. inv. 26727 lines 17–21

(from a collection of mythological genealogies; above, note 24).

55. Surber, *Meleagersage,* 16–18; Wilamowitz, *Kleine Schriften*, V 2, 88–90; West, *Hesiodic Catalogue*, 114f and 137f; cf. S. Radt on Soph. *Meleagros* (*TGrF* IV, p. 345).

56. West, *Hesiodic Catalogue*, 47f.

57. Ovid *Met.* 8.314 (generic name) and 8.362f (Enaesimus); Hyg. *Fab.* 173 (three names, two of which are corrupt, in a catalogue of heroes 'who went after the Calydonian boar'; for the transmitted text, which is ignored in H. J. Rose's deplorable edition (2nd edn, Leiden, 1963), see P. Lehmann, *Abh. Bay. Ak. Wiss.*, Phil.-hist. Kl. N. F. 23 (1944) 44).

58. Professor W. H. Willis has drawn my attention to an unpublished papyrus from the second century AD in the collection of Duke University (P. Robinson inv. 10), in which '[Ly]kaios and Eurymnos, sons of Hippokoon' appear in a long list of heroic names which I take to be a catalogue of Calydonian hunters. Since Lykaithos and Eurytos (Alcman fr. 1.2–9 Page = 3 Calame; Apollod. 3.124) are among the earliest attested Hippokoontids, the two names in the Duke papyrus could qualify as secondary variants (see the examples of variant names quoted above). In fact Lykaithos' name appears as Lykaios in the scholia of the Louvre papyrus of Alcman fr. 1.2, and as Lykos in most of the MSS of Apollod. 3.124.

59. Diod. 4.33.5–6, Apollod. 2.143–5 and 3.125, Paus. 3.15.3–5; Calame, this volume, Ch. 8, section 2.9.1.

60. Alcman fr. 1.2–12 Page = 3 Calame (five names preserved and several more lost; cf. H. Diels, *Hermes, 31* (1896) 342–5); Apollod. 3.124 (the longest list, with twelve names); Paus. 3.14.6–7 and 3.15.1 (a total of six names). At least two additional names can be found in Ovid and Hyginus (above, note 57), but the list of those Hippokoontids who participated in the Calydonian hunt need not have been identical with the more popular list of those slain by Herakles.

61. Thebros (= Sebros in Alcman's dialect, whence Paus. 3.15.1–2) corresponds to Tebros (Apollod. 3.124), Lykaisos (Alcman) to Lykaithos (Apollod.), and Enarsphoros (Alcman) lies behind Emarsphoros (MS of Apollod.) and Enaraiphoros (MSS of Paus.). Genuine variant names include Arēios (Alcman) versus Arēitos (Pherecydes of Athens *ap.* schol. Alcman; add to *FGrH* 3 F 124–9).

62. P. Med. Inv. 123 (late second century AD), edited by S. Daris in D. H. Samuel (ed.), *Proceedings of the Twelfth International Congress of Papyrology* (Toronto, 1970) 97–102 (forty-seven names originally, arranged by males and bitches, as in Hyginus; followed by another catalogue of mythological monsters and of paradoxical phenomena in nature); Aesch. F 245 Radt (four names); Apollod. 3.32 (interpolated fragments of one or more lists in hexameters; cf. J. U. Powell, *Collectanea Alexandrina*, Oxford, 1925, 71–2); Ovid *Met.* 3.206ff; Hyg. *Fab.* 181 (two catalogues of more than eighty names); cf. P. Oxy. 30.2509 (the fate of Aktaion's dogs after they killed their master). On the controversial attribution of the hexameters in Apollod. and in P. Oxy. 2509 to the Hesiodic *Catalogue*, see the different views of Renner, *HSCP, 82* (1978), 283–5 (with full bibliography) and West, *Hesiodic Catalogue*, 88. The practice of recording the names of dogs associated with mythical events goes back to the archaic period. The François vase and several other archaic vases with scenes of the Calydonian hunt record the names of numerous dogs.

63. Henrichs, 'Welckers Götterlehre'.

64. F. Graf, *Griechische Mythologie* (Munich and Zurich, 1985) 39–57; Burkert, *S&H*, 1–34; R. L. Gordon (ed.), *Myth, Religion and Society. Structuralist Essays by M. Detienne, L. Gernet, J.-P. Vernant and P. Vidal-Naquet* (Cambridge, 1981); L. Edmunds and A. Dundes, *Oedipus. A Folklore Casebook*, Garland Folklore Casebooks 4 (New York and London, 1984) 76–121 and 147–73.

65. The basis for all subsequent work on the Kallisto myth is R. Franz, *De Callistus fabula*, Leipziger Studien zur classischen Philologie 12 (Leipzig, 1890) 235–365, who valiantly reconstructs the Hesiodic, Arcadian, Callimachean and Eratosthenic versions and discusses Ovid's sources as well as his influence. Most of his reconstructions are vulnerable, but as a source collection Franz's monograph is unrivalled. Cf. T. Condos, 'The Katasterismoi of the Pseudo-Eratosthenes: A Mythological Commentary and English Translation' (Diss., University of Southern California, Los Angeles, 1970; unpublished, *Diss. Abstr.* 31 (1971) 6029A) 10–14 and 43–9 (largely an uninspired summary of Franz); P. Borgeaud, *Recherches sur le dieu Pan* (Rome, 1979) 41–69, esp. 49–55 (a comprehensive treatment of the Kallisto myth which ignores the specific nature of the sources and their relationship).

66. Cf. J. Martin, *Histoire du texte des Phénomènes d'Aratos* (Paris, 1956) 36–68 for a thorough discussion of the catasterismographic tradition.

67. C. Robert, *Eratosthenis Catasterismorum reliquiae* (Berlin, 1978) 47–200 (parallel text of Catast. Epit.; schol. Arat.; schol. Germ.; an inferior version of the Arat. Lat. which Robert wrongly believed to be another version of schol. Germ. and which is of no interest; and *Astr.*); E. Maass, *Commentariorum in Aratum reliquiae* (Berlin, 1898) 175–306 (parallel text of Arat. Lat. (unknown to Robert) and Catast. Epit.), 334–555 (schol. Arat.), 573–81 (Catast. Exc., codex Venetus Marcianus gr. 444 misc., after A. Oliveri, *Pseudo-Eratosthenis Catasterismi*, *Mythographi Graeci* III 1, Leipzig, 1897). In the meantime, the immediate ancestor of Ven. Marc. 444 has appeared (below, note 68); an augmented text of the schol. Arat. has been published by J. Martin, *Scholia in Aratum vetera*, Stuttgart, 1974 (users should be cautioned that Martin prints the *uncorrected* text of the MSS, which is informative but very misleading); and finally, a new edition of Hyginus' *Astr.* is now available (A. Le Bœuffle, *Hygin, L'Astronomie*, Paris, 1983) and yet another seems to be highly desirable (Le Bœuffle's text has a much smaller MS basis than that of Sister L. Fitzgerald, 'Hygini Astronomica' (Diss., St Louis University, 1967; unpublished, *Diss. Abstr.* 28 (1968) 3656A); cf. M. D. Reeve in L. D. Reynolds (ed.), *Texts and Transmission. A Survey of the Latin Classics* (Oxford, 1983) 187–9).

68. Catast. Exc. is known from codex Vaticanus gr. 1087 misc. (from which Ven. Marc. 444 was copied; see above, note 67), published by A. Rehm, *Eratosthenis Catasterismorum fragmenta Vaticana*, Programm des K. humanistischen Gymnasiums Ansbach für das Schuljahr 1898/99 (Ansbach, 1899), and from two other MSS (below, note 70).

69. Robert, *Eratosth.* 11–14.

70. Codd. Salmanticensis 233 (Q) and Scorialensis Σ III 3 (S), published by Martin, *Scholia in Aratum vetera*, 74–5 (S) and 90 (Q). Amphis' name is mentioned only in Q, where the Amphis version appears out of order and by itself, i.e. without versions I and III. S gives the full entry, i.e. I–III, but omits Amphis' name. All of the catasteristic *historiai* in S and some of those in Q seem to derive from the unepitomised collection of constellation myths which is the ancestor of Catast. Exc., but Q and S contain catasterisms which are lacking in cod. Vat. gr. 1087 (above, note 68), including that of Ursa Major.

71. Cf. Robert, *Eratosth.*, 31–2 and 237–48, who argues for Eratosthenes as the source of this erudition.

72. The best discussions are by G. Knaack, *RE* 6.1 (1907) 377–81 and G. A. Keller, *Eratosthenes und die alexandrinische Sterndichtung* (Diss., Zurich, 1946) 18–28. Keller believed, as did Wilamowitz, Robert, Rehm, Gürkoff and Solmsen before him, as well as Pfeiffer after him (*History*, 168), that the lost Greek original was the work of Eratosthenes. Neither the name of Eratosthenes nor the current title

Katasterismoi has MS support, but there can be no doubt that Hyginus (whoever he was) used a collection of constellation myths that bore Eratosthenes' name (cf. Martin, *Histoire*, 95–125). Schol. D (A, b) *Il.* 22.29 ascribes the story of Erigone's catasterism to Eratosthenes, presumably with his *Erigone* in mind (Keller). Even if the D-scholium (i.e. the Mythographus Homericus), like Hyginus, knew a collection of catasterisms ascribed to Eratosthenes, the ascription as such would hardly prove anything.

73. The extent of his knowledge is mirrored most accurately in the five representatives of Group A, viz. *Astr.*, Arat. Lat. and schol. Germ. on the Latin side, and schol. Arat. Q and S (above, note 70) on the Greek side.

74. By far the most methodological and compelling discussion of the relevant sources and their problems is W. Sale, 'The Story of Callisto in Hesiod', *Rhein. Mus.*, *105* (1962) 122–41, followed by the same author's 'Callisto and the Virginity of Artemis', *Rhein. Mus.*, *108* (1965) 11–35.

75. Franz, *De Callistus fabula*, excluded the catasterism from his Hesiodic version; A. Rehm, *Mythographische Untersuchungen über griechische Sternsagen* (Diss. Munich, 1896) 36–41 assigned it emphatically to Hesiod; Robert, *Eratosth.*, 238f insisted that Kallisto's bear transformation was conceptually inseparable from the constellation of that name and that her catasterism was indeed Hesiodic; Sale, 'Story', 140 concluded strictly on methodological grounds that the myth as told in the Hesiodic *Astronomy* may or may not have ended with the catasterism. Franz's idea that Callimachus invented it is utterly unfounded. Callimachus mentions the Great Bear more than once and connects it with Kallisto (*Hymn* 1.41; Pfeiffer on fr. 632; *Suppl. Hell.* fr. 250.9f Lloyd-Jones/Parsons). Such casual references may explain why version V is attributed to Callimachus by the Mythographus Homericus (above, note 5), whose ascriptions must never be taken at face value.

76. K. O. Müller, *Prolegomena zu einer wissenschaftlichen Mythologie* (Göttingen, 1825) 73–6 and 193f; cf. the posthumous second edition of *Die Dorier*, published as *Geschichten hellenischer Stämme und Städte*, II (Breslau, 1844) 376. Virtually all interpreters follow Müller and detach the catasterism from the myth proper.

77. On the Kallisto myth in Ovid see R. Heinze, 'Ovids elegische Erzählung' (1919), rep. in *Vom Geist des Römertums, Ausgewählte Aufsätze*, 3rd edn (Darmstadt, 1960) 308–403, esp. 385–8; B. Otis, *Ovid as an Epic Poet*, 2nd edn (Cambridge, 1970) 379–89.

78. Borgeaud, *Pan*, 50f as well as Burkert, *HN*, 86f and 91 make too much of the combined stories. In particular, the phrase 'Arkas married his mother unwittingly' (like Oedipus) in Catast. Exc. (above, note 68) is not remotely as significant as Burkert and, following him, Borgeaud (p. 55) suggest. The word 'married' is demonstrably a scribal interpolation, as the publication of S (above, note 70) has now confirmed. According to the original text of Catast., Arkas 'chased his mother' (*Astr.* and Arat. Lat.). On Lykaon see Buxton, this volume, Ch. 4, section 2.

79. Sale, 'Story', 125–33, and 'Callisto and Artemis', 22–5.

80. West, *Hesiodic Catalogue*, 91–3.

81. S. Radt (*TGrF* III, p. 216) suggests that Aeschylus 'may have followed Hesiod (fr. 163)' in his tragedy *Kallisto*, the content of which is unknown except for two words (F 98). This is to explain *obscurum per obscurius.*

82. Kallisto's seduction by Zeus posing as Artemis reappears in Apollod. 3.100, schol. Callim. *Hymn* 1.41 and Nonnus *Dion.* 2.122f, 33.289ff. Maass, *Commentariorum in Aratum reliquiae*, LXV f. argues that Nonnus, like Ovid, owed his knowledge of the Amphis version to the catasterismographic tradition. I doubt that the peculiar details of the Amphis version can be safely interpreted as a mythical reflection of initiation rites involving female homosexuality in the archaic period, a

view expressed by Calame, *Chœurs* I, 432f and Borgeaud, *Pan*, 53f. Artemis' own attachment to Kallisto would be a better clue to the existence of such practices than Zeus' female disguise.

83. Franz, *De Callistus fabula*, 283–97, who rests his case for Callimachean authorship on the Mythographus Homericus (above, note 75) and on a local (Argive?) version of the Kallisto myth, reported by Callimachus' pupil Istros (*FGrH* 334 F 75), which is similar to our versions V–VI.

84. Franz, *De Callistus fabula*, 343f; G. Maggiulli, 'Artemide-Callisto', in *Mythos. Scripta in honorem M. Untersteiner* (Genoa, 1970) 179–85; G. Arrigoni, 'Il maestro del maestro e i loro continuatori: mitologia e simbolismo animale in Karl Wilhelm Ferdinand Solger, Karl Otfried Müller e dopo', *Ann. Sc. Nor. Sup. Pisa*, ser. III, vol. 14 (1984) 937–1019, at 1018 (in a discussion of the modern study of the Kallisto myth; cf. T. Gelzer, 'Bachofen, Bern und der Bär', in R. Fellmann, G. Germann and K. Zimmermann (eds), *Jagen und Sammeln. Festschrift für Hans-Georg Bandi* (Bern, 1985) 97–120).Tzetzes' error was recognised by E. Scheer in his 1908 edition of schol. Lyc. *Alex.* 480 (= *FGrH* 262 F 12).

85. Kallisto's transformation into a bear *by Zeus* (Apollod. 3.101) is also reported by Hyg. *Astr.* 2.1.4 and Liban. *Narr.* 12 (vol. 8, p. 41f Förster), both of whom provide details not found in Apollodorus. Their Greek sources cannot be determined.

86. The connection goes back to K. O. Müller (above, note 76), *Die Dorier* II 384–92, and *Prolegomena* 73f, who obliterated the very distinctions from which the Kallisto myth draws its meaning when he identified Artemis with both Kallisto and the bear, Artemis' 'sacred animal' (an inadequate concept); cf. Arrigoni, 'Il maestro', 975–1019. On the Kallisto myth in relation to the *arkteia* see R. Arena, *Acme*, *32* (1979) 5–26; A. Henrichs, in J. Rudhardt and O. Reverdin (eds), *Le Sacrifice dans l'antiquité* (Vandœuvres-Geneva, 1981) 198–208; J. -P. Vernant, *Annuaire du Collège de France*, *81* (1980–1) 398–400, and *83* (1982–3) 451–6; Borgeaud, *Pan* 53–5. On the *arkteia* see S. G. Cole, *ZPE*, *55* (1984) 238–44 (with full bibliography); L. Kahil, 'Mythological Repertoire of Brauron', in Moon (ed.), *Ancient Greek Art and Iconography*, 231–44; M. B. Hollinshead, *AJA*, *89* (1985) 419–40; E. C. Keuls, *The Reign of the Phallus* (New York, 1985) 310–20; S. G. Cole and G. Arrigoni in Arrigoni (ed.), *Le Donne in Grecia* (Rome and Bari, 1985) 19–25, 101–4, with pls. 17–18.

87. L. Kahil, *Antike Kunst*, *20* (1977) 86–98, pl. 20; E. Simon, *Festivals of Attica. An Archaeological Commentary* (Madison, Wisconsin, 1983) 87f, pl. 25; Arrigoni, *Le Donne*, 21, pl. II.

88. West, *Hesiodic Catalogue*, 92 (Kallisto 'was killed in the story').

89. Sale, 'Callisto and Artemis', 29 (who tries, throughout his article, to separate the bear transformation from the shooting); A. Adler, *RE* 10.2 (1919) 1727 and 1729.

90. Franz, *De Callistus fabula*, 273–83, followed by Sale, 'Callisto and Artemis', 14f. The phrase '(Artemis) killed Kallisto' (*Certamen Homeri et Hesiodi* 118 Allen, written in the fifth century BC) does not imply, as both Franz and Sale think, that Kallisto was shot in human form. She retains her human name even after her bear transformation, as in Paus. 8.3.6f and Apollod. 3.101.

91. Cf. A. B. Cook, *Zeus. A Study in Ancient Religion*, II (Cambridge, 1925) 228 n 5, who reproduces both coin types (p. 229, figs 158–9).

92. For the four vases as well as the coins, see *LIMC* II 1 (1984) 'Artemis' nos. 1385–90 (L. Kahil), 'Arkas' nos. 1–5 (A. D. Trendall), and Arrigoni, 'Il maestro', 1016ff, where references to illustrations can be found.

93. A vase by the Niobid painter (*c.* 460 BC; *ARV* 604.51; E. Löwy, *JdI*, *47* (1932) 64, fig. 15), which shows Artemis taking aim at a woman carrying a baby

and trying to escape, has been tentatively connected with the Kallisto myth by R. M. Cook, *Niobe and Her Children* (Cambridge, 1964) ,13f. If interpreted correctly, this vase would be the earliest example of the dissociation of Kallisto's death from her animal transformation.

94. Boston MFA 10.185 = *LIMC* I 1 (1981) 'Aktaion' no. 15 (L. Guimond). The transformation of Aktaion is usually very graphic in representations from all periods, as Guimond's catalogue shows. See above, notes 25 and 62.

95. Burkert, *HN*, 12 – 34 and, on Aktaion, 111 – 14.

96. *Catast.* 32, pp. 162 – 7 Robert (above, note 67). But Hippe/Hippo, daughter of Cheiron, was transformed into a mare to save her from disgrace after she had been raped by Aiolos (other explanations for her animal transformation were given by Euripides and Callimachus); the catasterism followed the birth of her child Melanippe (*Catast.* 18).

I owe thanks to Seth Fagen, Jeffrey S. Rusten and Scott Scullion for their help and advice.

12
Greek Mythology:
A Select Bibliography (1965–1986)

Jan Bremmer

What follows is a personal sampling of the vast literature on Greek mythology. I start about the middle of the 1960s when the new approaches of structuralism and functionalism began to supersede the ruling fertility paradigm as developed by Mannhardt and Frazer, although some older and still valuable studies have not been omitted. What has been included here is designed to give access to the best or most inspiring recent studies; those interested in more complete listings should consult *L'Année philologique*.

1. Introductions, Handbooks, General Surveys, Bibliography

(a) Introductions

Kirk, G. S. (1970) *Myth. Its Meaning and Functions in Ancient and Other Cultures*, Berkeley and Cambridge.
—— (1974) *The Nature of Greek Myth*, Harmondsworth.
Burkert, W. (1981) 'Mythos und Mythologie', in *Propyläen Geschichte der Literatur*, vol. 1, 11–35, Berlin.
Detienne, M. (1981) *L'Invention de la mythologie*, Paris. (Note also the reviews by A. Momigliano, *Riv. Stor. It.*, *94* (1982) 784–7 and C. Grottanelli, *Hist. of Rel.*, *25* (1985) 176–9.)
Graf, F. (1985) *Griechische Mythologie*, Munich and Zurich. (English translation forthcoming.)

(b) Handbooks

Roscher, W. H. (ed.) (1884–1937) *Ausführliches Lexikon der griechischen und römischen Mythologie*, Leipzig.
Preller, L. (1894–1921) *Griechische Mythologie*, 4th edn, ed. C. Robert, Berlin.
Rose, H. J. (1953) *A Handbook of Greek Mythology*, 5th edn, London.
Grant, M. (1962) *Myths of the Greeks and Romans*, 2nd edn, Ohio and London.
—— and Hazel, J. (1973) *Who's Who in Classical Mythology*, London.

A Select Bibliography

Bonnefoi, Y. (1981) *Dictionnaire des Mythologies*, 2 vols, Paris. (Articles on Greek mythology by M. Detienne, N. Loraux, J.-P. Vernant and other members of the 'Paris' school.)

(c) General Surveys

Gruppe, O. (1921) *Geschichte der klassischen Mythologie und Religionsgeschichte während des Mittelalters im Abendland und während der Neuzeit*, Leipzig.

Vries, J. de (1961) *Forschungsgeschichte der Mythologie*, Freiburg and Munich.

Feldman, B. and Richardson, R. D. (1972) *The Rise of Modern Mythology 1680–1860*, Bloomington and London.

Vernant, J.-P. (1974) *Mythe et société en Grèce ancienne*, Paris, 195–250.

Burkert, W. (1980) 'Griechische Mythologie und die Geistesgeschichte der Moderne', *Entretiens Hardt*, *26*, Geneva, 159–99.

Detienne, M. (1981) *L'Invention de la mythologie*, Paris, 15–49.

Graf, F. (1985) *Griechische Mythologie*, Munich and Zurich, 15–57.

(d) Bibliography

Peradotto, J. (1973) *Classical Mythology. An Annotated Bibliographical Survey*, Urbana.

2. Myths and Mythical Themes

Arrigoni, G. (1977) 'Atalanta e il cinghiale bianco', *Scripta Philologa*, 1, 9–47.

Bouvier, D. and Moreau, P. (1983) 'Phinée ou le père aveugle et la marâtre aveuglante', *Rev. Belge Phil. Hist.*, *61*, 5–19.

Brelich, A. (1956) 'Theseus i suoi avversari', *SMSR*, *27*, 136–41.

—— (1955/7) 'Les monosandales', *La Nouvelle Clio*, *7–9*, 469–84.

—— (1958) *Glio eroi greci*, Rome.

—— (1958) 'Un mito "prometeico",' *SMSR*, *29*, 23–40.

—— (1969) *Paides e parthenoi*, Rome. (Initiation.)

—— (1969) 'Symbol of a Symbol', in J. M. Kitagawa and C. H. Long (eds) *Myths and Symbols. Studies in Honour of M. Eliade*, Chicago, 195–207. (Human sacrifice.)

—— (1969) 'Nireus', *SMSR*, *40*, 115–50.

—— (1970) 'La corona di Prometheus', in *Hommages à M. Delcourt*, Brussels, 234–42.

—— (1972) 'Nascita di miti', *Religione e civiltà*, 2, 7–80. (Eleusis.)

Bremmer, J. (1978) 'Heroes, Rituals and the Trojan War', *Studi Storico-Religiosi*, 2, 5–38.

—— (1983) 'Scapegoat Rituals in Ancient Greece', *HSCP*, *87*, 299–320. (Myth and ritual.)

—— (1984) 'Greek Maenadism Reconsidered', *ZPE*, *55*, 267–86.

Brisson, L. (1976) *Le Mythe de Tirésias*, Leiden.

—— (1982) *Platon, les mots et les mythes*, Paris.

Broek, R. v.d. (1972) *The Myth of the Phoenix*, Leiden.

Burkert, W. (1966) 'Kekropidensage und Arrephoria', *Hermes*, *94*, 1–25.

—— (1970) 'Jason, Hypsipyle, and New Fire at Lemnos', *CQ*, *20*, 1–16.

—— (1979) *Structure and History in Greek Mythology and Ritual*, Berkeley, Los Angeles, London.

—— (1982) 'Götterspiel und Götterburleske in altorientalischen und griechischen Mythen', *Eranos-Jb.*, *51*, 335–67.

————— (1983) *Homo necans. The Anthropology of Ancient Greek Sacrifical Ritual and Myth*, Berkeley, Los Angeles, London.

————— (1984) *Die orientalisierende Epoche in der griechischen Religion und Literatur*, Heidelberg.

Buxton, R. G. A. (1980) 'Blindness and Limits: Sophokles and the Logic of Myth', *JHS*, *100*, 22–37.

Calame, C. (1977) *Les Chœurs de jeunes filles en Grèce archaïque*, 2 vols, Rome. (Initiation.)

————— (1977) 'Mythe grec et structures narratives: le mythe des Cyclopes dans *l'Odyssée*', in B. Gentili (ed.), *Il mito greco*, Rome, 371–91.

————— (1977) 'L'Univers cyclopéen de *l'Odyssée* entre le carré et l'hexagone logiques', *Živa Antika*, *27*, 315–22.

————— (1982) 'Le Discours mythique', in J. -C. Coquet (ed.), *Sémiotique. L'Ecole de Paris*, 85–102.

————— (1983) 'L'Espace dans le mythe, l'espace dans le rite: Un example grec', *Degrés*, *35/6*, 1–15. (Myth and ritual, Theseus.)

————— (1985) 'Les figures grecques du gigantesque', *Communications*, *42*, 147–72.

Carlier, J. (1979) 'Voyage en Amazonie grecque', *Acta Ant. Hung.*, *27*, 381–405.

Conradie, P. J. (1977) 'The literary nature of Greek myths', *Acta Classica*, *20*, 49–58.

Corsano, M. (1979) 'Sparte et Tarente. Le mythe de fondation d'une colonie', *Rev. Hist. Rel.*, *196*, 113–40.

Delcourt, M. (1957) *Hephaistos ou la légende du magicien*, Paris.

————— (1981) *Oedipe ou la légende du conquérant*, 2nd edn, Paris.

Detienne, M. (1972) *Les Jardins d'Adonis*, Paris. English translation: *The Gardens of Adonis* (1977), Hassocks.

————— (1977) *Dionysos mis à mort*, Paris. English translation: *Dionysos Slain* (1979) Baltimore and London.

————— and Vernant, J.-P. (1978) *Les Ruses d'intelligence*, 2nd edn, Paris. English translation: *Cunning Intelligence in Greek Culture and Society* (1978), Hassocks.

Ellinger, P. (1978) 'Le gypse et la boue, I: Sur les mythes de la guerre d'anéantissement', *Quad. Urb. Cult. Class.*, *29*, 7–35.

————— (1984) 'Les ruses de guerre d'Artémis', *Cahiers du Centre Jean Berard*, *9*, 51–67.

Fehling, D. (1972) 'Erysichthon oder das Märchen von der mündlichen Überlieferung', *Rhein. Mus.*, *115*, 173–96.

Fontenrose, J. (1959) *Python: A Study of Delphic Myth and Its Origins*, Berkeley, Los Angeles, London.

————— (1960) *The Cult and Myth of Pyrrhos at Delphi*, Berkeley, Los Angeles, London.

————— (1966) *The Ritual Theory of Myth*, Berkeley, Los Angeles, London.

————— (1981) *Orion. The Myth of the Hunter and the Huntress*, Berkeley, Los Angeles, London.

Fauth, W. (1975) 'Zur Typologie mythischer Metamorphosen in der homerischen Dichtung', *Poetica*, *7*, 235–68.

Frontisi-Ducroux, F. (1975) *Dédale: mythologie de l'artisan en Grèce ancienne*, Paris.

Gernet, L. (1968) *Anthropologie de la Grèce antique*, Paris.

Gerritsen, W. P. (1984) 'De omgekeerde wereld van de Amazonen', in R. Stuip and C. Vellekoop (eds), *Middeleeuwers over vrouwen*, vol. 1, Utrecht, 157–76, 204–7.

Graf, F. (1978) 'Die lokrischen Mädchen', *Studi Storico-Religiosi*, *2*, 61–79.

————— (1979) 'Apollon Delphinios', *MH*, *36*, 1–22. (Theseus.)

————— (1979) 'Das Götterbild aus dem Taurerland', *Antike Welt*, *10*, 33–41.

A Select Bibliography

—— (1984) 'Women, War, and Warlike Divinities', *ZPE*, *55*, 245–54.

Haas, V. (1975) 'Jasons Raub des Goldenen Vliesses im Lichte hethitischen Quellen', *Ugarit-Forschungen*, *7*, 227–33.

—— (1978) 'Medea und Jason im Lichte hethitischen Quellen', *Act. Ant. Hung.*, *26*, 241–53.

Henrichs, A. (1978) 'Greek Maenadism from Olympias to Messalina', *HSCP*, *82*, 121–160. Also in G. Arrigoni (ed.), *Le donne in Grecia* (Rome and Bari, 1985) 241–74.

—— (1981) 'Human Sacrifice in Greek Religion: Three Case Studies', *Entretiens Hardt*, *27*, Geneva, 195–242.

Herter, H. (1973) 'Theseus', *RE*, Suppl. 13, 1045–238.

Hetzner, U. (1963) *Andromeda und Tarpeia*, Meisenheim.

Lefkowitz, M. R. (1986) *Women in Greek Myth*, London and Baltimore.

Lloyd-Jones, H. (1983) 'Artemis and Iphigeneia', *JHS*, *103*, 87–102.

Loraux, N. (1981) *Les Enfants d'Athéna*, Paris.

—— (1982) 'Ce que vit Tirésias', *L'Ecrit du temps*, *2*, 99–116.

—— (1982) 'Héraklès: le surmâle et le feminin', *Rev. franç. de psychanal.*, *46*, 697–729. Also in R. Schlesier (ed.), *Faszination des Mythos*, 1985, Stroemfeld, 167–208.

Massenzio, M. (1970) *Cultura e crisi permanente: la 'xenia' dionisiaca*, Rome.

Matthes, J. (1970) *Der Wahnsinn im griechischen Mythos*, etc., Heidelberg.

Nagy, J. F. (1981) 'The deceptive gift in Greek mythology', *Arethusa*, *14*, 191–204.

Nilsson, M. P. (1970) *The Mycenaean Origin of Greek Mythology*, 2nd edn, Berkeley, etc. (To be read with L. Gernet, *Les Grecs sans miracle*, Paris, 1982, 99–104, and Graf, *Mythologie*, 68–70.)

Pantel-Schmitt, P. (1977) 'Athéna Apatouria et la ceinture', *Annales ESC*, *32*, 1059–73.

Parker, R. C. T. (1983) *Miasma*, 375–92, Oxford. (Exile and purification of the killer in myth.)

Pellizer, E. (1982) *Favole d'identità — Favole di paura*, Rome.

—— (1983) 'Tre cavalli bianchi ed un cavallo bigio', in E. Pellizer and N. Zorzetti (eds), *La paura dei padri nella società antica e medievale*, 29–46, Rome and Bari.

Piccaluga, G. (1968) *Lykaon*, Rome.

—— (1974) *Minutal*, Rome. (Love between gods and mortals, Persephone, Adonis, Melanion and Timon.)

Prinz, F. (1979) *Gründungsmythen und Sagenchronologie*, Munich.

Rubin, N. Felson and Deal, H. M. (1980) 'Many meanings, one formula, and the myth of the Aloades', *Semiotica*, *29*, 39–52.

Rubin, N. Felson and Sale, W. M. (1983) 'Meleager and Odysseus: A Structural and Cultural Study of the Greek Hunting-Maturation Myth', *Arethusa*, *16*, 137–71.

Rudhardt, J. (1971) *Le thème de l'eau primordiale dans la mythologie grecque*, Bern.

—— (1981) 'Du mythe, de la religion grecque et de la comprehension d'autrui', *Rev. eur. des sciences soc.*, *19*, no. 58. (Myth, Prometheus, Persephone.)

—— (1982) 'De l'inceste dans la mythologie grecque', *Rev. franç. de psychanal.*, *46*, 731–763.

Sale, W. (1975) 'Temple Legends of the Arkteia', *Rhein. Mus.*, *118*, 265–84.

Segal, C. (1983) 'Greek Myth as a Semiotic and Structural System and the Problem of Tragedy', *Arethusa*, *16*, 173–98.

Sergent, B. (1984) *L'Homosexualité dans la mythologie grecque*, Paris.

Siegmund, W. (ed.) (1984) *Antiker Mythos in unseren Märchen*, Kassel.

Sourvinou-Inwood, C. (1974) 'The Votum of 477–6 B.C. and the Foundation Legend of Locri Epizephyrii', *CQ, 27*, 186–98.
—— (1979) 'The Myth of the First Temples at Delphi', *CQ, 29*, 231–51.
—— (1979) *Theseus as Son and Stepson*, London.
Stoneman, R. (1981) 'Pindar and the Mythological Tradition', *Philologus, 125*, 44–63.
Vernant, J.-P. (1965) *Mythe et pensée chez les Grecs*, Paris. English translation: *Myth and Thought among the Greeks* (1983), London.
—— (1974) *Mythe et société en Grèce ancienne*, Paris. English translation: *Myth and Society in Ancient Greece* (1980), Brighton.
—— (1985) *La Mort dans les yeux*, Paris. (Gorgo.)
—— and Vidal-Naquet, P. (1972) *Mythe et tragédie en Grèce ancienne*, Paris. English translation: *Tragedy and Myth in Ancient Greece* (1981), Brighton.
—— (1986) *Mythe et tragédie en Grèce ancienne* II, Paris.
Versnel, H. S. (1984) 'Gelijke monniken, gelijke kappen: Myth and Ritual, oud en nieuw', *Lampas, 17*, 194–246.
—— (1986) 'Apollo and Mars One Hundred Years After Roscher', *Visible Religion, 4*, 134–72.
Vian, F. (1963) *Les origines de Thèbes. Cadmus et les Spartes*, Paris.
—— (1968) 'La fonction guerrière dans la mythologie grecque', in J.-P. Vernant (ed.), *Problèmes de la guerre en Grèce*, Paris, 53–68.
Vidal-Naquet, P. (1983) *Le Chasseur noir*, 2nd edn., Paris.
Weiler, I. (1974) *Der Agon im Mythos*, Darmstadt.

3. Mythography

(a) Greek Mythography

See the study by Henrichs, this volume, Ch. 11.

(b) Modern 'Mythologists'

Heyne, C. G. (1729–1812): A. Horstmann, 'Mythologie und Altertumswissenschaft. Der Mythosbegriff bei Christian Gottlob Heyne', *Arch. f. Begriffsgesch., 16* (1972) 60–85.
Moritz, K. Ph. (1756–93): M. Boulby, *Karl Philipp Moritz: At the Fringe of Genius* (Toronto, Buffalo, London, 1980).
Creuzer, F. (1771–1858): N. -M. Munch, 'La "Symbolique" de Friedrich Creuzer', *Association des Publications près les Universités de Strasbourg, 155* (Paris, 1976) 60–9.
Solger, K. W. F. (1780–1819): G. Arrigoni, 'Il maestro del maestro e i loro continuatori: mitologia e simbolismo animale in Karl Wilhelm Ferdinand Solger, Karl Otfried Müller e dopo', *Ann. Sc. Norm. Sup. Pisa, 14* (1984) 937–1019.
Müller, K. O. (1797–1840): A. Momigliano, *Settimo contributo alla storia degli studi classici e del mondo antico* (Rome, 1984) 271–86.
Welcker, F. G. (1784–1868): A. Henrichs, 'Welckers Götterlehre', in W. M. Calder III *et al.* (eds), *Friedrich Gottlieb Welcker. Werk und Wirkung* (Stuttgart, 1986) 179–229.
Müller, F. M. (1823–1900): H. Lloyd–Jones, *Blood for the Ghosts* (London, 1982) 155–64.
Usener, H. (1834–1905): H. J. Mette, 'Nekrologie einer Epoche. Hermann

Usener und seine Schule', *Lustrum*, *22* (1979/80) 5–106; A. Momigliano, 'New Paths of Classicism in the Nineteenth Century', *History and Theory*, Beiheft 21 (1982) 33–48; A. Momigliano *et al.*, *Aspetti di Hermann Usener, filologo della religione* (Pisa, 1982) and the forthcoming review in *Mnemosyne* by J. Bremmer.

Rohde, E. (1845–98): H. Cancik, 'Erwin Rohde — ein Philologe der Bismarck-zeit', in *Semper apertus. 600 Jahre Universität Heidelberg* (Berlin, etc. 1986) 436–505.

Wilamowitz-Moellendorff, U. v. (1848–1931): A. Henrichs, '*Der Glaube der Hellenen:* Religionsgeschichte als Glaubensbekenntnis und Kulturkritik', in W. M. Calder III *et al.* (eds), *Wilamowitz nach 50 Jahren* (Darmstadt, 1985) 263–305.

Frazer, J. G. (1854–1941): J. Z. Smith, *Map is not Territory* (Leiden, 1978) 208–39; G. Wood, 'Frazer's magic wand of anthropology: interpreting "The Golden Bough"', *Arch. Europ. de Sociol.*, *23* (1982) 92–122; S. MacCormack, 'Magic and the Human Mind: A Reconsideration of Frazer's *Golden Bough*', *Arethusa*, *17* (1984) 151–76.

Otto, W. F. (1874–1958): H. Cancik, 'Die Götter Griechenlands 1929. W. F. Otto als Religionswissenschaftler und Theologe am Ende der Weimarer Republik', *Der altsprachliche Unterricht*, *27* (1984) 151–76; idem, 'Dionysos 1933. W. F. Otto, ein Religionswissenschaftler und Theologe am Ende der Weimarer Republik', in R. Farber and R. Schlesier (eds), *Die Restauration der Götter* (Würzburg, 1986) 105–23.

Gernet, L. (1882–1962): S. C. Humphreys, *Anthropology and the Greeks* (London, 1978) 76–106, 283–8; R. di Donato, 'Une Oeuvre, un itinéraire', in L. Gernet, *Les Grecs sans miracle* (Paris, 1983) 403–20.

Dumézil, G. (1898): C. S. Littleton, *The New Comparative Mythology*, 3rd edn (Berkeley, etc., 1982): A. Momigliano, 'Premesse per una discussione su Georges Dumézil', *Opus*, *2* (1983) 329–41 and *Riv. Stor. It.*, *95* (1983) 245–60.

Brelich, A. (1913–1977): A. Brelich, *Storia delle religioni: perchè?* (Naples, 1979) 21–115. (A moving autobiography.)

Notes on Contributors

Jan Bremmer, b. 1944, is Associate Professor of Ancient History at the University of Utrecht. He is the author of *The Early Greek Concept of the Soul* (1983) and the co-author (with Nicholas Horsfall) of *Studies in Roman Myth and Mythography* (1986). His articles on Greek myth and ritual include 'Greek Maenadism Reconsidered', *ZPE* 55 (1984).

Walter Burkert, b. 1931, is Professor of Classical Philology at the University of Zurich. His books and many articles on Greek religion, philosophy and archaic poetry include *Structure and History in Greek Mythology and Ritual* (1979), *Homo Necans. The Anthropology of Ancient Greek Sacrificial Ritual and Myth* (1983), *Die orientalisierende Epoche in der griechischen Religion und Literatur* (1984), and *Greek Religion. Archaic and Classical* (1985).

Richard Buxton, b. 1948, is Lecturer in Classics at the University of Bristol. He is the author of *Persuasion in Greek Tragedy* (1982) and *Sophokles* (1984). Amongst his other publications is 'Blindness and Limits: Sophokles and the Logic of Myth', *JHS* 100 (1980).

Claude Calame, b. 1943, is Professor of Greek at the University of Lausanne and Chairman of the Swiss Semiotic Association. His books and articles, often based on a semiotic approach, include *Les Chœurs de jeunes filles en Grèce archaïque* (1977), *Alcman* (1983) and *Le processus symbolique* (1983). He is the editor of *L'amore in Grecia* (1983).

Fritz Graf, b. 1944, teaches Classics at the University of Zurich. His publications on Greek religion include *Eleusis und die orphische Dichtung Athens* (1974), *Griechische Mythologie* (1985) and *Nordionische Kulte* (1985). He has also published various articles on emblematics and Latin literature.

Albert Henrichs, b. 1942, is Eliot Professor of Greek Literature at Harvard University. He edited *Die Phoinikika des Lollianus* (1972) and (with L. Koenen) the Cologne Mani Codex (*ZPE* 1975–82). His numerous articles on Greek religion and its study in modern times include 'Loss of Self, Suffering, Violence: the Modern View of Dionysus from Nietzsche to Girard', *HCSP* 88 (1984) and '*Der Glaube der Hellene*: Religionsgeschichte als Glaubensbekenntnis und Kulturkritik' in W. M. Calder III *et al.* (eds), *Wilamowitz nach 50 Jahren* (1985).

Robert Parker, b. 1950, is Fellow of Oriel College and Lecturer in Greek and Latin Languages and Literature at the University of Oxford. He is the author of *Miasma: Pollution and Purification in Early Greek Religion* (1983). He has also published 'Greek States and Greek Oracles' in *Crux. Studies presented to G.E.M. de Ste. Croix* (1985) and 'Greek Religion' in *The Oxford History of the Classical World* (1986).

Ezio Pellizer, b. 1942, is Professor of Greek at the University of Trieste. He is the author of *Favole d'identità — Favole di paura* (1982) and co-editor (with N. Zoretti) of *La paura dei padri nella società antica e medievale* (1983). He has also published various articles on archaic Greek poetry, notably 'Per una morfologia della poesia giambica arcaica' in AA.VV. *I Canoni letterari* (1981).

Christiane Sourvinou-Inwood, b. 1945, is a former Lecturer in Classical Archaeology, University of Liverpool. She is the author of *Theseus as Son and Stepson* (1979). Her articles on Greek religion and iconography include 'Persephone and Aphrodite at Locri: A Model for Personality Definitions in Greek Religion', *JHS* 98 (1978) and 'To Die and Enter the House of Hades: Homer, Before and After', in J. Whaley (ed.), *Mirrors of Mortality: Studies in the Social History of Death* (1981).

H. S. Versnel, b. 1936, is Professor of Ancient History at the University of Leiden. He is the author of *Triumphus* (1970) and the editor of *Faith, Hope and Worship* (1981). His many articles on Greek and Roman religion include 'Self-Sacrifice, Compensation and the Anonymous Gods', *Entretiens Hardt* 27 (1981).

Index

(Figures in parentheses refer to the numbered notes)

Achaeus 206f
Achilles 3, 14, 25
Acropolis 195–8, 210 (39)
Admetus 52, 81, 272 (49)
Adonis 86, 280f
Adrastus 52
adunata 141
Aegypus 51
Aeneas Tacticus 142
Aeolus 49f
Aeschylus 43, 99, 202, 231;
    and Orpheus 84, 99; *Bassarai*
    85–7
Agamemnon 28f, 50, 174f, 251
Agenor 166
Aglaosthenes 260
Aglaurus 195–7
agriculture 159, 161
Aigeus 170
Aigisthos 28f, 50
Aiolos 166–9, 249
Aipytos 2
aischrology 247
Ajax 11
Akastos 252
Akrisios 165, 175
Aktaion 73, 266
Alcestis 81
Alcman 2, 168, 172, 177, 254
Alcyope 108
Alkaios 156, 216f
Alkmene 172
Alkyone 249
Aloades 281
Amazons 280
Ameinias 107–13
Amphiaraus 94
Amphidamas 251
Amphis 259f
Amphitryon 29
Amyklai 154–78 *passim*
Amyklas 154–80 *passim*
Amyntor 2
Ancaeus 98
Anchises 1
Andania 160, 162, 169f, 183 (14),
    184 (37)

androgynos 115–17
Andromeda 28
Antaios/Ankaios 252
Anteros 107–19 *passim*
Anthesteria 142f
Antigone 41f
Antiochis 45
Anti(o)phemos 250f
Antisthenes 260
Antoninus Liberalis 243, 249, 252
Anu 123
Apaturia 268 (9)
Apharetids 172, 174, 177
Aphareus 154, 169, 172f
Aphrodite 122, 161
Apollo 80, 85, 93f, 96, 101, 114,
    133, 154, 164, 191, 263; Aiglatas/
    Asgelatas 247, 268 (11); and
    Claros 268 (11); and Crete 225;
    and Delphi 215ff; and Didyma
    247, 268 (11); and goats 238 (47);
    and Ion 207; and Poseidon 232;
    and stones 225; and water 222,
    237 (35); A. Daphnephorus 224;
    A. Delphinios 225; A. Gypaieus
    247, 269 (11); A. Lykeios 63; A.
    Patroos 213 (80)
Apollodorus of Athens 242, 246,
    250, 268 (6)
Apollodorus, Pseudo 243, 246, 268
    (6)
Apollonius Rhodius 95, 97, 245,
    251
Apsu 21
Arachne 73
Aratus 259
Arcadia 65–79, 164
Archilochus 101
Areios 273 (61)
Areithoos 2
Areitos 273 (61)
Arene 169, 172
Ares 46, 100
Arethousa 270 (25)
Argalos 154, 166, 184 (34)
Argia 175
Argiope 82

287

Argolid 175
Argonauts 1, 95–9, 253
Argos 154–74 *passim*
Aristobule 128
Aristodemus 155, 175
Aristophanes 114, 139–41
Aristotle 66f, 87, 140
Arkas 71, 73, 162, 258f, 261–6
Arktophylax 259–64
Arktos 261
Arnus 19
Arrephoria 121, 196
Artemidorus 260
Artemis 85, 128, 134, 163f; and
    Kallisto 258–67; A. Orthosia
    163; A. Tauropolus 104 (43), 230
Asclepiades of Tragilus 243
Asclepius 84, 94
Asios 176
Assassins 88
Astarte 28
Asteros 242, 249
Atalanta 279
Athena 26f; and Asteros 242; and
    Athens 187–207 *passim*; and
    Hephaestus 191; and Poseidon
    198–200, 203f, 232; and Zeus
    190–2; as Mycenaean goddess
    219f; A. Apaturia 281; A. Polias
    202, 204; A. Pronaia 218f; A.
    Victory 192
Athenian mythology 187–214
Atossa 47
Atreus 154
Attis 11
autochthony 156, 193–5
Autolykos 97f

Bacchic mysteries 86, 99, 101
Balandier, G. 136
Bastian, A. 10
Baubo 250
bear 264f
Berger, P. 137
Berserkir 88, 91
Boios 51
Bömer, F. 130, 134, 136
Boreads 96, 98, 204f
Bororo mythology 47f
Boulis 51
Brauro 250
Brelich, A. 98, 283
Burkert, W. 1f, 7, 48, 52, 69, 71,
    91, 121f, 124, 225, 255
Busiris 81, 251
Byblis 269 (12)

Calame, C. 5
Callimachus 4f, 245, 259, 261, 263
Calydonian Hunt 85, 97, 252–4
Candaules 47
cannibalism 49–54, 124, 128, 145,
    261
Carians 158
Castor 166, 170–4
catasterism 259ff
Cecrops 183 (20), 193–8
Cephalus 189f
cereal cultivation 159, 161
Chalkodon 251
Charybdis 46
Cheiron 95f, 124, 132f
Chimaera 46
Chione 202, 212 (64)
Ciconians 85, 87
Circe 51
Circumcelliones 141
Cleopatra 205
Cockaigne 134, 139, 141
comedy 139–42
Conon 87f, 92, 101, 108, 118,
    244–7
Cornford, F. M. 21
cosmogony 19–24, 29
Cratinus 260
Creusa 206f
Creuzer, F. 282
CuChulainn 3
culture heroes 17f
Cybele 100
Cyclopes 123, 144, 280
Cyrus 44f

Dactyls 92, 95
Daedalus 280
Danae 165
Danaoi 165
Danaos 165, 184 (30)
Delcourt, M. 42
Delos 200, 211 (57)
Delphi 41, 43, 45, 123, 202,
    215–41 *passim*
Demeter 48f, 50, 91, 122, 250; at
    Pheneos 268 (11); as Europa 271
    (33)
Demodocus 100

Demophon 197
Derveni papyrus 22–4, 96, 148 (28)
Deubner, L. 134, 160, 178, 189f,
    197
Deukalion 168
Diodorus Siculus 95
Diomede 165, 180
Diomedes 269 (13)
Dionysos 24, 46, 85, 99–101, 189,
    280f; and Delphi 235, 240 (73);
    D. Phallen 93; resistance to 216
Dionysius Scytobrachion 95, 245
Dioscuri 96, 160, 170–8
dog 63
Dorkeus 251
Dorus 207, 249
Dorykleus 251
dragon 17f, 25, 227
Dumézil, G. 283
Dundes, A. 12
Durkheim, E. 137
Dysaules 250

Echion 96
Echo 108–13 *passim*
ecstatic warriors 88, 91, 98f
Electra 29, 54
Eleusinian mythology 250f, 279
Eleusis 169f, 201–4
Eliade, M. 138
Elis 164
Elysium 140
Empedocles 49, 125, 128, 139
Enaesimus 273 (57)
Enaisphoros 273 (61)
Enceladus 193
Enkidu 24
Enuma elish 21, 23
Ephorus 92, 98
Epikaste 47, 51, 251
Epimenides 260
Eratosthenes 85, 260
Erechtheum 202
Erechtheus/Erichthonius 187–214
    passim; and Poseidon 202, 204;
    daughters of 197, 212 (66)
Erigone 275 (72)
Erinyes 46, 122
Eros 107ff, 268 (11)
Erysichthon 200, 211 (57)
Euenus 96
Euhemerus 96, 129, 140
Eumelos 153

Eumenides 200
Eumolpids 203
Eumolpus 201–3, 213 (68), 250
Eunous 141, 144
Euphemus 96, 184 (27), 272 (49)
Euripides 43, 50, 84, 94–6, 192,
    194, 202, 205, 207
Europa 41, 250
Eurotas 154–78 *passim*, 183 (19)
Eurydice 80–2
Eurydike 165
Eurymnus 273 (58)
Eurypylos 272 (54)
Eurysthenes 175
Euryte/Eureite 251
Eurytos 273 (58)
Evadne 164
exposure 43f

fairy-tale 6f, 98
Flood 161, 183 (19)
Fortuna Primigenia 144
fosterage 45, 54
François vase 252
Frazer, J. G. 121, 135–7, 247,
    268 (6), 283
Freud, S. 41, 53–5, 118
funeral games 52

Gaia 215ff
Gaster, T. 23
Ge 122, 250, 271 (31)
genealogy 153–86
Geriguiguiatago 47f
Gernet, L. 47, 283
gift 281
Gigantomachy 192
Gilgamesh 16, 26f
Gluckman, M. 136f
Glaucus 96
Golden Age 121–47 *passim*
Gorgo 26f, 46, 65, 269 (15)
Gorgophone 154, 166–70, 180
Graf, F. 3
Greek mythography 242–77; and
    paradoxography 245; and
    paroemiography 245
Greek mythology, age of 1–4; and
    cult 223; and genealogy 153–86;
    and history 215–17; and
    iconography 25–30; and Orient
    10–30; and other traditional tales
    6f; and ritual 23, 74, 121–52,

279f, 282; catalogues in 248–54; development of 4–6; gift-exchange in 231f; logic of 60; meaning of 188; metamorphosis in 73f; names in 45, 248–54; *see also* women
Gruppe, O. 134
Gyges 47

Hades 122, 124
Halirrhotius 211 (50, 56)
Harpalos 166
Harpalyke 50
Harrison, J. E. 121
head 190
Hecate 45, 100
Hegesippus of Mekyberna 246
Hekataeus 140, 153
Helen 2; and Sparta 160, 174f, 178
Helios 85f, 140, 268 (11)
Hellanicus 189
Hellen 168
Hephaestus 190, 194, 199
Hera 46, 66, 122, 161, 191; and Kallisto 263f; Hera Argeia 165
Herakleidai 153, 175–8
Herakleides 86, 95
Herakles 1, 14–19, 25, 29, 82, 84, 96, 98, 281; and Sparta 154, 172, 175, 178, 254
Hermes 85, 96, 130, 171, 177; and Cecropids 197; Hermes Charidotes 130
Hermesianax 50
Hermione 154, 174f, 180
Hermippus 91
Herodotos 91f, 177, 245
heroisation 51f
Herse 195f
Hesiod 3, 46, 48, 101, 153, 159, 168, 191; and Kallisto 259–65; and Kronos 19–23, 121–44 *passim; Catalogue of Women* 248f; *Theogony* 226, 229, 231
Hesperides 96
Hestia 122
Heyne, C. G. 244, 268 (8), 282
Hilaeira 173
Hippe/Hippo 277 (96)
Hippias 153
Hippodamus 140
Hippokoon 1, 154, 170–2, 251, 254
Hippokoontids 171f, 253f

Hippolytos 73
Homer 1f, 20
Homeric Hymn to Apollo 216f, 227f
homosexuality, ritual 86, 98, 107–13, 247, 281
Hooke, S. 121
Hultkrantz, Å. 83f
human sacrifice 122–47 *passim*, 279, 281
Humbaba 26f
hundred-handed giants 123, 144
hunting 159
Hyads 212 (66)
Hyakinthia 130, 165, 179, 184 (29), 186 (53)
Hyakinthides 212 (66)
Hyakinthos 154, 164–9
Hyginus 85f, 251f, 254, 259
Hylas 98
Hypsipyle 96

Iamboulos 140
Iamos 47, 164
Iapetus 122, 124
Idas 173f
Idmon 96
Ikarios 154, 170, 185 (40)
Illuyankas 20
incest 49–54, 112
Indo-European mythology 2
Indra 2f
infanticide 124
initiation 3, 27f, 47, 53f, 70–2, 80–106 *passim*; and Kallisto 279–81
Io 263
Ion 206
Ionia and Athens 206
Iphianassa 251
Iphiclus 97, 271 (36), 272 (54)
Iphidamas 251
Iphigeneia 251
Iphimede 251
Iuno 108f
Ixion 73

Jacoby, F. 134, 244
Jason 52, 95–7, 281
Jeanmaire, H. 47
Jocaste 47, 51–4, 251
Julian 125

Kadmos 41
Kalais 96, 205

Kalevala 84
Kallisto 254–67
Kanne, J. A. 244
Kares/Keres 142, 144
Keleos 250
Kerykes 197
Keryx 197
Kinaethon 176
Kirk, G. S. 7, 121f
Kleitos 269 (12)
Kleochareia 183 (12)
Kluckhohn, C. 121
Klymenos 50
Klytemnestra 28, 174f
Klytios 253
Knossos 162
Knut 47
Koan mythology 242, 249
Kometes 253
Kore 82
Koronis 184 (34)
Kouretes 124, 129, 249
Kranaos 183 (20), 200
Kresphontes 154, 175
Kristensen, W. B. 145
Kronia 23, 127–31
Kronos 16–22 *passim*, 121–52
  passim, 197, 234
Kumarbi 16–22 *passim*, 123, 133
Kynortas 154, 166–8, 184 (34)
Kypria 173
Kyrene 164

Labdacus 42, 53
Laios 42–5
Lakedaimon 154–80 *passim*
Lamia 46
Lang, A. 135
Lanternari, V. 138
Laothoe 156
Lapithes 165
Lapiths 160, 165
Larissa 50
laurel 224, 237 (35)
Leda 171, 176, 180
legend 6f
Leleges 154–83 (9) *passim*
Lelex 154–80 *passim*
Lemnian women 122
Leos, daughters of 197
Lerna 18
Lesbos 92
Leto 66

Leucippus 50, 173
Leukippidai 173
Leukothea 268 (11)
Lévi-Strauss, C. 12, 41, 48
Linforth, I. M. 85
Linos 99, 268 (11)
Liungmann, W. 10
Lokros 156
Lucian 92f, 140
Luckman, T. 137
Lugal-e 23, 35 (15)
lycanthropy 67f
Lykaios 273 (58)
Lykaithos 273 (58, 61)
Lykaon 69ff, 261f, 281
Lykos 169f, 273 (58)
Lynceus 98
lyre 85
Lysimachos 48

Macrobius 131
maenads 85f, 279, 281
magicians 94f
mania 100
Marduk 17, 21, 28
marriage 153–86 *passim*
Marsyas 73
maternal uncle 97
Medea 96
Medusa 46
Mekionike 164
Melanthos 268 (9)
Meleager 97, 252f, 281
Meles 107–11
Melqart 17
Menelaos 154, 160, 174
Merope 45
Meropis 242f, 249f
Messene 160, 165, 168f, 178, 180
Metis 191
Meuli, K. 97–9, 102 (6), 135, 137
Meyer, Ed. 134
Midas 269 (15)
Minos 162
mirror 112, 114
monosandaloi 98
Moritz, K.Ph. 282
Mopsos, 96f
mountains 44, 87
Müller, K. O. 255, 262, 282
Müller, M. 2, 48, 282
Musaeus 99, 101, 250f
Muses 4f, 93–101 *passim*; at

Delphi 240 (73)
music 80–106 *passim*
Myles 154, 159–61, 178, 183 (20)
Myrsilus 92–5, 260
Mythographus Homericus 243, 247, 249, 259, 263, 269 (17)

naiades 109, 159, 180
names 44f, 248–54
Narcissus 107–20, 268 (11)
Nausicaa 43
Neleus 169, 172
Nemesis 109
Neoptolemus 185 (48)
Nergal 17
Nestor 3, 172, 174
New Year festivals 142–5
Nilsson, M. P. 127, 134, 136, 143, 225
Ninurta/Ningirsu 14–29 *passim*
Nireus 279
Nonnus 45, 247 (Pseudo)
nymphs 159, 180, 249

Odysseus 51, 82, 85, 97, 281
Oedipus 41–59, 187
Oedipus complex 53–5
Oeneus 85
Oibalos 154–80 *passim*
Oinone 269 (12)
Olen 99, 101
olive 198f
omphalos 123, 225, 233–5
Orestes 52, 54, 154, 174–80; at Delphi 230f
Oriental mythology 10–40
Orion 266
Orithyia 189, 204f, 212 (64)
Orpheus 80–106, 251
Orphic mythology 22–4
Orphism 22–4, 50
Otto, W. F. 283
Ovid 50, 80, 85, 113f, 118, 245, 252, 254, 258, 262

Palaephatus 245
Pallantids 192
Pallene 269 (12)
Pamphus 100, 108
Panathenaea 143, 192, 204
Panchaia 140
Pandion 169, 207
Pandrosus 195f, 198

Panyassis 260
Paris 44, 269 (12)
parricide 45–53 *passim*, 124
Parthenius 243–6, 249
Patreus 166
Pausanias 88, 204, 246, 258, 263; and Sparta 153–77 *passim*
Pedias 183 (20)
Peisandros of Rhodos 18, 260
Pelasgians 158
Pelasgos 72
Pelias 169, 252
Pellana 154, 170, 185 (40)
Pelops 47
Peloria 130, 140, 144
Penelope 47, 51
Pentheus 73
Periboia 45
Periclymenus 96
Peridea 183 (12)
Perieres 154, 166–73, 184 (35)
Persephone 50, 85, 281
Perseus 26–9, 44, 154, 165f, 168, 175
Persians 126
Phaeacians 140
Phanocles 95
Phanodemus 200
Phemius 100
Pherecydes 132, 208
Philetas 50
Philochorus 95, 198
Philodemus 242, 250
Philostratus 92f
Phineus 205, 279
Phoebe 173, 225, 231
Phorbas 1
Piasos 50
Pindar 24, 96f, 123, 125, 163, 173, 193, 282
Pitane 163f
Plato 54, 81, 86, 114, 117, 140, 153
Plexippos 253
Pluto 85, 139
poets and Greek mythology 2–4
Pollux 170, 173f
Polybos 45
Polykaon 154–69, 178
Polyneices 41
Polyphemus 98
Poseidon 122, 124, 130, 147 (29), 156, 164; and Apollo 232; and Athena 198–200, 203f, 232; at

Delphi 220–32 *passim*; P.
   Genethlios 168
Posidaeja 221
Praxithea 202
Procris 190
Proitos 165
Prokaon 253
Prokles 175
Prometheus 279, 281
Propp, V. J. 11, 42, 44, 48, 98, 253
Prothoos 253
Pylos 172, 174
Pythagoras 89–92, 129
Pythia 155, 223–5, 233

reciprocity 111
reflexivity 111, 113
Rhadamantys 250
Rhea 122f, 128f
Robert, C. 45, 188, 259, 259f, 262
Rohde, E. 283
role reversal 135–42
Romulus and Remus 7, 44f
ritual; as symbolic language 74; of
   reversal 135–42; *see also* Greek
   mythology

sacrifice, of cakes 128; of maidens
   212 (66)
Samothrace 92, 96
Santas/Sandon 17
Sargon 44
Saturnalia 136, 144
'Saturnalian' festivals 129–31
Saturnus 125–9, 131, 145
Satyrs 249
Scylla 46
sea 44
Sebros 254
Semele 263
shamanism 82–101 *passim*
shepherds 43f
Simonides 84
Sirens 46, 96–9
Skira 143, 204
snake 193, 196
Solger, K. W. F. 282
Sophocles 43f, 125, 205
Soteira 196
Spartan mythology 153–86
Sparte 154–80 *passim*
Sphinx 46–8
Stesichorus 168

stripping 69f
Synoikia 143

Tages 94
Tantalos 73
Tartarus 123f
Taygete 154–80 *passim*
Taygetos 159f, 163, 171
Teiresias 73, 108, 279, 281
Teisamenos 154
Telamon 251
Teledike 183 (18)
Telegonus 51
Telekleides 139
Telemachos 51
Temenes 154, 175
Thamyris 99
Theban Cycle 1
Thebes 41–55 *passim*, 162
Thebros 273 (61)
Themis 122, 215–40 *passim*
Thera 164, 169
Therapne 160f, 164, 176
Theseus 3, 47, 187, 190, 279–82
Thestiadai 253
Thestios 170, 253
Thompson, S. 112
Thrace and Eleusis 203f, 271 (34);
   and hero-cult 268 (11); and
   Orpheus 86–92. 99f
three-functional ideology 178f
Thyestes 50
Tiamat 28
Timagoras 107–13
Tiphys 97f
Titanomachia 174
Titans 20–4, 122f, 173f, 192
Toxeus 253
trickery 64f, 175
Triopas 160, 178
triple crossroads 45
Triptolemos 250
Triton 96
Trophonios 250f
Tyndareus 154, 170–4, 179f, 184
   (25)
Typhoeus/Typhon 16, 20–3, 123,
   191f, 227f
tyrannos 51
Tyrtaios 153, 177

Ugarit mythology 28
Ullikummi 16–22 *passim*, 124

Urania 100
Uranos 19, 122f, 250, 270 (30), 271
  (31)
Ursa major 259–61, 274 (70)
Usener, H. 48, 254, 282f
Utopia 139–42

Vernant, J.-P. 54, 255
Virgil 80, 85

water 70
wedding poetry 2
Weidkuhn, P. 136
Welcker, F. G. 254, 283
werewolf 60–79, 98
Wilamowitz 127, 132, 134, 255, 283
wolf 60–79
women; and genealogy 153–86
  passim; as monsters 46; in myth

281; names of 45; of Thrace 85ff;
  suicide 52; washing 43f
Wotan/Odin 95

Xanthos 268 (9)

Zalmoxis 91f
Zetes 96, 205
Zethos 162
Zeus 14–22 *passim*, 85, 114f,
  122–5, 197, 202, 250, 261; and
  Athena 190–2; and Delphi
  227–33; and Kallisto 262–4; and
  Sparta 154–74 *passim*; Dictaean
  Z. 241 (77f); Z. Lakedaimon 163;
  Z. Lykaios 63, 69, 261; Z.
  Meilichios 133; Z. Olympios 133;
  Z. Peloros 130